Hezekiah in History and Tradition

Supplements

to

Vetus Testamentum

Editor in Chief

Christl M. Maier

VOLUME 155

The titles published in this series are listed at brill.nl/vts

Hezekiah in History and Tradition

By

Robb Andrew Young

BRILL

LEIDEN · BOSTON
2012

Library of Congress Cataloging-in-Publication Data

Young, Robb Andrew.
Hezekiah in history and tradition / by Robb Andrew Young.
p. cm. — (Supplements to Vetus Testamentum, ISSN 0083–5889 ; v. 155)
Includes bibliographical references and index.
ISBN 978-90-04-21608-2 (hardback : alk. paper)
1. Hezekiah, King of Judah. 2. Bible. O.T. Kings—Criticism, interpretation, etc. 3. Bible. O.T.
Isaiah I—Criticism, interpretation, etc. 4. Bible. O.T. Chronicles—Criticism, interpretation, etc.
5. Jews—History—953-586 B.C. I. Title.

BS580.H4Y68 2012
222'.54092—dc23

BS
580
.H4
Y68
2012

2012006802

This publication has been typeset in the multilingual "Brill" typeface. With over 5,100 characters
covering Latin, IPA, Greek, and Cyrillic, this typeface is especially suitable for use in the
humanities. For more information, please see www.brill.nl/brill-typeface.

ISSN 0083-5889
ISBN 978 90 04 21608 2 (hardback)
ISBN 978 90 04 22951 8 (e-book)

This book is printed on acid-free paper.

MIX
Paper from
responsible sources
FSC® C004472
www.fsc.org

PRINTED BY DRUKKERIJ WILCO B.V. - AMERSFOORT, THE NETHERLANDS

CONTENTS

Acknowledgements ix
Abbreviations xi

Introduction 1

PART ONE

HEZEKIAH VIA EXTRA-BIBLICAL MATERIAL

1 Regnal Years and Lineage 9
   1.1. The Regnal Years of Hezekiah 9
        1.1.1. Overview 9
        1.1.2. The Date of the Fall of Samaria 12
        1.1.3. The Date of the Fall of Jerusalem 18
        1.1.4. Regnal Years of the Latter Kings of Judah 21
   1.2. The Lineage of Hezekiah 24
        1.2.1. Relationship to Ahaz 24
        1.2.2. Relationship to Ataliah 28
   1.3. Conclusion 32

2 The Kingdom of Judah 35
   2.1. Assyrian Relations 35
   2.2. The Urbanization of Jerusalem 42
   2.3. The Siloam Tunnel 48
   2.4. The *LMLK* Seals 50
   2.5. Conclusion 58

3 Sennacherib's Third Campaign 61
   3.1. Archaeological Evidence 62
   3.2. The Number of Assyrian Campaigns 66
   3.3. Taharqo 73
   3.4. Historical Reconstruction 77
   3.5. Conclusion 86

PART TWO

HEZEKIAH IN THE BOOK OF KINGS AND FIRST ISAIAH

4 The Religious Reform 91
  4.1. Archaeological Evidence 93
    4.1.1. Arad 93
    4.1.2. Beer-sheba 95
    4.1.3. Lachish 97
  4.2. Biblical Evidence 101
    4.2.1. The Report in 2 Kgs 18:4 101
    4.2.2. The Report in 2 Kgs 18:22 104
  4.3. The Social Setting of the Reform 109
  4.4. Conclusion 120

5 The Relationship between 2 Kgs 18:13–20:19 and Isa 36–39 123
  5.1. Relative Priority of the Texts 123
    5.1.1. Annalistic Account A (2 Kgs 18:13–16) 123
    5.1.2. Prophetic Account B (2 Kgs 18:17–19:37/Isa 36–37) ... 126
    5.1.3. Hezekiah and Isaiah (2 Kgs 20/Isa 38–39) 133
  5.2. Editing of the Texts 136
    5.2.1. Source Division 136
    5.2.2. Literary Analysis 142
    5.2.3. The Secondary Nature of "The Fourteenth Year" 146
  5.3. Conclusion 150

6 The Messianic Oracles in First Isaiah 151
  6.1. Isa 8:23–9:6 152
    6.1.1. Overview 152
    6.1.2. Literary Extent and Structure 152
    6.1.3. Tense/Aspect Analysis 156
    6.1.4. Translation 158
    6.1.5. Function of Isa 9:5–6 159
    6.1.6. Literary and Historical Context 161
  6.2. Isa 11:1–9 164
    6.2.1. Overview 164
    6.2.2. Literary Extent 165
    6.2.3. The Significance of the "Shoot" 170
    6.2.4. Literary and Historical Context 177

6.3. Isa 7 and the Sign of Immanuel 181
    6.3.1. Overview 181
    6.3.2. The Identity of Immanuel 182
6.4. Conclusion 190

PART THREE

HEZEKIAH IN CHRONICLES

7 The Historical Reliability of 2 Chr 29–30 195
    7.1. The Rededication of the Temple (2 Chr 29) 197
        7.1.1. Authorship 197
        7.1.2. Material 202
    7.2. The Passover (2 Chr 30) 209
        7.2.1. Summary Statement 209
        7.2.2. Other Historical Objections 213
        7.2.3. Correspondence to Josiah's Passover and
              Deuteronomy 215
        7.2.4. Source Material 222
        7.2.5. The Second Month 227
    7.3. Conclusion 231

8 The Historical Reliability of 2 Chr 31–32 235
    8.1. The Reform and the Portions (2 Chr 31) 235
        8.1.1. The Reform 235
        8.1.2. Distribution of the Portions 238
        8.1.3. Historical Analysis of the Portions 244
    8.2. The Invasion of Sennacherib (2 Chr 32) 249
        8.2.1. Hezekiah's Defensive Measures (vv 3–6) 249
        8.2.2. Hezekiah's Achievements (vv 27–30) 253
    8.3. Conclusion 254

9 Hezekiah as a Second David/Solomon 257
    9.1. The Dynastic Promises to David and Solomon 259
        9.1.1. Conditional and Unconditional Material 259
        9.1.2. The Depiction of Solomon 263
    9.2. The Pro-Solomonic Source of Chronicles 267
    9.3. The Hezekian Provenance of the Source Material 276
    9.4. Conclusion 282

Summary and Future Directions 285

Appendix A 295
Appendix B 299
Bibliography 301
Author Index 335
Scripture Index 343
Subject Index 360

ACKNOWLEDGEMENTS

This monograph is a revised version of my Ph.D. thesis, submitted to the faculty of the Graduate School at Yale University in the spring of 2011. Writing on this particular topic has been a labor of love from start to finish, and I must first and foremost thank my advisors for suggesting it to me. Both Robert R. Wilson and John J. Collins have been of inestimable value in guiding my dissertation research, and the end product is far better for their forthright and discerning feedback.

The opportunity to pursue doctoral studies would not have been possible without the outstanding faculty at the Hebrew University of Jerusalem. I would like to extend my sincere thanks to Steven Fassberg, Wayne Horowitz, Matthew Morgenstern, and Baruch Schwartz for their erudition and encouragement. Special mention should also be made of my classmates Jeff Dinkelman and David Bremer, who were like a family to me and kept me motivated to finish what we started together.

The impetus for my decision to study in Israel was provided by Norman Stillman and Shmuel Shepkaru at the University of Oklahoma. They are to be commended for their open hearts and open minds in believing in me and setting me along the path to academic investigation of the Hebrew Bible.

It is only fitting that my family receive my warmest expression of gratitude. My brother Todd and my son Christopher have been supportive to the utmost despite the time I was forced to sacrifice away from them, and I look forward to being able to repay their kindness. My mother Shirley and father Andy were foundational in fostering my interest in Bible from an early age, and gave of themselves countless times over in order to assure that my needs were met as I worked to complete my various degrees. This work is dedicated to all of you.

ABBREVIATIONS

AASOR	Annual of the American Schools of Oriental Research
ÄAT	Ägypten und Altes Testament
ABL	Robert Francis Harper, *Assyrian and Babylonian Letters belonging to the Kouyunjik Collections of the British Museum* (Chicago: University of Chicago Press, 1892–1914)
ABS	Archaeology and Biblical Studies
AfOB	Archiv für Orientforschung, Beiheft
AHw	W. von Soden, *Akkadisches Handwörterbuch* (3 vols.; Wiesbaden: Harrassowitz, 1965–1981)
AJA	*American Journal of Archaeology*
ALASP	Abhandlungen zur Literatur Alt-Syrien-Palästinas und Mesopotamiens
ANET	J. B. Pritchard (ed.), *Ancient Near Eastern Texts Relating to the Old Testament* (3rd edition; Princeton, 1969)
AnOr	Analecta Orientalia
AOAT	Alter Orient und Altes Testament
ARAB	D. D. Luckenbill, *Ancient Records of Assyria and Babylonia* (2 vols.; Chicago: University of Chicago, 1926–27)
ArOr	*Archív Orientální*
AS	Assyriological Studies
ASOR	American Schools of Oriental Research
ASSF	Acta Societatis Scientiarum Fennicae
ATD	Das Alte Testament Deutsch
AThANT	Abhandlungen zur Theologie des Alten und Neuen Testaments
ATSAT	Arbeiten zu Text und Sprache im Alten Testament
AUM	Andrews University Monograph
AUSS	*Andrews University Seminary Studies*
AYB	Anchor Yale Bible Commentary
AYBD	David Noel Freedman (ed.), *Anchor Yale Bible Dictionary* (6 vols.; New Haven: Yale University Press, 2008)
BA	*Biblical Archaeologist*
BAIAS	*Bulletin of the Anglo-Israel Archaeological Society*
BAR	*Biblical Archaeology Review*
BASOR	*Bulletin of the American Schools of Oriental Research*
BAT	Die Botschaft des Alten Testaments

BEATAJ	Beiträge zur Erforschung des Alten Testaments und des Antiken Judentums
BEC	Books on Egypt and Chaldaea
BETL	Bibliotheca ephemeridum theologicarum lovaniensium
BEvT	Beiträge zur evangelischen Theologie
BFCT	Beiträge zur Förderung christlicher Theologie
BHK	Rudolph Kittel (ed.), *Biblia Hebraica* (3rd ed.; Stuttgart: Deutsche Bibelstiftung, 1945)
BHS	Karl Elliger and Wilhelm Rudolph (eds.), *Biblia Hebraica Stuttgartensia* (Stuttgart: Deutsche Bibelstiftung, 1983)
BHT	Beiträge zur Historischen Theologie
Bib	*Biblica*
BibOr	Biblica et Orientalia
BibSac	*Bibliotheca sacra*
BIFAO	*Bulletin de l'Institut français d'archéologie orientale*
BJRL	*Bulletin of the John Rylands Library*
BJS	Brown Judaic Studies
BLMJP	Bible Lands Museum Jerusalem Publications
BM	British Museum
BMECCJ	Bulletin of the Middle Eastern Culture Center in Japan
BN	*Biblische Notizen*
BZAW	Beihefte zur *Zeitschrift für die alttestamentliche Wissenschaft*
CAD	James Henry Breasted, Erica Reiner, and Martha Roth (eds.), *The Assyrian Dictionary of the Oriental Institute of the University of Chicago* (Chicago: Oriental Institute, 1956–2007)
CANE	Jack M. Sasson (ed.), *Civilizations of the Ancient Near East* (4 vols.; New York: Charles Scribner's Sons, 1995)
CB	Coniectanea Biblica, Old Testament series
CBQ	*Catholic Biblical Quarterly*
CdÉ	*Chronique d'Égypte*
CDL	Capital Decisions Limited
COS	William W. Hallo and K. Lawson Younger, Jr. (eds.), *The Context of Scripture: Canonical Compositions, Monumental Inscriptions, and Archival Documents from the Biblical World* (3 vols.; Leiden: Brill, 1997)
CR:BS	*Currents in Research: Biblical Studies*
CTN	Cuneiform Texts from Nimrud

CTU	Manfried Dietrich, Oswald Loretz, and Joaquín Sanmartín, *The Cuneiform Alphabetic Texts from Ugarit, Ras Ibn Hani and Other Places* (KTU 2nd ed.; ALASP 8; Münster: Ugarit-Verlag, 1995)
DDD	Karel van der Toorn, Bob Becking, and Pieter W. van der Horst (eds.), *Dictionary of Deities and Demons in the Bible* (2nd ed.; Leiden: Brill, 1999)
EdF	Erträge der Forschung
EgT	*Église et théologie*
EHS	Europäische Hochschulschriften
EncBib	E.L. Sukenik, U.M.D. Cassuto, H. Tadmor and Sh. Ahituv (eds.), האנציקלופדיה המקראית (*Encyclopaedia Biblica*) (9 vols; Jerusalem: Mosad Bialik, 1950–88) [Hebrew]
EncJud	F. Skolnik and M. Berenbaum (eds.), *Encyclopaedia Judaica* (2nd ed.; 22 vols.; Detriot: Thomson Gale, 2007)
EPRO	Études préliminaires aux religions orientales dans l'Empire romain
ETL	*Ephemerides Theologicae Lovaniensis*
ExpTim	*Expository Times*
FAT	Forschungen zum Alten Testament
FCSup	Fontes et commentationes, Supplement
FOTL	Forms of Old Testament Literature
FRLANT	Forschungen zur Religion und Literatur des Alten Testaments und des Neuen Testaments
FT	*Faith & Thought*
FTS	Freiburger theologische Studien
GAT	Grundrisse zum Alten Testament
GKC	E. Kautzsch (ed.), *Gesenius' Hebrew Grammar* (trans. A. E. Cowley; 2nd ed.; Oxford: Oxford University Press, 1910)
GTS	Gettysburg Theological Studies
GrTS	Grazer theologische Studien
HALOT	Ludwig Koehler, Walter Baumgartner, and J. J. Stamm, *The Hebrew and Aramaic Lexicon of the Old Testament* (trans. and ed. M. E. J. Richardson; 4 vols.; Leiden: Brill, 1994–99)
HANEM	History of the Ancient Near East Monographs
HAT	Handbuch zum Alten Testament
HBS	Herders biblische Studien
HBT	*Horizons in Biblical Theology*

HS	*Hebrew Studies*
HSO	Heidelberger Studien zum alten Orient
HSM	Harvard Semitic Monographs
HSS	Harvard Semitic Studies
HTKAT	Herders Theologischer Kommentar zum Alten Testament
HUCA	*Hebrew Union College Annual*
HUCM	Monographs of the Hebrew Union College
HTR	*Harvard Theological Review*
ICC	International Critical Commentary
IEJ	*Israel Exploration Journal*
IOS	Israel Oriental Studies
ISBE	G. W. Bromiley (ed.), *The International Standard Bible Encyclopedia* (4 vols.; Grand Rapids: Eerdmans, 1979–88)
ISFCJ	International Studies in Formative Christianity and Judaism
JAOS	*Journal of the American Oriental Society*
JARCE	*Journal of the American Research Center in Egypt*
JBL	*Journal of Biblical Literature*
JBMS	*Journal of Book of Mormon Studies*
JBR	*Journal of Bible and Religion*
JBS	Jerusalem Biblical Studies
JCS	*Journal of Cuneiform Studies*
JETS	*Journal of the Evangelical Theological Society*
JJS	*Journal of Jewish Studies*
JM	P. Joüon, *A Grammar of Biblical Hebrew.* (2 vols.; trans. and revised by T. Muraoka; Rome: Pontifical Biblical Institute, 1991)
JNES	*Journal of Near Eastern Studies*
JPOS	*Journal of the Palestine Oriental Society*
JPS	Jewish Publication Society
JQR	*Jewish Quarterly Review*
JRGZM	Jahrbuch des Römisch-Germanischen Zentralmuseums
JSOT	*Journal for the Study of the Old Testament*
JSOTSup	*Journal for the Study of the Old Testament*, Supplements
JSPSup	*Journal for the Study of the Pseudepigrapha*, Supplements
JSS	*Journal of Semitic Studies*
JSSEA	*Journal of the Society for the Study of Egyptian Antiquities*
KAH	Keilschrifttexte aus Assur historischen Imhalts
KAI	H. Donner and W. Röllig, *Kanaanäische und aramäische Inschriften* (2nd ed.; Wiesbaden, 1966–69)
KAT	Kommentar zum Alten Testament

KHC	Kurzer Hand-Commentar zum Alten Testament
KTU	Manfried Dietrich, Oswald Loretz, and Joaquín Sanmartín, *Die keilalphabetischen Texte aus Ugarit* (AOAT 24/1; Neukirchen-Vluyn, Neukirchener Verlag, 1976)
Lane	Edward William Lane, *Arabic-English Lexicon* (8 vols.; London, 1863–93; reprinted New York: Ungar, 1955–56)
LCL	Loeb Classical Library
LHB/OTS	Library of Hebrew Bible/Old Testament Studies
MC	Mesopotamian Civilizations
MDAIK	*Mitteilungen des deutschen archäologischen Instituts, Abteilung Kairo*
MHUC	Monographs of the Hebrew Union College
MS	Melammu Symposia
MThA	Münsteraner Theologische Abhandlungen
MVAG	Mitteilungen der Vorderasiatisch-Aegyptischen Gesellschaft
NAS95	New American Standard. The Lockman Foundation, 1995.
NCB	New Century Bible
ND	Nimrud Documents, signature of texts from ancient Kalḫu
NEA	*Near Eastern Archaeology*
NEAEHL	Ephraim Stern (ed.), *The New Encyclopedia of Archaeological Excavations in the Holy Land* (5 vols.; Jerusalem: Israel Exploration Society, 1993–2008)
NEASB	*Near Eastern Archaeological Society Bulletin*
NEchtB	Neue Echter Bibel
NJPS	New JPS translation. Jewish Publication Society 1st ed. 1985, 2nd ed. 1999
NRSV	New Revised Standard Version. Division of Christian Education of the National Council of the Churches of Christ in the United States of America, 1989
OBO	Orbis biblicus et orientalis
OBT	Overtures to Biblical Theology
OIP	Oriental Institute Prism / Oriental Institute Publications, University of Chicago
OLA	Orientalia Lovaniensia Analecta
OLZ	*Orientalistische Literaturzeitung*
OTL	Old Testament Library
OTS	Oudtestamentische Studiën
PBA	Proceedings of the British Academy
PEQ	*Palestine Exploration Quarterly*

PEFQS	*Palestine Exploration Fund Quarterly Statement*
PFES	Publications of the Finnish Exegetical Society
PJ	*Palästinajahrbuch*
PNAE	Karen Radner and Heather D. Baker (eds.), *Prosopography of the Neo-Assyrian Empire* (3 vols. of 2 parts; Helsinki: Neo-Assyrian Text Corpus Project, 1998–2011)
RA	*Revue d'Assyriologie*
RAI	Rencontre Assyriologique Internationale
RB	*Revue biblique*
RlA	Michael P. Streck, *Reallexikon der Assyriologie und Vorderasiatischen Archäologie* (16 vols.; Berlin: Walter de Gruyter, 1932-ongoing)
RSR	*Religious Studies Review*
RTR	*Reformed Theological Review*
SAA	State Archives of Assyria
SAAB	*State Archives of Assyria Bulletin*
SAAS	State Archives of Assyria Studies
SAOC	Studies in Ancient Oriental Civilization
SBA	Studies in Biblical Archaeology
SBLDS	Society of Biblical Literature Dissertation Series
SBLEJL	Society of Biblical Literature, Early Judaism and Its Literature
SBLMS	Society of Biblical Literature, Monograph Series
SBLSS	Society of Biblical Literature, Symposium Series
SBLWAW	Society of Biblical Literature, Writings of the Ancient World
SBOT	Sacred Books of the Old Testament
SBS	Stuttgarter Bibelstudien
SBT	Studies in Biblical Theology
SBTS	Sources for Biblical and Theological Study
SCM	Student Christian Movement
SEÅ	*Svensk Exegetisk Årsbok*
SH	Scripta Hierosolymitana
SHANE	Studies in the History of the Ancient Near East
SHCANE	Studies in the History and Culture of the Ancient Near East
SJT	*Scottish Journal of Theology*
SJOT	*Scandanavian Journal of Old Testament*
SOTS	Society for Old Testament Study
SPCK	Society for Promoting Christian Knowledge
SRB	Supplementi alla Rivista Biblica

StTh	*Studia Theologica—Nordic Journal of Theology*
SVC	*Studies in Visual Communication*
TA	*Tel Aviv*
TCS	Texts from Cuneiform Sources
TCT	Textual Criticism and the Translator
TDOT	G. Johannes Botterweck, Helmer Ringgren, and Heinz-Josef Fabry (eds.), *Theological Dictionary of the Old Testament* (trans. J. T. Willis, G. W. Bromiley, and D. E. Green; 17 vols. Grand Rapids: Eerdmans, 1974-ongoing)
TGUOS	*Transactions of the Glasgow University Oriental Society*
TLZ	*Theologische Literaturzeitung*
TPOA	J. Briend and M.-J. Seux, *Textes du Proche-Orient Ancien et histoire d'Israël* (Paris: Cerf, 1977)
TTZ	*Trierer theologische Zeitschrift*
TUAT	Otto Kaiser, Bernd Janowski and Gernot Wilhelm (eds.), *Texte aus der Umwelt des Alten Testaments* (Gütersloh: Gerd Mohn, 1982–)
TVG	Theologische Verlagsgemeinschaft
TynBul	*Tyndale Bulletin*
TZ	*Theologische Zeitschrift*
UBL	Ugaritisch-biblische Literatur
UCNES	University of California Near Eastern Studies
UCOP	University of Cambridge Oriental Publications
UF	*Ugarit Forschungen*
VT	*Vetus Testamentum*
VTSup	*Vetus Testamentum*, Supplements
WBC	Word Biblical Commentary
WeBC	Westminster Bible Companion
Wehr	Hans Wehr, *Arabic-English Dictionary: The Hans Wehr Dictionary of Modern Written Arabic* (4th ed.; ed. J. M. Cowan; Ithaca, N.Y.: Spoken Language Services, Inc., 1979)
WLQ	*Wisconsin Lutheran Quarterly*
WMANT	Wissenschaftliche Monographien zum Alten und Neuen Testament
ZAW	*Zeitschrift für die alttestamentliche Wissenschaft*
ZBK	Zürcher Bibelkommentare
ZDPV	*Zeitschrift des Deutschen Palästina-Vereins*
ZTK	*Zeitschrift für Theologie und Kirche*

INTRODUCTION

The Judean monarch Hezekiah, who reigned in the last quarter of the eighth century B.C.E., remains one of the most significant figures in the study of the Hebrew Bible. The echoes of his rule may be felt far beyond the biblical corpus itself, in both Assyrian annals and reliefs, archaeological finds, and rabbinic literature. His name is variously mentioned in no fewer than seven different biblical books, the annals of the Sargonid king Sennacherib, and a growing corpus of bullae.[1] His regnal accounts are not only the longest within the respective books of Kings and Chronicles, but the former is largely duplicated in the book of Isaiah. These eleven chapters of biblical material vastly overshadow the comparatively meager record of all other monarchs throughout the divided kingdom, rivaled only in scope by the legendary David and Solomon. A necessary

---

[1] 2 Kgs; 1–2 Chr; Isaiah; Jeremiah (15:4; 26:18–19); Hosea (1:1) Micah (1:1); Proverbs (25:1). The mention of him as the great-great-grandfather of Zephaniah in Zeph 1:1 is debated as being the same individual, while the references to Hezekiah in Ezra 2:16; Neh 7:21; 10:18[17] are to someone else altogether.

There are four variants of the name Hezekiah in the Hebrew Bible, attained by alternating the initial element as חזק or יחזק, and the final elements as either יהו- or יה-. The possible forms are, in frequency order: חִזְקִיָּהוּ (common throughout 2 Kgs 18–20; Isa 36–39; cf. 1 Chr 3:13; 2 Chr 29:18, 27; 30:24; 32:15; Jer 26:18–19); יְחִזְקִיָּהוּ (common throughout 2 Chr 29–32; cf. 2 Kgs 20:10; Isa 1:1; Jer 15:4); חִזְקִיָּה (2 Kgs 18:1, 10, 13–16; Prov 25:1; the debated Zeph 1:1); יְחִזְקִיָּה (Hos 1:1; Mic 1:1). In Assyrian cuneiform, the name is preserved as ¹Ha-za-qi-a-ú and ¹Ha-za-qi-a-a-ú, see George Smith, History of Sennacherib (London: Williams and Norgate, 1878) 61, 63, 68; Daniel David Luckenbill, The Annals of Sennacherib (OIP 2; Chicago: University of Chicago, 1924) 32–33, 77 (who reads a-a as ai). Based on the biblical evidence and in particular the extant bullae, the form חִזְקִיָּהוּ is to be preferred.

At least eight seal impressions have been recognized as originating from the court of king Hezekiah, made from three or perhaps four disparate seals. Another seven bullae name five different royal stewards (Amariah, Azariah, Domla, Ushna, Yehozarah) who identify themselves as a "servant of Hezekiah." For these artifacts, see Ruth Hestrin and Michal Dayagi, "A Seal Impression of a Servant of King Hezekiah," IEJ 24 (1974) 27–29; Nahman Avigad and Benjamin Sass, Corpus of West Semitic Stamp Seals (Jerusalem: Israel Academy of Sciences & Humanities, 1997) 172–73 no. 407; Robert Deutsch, Messages from the Past: Hebrew Bullae from the Time of Isaiah Through the Destruction of the First Temple (Tel Aviv: Archaeological Center Publication, 1997) 31 no. 2; 52–53, nos. 3–4 [Hebrew]; idem, "Lasting Impressions: New Bullae Reveal Egyptian-Style Emblems on Judah's Royal Seals," BAR 28/4 (Jul.–Aug. 2002) 42–51, 60; Frank Moore Cross, "King Hezekiah's Seal Bears Phoenician Imagery," BAR 25/2 (Mar.–Apr. 1999) 42–45, 60; G. M. Grena, Lmlk— A Mystery Belonging to the King, Vol. 1 (Redondo Beach, Cal.: 4000 Years of Writing History, 2004) 26 figs. 9–10.

consequence of this prominent exposure is that the Hezekiah of tradition gradually developed into a figure potentially far removed from the Hezekiah of history.

For all of his greatness, however, there is little that may be stated with certainty about this Judean ruler. His years of reign are disputed, and such chronological issues have raised questions in regard to his lineage. The strength and size of his empire has long been a matter of debate, along with the attribution and function of the ubiquitously preserved storage containers known as *lmlk* jars. Whether or not he instituted a cultic reform is no less divisive an issue in scholarship than ascertaining the number of campaigns Sennacherib made to Judah. Dissent persists as to whether any of the prophecies of Isaiah ben Amoz refer to Hezekiah, and exegetes remain skeptical as to whether his account in the ideologically motivated writings of the Chronicler has any historical value. Thus on the one hand, a thoroughgoing investigation into these perennial questions is partially justified.

Recent archaeological discoveries substantiating the expansion of the city of Jerusalem in the late eighth century B.C.E., as well as its corresponding growth in population, have renewed interest in the Judean kingdom under the reign of Hezekiah. Contemporary scholarship on economic conditions in the region has continued apace, along with data relating to decommissioned cultic sites of the period and the aforementioned *lmlk* jars. Questions have been raised as to the expanse of the Josianic empire and notable mainstays of biblical history have been feasibly antedated to the reign of Hezekiah, such as the legal core of Deuteronomy and the initial editing of the Deuteronomistic History.[2] These advances aid in placing Hezekiah in his proper context in history, while at the same time laying the groundwork for his depiction in later biblical tradition. In short, our picture of Hezekiah is not the same as it was even a decade ago. This

---

[2] The wealth of biblical research spawned by Martin Noth's ground-breaking work on the Deuteronomistic History over fifty years ago still nuances the proper distinction between the adjectives 'Deuteronomic' and 'Deuteronomistic', as scrutinized in Richard Coggins, "What Does 'Deuteronomistic' Mean?" in J. Davies, G. Harvey, and W. G. E. Watson (eds.), *Words Remembered, Texts Renewed: Essays in Honour of John F.A. Sawyer* (JSOTSup 195; Sheffield: Sheffield Academic Press, 1995) 135–48. I adhere to the delineation proffered by Norbert F. Lohfink, "Was There a Deuteronomistic Movement?" in L. S. Schearing and S. L. McKenzie (eds.), *Those Elusive Deuteronomists: The Phenomenon of Pan-Deuteronomism* (JSOTSup 268; Sheffield: Sheffield Academic Press, 1999) 38: "Deuteronomic" pertains to Deuteronomy, while "Deuteronomistic" pertains to material influenced by Deuteronomy.

second consideration, in conjunction with the first, warrants a comprehensive study.

This monograph aims to provide a detailed reworking of what may be asserted concerning the historical Hezekiah. The discipline of historical reconstruction is itself much maligned, particularly in regard to pre-exilic Israel. Texts chronicling this period are widely regarded as literary rather than historical texts, deemed to have been composed during the later Persian or Hellenistic periods. Such a temporal remove from the purported events described leaves the biblical text largely devoid of any historical content pertaining to the pre-exilic period, an elaborate myth concocted in the aftermath of exile.[3] The unavoidable ideological *Tendenz* inherent in all historiographic material has induced more extreme critics to advocate jettisoning the Hebrew Bible altogether as a tool for historical reconstruction, in favor of more impartial methods such as archaeology in which the subjectivity lies solely between the artifact and the scholar.[4]

---

[3] As summarized by Ernest Nicholson, "Current 'Revisionism' and the Literature of the Old Testament," in J. Day (ed.), *In Search of Pre-exilic Israel. Proceedings of the Oxford Old Testament Seminar* (JSOTSup 406; London: T&T Clark, 2004) 5–6. Among these "revisionist" scholars, Nicholson names Philip Davies, Niels Peter Lemche, Thomas L. Thompson, and Robert Carroll. Revisionists advocate such views as the non-existence of a united monarchy, and the fictitious nature of the figures of Saul, David, and Solomon.

For ongoing dialogue pertaining to the place of the Bible in historical reconstruction, other publications of interest include: Jacob Licht, "Biblical Historicism," in H. Tadmor and M. Weinfeld (eds.), *History, Historiography and Interpretation: Studies in Biblical and Cuneiform Literatures* (Jerusalem: Magnes Press, 1983) 107–20; Philip R. Davies and David M. Gunn (eds.), *"A History of Ancient Israel and Judah*: A Discussion of Miller-Hayes (1986)," *JSOT* 39 (1987) 3–63; Marc Zvi Brettler, *The Creation of History in Ancient Israel* (London: Routledge, 1995); Lester L. Grabbe (ed.), *Can a 'History of Israel' Be Written?* (JSOTSup 245; Sheffield: Sheffield Academic Press, 1997); V. Philips Long (ed.), *Israel's Past in Present Research: Essays on Ancient Israelite Historiography* (SBTS 7; Winona Lake, Ind.: Eisenbrauns, 1999); James Barr, *History and Ideology in the Old Testament: Biblical Studies at the End of a Millennium* (Oxford: Oxford University Press, 2000); Ernst Axel Knauf, "History, Archaeology, and the Bible," *TZ* 57/2 (2001) 262–68; Kenneth A. Kitchen, *On the Reliability of the Old Testament* (Grand Rapids: Eerdmans, 2003); Iain Provan, V. Philips Long, and Tremper Longman III, *A Biblical History of Israel* (Louisville: Westminster John Knox, 2003); James K. Hoffmeier and Alan Millard (eds.), *The Future of Biblical Archaeology: Reassessing Methodologies and Assumptions* (Grand Rapids: Eerdmans, 2004); Lester L. Grabbe, *Ancient Israel: What Do We Know and How Do We Know It?* (London: T&T Clark, 2007); H. G. M. Williamson (ed.), *Understanding the History of Ancient Israel* (PBA 143; Oxford: Oxford University Press. 2007).

[4] A question which succinctly encapsulates this skepticism is posed by Burke O. Long, "On Finding the Hidden Premises," *JSOT* 39 (1987) 10: "Should one even try to write a modern, critical history of Israel largely on the basis of a single amalgamated, culturally self-serving, and essentially private version of that history?"

It is to be readily admitted that there are acute methodological dangers involved in the process of historical reconstruction. As the conclusions of the scholar are unavoidably tainted by his or her presuppositions, one's position in this disputation should be well defined, and justified, at the outset of such an enterprise. In my opinion, taking an extreme stance on the historical value of the Hebrew Bible is methodologically unsound. At one end of the spectrum, studies which assert the complete trustworthiness of the biblical record run the risk of reconstructing erroneous history in the face of its ideologically motivated authors. Here the misstep is equating historiography with history, especially in regard to the stories of the pre-monarchic period in which comparative material is sorely lacking.[5] Several texts confess themselves to have been authored in a much later period, and the resulting anachronisms and contradictions, in concert with the author's cultural proclivities and literary aims, dictate that recorded events cannot be taken strictly at face value.[6] That ancient authors and scribes deliberately chose to whitewash their own history is ably demonstrated in the inner-biblical reinterpretation of earlier traditions and the selective editing of theologically difficult texts.[7]

---

[5] A case in point is the patriarchal period, on which see Thomas L. Thompson, *The Historicity of the Patriarchal Narratives: The Quest for the Historical Abraham* (BZAW 133; Berlin: W. de Gruyter, 1974); John Van Seters, *Abraham in History and Tradition* (New Haven: Yale University Press, 1975).

[6] For later, admitted authorship, note the following list of passages: Gen 12:6; 32:33[32]; 35:6 (הוּא בֵּית־אֵל); 36:31; Deut 2:21–22; 10:8; 34:6; Josh 4:9; 7:26; 8:28–29; 9:27; 10:27; 13:13; 14:14; 15:63; 16:10; Judg 1:21, 26; 6:24; 10:4; 14:4; 15:19; 18:12; 1 Sam 5:5; 6:18; 27:6; 30:25; 2 Sam 4:3; 6:8; 18:18; 1 Kgs 8:8; 9:21; 10:12; 12:19; 2 Kgs 2:22; 8:22; 14:7; 16:6; 17:23, 34, 41. The parenthetical comments in Deut 2:12; 3:11; 34:10; 1 Sam 9:9, for example, serve to explicate former situations for the contemporary reader. For anachronisms, note the following passages:
1. Gen 14:14, "He went in pursuit as far as Dan." Moses, in conservative circles the purported author, would not have known this as the name of the region because the tribe of Dan had not yet acquired its territory in the Promised Land.
2. Deut 1:1, "across the Jordan." is written from the standpoint of someone on the west side of the Jordan, a location where Moses never set foot.
For examples of contradictions in legal material, see Michael Fishbane, *Biblical Interpretation in Ancient Israel* (Oxford: Clarendon Press, 1985) 135–38, 206–208, 220, 223–25, 227–28, 251–52, 264–65, 270. For the harmonization of such conflicting passages in narrative, see Isaac Kalimi, *The Reshaping of Ancient Israelite History in Chronicles* (Winona Lake, Ind.: Eisenbrauns, 2005) 123–65. Thus in the estimation of Philip R. Davies, *In Search of 'Ancient Israel'* (JSOTSup 148; Sheffield: Sheffield Academic Press, 1992) 57, "There is no way to judge the distance between the biblical Israel and its historical counterpart unless the historical counterpart is investigated independently of the biblical literature."

[7] Fishbane, *Biblical Interpretation in Ancient Israel*; Yair Zakovitch, *Introduction to Inner-Biblical Interpretation* (Even-Yehuda: Reches, 1992) [Hebrew]. For examples of theologically motivated emendation, see Fishbane pp. 66–74.

At the other end of the gamut, studies which eschew the biblical text due to overt skepticism are resigned to constructing models which omit an important independent control and are thus potentially far removed from 'history'.[8] It is just the available quantity of these controls which limits the subjectivity of the researcher. Contrary to the assertion that biblical Israel is a purely literary construct, the biblical text rightfully remains our fundamental resource for reconstructing Israelite history.[9] The insufficiency of direct evidence for biblical claims cannot be summarily appropriated as validation of a story's fictitious character.[10] Instead, it is incumbent upon the scholar to measure such claims indirectly; to dismiss out of hand a detail lacking extra-biblical support is just as ingenuous as trusting it implicitly.[11] Careful scholarship has shown great success in being able to reconstruct earlier traditions from later texts, and biblical books knowingly composed in later periods may nonetheless preserve accurate details from antecedent eras.[12] For the very reason that gaps in the inscriptional, archaeological, sociological, and literary record do not permit complete, clear reconstruction of biblical history, it is the incorporation of all

---

[8] Strict reliance on extra-biblical documents is in turn hazardous, as they are likewise tendentious. Assyrian records for the eighth year of Esarhaddon, for instance, omit the defeat of the army in Egypt, a fact nevertheless confirmed by the Babylonian Chronicle. Alleviating the witness of the Bible removes a valuable counterpoint to other ancient Near Eastern writings, and in effect destabilizes the efforts of the historian. Surely weighing the propaganda and ideology of one system of texts versus another provides a more reliable means of reconstructing history from historiography.

[9] As recognized by John H. Hayes, "On Reconstructing Israelite History," *JSOT* 39 (1987) 7. The insistence of revisionist scholars on proof has been raised as the very lynchpin of their own theories, cf. Nicholson, "Current 'Revisionism'," 12–13; Barr, *History and Ideology in the Old Testament*, 100–101.

[10] Conveyed in the apposite scientific principle, "Absence of evidence does not equal evidence of absence."

[11] When the Bible is truly our only recourse for verifying a recorded event, what we can posit about the author is our single best criterion for evaluating its "history." Owing to the limited access by archaeologists to the Temple Mount, precisely in the location most likely to yield compelling evidence supporting the Solomonic era, alternative approaches for assessing the influence of the early monarchy have been more fruitful, such as that applied by Nadav Na'aman, "The Contribution of the Amarna Letters to the Debate on Jerusalem's Political Position in the Tenth Century BCE," *BASOR* 304 (1996) 17–27; Amihai Mazar, "The Spade and the Text: The Interaction between Archaeology and Israelite History Relating to the Tenth-Ninth Centuries BCE," in Williamson (ed.), *Understanding the History of Ancient Israel*, 143–71.

[12] The form-critical work of Hermann Gunkel on Genesis is notable in regard to scholarship, while the book of Chronicles exemplifies an example of the latter. The Bible is more historically accurate, particularly with regard to the late monarchical period, than is currently credited.

available data that affords the best opportunity for rational proposals by
the historian.

This book will commence with data outside of the biblical text which
may be brought to bear in reconstructing the historical Hezekiah, and
subsequently will proceed to augment this picture based on his portrayal
in the books of Kings, Isaiah, and Chronicles.[13] My objective is to focus
on those issues which either remain contentious in biblical scholarship,
or else have been resolved into a general consensus which needs to be
called into question. The conscious effort has also been made to turn this
copious volume into a general handbook on Hezekiah, so that general
bibliography on a particular aspect of his reign is readily accessible. As
each chapter will deal with a specific representation of this ruler, summaries of the corresponding history of scholarship will appear within their
appropriate context.[14] The goal of this work is for its findings to have as
profound an impact on Hezekiah studies as the selfsame ruler did upon
Israelite history.

---

[13] Biblical quotations in this book will generally follow the NAS95 translation, based
on its adherence to MT.

[14] In an effort to streamline the organization of this substantial work, exegesis in the
main text is restricted to the range of positions on a particular issue, while due credit for
those insights is reserved for the footnotes. Alleviating the mention of any and all scholars
in the body of this work facilitates the flow of discussion on a particular topic, while reinforcing the collegial academic notion that disagreements among scholars lie squarely with
their methodology and conclusions.

PART ONE

HEZEKIAH VIA EXTRA-BIBLICAL MATERIAL

CHAPTER ONE

REGNAL YEARS AND LINEAGE

The figure of Hezekiah is known primarily from the Bible, but there is relevant extra-biblical material that may also be brought to bear in fleshing out our understanding of this important Judean monarch. The intent of this and the next two chapters is to focus on those historical issues which are best resolved by recourse to this information. These data will provide a framework within which the biblical text may subsequently be analyzed.

Before Hezekiah can be properly discussed, it will first be necessary to place him chronologically. Despite the popularity of this sovereign, there is no consensus regarding when he actually came to the throne. For such a significant ruler, this is a deadlocked situation which must be addressed. Having ascertained the most probable regnal years for Hezekiah, it will then be possible to discuss his lineage, which has been called into question due to the aforementioned chronological issues surrounding his reign. There are also suggestions that have been raised in regard to potential relatives of Hezekiah that must be critically assessed.

1.1. The Regnal Years of Hezekiah

1.1.1. *Overview*

It is unfortunate that for such an important figure in biblical history, the years of reign of king Hezekiah are in dispute. The enterprise of chronological reconstruction is itself treated with skepticism, based on the inconsistent use by scholars of absolute durations and synchronisms attested in ancient records.[1] Rather than present an exhaustive review of the various academic positions regarding the dates of reign for Hezekiah, accompanied by detailed evaluation of these proposals which would ultimately be tedious for even the most riveted reader, this section will attempt to simplify the discussion by assessing the problem anew.

---

[1] For such studies, see the list provided in Leslie McFall, "Some Missing Coregencies in Thiele's Chronology," *AUSS* 30/1 (1992) 35 n. 1.

The diverse dates for Hezekiah's enthronement are the result of multiple, conflicting synchronisms within the biblical text. On the one hand are those scholars who give credence to 2 Kgs 18:9–10, whereby the fourth and sixth regnal years of Hezekiah are synchronized with the beginning and end of the conquest of Samaria, respectively. By correlating the siege and eventual capture of the capital city of Israel with Assyrian records, the installation of the Judean monarch falls in the date range of 727–724 B.C.E.[2] On the other hand are those who give priority to the chronological notice in 2 Kgs 18:13, in which the military campaign against Jerusalem by the Assyrian king Sennacherib transpired in "the fourteenth year of king Hezekiah." As this significant event is ubiquitously dated to 701, the first regnal year of Hezekiah is thus 715–714 B.C.E.[3]

---

[2] This has yielded the following reconstructed dates of reign for Hezekiah:
- Nisan 727—Adar 699 B.C.E., based on dating the fall of Samaria to 722. See Hayim Tadmor, "The Chronology of the First Temple Period: A Presentation and Evaluation of the Sources," in A. Malamat (ed.), *The World History of the Jewish People, First Series: Ancient Times. The Age of the Monarchies: Political History, Vol. 4/1* (Jerusalem: Massada Press, 1979) 58, 320 nn. 36–38; idem, "Chronology," *EncBib* 4.278–79 [Hebrew]; William Hamilton Barnes, *Studies in the Chronology of the Divided Monarchy of Israel* (HSM 48; Atlanta: Scholars Press, 1991) 154. Barnes is not explicit in designating the beginning of the regnal year, but does acknowledge that he follows the system of Tadmor, see pp. 114–16, 158 note r.
- Tishri 727—Elul 699 B.C.E., dating the fall of Samaria to late 722/early 721. See John H. Hayes and Paul K. Hooker, *A New Chronology for the Kings of Israel and Judah and Its Implications for Biblical History and Literature* (Atlanta: John Knox, 1988) 66–80.
- Nisan 725—Adar 697 B.C.E., dating the fall of Samaria to 720. See Gershon Galil, *Chronology of the Kings of Israel and Judah* (SHCANE 9; Leiden: E.J. Brill, 1996) 83–107. The results of this study, independently obtained, support his reconstruction.
- Nisan 725/4—Adar 697/6, dating the fall of Samaria to 721. See Joachim Begrich, *Die Chronologie der Könige von Israel und Juda und die Quellen des Rahmens der Königsbücher* (BHT 3; Tübingen: J.C.B. Mohr, 1929) 155–60.
- 724 B.C.E., dating the fall of Samaria to late 719/early 718. See M. Christine Tetley, *The Reconstructed Chronology of the Divided Kingdom* (Winona Lake, Ind.: Eisenbrauns, 2005) 162–64, 183–84. Tetley does not adhere to a Nisan- or Tishri-based regnal calendar, but instead reckons a king's first year of reign from his accession, see p. 118.
For earlier literature, consult Francolino J. Gonçalves, *L'expédition de Sennachérib en Palestine dans la littérature hébraïque ancienne* (Études bibliques, New Series 7; Paris: Librairie Lecoffre, 1986) 52–54.

[3] Those favoring this chronology, which dates Hezekiah's reign to 716/15–687/86, include: Edwin R. Thiele, "The Chronology of the Kings of Judah and Israel," *JNES* 3/3 (1944) 164; William F. Albright, "The Chronology of the Divided Monarchy of Israel," *BASOR* 100 (1945) 22; Nadav Na'aman, "Hezekiah and the Kings of Assyria," *TA* 21 (1994) 236–39. Na'aman's article is slightly nuanced from an earlier position he advocated ("Historical and Chronological Notes on the Kingdoms of Israel and Judah in the Eighth Century B.C.," *VT* 36/1 [1986] 83–92) whereby Hezekiah served as co-regent beginning in 728/27, but did not begin his sole reign until 715/14. As before, see Gonçalves, *L'expédition de Sennachérib*, 54–58, for additional bibliography.

It has long been observed that these two sets of biblical synchronisms cannot both be accurate, and those exegetes who favor one system of notices are compelled to invalidate the competing data.[4] Laudable attempts have been made to reconcile these opposing chronologies, but without broad acceptance.[5] This study contends that there is no basis for chronological reconstruction which relies upon the fourteenth year of Hezekiah in 2 Kgs 18:13. While the tendentious nature of this synchronism will be properly discussed in a later chapter, it will suffice here to note that it places the accession of Hezekiah after the fall of Samaria. Those scholars who advocate a late dating for the reign of Hezekiah must not only dismiss the synchronisms in 2 Kgs 18:9–10, but must also disregard the import of the immediate passage as a whole, which maintains that Hezekiah was still king during the final siege of the northern kingdom's capital city.[6]

---

[4] Reference, for example, the explanations in Yohanan Aharoni, "The Chronology of the Kings of Israel and Judah," *Tarbiz* 21 (1950) 97 [Hebrew]; Harold H. Rowley, "Hezekiah's Reform and Rebellion," *BJRL* 44/2 (1962) 410–13; Tetley, *Reconstructed Chronology of the Divided Kingdom*, 154–55 nn. 10–11.

[5] Both Julius Lewy, "Sanherib und Hizkia," *OLZ* 31 (1928) 158–59, and Allan K. Jenkins, "Hezekiah's Fourteenth Year: A New Interpretation of 2 Kings xviii 13–xix 37," *VT* 26/3 (1976) 284–98, argued for retaining the fourteenth year in 2 Kgs 18:13 by suggesting that it originally referred to Sargon's Palestinian campaign of 714–712, but was later associated with Sennacherib by a Deuteronomistic editor. This mediating position is discussed further in Gonçalves, *L'expédition de Sennachérib*, 58–60.

The fourteenth year is often emended to twenty-four under the justification of textual corruption, see James A. Montgomery, *A Critical and Exegetical Commentary on the Books of Kings* (ICC; New York: Charles Scribner's Sons, 1951) 480–518 (esp. 513–18); Aharoni, "The Chronology of the Kings of Israel and Judah," 96–97, and bibliography at M. Christine Tetley, "The Date of Samaria's Fall as a Reason for Rejecting the Hypothesis of Two Conquests," *CBQ* 64/1 (2002) 65 n. 28.

The extension of fifteen years of life granted to Hezekiah by the Lord in 2 Kgs 20:6 has prompted several scholars to suggest that the fourteenth year originally belonged in the story of the king's illness in 2 Kgs 20:1–11, but was secondarily imported into its current location. For proponents of this alternative, which has several variants, see the bibliography at Na'aman, "Historical and Chronological Notes on the Kingdoms of Israel and Judah," 84 n. 40. A more extreme position advanced by Max Vogelstein, *Biblical Chronology* (Cincinnati: Hebrew Union College, 1944) 2–6, is that a new era of calendar reckoning was established during the reign of Hezekiah, which commenced with his reform dated to 714/713 B.C.E. There is no express evidence for either view.

[6] See further Galil, *Chronology of the Kings of Israel and Judah*, 100–101, who notes no less than seven chronological data violated by placing Hezekiah's coronation in 715. The possibility of a co-regency has been a popular middle position. Under this proposal, the notice in 2 Kgs 18:13 is accommodated by synchronizing it with Hezekiah's sole reign, whereas the numerical data in vv 1, 9–10 refer to a co-regency with his father Ahaz. Such proponents include Owen C. Whitehouse, *Isaiah I–XXXIX* (New Century Bible; New York: Oxford University Press, 1905) 23; George W. Wade, *The Book of the Prophet Isaiah* (London: Methuen & Co., 1911) xl–xlii; Siegfried H. Horn, "The Chronology of King Hezekiah's Reign," *AUSS* 2 (1964) 40–52; Na'aman, "Historical and Chronological Notes on the Kingdoms of

While it is to be expected that certain synchronisms within the biblical record may be taken as suspect, to discount the historical value of the broader narrative by crediting such a crucial event to the wrong Judean ruler would be a grave methodological error.[7] The recording of such a momentous episode in the history of the divided kingdom should, at the very least, be trusted in its attribution to the reigning Judean king at the time.

Having taken a position as to the more reliable set of synchronisms in the biblical record with regard to Hezekiah, it does not necessarily follow that 2 Kgs 18:9–10 is to be blindly trusted. As with any chronological data, their value must be proven, not assumed. The approach taken here will be to ascertain the reliability of these synchronisms by triangulating the reign of Hezekiah via two independently datable events: the fall of Samaria and the fall of Jerusalem.

1.1.2. *The Date of the Fall of Samaria*

In order to determine the correct date for the conquest of the northern kingdom's capital, it is necessary to assess which Assyrian ruler was the

---

Israel and Judah," 84–85, 89; Leslie McFall, "Did Thiele Overlook Hezekiah's Coregency?" *BibSac* 146 (1989) 393–404.

Yet such a suggestion is baseless. Under at least some of these reconstructions, the duration of 29 years credited to Hezekiah is only meant to apply to his time as sole regent, in stark contrast to the many preceding examples in which the formula "he ruled as king for X years" records the cumulative years of a monarch's reign (i.e. co-regent plus sole regent). With his total throne tenure only partially provided under this scenario, the reader is left to infer how long Hezekiah actually held the Judean throne. The synchronism "in the Nth year," moreover, would have no consistent sense, as the formula must refer within the span of a few verses both to his co-regency (2 Kgs 18:9–10) and sole reign (2 Kgs 18:13). The reign of Uzziah is a pellucid case of a monarch who was in fact a co-regent multiple times, and thus his length of rule given as 52 years in 2 Kgs 15:2 cannot refer exclusively to his span as sole regent.

The synchronisms with the northern kingdom suggest that Hezekiah was co-regent with Ahaz for only two or three years, a duration insufficient to accommodate the incompatible dates in 2 Kgs 18. Hezekiah became king in the third year of Hoshea (2 Kgs 18:1). This was the 14th year of Ahaz, who was in his 12th year in the first year of Hoshea (2 Kgs 17:1). The first three regnal years of Hezekiah are thus roughly equivalent to years 14–16 of Ahaz, who reigned for a total of sixteen years (2 Kgs 16:2). In the end, the synchronism of 2 Kgs 18:13 cannot be justified via appeal to co-regency.

[7] As noted originally by Rowley, "Hezekiah's Reform and Rebellion," 411 n. 2, and seconded by Aharoni, "Chronology of the Kings of Israel and Judah," 96–97; Barnes, *Studies in the Chronology of the Divided Monarchy of Israel*, 83–84.

rightful conqueror of the city.[8] Very little is known about the reign of Shalmaneser V, who ascended to the throne after the death of Tiglath-pileser III (744–727 B.C.E.). Despite the paucity of information regarding his actual reign, the chronology of the Assyrian kings is well established thanks to multiple historical sources. Most relevant are the royal annals, which served as commemorative texts of the king's achievements and were periodically revised to accentuate or de-emphasize a particular aspect of his rule.[9] Secondly, the *limmu*-chronicle is a list of eponyms—imperial officials who gave their names to each year of the Assyrian calendar.[10] These concise entries enable verification of the chronology of recorded events, and provide an important corrective to the triumphal rhetoric of the royal inscriptions.[11]

---

[8] A summary of the various dates offered for this military victory:

– 723 B.C.E. See A. T. E. Olmstead, *History of Assyria* (New York: C. Scribner's Sons, 1923) 205; Edwin R. Thiele, *The Mysterious Numbers of the Hebrew Kings* (new rev. ed.; Grand Rapids: Zondervan 1983) 163–72; Bob Becking, *The Fall of Samaria: An Historical and Archaeological Study* (SHANE 2; Leiden: E.J. Brill, 1992) 53–55.

– late 722/early 721 B.C.E. Mordechai Cogan and Hayim Tadmor, *II Kings* (AYB 11; New York: Doubleday, 1988) 195–201; Hayes and Hooker, *New Chronology for the Kings of Israel and Judah*, 59–70; John H. Hayes and Jeffrey K. Kuan, "The Final Years of Samaria (730–720 BC)," *Bib* 72/2 (1991) 153–81, in which the biblical account is coordinated with the third of four submissions of Samaria; Barnes, *Studies in the Chronology of the Divided Monarchy of Israel*, 151–58; K. Lawson Younger Jr., "The Fall of Samaria in Light of Recent Research," *CBQ* 61/3 (1999) 461–82, who expressly dates the fall of the city to 722 B.C.E.

– 720 B.C.E. See Antti Laato, "New Viewpoints on the Chronology of the Kings of Juda and Israel," *ZAW* 98 (1986) 216–19; Nadav Na'aman, "The Historical Background to the Conquest of Samaria (720 BC)," *Bib* 71/2 (1990) 206–25; Gershon Galil, "The Last Years of the Kingdom of Israel and the Fall of Samaria," *CBQ* 57 (1995) 52–65. This is the date advocated by this study.

– 719 B.C.E. See Tetley, *Reconstructed Chronology of the Divided Kingdom*, 153–57.

[9] Each section of the annals is typically numbered by the *palû* of the king's reign, an Akkadian term meaning "term of office" and derived from Sumerian BALA. While it is known from the opening and closing sections of royal inscriptions and letters to refer to the entire reign of a king, it is more commonly used to indicate a single year of rule. For our purposes, we may consider it identical to a regnal year. For a detailed examination, see Hayim Tadmor, "The Campaigns of Sargon II of Assur: A Chronological-Historical Study," *JCS* 12 (1958) 26–32.

[10] For more information on the Assyrian eponym lists, see the introduction in Alan R. Millard, *The Eponyms of the Assyrian Empire 910–612 BC* (SAAS 2; Helsinki: Neo-Assyrian Text Corpus Project, 1994) 4–14.

[11] See Amélie Kuhrt, *The Ancient Near East c. 3000–330 BC* (2 vols.; London: Routledge, 1995) 2.473–78, who notes that among the historical sources should be included the inscriptions used as part of the architectural features of royal palaces. Additional evidence for events in the West during Shalmaneser V's reign may be found in Josephus, *Antiquities of the Jews*, 9.283–87, a narrative ultimately derived from Tyrian annals.

In addition to these Assyrian sources, the Babylonian Chronicle presents a year-by-year account—between the reigns of the Babylonian kings Nabu-naṣir (747–734 B.C.E.) and Šamaš-šum-ukīn (668–648 B.C.E.)—of political events as they affected the region of Babylonia. The most recent version of this text was copied in the 22nd year of the Persian king Darius (500 B.C.E.), but is considered to be a trustworthy account of facts and events from the years 744 to 668. The reign of Shalmaneser V is preserved in column 1, lines 27–32.[12] Based on this summary and the coterminous account in the Assyrian eponym list, the reign of Shalmaneser V has been reliably dated from Nisan 726–Adar 721.[13] He ascended to the throne in 25 Tebet 727, and died in Tebet 722 before completing his fifth regnal year.

The Babylonian Chronicle states succinctly of Shalmaneser: ^{uru}*Šá-ma-ra-ʾ-in iḫ-te-pi*. An issue of contention is the precise meaning of the verb *hepû*.[14] Those who assert that the notice is indeed crediting Shalmaneser

---

[12] Chronicle 1, as provided in A. Kirk Grayson, *Assyrian and Babylonian Chronicles* (TCS 5; Locust Valley, NY: J. J. Augustin, 1975) 73:

(27)   On the 25th day of the month Tebet, Shalmaneser (V) ascended the throne in Aššur
(28)   <and Akkad>. He ruined Samaria (^{uru}*Šá-ma-ra-ʾ-in iḫ-te-pi*).

(29)   Year 5: Shalmaneser died in the month of Tebet.
(30)   Shalmaneser ruled over Aššur and Akkad for five years.
(31)   On the 12th day of the month of Tebet, Sargon (II) ascended the throne in Aššur.
(32)   In the month of Nisan Marduk-apla-iddina (Merodach-baladan) ascended the throne in Babylon.

The document is arranged in a chronological order, and transverse lines are used to delineate individual units. Naʾaman, "Historical Background to the Conquest of Samaria," 210–11, is among those who feels that each unit represents a single year within the chronicle, and hence the ravaging of Samaria should be dated to Shalmaneser's accession year, 727 B.C.E. Becking, *Fall of Samaria*, 24, on the other hand, disagrees on the grounds that the traditional formula MU x, "in the xth year . . ." is not used to introduce the comment on Samaria, and was likely an "undated note" found in the Babylonian sources. I concur that an exact date cannot be concluded on the basis of these lines.

[13] Millard, *Eponyms of the Assyrian Empire*, 45–46 (Eng. p. 59).

[14] There are several factors within this short text which relate to the fall of Samaria, but these issues have been dealt with elsewhere and are not central to this study. Galil, *Chronology of the Kings of Israel and Judah*, 84–85, is one of the few scholars to split hairs on whether the word "Samaria" in line 28 refers to the city itself or to the entire northern kingdom, but to argue against the plain meaning of the determinative URU, "city" is to create problems which do not exist. On philological grounds, Hugo Winckler, *Die Keilinschriften und das Alte Testament* (3rd ed.; Berlin: Reuther & Reichard, 1903) 62–63, has claimed that the spelling of this city with a 'š' rules out its identification as Samaria, since Neo-Assyrian texts write the name with an 's'. Tadmor, "Campaigns of Sargon II," 39–40, has rebuffed this suggestion by noting that our chronicle is a Babylonian text rather than an Assyrian one. In Babylonian inscriptions, the Hebrew letter שׁ is indeed rendered

with an actual capture of the city have drawn their conclusions from parallels in royal inscriptions.[15] Yet these texts say nothing about actual victory, nor is there linguistic support for defining *hepû* as anything more than "to wreck, demolish, ruin" with respect to cities.[16] A more sound methodological approach is to perform analysis of the verb's meaning within the selfsame text before resorting to parallels elsewhere, since the deciding factor in interpreting a word should be its usage within the same corpus, if possible. The results of such an investigation show that *hepû* in the Babylonian Chronicle describes the mere plundering and ruination of cities, while their capture is indicated by verbs such as *ṣabātu* ("to seize"), *erēbu* ("to enter") and *kašādu* ("to reach, conquer").[17] In the end, the verb *hepû* does not yield convincing, let alone conclusive, evidence that this Assyrian king was the true conqueror of Samaria.[18]

By contrast, Sargon II asserts his claim to the conquest of Samaria in no fewer than eight different inscriptions.[19] A typical example may be seen

---

with the letter 'š'. The reading of the city's name here in line 28 as Šamara'in would appear to be the Babylonian rendering of the Aramaic שָׁמְרָיִן, which is attested in Ezra 4:10. For the orthography of Samaria in Neo-Assyrian texts, see Simo Parpola, *Neo-Assyrian Toponyms* (AOAT 6; Kevelaer: Butzon & Bercker, 1970) 302–303.

[15] As undertaken by Becking, *Fall of Samaria*, 24–25.

[16] As Becking himself admits: "From the parallels in the royal inscriptions it becomes clear that it [*hepû*] denotes the ruination of cities and/or countries and that it does not refer to a Pyrrhic victory" (*Fall of Samaria*, 25). Moreover, the examples brought by Becking do not support his conclusion. Instead, they are used to counter Na'aman's claim ("Historical Background to the Conquest of Samaria," 211) that *hepû* does not refer to the destruction of city walls.

The accepted definitions of Assyrian words are given in *CAD* and *AHw*. The verb *hepû* is defined generally in *CAD* Ḫ, 6.170–74 as "to break." *AHw* 1.340–41 concurs, with its definition of "zerschlagen." Among the typical examples which *CAD* cites regarding its use with cities is Sennacherib's statement *ištu* URU GN *aḫ-pu-ú*, "after I demolished Babylon" (OIP 2 137 = KAH 2 122:36).

[17] Na'aman, "Historical Background to the Conquest of Samaria," 211. For the meanings of these Akkadian words, consult the following: *ṣabātu* (*CAD* Ṣ, 16.5–41; *AHw* 3.1066–71); *erēbu* (*CAD* E, 4.259–73; *AHw* 1.234–37); *kašādu* (*CAD* K, 8.271–84; *AHw* 1.459–61).

[18] Given the weight it deserves, we may safely conclude that the Babylonian Chronicle corroborates the biblical account of Shalmaneser initiating a military campaign into the region and making Samaria a vassal state. The apocryphal book of Tobit credits Shalmaneser V with exiling the population of the Upper Galilee to Nineveh (Tob 1:1–2). As noted by Cogan and Tadmor, *II Kings*, 197 n. 6, the very fact that Sargon II is not mentioned in the chronology of the Assyrian kings in Tob 1:15 shows that the account is most likely influenced from the notice in 2 Kgs 17:6, and therefore has no independent historical value.

[19] The most recent editions of these inscriptions, updated from Younger, "Fall of Samaria in Light of Recent Research," 468 n. 31, are:

1. The Aššur Charter. Text: H. W. F. Saggs, "Historical Texts and Fragments of Sargon II of Assyria. 1: The 'Aššur Charter,'" *Iraq* 37/1 (1975) 11–20, pl. ix; trans. *ARAB* 2 §§133–35; *TPOA* 106–107; *TUAT* 1/4, 387; *COS* 2.295; Mordechai Cogan, *The Raging Torrent: Historical*

in what is known as the Great Summary Inscription, or *Prunkinschrift*, a text excavated at Khorsabad which provides details of the Assyrian ruler's military activities:

> I besieged and conquered Samaria (ᵘʳᵘ*Sa-me-ri-na al-me ak-šud*).
> I took as booty 27,290 people who lived there.
> I gathered 50 chariots from them,
> And I taught the rest (of the deportees) their skills.
> I set my governor over them, and
> I imposed upon them the (same) tribute as the previous king (Shalmaneser).

Unlike the Babylonian Chronicle surveyed previously, Sargon II actually asserts himself to be the conqueror of the city of Samaria (ᵘʳᵘ*Samerina . . . akšud*) and to have carried off its inhabitants. This boast is made several times throughout his inscriptions, lending weight to his claim. Unfortunately, the Great Summary Inscription is arranged according to the geographical proximity of the campaigns rather than their true chronological order, and hence cannot serve as a tool for dating his avowal to have overthrown the city.[20]

The annals state that the capital of Israel was conquered in Sargon's accession year, or 721 B.C.E.[21] Yet this assertion is not without problems,

---

Inscriptions from Assyria and Babylonia Relating to Ancient Israel (Jerusalem: Carta, 2008) 96–97.

2. The Khorsabad Annals. Text: Andreas Fuchs, *Die Inschriften Sargons II. aus Khorsabad* (Göttingen: Cuvillier, 1994) 82–188, esp. 87–89; trans. *ARAB* 2 §4; *ANET* 284; *TPOA* 108; *TUAT* 1/4, 379; *COS* 2.293–94; Cogan, *Raging Torrent*, 93–96.

3. The Great Summary Inscription (*Prunkinschrift*). Text: Fuchs, *Inschriften Sargons II*, 196–98; trans. *ARAB* 2 §55; *ANET* 284–86; *TPOA* 107–109; *TUAT* 1/4, 383–85; *COS* 2.296–97; Cogan, *Raging Torrent*, 82–89.

4. The Nimrud Prism, D and E. Text: C. J. Gadd, "Inscribed Prisms of Sargon II from Nimrud," *Iraq* 16 (1954) 179–82, pls. xlv, xlvi; trans. *TPOA* 109–110; *TUAT* 1/4, 382; *COS* 2.295–96; Cogan, *Raging Torrent*, 89–93.

5. The Cylinder Inscription. Text: Fuchs, *Inschriften Sargons II*, 34 lines 19–20; trans. *ARAB* 2 §§116–18; *TPOA* 112–13; *TUAT* 1/4, 386; *COS* 2.298; Cogan, *Raging Torrent*, 97–98.

6. The Small Summary Inscription (*Kleine Prunkinschrift*). Text: Fuchs, *Inschriften Sargons II*, 76; trans. *ARAB* 2 §80; *ANET* 285; *TUAT* 1/4, 385; *COS* 2.297.

7. The Palace Door (plaster work on the door) no. 4. Text: Fuchs, *Inschriften Sargons II*, 261; trans. *ARAB* 2 §99; *ANET* 284; *TUAT* 1/4, 386; Becking, *Fall of Samaria*, 27; *COS* 2.298.

8. The Bull Inscription. Text: Fuchs, *Inschriften Sargons II*, 63; trans. *ARAB* 2 §92.

[20] See A. T. E. Olmstead, *Assyrian Historiography: A Source Study* (Columbia, Mo.: University of Missouri, 1916) 36–42, esp. 40.

[21] There are three primary sources for the chronology of Sargon's reign. The first is the Eponym Chronicle, which is the sequentially arranged *limmu*-list mentioned in the

as Sargon closes the list of accolades in his first *palû* with the opening of the sealed harbor of Egypt.[22] The Assyrian king's initial contact with Egypt did not occur until his second regnal year, in which he defeated Sib'u "the *tartānu* of Egypt" and destroyed the city of Rafiah on the Egyptian border.[23] From this it has been concluded that the Khorsabad annals were similarly organized in a geographical rather than chronological sequence, and are hence unreliable for establishing dates. Historical reconstruction of the early years of Sargon's reign point to his completing the conquest of Samaria in late 720 B.C.E. during his second *palû*, having been forced to spend his initial year of rule securing his regime.[24]

In summary, the Assyrian royal inscriptions attribute the conquest of Samaria exclusively to Sargon II, which may be securely dated to 720 B.C.E. The most compelling Mesopotamian source which speaks to Shalmaneser's military involvement at Samaria is the Babylonian Chronicle, and its interpretation as a true conquest is inconclusive. If the foregoing analysis is accepted at face value, then Shalmaneser ravaged the city at some point during his reign.[25] The northern kingdom retained its vassal

---

previous section. Second is the Nineveh Prism, organized in annalistic form with each section numbered by the *palû* of the king's reign. Finally, the Khorsabad annals are the royal inscriptions found at Sargon's palace at Dur-Šarrukin. As often occurs in cases where crucial information is desired, these first two sources do not preserve events at the beginning of Sargon's reign. Even the Khorsabad annals are fragmentary here (specifically, in hall 2, plate 2, lines 11–17), with only four partial lines preserved out of the original seven. These lines are usually restored in light of the Great Summary Inscription, seen above, and another non-chronological text known as the Nimrud Prism.

[22] See lines 46–48 of the Nimrud Prism, from which the parallel content in the annals was restored. For Tadmor's reasoning that Sargon's scribes set the fall of Samaria in his accession year for literary-ideological reasons, see "Campaigns of Sargon II," 30–32.

[23] Lines 53–57 of the annals in A. G. Lie, *The Inscriptions of Sargon II, King of Assyria. Part 1: The Annals* (Paris: Librairie orientaliste Paul Geuthner, 1929) 8–9; Fuchs, *Inschriften Sargons II*, 90.

[24] As confirmed in lines 16–28 of the non-historiographical Aššur Charter, which expressly mentions a campaign undertaken to quell the rebellious Arpad and Samaria "in the second year of my reign." See also Tadmor, "Campaigns of Sargon II," 33–39.

[25] In agreement with the biblical notices of 2 Kgs 17:1–6; 18:9–12. The assumption that Shalmaneser V must be the conqueror in these texts due to the lack of explicit identification of "the king of Assyria" in 2 Kgs 17:6; 18:11 has been widely noted. The passage is typically treated as an exercise in historical telescoping, but in fact does not contradict the results obtained here. An analysis of the biblical accounts has been omitted because they are of limited value for chronological reconstruction beyond the synchronisms they contain. For discussion with older bibliography, see Cogan and Tadmor, *II Kings*, 195–201, 214–22; Becking, *Fall of Samaria*, 47–60; Younger, "Fall of Samaria in Light of Recent Research," 477–82.

status, however, only becoming an Assyrian province after the conquest overwhelmingly credited to Sargon II.[26]

1.1.3. *The Date of the Fall of Jerusalem*

The second date which factors into triangulating the regnal years of Hezekiah is that of the final Babylonian conquest of Jerusalem. This date has been variously championed as 586 or 587 B.C.E., and is another pivotal year in Israelite chronology which should be properly assessed.[27] Simply put, the erroneous date of 586 B.C.E. stems from the biblical dating of the breaking down of the walls of Jerusalem and the exile of its populace "on the seventh day of the fifth month, which was the nineteenth year of king Nebuchadrezzar."[28] According to Babylonian records, this monarch took the throne in September of 605, which makes Nisan 604–Adar 603 his first regnal year.[29] The nineteenth year of Nebuchadrezzar is thus Nisan 586–Adar 585, with the conquest of Jerusalem presumably dated to Av (July/August) of 586 B.C.E.

---

[26] It should be noted that many of the scholars who favor dating the fall of Samaria to 722 B.C.E. actually take a mediating position which permits them to credit Shalmaneser V with conquering the city, while at the same time acknowledging the conflicting evidence in Sargon's annals. Thus, for example, Mordechai Cogan, "Into Exile: From the Assyrian Conquest of Israel to the Fall of Babylon," in idem (ed.), *The Oxford History of the Biblical World* (New York: Oxford University Press, 1998) 244, claims: "After several encounters and a lengthy siege, Shalmaneser V (727–722) brought Samaria to its knees in the winter of 722. Only in 720, however, was the city's rebellious military and political leadership finally subdued by Sargon II (722–705)." This, in effect, provides independent confirmation of the chronology proposed here, in that the historical claim of Sargon to the capture of the city remains unassailable.

[27] Numerous scholars have weighed in on the matter, but for recent advocates of 586 B.C.E., see Gershon Galil, "The Babylonian Calendar and the Chronology of the Last Kings of Judah," *Bib* 72 (1991) 368–70 and bibliography there. For those favoring 587 B.C.E., reference Henri Cazelles, "587 ou 586?" in C. L. Meyers and M. O'Connor (eds.), *The Word of the Lord Shall Go Forth: Essays in Honor of David Noel Freedman in Celebration of His Sixtieth Birthday* (Winona Lake, Ind.; Eisenbrauns, 1983) 427–35. Jeremy Hughes, *Secrets of the Times: Myth and History in Biblical Chronology* (JSOTSup 66; Sheffield: Sheffield Academic Press, 1990) 229–32, lists eleven scholars who prefer the first date and eleven who prefer the second. Rodger C. Young, "When Did Jerusalem Fall?" *JETS* 47/1 (2004) 21–38, adds to the 587 camp Donald Wiseman and Kenneth Kitchen.

[28] 2 Kgs 25:8–11. The account is closely paralleled by Jer 52:12–15.

[29] Nebuchadrezzar acceded to the throne on the first of Elul, 605, cf. Grayson, *Assyrian and Babylonian Chronicles*, 99–100; D. J. Wiseman, *Chronicles of Chaldaean Kings (626–556 B.C.) in the British Museum* (London: Trustees of the British Museum, 1961) 68–69. Babylonian records thus date Nebuchadrezzar's 43-year reign from Nisan 604–Adar 561 B.C.E. See also Richard A. Parker and Waldo H. Dubberstein, *Babylonian Chronology: 626 B.C.–A.D. 75* (Providence: Brown University Press, 1956) 12.

This seemingly ironclad reconstruction, however, is based on Mesopotamian records which have been synchronized with the biblical text.
Taking the book of Kings on its own terms yields a slightly different chronology. The most secure way to begin such a reconstruction is to select an
absolute date which can be used as an anchor. For the later period of the
Judean monarchy, the best choice is the date of the battle of Carchemish,
which occurred in the 21st year of Nabopolassar, or 605 B.C.E.[30] According
to Jer 46:2, this fateful conflict between Pharaoh Neco II of Egypt and king
Nebuchadrezzar II of Babylon occurred "in the fourth year of Jehoiakim
the son of Josiah, king of Judah."[31] The fourth year of Jehoiakim is further
synchronized in Jer 25:1 with הַשָּׁנָה הָרִאשֹׁנִית of Nebuchadrezzar, which
according to these synchronisms must have been 605 B.C.E.[32] Rather than
counting the Babylonian monarch's reign from his first full year of rule
(Nisan 604–Adar 603), then, the book of Jeremiah anchors its dates to his
accession year.[33] This is not a discrepancy, but a perfectly valid alternative
for marking this king's reign. The significance of honoring this difference
will become clear in the following examples.[34]

2 Kgs 24:12 states that Jehoiachin was taken captive by Nebuchadrezzar
"the king of Babylon" in the eighth year of his reign (בִּשְׁנַת שְׁמֹנֶה לְמָלְכוֹ).

---

[30] Nabopolassar's accession occurred in the summer of 626 B.C.E. He reigned 21 years
(Nisan 625–Adar 604 B.C.E.), and died on the 8th day of Av, 605, cf. Grayson, *Assyrian and
Babylonian Chronicles*, 99, lines 1–5; Wiseman, *Chronicles of Chaldaean Kings*, 68–69. See
also Wiseman's introductory comments on the battle of Carchemish, 23–32.

[31] The accuracy of this synchronism remains largely unchallenged, although a notable detractor is Julius Lewy, *Forschungen zur alten Geschichte Vorderasiens* (MVAG 29/2;
Leipzig: J. C. Hinrichs, 1925) 28–37.

[32] This synchronism is lacking in LXX, but its originality is discussed and defended
in Jack R. Lundbom, *Jeremiah 21–36* (AYB 21B; New York: Doubleday, 2004) 242. Such an
important date in the ancient world, in which Nebuchadrezzar defeated the Egyptians at
Carchemish, was likely to be accurately recorded in any event.

[33] As affirmed by Hayim Tadmor, "Chronology of the Last Kings of Judah," *JNES* 15/4
(1956) 226–27. Hebrew הַשָּׁנָה הָרִאשֹׁנִית is a *hapax legomenon* whose precise meaning is
questioned, as "first year" could equally apply to a king's accession year or else to his first
full year of reign. For this reason, Tadmor claims it is inclusive of both, spanning "the
whole period from the accession of Nebuchadnezzar until the beginning of his second
regnal year" (p. 228 n. 11). Such an expansive position is not advocated in this study. Rather
than make unnecessary assumptions as to the meaning of this phrase, the approach taken
here is to assess its validity via both (a) corroboration with Mesopotamian records, and
(b) sustained accuracy within the biblical text.

[34] The subsequent examples pertain to the book of Kings, but the Deuteronomistic
influence within these chapters of Jeremiah is not disputed. Such expressions as עֲבָדָיו
הַנְּבִאִים "his servants the prophets" in Jer 25:4 are characteristic of Kings, cf. 2 Kgs 9:7;
17:13, 23; 21:10; 24:2.

The eighth year of Nebuchadrezzar, by biblical reckoning, would be Nisan 598–Adar 597, which may be compared with the following entry in the Babylonian Chronicles:

> Year 7, month Kislimu (Nov.–Dec.): The king of Akkad (Nebuchadnezzar) moved his army into Hatti land (Syria-Palestine), laid siege to the city of Judah, and the king took the city on the second day of the month Addaru (16 March 597). He appointed in it a (new) king of his liking, took heavy booty from it and brought it to Babylon.[35]

Because the Bible begins counting Nebuchadrezzar's official years of reign one year prior to the Mesopotamian records, the ruler's eighth year as claimed in the book of Kings and his seventh year as recorded in the Babylonian Chronicles are equivalent.[36]

This reveals an important void left in the chronology which adheres to 586 B.C.E. as the proposed date for the fall of Jerusalem. Since Jehoiachin was taken captive in Adar 597, Nebuchadrezzar did not allow the pending coronation of this rebellious leader. Zedekiah's reign is dated Nisan 596–Adar 585 under this reconstruction, meaning for those who adhere to this chronology that the year Nisan 597–Adar 596 is not attributed to any Judean king.[37] This is a necessary consequence of needing to

---

[35] BM 21946, as listed in *ANET*, 564; Grayson, *Assyrian and Babylonian Chronicles*, 102. Cf. Parker and Dubberstein, *Babylonian Chronology*, 27ff; Wiseman, *Chronicles of Chaldaean Kings*, 32–37; *TPOA* 138–41; *TUAT* 1/4, 402–404; *COS* 1.467–68; Jean-Jacques Glassner, *Mesopotamian Chronicles* (SBLWAW 19; Atlanta: Scholars Press, 2004) 226–31; Cogan, *Raging Torrent*, 201–10.

[36] Scholars who have not accounted for this distinction are impelled to reconcile the numerical variance via contrived explanation. Cogan and Tadmor, *II Kings*, 311, for instance, suggest that "It was some time later, as much as several months later, that the exiles actually left for Babylon." Yet 2 Kgs 24:12 states that Jehoiachin and his entire family surrendered to Nebuchadrezzar in his 8th regnal year, which has no connection to the departure of exiles for Babylon. The defeated king certainly did not give himself up months after the capture of the city, which would be required to support their position. They further suggest, following David Noel Freedman, "The Babylonian Chronicle," *BA* 19/3 (1956) 56, that Nebuchadrezzar left soon after the victory in order be in the capital for the New Year's celebration on the first of Nisan. As Jehoiachin was taken back to Babylon by Nebuchadrezzar himself (2 Kgs 24:15), the Judean monarch's exile would have begun at the end of the Babylonian ruler's seventh regnal year, by their own reckoning, directly contradicting their theory.

[37] Tadmor, "Chronology of the Last Kings of Judah," 230, labels 597 B.C.E. the "acc. year of Zedekiah." Under the reconstruction advocated in this study, Zedekiah was appointed by Nebuchadrezzar soon after Jehoiachin surrendered to the Babylonians, hence Nisan 598–Adar 597 represents his accession year, and Nisan 597–Adar 586 his first full regnal year. This is the time recorded in 2 Chr 36:10 as being "at the turn of the year" (לִתְשׁוּבַת הַשָּׁנָה). Other scholars would date Zedekiah's reign as Tishri 597–Elul 586, but for my preference of the Nisan-based new year for kings in Judah, see below.

pad an extra year into the timeline in order to account for the Bible's incremental variance from Mesopotamian reckoning with regard to Nebuchadrezzar's reign.

The correct date of 587 B.C.E. for the Babylonian conquest of Jerusalem may be further substantiated by examination of the end of the exile of Jehoiachin. His captivity began in the year in which he was taken prisoner, Nisan 598–Adar 597. According to 2 Kgs 25:27, Jehoiachin was released from prison "in the thirty-seventh year of the exile...in the year Evil-Merodach became king of Babylon."[38] The Babylonian monarch's name in Akkadian is Amēl-Marduk ("man of Marduk"), who succeeded his father Nebuchadrezzar in October of 562 B.C.E. and reigned for two years.[39] According to this verse, Jehoiachin was released on 27 Adar of Jehoiachin's 37th year, which by the reckoning employed here was Nisan 562–Adar 561. This was indeed the end of the accession year for Amēl-Marduk, who would not officially "take the hand of Bel" until the following month (Nisan 561). Those adherents to the capture of Jerusalem in 586 B.C.E. are obliged to admit that Jehoiachin's release from prison did not technically occur in his 37th year of exile.[40]

1.1.4. *Regnal Years of the Latter Kings of Judah*

It is thus preferable, in my opinion, to date the fall of Jerusalem to 587 B.C.E. Using this datum in conjunction with the date for the conquest of Samaria ascertained above, the lengths of reign in Kings may be compared to the duration independently attained for the remaining southern state. The reigns for the later Judean kings may be reconstructed as follows:

---

[38] Hebrew שְׁנַת מָלְכוֹ refers to the accession year for kings, synonymous with Akkadian *rēš šarrūti*, cf. *CAD* R, 14.285–86; *AHw* 2.975; Tadmor, "Chronology," 4.267–69 [Hebrew].

[39] Parker and Dubberstein, *Babylonian Chronology*, 12.

[40] Tadmor, "Chronology of the Last Kings of Judah," 230 n. 32: "Actually it was four or two days less than 37 full years, so that the Judean king was released on the eve of the New Year festival, when Amel-Marduk was to be formally enthroned." His dating of Jehoiachin's exile from Nisan 597 not only truncates the duration of the king's captivity from 37 to 36 full years, but also reckons 561 as the accession year of Amēl-Marduk. This conflicts with his own timeline which correctly computes 562 to be the 43rd and final regnal year of Nebuchadrezzar. The rounding in regard to Jehoiachin is not mentioned in his more widely read commentary, see Cogan and Tadmor, *II Kings*, 328–29.

King	Length of Reign	Accession Year	Regnal Years[41]
Hezekiah	29 years (2 Kgs 18:2)	726/early 725	Nisan 725–Adar 696
Manasseh	55 years (2 Kgs 21:1)	697/early 696	Nisan 696–Adar 641
Amon	2 years (2 Kgs 21:19)	642/early 641	Nisan 641–Adar 639
Josiah	31 years (2 Kgs 22:1)	640/early 639	Nisan 639–Adar 608
Jehoahaz	3 months (2 Kgs 23:31)	609 B.C.E.	(none)[42]
Jehoiakim	11 years (2 Kgs 23:36)	609 B.C.E.	Nisan 608–Adar 597
Jehoiachin	3 months (2 Kgs 24:8)	late 598 B.C.E.[43]	(none)
Zedekiah	11 years (2 Kgs 24:18)	early 597 B.C.E.	Nisan 597–Adar 586

[41] A crucial, and perennial, question pertains to the proper starting month of the new year for kings in the latter years of the kingdom of Judah. As it turns out, if one presumes that the three-month reign of Jehoahaz spanned the first of Tishri, then a Tishri-based royal calendar also adheres to the five synchronisms identified by Tadmor, "Chronology of the Last Kings of Judah," 226, for the final years of the kings of Judah:

Hezekiah	Tishri 726–Elul 697	Jehoahaz	Tishri 609–Elul 608
Manasseh	Tishri 697–Elul 642	Jehoiakim	Tishri 608–Elul 597
Amon	Tishri 642–Elul 640	Jehoiachin	(none)
Josiah	Tishri 640–Elul 609	Zedekiah	Tishri 597–Elul 586

Yet there are several reasons why Nisan reckoning should be preferred:
1. The three-month reign of Jehoahaz must be credited whereas the three-month reign of Jehoiachin must be ignored, which is inconsistent use of the data. The fact that the Bible reckons their reigns in terms of months is an indication that neither one was considered to have ruled a full year. Otherwise we would expect the reigns of other kings to be given the same accuracy, e.g.: ten years and seven months. Yet the reigns of other kings are given as full years despite their actual duration of rule.
2. The dates in Ezekiel are Nisan-based, and one must permit that multiple systems were in place in order to explain such a calendrical transition from Tishri to Nisan as early as the fifth year of Jehoiachin (Ezek 1:2). While this is possible, it is a more complicated scenario, and methodologically the simpler solution is always to be preferred.
3. Tishri reckoning permits that the dates for Nebuchadrezzar given in the Bible do not have to be dated from his accession year, but from the actual year of reign. Yet the reference to his eighth year in 2 Kgs 24:12 (equivalent to the seventh year of BM 21946) suggests that accession-year dating is intended, and requires no special pleading such as employed by other scholars noted previously.
4. The appointment of Zedekiah as king has been verified in this study as having occurred "at the turn of the year" (לִתְשׁוּבַת הַשָּׁנָה, 2 Chr 36:10). This idiom unquestionably refers to the spring, cf. 2 Sam 11:1 / 1 Chr 20:1; 1 Kgs 20:22, 26.

[42] Recall that according to accession-year dating, the year of accession is not counted as a year of reign. Since Jehoahaz was forcibly removed from the throne and deported to Egypt by Pharaoh Neco (2 Kgs 23:33), he failed to rule until Nisan of the following year and thus is not officially accorded a year of reign under this system.

[43] As shown in the Babylonian Chronicle, the three-month reign of Jehoiachin (three months and ten days according to 2 Chr 36:9) began in late Marcheshvan 598, ending in Adar 597 prior to the New Year for kings.

There are various synchronisms which serve to corroborate this timetable. Samaria falls in 720 B.C.E. according to this biblical chronology, in complete harmony with the Mesopotamian data assessed separately. The death of Josiah in 609 B.C.E. is another date that is almost universally recognized, and the exile of Jehoiachin occurs in Adar 597 just as claimed in the Babylonian Chronicle.[44] Finally, the 11th and final regnal year of Zedekiah aligns with the conquest of Jerusalem in Ab 587, with no years remaining unattributed to any Judean king.

Methodologically, this is a preferable approach in determining the regnal years of Hezekiah in that two unrelated termini have been selected, each evaluated without reference to the Judean king in question. The regnal formulae have been inserted into this framework only thereafter, not only for Hezekiah, but for all subsequent Judean rulers, and have been shown to conform with absolute precision to this previously ascertained data. This table establishes what no other reconstruction of the later Judean kingdom has heretofore accomplished: a chronology which adheres rigidly to the total lengths of reign given in the book of Kings, filling out with precision the timespan from the fall of the northern kingdom to that of the southern.[45] This reconstruction is in complete accord with both Mesopotamian and biblical data, with no emendation of any synchronisms or need to appeal to co-regencies.[46] Its straightforward

---

[44] Nevertheless, this date for Josiah still finds the occasional detractor. Paul K. Hooker and John H. Hayes, "The Year of Josiah's Death: 609 or 610 BCE?' in J. A. Dearman and M. P. Graham (eds.), *The Land that I Will Show You: Essays on the History and Archaeology of the Ancient Near East in Honour of J. Maxwell Miller* (JSOTSup 343; Sheffield: Sheffield Academic Press, 2001) 96–103, argue that Josiah was killed in 610 B.C.E. On the one hand, the primary text BM 21901 to which they appeal to support their position is inconclusive, as they themselves admit (p. 99). On the other, their reconstruction posits that Judah was without a ruler for almost nine months, and that the year 609 B.C.E. as a result "went unattributed in the Judean monarchical chronology" (p. 103).

The idea that Pharoah Neco II had to make two successive trips from Harran to Judah in order to establish Egyptian rule—the first to depose Jehoahaz II and the second to enthrone Jehoiakim as king—seems highly implausible and represents the kind of padding inherent in divergent chronologies. The uncredited regnal year in 609 lies open to the same criticisms raised in regard to the purported "accession year" of Zedekiah in 597 B.C.E. discussed previously.

[45] From 720 B.C.E. to 587 B.C.E. = 134 years inclusive. Adding in the first five regnal years of Hezekiah (because Samaria fell in his sixth year), we obtain 139 years, the total of the reckoned regnal years provided in the table.

[46] There is prevalent evidence for the recording of co-regencies under the divided kingdom, as discussed by Edwin R. Thiele, "The Question of Coregencies Among the Hebrew Kings," in E. C. Hobbs (ed.), *A Stubborn Faith. Papers on the Old Testament and Related Subjects Presented to Honor William Andrew Irwin* (Dallas: Southern Methodist University Press, 1956) 39–52; idem. "Coregencies and Overlapping Reigns among the Hebrew Kings,"

simplicity at once affirms that the regnal years for king Hezekiah are in all likelihood Nisan 725–Adar 696, while at the same time undergirding the accuracy of the preserved biblical records of the period.

1.2. The Lineage of Hezekiah

1.2.1. *Relationship to Ahaz*

The familial relationships of Hezekiah are known, as they are for all Judean monarchs, via the accession formulae provided in Kings and Chronicles. According to these records, Hezekiah was the son of Ahaz and Abiyah the daughter of Zechariah, and his only named offspring was his successor Manasseh.[47] It is also known that Hezekiah had daughters, who were deported to Nineveh along with servants of the Judean royal court in the aftermath of Sennacherib's third campaign.[48] As the detailed synchronisms for the reigns of Ahaz and Hezekiah raise questions in regard to their genealogical relationship, it behooves us to look more closely at these chronological data.

According to the biblical accounts, Ahaz ascended the throne at 20 years of age, and reigned for 16 years.[49] With the age at his death calculated to be 36, it strains credulity to see his son Hezekiah already aged 25 years at the time of his coronation. Ahaz would have fathered Hezekiah at the tender age of 11, and so various attempts have been made to resolve this numerical crux. Most commentators credit Ahaz with four additional years of co-regency alongside his father Jotham, which would make him closer to 15 years of age at the time Hezekiah was born.[50] Other scholars more or less accept the chronological data in the succession formulae, and

---

JBL 93 (1974) 174–200. The mathematical justification for a co-regency of Hezekiah with Ahaz was given previously. The reality of co-regencies is expressly affirmed in 2 Kgs 15:5, in which Azariah's illness required his son Jotham to assume the throne while his father was still alive.

[47] 2 Kgs 18:1–2; 20:21; 2 Chr 28:27; 29:1; 32:33. Chronicles provides the fuller name of אֲבִיָּה, which is shortened to אֲבִי in Kings. For the history of scholarship, see Richard S. Hess, "Issues in the Study of Personal Names in the Hebrew Bible," *CR:BS* 6 (1998) 169–92.

[48] DUMU.MUNUS.MEŠ-*šú* (*mārātišu*) "and his daughters," Rassam 58. Lines cited from the Rassam Cylinder in this monograph are according to the edition of Eckart Frahm, *Einleitung in die Sanherib-Inschriften* (AfOB 26; Vienna: Institut für Orientalisk der Universität, 1997) 53–55. My source for the edition of the Oriental Institute Prism is that of Daniel David Luckenbill, *The Annals of Sennacherib* (OIP 2; Chicago: University of Chicago, 1924) 34, at line iii 46.

[49] 2 Kgs 16:2; 2 Chr 28:1.

[50] The justification for this co-regency stems from the conflicting durations of Jotham's

take this to mean that Hezekiah was not the son of Ahaz but rather his sibling, both heirs to the throne of their father Jotham.[51]

There are many variables at play in this scenario which plague the chronologist attempting an accurate reconstruction of the reign of Ahaz. Much of these data are open-ended, meaning that an exegete may facilely select one synchronism as an anchor and then adjust all other dates accordingly. As there is no empirical means by which to determine the trustworthiness of the various synchronisms, a wholesale timeline for the entire divided monarchy would be required, aligned with key events in Mesopotamia whenever possible. Such a task is beyond the scope of this treatise, although such chronologies of kings of Israel and Judah have been undertaken on several occasions with mixed results. As my focus is on Hezekiah's genealogy, I shall restrict my purview in an attempt to resolve one singular question: is Hezekiah better seen as the son or brother of Ahaz?

There are indeed precedents in ancient Near Eastern royal accession for a fraternal successor to assume the title of 'son' from his forerunner.[52] Although it was imperative for rulers to have male offspring in order to guarantee the line of succession, it was inevitable that often these sons were too young to rule and to make state decisions at the time of their father's death. The choice was either to surround the youth with counselors who could advise the new king until he came of age, or else to choose a sibling of the former king who had already matured. Because of this eventuality, especially in the age of empires fraught with disease and warfare, it was infrequent to have lengthy cases of continuous succession from father to son. The longest known such example in the Assyrian king list is eleven generations, which makes all the more conspicuous the unbroken string of eighteen generations recorded in the Hebrew Bible from David to Jehoahaz, the son of Josiah.[53] The biblical claim is suspect not only for reasons of numerical incongruence but also owing to the ideological

---

reign, recorded as 16 years (2 Kgs 15:33) or 20 years (2 Kgs 15:30). The former is thus treated as his sole rule, and the latter as his co-regency with Ahaz.

[51] Donald V. Etz, "The Genealogical Relationships of Jehoram and Ahaziah, and of Ahaz and Hezekiah, Kings of Judah," *JSOT* 71 (1996) 50–53.

[52] Shigeo Yamada, "Notes on the Genealogical Data of the Assyrian King List," *Eretz-Israel* 27 (2003) 265*–275*.

[53] A string of continuous succession interrupted by the assignment of Eliakim/Jehoiakim to the Judean throne by Pharaoh Neco II in place of his brother Jehoahaz, cf. 2 Kgs 23:31–34; 2 Chr 36:1–4. The eleven continuous father-son generations in the Assyrian king list span from Aššur-rabi II to Shalmaneser IV, ca. 1010–772 B.C.E.

importance of the Davidic covenant, and for this reason the suggestion of
Hezekiah as a brother of Ahaz must be given serious consideration.[54]

Despite the initial attractiveness of this proposal, the weight of the biblical data does not readily support this interpretation. First of all, there
is little basis for appealing to a four-year co-regency for Ahaz with his
predecessor Jotham. Even if one accepts that the contradictory spans of
reign for Jotham—recorded as sixteen and twenty years, respectively—
are evidence of a four-year co-regency, it is expressly stated that Jotham
acceded to the throne while his own father, Azariah, was stricken with
leprosy.[55] Some, or perhaps all, of that residual four years must then be
credited to the beginning of Jotham's reign rather than to the end, leaving
one to wonder how Ahaz was ever credited with a full four years of con-
current dominion. In any event, the biblical synchronisms taken at face
value evince that Ahaz had a co-regency with Jotham up to twelve years
in duration, and such an extensive overlap in their reigns at once begs the
question as to their genealogical relationship.[56]

The connection between Ahaz and Hezekiah should only be questioned if the chronological data for the former can be demonstrated to
be reliable, but this turns out not to be the case. The age at his coronation is given variously as 20 or 25 years, with the latter as the minority

---

[54] The emphasis of the covenant made with David is exclusively on the father-son relationship, as may be seen in verses such as 2 Sam 7:12–14 (cf. 1 Chr 17:11–13); 1 Kgs 2:4; 3:6;
11:12. The concept is encapsulated in 1 Kgs 15:4, "But for David's sake YHWH his God gave
him a fief in Jerusalem, to raise up his son after him and to establish Jerusalem." The passing of kingship from one generation to the next was the true means of verifying the divine
promise. Progeny was also a sign of blessing (in Genesis alone, cf. Gen 17:16, 20; 22:17; 24:60;
26:4, 24; 28:3, 14; 30:6, 20; 48:9, 16), and so it would be more conducive to the king's reputation to avoid recording that he had no direct heir.

[55] 2 Kgs 15:5.

[56] There are two independent means of verifying this, notwithstanding the confused
chronology of the period. According to the first method, Ahaz began ruling in the 17th year
of Pekah (2 Kgs 16:1), and Hezekiah acceded to the throne in the 3rd year of Hoshea
(2 Kgs 18:1). Years 17–19 of Pekah plus years 1–2 of Hoshea accounts for only five years of
rule—keeping in mind that the northern kingdom utilized nonaccession-year dating and
hence year 20 of Pekah should not be counted—and so Ahaz must have been a co-regent
for some 11 years with Jotham and/or Hezekiah. If one ignores nonaccession-year dating,
one arrives at 12 years.

According to the second method, the first year of Hoshea was both the 20th year of
Jotham (2 Kgs 15:30) and the 12th year of Ahaz (2 Kgs 17:1). Because this was the last year of
Jotham's rule, year 12 of Ahaz's co-regency becomes the first year of his sole regency. Ahaz
was thus co-regent with his predecessor for roughly 12 years, or 11 years before becoming
sole regent.

reading.[57] The majority reading of 20 years is problematic in that this is a round number in the Hebrew Bible.[58] The 16-year length of reign for Ahaz is furthermore identical to that of his predecessor Jotham, a unique circumstance in the chronology of the divided monarchy. It is not feasible numerically that Ahaz, who began reigning in the 17th year of the Israelite king Pekah, could be in his 12th year by the first year of Hoshea.[59] If one wants to muddy the waters further, Hezekiah was 25 years old when he became king and reigned for 29 years, exactly as stated for Amaziah.[60] While the accuracy of Hezekiah's 29 years of reign may be substantiated, there is no empirical way to verify his age when he became king.

If Hezekiah were the brother of Ahaz, one is forced to resort to an ideological explanation for his designation as 'son' in the biblical text. But Ahaz is also said to have had another son by the name of Maaseiah, killed on the battlefield during an incursion into Judah by his northern adversary Pekah.[61] This was part of an anti-Assyrian alliance between Israel and Damascus which was crushed ca. 734–32 B.C.E. by Tiglath-pileser III. Virtually all commentators place this event early in the reign of Ahaz. For him to have had a son old enough to fight and die in the Syro-Ephraimite war is admittedly problematic, yet Maaseiah is a lesser-known, non-royal personage whose designation as son carries no ideological justification. Which is easier to accept, that both Hezekiah and Maaseiah were sons of Jotham later credited to Ahaz, or that Ahaz was already sufficiently mature to have borne sons by the time he came to the throne?

A final matter of import is the fact that not only is Ahaz recognized as the father of Hezekiah, but the name of the queen mother is also provided.[62] This is a pertinent detail which must be seen as having been falsified if Hezekiah is truly the son of Jotham. Moreover, although the acknowledgement of the queen mother is a standard part of the

---

[57] In LXX and Peshitta of 2 Chr 28:1, although 20 years is still maintained in verse 2 Kgs 16:2 of these witnesses.

[58] Cf. 1 Kgs 5:3[4:23]; 5:25[5:11]; 9:10 (Solomon's building); 9:11; 9:14/9:28/10:10 (100/400+20 talents of gold); 2 Kgs 4:42; passim. Some scholars would claim that Pekah's reign of 20 years is corrupt, which would raise the question as to why that value was chosen and preserved.

[59] 2 Kgs 16:1 cannot refer to the sole rule of Ahaz, since Jotham was still on the throne when Hoshea became king (2 Kgs 15:30). Hoshea's first year was the 12th year of Ahaz according to 2 Kgs 17:1, which likewise precludes the notice in v 16:1 (dated a mere three years earlier in northern reckoning) from referring to a co-regency.

[60] 2 Kgs 14:1–2.

[61] 2 Chr 28:5–8.

[62] 2 Kgs 18:2; 2 Chr 29:1.

succession formula in Kings, Ahaz is one of only two kings for whom the mother is not specified.[63] These observations suggest that not only should Hezekiah be rightfully seen as the legitimate offspring of Ahaz, but that Ahaz himself was more likely the brother of Jotham, both sons of Azariah whose lengthy 52-year reign prevented them from taking the throne until they were much older. Their mutual, protracted co-regency has already intimated this possibility, and the relatively short sole reign of Ahaz hints at an older king who was eligible to rule but had to wait his turn.

1.2.2. *Relationship to Ataliah*

An intriguing suggestion has been put forward regarding another potential relative of Hezekiah, based on the find of a royal tomb in the northwest palace at Nimrud (ancient Calaḫ). Of the two female bodies discovered in a single stone sarcophagus there, the lady designated Ataliah—according to inscriptions on the grave goods buried with the body—has been viewed as the mother of Sennacherib. If the name Ataliah is West Semitic and contains the Yahwistic theophoric ending, according to this proposal, then she may have been part of a diplomatic marriage to Judah and thus related to Hezekiah. Such an alliance would explain the relative leniency with which the king was treated by Sennacherib during his famed campaign of 701 B.C.E. against Judah.[64]

There are various reasons to question the claim of Ataliah's relationship as the mother of Sennacherib.[65] Most importantly, there is no express evi-

---

[63] Jehoram (2 Kgs 8:16–17) and Ahaz (16:2). For the expected formula, see that of Hezekiah in 18:2.

[64] As argued by Stephanie Dalley, "Yabâ, Atalyā and the Foreign Policy of Late Assyrian Kings," *SAAB* 12/2 (1998) 83–98. The ameliorated treatment of Hezekiah to which she refers stems from the standard practice by Assyrian kings of referring to those who rebel against the empire as guilty men or breakers of loyalty oaths. Furthermore, Sennacherib departed for his own country without capturing Jerusalem, collecting tribute (it was sent along only later), or deposing Hezekiah in favor of a puppet king.

It is worth noting that beyond the two royal figures, additional skeletons were found in the tomb which Dalley speculates "belong likewise to the same family, and may include those of daughters of Hezekiah deported by Sennacherib in 701" (p. 95). For archaeological information on the grave goods, as well as the accompanying inscriptions, see M.S.B. Damerji (ed.), *Gräber assyrischer Königinnen aus Nimrud* (JRGZM 45; Mainz: Verlag des Römisch-Germanischen Zentralmuseums, 1999).

[65] Most of the counterclaims raised in this paragraph are indebted to Sarah C. Melville, "Neo-Assyrian Royal Women and Male Identity: Status as a Social Tool," *JAOS* 124/1 (2004) 37–57.

dence to support such a linkage.[66] Ataliah does not refer to herself as the mother of Sennacherib, whereas queen mothers were wont to acknowledge both their husbands and sons. The estimated age of Ataliah's skeleton is thirty to thirty-five years, which makes her too young to have borne Sennacherib and yet to have lived so long into his reign.[67] Moreover, it is curious that Ataliah would share a sarcophagus with another corpse if she were indeed the consort of Sargon II and mother of Sennacherib.

If Ataliah is not a suitable candidate for the mother of Sennacherib, then there is little reason to see her influence over Assyrian policy toward Judah.[68] But the claim that Ataliah was Judahite is controversial as well. The name of Sargon's wife has been inscribed on the burial goods, twice as ᶠA-ta-li-a and once as ᶠA-tal-ia-a.[69] The assertion that this name contains the Yahwistic theophoric element is based on its similarity to the biblical name Athaliah (עֲתַלְיָהוּ), queen mother and brief ruler of Judah, buttressed by the names Ia-bi'di and ᴵHa-za-qi-ia-a preserved in Assyrian cuneiform.[70]

---

[66] Dalley herself provides no reasoning other than the fact that Ataliah was the consort (MÍ.É.GAL = segallu/sekallu) of Sargon II, which seems insufficient to justify the asseveration that "Atalyā was almost certainly the mother of Sennacherib" ("Yabâ, Atalyā," 97).

[67] The age of the queen's skeleton is based on Michael Schulz and Manfred Kunter, "Erste Ergebnisse der anthropologischen und paläopathologischen Untersuchungen an den menschlichen Skelettfunden aus den neuassyrischen Königinnengräbern von Nimrud," Gräber assyrischer Königinnen aus Nimrud, 118.

The queen mother lived at least twelve years into the reign of Sennacherib, based on a debt note dated 692 B.C.E., see Theodore Kwasman and Simo Parpola, Legal Transactions of the Royal Court of Nineveh, Part I: Tiglath-Pileser through Esarhaddon (SAA 6; Helsinki: Helsinki University Press, 1991) text 143. This figure could be extended by another decade based on a transfer of property from the perhaps recently deceased queen mother to the mother of the crown prince, documented in Laura Kataja and Robert Whiting (eds.), Grants, Decrees and Gifts of the Neo-Assyrian Period (SAA 12; Helsinki: Helsinki University Press, 1995) texts 21–23.

[68] Even as the mother of Sennacherib, the influence Ataliah could potentially wield over the empire's foreign policy is a debatable point. The appeal to a West Semitic princess would, in any case, be insufficient to account for Sennacherib's actions toward Hezekiah. As observed by John Wee in a Yale presentation on the subject (dated Oct. 31, 2006), a diplomatic marriage would not be a prime consideration if reprisal was necessary against a rebellious state. "Whether or not diplomacy continued, the foreign wife would have been expected to demonstrate greater loyalty to Assyria than to her home state, and to be willing to renounce the latter if there should be a conflict of interests."

[69] Ahmed Kamil, "Inscriptions on Objects from Yaba's Tomb in Nimrud," in Gräber assyrischer Königinnen aus Nimrud, 13–18.

[70] Dalley, "Yabâ, Atalyā," 94; Ran Zadok, The Pre-Hellenistic Israelite Anthroponymy and Prosopography (OLA 28; Leuven: Peeters, 1988) 168. For the source texts containing the personal names, see Dalley, "Yabâ, Atalyā," 94 n. 53; Reinhard Achenbach, "Jabâ und Atalja: zwei jüdische Konigstöchter am assyrischen Königshof?" BN 113 (2002) 29–30; K. Lawson Younger Jr., "Yahweh at Ashkelon and Calaḫ? Yahwistic Names in Neo-Assyrian," VT 52/2 (2002) 207–18.

It has been countered, however, that the Yahwistic theophoric is predominantly written in Neo-Assyrian as -ia-u/ú-, and that the examples cited are themselves exceptional.[71] These alleged linguistic similarities, moreover, only apply to the minority reading of ᶠA-tal-ia-a. The majority reading of ᶠA-ta-li-a speaks against a Yahwistic hypocoristicon, with the ending Ci-a being an unexpected form of the typical Ci-ia-.[72] There are no recognized Neo-Assyrian names bearing the Yahwistic theophoric ending in Ci-a, all attestations of which append a subsequent vowel Ci-a-a/u/ú. The ending -ia itself is well documented as far back as the Old Babylonian period, and thus gives pause to readily treating analogous forms in the Neo-Assyrian period as referring to the Israelite deity.[73] Based on the syllabic spelling, the hypocoristic ending more likely signifies the divine name Ea.[74]

The appeal to the biblical name Athaliah in itself complicates the picture as to the provenance of this unearthed queen of Sargon II. The meaning of עֲתַלְיָהוּ has not yet been satisfactorily traced to a Hebrew verbal root, whereas it is known from North Arabian dialects as well as Phoenician-Punic.[75] The latter is not surprising, given that Athaliah is generally

---

[71] Achenbach, "'Jabâ und Atalja," 31, and Younger, "Yahweh at Ashkelon and Calaḫ?" 209–14, 216–18, the latter of whom provides a table of twenty-four Yahwistic names in Neo-Assyrian cuneiform. Ia-bi'di has been variously argued as lacking the -u/ú- sign, as a misreading of the sign ia- for iu-, or else a name lacking the Yahwistic theophoric altogether. In the case of Luckenbill's rendering of ᵐHa-za-ki-ai-a from Sennacherib's Bull Inscriptions (bulls 2 and 3, line 21, in Annals of Sennacherib, 77), a supposedly better reading of Hezekiah's name has been supplied as ᴵHa-za-qi-a-a-ú by Riekele Borger, Babylonisch-Assyrische Lesestücke (2nd ed.; 3 vols.; AnOr 54; Roma: Pontificium Institutum Biblicum, 1979) 1.76 (no. 10).

[72] Based on the list of Neo-Assyrian names provided in Younger, "Yahweh at Ashkelon and Calaḫ?" 210–14. The only name in any way resembling the form Ci-a is ᴵḫi-il-qi-a-u, see Barbara Parker, "Administrative Tablets from the North-West Palace, Nimrud," Iraq 23/1 (1961) 27–28. Yet this name is also attested within the same corpus as ᴵḫi-il-qi-ia-u/ᴵḫi-il-qi-ia-(u), with the appended 'u' sign lacking in ᶠA-ta-li-a.

[73] Johann Jakob Stamm, Die Akkadische Namengebung (MVAG 44; Leipzig: J. C. Hinrichs, 1939) 113–14, 242–43.

[74] As suggested by Simo Parpola, PNAE 1/I, xxvii, "Since the divine element Aia/Ia occurring in WSem. names is spelled in exactly the same way as the NA Aia/Ia, showing the same predominance of a-a spellings, it is assumed that the same god is in question. This implies that the god Ea... continued to be venerated outside Mesopotamia proper in the first millennium as well."
Sennacherib strategically makes use in his own inscriptions of Ea, who was involved in the creation of humanity in the Enūma Eliš. The king boasts, "Ea provided me wide knowledge and granted me broad understanding, the equal of the sage Adapa" (Luckenbill, Annals of Sennacherib, 117). For further studies into the deity Ea and associated prosopography, see DDD, 125–26 and bibliography there.

[75] For linguistic data, see Younger, "Yahweh at Ashkelon and Calaḫ?" 218 n. 49.

considered to be the daughter of Omri, himself of Arabic or Canaanite descent.[76] Hence even if Ataliah from the royal grave at Nimrud could be argued as having a Yahwistic name, this would not assure her status as a Judahite princess from Jerusalem.[77] This casts even further doubt on the potential connection this figure would have to Hezekiah, and is too tentative, in my view, to maintain.[78]

Because the presumption has been made that the co-location of the two female skeletons within the same sarcophagus implies that they are from the same family, ascertaining the provenance of the second name is relevant as well.[79] The name Yabâ (^MIIa-ba-a) has been argued as West Semitic *yph "to be beautiful," based on the well-known alternation between b/p in Neo-Assyrian.[80] The roots *nby and *yhb have been posited as well, yet none of these etymologies makes a compelling case for a specifically Judean origin for this queen. The plethora of Assyrian personal names beginning with *Ia-* further speaks against confining the appellation in question to a particular geographic location.[81] Finally there is the fact that the shortened prefix *Ia-* is also attested as a feminine morpheme.[82]

---

[76] Based on the Arabic or Amorite origin of his name, see Winfried Thiel, "Omri," *AYBD* 5.17–20. Athaliah's parentage is disputed due to being called both a "daughter of Ahab" (בַּת־אַחְאָב, cf. 2 Kgs 8:18; 2 Chr 21:6) and "daughter of Omri" (בַּת־עָמְרִי, cf. 2 Kgs 8:26; 2 Chr 22:2). As this variance is not germane to our topic, we refer the reader to the analysis of Thiel, "Athaliah," *AYBD* 1.511–12.

[77] The inference is that the marriage to Sargon II must have been part of a diplomatic alliance, but as noted by John Wee (Yale presentation, Oct. 31, 2006): "The exoticness of a foreign wife, like Phoenician ivories or Neo-Hittite palace architecture, would have been a source of pride that added to the prestige of the Assyrian king (cf. the Semitic wives of Thutmose III in Egypt's initial phase of expansion into the Levant)."

[78] Space does not permit further appraisal of Dalley's argument, but there is caution that should be raised in the comparison of the queen's head dress to the *tefillin*, or phylactery, of later Jewish times. Moreover, the oracles of Isaiah to which she calls attention do not depict Assyria as a force for good but rather as an agent of Israel's destruction, and thus do not advance her position. In subsequent studies, she has taken a more focused stance in her defense, cf. Stephanie Dalley, "Recent Evidence from Assyrian Sources for Judaean History from Uzziah to Manasseh," *JSOT* 28/4 (2004) 387–401; eadem, "The Identity of the Princesses in Tomb II and a New Analysis of Events in 701 BC," in J. E. Curtis et al. (eds.), *New Light on Nimrud: Proceedings of the Conference on Nimrud 11th–13th March 2002* (London: British School of Archaeology in Iraq, 2008) 171–76.

[79] As argued by Dalley, "Yabâ, Atalyā," 95, "The name Yabâ very likely belongs in the same ethno-linguistic category as the name Atalyā, since they must have belonged to the same family." The suggestion was previously made by Damerji, *Gräber assyrischer Königinnen aus Nimrud*, 8 n. 37, but rejected by Karen Radner, "Ataia," *PNAE* 1/II, 433.

[80] Dalley, "Yabâ, Atalyā," 94.

[81] Knut L. Tallqvist, *Assyrian Personal Names* (ASSF 43/1; Helsinki, 1914) 90–93.

[82] The detection of the feminine morpheme is particularly perilous, as discussed by Scott C. Layton, *Archaic Features of Canaanite Personal Names in the Hebrew Bible*

Hence even if the name Yabâ could be convincingly demonstrated as West Semitic, its Judahite provenance is nonetheless highly speculative.

1.3. Conclusion

Although the dates of reign for king Hezekiah are a contentious issue, it is possible to resolve the impasse by means of chronological triangulation: selecting two independent events in Israelite history whose absolute dates are in accord with both biblical and extra-biblical evidence, which may then be correlated with the regnal years of the Judean ruler. The first date is that of the fall of the northern capital of Samaria, which is said to have transpired in the sixth regnal year of Hezekiah. The brief entry in the Babylonian Chronicle, ^{uru}Šá-ma-ra-'-in iḫ-te-pi, does not assert Shalmaneser V to have captured the city, but only to have wrought devastation upon it. His successor Sargon II, however, not only claims to have been the conqueror of Samaria, but to have deported its inhabitants in conformity with Assyrian military practice. As historical reconstruction of Sargon's reign places this incident in his second *palû*, the sixth regnal year of Hezekiah may be anchored in 720 B.C.E.

The second point of triangulation is that of the fall of Jerusalem to the Babylonians. This date has mistakenly been taken to be 586 B.C.E. by synchronizing "the nineteenth year of king Nebuchadrezzar" with Babylonian records. Yet by respecting the fact that the biblical record employs non-accession-year dating for this monarch, the capture of the Judean capital should rightfully be postdated to 587. There are 134 inclusive years from 720–587 B.C.E., beginning with Hezekiah's sixth regnal year. Adding in his five initial years of rule yields 139 years, which is in perfect agreement with the total regnal years provided in the biblical record for the latter kings of Judah. These data yield that 725 B.C.E. is the most accurate date that may be attained for Hezekiah's first year of reign.

There is little basis for seeing Hezekiah as the brother of Ahaz, a supposition prompted by the annalistic notice that Hezekiah was 25 years of age when he acceded to the throne, whereas Ahaz was only aged 36 at his death. The chronology of the period is difficult, and neither the assumption of sole rule nor a co-regency will permit the synchonisms of 2 Kgs 16:1; 17:1 to be reconciled. According to the book of Chronicles,

(HSM 47; Atlanta: Scholars Press, 1990) 241–45. The contrary points made here were previously presented by Achenbach, "'Jabâ und Atalja," 30–32.

Ahaz had another matured son named Maaseiah by the time of the Syro-Ephraimitic war, and the name of the queen mother is expressly given for Hezekiah. Because this maternal information is conspicuously lacking for Ahaz, and he was likely co-regent with his predecessor Jotham for some twelve years, it is more likely that Ahaz and Jotham were siblings, while Hezekiah was a direct descendant of Ahaz himself.

The female body of Ataliah, unearthed in a stone sarcophagus at Calaḫ, is highly questionable as a blood relative of Hezekiah or as the mother of Sennacherib. The expected promotion of herself as the queen mother is wanting, and the fact that her coffin is shared with another individual tells against this identification. The two forms of her name lack the Yahwistic theophoric -ia-u/ú- characteristic of Neo-Assyrian, but are in agreement with syllabic spellings of the name Ea which extend back to the Old Babylonian period. Even if the name could be proven as bearing a Yahwistic ending, its provenance as Judean would still be highly dubious. In any event, a theoretical West Semitic princess as part of a diplomatic marriage to Sargon II would have had no appreciable bearing on Sennacherib's policy toward Judah.

CHAPTER TWO

THE KINGDOM OF JUDAH

The focus of this chapter is the archaeological data relating to Hezekiah's capital city of Jerusalem and the breadth of his empire. It is only within the last generation that the debate over the size and extent of Jerusalem during the period of the monarchy has settled, prior to which the minimalist and maximalist interpretations of the archaeological record have held sway. The initial matter for investigation will be Judah's status in relation to Assyria, an important aspect of his rule to be treated in isolation before concentrating on the Judean kingdom itself.

The Siloam Tunnel is another controversial piece of evidence, traditionally admitted to be of Hezekian origin based on the brief references found in 2 Kgs 20:20 and 2 Chr 32:30. Yet recently even the paleography of its accompanying inscription has been questioned. The hundreds of examples of large storage containers, named *lmlk* jars according to the Hebrew word ubiquitously appearing in their accompanying seal impressions, must similarly be given consideration. Two key questions appertain to the *lmlk* jars: how reliably may they be said to have been initiated by Hezekiah himself, and what would have been their intended function?

2.1. Assyrian Relations

The relationship between Judah and Assyria during the reign of Hezekiah has been a matter of some debate. The southern Levantine state was of interest to the empire despite its tiny size, situated as it was along the important trade routes between Egypt and Mesopotamia. The Assyrianizing influence within the seal of a Hebrew servant attests to Judean recognition of Assyrian authority as early as the reign of Azariah/Uzziah, ca. 785–733.[1] The eighth century marks the first time that Judah is mentioned

---

[1] The seal of Shebanyau is catalogued in Nahman Avigad and Benjamin Sass, *Corpus of West Semitic Stamp Seals* (Jerusalem: Israel Academy of Sciences & Humanities, 1997) no. 3. Azariah has been equated with Azriyau (Assyrian ᵐ*Az-ri-a-⌈ú ⌉*, ᵐ*Az-ri-ia-a-ú*) as recorded in royal inscription Ann. 19*:1–12, but this association is debated. For the text and the various proposals see Hayim Tadmor, *The Inscriptions of Tiglath-pileser III King*

in Assyrian royal inscriptions, a testament to the successful expansion of the empire throughout this period.[2] During the imperial campaign through Syria-Palestine in 734–733 B.C.E., Hezekiah's father Ahaz voluntarily submitted to Tiglath-pileser III rather than join the anti-Assyrian coalition spearheaded by Pekah of Samaria and Rezin of Damascus.[3] In response, Damascus became a directly governed provincial center and Samaria was made an Assyrian province, but Judah retained its semi-independent vassal status.[4]

Following the brief reign of Shalmaneser V, his successor Sargon II (721–705 B.C.E.) was beset with difficulties securing his throne both at

---

of Assyria (Jerusalem: Israel Academy of Sciences and Humanities, 1994) 58–63, 273–76; *COS* 2.285; *PNAE* 1/I, 240. Regardless of the precise identification of Azriyau, it is sufficient to note that the Assyrian style of the official seal of Shebanyau connotes ties with the Assyrian court during the reign of Uzziah.

[2] Hayim Tadmor, "World Dominion: The Expanding Horizon of the Assyrian Empire," in L. Milano et al. (eds.), *Landscapes: Territories, Frontiers and Horizons in the Ancient Near East: Papers presented to the XLIV Rencontre Assyriologique Internationale Venezia, 7–11 July 1997. Part 1: Invited Lectures* (HANEM 3/1; Padova: Sargon, 1999) 55–62.

[3] Ahaz is referenced by his full name Jehoahaz (ᵐIa-ú-ḫa-zi ᵏᵘʳIa-ú-da-a+a, "Iauḫazi of Judah") in Summary Inscription 7:r.11' of Tiglath-pileser III among a list of various Syro-Palestinian kings bearing tribute, cf. *ARAB* 1.801; *ANET* 282; *COS* 2.289. For the text, see the edition of Tadmor, *Inscriptions of Tiglath-pileser III*, 170–71. The dates for this action have ranged from 735–33 B.C.E., reference his discussion on p. 277. The tribute is often equated with the "bribe" (שֹׁחַד) attributed to Ahaz by the Deuteronomist in 2 Kgs 16:7–8.

[4] For the biblical and Assyrian sources relating to this rebellion, known as the Syro-Ephraimitic War, see Stuart A. Irvine, *Isaiah, Ahaz, and the Syro-Ephraimitic Crisis* (SBLDS 123; Atlanta: Scholars Press, 1990). The typical model used to describe political relationships within the Assyrian empire has been popularized in such works as Herbert Donner, *Israel unter den Völkern* (VTSup 11; Leiden: E. J. Brill, 1964) 1–3, with a three-tiered structure in decreasing order of independence for the conquered territory:
(1) a vassal relationship marked by the payment of tribute and support for the Assyrian military machine;
(2) a vassal state marked by the installing of a ruler sympathetic to Assyrian interests, with increased burden of support for the empire and often reduced territory;
(3) a province marked by the incorporation of the kingdom directly into the empire with no autonomy.
Assyrian administration of these acquired regions is briefly surveyed in A. Kirk Grayson, "Assyrian Rule of Conquered Territory in Ancient Western Asia," *CANE* 2.959–68. The common two-tiered system of vassal and province is discussed in Jana Pečírková, "The Administrative Methods of Assyrian Imperialism," *ArOr* 55 (1987) 162–75; Peter Machinist, "Palestine, Administration of (Assyrian and Babylonian Administration)," *AYBD* 5.69–81. It has been brought to light, however, by Mordechai Cogan, "Judah under Assyrian Hegemony: A Reexamination of *Imperialism and Religion*," *JBL* 112/3 (1993) 406–410, that these clean categorizations are an over-simplification which "do not do justice to the wide spectrum of arrangements that developed between the conqueror and the conquered, especially in border and peripheral areas, particularly in the west" (p. 407).

home and abroad.[5] Upon subduing the rebellion of Merodach-baladan II
in Babylonia, backed by Elam, Sargon was able in his second regnal year
to turn his attention westward to the coalition of nations ranged against
him.[6] The alliance was defeated at the battle of Qarqar, and in the aftermath
Sargon swept through Israel and conquered Samaria.[7] In 716–15 B.C.E.,
the dynast undertook a campaign near the Egyptian border which has
been speculated to be commercially motivated.[8] Under the auspices of
the sheikh of the city of Laban, deportees were settled on the Brook of
Egypt, and Arabs were subsequently resettled in the region of Samaria.[9]
A third and final campaign to Palestine was necessary to quell a revolt led
by the Philistine city of Ashdod in 713–711 B.C.E., although Sargon himself
was not personally present. Despite the differing scholarly reconstructions
of this incursion, in broad strokes Sargon replaced the rebellious king of
Ashdod, Azuri, with his more pliant sibling Aḫimit.[10]

---

[5] The general history of Sargon's reign is chronicled in A. Kirk Grayson, "Assyria: Tiglath-
pileser III to Sargon II (744–705 B.C.)," in J. Boardman et al. (eds.), *The Cambridge Ancient
History Second Edition, Volume III Part 2: The Assyrian and Babylonian Empires and other
States of the Near East, from the Eighth to the Sixth Centuries B.C.* (Cambridge: Cambridge
University Press, 1991) 86–102; Amélie Kuhrt, *The Ancient Near East c. 3000–330 BC* (2 vols.;
London: Routledge, 1995) 2.497–99; "Sargon," *PNAE* 3/II (forthcoming).

[6] Among the rebellious cities mentioned in the annals are Arpad, Damascus, Gaza,
Simirra and Samaria, led by Yau-bi'di (Ilu-bi'di) of Hamath.

[7] Qarqar on the Orontes river is, of course, the same site at which Shalmaneser III
decisively routed a previous western coalition in 853 B.C.E. Whether the actions of Sargon
II at Samaria constituted actual conquest, as advocated in this study, or were merely a
mop-up operation, his involvement in the final days of the northern capital in 720 B.C.E.
is assured.

Isa 10:27–32 has been put forward as describing Sargon's approach to Jerusalem in the
context of this campaign. See Marvin A. Sweeney, "Sargon's Threat against Jerusalem
in Isaiah 10,27–32," *Bib* 75/4 (1994) 457–70; idem, *Isaiah 1–39, with an Introduction to the
Prophetic Literature* (FOTL 16; Grand Rapids: Eerdmans, 1996) 206–208; K. Lawson Younger,
Jr., "Sargon's Campaign against Jerusalem," *Bib* 77 (1996) 108ff. Sweeney appears to contradict himself, concluding "The present analysis of Isa 10:27–32 and the Assyrian records
indicates that Sargon's western campaign of 720 provides the best setting for the approach
to Jerusalem," (p. 208) after having previously stated "10:5–34 (+ 14:24–27) stems from the
period of Sargon II's invasion of the region to put down the Philistine revolt in 711 B.C.E."
(p. 204).

[8] Gerald L. Mattingly, "An Archaeological Analysis of Sargon's 712 Campaign against
Ashdod," *NEASB* 17 (1981) 47; Grayson, "Assyria: Tiglath-pileser III to Sargon II," 89.

[9] Hayim Tadmor, "The Campaigns of Sargon II of Assur: A Chronological-Historical
Study," *JCS* 12/3 (1958) 77–78; idem, "Philistia under Assyrian Rule," *BA* 29/3 (1966) 91–93;
Andreas Fuchs, *Die Annalen des Jahres 711 v. Chr. nach Prismenfragmenten aus Ninive und
Assur* (SAAS 8; Helsinki: Neo-Assyrian Text Corpus Project, 1998) 28–29; *COS* 2.293.

[10] In the Nineveh annal prism, Sargon's royal inscriptions record: "Together with the
rulers of Philistia, Judah, Edom, Moab, and those who live on islands and bring tribute
and *tamartu* gifts to my lord Aššur, they sent countless evil lies and unseemly speeches

What was the stance of Hezekiah toward Assyria at this time? In the undated Nimrud Inscription, Sargon proclaims himself to be "the subduer of the land Judah which is far away."[11] Such a boast, however, need not imply anything more than submission in the form of tribute.[12] This text has recently been argued as dating to late 717 or early 716 B.C.E., which would limit the context for Hezekiah's submission to Sargon's first five regnal years.[13] Germane to this discussion is the controversial provenance of the Azekah Inscription, which contains the partially restored name of Hezekiah and has been credited to both Sargon II and Sennacherib across five disparate years.[14] This fragmentary text seems to describe military reprisal against two cities under the control of the insurgent Hezekiah:

---

with their bribes to Pir'u, king of Egypt (a potentate, unable to save them) to set him at enmity with me and asked him to be an ally." Text: Fuchs, *Die Annalen des Jahres 711 v. Chr.*, 44–46, 73–74; Trans. *ARAB* 2 §§193–95; *ANET* 287; *TPOA* 114–15; *TUAT* 1/4, 381–82; Mordechai Cogan, *The Raging Torrent: Historical Inscriptions from Assyria and Babylonia Relating to Ancient Israel* (Jerusalem: Carta, 2008) 103–105.

The events of the Ashdod affair developed slowly over time, as may be seen in *COS* 2:294, 296–97, 300. This insurrection is the subject of Isa 20–22, and is discussed in Tadmor, "Campaigns of Sargon II," 79–80, 83–84, 92–95; idem, "Philistia under Assyrian Rule," 94–95; Anthony J. Spalinger, "The Year 712 B.C. and Its Implications for Egyptian History," *JARCE* 10 (1973) 95–101. The following essays related to the topic are all presented within the work of Andrew G. Vaughn and Ann E. Killebrew (eds.), *Jerusalem in Bible and Archaeology: The First Temple Period* (SBLSS 18; Leiden: Brill, 2003): James K. Hoffmeier, "Egypt's Role in the Events of 701 B.C. in Jerusalem," 226–29; K. Lawson Younger Jr., "Assyrian Involvement in the Southern Levant at the End of the Eighth Century B.C.E.," 240–44; J. J. M. Roberts, "Egypt, Assyria, Isaiah, and the Ashdod Affair: An Alternative Proposal," 265–83; Hoffmeier, "Egypt's Role in the Events of 701 B.C.: A Rejoinder to J. J. M. Roberts," 285–89.

[11] *mušakniš māt Iaudu ša ašaršu rûqu*, in the text edition of Hugo Winckler, *Die Keilschrifttexte Sargons, Vol. 1* (Leipzig: Eduard Pfeiffer, 1889) 168–73, with translations in *ARAB* 2 §§137–38; *ANET* 287; *TPOA* 110–11; *TUAT* 1/4, 287; *COS* 2.298–99; Cogan, *Raging Torrent*, 100–102. This is the only reference in Sargon's extant inscriptions to the subjugation of the kingdom of Judah.

[12] As noted by J. Maxwell Miller and John H. Hayes, *A History of Ancient Israel and Judah* (2nd edition; Louisville: Westminster John Knox, 2006) 404, the voluntary surrender of Cyprus in *ARAB* 2 §70 permitted Sargon to assert that he had "subdued seven kings of the land of Ia', a region of the land of Iadnana (Cyprus)."

[13] Nadav Na'aman, "The Historical Portion of Sargon II's Nimrud Inscription," *SAAB* 8/1 (1994) 17–20, based on analysis of the form and content of the historical section. See also Eckart Frahm, *Einleitung in die Sanherib-Inschriften* (AfOB 26; Vienna: Institut für Orientalisk der Universität, 1997) 231.

[14] The text is a combination of two originally separate fragments, K 6205 and BM 82–3-32, which were believed to be of purportedly different provenance (stemming from Tiglath-pileser III and Sargon II, respectively) until they were combined by Nadav Na'aman, "Sennacherib's 'Letter to God' on his Campaign to Judah," *BASOR* 214 (1974) 25–39. The initial attribution of K 6205 to Tiglath-pileser III was made by Paul Rost (ed.), *Die Keilschrifttexte Tiglat-Pilesers III* (2 vols., Leipzig: E. Pfeiffer, 1893) 1.18–21, ll. 103–19, at which time it was designated 3 R 9,2. Subsequent treatments may be found in Bob Becking,

the Judahite stronghold of Azekah, and an unnamed royal city in Philistia variously identified as Gath or Ekron.[15] The most compelling arguments for dating this inscription point to a date of 720 B.C.E. based on internal analysis, and this date may be buttressed by external data as well.[16]

The Fall of Samaria: An Historical and Archaeological Study (SHCANE 2; Leiden: E. J. Brill, 1992) 3 n. 8. The various dates proposed for the text are as follows:

- Sargon, 720 B.C.E. See Andreas Fuchs, *Die Inschriften Sargons II. aus Khorsabad* (Göttingen: Cuvillier, 1994) 314–15; Frahm, *Einleitung in die Sanherib-Inschriften*, 229–32. This is the date advocated in this study.
- Sargon, 715 B.C.E. Stefan Timm, *Moab zwischen den Mächten. Studien zu historischen Denkmälern und Texten* (ÄAT 17; Wiesbaden: Harrassowitz, 1989) 337 n. 19; 356 n. 50; Becking, *Fall of Samaria*, 3 n. 8; 54 n. 30.
- Sargon, 712 B.C.E. See Tadmor, "Campaigns of Sargon II," 80–84; Gershon Galil, "A New Look at the 'Azekah Inscription'," *RB* 102 (1995) 321–29; Mordechai Cogan and Hayim Tadmor, *II Kings: A New Translation with Introduction and Commentary* (AYB 11; New York: Doubleday, 1988) 262 n. 6; Jeremy Goldberg, "Two Assyrian Campaigns against Hezekiah and Later Eighth Century Biblical Chronology," *Bib* 80/3 (1999) 360–90; Miller and Hayes, *History of Ancient Israel and Judah*, 407.
- Sennacherib, 701 B.C.E. See Na'aman, "Sennacherib's 'Letter to God'"; idem, "Ahaz's and Hezekiah's Policy Toward Assyria in the Days of Sargon II and Sennacherib's Early Years," *Zion* 59/1 (1994) 5–30 [Hebrew]; Younger, "Assyrian Involvement in the Southern Levant," 238–40, 243, 245; Carl D. Evans, "Judah's Foreign Policy from Hezekiah to Josiah," in C. D. Evans, W. W. Hallo, and J. B. White (eds.), *Scripture in Context: Essays on the Comparative Method* (Pittsburgh: Pickwick Press, 1980) 160–61.
- Sennacherib, 689 B.C.E. See William H. Shea, "Sennacherib's Second Palestinian Campaign," *JBL* 104/3 (1985) 404–407; idem, "Jerusalem under Siege: Did Sennacherib Attack Twice?" *BAR* 25/6 (Nov.–Dec. 1999) 36–44, 64.

[15] Editions of the text may be found in Na'aman, "Sennacherib's 'Letter to God'"; Frahm, *Einleitung in die Sanherib-Inschriften*, 230, with translations in *TPOA* 123–24; *COS* 2.304–305; Cogan, *Raging Torrent*, 107–109. A relevant excerpt of the text is as follows:

> [Aššur, my lord, support]ed me [Sargon] and to the land of Ju[dah I marched. In] the course of my campaign, the tribute of the k[ings...] the district [of Hezek]iah of Judah...the city of Azekah, his stronghold...located on a mountain peak, like countless pointed i[ron] daggers...I conquered, I carried off its spoil...a royal [city] of the Philistines, which He[zek]iah had taken and fortified for himself. (*COS* 2:304)

Gath (Tell eṣ Ṣafi) was suggested by Na'aman as the Philistine "royal city," but more recently the consensus has shifted to Ekron, cf. Gershon Galil, "Judah and Assyria in the Sargonid Period," *Zion* 57 (1992) 111–33 [Hebrew]; idem, "Conflicts between Assyrian Vassals," *SAAB* 6 (1992) 55–63; idem, "New Look at the 'Azekah Inscription'," 321–29. For the purposes of this study, no precise identification is necessary.

[16] Na'aman, who assigned the text to Sennacherib and dated it to 701 B.C.E., himself admits: "There is no doubt that, stylistically and in lexicon, this text is especially close to the 'Letter to God' describing the campaign of Sargon II to Urartu in 714 B.C." ("Sennacherib's 'Letter to God'," 31). The tone of the letter is likewise far removed from that of the annalistic report of Sennacherib's campaign to Judah, which was "a doubtful success as far as the Assyrians were concerned" (p. 31). Tadmor, "Campaigns of Sargon II," 82; idem, "The Sin of Sargon," *Eretz-Israel* 5 (1958) 159–60 [Hebrew], has contributed that the spelling of the Assyrian god Aššur in the text as AN.ŠAR speaks to authorship under Sargon, since

According to 2 Kgs 18:8, Hezekiah "defeated the Philistines as far as Gaza and its territory, from watchtower to fortified city." This notice is situated early in the king's reign prior to the fall of Samaria, although it must be noted that royal achievements were often positioned as inaugural events.[17] Nonetheless, the notice makes clear that the editors of this material saw no correlation between these events and the later response of Sennacherib in 701 B.C.E. Hezekiah's timing for rebellion, while Sargon was otherwise occupied in securing his throne, is in accord with that of subject monarchs throughout the Assyrian empire, who felt that the time following the coronation of a new liege was the opportune moment for striving to throw off the imperial yoke. Most significantly, forced submission by Judah in 720 B.C.E. aligns with the chronology proposed herein for the fall of Samaria, which suggests that Judah was indeed part of the western coalition at this time and was likely aiding its northern neighbor in the face of Sargon's assault on the capital city.[18] Such a political move is only to be expected, as Hezekiah was all too aware of the previous deportations of the denizens of the north under Tiglath-pileser, and aspired to maintain good relations with Israel in the hope of future unification.[19] He could hardly expect Israel's support if he failed to back them in a time of crisis. This would provide the context for 2 Kgs 18:7, "And he rebelled

---

Sennacherib employed the traditional spelling of Aššur exclusively in historical texts, while reserving Anšar for building inscriptions and the literary genre.

Any attribution of the text to the Ashdod affair would appear unfounded based on the observation of Na'aman ("Sennacherib's 'Letter to God'," 30) that such letters were composed in the context of resounding military expeditions conducted personally by the king. Yet the king did not venture forth in that year, as confirmed by the chronological notice in Isa 20:1, "In the year that the commander-in-chief (tartān), who was sent by king Sargon of Assyria, came to Ashdod and fought against it and took it." For further arguments, see Younger, "Assyrian Involvement in the Southern Levant," 243.

[17] Comparison has been made to the reconstruction of Babylon credited to Esarhaddon in his rēš šarrūti, as examined by Mordechai Cogan, "The Chronicler's Use of Chronology as Illuminated by Neo-Assyrian Royal Inscriptions," in J. H. Tigay (ed.), Empirical Models for Biblical Criticism (Philadelphia: University of Pennsylvania Press, 1985) 197–209. The intent was to show that the pious ruler was concerned with the affairs of his god's city from his very first days upon the throne. The antedating of the fall of Samaria to Sargon's accession year for literary-ideological reasons has already been noted, see Tadmor, "Campaigns of Sargon II," 30–32.

[18] Such a reconstruction runs counter to the thesis of Paul K. Hooker, "The Kingdom of Hezekiah: Judah in the Geo-political Context of the Late Eighth Century BCE" (Ph.D. diss.; Emory University, 1993) 227–33, who surmises that in the aftermath of Sargon's opening of the bīt kāri in Egypt (720 B.C.E.), Hezekiah was given administrative control within Philistia as a reward.

[19] For Assyrian deportation practices, see Bustenay Oded, Mass Deportations and Deportees in the Neo-Assyrian Empire (Wiesbaden: Reichert, 1979).

against the king of Assyria and did not serve him," a notice again placed immediately prior to the account of Samaria's final days. A reprisal against Judah by Sargon would further substantiate the king's boast to be "the subduer of the land Judah which is far away."

These conclusions may be corroborated by suggestions in recent scholarship that Hezekiah was subsequently pro-Assyrian and actually aided the Assyrian juggernaut militarily as a client state.[20] This position is primarily based on two administrative letters excavated from Nimrud/Calaḥ and assigned to the reign of Sargon II.[21] The first is dated circa 716 B.C.E., and records the receipt of tribute at Nimrud from Egypt, Gaza, Judah, Moab and Ammon.[22] The second letter, badly damaged, is dated circa 715 B.C.E. and mentions Judeans in the context of a campaign in Urartu. Despite the laconic nature of the text, it suggests that Hezekiah was assisting the Assyrian military on campaign with levies.[23] More contentious is

---

[20] Hooker, "The Kingdom of Hezekiah" defends this position in regard to Sargon's first Palestinian campaign, but I would place this political alliance later. Stephanie Dalley, "Recent Evidence from Assyrian Sources for Judaean History from Uzziah to Manasseh," *JSOT* 28/4 (2004) 390, notes that "the relationship between Judah and Assyria may have resembled that of client and patron rather than that of oppressed vassal and harsh overlord." This would be consistent with Assyrian treatment of Phoenician territory due to its importance for commerce in the region, as well as potentially explain Sennacherib's treatment of Hezekiah. See the summary of Miller and Hayes, *History of Ancient Israel and Judah*, 404–407, who see 2 Kgs 18:8 as fitting into this picture.

[21] As discussed in Dalley, "Recent Evidence from Assyrian Sources" 388, and originally published by H. W. F. Saggs, *The Nimrud Letters, 1952* (CTN 5; London: British School of Archaeology in Iraq, 2001) 125–28, 219–21, pll. 24, 43. Although the letters are undated and must be assigned a time of authorship based solely on their content, the regnal years I advocate for Hezekiah encompass all of Sargon's reign, so precise dating is not an issue. Further bibliography for Nimrud letter 16 is provided in Younger, "Assyrian Involvement in the Southern Levant," 238 n. 11, who dates it between 720 and 715 B.C.E.

[22] ND 2765, in Saggs, *Nimrud Letters, 1952*, 219–21, pl. 43. He renders the relevant lines thus:

34	amēlṣīrānímeš mātmu-ṣur-a-a	The emissaries of Egypt,
35	mātha-za-ta-a-a mātia-ú-da-a-a	of Gaza, of Judah,
36	mātma-'a-ba-a-a mātba-an-am-ma-na-a-a	of Moab, cf the Ammonites,
37	ūm XII.KÁM* ina ālkal-ḫi e-tar-bu-u-ni	entered Calaḥ on the twelfth
38	m[a]-da-na-t[e]-šú-nu ina qatēll-šú-nu	(with) their tribute in their hands.

As Dalley, "Recent Evidence from Assyrian Sources," 388, rightly comments, Akkadian *mandattu/ma(d)dattu* is ambiguous and does not convey whether or not payment was given freely or under duress. See *CAD* M/1, 10.13–16 s.v. *maddattu*; *AHw* 2.572 s.v. *ma(d)dattu(m)*, mandattu.

[23] ND 2608, in Saggs, *Nimrud Letters, 1952*, 125–28, pl. 24. It should be noted that the identification of the geographical reference [KUR] [i]a-ú-da-a-a (line 9') is in dispute. Although Saggs is willing to entertain the possibility that the reference "may have denoted a contingent of troops from Judah operating with the Assyrians," his own position is more skeptical: "Although J. D. Hawkins, RLA, V, 273a, claims that Jaudu 'always denotes Judah',

the identification of Judean soldiers as part of the king's bodyguard in
a sculpture of Sennacherib from Nineveh, which would affirm that the
Assyrian monarch reckoned Hezekiah as a valuable ally.[24] This positive
stance is reflected and has been analyzed in the context of Isaiah's prophecies dealing with Egypt.[25]

The evidence, on balance, suggests that Hezekiah dared to challenge
Assyria early in his reign, confident in the expanding scope of his empire
into Philistine territory.[26] Although he ultimately failed, he was favorably
remembered in the biblical record for his defiant trust in YHWH, and for
his status as a deliverer to those in the north left behind after Sargon's
deportations. In the aftermath of 720 B.C.E., Hezekiah was forced to remain
passive and loyal to Assyria, not only for reasons of political expedience,
but also due to the formidable humanitarian and logistical issues arising
from the Israelites who had moved southward into Judah seeking refuge.
Hezekiah thus turned his attention internally to matters of state until the
death of Sargon, patiently awaiting the next opportunity to break away
from the grasp of his overlords.

2.2. THE URBANIZATION OF JERUSALEM

In the late eighth century B.C.E., the city of Jerusalem underwent a series
of expansions which transformed it from a small settlement to the largest
city in the divided kingdom. Since the early Bronze Age, the Jebusite hamlet had occupied the southern part of the eastern ridge later known as the
City of David, and by the Solomonic era likely had spread over the entire
hilltop, encompassing the Ophel and Mount Moriah.[27] The expansive

---

the fact that every other geographical reference in this letter is to the Urartian region or
north Syria suggests that the present reference is to a northern state rather than to biblical
Judah" (pp. 127–28).

[24] For this artistic work, see Richard D. Barnett, Erika Bleibtrau and Geoffrey Turner,
Sculptures from the South-West Palace of Sennacherib at Nineveh (2 vols.; London: British
Museum Press, 1998) 1.135; 2.473, 485, as briefly discussed in Dalley, "Recent Evidence from
Assyrian Sources," 391–92.

[25] Isa 19:23–24.

[26] In part, Hezekiah was seeking to retake territory in the Shephelah and Negev lost to
Philistia under Ahaz, as described in 2 Chr 28:18.

[27] The Ophel (עֹפֶל "hill," cf. parallelism in Isa 32:14, and references in Mic 4:8; Neh
3:26–27; 11:21; 2 Chr 27:3; 33:14) is the narrow promontory situated between the spur of the
City of David and the Temple Mount. The historicity of the Davidic and Solomonic empire
is a larger issue of contention beyond the scope of this monograph, and the role of Jerusalem at this time is still debated. For various positions based on recent archaeology, see

southwestern hill was the next logical area to accommodate subsequent growth, being at a higher elevation than the eastern ridge and bounded by the Hinnom Valley to the west, and the Transversal Valley to the north. For decades, insufficient archaeological evidence fueled the well-known debate concerning the date of expansion of the city onto the southwestern hill, with the minimalists advocating that the Jerusalem of biblical times was limited to the eastern ridge, while the maximalists favored the southwestern hillside as part of the city in the First Temple period.[28]

It is now well established that the urbanization of Jerusalem occurred in the late eighth century.[29] The city began to expand for the first time

---

the relevant articles in Vaughn and Killebrew (eds.), *Jerusalem in Bible and Archaeology*, with summaries at 343 n. 46, 417–22.

[28] The question as to when the fortified area of Jerusalem expanded from the eastern ridge to encompass the southwestern hill has given rise to various archaeological positions:

1. According to the "minimalist" view or the "one-hill theory," the city in biblical times was confined to the City of David and Mount Moriah. This view, prevalent among archaeologists in the mid-twentieth century, had among its proponents Michael Avi-Yonah, Nahman Avigad, and Kathleen Kenyon.

2. The "maximalist" view or "two-hills theory" credits the southwestern hill with being part of biblical Jerusalem. Its supporters have included Frederick Bliss, Gustaf Dalman, Archibald Dickie, Jan Simons, Louis-Hugues Vincent, and Ruth Amiran. Such dimensions, at the very least, concur with this study's findings on the current archaeological picture of the city.

3. The "super-maximalist" view, advocated by Gabriel Barkay, posits that the boundaries of Jerusalem during the late monarchy extended to the north and west, beyond the Ophel, City of David, and western hill.

The debate is summarized in Jan Simons, *Jerusalem in the Old Testament: Researches and Theories* (Leiden: E. J. Brill, 1952) 226–29; Michael Avi-Yonah, "Topography" in M. Avi-Yonah (ed.), *The Book of Jerusalem* (2 vols.; Jerusalem: Bialik Institute, 1956) 1.157–60 [Hebrew]; Hillel Geva, "The Western Boundary of Jerusalem at the End of the Monarchy," *IEJ* (1979) 84–85; Gabriel Barkay, "Jerusalem of the Old Testament Times: New Discoveries and New Approaches," *BAIAS* 5 (1985–86) 33–34, 40–41; Andrew G. Vaughn, *Theology, History, and Archaeology in the Chronicler's Account of Hezekiah* (ABS 4 Atlanta: Scholars Press, 1999) 59–61.

The slow process of archaeological discovery is chronicled in Hillel Geva, "Western Jerusalem at the End of the First Temple Period in Light of the Excavations in the Jewish Quarter," in Vaughn and Killebrew (eds.), *Jerusalem in Bible and Archaeology*, 183–208, with bibliography relevant to the debate at 185 n. 1. See also Nahman Avigad, *Discovering Jerusalem: Recent Archaeological Excavations in the Upper City* (Nashville: Thomas Nelson, 1983) 26–31. For history of scholarship, see Margreet Steiner, "The Archaeology of Ancient Jerusalem," *CR:BS* 6 (1998) 143–68.

[29] For an extensive list of recent field reports which support this consensus, see the bibliography at Ann E. Killebrew, "Biblical Jerusalem: An Archaeological Assessment," in Vaughn and Killebrew (eds.), *Jerusalem in Bible and Archaeology*, 330–31 n. 2. She concludes "The 'maximalist' proposal regarding the size of Jerusalem has been proven correct by the unambiguous evidence uncovered in the Jewish Quarter" (pp. 336–37). "Urbanization" here is employed in accordance with the discussions appertaining in William

from the eastern ridge, which comprised the core of the original Jebusite
village, toward the southwestern hill.[30] This was a substantial enlarge-
ment, as the hill alone, including its eastern slope overlooking the
Tyropoeon Valley, occupied approximately seventy-five percent, or 450
dunams, of the total land area of the city.[31] The settlement of this area
has been indirectly dated based on pottery assemblages in tombs exca-

---

G. Dever, "Social Structure in Palestine in the Iron II Period on the Eve of Destruction,"
in T. E. Levy (ed.), *The Archaeology of Society in the Holy Land* (New York: Facts on File,
1995) 416–30.

It is important to note that Jerusalem is acknowledged as the center of a full-fledged
state in the eighth century even by so-called "revisionist" scholars, cf. David W. Jamieson-
Drake, *Scribes and Schools in Monarchic Judah* (JSOTSup 109; Sheffield: Almond Press, 1991)
138–45; Ernst Axel Knauf, "King Solomon's Copper Supply," in E. Lipiński (ed.), *Phoenicia
and the Bible* (OLA 44; Leuven: Peeters, 1991) 171–84; Thomas L. Thompson, *Early History
of the Israelite People: From the Written and the Archaeological Sources* (SHANE 4; Leiden:
Brill, 1992) 409–11; Philip R. Davies, *In Search of 'Ancient Israel'* (JSOTSup 148; Sheffield:
Sheffield Academic Press, 1992) 67–70; Niels P. Lemche, "Is it Still Possible to Write a History of Israel?" *SJOT* 8 (1994) 183–84; Niels P. Lemche and Thomas L. Thompson, "Did Biran
Kill David? The Bible in the Light of Archaeology," *JSOT* 64 (1994) 3–22.

[30] As noted by Geva, "Western Jerusalem at the End of the First Temple Period," 198 n. 29,
this eighth-century dating does find a few detractors. Gabriel Barkay, "The Iron Age II–III,"
in A. Ben-Tor (ed.), *The Archaeology of Ancient Israel* (trans. R. Greenberg; New Haven:
Yale University Press, 1992) 367, opts for the ninth century as the beginning of the settlement of the southwestern hill. For those who postdate settlement to the seventh century,
see Magen Broshi, "The Expansion of Jerusalem in the Reigns of Hezekiah and Manasseh,"
IEJ 24 (1974) 21–23; A. Douglas Tushingham, *Excavations in Jerusalem 1961–1967, Vol. 1*
(Toronto: Royal Ontario Museum, 1985) 19–20; William G. Dever, Review of A. D. Tushingham,
Excavations in Jerusalem 1961–1967, Vol. 1. AJA 93/4 (1989) 611.

As one of the tentpoles for the later dating rests upon the contentious attribution of
assigning the end of Stratum III at Lachish to 597 B.C.E., a date of no later than the eighth
century for the settlement of the southwestern hill seems assured. More extreme positions
such as that of A. Douglas Tushingham, "The Western Hill of Jerusalem: A Critique of the
'Maximalist' Position," *Levant* 19 (1987) 137–43, who delays occupation of the entire western hill until the Herodian period, should be considered in light of the state of archaeology
at the time, whereby "most of the evidence from the Western Hill still awaits publication
and we have had to depend on what has been made available" (p. 143).

[31] As estimated by Geva, "Western Jerusalem at the End of the First Temple Period,"
206. For other numbers, see A. Douglas Tushingham, "The Western Hill of Jerusalem under
the Monarchy," *ZDPV* 95 (1979) 39–55; Shimon Gibson, "The 1961–1967 Excavations in the
Armenian Garden, Jerusalem," *PEQ* 119 (1987) 81–96; Dan Bahat, "Was Jerusalem Really
That Large?" in A. Biran and J. Aviram (eds.), *Biblical Archaeology Today, 1990: Proceedings
of the Second International Congress on Biblical Archaeology, Jerusalem, June 1990* (Jerusalem: Israel Exploration Society, 1993) 581–84; Doron Chen, Shlomo Margalit and Bargil
Pixner, "Mount Zion: Discovery of Iron Age Fortifications Below the Gate of the Essenes,"
in H. Geva (ed.), *Ancient Jerusalem Revealed* (2nd ed.; Jerusalem: Israel Exploration Society,
2000) 76–81; William M. Schniedewind, "Jerusalem, the Late Judaean Monarchy, and the
Composition of the Biblical Texts," in Vaughn and Killebrew (eds.), *Jerusalem in Bible and
Archaeology*, 383–84 n. 26.

vated in the Hinnom Valley as well as on the escarpment known as Ketef Hinnom.[32] The preference for rock-hewn tombs in this region rather than the traditional burial grounds utilized to the east of the City of David speaks to the emergence of a national elite at this time.[33] Residential dwellings were built further to the north of the southwestern hill, but outside of the city's fortifications.[34] There was also the addition of a smaller residential quarter on the eastern slopes of the City of David, an expansion which may have occurred earlier than that to the west.[35] Two of these areas are known by name—the Mišneh "Second" (Quarter) and the Makteš "Mortar/ Valley" (Quarter)—and significantly show up in the biblical record in texts pertaining to this period.[36] Population estimates for Hezekiah's Jerusalem

[32] Cf. Ruth Amiran, "The Necropolis of Jerusalem in the Time of the Monarchy," in *Judah and Jerusalem: The Twelfth Archaeological Convention* (Jerusalem: Israel Exploration Society, 1957) 65–72, and the following articles in Geva (ed.), *Ancient Jerusalem Revealed*: Amos Kloner and David Davis, "A Burial Cave of the Late First Temple Period on the Slope of Mount Zion," 107–10; Ronny Reich, "The Ancient Burial Ground in the Mamilla Neighborhood, Jerusalem," 111–15; Gabriel Barkay, "Excavations at Ketef Hinnom in Jerusalem," 93–106.

[33] As observed by Israel Finkelstein and Neil Asher Silberman, *The Bible Unearthed: Archaeology's New Vision of Ancient Israel and the Origin of Its Sacred Texts* (New York: Simon and Schuster, 2001) 245–46; Killebrew, "Biblical Jerusalem: An Archaeological Assessment," 337.

[34] Chronicled by Geva, "Western Jerusalem at the End of the First Temple Period," 207, who identifies this area as today's Christian and Muslim Quarters. For further discussion of this growth, see Shimon Gibson, "Ancient Jerusalem's Rural Landscape," *BAIAS* 3 (1983–84) 30–35; Shimon Gibson and Gershon Edelstein, "Investigating Jerusalem's Rural Landscape," *Levant* 17 (1985) 139–55; Gershon Edelstein and Ianir Milevski, "The Rural Settlement of Jerusalem Re-evaluated: Surveys and Excavations in the Reph'aim Valley and Mevasseret Yerushalayim," *PEQ* 126 (1994) 2–23; Avi Ofer, "'All the Hill Country of Judah': From a Settlement Fringe to a Prosperous Monarchy," in I. Finkelstein and N. Na'aman (eds.), *From Nomadism to Monarchy* (Jerusalem: Yad Izhak Ben-Zvi, 1994) 92–121; Vaughn, *Theology, History, and Archaeology*, 59–70; Finkelstein and Silberman, *The Bible Unearthed*, 245–46; Thomas L. Thompson (ed.), *Jerusalem in Ancient History and Tradition* (JSOTSup 381; London: T&T Clark International, 2003) 124, 130–31; Vaughn and Killebrew (eds.), *Jerusalem in Bible and Archaeology*, 209–18; 296–99; 334ff; 379ff.

[35] Whether or not these houses were originally extramural has been complicated by the find of a fortification wall on the lowermost slope of the eastern ridge. For articles arguing each side, see Donald T. Ariel and Alon De Groot, "The Iron Age Extramural Occupation at the City of David and Additional Observations on the Siloam Channel," in Donald T. Ariel (ed.), *Excavations at the City of David 1978–1985 Directed by Yigal Shiloh, Vol. V: Extramural Areas* (Qedem 40; Jerusalem: Institute of Archaeology, Hebrew University of Jerusalem, 2000) 155–69 [pro]; Ronny Reich and Eli Shukron, "The Urban Development of Jerusalem in the Late Eighth Century B.C.E.," in Vaughn and Killebrew (eds.), *Jerusalem in Bible and Archaeology*, 209–18 [con].

[36] 2 Kgs 22:14; 2 Chr 34:22; Zeph 1:10–11. מִשְׁנֶה in Neh 11:9 is sometimes read as a geographic reference as well.

vary based on the model employed, ranging from 6,000 at a conservative estimate to 20,000.[37]

The reasons for this sudden growth are varied as well, with many scholars favoring correlating the expansion of Jerusalem with the revolt of Hezekiah after the death of Sargon II.[38] The archaeological evidence from Stratum 12, however, suggests a decidedly non-military setting.[39] Not only is the construction of some houses extramural, such that domestic settlement more reasonably preceded the fortifications, but a portion of the wall around the western hill has been built over a row of these domiciles.[40] The appeal to economic motives merely trades one question for another, as the basis for either a burgeoning or stagnating economy is left wanting.[41] The documented residential growth on the southwestern hill dovetails with the demise of the northern kingdom after the fall of Samaria, which would have profoundly influenced the distribution of its

---

[37] Magen Broshi, "Estimating the Population of Ancient Jerusalem," in idem, *Bread, Wine, Walls and Scrolls* (JSPSup 36; London: Sheffield Academic Press, 2001) 110–20; Yigal Shiloh, "The Population of Iron Age Palestine in the Light of a Sample Analysis of Urban Plans, Areas, and Population Density," *BASOR* 239 (1980) 30; Magen Broshi and Israel Finkelstein, "The Population of Palestine in Iron Age II," *BASOR* 28 (1992) 47–60. I would personally favor the conservative estimates, based on the observations of Bahat, "Was Jerusalem Really That Large?" 583; Geva, "Western Jerusalem at the End of the First Temple Period," 206, pertaining to water sources as a limiting factor for the population of Jerusalem.

[38] As argued, for example, by Miller and Hayes, *History of Ancient Israel and Judah*, 411–16. Baruch Halpern explains this sudden influx as a state-mandated transferal of population to fortified centers on the eve of Sennacherib's campaign, in "Jerusalem and the Lineages in the Seventh Century BCE: Kinship and the Rise of Individual Moral Liability," in B. Halpern and D. W. Hobson (eds.), *Law and Ideology in Monarchic Israel* (JSOTSup 124; Sheffield: JSOT Press, 1991) 25–26.

[39] Avigad, *Discovering Jerusalem*, 55–56; Lynn Tatum, "Jerusalem in Conflict: The Evidence for the Seventh-Century B.C.E. Religious Struggle over Jerusalem," in Vaughn and Killebrew (eds.), *Jerusalem in Bible and Archaeology*, 296–97. Tatum, for example, describes the residential Lower Terrace House as being "marked by nicely stepped alleyways and a plastered drainage channel so well built as to be lined with hewn limestone slabs and covered with flagstones."

[40] Corroborated by the words of Isaiah ben Amoz: "And you counted the houses of Jerusalem and pulled down houses to fortify the wall; and you constructed a basin between the two walls for the water of the old pool" (Isa 22:10–11).

[41] Lawrence E. Stager, "The Archaeology of the Family in Ancient Israel," *BASOR* 260 (1985) 1–35, posits that as the availability of agricultural lands had reached a saturation point, urbanization was a necessary response to ensure the livelihood of the state's denizens. In contradistinction, Larry G. Herr, "The Iron Age II Period: Emerging Nations," *BA* 60/3 (1997) 155–57, sees Jerusalem as attracting new residents due to a thriving economy which afforded commercial opportunity. That two such extremes are hypothesized does not instill confidence in either position.

population throughout the divided kingdoms.[42] An abrupt influx of new inhabitants has been sustained via archaeological examination of the settlement and economic buildup of the Judean Shephelah, the Negev, as well as Jerusalem and its environs.[43] A secondary factor governing expansion of the city relates to necessary preparations against the reprisal of Sennacherib in the face of Hezekiah's rebellion. The fortification of the capital by a massive rampart, the so-called Broad Wall, is reliably dated to this period.[44]

[42] Suggested by Avigad, *Discovering Jerusalem*, 55; Broshi, "Expansion of Jerusalem in the Reigns of Hezekiah and Manasseh," 21–26; Broshi and Finkelstein, "Population of Palestine in Iron Age II," 47–60. Archaeological data from Jerusalem's extramural neighborhoods shows that the capital experienced sustained natural growth throughout the ninth and eighth centuries B.C.E., with the most drastic changes occurring during the reign of Hezekiah. This documented gradual expansion prompted Donald Ariel and Alon De Groot to conclude "the evidence does not support Broshi's historical reconstruction of a rapid expansion of Jerusalem in the 8th century BCE," because "If one accepts Broshi's reconstruction, one would expect to find that the construction of the extramural neighborhoods of Jerusalem was restricted to the second half of the 8th century BCE" ("Iron Age Extramural Occupation at the City of David," 162). This is needlessly limiting, however, as a brisk buildup within a concentrated period as surmised by Broshi does not preclude slower population growth at other times.
  This study advocates that the ostensibly competing models of Jerusalem's long-term gradual and short-term rapid expansion are indeed correct, as nuanced by Nadav Na'aman, "When and How Did Jerusalem Become a Great City? The Rise of Jerusalem as Judah's Premier City in the Eighth-Seventh Centuries B.C.E." *BASOR* 347 (2007) 21, "It is suggested that the growth of the city of Jerusalem was gradual, starting in the ninth century and accelerating in the eighth century B.C.E., culminating in the late eighth-early seventh centuries" (cf. idem, "The Growth and Development of Judah and Jerusalem in the Eighth Century B.C.E.: A Rejoinder," *RB* 116 [2009] 321–35). The various indications of peacetime settlement noted here, however, do not support his view that the capital's population increase should be attributed primarily to refugees seeking shelter from the Assyrians during Sennacherib's invasion of Judah.
[43] Vaughn, *Theology, History, and Archaeology*, 19–79. The increase in smaller agricultural installations and farms around Jerusalem is documented in Hayah Katz, "A Land of Grain and Wine...A Land of Olive Oil and Honey"—The Economy of the Kingdom of Judah (Jerusalem: Yad Ben-Zvi, 2008) 171–78 [Hebrew].
[44] 2 Chr 32:2–5. See Avigad, *Discovering Jerusalem*, 45–60; Nahman Avigad and Hillel Geva, "Iron Age II Strata 9–7," in Hillel Geva (ed.), *Jewish Quarter Excavations in the Old City of Jerusalem Conducted by Nahman Avigad, 1969–1982, Vol. 1: Architecture and Stratigraphy—Areas A, W and X–2, Final Report* (Jerusalem: Israel Exploration Society, 2000) 45–61. As there is some archaeological basis for both the refugees from the northern kingdom of Israel as well as from the Shephelah during the Assyrian campaigns, the older theory of Broshi, "Expansion of Jerusalem in the Reigns of Hezekiah and Manasseh," still holds up well.

2.3. The Siloam Tunnel

A project undertaken in tandem with building the fortification wall of the Second Quarter was the construction of a water supply system. The naturally occurring Gihon Spring lies in the Kidron Valley on the eastern slopes of the City of David.[45] Both the spring and its nearby drawing pool were flanked by guard towers of undressed cyclopean masonry, a fact which attests to the importance of ancient water sources.[46] Earlier kings had channeled the spring via a man-made conduit down to the Lower Pool at the southern tip of the City of David, whence it flowed into ditches used to irrigate agricultural terraces known as "the king's garden."[47] Such ostentatious projects involving water were commonplace in the ancient Near East.[48]

Prior to his rebellion against Sennacherib which prompted a retributive campaign against Judah, Hezekiah commanded to have a tunnel hewn which would lead the water from the Gihon Spring to a reservoir known

---

[45] In hydrological terms, the Gihon is commonly believed to be a syphon-type karstic spring, because it provides water in pulses or bursts rather than at a continuous, steady rate, see Simons, *Jerusalem in the Old Testament*, 163–64. This fact is reflected in the Hebrew name, which comes from גּוּח/גיח "to gush." On the various water-supply systems of Jerusalem, see *NEAEHL* 4.709–12.

[46] Ronny Reich and Eli Shukron, "Light at the End of the Tunnel," *BAR* 25/1 (Jan.–Feb. 1999) 22–33, 72; eidem, "The System of Rock-Cut Tunnels near Gihon in Jerusalem Reconsidered," *RB* 107/1 (2000) 5–17. Based on the stratigraphic evidence made available from their excavations, their dating of the Siloam Channel and Warren's Shaft to the Middle Bronze Age antedates the previous scholarly consensus by roughly one thousand years. Hence the original fortifications that protected Jerusalem and its waterworks stem, in their opinion, from the Canaanites in the second millennium B.C.E.

[47] 2 Kgs 25:4; Jer 39:4; 52:7; Neh 3:15. These are the שַׁדְמוֹת קִדְרוֹן, "terraces of the Kidron," (2 Kgs 23:4) as rendered by Philip J. King and Lawrence E. Stager, *Life in Biblical Israel* (Louisville: Westminster John Knox, 2001) 217. This conduit is designated Channel II, following the nomenclature of Louis-Hugues Vincent. The Lower Pool is identified with modern Birket el-Ḥamra, mentioned in the allocution of Isa 22:8–11.

[48] The irrigation networks constructed by Sennacherib were perhaps the most elaborate in the ancient world, intended to water his parks and orchards while permitting him to boast of his feats of hydraulic engineering. On this, see Thorkild Jacobsen and Seton Lloyd, *Sennacherib's Aqueduct at Jerwan* (OIP 24; Chicago: University of Chicago Press, 1935); Hayim Tawil, "The Historicity of 2 Kings 19:24 (= Isaiah 37:25): The Problem of *Yeʾōrê Māṣôr*," *JNES* 41/3 (1982) 195–206; Stephanie Dalley, "Nineveh, Babylon and the Hanging Gardens," *Iraq* 56 (1994) 45–58; eadem, "More about the Hanging Gardens," in L. Al-Gailani Werr et al. (eds.), *Of Pots and Plans: Papers on the Archaeology and History of Mesopotamia and Syria Presented to David Oates in Honour of his 75th Birthday* (Cambridge: MacDonald Institute, 2002) 67–73.

as the Pool of Siloam.[49] This hastily constructed tunnel was less vulnerable to enemy access, winding tortuously under the City of David toward the west. The collecting Pool of Siloam was also slightly northwest of the Lower Pool, safely ensconced between the defensive double circumvallation put in place by Hezekiah. These preparations, supported by archaeological evidence, are directly attributed to him in the Bible.[50] A monumental Hebrew inscription was incised at the south end of the tunnel to memorialize the achievement, whose paleography supports an eighth-century dating.[51]

---

[49] The Pool of Siloam is modern Birket Silwan, referenced in Isa 8:6; John 9:7. The later reuse of the Lower Pool after the blocking of the obsolete Channel II is discussed in Simons, *Jerusalem in the Old Testament*, 157–94, esp. 189–93; David Ussishkin, "The Water Systems of Jerusalem during Hezekiah's Reign," in M. Weippert and S. Timm (eds.), *Meilenstein: Festgabe für Herbert Donner zum 16. Februar 1995* (ÄAT 30; Wiesbaden: Harrassowitz Verlag, 1995) 289–307.
The first modern archaeologist to traverse this subterranean water supply system was Edward Robinson, *Biblical Researches in Palestine and the Adjacent Regions. A Journal of Travels in the Years 1838 & 1852* (2nd ed.; 3 vols.; London: John Murray, 1856) 1.337–43. A bibliography of preliminary reports from recent excavations may be found in Jane M. Cahill, "Jerusalem at the Time of the United Monarchy: The Archaeological Evidence," in Vaughn and Killebrew (eds.), *Jerusalem in Bible and Archaeology*, 17–18 n. 24.
[50] 2 Kgs 20:20; 2 Chr 32:2–6, 30. The actual length of Hezekiah's tunnel cited in scholarship varies somewhat, ranging from 512.5 meters to over 533 meters. The inscription itself has caused some dispute as to the original extent of Hezekiah's tunnel, since it gives the length as 1,200 cubits. While attempts have been made to reconcile the difference, as seen in David Ussishkin, "The Original Length of the Siloam Tunnel in Jerusalem," *Levant* 8 (1976) 82–95, the value preserved in the inscription is probably typological, see Ronny Reich and Eli Shukron, "On the Original Length of Hezekiah's Tunnel: Some Critical Notes on David Ussishkin's Suggestions," in A. M. Maeir and P. de Miroschedji (eds.), *"I Will Speak The Riddles Of Ancient Times" Archaeological and Historical Studies in Honor of Amihai Mazar on the Occasion of his Sixtieth Birthday* (Winona Lake, Ind.: Eisenbrauns, 2006) 2.795–800.
[51] A. H. Sayce, "The Ancient Hebrew Inscription Discovered at the Pool of Siloam in Jerusalem," *PEFQS* (1881) 141–54, with translations in *ANET* 321; *KAI* 186–88; *COS* 2.145–46. A selection of related studies is cited at T. C. Vriezen and A. S. van der Woude, *Ancient Israelite and Early Jewish Literature* (trans. Brian Doyle; Leiden: Brill, 2004) 9 n. 8. Despite the express biblical confirmation of Hezekiah's tunnel, as well as the paleographic studies done on the Siloam inscription, a subtle redating of the text to the reign of Manasseh has been advocated by Ernst Axel Knauf, "Hezekiah or Manasseh? A Reconsideration of the Siloam Tunnel and Inscription," *TA* 28 (2001) 281–87.
A more radical proposal dates the inscription to the Hasmonean period, see John Rogerson and Philip R. Davies, "Was the Siloam Tunnel Built by Hezekiah?" *BA* 59 (1996) 138–49. The claim has been soundly refuted by Ronald S. Hendel, "The Date of the Siloam Inscription: A Rejoinder to Rogerson and Davies," *BA* 59/4 (1996) 233–37; Jo Ann Hackett et al., "Defusing Pseudo-Scholarship: The Siloam Inscription Ain't Hasmonean," *BAR* 23 (Mar.–Apr. 1997) 41–50, 68; Stig Norin, "The Age of the Siloam Inscription and Hezekiah's Tunnel," *VT* 48/1 (1998) 37–48; Stephen Rosenberg, "The Siloam Tunnel Revisited," *TA* 25 (1998) 116–30.
More paleographic evidence has been provided in a recently discovered inscription from the City of David, documented in Ronny Reich and Eli Shukron, "A Fragmentary

The decision to change the course of the Gihon Spring was a drastic measure which would not have been taken lightly, owing to the extensive
engineering work involved and the consequent cessation of irrigating the
king's garden. The attribution of the tunnel is most reasonably assigned
to the reign of Hezekiah for the purpose of protecting Jerusalem's water
supply during the Assyrian blockade of 701 B.C.E.[52]

2.4. THE *LMLK* SEALS

The storage jars containing the seal impression *lmlk* (למלך, "belonging to
the king") are another significant, but controversial, indicator of the extent
of Hezekiah's kingdom.[53] These jar handles typically bear a four-winged

---

Palaeo-Hebrew Inscription from the City of David, Jerusalem," *IEJ* 58/1 (2008) 48–50. It has
been reliably dated to the eighth century based on pottery from this period in the thick
fill of its find location. The researchers concluded that "the script best resembles that of
the Siloam inscription" (p. 49).

[52] Miller and Hayes, *History of Ancient Israel and Judah*, 412, posit the construction of
the tunnel in tandem with the Ashdod affair, albeit without explanation. Tatum, "Jerusalem in Conflict," 297, sees the project as a peacetime effort effectuated along with the
expansion of Jerusalem in the years after the fall of Samaria. Ussishkin, "Water Systems of
Jerusalem," 301–303, followed by Dalley, "Recent Evidence from Assyrian Sources," 397–98,
favors that "the *raison d'être* of the tunnel has to be looked for in the field of hydrology,"
that is, to water the King's Garden. Yet the rapidly growing urban center already had an
adequate water supply which would not have been quantitatively increased by such a formidable engineering achievement. As with the double fortification wall, the only purpose
served by redirecting the flow of water from the Gihon Spring would have been defensive.
The biblical account implies the conjunction of both these undertakings in the context of
preparations for Sennacherib's invasion of Judah (2 Chr 32:1–5, 30), and there is no compelling reason to suggest otherwise.

[53] This translation is literal, but may be rendered more informally "royal property," as
suggested by Anson F. Rainey, "Wine from the Royal Vineyards," *BASOR* 245 (1982) 61. The
lmlk jars were technically designated as Lachish Type 484 jars by Olga Tufnell, *Lachish III:
The Iron Age* (2 vols.; London: Oxford University Press, 1953) 315–16 (text volume). Based
on the growing number of samples that have been uncovered, the *lmlk* jars have been
re-classified as Types SJO3 and SJO4 in the typology of Seymour Gitin, "The *lmlk* Jar-Form
Redefined: A New Class of Iron Age II Oval-Shaped Storage Jar," in Maeir and de Miroschedji (eds.), *"I Will Speak the Riddle of Ancient Times"*, 2.505–24.

The *lmlk* jar handles were initially discovered by Charles Warren in late 1868-early 1869,
and published in "Phoenician Inscription on Jar Handles," *PEQ* 2 (1870) 372. The first *lmlk*
jar handles bearing impressions with personal names were unearthed by F. J. Bliss and
R. A. S. Macalister, *Excavations in Palestine during the Years 1898–1900* (London: Committee
of the Palestine Exploration Fund, 1902) 106–23.

To date, the most thorough studies of the *lmlk* jars may be found in Peter Welten, *Die
Königs-Stempel: Ein Beitrag zur Militärpolitik Judas unter Hiskia und Josia* (Wiesbaden:
Otto Harrassowitz, 1969); Vaughn, *Theology, History, and Archaeology*, 81–167. The non-
academic, and lamentably derisive, work of G. M. Grena, *Lmlk—A Mystery Belonging to*

scarab beetle or a two-winged solar disc, with one of four geographic top-onyms inscribed underneath. Other seals bear personal names, presumed to be royal officials. Their distribution has been concentrated primarily in the Shephelah, most notably in Lachish, as well as in Jerusalem and Ramat Rachel. Urban settlements north of Lachish and Jerusalem also account for a large number of handles, with lesser concentration in the Negev and in Philistia.[54] They are a unique archaeological occurrence, being the only exemplar of jars with royal insignia known from the kingdom of Judah.[55]

It is only within the last quarter century that the accompanying impressions have been attributed predominantly to Hezekiah, having previously been credited to the reforms of Josiah.[56] Other consensus opinions have

---

the King, Vol. 1 (Redondo Beach, Cal.: 4000 Years of Writing History, 2004), is nevertheless useful for its extensive inclusion of previous scholarship.

[54] See further Nili Sacher Fox, *In the Service of the King. Officialdom in Ancient Israel and Judah* (HUCM 23; Cincinatti: Hebrew Union College Press, 2000) 219–20, and the chart of find spots in Vaughn, *Theology, History, and Archaeology*, 166. Chemical analysis of over one hundred *lmlk* jar handles has narrowed the actual production location to somewhere in the Shephelah, summarized in Hans Mommsen, Isadore Perlman and Joseph Yellin, "The Provenience of the *lmlk* Jars," *IEJ* 34 (1984) 89–113.

[55] As described by Fox, *In the Service of the King*, 216, "The *lmlk* seal impressions comprise the largest assemblage of archaeological data associated with an enterprise of the central government."

[56] Based on the diverse palaeographic styles on the seal impressions, David Diringer, "On Ancient Hebrew Inscriptions Discovered at Tell Ed-Duweir (Lachish)–II," *PEQ* 73/3 (1941) 89–109, distinguished three different sub-divisions. It was William F. Albright, *The Excavation of Tell Beit Mirsim, Vol. III: The Iron Age* (AASOR; New Haven: American Schools of Oriental Research, 1943) 74, followed by David Diringer, "The Royal Jar-Handle Stamps of Ancient Judah," *BA* 12/4 (1949) 70–86, who perceived this as evidence of three classes of *lmlk* jars ranging from the late 8th century to the early 6th century: Class I (Hezekiah), Class II (Manasseh), Class III (Josiah and subsequent kings through the first Babylonian deportation of 597 B.C.E.). For subtle refinements to these classifications, see Fox, *In the Service of the King*, 217–18, and bibliography there. The assignment of Lachish levels II and III to 586 B.C.E. and 597 B.C.E., respectively, by James L. Starkey, "Excavations at Tell Ed Duweir," *PEQ* 69 (1937) 236, bolstered the consensus of the time that the *lmlk* jars were material evidence of the Josianic reform.

It was not until the influential stratigraphic study of Lachish by David Ussishkin, "The Destruction of Lachish by Sennacherib and the Dating of the Royal Judean Storage Jars," *TA* 4 (1977) 28–57; idem, "Excavations at Lachish, 1973–77: Preliminary Report" *TA* 5 (1978) 1–97; idem, "Answers at Lachish," *BAR* 5/6 (Nov.–Dec. 1979) 16–39, confirming the earlier conclusions of Tufnell, *Lachish III*, 56–58, 95–98; eadem, "Hazor, Samaria, and Lachish: A Synthesis," *PEQ* 91 (1959) 90–105, that the dating of the *lmlk* jars reached a turning point. By demonstrating that Lachish Level III must have been the stratum destroyed by Sennacherib in 701 B.C.E., the seal impressions preserved within that layer should rightly be attributed to Hezekiah. Newer studies of eighth-century Judahite sites such as Tel Batash (Timnah) Stratum III and Stratum 12 of the City of David corroborate these findings, cf. George L. Kelm and Amihai Mazar, "Three Seasons of Excavations at Tell Batash—Biblical Timnah," *BASOR* 248 (1982) 29–30; Yigal Shiloh, *Excavations at the City of David I* (Qedem 19; Jerusalem: Institute of Archaeology, 1984) 28; idem, "Judah and Jerusalem in

gradually emerged, such as that the four- and two-winged scarab types cannot be readily distinguished diachronically,[57] and that those seals bearing the names of personal officials do not point to a different circumstance in the use of the jars.[58] The utilization of the *lmlk* storage jars continued into the seventh century, as well as a modest amount of production.[59] Even with these data reasonably well established, many questions still remain in the afterglow of considerable scholarship:[60] the precise location of the four geographic names;[61] the purpose connoted by these designations

---

the Eighth-Sixth Centuries B.C.E.," in S. Gitin and W. G. Dever (eds.), *Recent Excavations in Israel: Studies in Iron Age Archaeology* (AASOR 49; Winona Lake, Ind.: Eisenbrauns, 1989) 97–105. Stratigraphic layers are now commonly dated to the 8th century based on the seals, see p. 104 of the latter article.

[57] Originally proposed by Albright and Diringer, the four-winged seal was construed as a "pagan" Egyptian flying scarab which was replaced under the influence of Josiah's reform by a bird representing a flying scroll. The excavations at Lachish by Ussishkin nullified these conclusions, as evidenced by the fact that both the two-winged and four-winged varieties of seal impressions were found in Level III, whereas no *lmlk* seals have been discovered in Level II. It is clear, however, that the Type 484 jars with a rosette stamp should be attributed to a later period.

[58] Covered in Vaughn, *Theology, History, and Archaeology*, 90–93.

[59] A. Douglas Tushingham, "New Evidence Bearing on the Two-Winged *LMLK* Stamp," *BASOR* 287 (1992) 61–65; Oded Lipschits, Omer Sergi and Ido Koch, "Royal Judahite Jar Handles: Reconsidering the Chronology of the *lmlk* Stamp Impressions," *TA* 37/1 (2010) 8–9. The claim of continued production has been refuted by Vaughn, *Theology, History, and Archaeology*, 85–87, 95–110, but this position has not held in the face of more recent archaeological discoveries. A more nuanced stance arguing for continued use of the storage jars in the aftermath of Sennacherib's invasion is presented by Amihai Mazar, David Amit, and Zvi Ilan, "The 'Border Road' between Michmash and Jericho and the Excavations at Ḥorvat Shilḥah," *Eretz-Israel* 17 (1984) 248, 250 n. 46 [Hebrew].

[60] See the extensive bibliography assembled by Raz Kletter, "Temptation to Identify: Jerusalem, *mmšt*, and the *lmlk* Jar Stamps," *ZDPV* 118 (2002) 136.

[61] The identification of the four place names:

ḥbrn—Understood as king David's first capital, Hebron.

z[y]p—Popularly associated with Tell Zīf south of Hebron, and mentioned in Josh 15:55; 2 Chr 11:8. Another site by the same name in the Negev is a less likely candidate (Josh 15:24).

śwkh—Two locations are known by this name, one in the Shephelah east of Azekah (Ḥirbet 'Abbād, cf. Josh 15:35; 1 Sam 17:1), and the other in the Judean highlands (Ḥirbet Šuwēkē, cf. Josh 15:48; 1 Chr 4:18, suggested by Rainey, "Wine from the Royal Vineyards," 59). Due to the results of neutron activation analysis by Mommsen et al., "Provenience of the *lmlk* Jars," the former Judean town is preferable. See also the comments of Nadav Na'aman, "Hezekiah's Fortified Cities and the *LMLK* Stamps," *BASOR* 261 (1986) 12.

mmšt—An otherwise unattested geographic place name, and therefore the most debated. It was identified with Mampsis-Kurnub in the Negev highlands by William F. Albright, "The Administrative Division of Israel and Judah," *JPOS* 5 (1925) 45, but this site did not exist in the Iron Age. On the presumption that a royal storage program would have necessarily involved Jerusalem, H. L. Ginsberg, "MMŠT and MṢH," *BASOR* 109 (1948) 20–22, proposed *mmšt* as an elliptical form of *mmšlt* "[seat of] government." A similar conclusion was reached by Yohanan Aharoni, *The Archaeology of Eretz Israel: From the*

accompanying the king's seal;[62] when the jars ultimately fell out of use; their function. For the purposes of this book, the matter of function is the most relevant.

In the earlier period of research pertaining to the *lmlk* jars, when their dating was presumed to underscore the historicity of the Josianic reform, the argument was put forward that these storage vessels constituted a standardized system of weights and measures.[63] Once the *lmlk* jars were reassigned to the late eighth century, a new explanation had to be sought. Focusing on their distribution pattern in the fortified cities of the Shephelah and northern hill country of Judah—areas which would have been prime military targets during an Assyrian assault—it was advanced that the jars evinced the scope of Hezekieh's preparations to store provisions in the face of Sennacherib's imminent invasion.[64] This reasoning was subsequently followed and became the academic consensus.[65]

Prehistoric Beginnings to the End of the First Temple Period (ed. Miriam Aharoni; trans. Anson F. Rainey; Philadelphia: Westminster, 1978) 259, who availed himself of the accepted locations of the other three place names in order to triangulate the district capital in the northern hill country. The suggestion has persisted despite the rebuttals of Nahman Avigad, "New Light on the MSH Seal Impressions," *IEJ* 8 (1958) 118 n. 28, and Welten, *Königs-Stempel*, 150 n. 19. Kletter, "Temptation to Identify," 139–40, situates *mmšt* somewhere in the southern Judean highlands, based on proximity to the other sites. Most recently, the elusive town has been equated with Ramat Rachel, see Gabriel Barkay, "Royal Palace, Royal Portrait? The Tantalizing Possibilities of Ramat Rahel," *BAR* 32/5 (Sept.–Oct. 2006) 34–44; idem, "Ramat Rahel," *NEAEHL* 4.1261–67. For detailed discussion, see Welten, *Königs-Stempel*, 147–56.

[62] The meanings that have been attributed to the four locales inscribed upon the jar handles, as summarized in Mommsen et al., "Provenience of the *lmlk* Jars," 90–91, are as follows:
– Tax-collecting centers for administrative divisions of Judah.
– Supply centers or garrison towns to serve four defense zones.
– Royal estates which sent their produce to royal fortresses.
– Wine-producing centers or vineyards.
– Seats of royal offices for weights and measures.
– Sites of royal pottery workshops.
See further Welten, *Königs-Stempel*, 118–42; Nadav Na'aman, "Sennacherib's Campaign to Judah and the Date of the *lmlk* Stamps," *VT* 29/1 (1979) 61–86; Fox, *In the Service of the King*, 223–25.

[63] Developed by Frank M. Cross, "Judean Stamps," *Eretz-Israel* 9 (1969) 22*.

[64] Na'aman, "Sennacherib's Campaign to Judah and the Date of the *lmlk* Stamps," 75; idem, "Hezekiah's Fortified Cities and the *LMLK* Stamps," 12–14.

[65] Cf. Yohanan Aharoni, *The Land of the Bible: A Historical Geography* (Philadelphia: Westminster Press, 1979) 398–99; David Ussishkin, *The Conquest of Lachish by Sennacherib* (Tel Aviv: Institute of Archaeology, 1982) 50; Oded Borowski, "Hezekiah's Reforms and the Revolt Against Assyria," *BA* 58/3 (1995) 152–54; Halpern, "Jerusalem and the Lineages," 23; Lipschits, Sergi, and Koch, "Reconsidering the Chronology of the *lmlk* Stamp Impressions."

There are several objections that may be raised against this proposal. The lower distribution of *lmlk* jars in the Negev and southern Shephelah was accounted for under this invasion hypothesis as simply being outside of the supply chain.[56] If the geographic dispersement were intentional, however, the allocation of the *lmlk* jars under this theory should still be in direct proportion to the populations they served. It is problematic, then, that many of the Judean fortified cities in the days of Hezekiah—including prominent, centrally located Hebron, considered to be the crucial link in the distribution system—have such a low number of extant seals.[67] It makes little sense to stockpile storage jars at one location, only to transport virtually all of them elsewhere: a well-chosen distribution center for a military operation should have a correspondingly high number of containers.[68] The jars were also sent to agricultural, unfortified locations, where there would be few avenues to safeguard their sustainability.[69] Indeed, the need to specify the origin of each jar would hardly be relevant under circumstances in which the quantity, not quality, of supplies was of the utmost importance.[70] One is hard pressed to discern the need for over

---

[66] Na'aman, "Hezekiah's Fortified Cities and the *LMLK* Stamps," 17.

[67] Na'aman, "Hezekiah's Fortified Cities and the *LMLK* Stamps," 15, declares that Hebron "was selected to be the pivotal town in the distributional and defensive systems." His test case was the list of fifteen fortified cities in 2 Chr 11:6–10. As of August 13, 2011, only six excavated sites among those fifteen locations (Azekah, Beth-zur, Hebron, Lachish, Mareshah, and Sokoh) contain more then ten seals, based on the statistics compiled at the LMLK Research Website: <*http://www.lmlk.com/research/lmlk_corp.htm*>. Lachish boasts an impressive total of 415 seal impressions, whereas Hebron sports a meager thirteen.

[68] Such distribution locations should also be proximal to the place of manufacture of the jars themselves. As this locus has been isolated to the Shephelah by Mommsen et al., "Provenience of the *lmlk* Jars," most of the proposed sites for the geographic place names on the seals are poorly chosen militarily.

[69] Vaughn, *Theology, History, and Archaeology*, 141–46. As noted by Fox, *In the Service of the King*, 232–33 n. 142, Vaughn's survey of sites with *lmlk* impressions not destroyed by Sennacherib is not evidence against a military function for the storage jars, as the precise points of attack could not be known precisely beforehand.

[70] The actual contents of the jars is an open question. The prevalence of wine and oil in scholarly discussions as the likely commodity housed in the *lmlk* jars stems from early recommendations made by Cross, "Judean Stamps," 21*, as well as Tufnell and Avigad, see the references in Paul W. Lapp, "Late Royal Seals from Judah," *BASOR* 158 (1960) 22. Once the jars were no longer dated to the Josianic period, wine was summarily dismissed as the contents of the jars due to their presumed military function: "The hypothesis that the *lmlk* stamps indicated special brands of produce, namely wine ... presupposes a state of peace in the land, which would hardly accord well with the preparations for an impending war ... an emergency is certainly not the appropriate time to start the systematic recording of the origin of wine" (Na'aman, "Hezekiah's Fortified Cities and the *LMLK* Stamps," 14). Nevertheless, the early identifications have remained. The narrow mouth of the jars is indeed conducive to liquids, as observed by scholars such as Fox, *In the Service of the King*,

fifty engravers to spend their time embossing the jars in the face of military reprisal, or for the king to insist that the contents of the vessels rightfully belonged to the royal house if their function was to be apportioned among the people.[71]

It is now widely acknowledged that storage jars of the same typology had appeared in Israel by the late ninth or early eighth century B.C.E., and this system extended down to the Babylonian conquest.[72] As for the *lmlk* jars themselves, the sheer number of stamp impressions and corresponding unique seals used to make them testifies to an elaborate administrative network which had been in place for some time. The brief timespan typically postulated for this Hezekian program under the invasion hypothesis (704–701 B.C.E.) simply cannot accommodate the quantity and sophistication of the *lmlk* jars.[73] The procedure of marking the containers expressly as "royal property" and employing geographic place names tracking their points of origin speaks rather to a highly developed fiscal program necessitated by Judah's fluctuating socio-economic landscape in the eighth century.

The evidence suggests that the *lmlk* jars were part of a program of taxation, whereby the king took over the rural wineries and exacted money

---

227; Kletter, "Temptation to Identify," 140. Orna Zimhoni, "Two Ceramic Assemblages from Lachish Levels III and II," *TA* 17 (1990) 3–52, perceived clay stoppers that have retained the marks of leaves used to form airtight seals, as well as holes in other jars to permit air escape during fermentation. The evidence suggests that whereas fluids are the most likely candidate for the contents of the jars, grains cannot be excluded out of hand.

[71] Vaughn, *Theology, History, and Archaeology*, 123–26, provides a conservative estimate of 54. His discussions of the double-stamped impressions on pp. 112–17 suggest that their decipherment was indeed important. The palaeography of seals in general is of sufficient variance throughout the seventh and eighth centuries that caution must be exercised in their dating, as discussed in Andrew G. Vaughn, "Palaeographic Dating of Judean Seals and Its Significance for Biblical Research," *BASOR* 313 (1999) 43–64.

[72] The early "proto" jars are documented in Vaughn, *Theology, History, and Archaeology*, 138–40; Itzhack Shai and Aren M. Maeir, "The Pre-*LMLK* Jars: A New Class of Iron Age IIA Storage Jars," *TA* 30 (2003) 108–23; Gitin, "*lmlk* Jar-Form Redefined." For their continuity through the 6th century, see Gitin previously and Lipschits, Sergi, and Koch, "Reconsidering the Chronology of the *lmlk* Stamp Impressions."

[73] Vaughn, *Theology, History, and Archaeology*, 140–52, substantiates that this program enacted by royal decree extended over several years, and was not a last-minute effort. As stated by Lipschits, Sergi, and Koch, "Reconsidering the Chronology of the *lmlk* Stamp Impressions," 6: "It is implausible that such an elaborate system could develop in the three or four years between the revolt of Hezekiah and the Assyrian campaign. It is also hard to imagine that so complex a system of jar manufacture at a single centre, distribution for filling at a variety of agricultural estates and finally storage at royal hubs was developed and carried out on such a massive scale in a mere three years. The sizeable[sic] number of *lmlk* storage jars found compared, for example, to the number of rosette stamped jars, also testifies to the length of time this system must have been operative."

from them to ensure that revenue flowed into the royal treasury.[74] This would have been prompted on the one hand by the rapid growth of the kingdom at this time, and on the other by the role of Judah in supporting the imperial military as an Assyrian vassal.[75] Such an explanation provides a justification for the need to track the containers via the names of designated officials. This at once suggests a non-military setting, in which wine would still have been a luxury for those who could afford it, hence the value of inscribing the four regional wine-making locations, as well as the time needed to engrave them. During the revolt, the purpose of the jars would have been adapted based on more exiguous circumstances, which would account both for the types of seals that seem to have been done in haste, as well as those jar handles which conspicuously lack the royal seal.[76] With the economy drastically altered in the aftermath of the invasion, the jars would have continued to have been used until their lifespan had run out. This in fact may be seen in certain locales.[77] Coupled with the indications that the program was in use for some years, this points to the function of the *lmlk* jars as purely economic, ostensibly dealing with the new demands laid at Hezekiah's door due to repercussions from the fall of the northern kingdom.

A context anchored in the years following the immigration of northern refugees to Judah would likewise be commensurate with anthropological models which see agricultural buildup as a direct result of increases

---

[74] The dearth of *lmlk* jars in the Negev has been posited as due to a separate system of supply and taxation stemming from privately owned lands, suggested by Rainey, "Wine from the Royal Vineyards.'

[75] The latter option is the favored explanation of Lipschits, Sergi, and Koch, "Reconsidering the Chronology of the *lmlk* Stamp Impressions," 6–7, 27–28, but the rapid proliferation of the Type SJO jars would require under this theory a correspondingly greater burden of vassalage than, for instance, in the first half of the eighth century when the jars were first discovered. The correlation with the rise in agricultural estates and food production, on the other hand, suggests to me that the former was the overriding, if not exclusive, impetus.

[76] The so-called double-stamped seals need not all be posited as arising from an extreme emergency, as there is evidence to suggest that care was taken to ensure decipherment of a stamping deemed substandard, see Vaughn, *Theology, History, and Archaeology*, 112–17. The independent proposition of Kletter, "Temptation to Identify," likewise argues for seeing the archaeological data as supporting two separate phases in the lifecycle of the Type 484 jars: the first in a peaceful context prior to Hezekiah's revolt, and the second comprising the revolt itself (705–701 B.C.E.). It is puzzling, therefore, as to why he restricts his Stage 1 chronologically to "not much earlier; perhaps a matter of a few years" (p. 141) prior to Hezekiah's planned insurgency.

[77] Vaughn, *Theology, History, and Archaeology*, 139–40; Lipschits, Sergi, and Koch, "Reconsidering the Chronology of the *lmlk* Stamp Impressions."

in settlement population. Methods of food production that could support a larger populace would have been indispensable, and the rapid economic growth of the state through increased trade and tax revenue would translate directly into elevated political status and prestige for the king.[78] It would also explain the dual use of both the four-winged 'scarab' and two-winged 'sun' signs, which have some basis in being identified as the royal insignia of both the kingdoms of Israel and Judah, respectively.[79] Their usage would reflect the desire of Hezekiah to be seen as the ruler of a newly reunited kingdom, as well as the provider for the needs of his subjects.[80] A political agenda accompanying the administrative program also goes some way toward explaining the unique nature of royal insignia being employed on the storage jars, despite the likelihood of such government stockpiling earlier in the history of the monarchy.[81] The use of personal seals by government officials, in any event, is far more plausible in the context of economic trade than as part of a military effort.[82]

This reconstruction of the use of the *lmlk* seals is consonant with the evidence previously obtained in regard to the urbanization of Jerusalem; namely, that Hezekiah was a skillful leader who invested considerable resources in response to the socio-economic responsibilities of his

---

[78] For references to such studies, as well as pertinent citations, see the overview in Vaughn, *Theology, History, and Archaeology*, 19–21.

[79] A. Douglas Tushingham, "A Royal Israelite Seal (?) and the Royal Jar Handle Stamps," *BASOR* 200 (1970) 71–78 (part one) and *BASOR* 201 (1971) 23–35 (part two); idem, "New Evidence Bearing on the Two-Winged *LMLK* Stamp," 61–64. See further discussion in Fox, *In the Service of the King*, 220–22. As acknowledged by Kletter, "Temptation to Identify," 144, regarding his own theory, "The two-phases model does not explain the different distribution of two- and four-winged stamps." Independently, the same argument for reunification has been made in regard to the insignia on Hezekiah's seal impression, see Meir Lubetski, "King Hezekiah's Seal Revisited," *BAR* 27/4 (Jul.–Aug. 2001) 44–51, 59.

[80] The perennial image of the monarch as shepherd in ancient Near Eastern literature comes to mind, as this role was as fundamental to kingship as the establishment of justice. This suggestion has been applied to Josiah based on the older system of dating the seals, but the logic is all the more appropriate to Hezekiah whose kingdom truly encompassed the denizens of both Israel and Judah.

[81] As noted by Fox, *In the Service of the King*, 234, in her discussion of the novelty of the *lmlk* phenomenon, Solomon (1 Kgs 9:19, cf. 2 Chr 8:4, 6), Baasha (2 Chr 16:4), and Jehoshaphat (17:12) are credited with the building of storage facilities as well. This would seem to be the most reasonable interpretation for the ninth and early eighth-century storage receptacles surveyed by Vaughn, *Theology, History, and Archaeology*, 138–39, which have been classified as "prototype" *lmlk* jars.

[82] This new academic consensus supersedes the older view that the personal names were those of the potters themselves, see the survey in Vaughn, *Theology, History, and Archaeology*, 110–12, 161–65. For explanations of their purpose and significance, see Fox, *In the Service of the King*, 229–32.

proliferating domain. The sweeping measures which were taken during his rule point to a primary concern of ensuring the livelihood of his burgeoning subject base rather than plotting a coup to overthrow the tyrannical oppression of his Assyrian masters. Devoid of any martial role, the *lmlk* jars were a lucrative business venture to provide for the king's subjects and generate revenue for the royal treasury, all the while aggrandizing Hezekiah as the faithful shepherd and deliverer of his people.

2.5. Conclusion

Judah was sufficiently important to merit attention from Assyria throughout the reign of Hezekiah, which itself is a testament to the growth of the nation during the last quarter of the eighth century. The taking of Philistine cities by Hezekiah and subsequent forced tribute mentioned in the Azekah Inscription aligns well with the biblical notices of 2 Kgs 18:7–8, and points to the king's participation in the western coalition against Assyria in 720 B.C.E. Sargon, who successfully captured Samaria at this time, was able with the submission of Hezekiah to proclaim himself to be "the subduer of the land Judah which is far away." Thereafter Hezekiah was forced to be compliant and to assist his imperial masters, as revealed in two fragmentary letters from Nimrud. In the meantime, he had far more pressing matters demanding his attention at home, as he dealt with the humanitarian issues arising from the fall of the northern empire.

A consequence of the end of the northern kingdom was the transformation of Jerusalem from a small settlement into a major urban center. The capital city quickly swelled beyond the limited confines of the eastern ridge to encompass the southwestern hill, and residential dwellings were erected further north and on the eastern slopes of the City of David. This growth around Jerusalem and its environs was accompanied by similar economic buildup in the Judean Shephelah and the Negev. Such rapid expansion could not have occurred in the brief timeframe between Hezekiah's rebellion and the retaliation of Sennacherib, as favored by some scholars, and the archaeological evidence from Stratum 12 of Jerusalem confirms that this massive increase in construction was initially a peacetime effort. Along with the fortification wall around the Mišneh, or Second Quarter, Hezekiah undertook the hewing of the Siloam Tunnel to safeguard the city's water supply in the eventuality of future attack.

The Type 484 storage jars designated as *lmlk* "royal property" may now be securely placed under the auspices of king Hezekiah, thanks to the redating of the end of Level III at Lachish to 701 B.C.E. Their function as a form of military preparation is dubious. The narrow mouths of the jars are more conducive to wine or oil, and the time-consuming process of engraving the seals makes little sense in the context of impending warfare. The jars also show uneven distribution in regard to population, and were disseminated to locations which were militarily vulnerable. Rather, this would appear to have been a state-sponsored economic program which spanned several years, a systematic plan of taxation to coincide with the increase in settlement and agricultural buildup throughout the region. The scarab and sun insignia were indicative of the new, united kingdom that was being forged, with the generation of additional revenue strengthening the political center of the nation. The *lmlk* jars were of continued service to the country during wartime and thereafter, but they effectively came to an end after the reign of Hezekiah.

CHAPTER THREE

SENNACHERIB'S THIRD CAMPAIGN

It would be difficult to overstate the sheer amount of biblical scholarship that has been published on the topic of Sennacherib's campaign to Judah.[1] It is not only the longest account in the Hebrew Bible of any confrontation between Israel and Assyria, but is also the most detailed description preserved in cuneiform of an Assyrian campaign to the west.[2] Although any academic work has a responsibility to survey previous scholarship as a prelude to its own original contribution, in this case the length required

---

[1] As aptly phrased by Kenneth Kitchen, Review of William R. Gallagher, *Sennacherib's Campaign to Judah, New Studies. JSS* 47/1 (2002) 133, "During the past century, probably more pages have been published about the events of Sennacherib's campaign in Palestine in 701 BC than clay tablets were written at the time of the events themselves."

For older bibliographical surveys, see Leo L. Honor, *Sennacherib's Invasion of Palestine: A Critical Source Study* (New York: Columbia University Press, 1926); James A. Montgomery, *A Critical and Exegetical Commentary on the Books of Kings* (ICC; New York: Charles Scribner's Sons, 1951) 513ff; Hayim Tadmor, "Hezekiah," *EncBib* 3.99 [Hebrew]; Harold H. Rowley, "Hezekiah's Reform and Rebellion," *BJRL* 44/2 (1962) 395ff; Peter Machinist, "The *rab šāqēh* at the Wall of Jerusalem: Israelite Identity in the Face of the Assyrian 'Other'," *HS* 41 (2000) 152–53 n. 1; Hans Wildberger, *Isaiah 28–39: A Continental Commentary* (trans. Thomas H. Trapp; Continental Commentary; Minneapolis: Fortress Press, 2002) 359–60, 737–39.

[2] As pointed out by Hayim Tadmor, "Sennacherib's Campaign to Judah: Historiographical and Historical Considerations," *Zion* 50 (1985) 66 [Hebrew]. The Assyrian sources of Sennacherib's third campaign are given both in transliteration and translation in George Smith, *History of Sennacherib* (London: Williams and Norgate, 1878) 53–72; Daniel David Luckenbill, *The Annals of Sennacherib* (OIP 2; Chicago: University of Chicago, 1924); Eckart Frahm, *Einleitung in die Sanherib-Inschriften* (AfOB 26; Vienna: Institut für Orientalisk der Universität, 1997) 47–61; Walter Mayer, "Sennacherib's Campaign of 701 BCE: The Assyrian View," in L. L. Grabbe (ed.), *'Like a Bird in a Cage': The Invasion of Sennacherib in 701 BCE* (JSOTSup 363; London: Sheffield Academic Press, 2003) 168–200.

A critical discussion of the annals, along with their value as historical sources, may be found in Honor, *Sennacherib's Invasion of Palestine*, 1–12; Cornelius van Leeuwen, "Sanchérib devant Jérusalem," *OTS* 14 (1965) 245ff; Frederick Mario Fales (ed.), *Assyrian Royal Inscriptions: New Horizons in Literary, Ideological, and Historical Analysis* (Rome: Istituto per L'Oriente, 1981); Louis D. Levine, "Preliminary Remarks on the Historical Inscriptions of Sennacherib," in H. Tadmor and M. Weinfeld (eds.), *History, Historiography and Interpretation: Studies in Biblical and Cuneiform Literatures* (Jerusalem: Magnes Press, 1983) 58–75; Walter Mayer, *Politik und Kriegskunst der Assyrer* (ALASP 9; Münster: Ugarit-Verlag, 1995) 37–60.

for such a review would be detrimental.[3] The goal in retreading this ground is to take firm positions on those issues which remain contentious in academia, in the hope that new perspectives on this material will offer the chance of one day resolving such debates once and for all.

The bulk of the representation of Hezekiah in Kings relates to the narrative of Sennacherib's campaign against Jerusalem, and this will be the appropriate place to compare the biblical version of events with Assyrian records. Within the Deuteronomistic History, this confrontation is believed to be preserved in three discrete sources: a chronistic record in 2 Kgs 18:13b–16 (source A), and two prophetic narratives in 2 Kgs 18:17–19:37 (sources B$_1$ and B$_2$). The differing perspectives in these texts entail historical issues that need to be addressed, such as the question of one or two Assyrian campaigns, the dates of reign of Taharqo king of Kush, and the actual outcome of the confrontation between Hezekiah and Sennacherib.

3.1. ARCHAEOLOGICAL EVIDENCE

The landscape of Judah changed dramatically in the wake of the campaign of Sennacherib to Palestine. The archaeological record has preserved many details relating to the severity and scope of the event, although due to the interpretive nature of the discipline many of these facts have been variously understood. The field is also in a constant state of flux, with ongoing excavations that can dramatically alter the historical reconstruction of a particular site, compounded by field reports that are typically published in a gradual fashion over years or even decades. This section will undertake a brief survey of the sites and regions relevant to the period, in an effort to determine what conclusions may be drawn in accord with the detailed archaeological studies previously conducted.[4]

Lachish is the touchstone for ascribing comparable sites of the period, due to the recent consensus attained in the stratigraphic dating of the

---

[3] For laudable efforts by others, see Lester L. Grabbe, "Two Centuries of Sennacherib Study: A Survey," in idem (ed.), 'Like a Bird in a Cage', 20–36.

[4] Discussion of Jerusalem itself will be held in abeyance until the next chapter, where it rightfully becomes the singular focus. Owing to the discord which persists with regard to the proper designation for the period in question—Iron IIB, IIC, III—such archaeological terminology will be eschewed in the subsequent discussion. For the range of proposed schemes, see Lester L. Grabbe, "Introduction," in idem (ed.), 'Like a Bird in a Cage', 4.

end of Level III to 701 B.C.E.[5] Owing to the dense proportion of *lmlk* jar handles preserved within this destruction layer, and the independent evidence of personal seal impressions on many of these storage containers which evince a relatively short duration of production, layers at other sites preserving such seals may likewise be reliably dated to the late eighth century. The Assyrians set up camp southwest of the city, and Sennacherib himself oversaw the siege operations. In the monarch's "palace without rival" in Nineveh, the episode was memorialized in bold reliefs. The inner and outer walls of the massive fortifications of Lachish are evident, with the Assyrian battering rams brought near them on artificially constructed ramps. Torches were flung from atop the ramparts by the Judeans, while the Assyrian forces doused the fires with water and retaliated with sling-stones and arrows.[6]

The impressive siege earthworks remain visible to this day, being not only the sole surviving Assyrian siege ramp, but also the lone exemplar of such a military instrument in the ancient Near East. The ferocity of the final battle is amply substantiated by the hundreds of sling stones, iron arrowheads, and pieces of charred wood found at the critical juncture of the ramp and city wall. A counter-ramp was discovered inside the fortifications opposite the offensive slope employed by the attackers, as a means for the city residents to brace the rampart in the face of the imposing battering rams. After Lachish was taken, many captives were brutally impaled, and approximately 1500 massacred victims were buried in a cave outside the city. The municipality was ransacked and then deliberately set ablaze, and the debris within Stratum III of the site details this extensive conflagration. Despite not garnering a single mention in any of Sennacherib's monumental inscriptions, Lachish remains the best documented case for this leader's policy of handling rebellious cities in wartime.

---

[5] As established by David Ussishkin, "The Destruction of Lachish by Sennacherib and the Dating of the Royal Judean Storage Jars," *TA* 4 (1977) 28–57; idem, "Excavations at Lachish, 1973–77: Preliminary Report" *TA* 5 (1978) 1–97; idem., "Answers at Lachish," *BAR* 5/6 (Nov.–Dec. 1979) 16–39.

[6] On the palace reliefs, see Ussishkin, *The Conquest of Lachish by Sennacherib* (Tel Aviv: Institute of Archaeology, 1982); Richard D. Barnett, Erika Bleibtrau and Geoffrey Turner, *Sculptures from the South-West Palace of Sennacherib at Nineveh* (2 vols.; London: British Museum Press, 1998); Christoph Uehlinger, "Clio in a World of Pictures—Another Look at the Lachish Reliefs from Sennacherib's Southwest Palace at Nineveh," in Grabbe (ed.), *'Like a Bird in a Cage'*, 221–305. Archaeological sources for Lachish will be surveyed in the following section.

Other sites exhibiting evidence of Sennacherib's invasion:[7]

- Arad—The intervention of Sennacherib should be associated with the end of Stratum VIII.
- Beth-Shemesh—Stratum IIc contains many *lmlk* jars, and is considered to have been brought to an end during Sennacherib's campaign.
- Khirbet Rabud (Debir/Kiriath-Sefer)—Stratum II was destroyed by Sennacherib in 701, with many *lmlk* jar handles to assign its eighth-century date.
- Ramat Rachel—The remains of an impressive palace with a massive defensive wall have been found in Level VB, dated to the eighth century due to the approximately 170 *lmlk* jar handles and private seal impressions reminiscent of those at Lachish.
- Tel Batash—The partial destruction of the city at the end of Stratum III has been credited to the Assyrians in 701 B.C.E. This stratum contained a fortified area with an expansive edifice which has been conjectured as an administrative center. A substantial number of *lmlk* jars were preserved, including personal seal impressions matching those found at Azekah and Jerusalem.
- Tell Beit Mirsim—Recent studies on the pottery of the site have redated Stratum A2 to the eighth century, with its destruction attributed to Sennacherib.
- Tel 'Erani—The final report for the site has redated Stratum VI to the late eighth century due to its inclusion of *lmlk* jars along with other artifacts. This stratum is deemed to have ended in 701.
- Tell Judeideh (Moresheth)—At least 37 *lmlk* handles, including private seal impressions, were preserved in Iron IIB, and other late eighth-century pottery effectively date this layer to the reign of Hezekiah. This stratum ended in a massive conflagration which has been interpreted as from the hand of Sennacherib, and Mic 1:14 may depict this as well.
- Tel Ḥalif (Rimmon? or Hormah?)—The destruction of the fortified complex preserved in Stratum VIB has been dated to 701 based on the pottery assemblage there.

---

[7] This overview is indebted to the following studies, which provide extensive bibliography: Andrew G. Vaughn, *Theology, History, and Archaeology in the Chronicler's Account of Hezekiah* (ABS 4; Atlanta: Scholars Press, 1999) 19–79; Ephraim Stern, *Archaeology of the Land of the Bible, Vol. 2: The Assyrian, Babylonian, and Persian Periods (732–332 B.C.E.)* (New York: Doubleday, 2001) 130–65; Grabbe, "Introduction," 3–20.

- Tel Sheva—Stratum II, with a pottery assemblage highly reminiscent of that at Lachish III, is felt to have ended with Sennacherib's invasion, although this interpretation has been challenged.[8]

For sites not exhibiting evidence:

- Tell en-Naṣbeh (ancient Mizpah)—Although 87 *lmlk* seal impressions have been uncovered at the site, there is no evidence of conquest by Sennacherib's forces.
- Tell eṣ-Ṣafi (Tell Zafit)—*lmlk* seal impressions and a jar handle have been recovered here, but with no evidence of conflagration.
- Tell Jezer (Gezer)—Stratum V has been dated from the late eighth century, when the city served as an administrative center for the Assyrians. At least 31 *lmlk* handles have been recovered. As the end of Stratum V has been tied to the Babylonian conquest, the city does not appear to have been destroyed by Sennacherib.
- Tel Maresha—16 *lmlk* seal impressions uncovered.
- Tel Zakariah (ancient Azekah)—*lmlk* seal impressions found in Strata B and C. The so-called Azekah inscription should not be dated to 701 B.C.E. and thus has no bearing on the siege and conquest of the city described therein.

The strong correlation between destruction layers at various sites and the finding of *lmlk* jar handles provides indirect confirmation that these seal impressions are indeed an eighth-century Judean phenomenon. There is no other documented military retaliation against this small nation on the edge of the ancient world which would account for the sheer number of affected locations. At the same time, the data underscore the extent of the carnage wrought by Sennacherib in 701 B.C.E., as attested in his annals. The invasion was a forceful reprisal against the coalition of western states, with Judah as its particular target. Finally, the results of this brief archaeological survey affirm the breadth of Hezekiah's dominion. The number of active sites is strong evidence of the economic buildup throughout his kingdom during the latter half of the eighth century, as is the subsequent downturn in prosperity: out of 354 Judean settlements known to have

8 By Ernst Axel Knauf, "Who Destroyed Beersheba II?" in U. Hübner and E. A. Knauf (eds.), *Kein Land für sich allein* (OBO 186; Freiburg: Universitätsverlag 2002) 181–95.

been razed during Sennacherib's third campaign, only a scant 39 were rebuilt in the next century.[9]

3.2. THE NUMBER OF ASSYRIAN CAMPAIGNS

The exegete who undertakes the study of Sennacherib's campaign is faced with the perennial question as to whether the Sargonid made one or two military campaigns against Judah. The matter has never been satisfactorily resolved, and new articles continue to be published advocating both positions.[10] Because such evidence is lacking in the Assyrian annals,

---

[9] Stern, *Archaeology of the Land of the Bible*, Vol. 2, 142. This economic buildup is detailed in Vaughn, *Theology, History, and Archaeology*, 19–79.

[10] For proponents of a single campaign, see Eberhard Schrader, *Cuneiform Inscriptions and the Old Testament* (2 vols.; trans. O. C. Whitehouse; London: Williams and Norgate, 1885–88) 1.277–310; 2.1–27; James Frederick McCurdy, *History, Prophecy and the Monuments or Israel and the Nations* (3 vols.; London: Macmillan Company, 1894–1901) 2.276–321; William M. Flinders Petrie, *A History of Egypt From the XIXth to the XXXth Dynasties* (London: Methuen & Co., 1905) 3.296–97; Julius Wellhausen, *Prolegomena to the History of Ancient Israel* (trans. J. S. Black and A. Menzies; Edinburgh, 1885; repr. New York, 1957) 481–83; Luckenbill, *Annals of Sennacherib*, 9–14; Wilhelm Rudolph, "Sanherib in Palästina," *PJ* 25 (1929) 59–80; Herbert Haag, "La campagne de Sennachérib contre Jérusalem en 701," *RB* 58 (1951) 348–59; Merrill F. Unger, *Archeology and the Old Testament* (Grand Rapids: Zondervan, 1954) 267–71; André Parrot, *Nineveh and the Old Testament* (2nd ed.; SBA 3; trans. B. E. Hooke; New York: Philosophical Library, 1955) 51–63; Martin Noth, *The History of Israel* (2nd ed.; London: Adam & Charles Black, 1960) 265–69; Georg Fohrer, *Das Buch Jesaja* (3 vols.; ZBK; Zürich: Zwingli, 1960–64) 2.151–81; Rowley, "Hezekiah's Reform and Rebellion," with voluminous earlier bibliography at 406 n. 1; Walther Eichrodt, *Der Herr der Geschichte: Jesaja 13–23 und 28–39* (BAT 17,2; Stuttgart: Calwer, 1967) 225–60; Hayim Tadmor, "Judah from the Fall of Samaria to the Fall of Jerusalem," in H. H. Ben-Sasson (ed.), *A History of the Jewish People* (Cambridge, Mass.: Harvard University Press, 1976) 142–46.

In defense of multiple campaigns, see earlier bibliography at Rowley, "Hezekiah's Reform and Rebellion," 405–406 nn. 3–4; George Rawlinson, *The Five Great Monarchies of the Ancient Eastern World* (4 vols.; London: John Murray, 1864) 2.430–46; E. A. Wallis Budge, *A History of Egypt, from the End of the Neolithic Period to the Death of Cleopatra VII. B.C. 30, Vol. 6: Egypt Under the Priest-Kings and Tanites and Nubians* (BEC 14; London: Kegan Paul, Trench, Trübner & Co., 1902) 6.133–42; Kemper Fullerton, "The Invasion of Sennacherib," *BibSac* 63 (1906) 577–634; George Adam Smith, *Jerusalem, the Topography, Economics and History from the Earliest Times to A.D. 70* (2 vols.; London: Hodder and Stoughton, 1907–1908) 2.148–80; Alfred Jeremias, *The Old Testament in the Light of the Ancient East: Manual of Biblical Archaeology* (2 vols.; Theological Translation Library; London: Williams & Norgate, 1911) 222–28; Robert William Rogers, *Cuneiform Parallels to the Old Testament* (New York: Eaton and Mains, 1912) 337–39; George A. Barton, *Archaeology and the Bible* (Philadelphia: American Sunday-School Union, 1916) 471–76; William F. Albright, Review of A. T. E. Olmstead, *History of Palestine and Syria to the Macedonian Conquest. JQR* 24/4 (1934) 370–71; idem, "New Light from Egypt on the Chronology and History of Israel and Judah," *BASOR* 130 (1953) 8–11; idem, *The Biblical Period from Abraham to Ezra* (rev. ed.; New York: Harper & Row, 1963) 78ff; Jean Le Moyne, "Les deux ambassades de Sennachérib

historians turn primarily to the variegated accounts within 2 Kgs 18:13–19:37/Isa 36–37 in order to justify a second incursion. Rather than surveying the various possibilities for historical reconstruction in detail, this book will advocate that only one Palestinian campaign is supported based on the available data.[11]

Turning first to the extra-biblical evidence, it is crucial to recognize that Sennacherib's royal annals only mention one campaign to Judah. This in itself is decisive for most Assyriologists and Egyptologists, and to posit an additional military operation into the region in the face of this fact requires substantiation. Appeal has been made to the Azekah inscription as a product of the latter years of Sennacherib's rule. Its mention of the land of Judah, and preservation of a theophoric ending that has been restored as Hezekiah, would then infer a second campaign sometime after 689 B.C.E.[12] However, this text has already been deemed more

---

à Jérusalem: Recherches sur l'évolution d'une tradition," in *Mélanges bibliques rédigés en l'honneur d'André Robert* (Paris: Bloud & Gay, 1957) 149–53; Ernest W. Nicholson, "The Centralisation of the Cult in Deuteronomy," *VT* 13/4 (1963) 384–89; John Gray, *I & II Kings* (OTL; Philadelphia: Westminster Press, 1964) 599–607, although he largely retracts his statement in the 2nd ed. of 1970, pp. 657–69; van Leeuwen, "Sanchérib devant Jérusalem," 245–72; Roland de Vaux, *Jerusalem and the Prophets* (Cincinnati: Hebrew Union College Press, 1965) 16ff; idem, "Jérusalem et les prophètes," *RB* 73 (1966) 498–500; Siegfried H. Horn, "Did Sennacherib Campaign Once or Twice Against Hezekiah?" *AUSS* 4 (1966) 1–28; William H. Shea, "Sennacherib's Second Palestinian Campaign," *JBL* 104/3 (1985) 401–18; idem, "Jerusalem Under Siege: Did Sennacherib Attack Twice?" *BAR* 25/6 (1999) 36–44, 64; Christopher Begg, " 'Sennacherib's Second Palestinian Campaign': An Additional Indication," *JBL* 106/4 (1987) 685–86; A. Kirk Grayson, "Assyria: Sennacherib and Esarhaddon (704–669 B.C.)," in J. Boardman et al. (eds.), *The Cambridge Ancient History Second Edition, Volume III Part 2: The Assyrian and Babylonian Empires and other States of the Near East, from the Eighth to the Sixth Centuries B.C.* (Cambridge: Cambridge University Press, 1991) 109–11; Jeremy Goldberg, "Two Assyrian Campaigns against Hezekiah and Later Eighth Century Biblical Chronology," *Bib* 80 (1999) 361–74.

[11] For surveys of the various possibilities, see Honor, *Sennacherib's Invasion of Palestine*, 13–25, and the convenient chart on pp. 61–62; Rowley, "Hezekiah's Reform and Rebellion"; Horn, "Did Sennacherib Campaign Once or Twice against Hezekiah?"; John Bright, *A History of Israel* (4th ed.; Louisville: Westminster John Knox, 2000) 298–309; Paul-Eugène Dion, "Sennacherib's Expedition to Palestine," *EgT* 20 (1989) 12 n. 38, 15–18. The two-campaign theory is briefly discussed, but summarily dismissed, by Henry Trocmé Aubin, *The Rescue of Jerusalem: The Alliance between Hebrews and Africans in 701 BC* (New York: Soho Press, 2002) 335–36 n. 1, as "it lacks sufficient scholarly support to be included on this list of leading, still-current theories."

[12] As advocated by Shea, "Sennacherib's Second Palestinian Campaign," 401–18. His methodology is critically assessed by Frank J. Yurco, "The Shabaka-Shebitku Coregency and the Supposed Second Campaign of Sennacherib against Judah: A Critical Assessment," *JBL* 110/1 (1991) 39–45. The Azekah inscription has also been associated with the third campaign of Sennacherib, owing to its disputed date, see Mayer, *Politik und Kriegskunst der Assyrer*, 350–51.

suitable to the reign of Sargon II, in my opinion, and therefore should not be employed in reconstructing events under the reign of Sennacherib.

The archaeological record is likewise a deterrent to multiple campaigns, as the stratigraphy of pertinent sites evince only one destruction layer that can be dated to the period in question. Lachish Level III is pivotal to this analysis, in that this site is expressly mentioned within the prophetic source B₁ of the biblical account, considered by some exegetes to record the later expedition by Sennacherib into Judah. As discussed previously in reference to the *lmlk* jars, the end of this stratum may now be dated reliably to 701 B.C.E., after which time the site was abandoned and never rebuilt. The extensive frieze of the siege of the city preserved in Sennacherib's palace at Nineveh leaves no doubt that the destruction was absolute, and such savagery is only to be expected from the Assyrian army in their quest to use neighboring fortified towns as an appalling exemplar to force non-compliant monarchs into capitulation. Proponents of multiple campaigns are not only obliged to posit compelling historical reconstructions based on extant texts, but to bring their theories in line with this archaeological evidence as well.[13]

Thirdly, the two-campaign hypothesis requires dating Hezekiah's reign to ca. 715–686 B.C.E. based on the "fourteenth year" synchronism in 2 Kgs 18:13. The questionable nature of this key verse, moreover, has already been raised, and further support will be marshaled presently. If the first invasion did indeed transpire in 701 B.C.E., as most scholars concur, then Hezekiah must have ruled for several more years before Sennacherib was compelled to return. Yet as this study has endeavored to demonstrate, such a span does considerable violence to both Assyrian and biblical chronology, and cannot be sustained if the overall timeline from the conquest of Samaria to the fall of Jerusalem is to be upheld. The position heretofore advocated assigns Hezekiah's last year of rule to Nisan 697–Adar 696, which leaves insufficient time remaining after 701 to accommodate a second campaign.

Further chronological issues are apparent in attempting to date when Merodach-baladan would have sent emissaries to visit Hezekiah after his

---

[13] One could counter that the date assigned to the end of Level III is in fact incorrect, and that it should properly be 689 B.C.E. It is then incumbent upon the historian to justify why such a crucial military target as Lachish was excluded during Sennacherib's initial campaign.

illness as recorded in 2 Kgs 20:12/Isa 39:1.[14] He is described as מֶלֶךְ־בָּבֶל, and a time when this sheikh from the Chaldean tribe of Bīt-Yakin was securely in charge of Babylonia would indeed have afforded him the best opportunity to extend his diplomacy so far afield. By the year 700 B.C.E., Sennacherib had directed his attention toward Babylonia and had put its Chaldean rebels to flight. Merodach-baladan took refuge in Elam and died a few years later, with no occasion, reason, or ability to send a delegation to the tiny nation of Judah.[15] 2 Kgs 20:12–19 therefore cannot refer to events after 701 B.C.E., and thus is in no way conducive to the two-campaign theory.[16] Moreover, the fact that the Deuteronomistic editors saw this story as being of a piece with the foregoing tale of the capital city's deliverance from Sennacherib points to all of the traditions amalgamated

---

[14] The biblical name Merodach-baladan (Heb. מְרֹדַךְ בַּלְאֲדָן) is a localized rendering of Akkadian Marduk-apla-iddina, "Marduk has given an heir."

[15] A thorough introduction to this resilient leader may be found in John A. Brinkman, "Merodach-Baladan II," in *Studies Presented to A. Leo Oppenheim, June 7, 1964* (Chicago, 1964) 6–53; idem, "Marduk-apla-iddina," RlA 7.374–75; Eckart Frahm, "Sîn-aḫḫē-eriba" *PNAE* 3/I, 1119; Heather D. Baker, "Marduk-apla-iddina," *PNAE* 2/II, 705–11.

[16] The precise date of this mission to Hezekiah is in dispute, see Brinkman, "Merodach-Baladan II," 31–33; idem, *Prelude to Empire: Babylonian Society and Politics, 747–626 B.C.* (Philadelphia: University Museum, 1984) 57–60. Brinkman follows Edwin R. Thiele, *The Mysterious Numbers of the Hebrew Kings* (new rev. ed.; Grand Rapids: Zondervan, 1983) 173–76, in dating the end of the reign of Hezekiah to 687 B.C.E., timing the Babylonian embassy fifteen years earlier ca. 704–702 immediately prior to Sennacherib's third campaign. Joseph Blenkinsopp, *Isaiah 1–39* (AYB 19; New York: Doubleday, 2000) 458, likewise suggests 704–702 B.C.E., when Merodach-baladan was securely in charge of Babylonia, yet Sennacherib was still weak. As the fifteen years of extended life promised to Hezekiah cannot be proven to have originally been connected with the visiting delegation, these approximate dates are appealing in any event. The embassy in all likelihood would only have been motivated to travel so far for political reasons rather than due to Hezekiah's illness, so Francolino J. Gonçalves, *L'expédition de Sennachérib en Palestine dans la littérature hébraïque ancienne* (Études bibliques, New Series 7; Paris Librairie Lecoffre, 1986) 106 n. 16, 337.
If one correlates the story of Hezekiah's sickness with his "high chronology," however, then another possibility emerges for the timing of the embassy: 712 B.C.E., fifteen years prior to Hezekiah's last year of reign (Nisan 697-Adar 696) when Merodach-baladan was again on the throne in Babylonia (721–710 B.C.E.), cf. A. Kirk Grayson, "Assyria: Tiglath-pileser III to Sargon II (744–705 B.C.)," in Boardman et al. (eds.), *Assyrian and Babylonian Empires*, 86–102; Manfred Hutter, *Hiskija König von Juda* (GrTS 6; Graz: Universität Graz, 1982) 67–71; Rüdiger Liwak, "Die Rettung Jerusalems im Jahr 701 v. Chr," *ZTK* 83 (1986) 157. For some scholars this correlates well with Hezekiah's considered rebellion against Sargon at the side of Ashdod in 712 B.C.E., but this is often based on the subjective dating of the Azekah inscription, see e.g., Mordechai Cogan, *Imperialism and Religion: Assyria, Judah and Israel in the Eighth and Seventh Centuries B.C.E.* (SBLMS 19; Missoula, Mont.: Scholars Press, 1974) 66. Under this reconstructed biblical chronology, then, the Babylonian embassy had nothing to do with the rebellion against Sennacherib.

in 2 Kgs 18:13–20:19 as having their setting in 701.[17] The story of the Babylonian delegation, in the final analysis, bespeaks only a single Assyrian
campaign in the selfsame year.

It is important to ascertain whether different stories within the biblical text are retellings of the same event, regardless of how divergent their
storylines may be. One need only look at the manifold examples within
Pentateuchal source criticism—the giving of the law, the flood, the promise of a child to Abraham—to appreciate that dissimilar, even conflicting,
traditions need not necessarily imply a wholly separate happening. Such
variations may often be adduced as subject to the ideology of the author.
In such cases, the exegete must concentrate on literary similarities rather
than differences in order to properly assess this question.

At the outset, it may be observed that the annalistic report in
2 Kgs 18:13–16 is directly followed in v 17 by the sending of a military force
to Jerusalem, with no indication whatsoever of any lapse in time or of the
withdrawal of the Assyrian army.[18] The two-campaign hypothesis requires
that disparate occasions spanning several years have been telescoped, or
collapsed into a single event, but this is a dubious assumption. The pro-
tagonist and antagonist remain unchanged across this literary boundary,
and both are stationed in precisely the same respective geographic location: Sennacherib at Lachish, and Hezekiah in Jerusalem.[19] In both the
annalistic report and the longer prophetic accounts which follow, the city

---

[17] As evidenced by YHWH's promise to defend the city in 2 Kgs 20:6, as well as the fifteen
years of life promised to Hezekiah, which ostensibly occurred in his fourteenth year (2 Kgs
19:13; cf. 2 Kgs 18:2). Note that the temporal setting of these stories should not be confused
with their respective dates of composition, which are decidedly later.

[18] Notice how this is made expressly clear in the account of the conquest of Samaria in
2 Kgs 18:9–12, such that it is reasonable to ask whether the Shalmaneser in v 9 is the same
as "the king of Assyria" in v 11. Without the interposition of the crucial chronological notice
in v 10, such an inquiry would be methodologically unsound.

[19] Sennacherib is expressly said to be in Lachish in 2 Kgs 18:14, 17. Hezekiah is stated
as being in Jerusalem according to v 17, while his actions of stripping the materials from
the house of YHWH in vv 15–16 mandate the same location. Recognizing this congruity,
Fullerton, "Invasion of Sennacherib," 616–618, dismisses as coincidence the choice of Sennacherib to make his headquarters at Lachish during both invasions.

Allan K. Jenkins, "Hezekiah's Fourteenth Year: A New Interpretation of 2 Kings xviii 13–
xix 37," VT 26/3 (1976) 284–98, goes further afield in giving grounds for two campaigns
without attributing both to Sennacherib. By adopting the early chronology for Hezekiah's
reign, Jenkins proposes that at the time of the Ashdod revolt Hezekiah joined the rebellion. The inexplicable withdrawal of Assyrian troops from an advance on Jerusalem at
that time produced the biblical accounts of the miraculous deliverance of the city. After
the Sennacherib invasion of 701, Jenkins proposes, the latter campaign was interpreted in
light of the former, resulting in the telescoping of the two events and the association of
the deliverance report with the expedition of 701.

of Jerusalem is spared by the actions of Hezekiah. Despite the mismatched means by which this is achieved—the king's own initiative in the former, or his trusting intercession with the deity in the latter—the result is identical. To expect the deliverance of Jerusalem to have occurred twice under the same Judean king against his unchanged Assyrian overlord, with both parties acting from their selfsame physical locations, strains credulity.[20] This belief is further suspended by the additional datum that both the Assyrian annals and the biblical text refer to aid coming to Judah from its southern neighbor.[21] In broad strokes, then, the narratives play out in the same sequence, and ideological motivations can readily elucidate their varying presentations. In such a circumstance, recognizing parallel accounts is a preferable conclusion to asserting the telescoping of two broadly similar incidents.[22]

Another factor which has come into play in muddying the waters of historical reconstruction surrounding the number of Assyrian incursions into Judah is the independent account of the fifth-century B.C.E. Greek historian Herodotus of Halicarnassus. This tale, presumably preserved by the Egyptian priests, tells of the routing of Sennacherib's army at Pelusium by a horde of field mice, summoned by a priest of Hephaestus in the face of the cowardice of the Egyptian warriors.[23] While it has been argued that this passage developed from the biblical story in which the

---

[20] It is the assertion of Bright, *History of Israel*, 308, that one must posit two separate rescues for the city due to what he identifies as dichotomous perspectives within the prophecies of Isaiah. Logically, this is a *non sequitur*: multiple perspectives by the prophets do not mandate multiple outcomes to their prophecies.

[21] Rassam 43–45; OIP ii 78-iii 5; 2 Kgs 19:9. One is then led to more difficult questions such as why Sennacherib would employ a concordant military strategy on both occasions, or what would be the motivation for Hezekiah to choose to rebel again, barely a decade later according to the dates posited for the second campaign.

[22] The very fact that two independent traditions have been redacted together in itself indicates that the editors of the material saw them as referring to the same event. As a result, it is only natural that exegetes would find it productive to delve into synchronic readings of 2 Kgs 18:13–19:37, as done by Arie van der Kooij, "The Story of Hezekiah and Sennacherib (2 Kings 18–19): A Sample of Ancient Historiography," in J. C. de Moor and H. F. van Rooy (eds.), *Past, Present, Future: The Deuteronomistic History and the Prophets* (OTS 44; Leiden: Brill, 2000) 107–19.

[23] The story in Herodotus §2.141 is as follows:
"The next king was the priest of Hephaestus, whose name was Sethos...So presently came king Sanacharib against Egypt, with a great host of Arabians and Assyrians; and the warrior Egyptians would not march against him. The priest, in his quandary, went into the temple shrine and there bewailed to the god's image the peril which threatened him. In his lamentation he fell asleep, and dreamt that he saw the god standing over him and bidding him take courage, for he should suffer no ill by encountering the host of Arabia: 'Myself', said the god, 'will send you champions'."

angel of Yhwh acted as divine agent, with the actual devastation upon the
Assyrians enacted by a plague carried by the rodents themselves, such a
connection appears to be misguided and strained.[24] The field mice do not
bring about the death of a single Assyrian warrior, but rather render their
weaponry useless.[25]

Whether or not the story may be seen to be imbued with historical
memory, it lends little support to the two-campaign hypothesis.[26] The
linkage between this encounter and the biblical account lies in the mere
fact that Sennacherib's army faced a major setback. Yet because Esarhaddon is expressly known to have experienced a decisive defeat in his
first attempt to invade Egypt in 674, the name Sennacherib could well be
an incorrect attribution.[27] If it is feasible to propose multiple Egyptian

---

"So he trusted the vision, and encamped at Pelusium with such Egyptians as would follow him, for here is the road into Egypt; and none of the warriors would go with him, but
only hucksters and artificers and traders. Their enemies too came thither, and one night
a multitude of fieldmice swarmed over the Assyrian camp and devoured their quivers
and their bows and the handles of their shields likewise, insomuch that they fled the next
day unarmed and many fell. And at this day a stone statue of the Egyptian king stands in
Hephaestus' temple, with a mouse in his hand, and an inscription to this effect: 'Look on
me, and fear the gods.'"

For translation and commentary, see Alan B. Lloyd, *Herodotus Book II* (3 vols.; EPRO 43;
Leiden: E. J. Brill, 1975–88) 3.99–105, or the classic edition of W. G. Waddell, *Herodotus Book II*
(London: Bristol Classical Press, 1998) 93–94, 239–40. Pelusium was situated approximately
30 km to the southeast of modern Port Said, in the eastern extremes of Egypt's Nile Delta.
Hephaestus was the Greek name for Ptah, the god of Memphis, see Kenneth A. Kitchen,
"Egypt, the Levant and Assyria in 701 BC," in M. Görg (ed.), *Fontes atque Pontes: Eine Fest-
gabe für Hellmut Brunner* (ÄAT 5; Wiesbaden: Harrassowitz, 1983) 245.

[24] Mordechai Cogan and Hayim Tadmor, *II Kings: A New Translation with Introduction and Commentary* (AYB 11; New York: Doubleday, 1988) 251, drawing upon Alexander
Rofé, "Israelite Belief in Angels in the Pre-exilic Period as Evidenced by Biblical Traditions"
(Ph.D. diss.; Jerusalem: Hebrew University, 1969) 217 [Hebrew]. Honor, *Sennacherib's Invasion of Palestine*, 60, states "There are several Greek legends of a deliverance resulting from
the nibbling by mice of the enemies' weapons. The parallelism between these legends and
Herodotus II 141 is too close to be coincidental." Unfortunately, he does not cite any of
these other legendary tales.

[25] As observed by William R. Gallagher, *Sennacherib's Campaign to Judah: New Studies*
(SHCANE 18; Leiden: Brill, 1999) 250; Lester L. Grabbe, "Of Mice and Dead Men: Herodotus
2.141 and Sennacherib's Campaign in 701 BCE," in idem (ed.), *'Like a Bird in a Cage'*, 136.
Both offer respectful treatments of the Herodotus story as an independent source. For
other scholars who have wrestled with the historical value of the Herodotus story, see the
bibliography at Brevard S. Childs, *Isaiah and the Assyrian Crisis* (SBT II/3; London: SCM
Press, 1967) 101 n. 70.

[26] On this, see Gallagher and Grabbe cited previously, as well as Wilhelm Spiegelberg,
Die Glaubwürdigkeit von Herodots Bericht über Ägypten im Lichte der ägyptischen Denkmäler
(Heidelberg: C. Winter, 1926).

[27] Suggested by Sidney Smith, "Sennacherib and Esarhaddon," in J. B. Bury, S. A. Cook,
and F. E. Adcock (eds.), *The Cambridge Ancient History, Vol III: The Assyrian Empire*

encounters with the Assyrians within the context of a single campaign as has been done in various reconstructions, this is methodologically preferable to the more complicated alternative of a second imperial incursion into Palestine and the Sinai peninsula.[28] A biblical scholar must always be cognizant of whether conclusions are being based on the evidence or whether evidence is being used to support the conclusions. The data reinforcing multiple invasions have thus far been tangential and inferential, but there is one further bone of contention that must be brought under the microscope for analysis.

3.3. TAHARQO

The identity of Taharqo (biblical תִּרְהָקָה) is closely tied to the number of postulated campaigns.[29] According to 2 Kgs 19:9/Isa 37:9, it was "Tirhakah, king of Kush" who went forth to meet Sennacherib in battle. Because it

---

(1st ed.; Cambridge: Cambridge University Press, 1925) 74; Cogan and Tadmor, *II Kings*, 250–51. The attractiveness of this proposal hinges upon how well the proper name Sethon may be explained within the text. Lloyd, *Herodotus Book II*, 3.100, sees an original pronomen *S-b-t-k* (=Shebitku) with two assimilated consonants, while the hypothesis of J. von Beckerath, "Ägypten und der Feldzug Sanheribs im Jahre 701 v Chr." *UF* 24 (1992) 8, is that Sethon is derived from *stm*, the title of the high priest of Ptah in Memphis.

The defeat of Assyria by Egypt in 674 is ignored in the empire's own royal inscriptions, with a minor campaign to Babylonia substituted to save face. Our only knowledge of this military debacle is preserved in the Babylonian Chronicle (1 iv 16), which contains the terse report "The seventh year: on the fifth day of the month Adar the army of Assyria was defeated in Egypt." See A. Kirk Grayson, *Assyrian and Babylonian Chronicles* (TCS 5; Locust Valley, NY: J. J. Augustin, 1975) 84.

[28] These alternatives will be explored in the historical reconstruction below. Respecting the identity of Sennacherib within the passage, Frank J. Yurco, "Sennacherib's Third Campaign and the Coregency of Shabaka and Shebitku," *Serapis* 6 (1980) 234, contends that it is the toponym of Pelusium that is not reliable. Herodotus would have assumed that Pelusium, the entrance to Egypt in his own time, would have been the logical point of attack for a threat situated on the Egyptian border.

Josephus, *Antiquities*, 10.20, also refers to a lost text of Berossus, as translated by Ralph Marcus, *Josephus, Jewish Antiquities: Books IX–XI* (LCL; Cambridge, Mass: Harvard University Press, 1958) 166–67, "But Berosus, who wrote a History of Chaldea, also mentions King Senacheirimos and tells how he ruled over the Assyrians and how he made an expedition against all Asia and Egypt..." The tradition may have a Babylonian origin, based on the sources utilized by this late 4th-early 3rd cent. B.C.E. historian, see Robert Drews, "The Babylonian Chronicles and Berossus," *Iraq* 37 (1975) 39–55. It, too, may be explained in the context of Sennacherib's expedition of 701 and need not imply a second campaign.

[29] The usage of Taharqo rather than Tirhakah/Taharqa follows the theoretical reconstruction of Kushite name forms provided by Karl-Heinz Priese "The Kingdom of Kush: The Napatan Period," in S. Wenig (ed.), *Africa in Antiquity: The Arts of Ancient Nubia and the Sudan* (2 vols.; Brooklyn: Brooklyn Museum, 1978) 1.75–83.

has been established from Egyptian sources that Taharqo did not reign as Pharoah until 690 B.C.E., it is argued he could not have been ruler in 701 and thus the scenario arises for a second invasion.[30] Not only the office but the age of the leader is in dispute, being variously placed at roughly ten or twenty years of age in 701, the former deemed an age too young to wield military power.[31] Due to this apparent discrepancy, the biblical references have been viewed as anachronistic glosses due to the author's faulty memory.[32] On the other side stand those who defend the title "king of Kush" as proleptic, a titular form employed by Taharqo himself on his own stelae.[33]

Scholarship has been too reticent in accepting that Taharqo could have been a military commander directly involved in confronting Sennacherib in 701 B.C.E. The disputed reading of the Kawa stela which gave rise to the idea that Taharqo was only nine years old at this time is almost certainly in error, and it should be conceded that he was in fact closer to twenty.[34]

---

[30] Richard A. Parker, "The Length of the Reign of Amasis and the Beginning of the Twenty-Sixth Dynasty," *MDAIK* 15 (1957) 208–12.

[31] The age of Taharqo is based on a disputed reading of the Kawa stela, which states that Pharaoh Shebitku summoned the twenty year-old youth Taharqo north from Nubia. The younger age is claimed by M. F. Laming Macadam, *The Temples of Kawa: Oxford University Excavations in Nubia* (2 vols.; London: Oxford University Press, 1949) 1.18–20, while the older age is favored by Jean Leclant and Jean Yoyotte, "Notes d'histoire et de civilisation éthiopiennes: À propos d'un ouvrage récent," *BIFAO* 51 (1952) 17–29; Yurco, "Sennacherib's Third Campaign and the Coregency of Shabaka and Shebitku," 222–23; Kenneth Kitchen, *The Third Intermediate Period in Egypt (1100–650 B.C.)* (2nd ed.; Warminster, England: Aris & Phillips, 1986) 164–72, and further bibliography there.

[32] Rowley, "Hezekiah's Reform and Rebellion," 407–25; Beckerath, "Ägypten und der Feldzug Sanheribs," 3–8; Donald B. Redford, *Egypt, Canaan, and Israel in Ancient Times* (Princeton: Princeton University Press, 1992) 353 n. 163; Klaas A. D. Smelik, "King Hezekiah Advocates True Prophecy. Remarks on Isaiah xxxvi and xxxvii//II Kings xviii and xix," in idem, *Converting the Past. Studies in Ancient Israelite and Moabite Historiography* (OTS 28; Leiden: E. J. Brill, 1992) 105 n. 53; Dion, "Sennacherib's Expedition to Palestine," 24; Anthony J. Spalinger, "The Foreign Policy of Egypt Preceding the Assyrian Conquest," *CdÉ* 53 (1978) 40; Shea, "Sennacherib's Second Palestinian Campaign," 408–16; idem, "Jerusalem Under Siege: Did Sennacherib Attack Twice?" 36–44, 64; Gallagher, *Sennacherib's Campaign to Judah*, 221–22.

[33] As favored by Kenneth A. Kitchen, *Ancient Orient and Old Testament* (Chicago: Inter-Varsity Press, 1966) 82–84; idem, *Third Intermediate Period in Egypt*, xxxix–xlii, 158–61, 383–86, 552–59, 584–85; idem, "Egyptian Interventions in the Levant in Iron Age II," in W. G. Dever and S. Gitin (eds.), *Symbiosis, Symbolism, and the Power of the Past: Canaan, Ancient Israel, and Their Neighbors from the Late Bronze Age through Roman Palaestina* (Winona Lake, Ind.: Eisenbrauns, 2003) 127–28.

[34] As noted by Anson F. Rainey, "Taharqa and Syntax," *TA* 3 (1976) 38–41; James K. Hoffmeier, "Egypt's Role in the Events of 701 B.C. in Jerusalem," in A. G. Vaughn and A. E. Killebrew (eds.), *Jerusalem in Bible and Archaeology: The First Temple Period* (SBLSS 18; Leiden: Brill, 2003) 230–32. I would likewise concur that there was no six-year co-regency between

This would make him sufficiently mature to lead an army, especially in light of the fact that Shebitku exhibited a marked preference for him over the other young royals.[35] The appeal to prolepsis is likewise plausible, as far as it goes, yet it isn't necessary to resort to such special pleading. It is of no importance whatsoever whether Taharqo was Pharaoh in 701 B.C.E., which is needlessly made the central issue in the debate. As recorded in 2 Kgs 19:9/Isa 37:9, Taharqo is identified as "the king of Kush," and not the king of Egypt. Biblical Kush is widely recognized as a designation for Nubia or modern Sudan in general, positioned south of Semna at the second cataract of the Nile River, with its capital at Napata.[36] The title of Pharoah, in any event, was not exclusive in Egypt due to the multiple dynasties simultaneously in power in the late eighth century, such that modern Egyptologists differentiate them by geographic location.[37] There was in this period a confederation of kings and high chieftains who ruled smaller, local centers of power throughout Libya and Nubia, thus permitting Taharqo to be a king ruling from Napata while his brother Shebitku was recognized as a Pharaoh over Egypt.[38] Shabako and Shebitku are all but absent from the Nubian record, while the Ethiopian king list names Taharqo as ruler during the crucial year in question.[39] The fact of multiple

Shebitku and Taharqo, proposed by Macadam, *Temples of Kawa*, 1.17 n. 17, 19; Yurco, "Sennacherib's Third Campaign and the Coregency of Shabaka and Shebitku," but cogently rejected by Kitchen, *Third Intermediate Period in Egypt*, 164–72.

[35] Leclant and Yoyotte, "Notes d'histoire et de civilisation éthiopiennes," 18–20. Kenneth A. Kitchen, *Pharaoh Triumphant: The Life and Times of Ramesses II, King of Egypt* (Warminster, England: Aris & Phillips, 1982) 24, notes that Ramesses II received the position of commander-in-chief of the army at only age ten, and accompanied the army on foreign campaigns as early as fourteen or fifteen. Aubin, *Rescue of Jerusalem*, 112–13, points to Alexander the Great's success as a military commander at the tender age of eighteen.

[36] The use of the geographic designation Meluḫḫa (Kush) by Assyrian scribes seems to have been limited to Upper Egypt, cf. George Smith, *History of Assurbanipal* (London: Williams and Norgate, 1871) 48; R. Clover, *The Sabbath and Jubilee Cycle* (2nd ed.; Garden Grove, Calif.: Qadesh La Yahweh Press, 1995) 108–109. See further Donald B. Redford, "Kush," *AYBD* 4.109–11.

[37] See Kitchen, *Third Intermediate Period in Egypt*, 366ff. As seen in the name of his book, Egyptologists designate such times with a multiplicity of Egyptian rulers as "intermediate periods."

[38] That Taharqo was Shebitku's brother is predominant in scholarship, but László Török, *Kingdom of Kush: Handbook of the Napatan-Meroitic Civilization* (Leiden: Brill, 1997) 169–70, has put forward the view that they were cousins.

[39] As noted by Alan Gardiner, *Egypt of the Pharaohs: An Introduction* (Oxford: Clarendon Press, 1961) 342, "Considering the combined length of these two reigns, it is strange how seldom the names of Shabako and Shebitku are encountered. Apart from the pyramids at Kurru where they are buried and from a horse-cemetery in the same place, their Nubian home has hardly a trace of them to show."

kings is well attested in Egyptian sources and is evident in Sennacherib's own account of the battle of Eltekeh, which mentions both the "kings of the land of Egypt" and "the king of Meluḫḫa," or Kush.[40] Thus although Taharqo was not yet a Pharaoh, ruler of Egypt, there is no reason to doubt that he was both a skilled military leader and "the king of Kush" in 701 B.C.E.[41] The accuracy of the appellation מֶלֶךְ־כּוּשׁ in the Bible affirms that his involvement with Sennacherib in fact preceded his becoming Pharaoh in 690, a final, compelling piece of evidence which effectively undermines the two-campaign theory.[42]

The listing of Taharqo is given in Charles Fernand Rey, *In the Country of the Blue Nile* (London: Duckworth, 1927) 266, although the validity of this chronology is highly suspect. It is believed to be a creation of the 13th century, intended to establish the political credentials of the so-called Solomonid dynasty. For an academic attempt at reconstructing the rulers of Kush, see Derek A. Welsby, *The Kingdom of Kush: The Napatan and Meroitic Empires* (London: British Museum Press, 1996) 207–209, and bibliography there.

[40] As written in Sennacherib's annals (Rassam 43–44; OIP ii 78–83):

šarrānī māt Muṣuri	II 78	The kings of the land of Egypt,
ṣābī qašti narkabāt sisî	II 79	the bowmen [and] horse-drawn chariots
ša šar māt Meluḫḫi emūqī lā nibi	II 80	of the king of Meluḫḫa, innumerable forces
ikterūnimma illikū rēṣūssun	II 81	banded together, and came to their assistance.
ina tamirti Altaqû	II 82	In the environs of Altaqû,
ellāmū'a sidru šitkunū	II 83	they set battle lines in place before me.

Text-critically, the Rassam Cylinder has only the singular LUGAL KUR *Mu-uṣ-ri*, "king of the land of Egypt." Meluḫḫa originally depicted an area in Iran and India, according to Ignace J. Gelb, "Makkan and Meluḫḫa in Early Mesopotamian Sources," *RA* 64 (1970) 1–8, but by the time of Sargon II the toponym was employed for Nubia. I take the reading "king of Meluḫḫa" at face value and therefore see no need for the suggestion of Yurco, "Sennacherib's Third Campaign and the Coregency of Shabaka and Shebitku," 225, that this designation was merely to distinguish Nubian from Egyptian charioteers.

[41] As noted by Leclant and Yoyotte, "Notes d'histoire et de civilisation éthiopiennes," 19 n. 2, the term *hwn nfr*, "young man" which Taharqo uses to describe himself at the time of his summoning by Shebitku may imply military prowess, being "the ancient designation for elite troops."

[42] The mistranslation of מֶלֶךְ־כּוּשׁ as "king of Egypt" has been the basis for much of the needless speculation surrounding the two-campaign theory, note the synopsis of Shea, "Sennacherib's Second Palestinian Campaign," 416, "On the surface, reference to Tirhakah as king of Egypt in 2 Kgs 19:9 poses a further problem, since he did not come to the throne of Egypt until 690."

3.4. Historical Reconstruction

The timing of Sennecharib's third campaign is one of the most certain details in biblical chronology.[43] The appointed heir of Sargon II reigned from Nisan 704-Adar 680, a total of 23 years.[44] The Assyrian inscription known as the Bellino Cylinder is dated to the third regnal year of Sennacherib (Nisan 702-Adar 701), and mentions only his first two military expeditions.[45] The earliest record of the third campaign has been preserved in the Rassam Cylinder, which is dated to his fifth regnal year (Nisan 700-Adar 699).[46] This inscription also records the famous monarch's fourth expedition, which precludes his third campaign from extending far into the year 701 B.C.E. At a most generous estimate, then, Sennacherib's third campaign began no earlier than the middle his third year (late spring/summer of 702), and had to be concluded by the middle of his fourth year (late spring/summer of 701).[47]

Philistia had been an Assyrian vassal since the time of Tiglath-pileser III, although three Assyrian expeditions were necessary during the reign of Sargon II to maintain order. By the end of the latter's reign, there were two

---

[43] Gallagher, *Sennacherib's Campaign to Judah,* doesn't even bother to justify the date of 701 B.C.E. for the third campaign, as shown from the very first sentence of his introduction (p. 1), "In 701 B.C. Sennacherib, king of Assyria, led his army against some rebels in the western part of his empire." Henry C. Rawlinson, *A Commentary on the Cuneiform Inscriptions of Babylonia and Assyria* (London: John W. Parker, 1850) dated the attack on Judah to 700 B.C.E., but this was already corrected to 701 in the 2nd edition of 1870. By 1878, Wellhausen had dated the invasion correctly to 701 B.C.E.

[44] According to Hayim Tadmor, "The Campaigns of Sargon II of Assur: A Chronological-Historical Study (Conclusion)," *JCS* 12/3 (1958) 97, Sennacherib ascended to the throne on Abu (July/Aug.) 12 in the 17th regnal year of his father Sargon II (Nisan 705-Adar 704). As the native Mesopotamian practice was to begin counting years of rule from the year after succession, his first official regnal year was 704/703, Nisan reckoning. According to *ANET*, 302, he was slain by one of his rebellious sons on Tebetu (Dec./Jan.) of 681. Since he had survived past Nisan, the full year Nisan 681–Adar 680 would have been accorded to him as well. For convenience, I am using transliterations of month names from Hebrew (Nisan, Adar) rather than from Akkadian (Nisânu, Addaru).

[45] See *ARAB*, 2.438 for the cylinder text. The inscription is dated to the eponymy of Nabuli of Arbailu. Officials were used to date each year of the Assyrian calendar, and this eponym list, or *limmu*-chronicle, is an important tool for verifying Mesopotamian chronology. For more information, see the introduction in Alan R. Millard, *The Eponyms of the Assyrian Empire 910–612 BC* (SAAS 2; Helsinki: Neo-Assyrian Text Corpus Project, 1994) 4–14.

[46] The cylinder is so-named after its excavator, and is dated to the *limmu* of Metunu. See Riekele Borger, *Babylonisch-assyrische Lesestücke* (2nd ed.; 3 vols.; AnOr 54; Roma: Pontificium Institutum Biblicum, 1979) 1.64–5 for a listing of cylinder copies, and Frahm, *Einleitung in die Sanherib-Inschriften,* 47–61 for the text.

[47] Logic along these same lines was presented by Honor, *Sennacherib's Invasion of Palestine,* 4.

Assyrian provinces in Philistia: Dor and Ashdod, as well as a faithful king in Gaza and a clearly defined border with Egypt. After Sargon's untimely death on the battlefield in the remote region of Tabalu, widespread rebellion erupted throughout the empire. It extended from Ellipi and Media in the east to Lulî of Tyre in the west, who controlled the Phoenician coast. Ashkelon and Ekron were among the Philistine cities to rise up against Assyria, and Ammon, Moab and Edom may have joined the revolt.

Hezekiah chose to rebel, although his reason is not clear.[48] Certainly there was the onerous millstone of vassaldom, but as this was a perennial situation for all subjugated lands, it cannot account for the timing itself. Sargon had undertaken expansions which had placed a strain on the empire and had depleted its manpower. The epidemic that struck Assyria just as the king's new capital of Dur-Šarrukin was approaching completion may have further exacerbated military readiness.[49] Vassals often rebelled at the time of succession in order to test the mettle of their imperial masters, and Sargon's demise caused a spectacular ripple effect throughout the empire.[50] Sennacherib's actions after ascending the throne could easily have been mistaken for cowardice, having abandoned Dur-Šarrukin as a bad omen and initially refusing to take the hand of Bel in Babylon. In 704, he subsequently lost control of Babylonia and was perceived as weak.[51] Hezekiah along with other countries in the west may well have coordinated an alliance with Merodach-baladan II, and so the time was as opportune as it would ever be.

The importance of the expedition for Sennacherib as a military commander is evident in the fact that it was the only military offensive in the west which he personally initiated.[52] The broad outline of events during the third campaign is apparent from his annals, and is typically divided

---

[48] The full gamut of possibilities is surveyed in Gallagher, *Sennacherib's Campaign to Judah*, 263–74.

[49] Letters by Sargon complaining of this shortage may be found in Simo Parpola, *The Correspondence of Sargon II, Part I: Letters from Assyria and the West* (SAA 1; Helsinki: University of Helsinki Press, 1987) 115–16 no. 143; 188 no. 241. The correlation between the epidemic (Akkadian *mūtānu*) and military strength was suggested by Wolfram von Soden, "Sanherib vor Jerusalem 701 v. Chr.," in H.-P. Müller, *Bibel und Alter Orient. Altorientalische Beiträge zum Alten Testament von Wolfram von Soden* (BZAW 162; Berlin: Walter de Gruyter, 1985) 155.

[50] See the chronicle entries in Grayson, *Assyrian and Babylonian Chronicles*, 76, I ii 6'; Millard, *Eponyms of the Assyrian Empire*, 60, B6 r. 8–11.

[51] On this, see Louis D. Levine, "Sennacherib's Southern Front: 704–689 B.C.," *JCS* 34/1,2 (1982) 29–40.

[52] Hayim Tadmor, "World Dominion: The Expanding Horizon of the Assyrian Empire," in L. Milano et al. (eds.), *Landscapes: Territories, Frontiers and Horizons in the Ancient Near*

into three phases based on geography: Phoenicia, Philistia, and Judah.[53] In phase one, Sennacherib swept southward along the Phoenician coast, forcing the rebellious Lulî "king of Sidon" to flee to Cyprus where he later died. The puppet leader Tuba'alu was appointed in his place, and eight "kings of the west" submitted to Sennacherib at Ushu, or ancient Tyre.[54] In phase two, the principal strongholds of Assyrian resistance in Philistia were Ashkelon and Ekron. Ṣidqa, the king of Ashkelon, was deposed and replaced by Šarru-lū-dāri, "the son of Rukibtu, their former king."[55] The officials, nobles, and citizens of Ekron had bound their pro-Assyrian king, Padî, and had turned him over to Hezekiah for safekeeping.[56] They had, moreover, established an alliance with the Egyptians who came to their aid at the battle of Eltekeh. The Egyptian resistance was unable to halt the Assyrian army, as evidenced by the fact that Ekron was taken and those rulers responsible for handing over Padî were punished by impalement.[57]

East: Papers presented to the XLIV Rencontre Assyriologique Internationale Venezia, 7–11 July 1997. Part 1: Invited Lectures (HANEM 3/1; Padova: Sargon, 1999) 61.

[53] The extant annals from this noteworthy Sargonid are arranged according to date with corresponding critical editions in K. Lawson Younger Jr., "Assyrian Involvement in the Southern Levant at the End of the Eighth Century B.C.E.," in Vaughn and Killebrew (eds.), *Jerusalem in Bible and Archaeology*, 245 n. 40. From a literary standpoint, Younger prefers to classify the expedition as having only two phases: Phoenicia and the Southern Levant (Philistia and Judah).

[54] This submission is recorded in Rassam 36–38, and Bull 4, lines 19–20. For the latter, see Smith, *History of Sennacherib*, 65; Luckenbill, *Annals of Sennacherib*, 69; Frahm, *Einleitung in die Sanherib-Inschriften*, 116–18, with additional bibliography. It has been equated with another bull inscription by John Malcolm Russell, *The Writing on the Wall: Studies in the Architectural Context of Late Assyrian Palace Inscriptions* (MC 9; Winona Lake, Ind.: Eisenbrauns, 1999) 262–65. As noted by Gallagher, *Sennacherib's Campaign to Judah*, 95, "This first episode establishes the themes which occur repeatedly in the third campaign account. The readers are shown the futility of opposing the Assyrian king, the Assyrian king's ability to penetrate into the heart of the enemy's strongholds and his ability to replace hostility with proper order."

[55] The antecedent of "former king" is not made explicit, but it is more reasonable to identify this monarch as Rukibtu, see Gallagher, *Sennacherib's Campaign to Judah*, 118–19.

[56] The violation of the oath (*adê/māmītu*) taken by the people was an egregious offense, as exemplified in several Assyrian texts. See further Hayim Tadmor, "Treaty and Oath in the Ancient Near East: A Historian's Approach," in G. M. Tucker and D. A. Knight (eds.), *Humanizing America's Iconic Book* (Chico, Calif.: Scholars Press, 1982) 125–52; idem, "Autobiographical Apology in the Royal Assyrian Literature," in Tadmor and Weinfeld (eds.), *History, Historiography and Interpretation*, 36–57; Tzvi Abusch, "The Socio-Religious Framework of the Babylonian Witchcraft Ceremony Maqlû, Part 1," in idem (ed.), *Riches Hidden in Secret Places. Ancient Near Eastern Studies in Memory of Thorkild Jacobsen* (Winona Lake, Ind.; Eisenbrauns, 2002) 27–32.

[57] If the Egyptian counter-offensive came after the capture of Ekron, it was poorly timed and of little benefit to those whom they had pledged their allegiance. The chronology of the annals in this regard is plausible. The true outcome of the confrontation has

The final phase of the campaign was centered in Judah for the express purpose of retribution toward Hezekiah. Sennacherib claims to have captured forty-six walled cities and their surrounding villages.[58] Lachish was taken in dramatic fashion, with the conquest of the city proudly memorialized among the dynast's palace reliefs at Nineveh and the siege ramp set up by the Assyrians still visible today at the site.[59] From this base of operations, an embassage including the *rab šāqê*, or chief cupbearer, was dispatched to Jerusalem in order to negotiate Hezekiah's surrender. The city was never besieged as has been intimated in some historical reconstructions, the characteristic Assyrian term for the practice (*lamû*) not being applied to Jerusalem.[60] Rather, the burgeoning settlement was enclosed (*eṣēru*) by fortifications (*birātu*, Sumerian URU.ḪAL-ṢU-MEŠ) in order to control access points and to restrict the freedom of movement of its citizens.[61] With the intractability of Sennacherib's resolve firmly punctuated by the decimation of the Judean countryside and the capital itself effectively blockaded, the persuasive propaganda and threatening tactics had their intended effect, forcing Hezekiah to accede to his Assyrian overlord.

long been debated by historians, as it has implications for Sennacherib's timing in withdrawing from the region.

[58] Rassam 49–51; OIP iii 18–23.

[59] Bibliography for the palace reliefs was presented previously in n. 6.

[60] *AHw* 1.541; *CAD* L, 9.69–77. The rendering of URU.ḪAL-ṢU-MEŠ as "earthworks" by A. Leo Oppenheim in his translation of Sennacherib's third campaign (*ANET*, 287–88) implies an aggressive siege, a rendering followed by other scholars such as Siegfried Herrmann, *A History of Israel in Old Testament Times* (2nd ed.; trans. J. Bowden; London: SCM Press, 1981) 258; and Mordechai Cogan in *COS* 2.303.

[61] Arie van der Kooij, "Das assyrische Heer vor den Mauern Jerusalems im Jahr 701 v. Chr," *ZDPV* 102 (1986) 93–109; Gallagher, *Sennacherib's Campaign to Judah*, 133; Ludwig Massmann, "Sanheribs Politik in Juda. Beobachtungen und Erwägungen zum Ausgang der Konfrontation Hiskias mit den Assyrern," in U. Hübner and E. A. Knauf (eds.), *Kein Land für sich allein* (OBO 186; Freiburg: Universitätsverlag, 2002) 167–80; Mayer, "Sennacherib's Campaign of 701 BCE," 179–81; Stephanie Dalley, "Recent Evidence from Assyrian Sources for Judaean History from Uzziah to Manasseh," *JSOT* 28/4 (2004) 392.

For an expansive list of the techniques employed by Assyria when conquering a city, refer to Israel Eph'al, "Ways and Means to Conquer a City, Based on Assyrian Queries to the Sungod," in S. Parpola and R. M. Whiting (eds.), *Assyria 1995: Proceedings of the 10th Anniversary Symposium of the Neo-Assyrian Text Corpus Project, Helsinki, September 7–11, 1995* (Helsinki: Neo-Assyrian Text Corpus Project, 1997) 49–53, esp. 50, conveniently charted by Younger, "Assyrian Involvement in the Southern Levant," 260. See also Israel Eph'al, "On Warfare and Military Control in the Ancient Near Eastern Empires: A Research Outline," in Tadmor and Weinfeld (eds.), *History, Historiography and Interpretation*, 88–106; JoAnn Scurlock, "Neo-Assyrian Battle Tactics," in G. D. Young et al. (eds.), *Crossing Boundaries and Linking Horizons: Studies in Honor of Michael C. Astour on His Eightieth Birthday* (Bethesda: CDL, 1997) 491–517.

His tribute, however, had to be sent to Nineveh after Sennacherib's departure, a sudden withdrawal that may never be adequately understood.[62]

A central question in the reconstruction of events is the timing of the battle of Eltekeh, the only open-field battle during the campaign due to the rarity of Assyrian rebels daring to oppose their imperial masters militarily.[63] In the annals, it provides the only tantalizing hint as to why Sennacherib might have been forced to withdraw from the region, and yet this aid from the southern allies of the coalition is timed prior to the blockade of Jerusalem whereas in the Hebrew Bible it is distinctly after. Five reasons have been put forward to favor the placement of the battle of Eltekeh in the middle, rather than at the end, of the campaign:[64]

(1) While it has long been recognized that the Assyrian annals do not relate events in a strictly chronological order, deviation from this organizing principle should be discernible on both literary and ideological grounds.[65]

---

[62] But as noted by Mayer, "Sennacherib's Campaign of 701 BCE," 181, the fact that Hezekiah had to send his tribute "after me to Nineveh" is not proof in itself of a hasty retreat, as the king would return to his palace ahead of the slow-moving caravans of booty and await their arrival.

[63] Eltekeh was the first of four levitical cities in the Danite allotment (Josh 21:23), although it does not appear in the corresponding list in Chronicles (1 Chr 6:51–54[66–69]). Its location is unknown, and various sites have been suggested. William F. Albright, "Researches of the School in Western Judaea," *BASOR* 15 (1924) 8, identified the site with Khirbet el-Mukenna' (Heb. Tel Miqne), a location which has since been widely accepted as biblical Ekron due to the 1957 survey by Joseph Naveh, "Khirbet al-Muqanna'—Eqron: An Archaeological Survey," *IEJ* 8 (1958) 87–100, 165–70. Eltekeh is now equated with Tell esh-Shallaf or with Tell Melât, cf. Benjamin Mazar, "The Cities of the Territory of Dan," *IEJ* 10 (1960) 72–77; Nadav Na'aman, *Borders and Districts in Biblical Historiography: Seven Studies in Biblical Geographical Lists* (JBS 4; Jerusalem: Simor, 1986) 108 n. 49.

[64] Gallagher, *Sennacherib's Campaign to Judah*, 123–25.

[65] In the third campaign there are clear examples of this phenomenon. Two such examples of chronological displacement are cited at Younger, "Assyrian Involvement in the Southern Levant," 249 n. 49, cf. W. J. Martin, "'Dischronologized' Narrative in the Old Testament," in *Congress Volume, Rome 1968* (VTSup 17; Leiden: E. J. Brill, 1969) 179–86. Gallagher challenges that "People who hold that the chronological order of the annals has been so drastically altered for the Egyptian battle should give an explanation as to why the Assyrian scribe chose to present the material in this manner" (*Sennacherib's Campaign to Judah*, 123). In response, Ernst Axel Knauf, "701: Sennacherib at the Berezina," in Grabbe (ed.), *'Like a Bird in a Cage'*, 141–49, counters that the battle of Eltekeh belongs at the very end of the campaign because the "present finale, the submission of Hezekiah, makes better reading and bestows on Sennacherib more glory, praise and honor to take back with him to Assyria than the 'Peace Conference of Ekron' would have left him in case it had been reported."

It is to be seriously doubted how a depiction of a strategic military engagement, cast with strong literary allusions to the mythical battle by Marduk against chaos in the Enūma

(2) Tell esh-Shallaf, the commonly accepted site of Eltekeh, is too far north for the Egyptian army to have penetrated so late in the campaign.

(3) With regard to Taharqo's approach mentioned in 2 Kgs 19:9a, 36, there is no battle recorded, but only a report.

(4) It would have been poor timing and military strategy for Egypt, with so much advance notice to prepare for the intervention of Sennacherib in Palestine, to wait to confront the Assyrian army until after Ashkelon had capitulated and both Ekron and Lachish had been decimated, the very point at which Hezekiah was ostensibly negotiating a surrender.

(5) In Jerusalem the *rab šāqê* refers to Egypt as a "crushed reed" (2 Kgs 18:21), an Akkadian simile used to refer to defeated enemies, which at face value can only mean that this ally had already been confronted and subdued.

To this may be added that timing the battle of Eltekeh at the climax of the campaign requires moving the whole affair with Ekron to the end as well. There is not merely a literary chiasm with the Ekronite rebellion book-ending the battle, but the Egyptians seem to have disrupted the Assyrian attack on the city when "they came to their assistance" (*illikū rēṣūssun*), and the vengeance taken on the Ekronites can only be concluded when the defensive stand has been put down.[66] If the Assyrians are still pressing their attacks on the populace at the end of the campaign, however, then the preceding battle has not been decisive by any measure.

For those who favor moving the battle of Eltekeh to the end of the campaign, there is an unspoken assumption that it was a strategic military defeat, or at least a major setback, which prompted Sennacherib to withdraw from the region.[67] Although the five written sources available to

---

Eliš, would fail to be the high point of the action. For this transferring of the battle to the cosmic realm, viewed as one of three major rhetorical peaks in Sennacherib's annals, see Elnathan Weissert, "Creating a Political Climate: Literary Allusions to Enūma Eliš in Sennacherib's Account of the Battle of Halule," in H. Waetzoldt and H. Hauptmann (eds.), *Assyrien im Wandel der Zeiten* (HSO 6; Heidelberg: Heidelberger Orientverlag, 1997) 191–202. Gallagher, *Sennacherib's Campaign to Judah*, 120–21, also sees literary allusions in the Ekron episode to the Legend of Etana.

[66] Rassam 43; OIP ii 73–iii 11. The literary chiasm is discussed in Younger, "Assyrian Involvement in the Southern Levant," 249. For the grammatical issue with this cited line, see idem, 251–52 n. 58. For the record, I favor the interpretation of Gallagher, *Sennacherib's Campaign to Judah*, 116.

[67] Part of this justification stems directly from the annals, in its staid, prosaic presentation of the engagement. As noted by Hayim Tadmor, "Philistia under Assyrian Rule,"

us which have been connected to the invasion of 701 B.C.E. are diverse in their explanations as to what actually transpired, of one thing they are in complete agreement: it was not a military engagement which signaled the end of Sennacherib's reign of destruction.[68] Both the annals and source A of 2 Kings provide no explanation, but give no credence to an Egyptian victory. The prophetic source B₁ states that it was merely news of the advance of Taharqo which made the Sargonid take flight, which squares with a non-military explanation for the withdrawal.[69] The annals further confirm that Taharqo, "the king of Meluḫḫa," was not present at Eltekeh but only some of his forces, hence the biblical and Assyrian texts are in agreement that there was no direct encounter with the Nubian leader.[70]

As for the prophetic source B₂ and the independent tale of Herodotus, something altogether supernatural is to be credited with the defeat of the Assyrian army, a matter which for all intents and purposes could only be attributed to the divine sphere. There are many reasons why an army might be forced to turn back from an offensive: bad weather, plague, lack of supplies, low morale, or an exigency elsewhere in the kingdom.[71] It should be said that only a means of deliverance unrelated to conventional warfare, at such a fortuitous moment that tradition credited it to divine intervention, can justify the legendary status that the story has

---

BA 29/3 (1966) 97, there are no specific numbers given of prisoners taken, no booty listed, and no mention of any pursuit of the routed enemy.

[68] These five written sources are: the Assyrian annals (in particular the Rassam Cylinder and the Oriental Institute Prism), Herodotus §2.141, and the three separate traditions considered by many scholars to underly 2 Kgs 18:13–20:19.

[69] If the matter were merely an issue of military strength, it seems strange on the face of it as to why the implacable imperial army would retreat at the prospect of impending confrontation. Sennacherib would reasonably be expected to flee if his forces were somehow outmatched, more sensible after a skirmish in which the army had taken losses and dispersed itself fearing further reprisal. Again, Eltekeh would appear to loom large as an earlier standoff in the campaign. Due to the ascendancy of the Nubian dynasty— sufficiently strong under Taharqo that the Babylonian Chronicle reports his successful repulsion of Esarhaddon during the Sargonid's first campaign to Egypt—there is credence to the idea that even a report of the Nubian king's approach would have been worrying to Sennacherib.

[70] Rassam 43–44; OIP ii 78–83, highlighted previously.

[71] Sennacherib was forced to turn back by heavy rain and snow storms in the month of Tebetu (Dec./Jan.) during his seventh campaign, see *ARAB* 2.155, #351. The epidemic which struck Assyria during the reign of Sargon II is recorded in the Babylonian Chronicle (1 ii 5'), "The fifteenth year ... there was plague (*mūtānu*, lit. 'death') in Assyria." See Grayson, *Assyrian and Babylonian Chronicles*, 76. The scorched-earth policy of Assyria would also have been a factor, as noted by Knauf, "701: Sennacherib at the Berezina," 147 n. 16, "Nothing destroys an army more quickly and more thoroughly than a systematically devastated region supposed to feed it."

attained in its various transmitted forms.[72] Other ancient texts affirm
that such descriptions are rightly to be classified as beyond the purview
of mere martial conflict, and it is the duty of the scholar to respect that
distinction.[73] While we may never know or understand what prompted
the retreat of the imperial army, it would be an exegetical error to reduce
it to the simplistic explanation of being defeated in combat. The battle
of Eltekeh was not the reason for Sennacherib's return to Nineveh, and
should not be placed at the end of the campaign.

The miraculous deliverance of Jerusalem as recorded in 2 Kgs 19:35/
Isa 37:36 does not claim to be an eyewitness account, and its inclusion at
the end of the blockade narrative serves a literary motivation quite apart
from the accurate reporting of historical events. The slaying of 185,000
within the enemy camp by the angel of YHWH represents an attempt
to harmonize the failure of Sennacherib to take Jerusalem with Isaiah's
prophecy of the army's defeat before Zion.[74] Rather than recording the
withdrawal of the Assyrian troops, the divine intervention preserved in
the biblical text accords with the promise that the cloak of every warrior would be rolled in blood, and that all the trees of the enemy king's
forest would be chopped down.[75] The destruction of the Assyrian army
by the angel was hence a means to ensure the veracity of Isaiah's prophetic word.[76] Its presence is the result of Isaiah's prophecies regarding
the demise of Assyria having been composed before, not after, Sennacherib's invasion.[77]

---

[72] In attempting to deal with the realia of this explanation, Alan R. Millard concludes:
"Penetrating beyond the words of the text to seek for an explanation in terms of the natural world is unprofitable ... the historian has no alternative but to admit that something
happened which is beyond his resources to comprehend" ("Sennacherib's Attack on Hezekiah," *TynBul* 36 [1985] 77).

[73] See examples in Moshe Weinfeld, "Divine Intervention in War in Ancient Israel and
in the Ancient Near East," in Tadmor and Weinfeld (eds.), *History, Historiography, and
Interpretation*, 121–47; Alan R. Millard, "The Old Testament and History: Some Considerations," *FT* 110/1,2 (1983) 34–53.

[74] Isa 10:24–34.

[75] Isa 9:3–4[4–5]; 10:17–19, 33–34.

[76] Independently, this is Peter Machinist's own view regarding Nahum: "Indeed, the
inclusion in the Biblical canon of Nahum, along with other texts proclaiming the thesis,
like Zephaniah 2:13–15, Zechariah 10:8–12, and Jeremiah 50:17–20, must be understood as
the intent to confirm the initial vision of Isaiah and his era: to see in the period of Assyrian
collapse the theological counterpoint to the earlier period, when Assyria was ascendant"
("Assyria and Its Image in the the First Isaiah," *JAOS* 103/4 [1983] 736).

[77] Additional argumentation for this dating will be provided in my chapter on First
Isaiah.

If there is any additional insight that may be made into a possible solution, it should be centered on the fact that Hezekiah himself represents the climatic conclusion of the third campaign in Sennacherib's annals. The emphasis is made clear via the threefold identification of the Judahite—ᵐHazaqiau, šâšu, and šū ᵐHazaqiau—each reference in an increasingly focused concentric circle moving from the Judean countryside to the blockade of Jerusalem and finally to the king himself.⁷⁸ The victory over the Ekronites, regardless of when it occurred chronologically, would certainly have provided a more resounding finale to the annals by defeating the forces of chaos and restoring order to the realm. The placement of the Hezekiah episode at the end of the campaign is doubtless because the Judean king was the ringleader for the resistance, and the subjugation of the mightiest foe at the climax of the epic was the logical means of reinforcing the invincibility of the Assyrian king.⁷⁹

Yet according to Sennacherib, Hezekiah "did not submit to my yoke" and as an adversary was *šepṣu mitru* "tough and powerful."⁸⁰ For an Assyrian king to bestow such an accolade upon an enemy is extremely unusual, and diametrically opposed to the enterprise of imperial propaganda. Sennacherib only employs this expression two other times, in reference to peoples who had been difficult to subdue.⁸¹ By asserting the Judean's staunch tenacity and by having the campaign account end directly before

---

⁷⁸ As noted by Younger, "Assyrian Involvement in the Southern Levant," 250.

⁷⁹ I find this explanation more satisfying than that of Tadmor, "Sennacherib's Campaign to Judah," 71, 73, who argues that scribes progressed from easy victories to harder ones. Regardless of how difficult a victory might have been to achieve, it was of little propogandistic value if the enemy himself were of no account. A man is measured by his enemies.

⁸⁰ *šepṣu mitru* ᵐHa-za-qí-a-a-ú šarrišu ušakniš šēpū'a "The tough and powerful Hezekiah, its [Judah's] king, I brought to submission at my feet," Bull 1 line 21; Bulls 2–3 line 21. For editions, translations and studies, see Frahm, *Einleitung in die Scnherib-Inschriften*, 115–16. The reading here is in agreement with *ARAB* 2.148; *CAD* M/2, 10.139–40, s.v. *mitru* A; Gallagher, *Sennacherib's Campaign to Judah*, 130, over against *šepṣu bēru*, rendered as "offenkundiger Aufrührer" (*AHw* 1.130, s.v. *bīru* I) and "notoricus rebel" (Mayer, "Sennacherib's Campaign of 701 BCE," 194). The reading *bēru* follows the transliterations of Smith, *History of Sennacherib*, 68; Luckenbill, *Annals of Sennacherib*, 77 ll. 20–22; Borger, *Babylonisch-assyrische Lesestücke*, 1.76, but I personally can find no lexical gloss for *bēru/bīru* that even approaches the glosses cited above.

Some editions such as that of Smith connect the epithet with the preceding reference to Judah, but it is better retained with Hezekiah: although adjectives typically follow nouns in Akkadian, it is not an inviolable rule, and normal word order has already been contravened in the preceding sentence, beginning as it does with a verb (*ušalpit*). Because the translations for this verb differ as well, I personally prefer "devastated, laid waste" as the rendering of *lapātu* (Š pret).

⁸¹ Gallagher, *Sennacherib's Campaign to Judah*, 142 n. 71.

the walls of Jerusalem, Sennacherib in effect credits his formidable opponent for his own failure to take the city.[82] This Assyrian perspective is perfectly in line with the biblical traditions in the A and B sources which, despite their differing resolutions to the crisis, nonetheless concur in correlating Hezekiah's actions with the withdrawal of the enemy. In the final analysis, it would seem that Hezekiah himself was a pivotal reason for the redemption of Jerusalem.[83]

3.5. Conclusion

Sennacherib's third campaign, conducted in order to quell unrest in the western part of his empire, was both Hezekiah's darkest hour and peerless shining moment. There was only one expedition by Sennacherib to Judah, based on both Assyrian records and archaeological data. The chronology of Hezekiah's reign, previously affirmed, allows insufficient time for a return expedition during his lifetime. The diplomatic mission of Merodach-baladan offers no support for multiple invasions, as the Chaldean was in hiding in Elam from approximately 700 B.C.E. until his death. The differing presentations of the campaign preserved in the Bible feature identical principal characters in the same respective geographical locations, with Jerusalem in crisis and ultimately spared. By all accounts, these texts preserve separate traditions of the same historical event.

Although Taharqo was not yet a pharaoh of Egypt in 701 B.C.E., he was certainly old enough to be serving as a military commander. The Deuteronomistic History is all too aware of the precise meaning of פַּרְעֹה מֶלֶךְ־מִצְרַיִם, and the fact that Taharqo is not designated in this manner attests to the historical accuracy of the biblical text in this regard. Both Assyrian records and the parallel versions in the book of Kings and First Isaiah

---

[82] For discussion of Hezekiah's status in the eyes of Sennacherib, cf. Gallagher, *Sennacherib's Campaign to Judah*, 38, 130, 141–42; Younger, "Assyrian Involvement in the Southern Levant," 253.

[83] One hint at Hezekiah's brilliance as a strategist was to prevent the Assyrian army's access to water supplies by stopping up local streams, as recorded in 2 Chr 32:3–4. Redirecting the flow of the city's own water source within its walls prevented Sennacherib from commandeering the natural resource as a means to starve out the incarcerated population, and we may presume that food had been hoarded as well. The additional fortifications put in place, such as the archaeologically verified Broad Wall, would have made the prospect of a siege daunting. Hezekiah had long before planned to rebel with plenty of time to prepare his capital city, and with restricted access to regional water and advance news of reinforcements headed by the dominant Nubian empire, it would have been prudent for Sennacherib to assess the merits of lingering to finalize the campaign.

distinguish between a Pharaoh of Egypt who personally engaged Sennacherib, and a king of Kush who did not.[84] Still some ten years prior to ascending to power over Egypt, Taharqo was in all likelihood the "king of Kush" as claimed in 2 Kgs 19:9/Isa 37:9.

The battle of Eltekeh makes sense as having taken place in the middle of the campaign precisely where it is depicted in Assyrian records. The *rab šāqê* refers to Egypt as a "crushed reed" in 2 Kgs 18 21/Isa 36:6, which dovetails well with the mention of the LUGAL KUR *Muṣri* at Eltekeh in the account of Sennacherib's third *palû*. Jerusalem was blockaded rather than beseiged, and Hezekiah was forced under duress to spare the capital city by paying a substantial sum to Sennacherib. None of the extant versions provide the specific rationale for the withdrawal of the imperial army from the region, but all are in agreement that it was not a military engagement which brought an end to the campaign. While the departure was ostensibly due to the potential for a direct encounter with Nubian forces, Hezekiah's extensive preparations for the Assyrian invasion may well have been the primary deterrent against Sennacherib's continued assault on Jerusalem.

---

[84] Rassam 43–44; OIP ii 78–83; 2 Kgs 18:21; 19:9/Isa 36:6; 37:9.

PART TWO

HEZEKIAH IN THE BOOK OF KINGS
AND FIRST ISAIAH

CHAPTER FOUR

THE RELIGIOUS REFORM

Perhaps the most contentious matter in reconstructing the world of Hezekiah relates to the cultic reform credited directly to him in the Bible. The
question of its historicity has long divided the academic community.[1]

---

[1] For those who accept the historicity of the reform and have proposed explanations
to justify its implementation, see Harold H. Rowley, "Hezekiah's Reform and Rebellion,"
BJRL 44/2 (1962) 425–31, with earlier literature; the bibliography provided by Hermann
Spieckermann, *Juda unter Assur in der Sargonidenzeit* (Göttingen: Vandenhoeck &
Ruprecht, 1982) 174 n. 34; Moshe Weinfeld, "Cult Centralization in Israel in the Light of
a Neo-Babylonian Analogy," *JNES* 23 (1964) 202–12; idem, *Deuteronomy 1–11* (AYB 11; New
York: Doubleday, 1991) 156–62; John W. McKay, *Religion in Judah under the Assyrians* (SBT
2/26; London: SCM Press, 1973) 15–17; Baruch Halpern, "Jerusalem and the Lineages in the
Seventh Century BCE: Kinship and the Rise of Individual Moral Liability," in B. Halpern
and D. W. Hobson (eds.), *Law and Ideology in Monarchic Israel* (JSOTSup 124; Sheffield:
JSOT Press, 1991) 47–48, 65–70; Gösta W. Ahlström, *Royal Administration and National
Religion in Ancient Palestine* (SHANE 1; Leiden: E. J. Brill, 1982) 65–68; Ze'ev Herzog et al.,
"The Israelite Fortress at Arad," *BASOR* 254 (1984) 1–34; Menahem Haran, *Temples and
Temple-Service in Ancient Israel* (2nd ed.; Winona Lake, Ind.: Eisenbrauns, 1985) 132–42;
Francolino J. Gonçalves, *L'expédition de Sennachérib en Palestine dans la littérature hébra-
ïque ancienne* (Études bibliques, New Series 7; Paris: Librairie Lecoffre, 1986) 73–88, 100–101,
with earlier literature; Mordechai Cogan and Hayim Tadmor, *II Kings* (AYB 11; New York:
Doubleday, 1988) 218–20; Richard H. Lowery, *The Reforming Kings: Cults and Society in
First Temple Judah* (JSOTSup 120; Sheffield: JSOT Press, 1991) 142–68; Oded Borowski,
"Hezekiah's Reforms and the Revolt Against Assyria," *BA* 58/3 (1995) 148–55; Ze'ev Herzog,
"The Date of the Temple at Arad: Reassessment of the Stratigraphy and the Implications
for the History of Religion in Judah," in A. Mazar (ed.), *Studies in the Archaeology of the Iron
Age in Israel and Jordan* (JSOTSup 331; Sheffield: Sheffield Academic Press, 2001) 156–78;
J. Maxwell Miller and John H. Hayes, *A History of Ancient Israel and Judah* (2nd edition;
Louisville: Westminster John Knox, 2006) 413–15; Israel Finkelstein and Neil Asher Silber-
man, "Temple and Dynasty: Hezekiah, the Remaking of Judah and the Rise of Pan-Israelite
Ideology," *JSOT* 30/3 (2006) 259–85.
    In the opposing camp stand those who, on the whole, regard the reform as a retrojec-
tion of the sweeping cultic measures undertaken by Josiah almost a century later. On
this, see the references at Julius Wellhausen, *Prolegomena zur Geschichte Israels* (6th ed.;
Berlin: W. de Gruyter, 1905) 25, and Rowley, "Hezekiah's Reform and Rebellion," 425 n. 1; the
bibliography of Spieckermann, *Juda unter Assur in der Sargonidenzeit*, 174 n. 34; references
at Gonçalves, *L'expédition de Sennachérib*, 74 nn. 83, 85–86; Hans D. Hoffmann, *Reform
und Reformen: Untersuchungen zu einem Grundthema der deuteronomistischen Geschichtsschreibung* (AThANT 66; Zürich: Theologischer Verlag, 1980) 146–55; Ernst Würthwein, *Die
Bücher der Könige. 1. Kön. 17–2. Kön. 25.* (ATD 11/2; Göttingen: Vandenhoeck & Ruprecht,
1984) 411–412; Herbert Donner, *Geschichte des Volkes Israel und seiner Nachbarn in
Grundzügen* (2 vols.; GAT 4; Göttingen: Vandenhoeck & Ruprecht, 1986) 2.332; Lowell K.
Handy, "Hezekiah's Unlikely Reform," *ZAW* 100/1 (1988) 111–115; Ludger Camp, *Hiskija und*

Early in the summation of his reign given in the book of Kings, we are told: "He removed the high places and broke down the [sacred] pillars and cut down the Asherah. He also broke in pieces the bronze serpent that Moses had made, for until those days the sons of Israel burned incense to it; and it was called Nehushtan" (2 Kgs 18:4). Later in the account of the speech of the *rab šāqê* before the walls of Jerusalem, the spokesman for the Assyrian king declares of YHWH: "Is it not He whose high places and whose altars Hezekiah has taken away, and has said to Judah and to Jerusalem, 'You shall worship before this altar in Jerusalem'?" (v 22).

The archaeological evidence potentially relating to this religious reformation will be the last of the extra-biblical material marshaled in this study. The sites placed under scrutiny in this investigation are those whose stratigraphic record preserves the use of sanctuaries during the eighth century B.C.E., notably Tel Arad and Tel Beer-sheba. The controversial sanctuary at Lachish will also be considered before attempting a final evaluation.[2] Analysis will continue with the biblical text, specifically the aforementioned consequential verses of Kings. The extensive coverage of his cultic program in Chronicles will be considered in a separate chapter. Finally, the historical likelihood of this initiative will be assessed by exploring a probable social setting.

Hiskijabild: Analyse und Interpretation von 2 Kön 18–20 (MThA 9; Altenberge: Telos, 1990) 274–87; Nadav Na'aman, "The Debated Historicity of Hezekiah's Reform in the Light of Historical and Archaeological Research" *ZAW* 107 (1995) 179–95; Lisbeth S. Fried, "The High Places (*Bāmôt*) and the Reforms of Hezekiah and Josiah: An Archaeological Investigation," *JAOS* 122/3 (2002) 437–65; Diana Edelman, "Hezekiah's Alleged Cultic Centralization," *JSOT* 32/4 (2008) 395–434.

[2] A fourth cultic site from Iron Age II Judah has been identified at Tel Halif, see Paul Jacobs and Oded Borowski, "Notes and News: Tell Halif, 1992," *IEJ* 43 (1993) 66–70; Borowski, "Hezekiah's Reforms and the Revolt Against Assyria," 148–55. According to its excavator, the site preserves a four-room house, whose rear broad-room had been converted to serve as a shrine. Its destruction is attributed to Sennacherib in 701 B.C.E., and thus the house fits the rough timeline of sites potentially affected during the reign of Hezekiah. Due to the domestic nature of the shrine, however, it has little bearing on the issue of state religion. It is to be expected that the *Volksreligion* would have continued to reflect more broad-based Canaanite religious practices, cf. Rainer Albertz, *A History of Israelite Religion in the Old Testament Period* (2 vols.; trans. J. Bowden; OTL; Louisville: Westminster/John Knox, 1994) 1.17–21, 94–103, 186–195; Patrick D. Miller, *The Religion of Ancient Israel* (London: SPCK, 2000) 46–105; Ziony Zevit, *The Religions of Ancient Israel: A Synthesis of Parallactic Approaches* (London: Continuum, 2001) 662–63; Mark S. Smith, *The Early History of God: Yahweh and the Other Deities in Ancient Israel* (2nd ed.; Grand Rapids: Eerdmans, 2002) 1–14.

4.1. Archaeological Evidence

4.1.1. *Arad*

The Yahwistic temple at Arad was discovered in the 1960s and was initially dated to the tenth century B.C.E. (Stratum XI), when the earliest walled fortress was erected. Its courtyard, including the altar, was completely covered with a fill approximately one meter in depth. The first reports of the sanctuary's excavation claimed that the large altar in the courtyard had been abolished in the late eighth century (Stratum VIII), presumably due to the abolition of sacrifice under Hezekiah. The temple itself stood until the late seventh century (Stratum VI), when it was decommissioned during the reign of king Josiah.[3] The Arad team later emended its findings and argued that both the altar and shrine were removed in Hezekiah's time.[4] In the process of final publication of the site and its finds, the dating of the temple was once again modified: the shrine and its associated altar were confirmed as having been abandoned at the same time, but earlier in the eighth century (Stratum IX). There was no sanctuary in the fortress of the late eighth century (Stratum VIII), which is dated coterminous with Sennacherib's campaign of 701 B.C.E.[5] These results may be expressed in tabular form as follows:[6]

Terminus of	Initial dating	Later dating	Final dating
altar	Stratum VIII	Stratum VIII	Stratum IX
shrine	Stratum VI	Stratum VIII	Stratum IX

Due to the discontinuity of the analysis and the straightforward correlations drawn between the archaeological data and the biblical material, these conclusions have not gone unchallenged. Some scholars assert no linkage whatsoever between the decommissioning of the Arad sanctuary

---

[3] As reported by the lead excavator Yohanan Aharoni, "Arad: Its Inscriptions and Temple," *BA* 31 (1968) 26.

[4] After the death of Aharoni, the revised interpretation was published in Herzog et al., "Israelite Fortress at Arad," 1–34.

[5] Herzog, "Date of the Temple at Arad," 156–78; idem, "The Fortress Mound at Tel Arad: An Interim Report," *TA* 29 (2002) 3–109.

[6] The latest stratigraphical analysis with revised dates, prior to the as-yet unpublished final report on the site, may be found in Herzog, "Fortress Mound at Tel Arad," 11–14.

and the Hezekian reform, preferring to date the very construction of the shrine to Stratum VIII.[7] Others accept the revised stratigraphy of the excavation team with regard to the founding of the sanctuary, but aver that it continued in use until after the end of Stratum IX.[8] More subtle arguments maintain that the site was decommissioned rather than destroyed and may have been in the hands of the enemy, who nonetheless treated the foreign holy place with utmost respect.[9]

Even for those who accept the dating of the stratigraphy, it is still preferable to explicate the burial of the sanctuary as a preemptive move to safeguard its sacred components in the face of enemy attack.[10] If this is correct, then preventing defilement in this manner was a stratagem to assure reuse of the shrine. This is at once questionable, since the sanctuary complex at Arad was never restored. It would be a simple matter

---

[7] David Ussishkin, "The Date of the Judean Shrine at Arad," *IEJ* 38/3 (1988) 142–57.

[8] Edelman, "Hezekiah's Alleged Cultic Centralization," 395–434.

[9] With regard to the sanctuary at Arad, Nadav Na'aman, "No Anthropomorphic Graven Image: Notes on the Assumed Anthropomorphic Cult Statues in the Temples of YHWH in the Pre-Exilic Period," *UF* 31 (1999) 406, has suggested that prior to its careful burial, signs of desecration and destruction might have been removed from the complex. Such a proposal contradicts the blatant destruction and abandonment of cultic sites he himself surveys in "Debated Historicity of Hezekiah's Reform," 187–88. Similarly Edelman, "Hezekiah's Alleged Cultic Centralization," speculates that the relatively pristine condition of the sanctuary remains at Arad and Beer-sheba may be due to their fortifications having been taken by the enemy "without the entire interior area catching fire" or "without attack or destruction" (pp. 409, 421). In her estimation, "The newcomers appear to have respected the sanctity of the defeated deity to the extent that they decommissioned his temple, burying it and certain cultic appurtenances" (p. 409). Yet this is inconsistent with her own assessment of the alleged cultic sites surveyed by Na'aman, which she acknowledges were clearly destroyed and hence "do not offer parallels to internally decommissioned temples that had not been desecrated" (p. 416). These data speak to a systematic program of cultic desecration by invading armies. It is further contrary to the report in Sennacherib's annals (OIP iii 19–31), and to that of Assyrian policy in general. Methodologically speaking, a position which is able to accommodate the archaeological record while respecting the Assyrian and biblical accounts seems preferable.

[10] Fried, "High Places (*Bāmôt*) and the Reforms of Hezekiah and Josiah," 447. She sees this as the only possible option because the lack of destruction by fire indicates that the temple complex was buried prior to the conflagration which marked the end of Stratum IX, whereas the alternative she claims is preferred by Herzog—"the sanctuary was buried *after* having survived the destruction which destroyed the tell" (emphasis mine)—is untenable. Herzog, in fact, does not take a position in the original Hebrew ("The Temple at Arad and Its Parallels," in idem, *Arad: The Arad Fortresses* [Tel Aviv: Hakkibutz Hammeuchad, 1997] 202–203), and even accords with her own stance in his later English article, "Fortress Mound at Tel Arad," 66: "It is unreasonable to assume that the temple was spared the damage caused by the destruction of Stratum IX. I, therefore, prefer to interpret the data as pointing to willful cancellation a *short time before* the destruction of the fortress" (emphasis mine).

to reconsecrate defiled objects for renewed use, and a demolished altar could be rebuilt.[11] Other sites which have been argued as temples, moreover, were buried only after having been destroyed.[12] This is an indication that burial was a means of permanently ridding oneself of an object, akin to human burial or the removal of idols. The sheer depth of the fill at Arad, at nearly one meter, reinforces this idea.[13] It is significant, furthermore, that despite the variance in dating the terminus of the shrine and altar by the excavation team, the subsequent recalibration of the dates in response to assimilating the archaeological data has nonetheless been consistently earlier chronologically.[14] This fact in itself gives pause to the opposing positions which seek to postdate part or all of the sanctuary to Stratum VIII or later.

4.1.2. *Beer-sheba*

The large horned altar discovered in 1973 at Beer-sheba presents a second potential case study. It was found dismantled within an eighth-century pillared storehouse complex, its ashlar stones used to make repairs there as well as to the retaining walls of the glacis. The altar was originally surmised to have stood within a sanctuary, although such an edifice is no longer discernible. The altar is considered to have been constructed in the ninth century B.C.E. (Stratum III), while the storehouse was eventually destroyed at the hands of Sennacherib in 701 (end of Stratum II). The excavator proposed that the altar was demolished in the reign of Hezekiah as a concomitant of repairing the building, a direct corroboration of his religious reform.[15]

---

[11] In the case of the Stratum X temple, this was apparently done after it was destroyed in a conflagration, see Herzog, "Fortress Mound at Tel Arad," 58–59. It was a known ancient Near Eastern practice to rededicate defiled sanctuaries, just as Aššurbanipal purified the cultic centers of Babylon, Kutha, and Sippar, as recorded in Rassam Cylinder iv 86–87. What was to be avoided at all costs, however, was the removal of the divine images. Although new ones could be refashioned, the originals were intrinsically of inestimable value.

[12] As surveyed by Naʾaman, "Debated Historicity of Hezekiah's Reform," 187–88, but see the cautious response of Edelman, "Hezekiah's Alleged Cultic Centralization," 412–16.

[13] Inasmuch as the stela was laid on its flat side and the incense altars were placed in an even deeper pit, a depth of one meter was more than sufficient to cover the objects completely with earth.

[14] Exemplified in the table of proposed dates for the altar and shrine previously presented.

[15] Yohanan Aharoni, "The Horned Altar of Beer-sheba," *BA* 37 (1974) 2–6; idem, "Excavations at Tel Beer-sheba, Preliminary Report of the Fifth and Sixth Seasons, 1973–1974," *TA* 2 (1975) 154–56.

Several aspects of these conclusions have come under fire. At the most
basic level, there is dispute as to whether Tel Beer-sheba is in fact biblical Beer-sheba.[16] A second fulcrum of dissension is whether the end of
Stratum II should be dated to the time of Sennacherib in 701 B.C.E.[17] The
traces of fire detected on the four horns of the altar have been questioned
as residue from incense burning rather than from animal sacrifices.[18] The

---

[16] The site has been identified as the Shema/Sheba of Josh 15:26; 19:2, while biblical
Beer-sheba is thought to be the modern civilian settlement of Bir es-Sebaʿ some five kilo-
meters distant, cf. Albrecht Alt, "Beiträge zur historischen Geographie und Topographie
des Negeb, III: Saruhen, Ziklag, Horma, Gerar," *JPOS* 15 (1935) 320–21; Félix-Marie Abel,
Géographie de la Palestine (2 vols.; Paris: Lecoffre, 1933–38) 2.263; Martin Noth, *Das Buch
Josua* (2nd ed.; HAT I/7; Tübingen: J.C.B. Mohr, 1953) 93; Nadav Naʾaman, "The Inheritance
of the Sons of Simeon," *ZDPV* 96 (1980) 149–51; Mervyn D. Fowler, "The Excavation of Tell
Beer-sheba and the Biblical Record," *PEQ* 114 (1982) 7–11.
The rejoinder to this claim is that the tell represents the only viable location in the
region of modern Beer-sheba for a major fortified administrative center of the Iron Age.
The fact that a nearby small settlement might have borne that name in antiquity is not
problematic, as doublets of ancient sites are well known. Multiple sites have been conflated
with a phonetically similar Arabic name, the modern toponym being identified based on
linguistic homophonia. A more recent proposal has equated Tel Beer-sheba with biblical Ziklag, see Volkmar Fritz, "Where is David's Ziklag?" *BAR* 19/3 (May–Jun. 1993) 58–61,
76. The preference for maintaining the assignment of biblical Ziklag with Tel Seraʿ (Tell
esh-Shariʿah), however, is provided by Anson F. Rainey, "Ziklag," *ISBE* 4.1196b, and reiterated in idem, "Hezekiah's Reform and the Altars at Beer-sheba and Arad," M. D. Coogan,
J. C. Exum, and L. E. Stager (eds.), *Scripture and Other Artifacts: Essays on the Bible and
Archaeology in Honor of Philip J. King* (Louisville: Westminster John Knox, 1994) 337.
[17] Nadav Naʾaman, "Sennacherib's Campaign to Judah and the Date of the lmlk Stamps,"
VT 29/1 (1979) 74–75; idem, "The Brook of Egypt and Assyrian Policy on the Border of Egypt,"
TA 6/1–2 (1979) 82–83, has favored that Stratum II should be dated prior to Sennacherib's
campaign. On the opposing side, Kathleen M. Kenyon, "The Date of the Destruction of
Iron Age Beer-sheba," *PEQ* 108 (1979) 63–64; Ernst Axel Knauf, "Who Destroyed Beersheba
II?" in U. Hübner and E. A. Knauf (eds.), *Kein Land für sich allein* (OBO 186; Freiburg:
Universitätsverlag, 2002) 180, 191, and Edelman, "Hezekiah's Alleged Cultic Centralization,"
421, opt to date Stratum II to the reign of Manasseh, destroyed by the Arab sheikh Asuhili
ca. 679 B.C.E.
The pottery repertoire of Stratum II has already been shown to be comparable to that of
Lachish III and Arad VIII by Miriam Aharoni and Yohanan Aharoni, "The Stratification of
Judahite Sites in the 8th and 7th Centuries B.C.E.," *BASOR* 224 (1976) 73–90. The fact that
pottery from Stratum III shares similar characteristics is not as significant as the disappearance of this distinctive type altogether. The one *lmlk* seal impression recovered from Tel
Beer-sheba in fact came from Stratum II. While the paucity of seals at Beer-sheba compared to that at Lachish has been called upon as evidence that Stratum II should not be
dated to the time of Hezekiah (Naʾaman above followed by Edelman, "Hezekiah's Alleged
Cultic Centralization," 421), this matter has been satisfactorily explained as being due to a
different supply chain for southern cities as opposed to those in the Shephelah and the hill
country, see Anson F. Rainey, "Wine from the Royal Vineyards," *BASOR* 245 (1982) 59–61.
[18] Yigael Yadin, "Beer-sheba: The High Place Destroyed by King Josiah," *BASOR* 222
(1976) 11; Fowler, "Excavation of Tell Beer-sheba and the Biblical Record," 8–9; idem, "Excavated Incense Burners," *BA* 47 (1984) 183–86. It is the contention of Niels H. Gadegaard,

original location of the altar is a further controversial issue, with an alternative location proposed in the courtyard of House 430 beside the city gate.[19]

Even if the end of Stratum II is dated to 701 B.C.E., it merely establishes a *terminus a quo* for the secondary use of the altar stones. There is no destruction layer separating Strata III and II, and the pottery within both of these layers is highly reminiscent of Lachish Level III.[20] As Stratum IV was destroyed no later than the early part of the ninth century, that leaves a span of roughly a century and a half for the ashlars of the altar to have been retasked throughout the site for other purposes. It is also of note that one of the fragments was found in a portion of the retaining wall dated to Stratum III, although this does not preclude that this rampart had fallen into disrepair and was only stabilized at a later time with materials properly belonging to Stratum II.[21]

4.1.3. *Lachish*

The site of Lachish has recently been brought into the discussion as well, owing to a reassessment of its stratigraphy. A small broad-room with benches along the walls and containing a stone altar and various cult vessels was identified as a Judahite sanctuary by its excavator, complete with an object classified as a *bāmâ*.[22] The shrine was interpreted as

---

"On the So-Called Burnt Offering Altar in the Old Testament," *PEQ* 110 (1978) 35–45, that the altars at Arad and Beer-sheba were too insubstantial to maintain a fire of sufficient heat or duration to consume a sheep or goat.

[19] This alternate location was proposed by Yadin, "Beer-sheba: The High Place Destroyed by King Josiah"; Hershel Shanks, "Yigael Yadin Finds a Bama at Beer-Sheva," *BAR* 3/1 (Mar. 1977) 3–12. For rebuttal, see Ze'ev Herzog, Anson F. Rainey, and Shmuel Moshkovitz, "The Stratigraphy of Beer-sheba and the Location of the Sanctuary," *BASOR* 225 (1977) 49–58; Anson F. Rainey, "Beer-Sheva Excavator Blasts Yadin—No Bama at Beer-Sheva," *BAR* 3/3 (Sept. 1977) 18–21, 56. Although the four-horned altar would indeed seem to have been too unwieldy to fit inside the courtyard adjacent to House 430, as argued by Rainey, "Hezekiah's Reform and the Altars at Beer-sheba and Arad," 339–48, the presence of two limestone incense altars discovered *in situ* within this building suggest that it nevertheless did serve a cultic function, see Ephraim Stern, "Limestone Incense Altars," in Y. Aharoni (ed.), *Beer-Sheba I: Excavations at Tel Beer-Sheba, 1969–1971 Seasons* (Givatayim-Ramat Gan: Peli Printing Works Ltd., 1973) 52–53, pls. 29, 52.

[20] Fried, "High Places (*Bāmôt*) and the Reforms of Hezekiah and Josiah," 447, prefers to speak of a single layer, which she designates Stratum III/II.

[21] Aharoni, "Excavations at Tel Beer-sheba," 154.

[22] The form and function of the biblical בָּמָה has been the subject of much scholarly discussion, see Philip J. King and Lawrence E. Stager, *Life in Biblical Israel* (Louisville: Westminster John Knox, 2001) 320–22; Fried, "High Places (*Bāmôt*) and the Reforms of Hezekiah and Josiah," 437–43; Patrick H. Vaughn, *The Meaning of 'bēmâ' in the Old Testament.*

having been destroyed in a conflagration at the end of Level V, dated to the tenth century.[23] A later examination of the remains surmised that the walls and floor of the sanctuary itself belonged to no less than four different stratigraphic layers, and that no trace of destruction by fire could be detected. The associated cultic objects were presumed to have been in a pit due to their circular layout, which was filled in as part of Level IV prior to the construction of a subsequent walled, paved palace courtyard assigned to Level III.[24] The date of burial of the cult vessels themselves has been questioned, in that their deposition could equally have been in Level III during the construction of the courtyard. Such a chronology would permit the sealing of the objects under the courtyard to be linked to the closure of sanctuaries under the reform of Hezekiah.[25]

The possibility that the inhumation of these ritual paraphernalia may have ensued during the reign of king Hezekiah is intriguing, but ultimately unverifiable. While the claim that the broad-room suffered no impairment due to fire could suggest an internal decommissioning of the shrine, this is certainly not the only possibility, and even this detail is not beyond contention. Even if the dating could be reliably established, it would still be highly conjectural to posit a link between this event and cultic reform: the range of disputed dates assigned to the shrine, whether Level V or Level IV, are well before the reign of Hezekiah. It may be that the nearby pit of whole and broken מַצֵּבֹת could help to clarify the issue, but the

A Study of Etymological, Textual and Archaeological Evidence (SOTS 3; Cambridge: Cambridge University Press, 2009); Beth Alpert Nakhai, Archaeology and the Religions of Canaan and Israel (ASOR Books 7; Boston: ASOR, 2001) 161–200 and bibliography there.

[23] Building 49, as discussed in Yohanan Aharoni, Investigations at Lachish: The Sanctuary and the Residency (Lachish V) (Tel Aviv: Institute of Archaeology, 1975) 26–32, pls. 3–6, 60.

[24] David Ussishkin, "The Level V 'Sanctuary' and 'High Place' at Lachish. A Stratigraphic Analysis" in C. G. den Hertog, U. Hübner and S. Münger (eds.), Saxa Loquentur: Studien zur Archäologie Palästinas/Israels (AOAT 302; Münster: Ugarit-Verlag, 2003) 205–11. The vessels themselves are typologically difficult to date, see Orna Zimhoni, Studies in the Iron Age Pottery of Israel: Typological, Archaeological and Chronological Aspects (Tel Aviv: Institute of Archaeology, 1997) 62.
Level IV is dated to the ninth-early eighth century B.C.E., while Level III is dated to 701. It should not be forgotten that Level III at one time was predominantly viewed to have been destroyed in 597 B.C.E. Fortunately the matter has been resolved, with later excavations demonstrating conclusively that Sennacherib should be credited with the stratum's destruction, in David Ussishkin, "The Destruction of Lachish by Sennacherib and the Dating of the Royal Judean Storage Jars," TA 4 (1977) 28–57.

[25] Finkelstein and Silberman, "Temple and Dynasty," 272–73. Such ritual burial of sanctified objects is an old and widespread custom, see David Ussishkin, "The Syro-Hittite Ritual Burial of Monuments," JNES 29/2 (1970) 124–28.

dating of these objects is disputed as well.[26] For the purposes of this study, the sanctuary at Lachish is of little value in ascertaining the historicity of a reported bulk closure of ritual centers in the eighth century.

Lachish still has a bearing on the broader discussion of cultic reform, however, in the reliefs at Nineveh depicting booty from the Judean city being brought before Sennacherib during his third campaign. The identification of shortened posts among this plunder as possible incense burners raises a question as to the historicity of the reform.[27] While it is certainly a valid observation that incense burning would have remained a permissible act even after the enactment of the reform, this only serves to highlight the conspicuous nature of the buried incense stands at Arad. There would seem to be a resolution to the crux, however. The description of the incense altar in Exodus suggests that, as with most other aspects of cultic worship, there was but one ritually acceptable way of performing the act.[28] The burning of incense within a censer atop a stand, however, is of an altogether different order, and would not have been cultically sanctioned.[29] If the identification of the objects in the Lachish reliefs as incense burners is maintained, then their use is likely to have been independent

---

[26] Aharoni, *Investigations at Lachish*, 31; John S. Holladay, "Religion in Israel and Judah Under the Monarchy: An Explicitly Archaeological Approach," in P. D. Miller, P. D. Hanson, and S. D. McBride (eds.), *Ancient Israelite Religion: Essays in Honor of Frank Moore Cross* (Philadelphia: Fortress Press, 1987) 254. Aharoni notes that "From their appearance it seems that after being deliberately defaced and broken, they were carefully buried."

[27] Na'aman, "Debated Historicity of Hezekiah's Reform," 191–93; idem, "No Anthropomorphic Graven Image," 404–405.

[28] Exod 30:1–10 (P). Such an appeal to material within the Priestly Code does not have direct implications for this proposal, as it has long been recognized that the age of the priestly traditions may be much older than their time of composition. It should be noted, however, that both P and the Holiness Legislation (H) bear witness to their pre-exilic provenance, on which see Jacob Milgrom, *Leviticus 17–22* (AYB 3A; New York: Doubleday, 2000) 1319–64.

[29] As noted by Jacob Milgrom, "Does H Advocate the Centralization of Worship?" *JSOT* 88 (2000) 68–70, who suggests that "the survival of the Arad incense altars may be an indication that Hezekiah's reform only affected sacrificial not incense altars" (p. 70). There is a distinction to be made between incense altars and incense burning in general. The latter could be achieved in sundry forms as long as there was some sort of bowl that could withstand burning, as discussed in Kjeld Nielsen, *Incense in Ancient Israel* (VTSup 38; Leiden: E. J. Brill, 1986) 68–73, cf. p. 3.
The incense altars at Arad conform closely to the pattern described in Exod 30:1, as shown by Nielsen, p. 47. That an altar for burning incense is described, with no attention given whatsoever to incense burning in other forms, suggests that burning in this fashion was more "official," see pp. 29, 51. With this understanding, a cultic reform could require removal of incense burned in such a manner, while still permitting the act on cultic stands or censers. Hence it was not the practice of incense burning that was at issue, but the manner of implementation.

of any purportedly operating sanctuary. Indeed, their position within the procession of plunder intimates that they may have come from the royal palace.[30]

In evaluating the archaeological data as a whole, it is well recognized that there can never be conclusive proof that the dismantling of the altars and sanctuaries discussed above is directly due to the religious reform credited in the Bible to king Hezekiah. Yet this fact is consistent with the challenge inherent in archaeology in general, in that the discipline can only tell us what has happened and when, whereas the final interpretation of events must rely upon harmonious integration with other sources.[31] In the case of the evidence surveyed here, it is telling that these are the only known exemplars in Israelite culture of deliberately decommissioned temples which have not been desecrated.[32] Although there are many possibilities which could account for each respective situation, the fact that multiple sites from the same period exhibit this phenomenon speaks to factors which should not be attributed solely to a minimal, localized cause.[33] While the diverse means by which the sanctuaries of Arad and

---

The likelihood that only certain formal aspects of Yahwistic worship were prohibited also provides an answer to the counterargument raised by Nadav Na'aman, "The Abandonment of Cult Places in the Kingdoms of Israel and Judah as Acts of Cult Reform," *UF* 34 (2002) 588, concerning the complete, yet unburied bowls at loci 380, 383, and 788 in the temple courtyard at Arad. The preservation of such bowls in Stratum IX, on the contrary, may be considered as *evidence* of centralization, since they attest to only minimal practices in the aftermath of the sanctuary's inhumation.

[30] As noted by David Ussishkin, *The Conquest of Lachish by Sennacherib* (Tel Aviv: Institute of Archaeology, 1982) 105, 107, who classifies these objects as royal regalia, "ceremonial symbols of state from the local Judahite governor's palace."

[31] This linkage is typically referred to as "spade and text" or "Bible and spade." The interdependence of archaeology and biblical scholarship is well recognized by David Ussishkin, "Archaeology of the Biblical Period: On Some Questions of Methodology and Chronology of the Iron Age," in H. G. M. Williamson (ed.), *Understanding the History of Ancient Israel* (PBA 143; Oxford: Oxford University Press, 2007) 131–35.

[32] A supporting point inadvertently provided by Na'aman, "Debated Historicity of Hezekiah's Reform," 187–88, whose sees the destruction and abandonment of other Iron Age II shrines as analogous to the data obtained from Arad and Beer-sheba. Yet of the examples he brings (Megiddo, Taanach and Tel 'Amal in the north; Lachish in the south), all of them by his own admission were destroyed. It is this fact, rather than "the biblical history and the assumption of its fundamental correctness" (p. 281), which accounts for not relating them to any type of cultic reform. These locations are not secure examples for decommissioned sanctuaries in any case, as discussed by Edelman, "Hezekiah's Alleged Cultic Centralization," 412–16.

[33] Some are which are hypothesized by Edelman, "Hezekiah's Alleged Cultic Centralization," 416, "So we are left to wonder if irreversible sacrilege was possible, whether in some instances survivors could not afford to rebuild their shrines and did not consider them to be essential and so chose to bury them out of respect for their holiness, or whether

Beer-sheba have been decommissioned is a crucial indicator for some scholars that the underlying circumstances must therefore have differed as well, the fact that neither site was rebuilt and rededicated is equally meaningful.[34] This suggests, on the contrary, that a preferable method-ology would be to look to the same explanation for the closing of these cultic sites. Given the epoch in question, this leaves Hezekiah's reform as a viable possibility.

4.2. BIBLICAL EVIDENCE

4.2.1. *The Report in 2 Kgs 18:4*

Early in the account of Hezekiah's reign, there is a terse notice of his activ-ities in extirpating foreign elements from Israelite cultic worship:

הוּא ׀ הֵסִיר אֶת־הַבָּמוֹת וְשִׁבַּר	He removed the high places and broke down
אֶת־הַמַּצֵּבֹת וְכָרַת אֶת־הָאֲשֵׁרָה	the [sacred] pillars and cut down the
וְכִתַּת נְחַשׁ הַנְּחֹשֶׁת אֲשֶׁר־עָשָׂה	Asherah. He also broke in pieces the bronze
מֹשֶׁה כִּי עַד־הַיָּמִים הָהֵמָּה הָיוּ	serpent that Moses had made, for until those
בְנֵי־יִשְׂרָאֵל מְקַטְּרִים לוֹ וַיִּקְרָא־	days the sons of Israel burned incense to it;
לוֹ נְחֻשְׁתָּן׃	and it was called Nehushtan.

As is well known, the putative measures instigated by the king in verse 4a are scrupulously aligned with Deuteronomistic theology, which at once makes them historically suspect. Aberrant cultic practices relating to the מַצֵּבֹת, בָּמוֹת, and אֲשֵׁרִים are traced by the Deuteronomist back to Rehoboam, are temporarily suspended during the reigns of Asa and Heze-kiah, renewed with vigor by Manasseh, and see their climactic undoing

---

a change in population at one or more sites might have led to the elimination of the worship of deities of the former group in favour of the introduction of gods of the new group."

[34] Such an objection is lodged by Edelman, "Hezekiah's Alleged Cultic Centralization," 420–21. The basis for presuming a common means of decommissioning is not evident. If these scholars postulate a select group of individuals who were responsible for enforcing a cultic reform, such an expectation is plausible. But if a royal edict were to be declared which merely demanded the removal (הֵסִיר) of Yahwistic sanctuaries beyond Jerusalem, any of the disparate possibilities for accomplishing this (dismantling, burial, etc.) by the personnel of each worship center would be in compliance, a fact independently noted by Milgrom, "Does H Advocate the Centralization of Worship?" 70. Methodologically, a position should not be rejected based on undue suppositions; rather, the position remains valid as long as reasonable explanations remain to account for the available evidence.

at the hands of king Josiah.[35] The otherwise unattested mention of the
Nehushtan, however, has sparked several studies which, although speculative, have served to corroborate its ancient origins.[36] The unique
description of the cult of the bronze serpent, remarkable in light of the
Deuteronomistic preoccupation with deviations from its touchstone of
Yahwistic worship, has led scholars to a consensus that this verse indeed
preserves legitimate archival material.

A grammatical argument has been made for the secondary nature of
the removal of Canaanite cult objects in the first half of the verse, based
on the use of the copula *waw* with the perfective (וְכִתַּת) at the beginning
of verse 4b. The logic runs that the *waw*-consecutive should be expected
at this point, and its absence indicates that a centralization in strict
accordance with Deuteronomomic law has been prefixed to an original
annalistic note pertaining to the purgation of the Nehushtan.[37] It is not
clear whether the expectation of these scholars is driven by the preceding
disjunctive *athnah*, or else by the idea that the *waw*-copulative plus

---

[35] Cf. 1 Kgs 14:23; 15:12–13; 2 Kgs 21:3-7; 23:6, 8, 13–14. For the underlying Deuteronomic
laws, see Deut 7:5; 12:3 and the skepticism of Na'aman, "Debated Historicity of Hezekiah's
Reform," 179–95.

[36] The proposals for the provenance of the Nehushtan have been many and varied.
Harold H. Rowley, "Zadok and Nehushtan," *JBL* 58/2 (1939) 113–41, proposes that it was
a Zadokite cult symbol; John Gray, "The Canaanite God Horon," *JNES* 8/1 (1949) 27–34,
sees it as a symbol of healing related to the Canaanite god Horon; Karen R. Joines, "The
Bronze Serpent in the Israelite Cult," *JBL* 87/3 (1968) 245–46, accentuates the ties between
serpents and Canaanite fertility cults; Saul Olyan, *Asherah and the Cult of Yahweh in Israel*
(SBLMS 34; Atlanta: Scholars Press, 1988) 70–71, posits that Nehushtan was in fact a cult
symbol of Asherah; the possible origins discussed in Heinz-Josef Fabry, "נחשת," *TDOT*
9.370–80 are Mosiac, Davidic, Egyptian, Babylonian, Canaanite, and Phoenician. The most
extensive study pertaining to the Nehushtan is that of Kristin A. Swanson, "Hezekiah's
Reform and the Bronze Serpent" (Ph.D. diss.; Vanderbilt University, 1999), who identifies
it as an Egyptian symbol.
On a text-critical note, Peshitta, Targum, and Lucianic recension of LXX read the plural:
וַיִּקְראוּ לוֹ נְחֻשְׁתָּן. Such a form is extremely rare: the singular וַיִּקְרָא לְ is the standard way
of rendering the passive in MT, and all attestations of וַיִּקְראוּ immediately followed by the
preposition לְ are active. Thus the rendering in LXX suggests that the local populace had
named the cultic image, whereas MT is ambiguous and could refer to Hezekiah, Moses,
or generally "it was called." The textual issues within this verse are covered in far greater
detail in Swanson, "Hezekiah's Reform and the Bronze Serpent," 22–72, than will be feasible here.

[37] McKay, *Religion in Judah under the Assyrians*, 84 n. 5; Diethelm Conrad, "Einige
(archäologische) Miszellen zur Kultgeschichte Judas in der Königszeit," in A.H.J. Gunneweg
and O. Kaiser (eds.), *Textgemäss: Aufsätze und Beiträge zur Hermeneutik des Alten Testaments* (Göttingen: Vandenhoeck & Ruprecht, 1979) 28–32; Hoffmann, *Reform und Reformen*, 151–55; Spieckermann, *Juda unter Assur in der Sargonidenzeit*, 174–75, 420; Na'aman,
"Debated Historicity of Hezekiah's Reform," 181–83.

perfective is altogether erroneous.[38] Yet not only does verse 4a lack reso-
nance with Deuteronomy,[39] there is no grammatical problem with the
verbal form וְכִתַּת, following consistently as it does the verbal sequence
הֵסִיר ... וְשִׁבַּר ... וְכָרַת.[40] If the grammatical explanation were to carry any

---

[38] The *waw*-consecutive form anticipated at this point by some exegetes may be seen
after the *athnaḥ* in a narrative sequence preceded by *waw* plus perfective, cf. Gen 49:23;
1 Sam 17:38; 1 Kgs 6:32; 2 Kgs 11:1; 14:7, 14; Neh 13:30. The verbal sequence in the highly
reminiscent 2 Kgs 23:14 likely accords with their expectations. For a synopsis of the scholarly debate surrounding the *waw* plus perfective, see McKay, *Religion in Judah under the
Assyrians*, 84 n. 5, and the more recent summary by Swanson, "Hezekiah's Reform and the
Bronze Serpent," 30–41. Extensive lists of non-iterative *wᵉqatal* forms are provided in Samuel Rolles Driver, *A Treatise on the Use of the Tenses in Hebrew and Some Other Syntactical
Questions* (4th ed.; Grand Rapids: Eerdmans, 1998) 158–64; John Huesman, "The Infinitive
Absolute and the *Waw*+Perfect Problem," *Bib* 37 (1956) 410–34 Spieckermann, *Juda unter
Assur in der Sargonidenzeit*, 125–28.
  McKay suggests emending הָאֲשֵׁרָה to הָאֲשֵׁרִים in order that וְשִׁבַּר and וְכָרַת may
be regarded as *waw*-consecutive forms expressing the repetitive or frequentative, see
2 Kgs 23:14. While this emendation to הָאֲשֵׁרִים may well be correct based on the plural
attested in LXX, Peshitta, the Vulgate, and one medieval manuscript, there is no need for
seeing v 4a as an expansion based on the shorter *Vorlage* preserved in LXX, as suggested
by E. W. Todd, "The Reforms of Hezekiah and Josiah," *SJT* 9 (1956) 290. The distributed
rendering of the verb ἐξωλέθρευσεν in LXX is due to its ability to convey generally the more
precise nuances of Hebrew וְכָרַת and וְכִתַּת. The reading of MT is preferable.
[39] As noted by Milgrom, "Does H Advocate the Centralization of Worship?" 69,
Hezekiah's reform in fact deviates from the stipulations of Deuteronomic law, in that the
king only removed the altars (הֵסִיר) but did not expressly tear them down (נָתַץ/נָתַץ), and
merely cut down the Asherahs (כָּרַת) rather than burning them (שָׂרַף), cf. 2 Kgs 18:4 and
Deut 12:3. Josiah, however, who strictly fulfilled the "book of the covenant," does both, cf.
2 Kgs 23:6, 8, 26. For further differences, see Haran, *Temples and Temple-Service in Ancient
Israel*, 136–40.
[40] Grammarians have long debated as to whether *waw* plus perfective represents glos-
sation, corruption, or a breakdown of classical Hebrew style. Rather than seeing the form
as late or peculiar to annalistic writing, I follow those scholars who believe the construction to be ancient, a valid linguistic phenomenon which stands alongside the *waw*-con-
secutive. Although more ubiquitous in Late Biblical Hebrew, it is certainly attested in the
classical period as well, see Jan Joosten, "The Disappearance of Iterative WEQATAL in the
Biblical Hebrew Verbal System," in S. E. Fassberg and A. Hurvitz (eds.), *Biblical Hebrew in
Its Northwest Semitic Setting: Typological and Historical Perspectives* (Jerusalem: Hebrew
University Magnes Press, 2006) 135–47.
  Restricting usage solely to analogous cases in which the iterative *waw* plus perfective
follows an *athnaḥ*, the following clear instances may be cited in narrative: Gen 37:3; 38:5;
Exod 38:28; Num 10:17, 21; 21:20; Judg 16:18; 1 Sam 2:22; 5:7; 27:9; 2 Sam 19:17; 1 Kgs 6:35;
9:25; 12:32; 14:27; 20:21; 21:12; 2 Kgs 3:15; 18:4; 23:8; Ezek 40:24, 35; 42:15; Job 1:1; Esth 9:24–25;
Dan 2:12–13; 3:8, 21; 5:3–4, 29; 6:24 (all Aramaic); Ezra 4:24; 6:1, 14 (all Aramaic); 8:36; Neh
13:1; 1 Chr 7:21; 8:7; 2 Chr 12:10. For more subjective cases in which the *waw* preceding the
perfect may be argued as consecutive rather than iterative, cf. Gen 34:5; 1 Sam 16:14; 2 Kgs
3:4; 1 Chr 9:26.
  Although there is some attractiveness to the suggestion of both Huesman, "Infinitive
Absolute," and Jeremy Hughes, "Post-Biblical Features of Biblical Hebrew Vocalization," in
S. E. Balentine and J. Barton (eds.), *Language, Theology, and the Bible: Essays in Honour of

weight whatsoever, it would similarly undermine the reform of Josiah as well, where the construction is more widely attested.[41]

4.2.2. *The Report in 2 Kgs 18:22*

The other reference to the cultic reform of Hezekiah is contained in the words of the *rab šāqê* before the walls of Jerusalem:[42]

וְכִי־תֹאמְר֣וּן אֵלַ֔י אֶל־יְהוָ֥ה אֱלֹהֵ֖ינוּ
בָּטָ֑חְנוּ הֲלוֹא־ה֗וּא אֲשֶׁ֨ר הֵסִ֤יר
חִזְקִיָּ֙הוּ֙ אֶת־בָּמֹתָ֣יו וְאֶת־מִזְבְּחֹתָ֔יו
וַיֹּ֤אמֶר לִֽיהוּדָה֙ וְלִיר֣וּשָׁלַ֔ם לִפְנֵ֛י
הַמִּזְבֵּ֥חַ הַזֶּ֖ה תִּֽשְׁתַּחֲו֑וּ בִּירוּשָׁלָֽם׃

But if you say to me, 'We trust in Yнwн our God,' is it not He whose high places and whose altars Hezekiah has taken away, and has said to Judah and to Jerusalem, 'You shall worship before this altar in Jerusalem'?

Scholarship is again divided as to the authenticity of the quotation. Those who see the verse as integral to the speech of the *rab šāqê* are balanced by others who classify the report as a gloss or part of the Deuteronomistic redaction.[43] The arguments are typically grammatical, and center on the ways in which the verse deviates from the structure of the Assyrian messenger's inner speech.[44] The verse itself, however, is tightly integrated into

---

James Barr (Oxford: Clarendon Press, 1994) 69, that many cases of the perfective preceded by the copula *waw* may instead be revocalized as infinitive absolutes, many *hifîl* forms with *plene* spelling would require consonantal emendation. It is even less appealing to classify this broad phenomenon as later Aramaic interpolation, as is done in GKC §112pp.

[41] See the discussion in McKay, *Religion in Judah under the Assyrians*, 97 n. 5. In particular, 2 Kgs 23:8 contains the *waw* plus perfective (וְנָתַץ) immediately after the disjunctive *athnaḥ*, just as in our verse under consideration.

[42] Isa 36:7 reads כִּי־תֹאמַר at the beginning of the verse, and omits בִּירוּשָׁלָם at the end.

[43] For a summary of scholarship, see Gonçalves, *L'expédition de Sennachérib*, 390–92, nn. 85–88.

[44] Typical are the observations of Na'aman, "Debated Historicity of Hezekiah's Reform," 183, who notes regarding the first speech of the *rab šāqê* (2 Kgs 18:19–25):

"(a) All passages open with the time adverb 'now' (*'attāh*), except for v. 22.
(b) All other passages address Hezekiah in the second person singular, whereas v. 22 addresses the delegation in the second person plural.
(c) Whereas the other passages address Hezekiah in the second person, this passage refers to him in the third person."

In response, v 22 does not begin a new "passage" as asserted in (a), but is rather a continuation of v 21 building upon the theme of trust. The biblical versification belies the fact that vv 21–22 comprise a single statement. Hence the mention of the reform does indeed begin with עַתָּה. This Hebrew word is normally reserved for cause and effect relationships in any event, and is highly unusual functioning as an adversative (see 1 Kgs 12:11).

Regarding point (b), the purpose of the *rab šāqê* before the walls of Jerusalem was not merely to convey a formal message to the king, but to instill fear among the populace by ensuring that they heard as well, see vv. 26–28. The subsequent dialogue demonstrates

the surrounding context and in no way suggests a gloss, building as it does upon the all-important theme of trust in the discourse, conforming to the *rab šāqê*'s presentation technique elsewhere in quoting Hezekiah, and adhering to the principles of Assyrian propaganda.[45] If this is accepted, then the accuracy of this brief report gains additional currency. It would have negated the credibility of the author's account to attribute such a major but non-existent reform to Hezekiah, in light of the details of his reign readily known over a century later.[46]

----

that at no time were the words of the cupbearer to be construed as private, since it would be a political failure on the part of Assyria to forego an occasion to employ its propaganda to maximum effect. In this case, the *rab šāqê* has taken the opportunity to undermine the faith of Hezekiah's own messengers in the course of his formal address to the king. While the words to the Judean delegation could be construed as anomalous when concentrating on the first speech of the *rab šāqê*, they are in accord with the message and function of the oration as a whole.

Point (c) does not bring any new evidence to bear, but is rather a corollary of point (b): if the delegation is addressed in the second person in v 22, Hezekiah of necessity must be addressed in the third person. The issue of alternating person, or *Numeruswechsel*, is itself a thorny problem, having been employed for years in the study of Deuteronomy to discern different literary strata. There, scholarship has, in the main, moved away from explaining most instances of this phenomenon as being literary-critical indicators, but rather as "citations" of set Deuteronomic phrases (so Christopher T. Begg, "The Literary Criticism of Deut 4,1–40: Contributions to a Continuing Discussion," *ETL* 56 [1980] 10–55) or as a stylistic device to create contrast or heighten the tension (Weinfeld, *Deuteronomy 1–11*, 15–16). *Numeruswechsel* in biblical passages is discussed in Kevin L. Barney, "Enallage in the Book of Mormon," *JBMS* 3/1 (1994) 113–147, with an appendix showing the distribution of 188 number switches that occur within the context of a single verse in the KJV. It also occurs in the Book of the Covenant (see Exod 22:20–23), the legal corpus which underlies many of the Deuteronomic laws. For the ancient Near Eastern evidence, see Weinfeld, *Deuteronomy 1–11*, 15–16.

[45] The theme of misplaced trust (root בטח) is prevalent in Assyrian inscriptions and recurs throughout the chapter, cf. 2 Kgs 18:5, 19–22, 24, 30, and the positive application in v 5. Hezekiah is quoted directly three times within the speech by the *rab šāqê* (2 Kgs 18:22, 29, 32). As to propaganda, the removal of the altars of YHWH recalls the Mesopotamian motif of divine abandonment, in which the deity willingly removes his protection from a city or land in order to permit it to be taken by the enemy (cf. vv 18:25, 33–35).

On this latter topic, see Harold D. Lasswell, Daniel Lerner, and Hans Speier (eds.), *Propaganda and Communication in World History, Vol. 1: The Symbolic Instrument in Early Times* (Honolulu: University Press of Hawaii, 1979); Julian Reade, "Ideology and Propaganda in Assyrian Art," in M. T. Larsen (ed.), *Power and Propaganda: A Symposium on Ancient Empires* (Mesopotamia 7; Copenhagen: Akademisk Forlag, 1979) 329–43; Irene Winter, "Royal Rhetoric and the Development of Historical Narrative in Neo-Assyrian Reliefs," *SVC* 7/2 (1981) 2–38; Hayim Tadmor, "Propaganda, Literature, Historiography: Cracking the Code of the Assyrian Royal Inscriptions," in S. Parpola and R. M. Whiting (eds.), *Assyria 1995: Proceedings of the 10th Anniversary Symposium of the Neo-Assyrian Text Corpus Project* (Helsinki: Neo-Assyrian Text Corpus Project, 1997) 325–38.

[46] Jer 26:17–19. This point was articulated by Moshe Weinfeld, *From Joshua to Josiah: Turning Points in the History of Israel from the Conquest of the Land until the Fall of Judah* (Jerusalem: Magnes Press, 1992) 160 n. 15 [Hebrew]. The analysis of Gonçalves, *L'expédition*

It is not, moreover, to be assigned to a layer of Deuteronomistic editing, as its justification for the purgation of cultic sites evinces a rationale not otherwise manifested in the theology of this literary school. While a fundamental tenet of Deuteronomy is the worship of YHWH solely at "the place which He shall choose," there is no corresponding command to destroy other Yahwistic places of worship.[47] This suggests that the report preserved in the words of the *rab šāqê* was written very close in time to the events described.[48] That 2 Kgs 18:4, 22 are likely of dissimilar provenance underscores the possibility that their independent accounts of a cultic reform under Hezekiah have historical underpinnings.[49]

Some of the scholars who see no historical basis for Hezekiah's reform have made recourse to the alternating pattern of good and bad rulers exhibited in the Kings narrative spanning from Ahaz-Hezekiah-Manasseh-Josiah. Under this scheme, the righteous Hezekiah is being juxtaposed with the objectionable cultic and military undertakings imputed to his predecessor Ahaz, who "walked in the way of the kings of Israel" by conducting child sacrifice and performing cultic acts at indiscriminate locations, coupled with replicating a foreign altar and setting aside the bronze altar for his own personal use.[50] To balance this portrayal, a reform was ascribed to Hezekiah which limned restitution of proper cultic worship. The same literary technique was similarly employed in recounting the

---

de Sennachérib, 390–91, likewise affirms that the *rab šāqê*'s criticism in this verse is not a later gloss but rather part of the original narrative.

[47] Deut 12:13, for instance, expressly refers to competing cultic installations used for offerings to the Israelite deity. Rather than forbidding their existence, however, their religious authority is negated because those sites have not been chosen.

[48] An early date is typically argued for the *rab šāqê*'s speech as a whole, further supporting the unity of v 22 with its context. The antiquity of this material, labeled B₁ in scholarship, will be explored in further detail in the next chapter. For the moment, note the conclusions of Cogan and Tadmor, *II Kings*, 243, regarding this account: "B₁ bears the markings of authentic events, close to the time of Sennacherib's invasion; inasmuch as persons, places, situations are all vividly recalled, it would seem that B₁ was composed under the impress of the events themselves."

[49] As noted by Weinfeld, "Cult Centralization in Israel," 206–209, it is unthinkable that such a thinly veiled condemnation of Hezekiah's policies would have been perpetuated by the Deuteronomistic school.

[50] 2 Kgs 16:3–4, 10–16. The contrast formed by the paratactic juxtaposition of Ahaz and Hezekiah has been argued, among others, by Peter R. Ackroyd, "The Biblical Interpretation of the Reigns of Ahaz and Hezekiah," in W. B. Barrick and J. R. Spencer (eds.), *In the Shelter of Elyon: Essays on Ancient Palestinian Life and Literature in Honor of G.W. Ahlström* (JSOTSup 31; Sheffield: JSOT Press, 1984) 247–59; Hayim Tadmor and Mordechai Cogan, "Ahaz and Tiglath-Pileser in the Book of Kings: Historiographic Considerations," *Bib* 60 (1979) 505–506; Stuart A. Irvine, *Isaiah, Ahaz, and the Syro-Ephraimitic Crisis* (SBLDS 123; Atlanta: Scholars Press, 1990) 89–90.

abominable cultic acts, and their subsequent undoing, by Manasseh and Josiah, respectively.[51] This generalized structure is complicated, however, by the closing pericope of the Hezekiah arc in Kings. This passage paints Hezekiah in a particularly bad light, which disrupts the neat, alternating literary sequence of wicked and righteous royal behavior. If the negative story may itself be justified as highly tendentious, it increases the likelihood that the positive portrayal of Hezekiah, including his cultic reform, may be given some measure of historical credence.[52] Methodologically, the acknowledgment of a broad literary pattern is an exiguous criterion for determining the historical value of discrete elements within the narrative.

The report in the words of the *rab šāqê* in v 22 amounts to a volitional act of centralization, a deliberate and systematic program of permanently closing down Yahwistic cult centers beyond Jerusalem. This verse clarifies that the cultic installations (בָּמוֹת) removed by Hezekiah were not those of foreign deities, but those used for the worship of YHWH. This is consistent with the usage of the term throughout most of Kings, which is concerned with illegitimate Yahwistic worship.[53] Verse 4 clarifies that the YHWH cult in particular was the focus by the annalistic recollection of the removal of the Nehushtan "the bronze serpent that Moses had made." Thus the eradication of competing cults was in no way the purpose of Hezekiah's actions, and the prolific iconography on seals and bullae from the period confirm this premise.[54] He is never described as having removed foreign priests, or having razed the high places or altars of foreign deities. If the

---

[51] The appeal of this purported literary scheme is further marred by the reign of Amon (2 Kgs 21:19–26; 2 Chr 33:21–25), sandwiched between Manasseh and Josiah.

[52] Unless these dissimilar portrayals are mutually written off as purely literary inventions, then one must bear more historical value for reconstruction than the other. As the analysis of 2 Kgs 20 provided in the following chapter will argue for its inclusion in Kings as the primary motivation for its composition, this leaves the favorable depiction as the more likely locus for research into the historical Hezekiah.

[53] As noted by Mordechai Cogan, *I Kings* (AYB 10; New York: Doubleday, 2000) 184, "The overwhelming majority of references to *bāmôt* associate them with the illicit worship of YHWH, which continued after the Temple in Jerusalem was built." Here I concur with Na'aman, "Debated Historicity of Hezekiah's Reform," 181, that it is an "appellation for forbidden open cult place…counterposed in Dtr. literature to the temple of Jerusalem." The term, therefore, need not apply solely to foreign sanctuaries

[54] Observed by scholars such as Frank Moore Cross, "King Hezekiah's Seal Bears Phoenician Imagery," *BAR* 25/2 (Mar.–Apr. 1999) 42–45, 60: "From the evidence thus far available, it appears that the reforms of Josiah were more rigorous in their aniconic thrust than those of Hezekiah."

extended account of Josiah's reform has any validity, it corroborates that such worship sites were still in existence even after Hezekiah's reign.[55]

An important distinction between the reforms of the respective kings may be discerned by appreciating the intent of Josiah's reform. He is prompted to act in response to the dire portent of Huldah the prophetess, who conveys on behalf of YHWH: "Because they have forsaken Me and have burned incense to other gods that they might provoke Me to anger with all the work of their hands, therefore My wrath burns against this place, and it shall not be quenched" (2 Kgs 22:17). This, in effect, is precisely what Josiah proceeds to do, in a detailed path of destruction inserted into the covenant ceremony of 2 Kgs 23:1–3, 21–23. Every location selected by Josiah either belongs to a foreign cult, or hosts an illicit means of worshipping YHWH. Not a single shrine or sanctuary is destroyed for being a *place* of worship other than the Temple in Jerusalem; all devastation is triggered by an illegitimate *form* of worship.[56] The statement in 2 Kgs 23:24 affirms that his actions rightfully fulfilled "the words of the law which were written in the book that Hilkiah the priest found in the house of YHWH," yet the same verse only lauds him for the removal of abominable elements from the land. In short, Josiah's reform was not concerned with centralization, but the extirpation of foreign cults.[57] This is a crucial distinction between the reforms of the two kings, which casts further doubt upon the assertion that the reform of Hezekiah is merely a retrojection of the latter.[58]

---

[55] 2 Kgs 23:12–13, in reference to "the altars on the roof of the upper chamber of Ahaz" and "the high places … which king Solomon of Israel had built." The former altars were not necessarily constructed by Ahaz but by "the kings of Judah," yet as Manasseh is expressly mentioned in the second half of v 12, these kings must pre-date Hezekiah.

[56] Contrast this with the reform notices of Hezekiah, in which the same cultic installations are not removed for any given offense, but simply because they exist. Even the ingathering by Josiah of all the priests from the cities of Judah (v 23:8) is due expressly to their having burned incense at the high places where they served. Deviations from Deuteronomic law in the handling of these provincial priests is further noted by John Gray, *I & II Kings* (OTL; 2nd ed.; London: SCM, 1970) 734–35.

[57] A differentiation of *Kultusreinheit* versus *Kultuseinheit* highlighted in the influential study of Theodor Oestreicher, *Das deuteronomische Grundgesetz* (BFCT 27/4; Gütersloh: C. Bertelsmann, 1923) 37–58.

[58] It is thus the intrinsic link between Josiah and Deuteronomy in scholarship that has perpetuated his reform as an exercise in centralization.

4.3. THE SOCIAL SETTING OF THE REFORM

Additional means of substantiating a religious reform in the time of Hezekiah, and the centralization of the cult in particular may be obtained by ascertaining the most suitable social setting for such a revision. Various explanations have been proposed, the bulk of them accounting for the reform in some measure as a response to the dominance of the Assyrian empire. An early view was to see the closure of cultic centers as an act of open rebellion, a deliberate attempt to repudiate the worship of Assyrian gods which had presumably been forced on subject nations by their imperial masters.[59] It is now widely held that there was no imposition of the cult of Aššur within its wholly controlled provinces, much less in autonomous vassal states such as Judah.[60]

---

[59] Oestreicher, *Das deuteronomische Grundgesetz*, 54–56; Todd, "Reforms of Hezekiah and Josiah," 291; Rowley, "Hezekiah's Reform and Rebellion," 425; John Bright, *A History of Israel* (4th ed.; Louisville: Westminster John Knox, 2000) 279, 282–84; Jonathan Rosenbaum, "Hezekiah's Reform and the Deuteronomistic Tradition,' *HTR* 72.1/2 (1979) 37–38.

[60] As was popularized by the late nineteenth-century works of George Rawlinson, and subsequently by Oestreicher, *Das deuteronomische Grundgesetz*, 38; A. T. E. Olmstead, *History of Palestine and Syria to the Macedonian Conquest* (New York: C. Scribner's Sons, 1931) 452. See the various examples presented by Stephanie Dalley, "Recent Evidence from Assyrian Sources for Judaean History from Uzziah to Manasseh," *JSOT* 28/4 (2004) 397, who observes, "Religious tolerance is a particular hallmark of Assyrian control." This position was cogently argued in the seminal monographs of McKay, *Religion in Judah under the Assyrians*; Mordechai Cogan, *Imperialism and Religion: Assyria, Judah and Israel in the Eighth and Seventh Centuries B.C.E.* (SBLMS 19; Missoula, Mont.: Scholars Press, 1974); idem, "Judah under Assyrian Hegemony: A Reexamination of *Imperialism and Religion*," *JBL* 112/3 (1993) 403–414. A notable detractor is Spieckermann, *Juda unter Assur in der Sargonidenzeit*, who feels that all areas under Assyrian hegemony were impelled to worship Assyria's gods. The question of the intrusion of state religion into annexed regions has such profound implications for understanding the basis for cultic reform in Judah that it should not be lightly brushed aside.

Spieckermann sees the removal of native deities as a necessary first step to introducing imperial gods into conquered territories via interruption of local worship. Yet spoliation, or plundering, of divine images by Assyria was a formal means of acknowledging the submission of the subjugated nation, based on the ancient Near Eastern tradition that a city or state could only collapse once its protecting deity had departed. The absence of the local gods would encourage fealty and prevent uprisings (e.g., Num 14:39–45, when the Israelites try to take the hill country without the presence of YHWH). Furthermore, the example which Cogan brings regarding the agreements reached with the Arabian tribes over the return of their divine images ("Judah under Assyrian Hegemony," 408) suggests that a key reason for the policy of plundering divine images was to employ them as a bargaining chip for ensuring the conduct of the subjugated peoples. The fact that local deities were carefully preserved by the ruling power, holding out hope for the repatriation of the original, time-honored cult statue, thus speaks to a more rudimentary, and essential, motive than the imposition of foreign worship: that of preventing active resistance.

For many scholars, the objective of the reform was to secure the kingdom in anticipation of Sennacherib's impending retaliation. This economic argument defends the abolition of cultic centers beyond the capital city as a means to prevent the imperial army from acquiring their material wealth.[61] Any gold, silver, or offerings from these regional temples would have been kept safe from plunder, safely ensconced within Jerusalem or other defensible cities for the king to avail himself of should the Judean state ultimately need to capitulate and pay off its aggressor.[62] Another, related interpretation sees the decommissioning of outlying sanctuaries as a means to ensure the loyalty of the populace.[63] According to this model, the removal of divine images would prevent their capture and use by the Assyrians as propaganda, while at the same time forestalling potential defection to the totalitarian regime by increasing dependence on the capital city and making it a political religious center.[64]

Both of these positions are subject to the same criticism. While safeguarding the financial holdings or divine images of the cultic installations

---

It is difficult to see what would have been gained by adopting a program of compulsory worship toward foreign gods. On the one hand, it could only foment greater antipathy toward the imperial administration, yielding more uprisings and greater political unrest. On the other hand, it would have needlessly consumed administrative resources better utilized in assuring that everyone contributed toward the onerous taxes and resources demanded by the empire. Religious coercion would not ensure, or even necessarily contribute, toward a more compliant subjugated territory, and could never be more effective than the threat of military action at keeping the anti-Assyrian parties in check. In short, if there were nothing to be gained by the increased overhead of enforcing obedience to a program of imperial worship, the efficient and power-conscious Assyrians were hardly likely to employ it as a strategy in their quest for the continued expansion of the realm. In the end, the removal of local deities is better explained as serving the political purpose of perpetuating Assyrian sovereignty than as a religious effort to interrupt the cult in order to demand the veneration of newly introduced imperial deities.

[61] Handy, "Hezekiah's Unlikely Reform," 111–115; Lowery, *Reforming Kings*.

[62] Handy, "Hezekiah's Unlikely Reform," 113, notes that territory from Judah was redistributed by Sennacherib to the more loyal Philistine kingdoms, based on the Assyrian annals, cf. Rassam 53; OIP iii 32–34. It is not necessary, however, to presume that the Assyrians would have "allowed the provisions of sanctuaries in confiscated areas to be given over to the Philistines."

[63] Theodore H. Robinson and W. O. E. Oesterley, *A History of Israel* (2 vols.; Oxford: Clarendon Press, 1932) 1.392–93; Weinfeld, "Cult Centralization in Israel," 205–206; Hanoch Reviv, "The History of Judah from Hezekiah to Josiah," in A. Malamat (ed.), *The World History of the Jewish People. The Age of the Monarchies: Political History, Vol. 4/1* (Jerusalem: Massada Press, 1979) 194; Ahlström, *Royal Administration and National Religion*, 66; Gonçalves, *L'expédition de Sennachérib*, 88; Smith, *Early History of God*; Halpern, "Jerusalem and the Lineages," 26–27.

[64] For Mesopotamian precedents of this practice, see the sources collected in Cogan, *Imperialism and Religion*, 30–34.

could be seen as a prudent measure in the face of an advancing enemy, wholesale closure of these centers of worship would not have been a requisite response.[65] The removal of the cultic paraphernalia and cessation of the cult in outlying areas at such a time would more likely have signaled to the people that YHWH was unable to protect them, and had abandoned them to their fate before "the terrifying appearance of the weapon of Aššur."[66] It is difficult to comprehend how the discontinuation of the local sanctuaries would strengthen the resolve of Judah's denizens in the face of invasion. The biblical account, moreover, expressly describes the altars and high places not as having been merely closed or decommissioned, but as having been violently eradicated.[67] The destruction of these cultic centers does not point to any provisional action in a time of war, but rather to a deliberate, permanent change.[68] The explanations

---

[65] Comparable sentiment has been expressed by Cogan and Tadmor, *II Kings*, 219, "At a time when efforts were being directed toward the physical fortification and provisioning for war, wise counsel would not have recommended cult reforms." Their statement is a rejoinder to the position of Weinfeld, "Cult Centralization in Israel," who sees a Mesopotamian parallel in the decision of Nabonidus to transfer the gods from their local sanctuaries to Babylon on the eve of the Persian siege by Cyrus in 539 BCE. Rather than viewing this merely as a reactionary measure to prevent the spoliation of the Babylonian cult statues, however, Weinfeld proposes that it was a pretext for centralizing the cult. This suggestion has been rejected by Cogan, *Imperialism and Religion*, 33 n. 67; William W. Hallo, "Cult Statue and Divine Image: A Preliminary Study," in W. W. Hallo, J. C. Moyer, and L. G. Perdue (eds.), *Scripture in Context II: More Essays on the Comparative Method* (Winona Lake, Ind.: Eisenbrauns, 1983) 14–15; Paul-Alain Beaulieu, "An Episode in the Fall of Babylon to the Persians," *JNES* 52/4 (1993) 257; Edelman, "Hezekiah's Alleged Cultic Centralization," 427–28.

[66] Rassam 34; OIP ii 45, passim. This was, in fact, the angle being played by the Assyrian embassage in order to undermine support for Hezekiah's policies and compel the populace to capitulate. As noted by Zevit, *Religions of Ancient Israel*, 659, "Rabshaqeh's logic was that in the absence of the many altars and places of worship eliminated by Hezekiah, Judah was actually weaker than before and that restricting YHWH worship to the single Jerusalem altar was an act of disrespect to the national deity."

The case developed here is similarly employed by Edelman, "Hezekiah's Alleged Cultic Centralization," 426. I concur with her sentiment that there is no basis for the suggestion of Lowery, *Reforming Kings*, 151–57, that centralization was effectuated in order to limit the amount of tithes collected at the sanctuaries and thereby reduce the amount of Assyrian tribute. It is not readily apparent to me, however, that any other economic theories imply "Hezekiah closed down rural sanctuaries where taxes used to be paid in order to eliminate skimming by local priests" ("Hezekiah's Alleged Cultic Centralization," 427).

[67] 2 Kgs 18:4, 22; 2 Chr 31:1.

[68] Such reasoning formed the basis on which Yehezkel Kaufmann, *The History of Israelite Religion* (8 vols.; Tel Aviv: Bialik Institute-Dvir, 1937–56) 1.96 [Hebrew], refuted the view of Oestreicher, *Das deuteronomische Grundgesetz*, that the high places were only temporarily defiled to preclude the advancing Assyrians from employing the autochthonous deities for sacrificial purposes, thereby obtaining the religious sympathies of the local populace.

proposed by scholars in the face of Assyrian threat hence do not account
for the militant nature of the cultic reform. What is required, then, is a
social setting which is consonant with a radical, dramatic upheaval in the
geo-political landscape of Judah.

The first stream of interpretation which fits this criterion advocates
that centralization was but a *de facto* occurrence in the aftermath of
Sennacherib's invasion, a repercussion of the Judean state having been
reduced to the environs of Jerusalem.[69] The initial drawback to this stance
is that it is directly contradicted by the biblical record, which maintains
that worship was concentrated in Jerusalem prior to the momentous
conflict with Assyria in 701 B.C.E.[70] Secondly, it must contend with the

---

[69] J. Skinner according to Todd, "Reforms of Hezekiah and Josiah," 289–90; Victor
Maag, "Erwägungen zur deuteronomischen Kultzentralisation," *VT* 6/1 (1956) 18; Ernest W.
Nicholson, "The Centralisation of the Cult in Deuteronomy," *VT* 13/4 (1963) 385; K. Fullerton according to Leo L. Honor, *Sennacherib's Invasion of Palestine: A Critical Source Study*
(New York: Columbia University Press, 1926) 76 n. 57; Kristin A. Swanson, "A Reassessment
of Hezekiah's Reform in Light of Jar Handles and Iconographic Evidence," *CBQ* 64 (2002)
460–69; Edelman, "Hezekiah's Alleged Cultic Centralization," 395–434.

Based on her identification of Nehushtan as an Egyptian royal symbol, as well as the
winged scarab and sun disk known from the *lmlk* seals, Swanson, "Reassessment of Hezekiah's Reform," sees the absence of these insignia in the later archaeological record as
part of a broader removal of royal symbolism instigated by Hezekiah, a form of capitulation to express his loyalty to Sennacherib. It is debatable to what extent the removal of
royal symbolism should be seen as analogous to the abolition of religious centers: even if
Swanson's contribution is valid with regard to the waning of royal imagery after 701 B.C.E.,
it does not preclude a cultic reform from having occurred at a different time under different circumstances. See further review of her argument by Hershel Shanks, "The Mystery
Nechushtan," *BAR* 33/2 (Mar.–Apr. 2007) 58–63.

[70] 2 Kgs 18:22 within the speech of the *rab šāqê*, previously argued as having been composed not long after the invasion. Nicholson, "Centralisation of the Cult in Deuteronomy,"
384–87, respects this datum in dismissing the idea that centralization occurred after the
miraculous deliverance of Jerusalem. He is still able to maintain that Hezekiah's reform
was precipitated by Sennacherib's invasion in 701 B.C.E., however, by appealing to a second campaign by Sennacherib in 688. It was during this second military incursion that
the Assyrians actually failed to take the Judean capital. Nicholson already acknowledges
the challenge by H. H. Rowley to such a reconstruction, and my own position has been
presented previously.

In recognizing that the dating of Hezekiah's cultic reforms in Chronicles to his first regnal year exhibits a well-known Mesopotamian *Tendez*, Edelman, "Hezekiah's Alleged Cultic Centralization," 400, proposes an explanation: "Another consideration could have been
a desire to eliminate the possibility that the reforms took place after 701 BCE, because then
they would not have been the voluntary initiative of Hezekiah but the natural outcome of
his having lost control over a large portion of Judah." Even if the cultic reforms credited to
Hezekiah did not occur in the first year of his reign, there is no foundation for dating them
twenty years later. This suggestion implicitly rejects not only the dating but also the very
details of the reform in Chronicles, as it would be inconsistent to anticipate that "the sons
of Israel provided in abundance the first fruits of grain, new wine, oil, honey and of all the

archaeological evidence from sites such as Arad, proposing explanations which must necessarily avoid all implication of Hezekiah's reform yet are ultimately themselves no more cogent.[71] The fact that the Assyrian army had devastated much of Judah did not mean that no more cultic sites existed, and a post–701 reformation of the cult still requires a justification as to the voluntary decommissioning of those remaining sanctuaries if the biblical description is to be respected.[72]

---

produce of the field" (2 Chr 31:5) in the wake of the Assyrian army's wholesale desolation of the land (cf. Rassam 49–51; OIP iii 18–27).

[71] Nicholson, "Centralisation of the Cult in Deuteronomy," 385–86, marshals Zeph 1:4–6, 8–9; 2 Kgs 23:4–20; Jer 3 in order to give credence to the idea that Hezekiah was constrained to abolish the high places due to foreign cults established by those brought in by the Assyrians from other parts of the empire. If these non-Yahwistic practices were truly so politically and religiously dangerous that they served as the impetus for the cultic reformation, then they must have taken root very quickly for the king to have considered them a threat before the end of his reign, which was already in its 24th year in 701 B.C.E. Yet Nicholson only views Hezekiah as being in the middle of his reign, accepting the regnal years 715–687 B.C.E. proposed by Albright.

Maag, "Erwägungen zur deuteronomischen Kultzentralisation," sees centralization not as the direct result of the diminishment of Judah's territory, but rather as having been inspired by the failure of Assyria to take Jerusalem: "Die aktive Kraft zur Zentralisation lag in der glaubensmässigen Verarbeitung der Tatsache von Jerusalems Verschonung im Jahre 701" (p. 18). Such a basis is ostensibly devoid of political inducement, which is more problematic to attribute to a royal initiative. Neither does it provide any religious underpinning for the reform: if Jerusalem had been spared while numerous outlying sanctuaries were still operable, how was this perceived as a divine directive to close them down?

Edelman, "Hezekiah's Alleged Cultic Centralization," 409, accounts for the archaeological evidence at Arad by theorizing, "The newcomers appear to have respected the sanctity of the defeated deity to the extent that they decommissioned his temple, burying it and certain cultic appurtenances." The implausibility of this suggestion has already been discussed, see n. 9. It is worth noting that all of the proposals surveyed and rejected by Edelman in her conclusion are all variations of the model of military preparation in advance of Sennacherib's invasion. She does not present any counter-arguments to nullify the refugee model which we will be considering next, which also sees Jerusalem as the *de facto* cultic center in the aftermath of the fall of the north.

[72] The attitude of Edelman, "Hezekiah's Alleged Cultic Centralization," toward the biblical account of Hezekiah's reform is to discount its historicity altogether, being the work of a later author or editor of Kings who "had no need to concern himself with the historical details" (p. 425) and chose to credit Hezekiah with centralization when the territory of the kingdom of Judah was curtailed after Sennacherib's predations. Her article is largely concerned with discrediting the archaeological testimony from Arad, Lachish, and Beersheba because "the post–701 situation provides a more plausible setting for the closure of such sanctuaries, when one and perhaps all three sites were lost from Judahite control" (p. 406). Under her reconstruction, these sites were taken over in 701 B.C.E. by the Philistines or Assyrians, who eliminated the functioning cult places of their own accord. As has been argued, there is little basis for completely rejecting the two independent reports of cultic centralization preserved in Kings.

An alternative social setting for Hezekiah's reform would be in the aftermath of the fall of the northern kingdom in 720 B.C.E. In this, there is already corroboration with the biblical sources, which fix the implementation of his program early in his reign.[73] The basis typically postulated is inherently political, with the goal of strengthening the central authority of the king while weakening the power base of clan leadership in the countryside.[74] It also would shore up Jerusalem as a rival cult place to Bethel, to which pilgrimages may still have been made.[75] The economic rationale for centralization, moreover, while problematic in the context of preparations for Assyrian invasion, is meaningful when considered in light of the political fallout from the decimated northern kingdom. The vast influx of refugees from the north which resulted in the burgeoning population growth of the Judean capital in the last quarter of the eighth century would in turn have posed extensive humanitarian challenges.[76] The collection of tax revenues from the rural sanctuaries would have remained relatively unchanged, whereas the rapid urbanization of Jerusalem necessitated a fiscal reform to ensure a larger proportion of taxes assessed. The permanent abandonment of other cultic centers of worship could be argued, in addition to all that has been proposed, as a means to ensure that more revenue streamed into the capital city even as the state religion was transformed into a royal cult.[77]

---

[73] Even if we may rightly question the attribution of the reform to the first regnal year of Hezekiah, the setting of 2 Chr 31:1 with "all Israel" tearing down the altars of their own accord—without any regard to Assyrian threat or obligation—supports an earlier date for the event. 2 Chr 30:6, 9 likewise refers to multiple kings who have led the northern kingdom into captivity, which suggests that the overture is in the aftermath of exile.

[74] Halpern, "Jerusalem and the Lineages," 26–27.

[75] See Finkelstein and Silberman, "Temple and Dynasty," 274–75. The argumentation of Herzog et al., "Israelite Fortress at Arad," 21 is somewhat further afield. The authors suggest that the abolition of cult places in Judah was equanimity on the part of Hezekiah for the shrines he was demanding the northern residents to abandon.

As explained by Harold Brodsky, "Bethel," *AYBD* 1.710–12, "Two factors, somewhat interrelated, are responsible for the importance of Bethel: (1) it was associated with a religious sanctuary; and (2) it lay along a crossroads and near a physical and political frontier that divided the central hill country of Palestine into two parts." For more, see Jules Francis Gomes, *The Sanctuary of Bethel and the Configuration of Israelite Identity* (BZAW 368; Berlin: Walter de Gruyter, 2006).

[76] As argued by W. Eugene Claburn, "The Fiscal Basis of Josiah's Reforms," *JBL* 92/1 (1973) 11–22. His conclusions are oriented toward the Josianic reform, but would seem more credible within the scope of Hezekiah's reign. It is little wonder, then, that such exhortations are found in Deuteronomy for the citizens of the state to take upon themselves the responsibility to care for the widow, orphan, alien, and Levite, cf. Deut 24:19–21; 26:12–13.

[77] In investigating the closure of the temple at Arad, Conrad, "Einige (archäologische) Miszellen," 28–32, occupies a middle position which sees no basis for centralization in

This proposal becomes more plausible in the light of recent studies which point to a similar setting for the composition of the earliest layer of Deuteronomic legislation.[78] The nascent origins of Deuteronomic ideology lay in the north, with the zeal of the prophets to purify the Israelite cult from pagan elements, and to abstain from the proliferation of sacrificial altars.[79] This in itself is significant, as studies have tied the program of Hezekiah to prophetic influence independently of appreciating the connections with Deuteronomic thought.[80] It should not be overlooked that the conditionality of the covenant, upon which so much stress is placed in Deuteronomy, was previously affirmed by the prophets in the north, and would have become a firmly entrenched theological position in the aftermath of northern exile.[81] The exhortations placed on the lips of Moses

---

Hezekiah's efforts at religious reform, but rather in the new social and economic conditions resulting from the conquest of the northern kingdom in 720 B.C.E. As this study aims to demonstrate, there is no compelling reason why both reconstructions cannot be viable.

Nicholson, "Centralisation of the Cult in Deuteronomy" 384, incorporates a nationalistic motivation, based on the desire of those who sought the reunification of all Israel to reconstitute Jerusalem as the nation's religious center. This would be, in effect, a reapplication of the loyalty argument discussed earlier, situated during the vicissitudes of Sennacherib's invasion.

[78] Nicholson, "Centralisation of the Cult in Deuteronomy"; H. L. Ginsberg, *The Israelian Heritage of Judaism* (New York: Jewish Theological Seminary, 1982) 115–16; Weinfeld, *Deuteronomy 1–11*, 44–57; James Philip Ashmore, "The Social Setting of the Law in Deuteronomy" (Ph.D. diss.; Duke University, 1995); Robert R. Wilson, "Deuteronomy, Ethnicity, and Reform: Reflections on the Social Setting of the Book of Deuteronomy," in J. T. Strong and S. S. Tuell (eds.), *Constituting the Community: Studies on the Polity of Ancient Israel in Honor of S. Dean McBride Jr.* (Winona Lake, Ind.: Eisenbrauns, 2005) 107–23. It would be going too far, however, to assert that the book of Deuteronomy preceded Hezekiah's reform and was the impetus for it, as originally claimed by Ernst Sellin, *Introduction to the Old Testament* (trans. W. Montgomery; London: Hodder & Stoughton, 1923) 73ff.

[79] Weinfeld, *Deuteronomy 1–11*, 44–50.

[80] As noted by S. R. Driver in the introduction to Franz Delitzsch, *Biblical Commentary on the Prophecies of Isaiah, Vol. I* (Edinburgh: T.&T. Clark, 1892) xv, Wellhausen considered "Deuteronomy as being, in form, the work of a prophet of the age of Hezekiah, and allowing that ceremonial law was not probably cast into its present shape until a date later still." See McKay, *Religion in Judah under the Assyrians*, 15–17, who makes two separate proposals for the influence on Hezekiah's reform activity, pertaining to the prophets Micah and Isaiah, and the Deuteronomists who fled from the north into Judah, respectively. Prophetic influence has been posited more recently by others such as Claudemiro Francisco Mariottini, "The Problem of Social Oppression in the Eighth Century Prophets" (Ph.D. diss., The Southern Baptist Theological Seminary, 1983); William Dever, *Did God Have a Wife? Archaeology and Folk Religion in Ancient Israel* (Grand Rapids: Eerdmans, 2005) 269.

[81] Deut 6:25; 8:19; 11:13–15, 22–28; 13:18–19[17–18]; 15:4–5; 17:8–9; 28; 30:1–10, 15–20. The inevitability of judgment for the north had already been augured in the allocutions of Hosea against idolatry, and in those of Amos against social injustice. As noted by Nicholson, "Centralisation of the Cult in Deuteronomy," 383–84: "But the tragedy which had befallen the Northern kingdom would have provoked much heart searching in Judah

would doubtless have held a similar urgency in the hearts of his southern audience, faced with the reality of a vengeful God who was willing to cast his chosen people from his sight for continued disobedience.

With this background in mind, is it possible to infuse the political motive for centralization with a religious basis. In this, the older scholarly view which saw centralization as a means to discontinue syncretistic practices at the high places has merit.[82] A fundamental weakness of this position has been that there was no reason to justify why this point in Israelite history was preferable for such a reformation than any other, but in fact the second half of the eighth century conforms to the attitude toward the purification of the cult already existing in northern Israel.[83] It is furthermore unreasonable to expect that such a brilliant statesman as Hezekiah would have gone to such great lengths in preparing the city of Jerusalem for the swell of inhabitants cascading from the north, while neglecting to take the necessary measures to ensure its populace a strong religious basis

---

for it would have seemed to many that the fate of the northern people was nothing less than Yahweh's judgement upon their apostasy and idolatry."

[82] Rudolf Kittel, *Geschichte des Volkes Israel, 2. Band: Das Volk in Kanaan* (2nd ed.; Gotha: Friedrich Andreas Perthes, 1909) 493–501; and reaffirmed in newer studies such as Albertz, *History of Israelite Religion*, 1.180. I find somewhat forced the demurral by Weinfeld, "Cult Centralization in Israel," 203, that syncretism could not have been at issue because the temple in Jerusalem would necessarily need to have been destroyed as well in order to ensure a permanently purified cult. He seems to have become more amenable later to the possibility that religious ideology, as well as political circumstances, were responsible for Hezekiah's reform, see Weinfeld, *Deuteronomy 1–11*, 44–47.

The very notion of syncretism has been questioned in recent scholarship, due to its more sophisticated comprehension of Canaanite religion and critical stance toward the religion of Israel. It is commonplace to view Israelite folk religion as an extension of Canaanite culture itself, rather than having borrowed supposedly pagan practices under the influence of its neighbors, cf. Olyan, *Asherah and the Cult of Yahweh in Israel*, 5, 8; Michael D. Coogan, "Canaanite Origins and Lineage: Reflections on the Religions of Ancient Israel," in Miller, Hanson, and McBride (eds.), *Ancient Israelite Religion: Essays in Honor of Frank Moore Cross*, 115–24; Susan Ackerman, *Under Every Green Tree: Popular Religion in Sixth-Century Judah* (Atlanta: Scholars Press, 1992) 213–217; Miller, *Religion of Ancient Israel*, 57–62; Mark S. Smith, "Ugaritic Studies and Israelite Religion: A Retrospective View," *NEA* 65/1 (2002) 17–29. Despite the rightful stress on the many similarities between Canaanite and Israelite religion, however, there may still be argued a place for syncretism in the development of the latter. I side in this regard with the definition of syncretism provided by Dever, *Did God Have a Wife?*, 269: "The essential meaning is to incorporate various beliefs, some of which may once have been contradictory, into a fusion on the basis of other beliefs held in common."

[83] Weinfeld, *Deuteronomy 1–11*, 44–50. This permits the inclusion of the view of McKay, *Religion in Judah under the Assyrians*, 17–18, who sees Hezekiah's reform as a form of puritan religious enthusiasm under the influence of Deuteronomists from the north and receptive Yahwists in the south.

for the *de facto* center of Yahwistic worship.[84] Such a sweeping change would not have raised the ire of Judah's Assyrian overlords, as the empire was prone to leave their territories to control their own religious practices. This proposal has the additional advantage of respecting the depiction of Hezekiah's actions as a legitimate removal of foreign elements from the Yahwistic cult, an undertaking which has unjustifiably been argued as tendentious.[85] Thus while attempts have been made to appeal to other legal corpora as reflecting the measures imposed by Hezekiah, the enactments of Deuteronomy are the most harmonious.[86]

---

[84] The insight of Miller and Hayes, *History of Ancient Israel and Judah*, 415, is apt: "In addition, the religion of the state could be more adequately supervised and the capital city benefit from the economy associated with official religion."

[85] Based on its strict adherence to the commandments of Deuteronomy, as discussed in Na'aman, "Debated Historicity of Hezekiah's Reform," 181–83. Such a conclusion stems from the close association between Deuteronomy and the reform of Josiah in modern scholarship, which necessitates a theological justification for the attribution of such a reform to Hezekiah. But if the legal core of Deuteronomy was indeed composed during the reign of Hezekiah or soon thereafter, and the summary information regarding Hezekiah in 2 Kgs 18:1–6 dates to a similar period or even later, then 2 Kgs 18:4 bears such a strong resemblance to Deuteronomic law because Hezekiah was seen as adhering to it to the letter.

[86] Scholars who accept the historicity of Hezekiah's reform have sought other alternatives for its legal basis. Albertz, *History of Israelite Religion*, 1.180–86, credits the reform to the Book of the Covenant, whose composition he dates to the end of the eighth century. Placing the literary creation of this legal corpus in the pre-state period, however, remains on better footing, as amply demonstrated by Shalom M. Paul, *Studies in the Book of the Covenant in the Light of Cuneiform and Biblical Law* (VTSup 18; Leiden: E.J. Brill, 1970), esp. 43–45.

Menahem Haran, "Behind the Scenes of History: Determining the Date of the Priestly Source," *JBL* 100/3 (1981) 321–33; idem, *Temples and Temple-Service in Ancient Israel*, 140–148, marshaled arguments for seeing the reform as based on the ideology of the Priestly source. A key presupposition in his proposal is that "P takes cult centralization for granted" (p. 145), a long-standing idea firmly entrenched in biblical scholarship by Karl H. Graf, *Die Geschichtlichen Bücher des Alten Testaments* (Leipzig: T.O. Weigel, 1866) 51–66; Abraham Kuenen, *Historisch-kritische Einleitung in die Bücher des alten Testaments, I/1* (Leipzig: Otto Schulze, 1885) 203–14, 251ff, and ultimately Wellhausen, *Prolegomena zur Geschichte Israels*, 17–52. Space does not permit an adequate response to this important question, but chinks in the armor of this position may nonetheless be demonstrated.

Wellhausen, who championed the lateness of the Priestly Code relative to the laws of Deuteronomy, upheld that the Holiness Legislation was an earlier stratum of priestly laws that did not presuppose centralization: "Leviticus 17ff attaches great importance to unity of worship. It is still a demand, not a presupposition (17:8ff, 19:30, 26:2); the motive of it is to guard against heathen influences and to secure the establishment of a monotheism without images" (*Prolegomena*, English trans., 377). Modern research concurs that there is no basis for centralization in H, as commendably shown by Milgrom, "Does H Advocate the Centralization of Worship?" The fact that H provides for Levitical cities is compelling evidence that it is advocating regional support for the Levites wherever they happen to serve. The Holiness Legislation is expressly aware of and permits cultic places, altars and

Dating the legal core of the book of Deuteronomy to the reign of Hezekiah or soon after not only explains the vast amount of northern traditions which have been incorporated into the work, but permits the story relating the discovery of the book of the law by Josiah to be read at face value, and allows sufficient time for the development of the complex compositional history of the text.[87] If the prevailing logic holds true that

---

sanctuaries (Lev 26:30–31, despite the efforts of some to emend the text), affirming that God is "in the camps" (= all cities), and demanding only that foreign sites of worship be removed (Num 33:52). None of these places of religious practice (בָּמָה, חַמָּן, מִקְדָּשׁ) are even mentioned in D, having been deemed unacceptable forms of worship.

Yet unwittingly, Wellhausen also acknowledged that P knew nothing of a central sanctuary as well, as it is now generally believed that H represents a later literary stratum of priestly legislation than P, see Israel Knohl, *The Sanctuary of Silence: The Priestly Torah and the Holiness School* (Minneapolis: Fortress Press, 1995), in addition to Milgrom above. From its more sophisticated chiastic forms to further restrictive definitions of sacrificial slaughter and priesthood, H reveals itself to be dependent upon the Priestly source. If P truly mandated a central sanctuary, we are at a loss to explain why H would deviate from that sanction. See further Milgrom, *Leviticus 17–22*, 1503–14. This leaves the door open for future scholarship to ultimately settle whether H or D is indeed the latest stratum of Israelite legal corpora. While I personally see H as antedating Deuteronomy, see Jeffrey Stackert, *Rewriting the Torah: Literary Revision in Deuteronomy and the Holiness Legislation* (FAT 52; Tübingen: Mohr Siebeck, 2007) for the priority of D.

[87] Ever since the proposal of W. M. L. de Wette, "Dissertatio critico-exegetica qua Deuteronomium a prioribus pentateuchi libris diversum, alius cuiusdam recentioris auctoris opus esse monstratur" (Ph.D. diss.; Jena, 1805), that the book of the law found in the Temple by Hilkiah was, in fact, the book of Deuteronomy, scholarship has responded favorably to his contention that the book was commissioned by Josiah as a "pious fraud" to further his agenda of religious reform. Such an extreme stance need not be taken. The position advocated here aligns with similar conclusions independently reached by Paul-Eugène Dion, "Sennacherib's Expedition to Palestine," *EgT* 20 (1989) 25, "If this [source B₁] narrative is really pre-Josianic, its contention that Hezekiah removed the local shrines of YHWH must reflect an opinion preceding in time the discovery of the Book of the Law; it can be based, in particular, on an early version of Kings culminating in Hezekiah's reform (2 Kgs 18:3–4)."

For overviews of the various theories which posit Josianic, exilic, and post-exilic layers to Deuteronomy, see the surveys of Horst D. Preuss, *Deuteronomium* (EdF 164; Darmstadt: Wissenschaftliche Buchgesellschaft, 1982) 1–74; Steven L. McKenzie, *The Trouble With Kings: The Composition of the Book of Kings in the Deuteronomistic History* (VTSup 42; Leiden: E. J. Brill, 1991); Thomas C. Römer, "The Book of Deuteronomy," in S. L. McKenzie and M. P. Graham (eds.), *The History of Israel's Traditions: The Heritage of Martin Noth* (JSOTSup 182; Sheffield: JSOT Press, 1994) 178–212; Erik Eynikel, *The Reform of King Josiah and the Composition of the Deuteronomistic History* (OTS 33; Leiden: E.J. Brill, 1996) 7–31; Thomas C. Römer and Albert de Pury, "Deuteronomistic Historiography (DH): History of Research and Debated Issues," in A. de Pury, T. C. Römer, and J.-D. Macchi (eds.), *Israel Constructs Its History: Deuteronomistic History in Recent Research* (JSOTSup 306; Sheffield: JSOT Press, 2000) 24–141.

This study eschews the proposed nomistic (DtrN) and prophetic (DtrP) layers of the Deuteronomistic History advanced by the so-called Smend/Göttingen school. For recent critiques of this critical approach, see Hoffmann, *Reform und Reformen*; Iain W. Provan,

codified biblical law reflects the world of its time rather than introducing heretofore unknown legislation—that is, real-world practices precede written law and not vice versa[88]—then it is significant that Hezekiah's centralization is never vindicated with recourse to Deuteronomic commandments, but may be explained based entirely on the exigencies of his reign.[89] The fact that the cultic reformation of Hezekiah is never conducted in conformance with "the book of the covenant" as seen in the account of Josiah speaks against the overtly tendentious nature of its presentation, and suggests a kernel of historicity.[90] Finally, as amply demonstrated in the preceding survey of eighth-century Judah and Jerusalem, the kingdom of Hezekiah was by all accounts considerably stronger than that of Josiah.[91] This further complicates any historiographic or theological

---

Hezekiah and the Books of Kings: A Contribution to the Debate about the Composition of the Deuteronomistic History (BZAW 172; Berlin: Walter de Gruyter, 1988); Mark A. O'Brien, *The Deuteronomistic History Hypothesis: A Reassessment* (OBO 92; Freiburg: Universitätsverlag, 1989); McKenzie, *Trouble With Kings*. For an attempt at a synthesis, see William M. Schniedewind, "The Problem with Kings: Recent Study of the Deuteronomistic History," *RSR* 22/1 (1996) 22–27.

[88] Articulated by Weinfeld, "Cult Centralization in Israel," 204: "Generally considered, religio-cultural phenomena in Israel and the ancient world were not the products of abstract ideas; on the contrary, such concepts and principles as existed were outgrowths of practical religious reality: monotheistic consciousness was based on and strengthened by the worship of one god (monolatry) and not vice versa." The view that 2 Kgs 18:4a is a tendentious editorial addition stems from the presumption that its purported reform was meant to depict Hezekiah in strict obedience to Deuteronomic law. Yet it is possible, although ultimately unprovable, that the description of Hezekiah's cultic purgations here so closely mirrors Deuteronomy because his delineated actions in fact occurred first, and the corresponding laws were only subsequently written to reflect the realia of the king's ambitious royal program consolidating Yahwistic worship. With the historicity of the reform typically cast in doubt, this possibility has not been seriously considered.

[89] As noted by Weinfeld, *Deuteronomy 1–11*, 65, "Indeed, the decisive difference between the reform of Hezekiah and that of Josiah lies in the fact that the former was not authorized by a book, whereas in the latter it is emphasized several times that the actions were performed in accordance with the book found in the House of YHWH (2 Kgs 23:3, 21, 24)."

[90] As discussed previously in n. 39. These facts have led scholars such as Weinfeld to posit that the eradication of foreign cults by Josiah preceded the discovery of the book of the Torah, see *Deuteronomy 1–11*, 69–74. This is in accord with the dating of Josiah's reform in 2 Chr 34:6–7 to his twelfth year, whereas the law book was not discovered in the Temple until his eighteenth year (2 Chr 35:1–18; cp. 2 Kgs 22:3–10). If correct, this suggestion would favor those exegetes who feel that the account of Josiah's reform in Kings is, in fact, more tendentious than the brief reports concerning Hezekiah in 2 Kgs 18:4, 22, and at the same time support the view that there are indeed accurate, unique, historical data preserved in Chronicles.

[91] Rosenbaum, "Hezekiah's Reform and the Deuteronomistic Tradition," 23–43; Nadav Na'aman, "The Kingdom of Judah under Josiah," *TA* 18 (1991) 3–71; Marvin A. Sweeney, *King*

explanations for artificially projecting Josiah's cultic purification back to the time of Hezekiah, and permits the latter's reform to stand on its own as a legitimate, *bona fide* historical reality.

4.4. CONCLUSION

The archaeological evidence for Hezekiah's reform is ultimately inconclusive. Tel Arad, Tel Beer-sheba, and Lachish are all potential candidates for investigation, but each site poses its own interpretive difficulties. The shrine at Lachish predates the reign of Hezekiah by some time, and the associated cultic vessels found in a circular layout there cannot with any certainty be assigned to Level III. If incense burners are indeed among the plunder being paraded before Sennacherib in the Lachish reliefs, they are better viewed as royal or ceremonial rather than cultic, and thus have no bearing on the question of religious reform. The storehouse at Tel Beer-sheba containing ashlars from a horned altar may well have been destroyed in 701 B.C.E. (Stratum II), but the stones themselves may have been secondarily used for some time beforehand. The lack of a destruction layer separating Strata III and II, as well as the altar fragment found in the retaining wall of the glacis and dated to Stratum III, makes it debatable as to whether Tel Beer-Sheba preserves any evidence of Hezekiah's reform.

Of the three, the sanctuary at Tel Arad is most reliably dated to the eighth century with a conflagration layer in 701 B.C.E., but even this has not gone unchallenged. The burial of the courtyard and altar prior to the destruction of the site does not appear to have been for the sake of preservation, as it was not rebuilt and its cultic objects never reclaimed. This temple was not reconsecrated despite having survived intact and hence its inhumation would appear to have been intended as permanent, in keeping with the ancient Near Eastern practice of burying ritual objects. While Arad offers the most tantalizing glimpse of what could possibly be classified as a legitimate decommissioning, it falls short of historical proof. With the archaeological data exhausted, attention must be turned to the biblical record.

Josiah of Judah: The Lost Messiah of Israel (Oxford: Oxford University Press, 2001) 6–7. Note the succinct summary of Na'aman, "Debated Historicity of Hezekiah's Reform," 190, "Yet it must be emphasized that in all matters relating to the extent of its borders, its strength of settlement and its economic power Josiah's kingdom was considerably weaker than the kingdom which had existed in the eighth century BCE."

The biblical picture of Hezekiah further solidifies the Mesopotamian evidence which casts him as a savvy and perspicacious statesman who took calculated risks to augment the strength of his empire. The two brief references to centralization in the book of Kings are not to be readily dismissed as retrojections of a later Josianic reformation. The removal of the Nehushtan in 2 Kgs 18:4 is too specific to be a mere blatant alignment with Deuteronomic theology, and must bear historical underpinnings. The second half of this verse, furthermore, is not in accordance with Deuteronomic law, and contains no grammatical issues which might betray editorial activity. The same tight literary cohesion of the centralization described in 2 Kgs 18:22 favors its originality in the taunting speech of the *rab šāqê*, while its rationale for removing Yahwistic places of worship is such an important differentiator from Deuteronomic thought and the reforms of Josiah that it should properly be seen as evidence of national memory. The most logical social setting for Hezekiah's reform lies as an aftereffect of the influx of northern refugees caused by the fall of the kingdom of Israel in 720 B.C.E. Whether one attempts an economic, political, or religious justification, this scenario compellingly accommodates them all, while at the same time dovetailing with the *Sitz im Leben* of the earliest stratum of the book of Deuteronomy.

CHAPTER FIVE

THE RELATIONSHIP BETWEEN 2 KGS 18:13–20:19 AND ISA 36–39

The largely identical blocks of material found in 2 Kgs 18:13–20:19 and Isa 36–39 give rise to various redaction-critical questions. The intent of this chapter is to ascertain the original literary setting for this content and to reconstruct the process of editing which resulted in its current reduplication. The account of Sennacherib's blockade of Jerusalem is widely recognized as being composed of multiple sources, although some recent studies have favored the unity of the text. This debate invites a reassessment of the issue.

The stories relating to the audience of Isaiah ben Amoz with the king are also relevant for interpreting the character of Hezekiah. The juxtapositioning of the respective stories of the monarch's illness and the Babylonian embassy produce a contrasting portrayal of Hezekiah within these pericopes. The latter is the only text preserved in the Hebrew Bible which casts a decidedly negative shadow on the monarch. The extent to which this can be accounted for within each respective literary setting must be examined.

5.1. Relative Priority of the Texts

5.1.1. *Annalistic Account A (2 Kgs 18:13–16)*

An analysis of 2 Kgs 18:14–20:19 cannot be separated from the question of the priority of this block of material in relation to its counterpart in Isa 36–39. The two passages are not identical but are so strikingly similar that one has clearly influenced the other, or else they have both drawn upon earlier, common traditions. For most of the twentieth century, the predominant opinion in biblical scholarship has been that the book of Kings is the rightful literary origin of these texts, which were extracted and added to the book of Isaiah in order to serve as an historical appendix.[1]

---

[1] For this position, see D. Wilhelm Gesenius, *Der Prophet Jesaic* (4 vols.; Leipzig, 1820–29) 2.932ff; Francolino J. Gonçalves, *L'expédition de Sennachérib en Palestine dans la littérature hébraïque ancienne* (Études bibliques, New Series 7; Paris: Librairie Lecoffre, 1986)

More recently, in the light of literary- and redaction-critical studies of the book of Isaiah, there has been a return to the pre-critical view whereby this biblical work is the rightful setting for this block of material, with secondary editing into the book of Kings.[2] The debate remains open with no consensus.

The beginning of these extended stories relating to Sennacharib's third campaign contains a synchronism to the reign of Hezekiah, at which time "Sennacherib king of Assyria came up against all the fortified cities of Judah and seized them" (2 Kgs 18:13/Isa 36:1). This notice is followed by a terse description in Kings of Hezekiah's acquiescence to his Assyrian overlord in the face of the razing of the land (vv 14–16), a report noticeably lacking in the book of Isaiah. The direction of literary dependence has been maintained in both directions, with the shorter account in Isaiah argued as an indication of the priority of Kings or else construed as evidence that Isa 36:1 was the original introduction to the longer prophetic accounts which follow.[3] The fact that opposing conclusions may be reached in analyzing the same text is at once methodologically suspect. The provenance of the material can only be properly determined by assessment of both the positive and negative literary evidence: the plus must be shown to have close association to its literary context, while there must be justification for the removal of that text in the case of the minus.

---

343 n. 60; Antti Laato, *Who Is Immanuel? The Rise and the Foundering of Isaiah's Messianic Expectations* (Åbo: Åbo Academy Press, 1988) 271–96; Christof Hardmeier, *Prophetie im Streit vor dem Untergang Judas* (BZAW 187; Berlin: 1990) 124–26; August H. Konkel, "The Sources of the Story of Hezekiah in the Book of Isaiah," *VT* 43/4 (1993) 462–82; H. G. M. Williamson, *The Book Called Isaiah: Deutero-Isaiah's Role in Composition and Redaction* (Oxford: Clarendon Press, 1994) 189–211; idem, "Hezekiah and the Temple," in M. V. Fox et al. (eds.), *Texts, Temples, and Traditions: A Tribute to Menahem Haran* (Winona Lake, Ind.: Eisenbrauns, 1996) 47–52; Marvin A. Sweeney, *Isaiah 1–39 with an Introduction to Prophetic Literature* (FOTL 16; Grand Rapids: Eerdmans, 1996) 477–83; Raymond E. Person, *The Kings-Isaiah and Kings-Jeremiah Recensions* (BZAW 252; Berlin: W. de Gruyter, 1997) 5–79; Hans Wildberger, *Isaiah 28–39: A Continental Commentary* (trans. Thomas H. Trapp; Continental Commentary; Minneapolis: Fortress Press, 2002) 360–68.

2 Roy F. Melugin, *The Formation of Isaiah 40–55* (BZAW 141; Berlin: W. de Gruyter, 1976) 177–78; Peter R. Ackroyd, "An Interpretation of the Babylonian Exile: A Study of II Kings 20, Isaiah 38–39," *SJT* 27 (1974) 329–52; idem, "Isaiah 36–39: Structure and Function," in W. C. Delsman et al. (eds.), *Von Kanaan bis Kerala: Festschrift für Prof. Mag. Dr. Dr. J. P. M. van der Ploeg* (AOAT 211; Neukirchen-Vluyn: Neukirchener Verlag, 1982) 3–21; Klaas A. D. Smelik, "Distortion of Old Testament Prophecy: The Purpose of Isaiah xxxvi and xxxvii," in *Crises and Perspectives: Studies in Ancient Near Eastern Polytheism, Biblical Theology, Palestinian Archaeology and Intertestamental Literature* (OTS 24; Leiden: E. J. Brill, 1986) 70–93.

3 For extensive bibliography, see Gonçalves, *L'expédition de Sennachérib*, 355–61.

There are four reasons supporting the position that 2 Kgs 18:13–16 is original to the book of Kings.[4] First and foremost, the date formula in v 13 is attested elsewhere in the Deuteronomistic History, particularly in regard to accounts of invasions, yet is otherwise unknown in prophetic stories. Secondly, the fourteenth-year synchronism in this verse combined with the extension of fifteen years of life granted to Hezekiah in 2 Kgs 20:6/Isa 38:5 is inherently tied to the datum of the king's length of reign as twenty-nine years. As this total duration of rule is mentioned only in 2 Kgs 18:2, an element of the consistent accession formula used throughout the history of the monarchy, it lends weight to the impression that the overall chronological framework of the Hezekiah narratives was structured for its inclusion within the book of Kings.[5] Thirdly, the short annalistic account of 2 Kgs 18:14–16 is unintelligible without the introductory note of Sennacherib's taking of the fortified cities of Judah in v 13. The pericope shares with the preceding notice the context of the whole country, whereas both are equally devoid of interest in Jerusalem, the focal region of the following prophetic narratives. Finally, there is a striking parallel to this passage in 2 Kgs 16:5, 7–9, in which during a time of military crisis, Ahaz is compelled to give to the king of Assyria "the silver and gold that was found in the house of YHWH and in the treasuries of the king's house" (16:8, cf. 18:15).[6] This passage pertaining to the Syro-Ephraimitic war is considered integral to the Deuteronomistic History, and moreover its introduction is seen as being of a piece with the remainder of the story. In light of these facts, 2 Kgs 18:13 is best assigned to the book of Kings, with vv 14–16 as an

---

[4] Most of these insights have been articulated previously by Gonçalves, *L'expédition de Sennachérib*, 355–61. Missing from this list are justifications such as that of Christopher R. Seitz, *Zion's Final Destiny: The Development of the Book of Isaiah* (Minneapolis: Fortress Press, 1991) 51–61, who argues that the antiquity of 2 Kgs 18:13–16 speaks against its being a later addition to the Kings account. This is tantamount to saying that early material cannot be incorporated into later texts, which has been soundly disproven in studies of the sources of the books of Chronicles, for example. The antiquity of a text cannot be an overt indicator of its editorial placement into a composite work.

It should be noted that "original" in this context does not necessarily mean that the text was composed *de novo* for its current location, but that its current form conveys an editor's intent for express inclusion there. This does not rule out the possibility of underlying sources having been utilized in order to construct the text, as is commonly presumed with regard to the book of Kings, see Mordechai Cogan, *I Kings* (AYB 10; New York: Doubleday, 2000) 89–95.

[5] Also noted by Jeremy Hughes, *Secrets of the Times: Myth and History in Biblical Chronology* (JSOTSup 66; Sheffield: Sheffield Academic Press, 1990) 212.

[6] For convenience, the two texts are presented here in parallel:

original continuation of the narrative which was later excised from the
book of Isaiah. The corresponding 'negative evidence' will be presented
in my reconstruction of the editing of this material.

5.1.2. *Prophetic Account B (2 Kgs 18:17–19:37 / Isa 36–37)*

The prioritization by scholars of the version of the Jerusalem blockade in
Kings has been supported by appeal to Jer 52, which is virtually identical to 2 Kgs 24:18–25:30. In this case, the editorial note closing the previous chapter—"Thus far are the words of Jeremiah" (Jer 51:64)—is seen as
an indication that longer prophetic collections which had substantially
reached their present form could be closed by utilizing other historical
sources which served to verify the words of the prophet himself.[7] Yet the
analogy does not hold up very well: the book of Isaiah lacks a clear break
which would signal that the preceding collections had all but crystallized,
nor does the transition into narrative bring the prophet's message to an

2 Kgs 18:13–16	2 Kgs 16:5, 7–9
[18:13]Now in the fourteenth year of King Hezekiah, Sennacherib king of Assyria came up against all the fortified cities of Judah and seized them. [14]Then Hezekiah king of Judah sent to the king of Assyria at Lachish, saying, "I have done wrong. Withdraw from me; whatever you impose on me I will bear." So the king of Assyria required of Hezekiah king of Judah three hundred talents of silver and thirty talents of gold. [15]Hezekiah gave [him] all the silver which was found in the house of Yнwн, and in the treasuries of the king's house.	[16:5]Then Rezin king of Aram and Pekah son of Remaliah, king of Israel, came up to Jerusalem to [wage] war; and they besieged Ahaz, but could not overcome him. [7]So Ahaz sent messengers to Tiglath-pileser king of Assyria, saying, "I am your servant and your son; come up and deliver me from the hand of the king of Aram and from the hand of the king of Israel, who are rising up against me." [8]Ahaz took the silver and gold that was found in the house of Yнwн and in the treasuries of the king's house, and sent a present to the king of Assyria.
[16]At that time Hezekiah cut off [the gold from] the doors of the temple of Yнwн, and [from] the doorposts which Hezekiah king of Judah had overlaid, and gave it to the king of Assyria.	[9]So the king of Assyria listened to him; and the king of Assyria went up against Damascus and captured it, and carried [the people of] it away into exile to Kir, and put Rezin to death.

While the phrase "your servant and your son" has been written off as a Deuteronomistic
creation by Mordechai Cogan and Hayim Tadmor, *II Kings* (AYB 11; New York: Doubleday,
1988) 187, linkages with international treaty language have been delineated by Burke O.
Long, *2 Kings* (FOTL 10; Grand Rapids: Eerdmans, 1991) 177.

7 For example, Wildberger, *Isaiah 28–39*, 360–61.

end.[8] Most telling is the fact that nothing in Isa 36–39 is expressly foretold in the prophecies of Isaiah ben Amoz, hence the literary function of these chapters is altogether different from that of the closing chapter of Jeremiah. The appeal to Jer 52, then, does little to advance the argument for the originality of the material in Kings.

There are, moreover, peculiarities within the Kings account. It is not only the sole text in Kings featuring one of the writing prophets, but is also the lone southern story with a narrative containing a prophet.[9] This section contains the only poetic material in Kings and is the annalistic work's most detailed event, with three distinct chapters relating in some way to the Assyrian threat against Jerusalem. The discordant literary style has long been noted, with the ubiquitous trademarks of Deuteronomic thought noticeably wanting.[10] By all rights, the extensive propaganda

---

[8] The Peshitta actually contains a notice following Isa 38:8 stating *šlm ʾšʿy*, "Isaiah ends (here)." This editorial notation was based on the belief that Hezekiah was the author of what followed in v 9, "a writing of Hezekiah." In addition to Jer 51:64 already mentioned, Wildberger, *Isaiah 28–39*, 360, notes a similar phenomenon in Ps 72:20 and Job 31:40.

[9] Such observations have been noted by Smelik, "Distortion of Old Testament Prophecy," 70–93. Jonah, of course, is not an exception. Although the character of that prophetic work was identified by tradition with Jonah ben Amittai, a contemporary of Jeroboam II king of Israel (2 Kgs 14:25), the book itself dates from a later period.

This fact ties into the observation made by Yair Zakovitch, "Elijah and Elisha in the 'Praise of Israel's Great Ancestors' (Ben Sira 47:36–48:19)," in M. Garsiel et al. (eds.), *Studies in Bible and Exegesis, Vol. 5. Presented to Uriel Shimon* (Ramat Gan: Bar Ilan University Press, 2000) 177 [Hebrew], that there is no prophecy in the kingdom of Judah as long as the kingdom of Israel hangs in the balance. At the beginning of the kingdom of Judah, there is mentioned Shemaiah the man of God, who forbids Judah to fight with the sons of Israel, their brothers (1 Kgs 12:22–24), but he considers these verses as a late addition from the book of Chronicles (2 Chr 11:2–4). Henceforth the only prophetic activity mentioned is in the kingdom of Israel: even when the man of God leaves Judah, he goes to prophesy to the kingdom of Israel (1 Kgs 13). In his footsteps prophesy Ahijah of Shiloh (to the house of Jeroboam, 1 Kgs 14:5–10; 15:29–30); Jehu the son of Hanani (to the house of Baasha, 1 Kgs 16:1–4, 7, 12); Elijah; Micaiah ben Imlah (to Ahab, 1 Kgs 22:7–28); Elisha; Jonah ben Amittai (to Jeroboam II, 2 Kgs 14:25).

Only after the fall of the kingdom of Israel does the author of Kings turn his gaze toward the activity of the prophets in Judah: Isaiah who was active in the days of Hezekiah (2 Kgs 19–20); a general mention of "his servants the prophets" through whom God revealed that the end of Jerusalem would come due to the sins of Manasseh (21:10–15); Hulda the prophetess who foretold the imminent end of the kingdom to Josiah, but informed him that he would die in peace because of his righteousness (22:14–20). The prophets are mentioned again in 2 Kgs 23:2 when Josiah cuts a covenant before YHWH, although the reading "Levites" in 2 Chr 34:30 and in other manuscripts may be preferable. Either way, the prophets are not mentioned again in the book of Kings after the days of Josiah, because the die had already been cast and there was no hope of salvation via repentance.

[10] As noted long ago by Franz Delitzsch, *Jesaja* (5th ed.; TVG; Giessen: Brunnen, 1984) 368, "Ueberhaupt ist es undenkbar, daß der Verf. des Königsbuchs ihn geschrieben habe, denn einerseits weist er durch die Wörtlichkeit der mitgetheilten prophetischen

speech delivered by the *rab šāqê*, followed by the assertive response of Isaiah ben Amoz, appears to be imported from elsewhere rather than integral to the book.

Modern studies have already moved in this direction, citing various points which corroborate the priority of the book of Isaiah. Most notable are the connections with Isa 7, which utilize an imminent military attack on Jerusalem as a means to draw a contrast between the doubt of Ahaz and the righteous actions of Hezekiah: the commencement of each narrative with the incursion of an invading army (Isa 7:1; 36:1), the geographical locus of the upper pool on the highway to the fuller's field (Isa 7:3; 36:2), the respective distress of both monarchs (Isa 7:2; 37:1–4), and their receiving an oracle of assurance in tandem with a confirming sign (Isa 7:4–9, 11; 37:6–7, 30).[11] The extensive knowledge of Assyrian practices and terminology in Isa 36–37 has also been detailed, which dovetails well with the same observation made independently for the prophecies in First Isaiah.[12]

Reden auf eine schriftliche Quelle, andererseits fehlt ihm jenes deuteronomische Gepräge, an welchem die selbständig eingreifende Hand dieses Verf. kenntlich ist." The investigation into Deuteronomic thought and terminology has blossomed into an academic field in its own right, spawned by the seminal study of Moshe Weinfeld, *Deuteronomy and the Deuteronomic School* (Oxford: Clarendon Press, 1972).

[11] Noted in numerous studies ranging from Otto Eissfeldt, *Einleitung in das Alte Testament* (3rd ed.; Tübingen: J. C. B. Mohr, 1964) 198 (already noted in the 2nd ed. of 1956, p. 176), to Edgar W. Conrad, "The Royal Narratives and the Structure of the Book of Isaiah," *JSOT* 41 (1988) 67–81; idem, *Reading Isaiah* (OBT; Minneapolis: Fortress Press, 1991) 34–51, who posits that "The two narratives follow the same fixed sequence of motifs and are similar to what Robert Alter identifies as a recurring 'type-scene,' a technique of repetition in Hebrew narrative that is a major indication of structural unity in the Book of Isaiah" (*Reading Isaiah*, 36). Conrad's claim that each narrative records the sparing of both the king and city is to be contested, as Isa 7:15–25 relate merely the oracle given by Isaiah rather than any resultant outcome. It is also to be appreciated that both narratives are composite texts, in particular with regard to their endings, such that a straight synchronic comparison at this point is best avoided.

[12] For the reflection of Assyrian speech and propaganda in these chapters see Chaim Cohen, "Neo-Assyrian Elements in the First Speech of the Biblical *Rab-šāqê*," IOS 9 (1979) 32–48; Cogan and Tadmor, *II Kings*, 229ff; William R. Gallagher, *Sennacherib's Campaign to Judah: New Studies* (SHCANE 18; Leiden: Brill, 1999) 187ff; Peter Machinist, "The *rab šāqêh* at the Wall of Jerusalem: Israelite Identity in the Face of the Assyrian 'Other'," HS 41 (2000) 151–68; Peter Dubovský, *Hezekiah and the Assyrian Spies: Reconstruction of the Neo-Assyrian Intelligence Services and its Significance for 2 Kings 18–19* (BibOr 49; Rome: Pontifical Biblical Institute, 2006) 238–41. The examination of the Neo-Assyrian empire as seen through the eyes of First Isaiah was undertaken by Machinist, "Assyria and Its Image in the the First Isaiah," *JAOS* 103/4 (1983) 719–37.

These studies are more compelling than those which eschew an Assyrian background in the words of the *rab šāqê* for more common biblical language, cf. Ehud Ben Zvi, "Who Wrote the Speech of the Rabshekeh and When?" *JBL* 109/1 (1990) 79–92; Dominic Rudman, "Is the Rabshakeh also among the Prophets? A Rhetorical Study of 2 Kings XVIII 17–35,"

An important leitmotif in the speech of the *rab šāqê* is that of misplaced trust.[13] A form of the root בטח occurs seven times in the span of twenty-nine verses, yet only two other times in the book of Kings.[14] By contrast, its usage is much more balanced within the book of Isaiah, occurring ten additional times in Isa 1–35, and five times in Isa 40–66. Some of this usage is even attributed to Isaiah ben Amoz, who warned Judah against relying upon Egypt for safety and trusting (וַיִּבְטְחוּ) in its chariots and horsemen.[15] This very idea is derided by the *rab šāqê*, who mocks the confidence of the people in this "crushed reed" by saying "How can you rely (וַתִּבְטַח) upon Egypt for chariots and for horsemen?"[16] This undermining of trust is prevalent in Neo-Assyrian inscriptions—expressed via *takālu* "to trust" and its substantive *tukultu*—which demonstrates a keen awareness of Assyrian

---

VT 50/1 (2000) 100–10. A few select examples will suffice to demonstrate the Assyrian influence in 2 Kgs 18:13–20:19 / Isa 36–37:

–   The epithet which the *rab šāqê* ascribes to Sennacherib in 18:19 (הַמֶּלֶךְ הַגָּדוֹל מֶלֶךְ אַשּׁוּר) is similar to his early royal inscriptions which open with *šarru rabû šarru dannu šar māt Aššur*.

–   The *rab šāqê* calls Egypt a crushed reed (הַקָּנֶה הָרָצוּץ הַזֶּה) in 18:21, equivalent to Akkadian *qanâ ḥašāšu/ḥuššušu* which occasionally occurs in similes of defeating enemies. The use of parables is known from Assyrian royal correspondence, see Esarhaddon's letter to the Babylonians (ABL 403).

–   The *rab šāqê*'s second speech in 2 Kgs 18:28–35 is similar in structure to an Assyrian text designated ABL 301, a letter from Aššurbanipal to the Babylonians during the rebellion of his brother Šamaš-šum-ukin.

–   The phrase אֱלֹהֵי הָאֲרָצוֹת in 2 Kgs 18:35 is an Akkadianism of *ilāni mātāti*, found in Esarhaddon's inscriptions and loyalty oaths. The broader expression כָּל־אֱלֹהֵי הָאֲרָצוֹת may be compared to *ilāni mātāti kališunu*.

–   The theme of the second speech is the inability of anyone to rescue the Jerusalemites, which appears nine times via the *hifil* of the root נצל, "to save.' The closest equivalents in Akkadian are *eṭēru* and the Š of *ezēbu*, both of which appear in texts of Sargon II. The themes of misplaced trust and not being saved are juxtaposed just as in the speech of the *rab šāqê*. Based on Egypt's inability to aid Philistia, Sargon mocks Pharaoh as *malku lā mušēzibišunu*, "a king who cannot save them," in Nineveh Annal Prism VII.b line 31. For an edition of the text, see Andreas Fuchs, *Die Annalen des Jahres 711 v. Chr. nach Prismenfragmenten aus Ninive und Assur* (SAAS 8; Helsinki: Neo-Assyrian Text Corpus Project, 1998) 44–46, 73–74, and *ARAB* 2 §§193–95; *ANET* 287; *TPOA* 114–15; *TUAT* 1/4, 381–82; Mordechai Cogan, *The Raging Torrent: Historical Inscriptions from Assyria and Babylonia Relating to Ancient Israel* (Jerusalem: Carta, 2008) 103–105, for translations.

[13]   An important theme discussed in Moshe Weinfeld, "Cult Centralization in Israel in the Light of a Neo-Babylonian Analogy," *JNES* 23 (1964) 207–208; Cohen, "Neo-Assyrian Elements," 39–41; Gonçalves, *L'expédition de Sennachérib*, 410–12; John W. Olley, "'Trust in the 'Lord': Hezekiah, Kings, and Isaiah," *TynBul* 50/1 (1999) 59–77.

[14]   2 Kgs 18:19, 20, 21, 22, 24, 30; 19:10; cf. Isa 36:4, 5, 6, 7, 9, 15; 37:10. The sole outliers are 1 Kgs 5:5[4:25]; 2 Kgs 18:5. It is noteworthy that the latter of these two occurrences relates to the assessment of Hezekiah himself.

[15]   Isa 30:1–5; 31:1.

[16]   2 Kgs 18:19–24.

propaganda in these biblical texts.[17] Furthermore, this notion forges a stronger bond with the earlier narrative in Isa 7 featuring Ahaz, who is expressly told by the prophet: אִם לֹא תַאֲמִינוּ כִּי לֹא תֵאָמֵנוּ (v 9).

The declaration of the *rab šāqê* that Yhwh himself had sent the Assyrian king against the land in order to destroy it establishes another connection with Isaianic thought.[18] Throughout the book of Isaiah, the prophet

---

[17] For Akkadian *takālu* see *CAD* T, 18.63–68; *AHw* 3.1304–5. Gallagher, *Sennacherib's Campaign to Judah*, 190–91, seems to have a problem with the specific mention of Hezekiah's trust in Yhwh, but Assyrian texts do employ phrases such as *ilānī tiklišunu*, "the gods, their objects of trust."

The contention that the speech of the *rab šāqê* preserves historical memory is given additional currency by the fact that Sennacherib's annals (Rassam 43; OIP ii 78–81) make paramount the unholy motive of misplaced trust in the description of the *kitru* alliance between Ekron and Egypt, see Mario Liverani, "Kitru, Katāru," *Mesopotamia* 17 (1982) 43–66. The observation of K. Lawson Younger Jr., "Assyrian Involvement in the Southern Levant at the End of the Eighth Century B.C.E.," in A. G. Vaughn and A. E. Killebrew (eds.), *Jerusalem in Bible and Archaeology: The First Temple Period* (SBLSS 18; Leiden: Brill, 2003) 252–53, is apt: "The religious overtones with the issue of 'trust in the deity' playing a significant role in each demonstrate the inherent religious or theological flavor of all ancient Near Eastern history writing."

[18] 2 Kgs 18:25. Some scholars find problematic the claim of the *rab šāqê* that Yhwh sent the Assyrians to destroy Judah, but we know that imperial oaths in both the eighth and seventh centuries included the gods of contracting partners as witnesses and protectors. The Assyrians in their treaties regarded the vassals' deities as overseers and defenders of their interests. The vassal gods were accountable to Aššur, and within this subjugation, they could have worked on Aššur's side. This relates to the phenomenon of divine abandonment—the desertion of the enemy's own gods, leading to its downfall—covered in detail in Mordechai Cogan, *Imperialism and Religion: Assyria, Judah and Israel in the Eighth and Seventh Centuries B.C.E.* (SBLMS 19; Missoula, Mont.: Scholars Press, 1974).

This does not seem to be far afield from the justification of Sennacherib for the theft of the statue of Marduk from Babylon in 689 by saying that Marduk was angry with the Babylonians, see Daniel David Luckenbill, *The Annals of Sennacherib* (OIP 2; Chicago: University of Chicago, 1924) 83–84 (lines 46–54) and discussion in John A. Brinkman, "Sennacherib's Babylonian Problem: An Interpretation," *JCS* 25/2 (1973) 94–95. Similarly, Sargon II claimed that his conquest of Babylon came about as a call of Marduk to rescue the Babylonians from the illegal rule of Merodach-baladan (*ARAB* 2.31). Cyrus states in his Babylonian inscription that he was called by Marduk "to march against his city" (*ANET*, 315). Whatever the Assyrian agenda was, they were certainly willing to exploit local beliefs in order to advance their cause.

Stephanie Dalley, "Yabâ, Atalyā and the Foreign Policy of Late Assyrian Kings," *SAAB* 12/2 (1998) 88, contends that from ca. 740 B.C.E., the Judean king swore loyalty oaths by Yhwh and the Assyrian gods which bound the current king, his sons and grandsons to Assyria. This meant that the king could not renege without alienating Yhwh, and his enemies must depose him if they wanted him to change his allegiance (see Ezek 17). The argument has been made, then, that Yhwh sent Sennacherib against Judah due to Hezekiah's breach of loyalty to Assyria, but Hayim Tadmor contends that Hezekiah was not under a loyalty oath when he rebelled, see "Treaty and Oath in the Ancient Near East: A Historian's Approach," in G. M. Tucker and D. A. Knight (eds.), *Humanizing America's Iconic Book* (Chico, Calif.: Scholars Press, 1982) 150–51.

declares that the nations of the world may be used to accomplish God's purpose.[19] Of particular interest is Isa 10:5–19, considered by many commentators to be an authentic prophecy from the son of Amoz.[20] Just as in the Sennacherib narrative shared by Kings and Isaiah, this text asserts that the gods of the nations are powerless to intervene.[21] In both cases, YHWH is compelled to act on behalf of his chosen people due to the pride of the Sargonid king, who boasts of his own accomplishments without acknowledging the sovereignty of the Lord.[22] Because the Israelite deity is the supreme ruler of the nations, the Assyrian empire is but an instrument of punishment, acting at YHWH's behest.[23] The arrogation of power by Sennacherib is the very reason for his failure to take the the city, and thus the sparing of Jerusalem can only be understood against the backdrop of Isaian ideology.

Another ideological connection relates to the status of idols. Throughout the Deuteronomistic History the efficacy of idols is maintained. As with consulting mediums and spiritists, these mantic devices are not

---

[19] Isa 8:5–8; 10:5–11; 14:24–27. As observed by Delitzsch, *Jesaja*, 373, "In v. 10 (Jes. XXXVI) erscheint der proph. Ged. daß Assur Jehovah's Werkzeug ist (10,5 u.ö.), in des Assyriens eigenem Munde. Das läßt sich begreifen, aber unleugbar ist die jes. Farbung." The conception of Assyria as God's instrument is important in the prophecies of Isaiah, resolving an issue of theodicy in which foreign emperors saw themselves as having been given a divine mission to rule their vast empires. The prophet ostensibly acknowledges this call, but at the same time co-opts their understanding and subsumes it to the will of YHWH himself. This ideological reversal, characteristic of Isaiah, is evident when comparing his prophecy to Assyrian royal inscriptions, see the example in Moshe Weinfeld, "The Protest against Imperialism in Ancient Israelite Prophecy," in S. N. Eisenstadt (ed), *The Origins and Diversity of Axial Age Civilizations* (Albany: State University of New York Press, 1986) 176. While the actions of Assyria toward Israel may have been deemed by the prophet as a divine mission invoked by the Lord, Isaiah was nevertheless able to hold the Assyrian king responsible for his own human actions performed in fulfillment of it. Thus the dynast could still be held accountable for his haughty behavior in taking credit for his many victories, even as the results of his sweeping campaigns could be construed as receiving divine sanction.

[20] Edward J. Kissane, *The Book of Isaiah* (2 vols.; Dublin: Browne & Nolan, 1941–43) 1.123; Brevard S. Childs, *Isaiah* (OTL; Louisville: Westminster John Knox, 2000) 91; Hans Wildberger, *Isaiah 1–12: A Commentary* (trans. Thomas H. Trapp; Continental Commentary; Minneapolis: Fortress Press, 1991) 415; John Skinner, *The Book of the Prophet Isaiah Chapters I–XXXIX* (2nd ed.; Cambridge: Cambridge University Press, 1915) 92; Sweeney, *Isaiah 1–39*, 204, 210. This is in line with 19th-century scholarship, as summarized by Franz Delitzsch, "most modern commentators agree in assigning it to the time of Hezekiah, because chap. x. 9–11 represents the conquest of Samaria as having already taken place" (*Biblical Commentary on the Prophecies of Isaiah, Vol. I* [Edinburgh: T.&T. Clark, 1892] 259).

[21] Isa 10:10–11; cf. 2 Kgs 18:30–35; 19:10–13 / Isa 36:15–20; 37:10–13.

[22] Isa 10:8–14; cf. 2 Kgs 19:21–24 / Isa 37:22–25.

[23] Isa 10:5–6, 15; cf. 2 Kgs 19:25–28 / Isa 37:26–29. For further development of this theme, see Baruch Levine, "Assyrian Ideology and Israelite Monotheism," *Iraq* 67/1 (2005) 411–27.

forbidden because they are ineffective, but because they are an acceptable means of divination for the nations.[24] It is this fact which makes them unacceptable for Israel, since the holy people of God must set themselves apart from the surrounding peoples. The prophet Isaiah feels differently: idols are but the work of men's hands devoid of power.[25] This perception is similarly affirmed in Hezekiah's supplication within the temple, when he reports that the kings of Assyria have managed to cast the idols of their conquered territories into the fire "for they were not gods but the work of men's hands, wood and stone. So they have destroyed them" (2 Kgs 19:17–18).

The conception of a remnant strengthens the affinity between the Sennacherib narrative and the book of Isaiah.[26] It is mentioned in Hezekiah's plea to Isaiah that he offer "a prayer for the remnant (הַשְּׁאֵרִית) that is left" (2 Kgs 19:4), and is central to the sign Isaiah provides in 2 Kgs 19:30–31. Here the prophet pledges in the name of YHWH that "The surviving remnant of the house of Judah (פְּלֵיטַת בֵּית־יְהוּדָה הַנִּשְׁאָרָה) will again take root downward and bear fruit upward. For out of Jerusalem will go forth a remnant (שְׁאֵרִית), and out of Mount Zion survivors (פְּלֵיטָה)." All three of these designations are prominent in the ideology of Isaiah, where in the context of warfare and defeat, the prospect of annihilation was very

---

[24] Judg 17–18 (idols); 1 Sam 28:3–19 (divination). Note also the extraordinary text relating to the potency of child sacrifice in 2 Kgs 3:26–27.

[25] Isa 2:8, 20, cf. Isa 42:17; Jer 10:3–5; 51:17.

[26] On the concept of the surviving remnant, see George W. Anderson, "Some Observations on the Old Testament Doctrine of the Remnant," *TGUOS* 23 (1969–70) 1–10; Ronald E. Clements, "שָׁאַר, šāʾar," *TDOT* 14.272–86, and bibliography there; Rudolf Kilian, "Der Rest in der Verkündigung Jesajas" in idem, *Jesaja 1–39* (EdF 200; Darmstadt: Wissenschaftliche Buchgesellschaft, 1983) 27–39; Gerhard F. Hasel, "'Remnant' as a Meaning of *ʾaḥarît*," in L. T. Geraty (ed.), *The Archaeology of Jordan and Other Studies* (Berrien Springs, Mich.: Andrews University Press, 1986) 511–524; Lester V. Meyer, "Remnant," *AYBD* 5.669–71; Heide-Marie Pfaff, *Die Entwicklung des Restgedankens in Jesaja 1–39* (EHS 561; Frankfurt am Main: Peter Lang, 1996); Rolf Rendtorff, "Israels 'Rest'. Unabgeschlossene Überlegungen zu einem schwierigen Thema der alttestamentlichen Theologie,", in A. Graupner, H. Delkurt, and A. B. Ernst (eds.), *Verbindungslinien. Festschrift für Werner H. Schmidt zum 65. Geburtstag* (Neukirchen-Vluyn: Neukirchener Verlag, 2000) 265–279; Sara Japhet, "The Concept of the 'Remnant' in the Restoration Period. On the Vocabulary of Self-definition," in F.-L. Hossfeld and L. Schwienhorst-Schönberger (eds.), *Das Manna fällt auch heute noch. Beiträge zur Geschichte und Theologie des Alten, Ersten Testaments. Festschrift für Erich Zenger* (HBS 44; Freiburg: Herder, 2004) 340–361; Gerald Emem Umoren, *The Salvation of the Remnant in Isaiah 11:11–12: An Exegesis of a Prophecy of Hope and Its Relevance Today* (Boca Raton, Fl.: Dissertation.com, 2007); Joel Willitts, "The Remnant of Israel in 4QpIsaiahª (4Q161) and the Dead Sea Scrolls," *JJS* 57/1 (2006) 11–25.

real for not only Judah but for other nations as well.[27] The sign of Isaiah shares the idea with the prophetic book that the remnant is something positive, representing the continuation of the life of the community and constituting the saving activity of YHWH.[28] This is entirely counter to the Deuteronomistic perspective in Kings, where the Lord avers "I will abandon the remnant (שְׁאֵרִית) of my inheritance and deliver them into the hand of their enemies, and they will become as plunder and spoil to all their enemies" (2 Kgs 21:14).

There are also linguistic ties to the book of Isaiah within the prophet's response to Hezekiah. Within the Deuteronomistic History as a whole, the expression בַּת־צִיּוֹן only occurs in 2 Kgs 19:21, framed within Isaiah's response to Hezekiah's prayer. Throughout the Hebrew Bible it appears thirty-one times, with six of those contained in First Isaiah. The title קְדוֹשׁ יִשְׂרָאֵל in v 22 is again unique within the Deuteronomistic History, and yet twenty-five of its thirty-one occurrences appear in the book of Isaiah. The forests of Lebanon and the rivers of Egypt, featured in vv 23–24, are also common prophetic imagery employed by the son of Amoz.[29] The weight of the evidence surveyed here suggests that the narrative of the blockade of Jerusalem was originally composed in Isaianic circles, and is therefore secondary in the book of Kings.

5.1.3. *Hezekiah and Isaiah (2 Kgs 20 / Isa 38–39)*

A key argument for maintaining the priority of Isaiah for the latter chapters of the Hezekiah arc is the so-called 'bridge theory': that is, Isa 38–39 is intended as a transitional narrative leading into Second Isaiah. Without a

---

[27] noun שְׁאָר: Isa 7:3; 10:19–22; 11:11, 16; 14:22; 16:14; 17:3; 21:17; 28 5.
   noun שְׁאֵרִית: Isa 14:30; 15:9; 37:4, 32.
   perfect נִשְׁאַר and participle נִשְׁאָר: Isa 4:3; 17:6; 24:6, 12; 37:31
   noun פְּלֵיטָה: Isa 4:2; 10:20; 15:9; 37:31–32.
For a remnant in reference to other nations, cf. Isa 14:22 (Babylon); 14:30 (Philistia); 15:9; 16:14 (Moab); 17:3 (Syria); 21:17 (the Kedarite Arabs). Because survival was foremost in the face of military conflict, it is questionable to speculate whether "Isaiah took over the idea from Amos" as suggested by Joseph Blenkinsopp, *Isaiah 1–39* (AYB 19; New York: Doubleday, 2000) 110. The universality of the idea is readily plausible under any of the three views briefly mentioned by Meyer, "Remnant," *AYBD* 5.671.

[28] Cf. Isa 10:20–22; 11:11, 16; 17:3; 28:5, in addition, of course, to Isa 37:4, 31–32. The remnant is well attested in eighth-century prophecy, supporting its authenticity in Isaian oracles. For such passages in Amos, see Gerhard F. Hasel, *The Remnant* (AUM 5; Berrien Springs, Mich.: Andrews University, 1972) 173–215, as well as Paul R. Noble, "The Remnant in Amos 3–6: A Prophetic Paradox," *HBT* 19/2 (1997) 122–147.

[29] For the forests of Lebanon, see Isa 2:13; 10:34; 14:8; 29:17; 32:9; 35:2. For the rivers of Egypt, cf. Isa 7:18; 19:6–8, 23:3, 10.

doubt, there is intentionality with regard to the placement of the Babylonian embassy and the judgment against Hezekiah which foretells the end
of Judah, both of which immediately precede the promises of return and
restoration that begin in Isa 40. It has long been observed that Isa 38:6,
"I will deliver you and this city from the hand of the king of Assyria; and
I will defend this city," seems to place the events of Hezekiah's illness prior
to the deliverance of Jerusalem. An additional error in continuity occurs
in Kings within the annalistic source A, according to which Hezekiah
paid the heavy indemnity to Assyria (2 Kgs 18:14–16). There would subsequently have been precious little for Hezekiah to display to the visiting
Babylonians, a problem lacking in the book of Isaiah due to the absence
of this ancient source.[30] Hence the ordering of the material is seemingly
incoherent in the chronologically structured book of Kings, whereas in the
book of Isaiah such a literary framework more clearly serves as a link to
the exilic setting of the subsequent prophetic material.[31]

In response, it must be stated at the outset that regardless of which
book may be claimed as the original mooring for these stories, the same
underlying issue of chronological sequence within these successive texts
remains. Thus the motivation for the editor in determining their current
placement was for reasons other than strict temporal order. With this in
mind, there is little point in appealing to such issues in continuity when
assessing the provenance of the stories. Because it was sufficiently important for the redactor to ostensibly upset the clear chronology established
within these texts, the proper bellwether of their origin is to be found by
testing which literary environment best justifies this rearrangement.

With this in mind, the stories in Isa 38–39 of Hezekiah's illness and
the Babylonian delegation who come to pay their respects can only be
argued as having literary ties with the book of Isaiah by looking forward.
These two chapters do not accord with the prophet Isaiah's Zionist theology, which advocates the inviolability of Jerusalem and the favored
status of YHWH's chosen ruler.[32] It furthermore is a stark *volte-face* from

---

[30] As noted by Blenkinsopp, *Isaiah 1–39*, 286, and others.

[31] A key point advanced by Smelik, "Distortion of Old Testament Prophecy," 74, "We
have to conclude that the present arrangement of the Hezekiah-narratives is only understandable from the perspective of the book of Isaiah, not from that of Kings."

[32] A motif within the larger Zion tradition, in which YHWH the great king chose Jerusalem as his dwelling place and protects it from his enemies. For studies relating to this
tradition, see John H. Hayes, "The Tradition of Zion's Inviolability," *JBL* 82/4 (1963) 419–26;
Ronald E. Clements, *God and Temple: The Idea of the Divine Presence in Ancient Israel*
(Philadelphia: Fortress Press, 1965) 40–78; J. J. M. Roberts, "The Davidic Origin of the Zion

the depiction of Hezekiah in the preceding two chapters, which serve to paint the Judean monarch as trusting in the Lord in the face of an enemy, unlike his predecessor Ahaz. Rather, the villified Ahaz is now seen to be more righteous than Hezekiah, the latter of whom has committed a crime deemed so heinous that the kingdom is torn from him.

It must also be admitted that the evidence supporting connections between Isa 38–39 and Deutero-Isaiah are tenuous at best, being limited primarily to the theme of exile. While this linkage is certainly valid, the scholar is also obligated to seek associations at the linguistic level as well, and yet such data are meagre.[33] The more closely one examines the text, in fact, the more one is able to discern connections with the book of Kings. The oracle of Isaiah in 2 Kgs 20:17–18 is pivotal to the overall prophecy-fulfillment scheme of that work as a whole: the proclamation in verse 17, "All that is in your house, and all that your fathers have laid up in store to this day will be carried to Babylon" is brought to fruition in 2 Kgs 24:13; 25:13–17, while the promise that "Your sons...will be taken away and will become officials in the palace of the king of Babylon" in verse 18 foreshadows the fates of Jehoiachin and Zedekiah which close the book.[34] Deutero-Isaiah, by contrast, evinces scant interest in the temple, and absolutely

---

Tradition," *JBL* 92 (1973) 329–44, and bibliography there; idem, "Zion in the Theology of the Davidic-Solomonic Empire," in T. Ishida (ed.), *Studies in the Period of David and Solomon and Other Essays. Papers Read at the International Symposium, Tokyo, 5–7 December, 1979* (Winona Lake, Ind.: Eisenbrauns, 1982) 93–108; Moshe Weinfeld, "Zion and Jerusalem as Religious and Political Capital: Ideology and Utopia," in R. E. Friedman (ed.), *The Poet and the Historian: Essays in Literary and Historical Biblical Criticism* (HSS 26; Chico, Calif.: Scholars Press, 1983) 75–115; Ben C. Ollenburger, *Zion the City of the Great King: A Theological Symbol of the Jerusalem Cult* (JSOTSup 41; Sheffield: JSOT Press, 1987); Boyo G. Ockinga, "The Inviolability of Zion—A Pre-Israelite Tradition?" *BN* 44 (1988) 54–60.

[33] Literary links between the poem in Isa 37:23–29 and Deutero-Isaiah have been claimed by Ackroyd, "Isaiah 36–39," 112, and Joseph W. Groves, *Actualization and Interpretation in the Old Testament* (SBLDS 86; Atlanta: Scholars Press, 1987) 198–99. The rebuttals offered by Wildberger, *Isaiah 28–39*, 360–68, and Williamson, *Book Called Isaiah*, 195–97, are sufficient to cast extreme doubt on this proposal. Williamson dismisses the "bridge theory" on the lines that one should expect stronger literary connections if such were truly the case. A questionable methodology is employed by Seitz *Zion's Final Destiny*, 83–86, 91–92, who rejects the idea on the presumption that Isa 36–39 predates Deutero-Isaiah.

[34] Noted in studies of this material by Ronald E. Clements, *Isaiah and the Deliverance of Jerusalem* (JSOTSup 13; Sheffield: JSOT Press, 1980) 52–71; idem, "The Isaiah Narrative of 2 Kings 20:12–19 and the Date of the Deuteronomic History," in A. Rofé and Y. Zakovitch (eds.), *Isac Leo Seeligmann Volume. Essays on the Bible and the Ancient World* (3 vols.; Jerusalem: E. Rubinstein, 1983) 3.209–20; Christopher T. Begg, "2 Kings 20:12–19 as an Element of the Deuteronomistic History," *CBQ* 48 (1986) 27–38; idem, "The Deuteronomistic Retouching of the Portrait of Hezekiah in 2 Kgs 20,12–19," *BN* 38/39 (1987) 7–13; Childs, *Isaiah*, 262.

none in the royal family.[35] Recent text-critical studies likewise concur that the Greek texts behind Kings serve as the oldest sources for the story.[36] It remains, then, to explain how this non-chronological arrangement of material, in which the stories of Hezekiah's illness and the Babylonian delegation follow the blockade and deliverance of Jerusalem, serves foremost the purposes of the Deuteronomistic editors.

The investigation into the relationship between 2 Kgs 18:13–20:19 and Isa 36–39 has yielded somewhat different results than those obtained in previous studies. Rather than assigning this tradition complex entirely to a single book, its provenance would appear to extend to multiple literary locales. The brief, annalistic report of 2 Kgs 18:13–16 belongs squarely within the Deuteronomistic History, based on its characteristic synchronism associated with a significant event, the unity of the account, and the similarity it shares with 2 Kgs 16:5, 7–9. By contrast, 2 Kgs 18:17–19:37/Isa 36–37 shows itself to be consonant with the terminology, ideology, and literary themes of the book of Isaiah. Finally, 2 Kgs 20/Isa 38–39 betrays its origin in Kings.[37] The next step in this literary analysis will be to reconstruct the process of editing these aggregate narratives into the respective books.

5.2. Editing of the Texts

5.2.1. *Source Division*

The blockade of Jerusalem by the Sargonid Sennacherib was the event of greatest import up until that time in Israelite history. Court scribes assigned to the king, or else those trained to preserve the oracles of the

---

[35] The word בַּיִת, "house" occurs only six times in Second Isaiah, and never refers to the temple. Only Isa 44:28 discusses rebuilding the temple (הֵיכָל) and Jerusalem, with Cyrus acting as God's agent. By this period in the nation's history, in which any foreign power could be used as the agent of Yнwн for accomplishing his purpose, the Lord's anointed no longer had to be the king of Israel.

[36] See Konkel, "Sources of the Story of Hezekiah," 462–82, whose conclusions pertain to the entire invasion arc of Sennacherib, yet derive largely from analysis of the stories surrounding Hezekiah's illness.

[37] Previous research has indirectly verified these conclusions, if one observes that the identified links between Isa 36–39 and earlier chapters of the book are contained almost exclusively within chaps. 36–37, whereas linkage with Deutero-Isaiah is supported predominantly via Isa 38–39. Here I concur with Williamson, *Book Called Isaiah*, 194, in regard to the former material: "The conclusion that we are dealing with material drafted in some sort of close association with Isaianic circles is an important step in the investigation."

prophets, would have been on hand to record events as they transpired.[38]
The information would have been of value subsequently for either official
annals or prophetic collections. So it is not surprising for such a watershed event that multiple accounts have come down to us preserved in
the Hebrew Bible. The synchronic form of 2 Kgs 18:17–19:37/Isa 36–37 has
long been recognized as composed of two prophetic stories that have
been redacted together. They were originally divided into 2 Kgs 18:17–19:9a
(B₁) and 19:9b-37 (B₂), with later revision into 2 Kgs 18:17–19:9a, 36–37 and
19:9b-35.[39] Scholarship has, for the most part, accepted this latter separation of the prophetic material.[40]

---

[38] In the case of Sennacherib's campaign, we read that Shebna the scribe was on hand
when the *rab šāqê* spoke on behalf of his Assyrians masters (2 Kgs 18:18, 37; 19:2 / Isa 36:3,
22; 37:2). In the Assyrian empire, it was common practice for a royal scribe to accompany
the king on military engagements. They are depicted on monuments recording events in
both cuneiform as well as alphabetic script, see Hayim Tadmor, "Propoganda, Literature,
Historiography: Cracking the Code of the Assyrian Royal Inscriptions," in *Assyria 1995:
Proceedings of the 10th Anniversary Symposium of the Neo-Assyrian Text Corpus Project*
(Helsinki: Neo-Assyrian Text Corpus Project, 1997) 329. Additional royal records are known
to have been kept thanks to the notices of the Chronicles of the Kings of Judah periodically
announced in the Deuteronomistic History (e.g., 2 Kgs 20:20).
   The popular example of a scribe working in prophetic circles is Baruch, on behalf of
Jeremiah (Jer 36:4–32). As I concur with Weinfeld, "Cult Centralization in Israel," 207–
209, and others that source B₁ stems from a prophetic provenance, it provides additional
ammunition against those critics who see the silence of the prophets Isaiah and Micah
concerning the reform as evidence for its non-historicity. See the rejoinder by Jacob Milgrom, "Does H Advocate the Centralization of Worship?" *JSOT* 88 (2000) 69.
[39] The original division was proposed by Bernhard Stade, "Miscellen. 16. Anmerkungen
zu 2 Kö. 15–21," *ZAW* 6 (1886) 172–86; idem and Friedrich Schwally, *The Book of Kings*
(SBOT 9; Leipzig: J.C. Hinrichs, 1904) 50–52. Although Brevard Childs is traditionally credited with the revision of these sources in *Isaiah and the Assyrian Crisis* (SBT II/3; London:
SCM Press, 1967) 69–103, he himself acknowledges that this separation had been done previously by others such as Kittel, Marti, and Skinner (p. 74). More recently, Childs favors the
dependence of B₂ upon B₁ rather than maintaining them as independent literary sources
(*Isaiah*, 263).
[40] A recent defender is Nadav Na'aman, "Updating the Messages: Hezekiah's Second
Prophetic Story (2 Kings 19.9b-35) and the Community of Babylonian Deportees," in
L. L. Grabbe (ed.), *'Like a Bird in a Cage': The Invasion of Sennacherib in 701 B.C.E.* (JSOT-
Sup 363; London: Sheffield Academic Press, 2003) 201–20. Notable detractors are Seitz,
Zion's Final Destiny; Klaas A. D. Smelik, "King Hezekiah Advocates True Prophecy. Remarks
on Isaiah xxxvi and xxxvii//II Kings xviii and xix," in idem, *Converting the Past. Studies
in Ancient Israelite and Moabite Historiography* (OTS 28; Leiden: E. J. Brill, 1992) 70–93;
Gallagher, *Sennacherib's Campaign to Judah*, 143–59. For other modifications to the divi-
sions identified by Stade and Childs, see Paul S. Evans, *The Invasion of Sennacherib in the
Book of Kings. A Source-Critical and Rhetorical Study of 2 Kings 18–19* (VTSup 125; Leiden:
Brill, 2009) 13–14 n. 62.

But this division is not eminently satisfying. While the B₂ source is clearly a unified narrative, leading from the threat relayed by the messengers to Hezekiah's prayer and Isaiah's response from the Lord, the B₁ source can only be followed with difficulty. The narrative begins with a surfeit of verbs meticulously chronicling the actions of Sennacherib sending his trusted emissaries to Jerusalem along with his army: וַיַּעֲלוּ וַיָּבֹאוּ יְרוּשָׁלַ͏ִם וַיַּעֲלוּ וַיָּבֹאוּ וַיַּעַמְדוּ, "and they went up and they came (to) Jerusalem, and they went up and they came and they stood." The need for such meaningless repetition to describe such a mundane task is perplexing.

This excess of activity is met with conflicting locations for the meeting between the respective parties. According to 2 Kgs 18:17, this rendezvous for the purposes of diplomacy was stationed at "the conduit of the upper pool, which is on the highway of the fuller's field." Though the exact location of this conduit has been given scholarly treatment, it remains unknown. Based on the combined data that one had to "go out" in order to reach it, and that it was located along a highway, however, it must have been some distance outside the city.[41] This is to be contrasted with the geographical setting of vv 26–27, which transpires directly before the city walls, sufficiently close that the *rab šāqê* can speak directly to the fearful populace listening atop them.

The addressee is a further issue. The emissaries dispatched by Sennacherib appear to have been assigned to speak only to the Judean king, for "they called to the king" and begin their declaration with "Say now to Hezekiah" (2 Kgs 18:18–19). And yet, in the second speech of the *rab šāqê*, he denounces the idea of such a singular audience, "Has my master sent me only to your master and to you to speak these words, [and] not to the men who sit on the wall...?" (v 27). The contrast is just as stark as the actions of Hezekiah's delegates themselves. When they are receiving the

---

[41] Cf. וַיֵּצֵא אֲלֵהֶם in 2 Kgs 18:18; צֵא־נָא in Isa 7:3. The location of the upper pool on the Fuller's Field Road (cf. Isa 7:3) is not known, but see Millar Burrows, "The Conduit of the Upper Pool," *ZAW* 70 (1958) 221–27; Benjamin Mazar, "Jerusalem," *EncBib* 3.824, 827–28; John Gray, *I & II Kings* (2nd ed.; OTL; Philadelphia: Westminster Press, 1970) 679–81, for a survey of the suggestions. Burrows concurs with the conclusions reached here, but due to reading 2 Kgs 18:17–19:9a as a single source, he unfortunately harmonizes the evidence: "In II Kings 18 the Assyrian envoys obviously remained outside the city wall but near it, where the people sitting on the wall could hear what they said (vv. 26f.). Some portion of the highway of the fuller's field and the conduit of the upper pool must therefore have been close to the foot of the wall" (pp. 221–22).

word intended for the king, they politely await for the *rab šāqê* to deliver his demands. Yet in the second speech, directed toward the populace, the Judean liaisons are quick to try and silence the selfsame designated Assyrian spokesperson. One wonders, if the narrative is truly unified, why the emissaries of Hezekiah are so patient as to allow the *rab šāqê* to complete one full speech before beseeching him not to speak in the native language of the Israelites.

A final concern with regard to the continuity of the B₁ source as currently identified pertains to Hezekiah's receipt of the word from the *rab šāqê*. His delegates come to him with their clothes torn to report what they have heard, at which time Hezekiah tears his own clothes, covers himself with sackcloth, and enters the temple. A slightly different set of individuals are then expressly named, commanded to be covered with sackcloth, and then promptly sent off to inquire of the Lord through the prophet Isaiah. While the recounting of different servants, who are apparently not sufficiently humbled by having their clothes torn that they likewise need to be covered in sackcloth, is in itself curious, the main issue relates to the phrase וַיְהִי כִּשְׁמֹעַ הַמֶּלֶךְ חִזְקִיָּהוּ in 2 Kgs 19:1. There are only six instances in the Hebrew Bible of someone hearing without reference to a direct object, and in each of the other five cases there is no agent required to convey what has been heard.[42] That is, the grammatical use of שָׁמַע without a direct object elsewhere in Scripture indicates that word has reached the recipient by virtue of its import alone.[43]

With these observations in mind, the prophetic source B may be divided into the following essentially complete narratives, each with the corresponding characteristics. The complete division is detailed in Appendix A.[44]

---

[42] Josh 9:1; 11:1; 1 Kgs 12:2; 15:21; 19:13; 2 Kgs 19:1; cf. Isa 37:1; 2 Chr 10:2; 16:5.

[43] The idea is akin to the situation in the book of Jonah, as the message of the imminent fall of Nineveh is proclaimed in the streets: "When the word *reached* (וַיִּגַּע) the king of Nineveh..." (Jon 3:6).

[44] Although the results achieved here differ from those attained by Stade and Childs, they nonetheless serve to affirm their source-critical analyses. If the B₂ narrative is complete in itself and independent of B₁, then it cannot be a secondary addition to the latter as maintained by Hardmeier, *Prophetie im Streit*, 15, 157–59. Furthermore, the mutual starting point for these stories reinforces the position that source A indeed stands apart from them both. There is hence no basis for reading A and B₁ as a unified whole (2 Kgs 18:13–19a, 36–37), nor need to explain why Sennacherib does not withdraw following v 16 (pace *Prophetie im Streit*, 154–56).

B₁ (2 Kgs 18:17a, 26–36; 19:1–9a, 36–37)	B₂ (2 Kgs 18:17b–25, 37; 19:9b–35)
• The *rab šāqê* arrives in Jerusalem (18:17a). Hezekiah's delegates are on hand to speak to him.	• The Assyrian delegation comes to the conduit of the upper pool outside of Jerusalem, and Hezekiah's emissaries go out to meet them (18:17b–18).
• The *rab šāqê* is stationed before the walls of the city, to address the populace directly (18:26).	• The message of the Assyrian delegation is for Hezekiah himself (18:18, 19).
	• Hezekiah's emissaries relay the message, showing their emotion spontaneously (18:37).
	• When the king does not respond, more messengers are sent to contact him (19:9b).
• The *rab šāqê* taunts the Lord (18:30, 35).	• The messengers taunt the Lord in a second, direct address (19:10–13).
• Hezekiah hears of the message (on his own) and enters the temple (19:1).	• Hezekiah reads the scroll of the messengers and enters the temple to pray (19:14–19).
• Hezekiah sends emissaries to Isaiah, commanding them to demonstrate their anguish by wearing sackcloth (19:2).	
• Isaiah gives the Lord's reply (19:6–7).	• Isaiah gives the Lord's reply (19:20–34).
• The Assyrian army retreats upon hearing that Taharqo of Kush is approaching (19:8–9a, 36–37).	• The Assyrian army is decimated by the angel of YHWH (19:35).

This new proposal for the separation of the two accounts provides greater continuity, resolving the difficulties inherent in 2 Kgs 18:17–19:9 discussed above. In source B₂, the emissaries of Hezekiah have been dispatched to meet with the Assyrian delegation for the express purpose of obtaining their message for the king, hence their willingness to listen to the bombastic demands of the enemy. The servants of Hezekiah are explicitly described as returning to the king in order to relay the Assyrian message, in accordance with their function. In source B₁, however, these same emissaries have the more pressing issue of not wanting to incite panic within the city walls, as the *rab šāqê* intends to address the populace directly. The request that the the *rab šāqê* speak in Aramaic is brazenly brushed aside, and the subsequent threats proclaimed before the denizens of the capital city reach Hezekiah of their own accord.

This delineation would seem to be supported via textual criticism as well. The opening verse of the prophetic account varies slightly between Kings and Isaiah:

2 Kgs 18:17	Isa 36:2

2 Kgs 18:17

וַיִּשְׁלַח מֶֽלֶךְ־אַשּׁוּר אֶת־תַּרְתָּן
וְאֶת־רַב־סָרִיס וְאֶת־רַב־שָׁקֵה מִן־
לָכִישׁ אֶל־הַמֶּלֶךְ חִזְקִיָּהוּ בְּחֵיל
כָּבֵד יְרוּשָׁלָ͏ִם וַיַּעֲלוּ וַיָּבֹאוּ יְרוּשָׁלַ͏ִם
וַיַּעֲלוּ וַיָּבֹאוּ וַיַּעַמְדוּ בִּתְעָלַת
הַבְּרֵכָה הָעֶלְיוֹנָה אֲשֶׁר בִּמְסִלַּת
שְׂדֵה כוֹבֵס:

Isa 36:2

וַיִּשְׁלַח מֶֽלֶךְ־אַשּׁוּר אֶת־רַב־שָׁקֵה
מִלָּכִישׁ יְרוּשָׁלַ͏ְמָה אֶל־הַמֶּלֶךְ חִזְקִיָּהוּ
בְּחֵיל כָּבֵד וַיַּעֲמֹד בִּתְעָלַת הַבְּרֵכָה
הָעֶלְיוֹנָה בִּמְסִלַּת שְׂדֵה כוֹבֵס:

The variant in Isaiah mentions only the *rab šāqê*, whereas Kings adds the *tartānu* and the *rab ša-rēši*.[45] The following verbs in each respective version are in agreement numerically, with וַיַּעֲמֹד in Isaiah and וַיַּעֲלוּ וַיָּבֹאוּ, etc. in Kings. The going forth of the delegation in each book is also in accord with its respective Assyrian counterpart, being וַיֵּצֵא אֵלָיו in Isaiah but וַיֵּצֵא אֲלֵהֶם in Kings. Rather than argue for the priority of one reading over the other, I would suggest that both are original, preserving to some degree the *Urtext* of the underlying B₁ and B₂ accounts. Isa 36:2 represents the B₁ version, in which only the *rab šāqê* appears, the sole Assyrian spokesman designated to impel the populace to flee or else turn on their leaders. This is the reason that Eliakim, Shebnah and Joah address only the *rab šāqê* in their request, and that only he is reported as leaving Jerusalem.[46] 2 Kgs 18:17 exhibits the B₂ version, in which Sennacherib sends multiple messengers to negotiate with Hezekiah. This is affirmed by the fact that after failing to obtain a reply, וַיָּשָׁב וַיִּשְׁלַח מַלְאָכִים אֶל־חִזְקִיָּהוּ, "he sent messengers again to Hezekiah" (2 Kgs 19:9). At the editing stage, however, there was no possible way to harmonize the numerical disparity, as only one choice of messenger could be initially dispatched by Sennacherib. The book of Isaiah elected to begin its account with the B₁ version in the singular, whereas Kings opted for the B₂ version in the plural.[47]

---

[45] For discussion of these Assyrian titles, see Hayim Tadmor, "Rab-sārîs or Rab-shakeh in 2 Kings 18," in C. L. Meyers and M. O'Connor (eds.), *The Word of the Lord Shall Go Forth: Essays in Honor of David Noel Freedman in Celebration of His Sixtieth Birthday* (Winona Lake, Ind.: Eisenbrauns, 1983) 279–85.

[46] The addressing of the *rab šāqê* occurs in 2 Kgs 18:26/Isa 36:11, and his leaving in 2 Kgs 19:8/Isa 37:8. The fact that the *rab šāqê* departs from Lachish (2 Kgs 18:17/Isa 36:2) and later learns that Sennacherib has moved on from there is further evidence of continuity within the B₁ source.

[47] This distinction is reflected in the division of sources provided in Appendix A. It is also likely that 2 Kgs 18:17 in LXX reflects the earliest extant version of the B₂ introduction, lacking the superfluous verbs found in MT. Having separated the two accounts based on

The source division proposed here has important implications for historical reconstruction of the events themselves. Because these two narratives follow in broad strokes the same basic script, they should be seen as preserving the same historical memory.[48] This obviates the need to seek within them evidence of more than one Assyrian campaign into Judah. It is the current consensus opinion in biblical scholarship for the separation of these accounts that has, in part, permitted claim to be made for multiple incursions into the region.

5.2.2. *Literary Analysis*

With the two narratives isolated in this manner, the literary purpose of each comes into stark relief. Both traditions are intent on demonstrating that the trust Hezekiah placed in Yhwh played a key part in the salvation of the city, yet each one achieves this goal in a different way.[49] The B_1 narrative has the *rab šāqê* addressing the people directly, in credible imitation of the classic Assyrian method of propaganda, and the king responds in fear by entering the temple. He cannot importune the deity directly, however, and must send Isaiah to ascertain a response from the Lord. In the B_2 account, Hezekiah is even more strongly in focus. The Assyrian

---

the primary criteria of continuity, duplication, and contradiction, even stylistic variations serve to affirm the division of sources proposed here. Hezekiah's delegates are referred to consistently in source B_2 as "Eliakim the son of Hilkiah, who was over the household, and Shebnah the scribe and Joah the son of Asaph the recorder" (18:18, 37). As with the identification of the documents of the Pentateuch, signs of literary discord are evident in duplications, contradictions, discontinuity, and inconsistency of style and literary characteristics. Authorial style is pertinent to such literary-critical investigation, but should never be the determining factor in isolating narrative strands. See further David M. Carr, *Reading the Fractures of Genesis: Historical and Literary Approaches* (Louisville: Westminster John Knox, 1996) 23–40.

[48] The duplication of these accounts speaks against them being mere fallacious propaganda composed at the same point in time for the same literary purpose, as required by Hardmeier, *Prophetie im Streit*. He proposes that the Hezekiah-Sennacherib narrative is unified and wholly fictitious, written in 588 B.C.E. as polemic against the message of Jeremiah to submit to the Babylonian yoke. The lack of any compelling explanation under this view for the survival of the narrative in the wake of the Babylonian conquest of 587 and the subsequent vindication of Jeremiah's message has been labelled as its "fatal flaw" by Christopher R. Seitz in his review of *Prophetie im Streit*, see *JBL* 110 (1991) 511–13.

[49] For the form and intent of these narratives, as well as the theological development within them and their historical value, cf. Childs, *Isaiah and the Assyrian Crisis*, 73–103; Richard R. Deutsch, *Die Hiskiaerzählungen. Eine formgeschichtliche Untersuchung der Texte Js 36–39 und 2R 18–20* (Basel: Basileia, 1969); Clements, *Isaiah and the Deliverance of Jerusalem*; Paul-Eugène Dion, "Sennacherib's Expedition to Palestine," *EgT* 20 (1989) 5–25; Machinist, "The *rab šāqēh* at the Wall of Jerusalem," 151–68; Na'aman, "Updating the Messages," 201–20.

delegation is sent to negotiate with him personally, but after Hezekiah fails to answer their first dialogue discrediting Judah's alliance with Egypt, a second set of messengers is dispatched to him directly in order to assure the placid ruler that the gods of the empire's conquered lands were helpless to stand in the way of the might of Assyria. This ominous threat has the desired effect, and Hezekiah enters the temple to beseech YHWH to deliver his people as a means to exhibit his great power before all other kingdoms. Isaiah is no longer necessary as a conduit to the deity, but relays an assurance from the Lord in answer to the ruler's prayer. In both accounts, YHWH responds favorably to Hezekiah's entreaty, Assyria is denounced as having committed blasphemy, and the crisis is in some way divinely averted. As with other biblical stories both inside and outside of the Pentateuch, individual traditions which were felt to be recounting the same event were edited together for maximal preservation of the material.[50] The similarities that each source shares with the story of Ahaz in Isa 7 suggest that they were edited together for inclusion in the book of Isaiah.

The stories relating to Hezekiah's illness—both the extension of fifteen years granted to him after his earnest prayer (2 Kgs 20:1–11/Isa 38) and the subsequent visit by the Babylonian embassy in order to ascertain his welfare (2 Kgs 20:12–19/Isa 39)—have been posited in this chapter on literary grounds as being original to the book of Kings. Issues of continuity that arise from their current placement, discussed previously, point to redactional intentionality, meaning that these texts served a broader purpose within the overall scope of the original book into which they were edited.[51] The appearance of these texts within two biblical books, moreover, implies that this intent is primary in one work but only secondary in the other. The burden of proof is upon whomever would argue for the book of Kings as primary, as the threat of exile arranged immediately prior to the exilic promises of Second Isaiah has been readily seen as evidence that they were originally composed for their current location in the book of Isaiah.

---

[50] Within the Deuteronomistic History this is evident in the crossing of the Jordan in Josh 3–4, and most notably in the story of David and Goliath in 1 Sam 17. For the latter, see Emanuel Tov, *The Text-Critical Use of the Septuagint in Biblical Research* (2nd ed.; JBS 8; Jerusalem: Simor, 1997) 250–52 and bibliography there.

[51] Childs, *Isaiah*, 264, among others, has noted that "Chapter 33 is only very loosely related to chapters 36 and 37 by means of a vague chronological formula, 'in those days'." This is as we would expect if two disparate blocks of material have been edited together.

Exegetes have claimed that there is an alternating pattern of good and bad rulers exhibited in the Kings narrative spanning from Ahaz-Hezekiah-Manasseh-Josiah, but this is only achieved by a selective reading of these respective reigns. The placement of a negative value judgment on the otherwise righteous Hezekiah at the very end of his tenure as king suggests that the editor desired to cast a negative shadow over his entire rule, in a manner consistent with, not contrasting, the evaluation of his peers. Beginning with Ahaz and continuing through Manasseh, the Judean monarchs are given condemning evaluations of an escalating nature, such that the reader is in no way uncertain as to the just decision of the Lord to bring about the downfall of the southern kingdom. A true pattern of alternating good and bad kings would be—and evidently was—ideologically problematic for the Deuteronomist. In the face of such weight being placed on the conduct of the Lord's anointed rulers, why did God not spare his chosen city and its inhabitants from the Babylonian conquest in the wake of such a faithful and obedient king as Hezekiah?[52] The strategic positioning of this regent's tale of hubris at the end of the Hezekian arc in Kings resolves this crux: even the great Hezekiah was not wholly righteous, and his actions divinely signaled the end of his kingdom.[53]

This is the quintessential reason why the final story introduces the Babylonian delegation: to ensure that the divine punishment meted out against Hezekiah is strictly measure-for-measure in accordance with justice elsewhere in the Hebrew Bible. Just as Hezekiah revealed to the Babylonians "all that is in my house; there is nothing among my treasuries

---

[52] 2 Kgs 18:3, 5–6. Josiah is similarly cast as a righteous king, but in his case there need not be any corresponding denigration of his character because the fate of the kingdom had already been decreed and its situation was without remedy. For the Deuteronomist, the fact that God had irrevocably ordained that Jerusalem would fall was not an issue; that he could do so in the aftermath of such a righteous king, on the other hand, was.

[53] This is not to negate, however, the possibility of an actual historical event underlying the tale. Based on 2 Kgs 20, it is generally presumed that Hezekiah and other countries in the west probably coordinated an alliance with Merodach-baladan II. According to Josephus, *Antiquities*, 10.30–31, Hezekiah was a "friend and ally" of Merodach-baladan. The disputed date of his mission to Hezekiah has been discussed previously, see chap. 3 n. 16. For another interpretation of this display, see Boyo G. Ockinga, "Hiskias 'Prahlerei.' Ein Beitrag zur Interpretation von 2 Könige 20, 12–19/Jesaja 39, 1–8," in M. Görg (ed.), *Fontes atque Pontes: Eine Festgabe für Hellmut Brunner* (ÄAT 5; Wiesbaden: O. Harrassowitz , 1983) 342–46. It is further afield, however, to speculate that Hezekiah's boil was due to bubonic plague and thus evidence of how the Assyrian army was defeated, as claimed by Margaret Barker, "Hezekiah's Boil," *JSOT* 95 (2001) 31–42. The promise of YHWH to deliver the city precedes the divine response to the king of Assyria (cf. 2 Kgs 20:6/Isa 38:6), and so Hezekiah's illness was in no way connected with the fate of Sennacherib's forces.

that I have not shown them" (2 Kgs 20:15/Isa 39:4), so the corresponding judgment becomes "all that is in your house and all that your fathers have laid up in store to this day will be carried to Babylon; nothing will be left" (2 Kgs 20:17/Isa 39:6).[54] This verdict is never realized in the book of Isaiah, but serves as strategic foreshadowing of the end of the book of Kings. The strict adherence to *lex talionis* ensures that the reader recognizes that the fate of the nation stems directly from the hand of God, even as it underscores the accuracy of fulfilled prophecy which plays a vital role in the literary structure of the Deuteronomistic History.[55]

If this proposal is sufficient to explain how the positioning of the embassy pericope serves the purposes of the Deuteronomistic editor, it simultaneously elucidates why its later appropriation by Isaian tradents only serves as a weak bridge into Second Isaiah: the placement there was

---

[54] The claim of Marc Zvi Brettler, "2 Kings 24:13–14 as History," *CBQ* 53 (1991) 549, that 2 Kgs 24:13–14 "are of no historical value for writing the history of the exiles of 597 or 587/6" in no way undermines this view. Further connections between the oracles of Isaiah and the Babylonian conquest are surveyed by Ronald E. Clements, "The Prophecies of Isaiah and the Fall of Jerusalem in 587 B.C.," *VT* 30/4 (1980) 421–36.

[55] As noted by Wildberger, *Isaiah 28–39*, 477. The Deuteronomistic History regularly notes fulfillment of the prophetic word via the rubric "in accordance with the word of YHWH, which (the prophet spoke)," cf. 1 Kgs 2:27; 12:15; 13:26; 14:18; 15:29; 16:12; 17:16; 22:38; 2 Kgs 2:22; 4:44; 7:16–18; 14:25; 23:15–17; 24:13. Such asseverations conform to the Deuteronomic test of true prophecy given in Deut 18:22. For this key aspect of Deuteronomistic historiography, see the seminal study of Gerhard von Rad, "The Deuteronomic Theology of History in I and II Kings," in idem (ed.), *The Problem of the Hexateuch and Other Essays* (trans. E. W. Trueman Dicken; Edinburgh: Oliver & Boyd, 1966) 205–21, as well as idem, *Studies in Deuteronomy* (SBT 9; London: SCM Press, 1953) 74–91.
　　See also the summarizing words of the editor of Kings concerning the activity of the prophets in the kingdom of Israel: "Yet YHWH warned Israel and Judah through all His prophets [and] every seer, saying, 'Turn from your evil ways and keep My commandments, My statutes according to all the law which I commanded your fathers and which I sent to you through My servants the prophets.' However, they did not listen" (2 Kgs 17:13–14). The direct connection between failure to obey the prophets and the destruction of the northern kingdom is reinforced in v 23: "until YHWH removed Israel from His sight, as He spoke through all His servants the prophets. So Israel was carried away into exile from their own land to Assyria until this day."
　　Such literary artistry is also evident in the J narrative of Gen 16, in which Abram and Sarai are responsible for mistreating Hagar the Egyptian. The act comes on the heels of God's warning that Abram's descendants would be enslaved (עָבַד) and oppressed (עִנּוּ) in a land not theirs (Gen 15:13, likely redactional). Just as the Israelites oppressed (וַתְּעַנֶּהָ, Gen 16:6) the Egyptian maidservant, so the Israelites themselves would be enslaved (עָבַד, Exod 1:13–14) and oppressed (עִנָּה, Exod 1:11–12) by the Egyptians. As in Kings, a key transgression by a leader among God's chosen people leads to consequences for the society as a whole, pronounced according to a standard of measure-for-measure and brought to fruition at the end of the respective book.

prompted principally due to the theme of exile, which otherwise has little connection to the subsequent oracles of Isaiah.

5.2.3. *The Secondary Nature of "The Fourteenth Year"*

According to the reconstruction proposed here, the book of Kings was the starting point for redacting the sources of the onslaught against Jerusalem and its deliverance together with the stories of Hezekiah's illness and the diplomatic visit by the Babylonians. The bridging of this material into a composite whole was achieved in part by the opening words of 2 Kgs 20, בַּיָּמִים הָהֵם, which serve to make the following pericope a smaller, con-current episode within the broader, preceding narrative of the blockade. Rather than disrupt the flow of the foregoing chapters by inserting the separate story of Hezekiah's illness into its purportedly proper temporal location, the editor instead chose to juxtapose the heterogeneous texts while marking their simultaneity.[56]

The seemingly anachronistic promise in v 6, "I will deliver you and this city from the hand of the king of Assyria," is hence chronologically correct. At the same time, because this verse functions to tie unequivocally 2 Kgs 20 with the previous material, it is suspect from a redactional standpoint. On the one hand, the divine deliverance of Jerusalem from Sennacherib is part of YHWH's promises made to Hezekiah because "I have heard your prayer" (v 5). Yet Hezekiah does not pray for the salvation of his city or his people in v 3, only for the sparing of his life in accordance with his righteous behavior. It is further troubling that Hezekiah would choose to focus on his own predicament if the tale were truly set during Sen-nacherib's advance on the city. The secondary nature of v 6 is affirmed by means of v 8, in which Hezekiah asks for confirmation of the Lord's vow, yet repeats only the assurances given in v 5: being healed and going up to the temple on the third day.[57] With the editorial addition in v 6 excised,

---

[56] This narrative technique is employed elsewhere in the Hebrew Bible for those cases in which stories overlap chronologically but must of necessity be related consecutively. A case in point is 2 Sam 3:6–21, set "during the war between the house of Saul and the house of David." This war has already been related to the reader in the preceding chapter. Its lengthy duration and the downfall of Saul's followers are declared outright in v 3:1, yet thereafter "Abner was making himself strong in the house of Saul." The texts are thus concurrent, not sequential.

[57] One could argue in light of the disparaging of Hezekiah's character in 2 Kgs 20:12–19 that the monarch's selfish nature is being insinuated here as well, but this interpretation is at odds with the manner in which he is treated by both prophet and deity. The possibility of editorial insertion is more reasonable at this juncture than implied polemic.

the story reads smoothly and shows itself to be truly independent of the surrounding material.

The grafting together of these texts was finalized via 2 Kgs 18:13, the introduction to the annalistic source A which has already been argued as original to the Deuteronomistic History. Because "the fourteenth year" in this verse neatly ties the promise that YHWH will "add fifteen years" (v 20:6) to the datum of Hezekiah's reign as being twenty-nine years, it has been conjectured that it originally served as the introduction to the story of the monarch's illness and recovery in chapter 20.[58] Apart from this numerical justification, the weight of evidence places this suggestion in doubt. The inclusion of this regnal year marks the beginning of the extended narrative relating Sennacherib's campaign against Judah, and there is no textual basis within verse 18:13 itself for asserting any sort of literary seam. Regnal years are furthermore not utilized in Kings for dating prophetic narratives, whereas incursions by foreign rulers typically entail such a chronological note.[59]

The suspect nature of the synchronism in verse 18:13 is widely known, as it cannot be reconciled with Hezekian chronology either in terms of his co-regency or sole rule. There is no need to question whether the length of reign for Hezekiah in 2 Kgs 18:2 has been updated as a result of verse 13, as the accuracy of the former datum has already been established in this book. As this unreliable synchronism signals the advent of the biblical version of the Assyrian campaign and also has a clear chronological connection to the "fifteen years" of the redactional verse 20:6, it points to "the fourteenth year" in 2 Kgs 18:13 as being another addition, an emendation made to a pre-existing synchronism at the time of editing the narratives

---

[58] Hayim Tadmor and Mordechai Cogan, "Hezekiah's Fourteenth Year: The King's Illness and the Babylonian Embassy," *Eretz-Israel* 16 (1982) 198–201 [Hebrew]; Manfred Hutter, *Hiskija König von Juda* (GrTS 6; Graz: Universität Graz, 1982) 67–69; Cogan and Tadmor, *II Kings*, 228, 260–63; Eberhard Ruprecht, "Die ursprüngliche Komposition der Hiskia-Jesaja-Erzählungen und ihre Umstrukturierung durch den Verfasser des deuteronomistischen Geschichtswerkes," *ZTK* 87 (1990) 33–52, 65–66.

It should be noted that such a rearrangement of the synchronic text produces even more problems, as YHWH would be promising to deliver the city from the king of Assyria (20:6 as currently numbered) prior to the beginning of the Jerusalem blockade. The current order of the chapters is preferred: when two narratives are intended to run concurrently, the one with the more extended timeframe is presented first so that the other may be more logically slotted into its temporal context.

[59] These protestations have been ably noted by Nadav Na'aman, "Hezekiah and the Kings of Assyria," *TA* 21 (1994) 237. It has already been observed that the prophetic narrative surrounding king Ahaz in Isa 7—often seen as the counterpart to the faithful depiction of Hezekiah in Isa 36–39—lacks such a synchronism as well.

together.[60] With the story of Hezekiah's illness and the judgment resulting from the king's hubris needing to be at the end of the Hezekian arc
for the ideological purposes of the Deuteronomistic editor, the original
chronological notice at 18:13 was changed to reflect that the timing for
the invasion was roughly coincident with Hezekiah's illness and the Babylonian embassy, reinforced by its redactional counterpart in v 20:6. The
"fourteenth year" in the former verse is hence an intentional change and
not a corruption, but neither does it have any historical value, being an
editorial notation for the expedient of continuity.[61]

At some point after the editing together of the composite textual block
of 2 Kgs 18:13–20:19, these conglomerate traditions were incorporated back
into the book of Isaiah. Several changes were made as a result, one of
which was likely the transposition of the pre-existing Hezekiah narratives
in Isaiah to their current location immediately preceding Second Isaiah.
The decree of exile by the prophet himself was eminently useful for the
redactors of the book, cementing the authority of the son of Amoz while
forming an apposite literary bridge to the following promises of return.
With the newly combined material at some literary remove from the story
of Ahaz in Isa 7, it would be left to modern exegetes to rediscover the
intentional linkages between these contrasting stories.

A second, widely recognized change was the excision of the annalistic
source A from Isa 36, such that the expedition of Sennacherib "against all
the fortified cities of Judah" in verse 1 is jarringly trailed by an exclusive
focus on Jerusalem and the showdown between Hezekiah and the *rab
šāqê*.[62] The usual justification for this omission is on ideological grounds,

---

[60] Here I differ subtly from Na'aman, whose arguments aim to demonstrate that "2 Kgs
18:13 is an integral part of the description in 2 Kgs. 18:13 ff." ("Hezekiah and the Kings of
Assyria," 237). While the inclusion of the chronological notice itself may rightly be argued
as original, his evidence points to the fourteenth year within that selfsame notice as being
from the hand of an editor rather than an author.

[61] This conclusion serves as a rejoinder to the justification of J. J. M. Roberts for the
priority of 2 Kgs 18:13 given in "Egypt, Assyria, Isaiah, and the Ashdod Affair: An Alternative
Proposal," in Vaughn and Killebrew (eds.), *Jerusalem in Bible and Archaeology*, 270–71 n. 20.
The possibly of appealing to a co-regency in order to explain these numbers has likewise
been investigated in my opening chapter, and found wanting.

[62] Naturally this literary justification is not without its share of detractors, who prefer
to make their case via appeal to textual criticism. In this instance, it is the longer form of
Hezekiah's name (חִזְקִיָּהוּ) which appears in Isa 36:1, just as in the successive prophetic
stories. The majority of the Kennicott manuscripts for 2 Kgs 18:13, as found in Benjaminus Kennicott, *Vetus Testamentum Hebraicum: cum variis lectionibus* (2 vols.; Oxonii:
e typographeo Clarendoniano, 1776–80) 1.672, likewise reflect this longer form, as opposed
to the shorter reading חִזְקִיָּה in vv 14–16. For the priority of Isaiah based on this reading,

with the portrayal of Hezekiah as a submissive vassal being thought by the editors as too damaging to his royal image. It is also equally plausible, and perhaps more compelling, to posit that the withdrawal of Sennacherib due to Hezekiah's own initiative detracted from the grandeur of Yhwh's distinct resolutions to the crisis within the respective prophetic sources, each response foretold by the prophet Isaiah and therefore more affirming of prophetic authority.

Other minor editorial changes would have been made at this juncture, or as the result of the independent growth of the respective material. Hezekiah's prayer in Isa 38:9–22 is a pertinent case in point: was it incorporated into the text by a later scribal tradent who felt it necessary to emphasize the piety of Hezekiah through prayer, or did the editors of Isa 36–39 deem it necessary to make this material from Kings more suitable to their purposes before it could be subsumed into the book of Isaiah?[63] Once both books were transmitted within scribal circles, cross-pollination between the texts would always have been possible, such as the gloss in 2 Kgs 20:11, described as an "assimilation to the Isaiah text."[64] It is this very aspect of textual growth which has yielded the seeming impasse with regard to the priority of this material. Due to the long process of

---

see Stig Norin, "An Important Kennicott Reading in 2 Kings xviii 13," *VT* 32/3 (1982) 337–38, with corresponding rebuttal by Gonçalves, *L'expédition de Sennacherib,* 355 n. 2, 356–57.

[63] The latter possibility is favored by Konkel, "Sources of the Story of Hezekiah," 482, "Comparison of the differences of the pre-masoretic text of Kings, especially as seen in *kaige*, shows us how the story of Hezekiah has been theologically adapted for its inclusion in Isaiah. An examination of the major modifications of Isa. xxxvii indicates that the addition of the poem and the abbreviation and alteration of the Hezekiah story were part of the same process with the same theological goals."

Prayers have long been viewed as later additions to biblical books for the purpose of idealizing their characters, as may be demonstrated in the prayers of Daniel's friends in the fiery furnace, or those of Mordechai and Esther in the Greek additions to Esther. On these specific prayers, see respectively John J. Collins, *Daniel* (Hermeneia; Minneapolis: Fortress, 1993) 195–207, and Carey A. Moore, *Daniel, Esther and Jeremiah: The Additions* (AYB 44; Garden City, N.Y.: Doubleday, 1977) 39–76, 153ff, 203–15. The prayers of Hannah (1 Sam 2:1–10) and Jonah (Jon 2:1–9) are also widely held to be later additions, but in the case of Jonah the situation is of greater literary complexity, see Jonathan Magonet, "Jonah, Book of," *AYBD* 3.939–40. For a more extensive survey of prayer in both the pre-exilic and Second Temple period, consult Judith H. Newman, *Praying by the Book: The Scripturalization of Prayer in Second Temple Judaism* (SBLEJL 14; Atlanta: Scholars Press, 1999).

[64] Williamson, *Book Called Isaiah,* 207. Its counterpart is in Isa 38:8. For a synoptic comparison of the variants between 2 Kgs 18:13–20:19 and Isa 36–39, see Wildberger, *Isaiah 28–39,* 481–93. Here the comment of Childs, *Isaiah,* 262, is apt: "However, what now seems evident is that from an original nucleus the tradition was shaped in different ways by the editors of both Kings and Isaiah. In the present parallel form one can see redactional elements from both of these tradents. The shaping process thus moved in both directions."

transmission of each book, the underlying *Urtext* can only be hypothetically reconstructed.[65]

5.3. CONCLUSION

The relationship between 2 Kgs 18:13–20:19 and Isa 36–39 is a beguiling compositional question, and the procedure employed in this chapter has been to try and ascertain the appropriate literary context for each respective block of material. The brief, annalistic source A of 2 Kgs 18:13–16 is at once at home in the book of Kings, sharing its synchronisms and terminology. It may have been excised from the book of Isaiah due to its human resolution to the Assyrian crisis which detracted from the efficacy of the prophetic word and the sovereign power of YHWH. A new delineation of the prophetic B_1 and B_2 sources has been proposed based on the inconsistencies that assail that currently predominant theory. While lacking the prosaic tone of the annalistic report, they nonetheless have historical value and appear to have been preserved and disseminated by circles close to the prophet Isaiah.

The stories of Hezekiah's illness and the visit of the Babylonian embassage have been argued as having their origin in the book of Kings, owing to the measure-for-measure punishment which undergirds the prophecy-fulfillment schema throughout the Deuteronomistic History, as well as the disparagement of the character of Hezekiah necessary to account for the Babylonian conquest. The original synchronism in 2 Kgs 18:13 was emended and verse 20:6 was inserted in order to bring these latter tales into chronological intersection with the rest of the Sennacherib invasion arc. The resulting amalgamation of 2 Kgs 18:17–20:19 was pressed into service as the proem to Second Isaiah owing to the son of Amoz having foretold of the exile.

The biblical traditions of Sennacherib's third campaign to Judah imbued the regent with qualities beyond those previously ascribed to YHWH's anointed rulers. The prophecies of Isaiah also played a pivotal role in transforming Hezekiah in the eyes of his subjects, and are the focus of the next chapter.

---

[65] Wildberger, *Isaiah 28–39*, 361–63, favors the textual priority of Isaiah, countering the stance of Gesenius, *Der Prophet Jesaia*, 2.932–36, taken on the originality of the text of Kings. More recent studies such as Konkel, "Sources of the Story of Hezekiah," rightly incorporate into their textual criticism the pre-Masoretic text of Kings.

CHAPTER SIX

THE MESSIANIC ORACLES IN FIRST ISAIAH

Building upon the royal ideology evidenced in the psalms and in the Deuteronomistic History, there are prophecies preserved in First Isaiah which reflect the hope and expectation for a righteous ruler. The intent of this chapter is to determine whether any of the oracles in First Isaiah that may be traced with some certitude back to Isaiah ben Amoz were proclaimed with Hezekiah in mind. A select core of these prophecies came to form an integral part of the foundation for later messianic expectation, and as such have been the subject of perennial studies. Rather than analyze these oracles in their canonical order, exposition shall instead proceed with content that is more widely accepted in its attribution to the Judean king.

The first oracle to be examined will be that of Isa 8:23–9:6, with its famed climactic announcement that "a child will be born to us." The most formidable issue confronting any exegete dealing with this passage is the proper rendering of the aspect of the verbs. The interpretation of the passage is also greatly dependent on verse 23, which turns on the function of the words הָרִאשׁוֹן and הָאַחֲרוֹן and the verbs used in conjunction with them. Another issue of crucial importance for the purpose of exegesis is whether Isa 9:5–6 reflects a birth announcement or a proclamation of enthronement. Guided by the results of these inquiries, the historical context of the prophecy may be brought to light.

Secondly, Isa 11:1–9 contains a depiction of an ideal future ruler, which by the time of the Dead Sea Scrolls had become a fundamental prooftext for messianic expectation. Its Isaianic authenticity is widely disputed due to its consistent use of future tense verbs, idyllic presentation, and the presumption that the "stump" of Jesse refers to a Davidic line that had already been cut off. Other scholars have argued for Josiah as the intended referent, taking the stump as an allusion to the assassination of his father Amon. It is hoped that some progress may be made with regard to isolating its applicability to Hezekiah.

The final oracle under scrutiny will be the sign of Immanuel given to Ahaz in Isa 7:10–17. The promised child born to the עַלְמָה during the Syro-Ephraimitic crisis has often been associated with Hezekiah due to Ahaz as the chosen recipient of the oracle, while some consider the infant to be one of Isaiah's own children. The likelihood of these possibilities will be surveyed in an attempt to ascertain the identity of Immanuel himself.

6.1. Isa 8:23–9:6

6.1.1. *Overview*

The consensus of modern scholarly exegesis relating to Isa 8:23–9:6 has swung back and forth as if on a pendulum.[1] Traditionally, this prediction of the end of Assyrian oppression, followed by the seeming announcement of the birth of a royal child, was deemed to be authentically Isaian with a messianic intent, but at the turn of the last century interpretation pushed the date of the passage into the post-exilic period. By the middle of the twentieth century, the predominant opinion had shifted back to that of an accession oracle for a Judean king stemming from the prophet Isaiah himself, with the promised ruler widely viewed to be king Hezekiah. More recently, redaction criticism has raised the possibility that the prophecy stems from the time of Josiah and in fact refers to him.[2]

The purpose of this section is to focus on one particular aspect of Isa 8:23–9:6: to determine whether or not Hezekiah is intended as the individual highlighted at the culmination of the prophecy. The extent to which this text has been analyzed in biblical studies is considerable, and there is little need to attempt another end-to-end exegesis which could only revisit what has been said many times over in previous studies. Instead, this exposition will concentrate on those exegetical insights which are felt both to contribute something new to the discussion, and to aid in moving scholarship forward in resolving the question at issue.

6.1.2. *Literary Extent and Structure*

In the examination of a biblical text, the first step methodologically is to assess the extents of the literary unit. In this case, Isa 9:6 clearly serves as the end of the passage, which may be verified by its closing, almost

---

[1] In English Bibles, this passage is assigned to Isa 9:1–7. For ease of citation, all references to these verses in the subsequent discussion will be exclusively based on the Hebrew.

[2] For a review of critical scholarship of the passage, see Antti Laato, *Who Is Immanuel? The Rise and the Foundering of Isaiah's Messianic Expectations* (Åbo: Åbo Academy Press, 1988) 173–96; Paul D. Wegner, *An Examination of Kingship and Messianic Expectation in Isaiah 1–35* (Lewiston, N.Y.: Edwin Mellen, 1992) 139–40.

liturgical formula, and the new word from YHWH (דְּבַר) introduced in the subsequent verse. The Masoretic closing paragraph marker סתומה after verse 6 concurs with this analysis. The beginning of the oracle is more contested, but there are strong poetic connections with verses from the preceding chapter. The עַם הַהֹלְכִים בַּחֹשֶׁךְ in Isa 9:2 are the same people אֲפֵלָה מְנֻדָּח "driven away into darkness" in v 8:22, and despite their differing forms, the conceptions of gloom and anguish are clearly shared between vv 22–23.[3] These latter two verses are, in turn, of a piece with vv 19–21, all centered on a hypothetical disputation with Isaiah and his sons (אֲלֵיכֶם, v 19) over the efficacy of mediums and sorcerers rather than YHWH and his prophetic signs. As the prophet and his house are the subject of vv 16–18, the entirety of the oracle properly spans Isa 8:16–9:6.[4]

The vision thus begins with Isaiah's faithful response to "wait for YHWH" (v 17), followed by the Lord's admonition of those who would place their trust in other divinatory methods. God assures that they will be נִקְשֶׁה וְרָעֵב "hard-pressed and famished" (v 21), facing צָרָה וַחֲשֵׁכָה "distress and darkness" (v 22). The interpretation of Isa 8:23 hinges on the function of the words הָרִאשׁוֹן and הָאַחֲרוֹן and their respective verbs. In the Hebrew Bible, when רִאשׁוֹן and אַחֲרוֹן are used together, their purpose is to produce:

(1) a temporal sequence: 'first X ... then Y'[5]
(2) a temporal contrast: 'the latter will be different than the former'[6]
(3) entirety, completeness[7]

---

[3] Cf. מָעוֹף צוּקָה in v 22; לָאֲשֶׁר מוּצָק לָהּ in v 23. Note that by linking Isa 8:22 with 9:1, there is no need to become embroiled in the tedious debate over the inclusion of v 8:23, see Albrecht Alt, "Jesaja 8, 23–9, 6. Befreiungsmacht und Krönungstag," in W. Baumgartner (ed.), *Festschrift Alfred Bertholet zum 80. Geburtstag gewidmet* (Tübingen: Mohr/Siebeck, 1950) 29–49; A. S. van der Woude, "Jesaja 8, 19–23a als literarische Einheit," in J. van Ruiten and M. Vervenne (eds.), *Studies in the Book of Isaiah: Festschrift Willem A. M. Beuken* (BETL 132; Leuven: Leuven University Press, 1997) 129–36.

[4] As recognized by Edward J. Kissane, *The Book of Isaiah* (2 vols.; Dublin: Brown and Nolan, 1941–43) 1.104–107; Marvin A. Sweeney, *Isaiah 1–39 with An Introduction to Prophetic Literature* (FOTL 16; Grand Rapids: Eerdmans, 1996) 175–88.

[5] Deut 13:10; 17:7; 1 Kgs 17:13; Jer 50:17. See further Patrick D. Miller, "Meter, Parallelism, and Tropes: The Search for Poetic Style," *JSOT* 28 (1984) 106. Some English translations of Jer 50:17 relate רִאשׁוֹן and אַחֲרוֹן to the respective foreign kings, cf. NAS and NIV. But KJV, (N)RSV, JPS perceive correctly that the emphasis is not on the kings themselves, but rather on a temporal sequence of escalating events. As noted by Jack R. Lundbom, *Jeremiah 37–52* (AYB 21C; New York: Doubleday, 2004) 396, "Envisioned here is progressive destruction: Assyria consumed the flesh, and Babylon gnawed the bones."

[6] Hag 2:9; Ruth 3:10; Dan 11:29.

[7] Isa 41:4; 44:6; 48:12; Eccl 1:11; Neh 8:18, all occurrences in Chronicles.

Because the two words are constrained to these distinct meanings when appearing in the same context, such referents for רִאשׁוֹן and אַחֲרוֹן as two Israelite kings,[8] two Assyrian kings,[9] or the collective northern kingdom are precluded.[10] Based on the attested occurrences of רִאשׁוֹן and אַחֲרוֹן, their utilization to express totality is exclusively exilic or post-exilic. Since scholarship overwhelmingly concurs that this passage is pre-exilic, the linguistic data favor a temporal interpretation for these words. The time-based nature of the passage is further supported by the explicit inclusion of עֵת.[11]

Are רִאשׁוֹן and אַחֲרוֹן intended to convey a temporal sequence or contrast? The verbs הֵקַל and הִכְבִּיד, if the consonantal text be accepted, are intuitively antithetical in meaning.[12] Appealing to comparative evidence, in every other verse in the Hebrew Bible in which the roots קלל and כבד

---

[8] H. L. Ginsberg, "An Unrecognized Allusion to Kings Pekah and Hoshea of Israel," *Eretz-Israel* 5 (1958) 61*–65*; Stuart A. Irvine, *Isaiah, Ahaz, and the Syro-Ephraimitic Crisis* (SBLDS 123; Atlanta: Scholars Press, 1990) 222–25.

[9] Godfrey Rolles Driver, "Isaianic Problems," in G. Wiessner (ed.), *Festschrift für Wilhelm Eilers* (Wiesbaden: Otto Harrasowitz, 1967) 46–49.

[10] J. A. Emerton, "Some Linguistic and Historical Problems in Isaiah VIII. 23," *JSS* 14 (1969) 158–60.

[11] It has been observed by Ginsberg, "An Unrecognized Allusion"; Emerton, "Problems in Isaiah VIII. 23" and others that עֵת is a feminine noun while the following adjectives are masculine, and this grammatical inconsistency has led to their respective proposals for רִאשׁוֹן and אַחֲרוֹן as referents to various people as noted above. However, עֵת is attested in the plural with both masculine endings (עִתִּים, common) and feminine (עִתּוֹת, cf. Ps 9:10[9]; 10:1; 31:16[15]). In the Lachish Letters, the masculine form of עֵת appears: ירא את אדני את העת הזה שלם יהוה, literally "May YHWH cause my lord to see well-being at this time" (letter 6, line 1). Such examples suggest that עֵת is to be classified as one of the Hebrew nouns that is not of fixed gender (cf. GKC §122d, l, o).

[12] C. F. Whitley, "The Language and Exegesis of Isaiah 8 16–23," *ZAW* 90 (1978) 34–37, prefers to read the adjectives רִאשׁוֹן and אַחֲרוֹן as feminine in gender. He emends כָּעֵת הָרִאשׁוֹן הֵקַל to כָּעֵת רִאשׁוֹנָה קַל, and asserts dittography in the case of the needed *heh* after הָאַחֲרוֹן. He thus renders "at the former time he hastened," appealing to LXX ταχὺ ποίει and Peshitta ܐܣܬܪܗܒ. Both textual witnesses, however, seem to be making sense of MT, rendering a causative: "cause/make haste."

Although Whitley's suggestion might at first appear to make better sense of the locative endings in the verse (אַרְצָה), there are other possibilities to account for this situation. The affix *heh* could be possessive (אַרְצָה, "her land") referring to the feminine subject לָהּ as vocalized in MT, or else evidence of the old accusative case ending, artifacts from the proto-Semitic system which may still be seen vestigially in Biblical Hebrew, see Bruce K. Waltke and M. O'Connor, *An Introduction to Biblical Hebrew Syntax* (Winona Lake, Ind.: Eisenbrauns, 1990) 127–28.

Alternatively, the final *heh* could be a misplaced definite article belonging to the respective following proper nouns. There are several instances in the Hebrew Bible of the phrase "land of PN" in which the toponym occurs both with and without the definite article, cf. the typical אֶרֶץ הַגִּלְעָד, also attested as אֶרֶץ גִּלְעָד (Num 32:1; 1 Kgs 4:19; Zech 10:10; 1 Chr 5:9) and the common אֶרֶץ גֹּשֶׁן, occurring once as אֶרֶץ הַגֹּשֶׁן (Josh 11:16).

appear, they serve to contrast rather than complement each other.[13] These
verbs correspond, respectively, to the dichotomous themes of darkness
and light in the two halves of the prophecy, and serve to corroborate its
literary extent ascertained previously. The antithesis between הֵקַל "to
belittle, treat with contempt" and הִכְבִּיד "to honor" is therefore to be
expected.

According to this understanding, the verse depicts a temporal contrast:
a prior situation of despair is being reversed, presumably by the Lord
himself.[14] Of necessity, the subject cannot be a single Assyrian king conducting two successive invasions.[15] Such an interpretation falters in any
case due to the fact that no foreign monarch is mentioned anywhere in
the surrounding context. Isa 8:23 thus serves as the crucial bridge between
the two halves of the Isaianic oracle, and is the proper introduction to the
hopeful material which follows. The optimistic stance taken toward the
northern kingdom begins precisely here, and Isa 9:3–4 similarly presume
YHWH as the subject.

Having identified the extent of the poetic unit, a determination of its
structure is the next logical step. In the interests of space, I shall restrict
myself to the second half of the oracle which contains our focal text. With
Isa 8:23 serving as the superscription to the prophecy, the subsequent six
verses justify the statement that the condition of the land of Zebulun and
Naphtali is no longer bleak. Isa 9:1–2 relate directly to the inhabitants of
the land, vv 3–4 to the end of foreign oppression and vv 5–6 to a royal
child. Verses 3–5 all begin with כִּי clauses, which elaborate reasons for the
rejoicing of the nation.[16] A light has shone upon the people and they are

---

[13] 1 Sam 2:30; 2 Sam 6:22; 1 Kgs 12:4, 10; Isa 23:9; 2 Chr 10:4, 10. As noted by Paul D.
Wegner, "What's New in Isaiah 9:1–7?" in D. G. Firth and H. G. M. Williamson (eds.), *Interpreting Isaiah. Issues and Approaches* (Downers Grove, Ill.: InterVarsity Press, 2009) 240,
"The *hiphil* forms of *qālal* are consistently used as 'to treat with contempt' when referring
to countries or people. Thus the rendering 'to treat leniently' for verse 8:23b, as some scholars have suggested, is extremely unlikely."

[14] It should be noted that part of the difficulty for scholars in making this determination has been the delineation between Isa 8:23 and the preceding material.

[15] The position of Whitley, "The Language and Exegesis of Isaiah 8 16–23."

[16] I prefer to see the first and second clauses as interrelated based on their subject matter, although the latter is not grammatically dependent on the former. It is the contention
of John D. W. Watts, *Isaiah 1–33* (WBC 24; Waco, Texas: Word Books, 1985) 128–38, that
the three כִּי particles in vv 3–5 are to be rendered as "if," connoting "contingencies that
must be met for the announcement to be true." Understood in this manner, the passage no
longer comprises a promise. With little justification, Watts approaches the book of Isaiah
as a drama in which YHWH and his "aides" heaven and earth are the principal characters.
He reads Isa 8:23–9:6 not as stemming from the mouth of the prophet, but from a range

to rejoice, because their subjugation is at an end and a new, Davidic ruler will reign over them in peace.

6.1.3. *Tense/Aspect Analysis*

The most formidable issue confronting any exegete dealing with this passage is the proper rendering of the aspect of the verbs.[17] The text is predominantly written using perfective aspect,[18] interspersed with two *yiqtol* forms, two *wayyiqtol* forms and a single *wᵉqatal*.[19] Those scholars who prefer to translate the passage in the future appeal to the nebulous grammatical term known as the 'prophetic perfect', defined as future action depicted as though it has already transpired.[20] The two *yiqtol* forms and the sole *wᵉqatal* are used to undergird this interpretation. Even if the prophecy is attributed to Isaiah ben Amoz, it is argued, he nevertheless was anticipating a future ruler.[21] Closer examination of the text itself gives pause to readily accepting this impending timeframe. The two *wayyiqtol* verbs in the pivotal verse 9:5 leave no doubt that the child has already been born and provided with a name, in agreement with the preceding passive *qal*

---

of bystanders and officials who take turns speaking as if in an oratorio. The doubts that may be cast upon this approach are similar to those voiced in reviews of Klaus Baltzer, *Deutero-Isaiah: A Commentary on Isaiah 40–55* (trans. M. Kohl; Hermeneia; Minneapolis: Fortress Press, 2001), who reads Second Isaiah as a liturgical drama in six acts.

[17] Although my preference is to treat the Hebrew verbal system as primarily aspectual rather than based on tense, I will occasionally retain the tense-based labels of "past" and "future" for the sake of clarity. The problems inherent in a clear division between these choices is highlighted most notably in Leslie McFall, *Enigma of the Hebrew Verbal System: Solutions from Ewald to the Present Day* (Sheffield: Almond Press, 1982).

[18] Ten occurrences: Isa 8:23 (2x); 9:1 (2x); 9:2 (3x); 9:3 (1x); 9:5 (2x).

[19] *yiqtol*: יָגִילוּ (9:2) and תַּעְשֶׂה (9:6); *wayyiqtol*: וַיִּקְרָא and וַתְּהִי (9:5); *wᵉqatal*: וְהָיְתָה (9:4).

[20] GKC §106m–o; JM §112g–h. It is generally accepted that "prophetic perfect" is a misnomer since examples may be cited in other genres, and the need for such terminology reflects the weakness of a tense-based approach to the Hebrew verbal system. A recent study with updated bibliography is that of Max Rogland, *Alleged Non-Past Uses of* Qatal *in Classical Hebrew* (Assen: Royal Van Gorcum, 2003). For those who render this passage via prophetic perfects, see GKC and JM (cited above); Samuel Rolles Driver, *A Treatise on the Use of the Tenses in Hebrew and Some Other Syntactical Questions* (4th ed.; Grand Rapids: Eerdmans, 1998) 4; John Skinner, *The Book of the Prophet Isaiah Chapters I–XXXIX* (2nd ed.; Cambridge: Cambridge University Press, 1915) 81, 83; Frank M. Cross, *Canaanite Myth and Hebrew Epic* (Cambridge, Mass.: Harvard University Press, 1973) 263; G. L. Klein, "The 'Prophetic Perfect'," *JNSL* 16 (1990) 52–53.

[21] Otto Eissfeldt, *Einleitung in das Alte Testament* (3rd ed.; Tübingen: J.C.B. Mohr, 1964) 428–29. Eissfeldt is skeptical of its authenticity, however, deeming it non-genuine ("Unechtheit").

יָלַד and *nifal* נִתַּן.[22] One could further appeal to the subsequent descriptions of his kingdom, which are said to be in force מֵעַתָּה וְעַד־עוֹלָם.[23]

Additional weight may be brought to bear by examination of other textual witnesses. Among the ancient translations, LXX, the Great Isaiah Scroll (1QIsaᵃ), Syriac, and Vulgate all faithfully render this oracle in the past tense.[24] Notable in this regard are the scribal traditions of LXX Isaiah and 1QIsaᵃ, which did not hesitate to switch the tense/aspect of perfect verbs when it was felt to suit the context.[25] Neither translation alters the tense of a single verb in this passage.[26] The prophetic perfect is itself an infrequent, even debated phenomenon, and such a tight cluster of perfect verbs with future meaning is unprecedented in the Hebrew Bible.[27]

---

[22] Most critical editions emend וַיִּקְרָא to the *nif'al* וַיִּקָּרֵא with LXX, Syriac, and Vulgate, which makes more sense contextually. 1QIsaᵃ 9:5 reads וקרא, which should not be mistaken for an inverted perfect owing to the unemended *wayyiqtol* form ותהי immediately preceding. The *wayyiqtol* form was perfectly acceptable within the scribal practice of the Qumran community, and therefore this reading, if not original, may reflect the adaptation of a seemingly irregular form to the context, as discussed in Emanuel Tov, *Textual Criticism of the Hebrew Bible* (2nd ed.; Minneapolis: Fortress Press, 1992) 107–111. In this case, there is no one expressly stated within the prophecy to name the child, and hence the impersonal form וְקָרָא־שְׁמוֹ was adopted instead, see Gen 11:9; 19:22; 25:30; 27:36; 29:34; 50:11 (Gen 31:48; 33:17 are ambiguous); Exod 15:23; Josh 7:26 Judg 15:19; 2 Sam 5:20 (cf. 1 Chr 14:11).

[23] Caution must be exercised here, however, for although the adverb עַתָּה ubiquitously means "now," it may also refer to an impending occasion. The expression מֵעַתָּה וְעַד־עוֹלָם is typically anchored in the present day of the speaker, cf. Isa 59:21; Ps 113:2; 115:18; 121:8; 125:2; 131:3. Note however Mic 4:6–7, in which the time reference is clearly established as the future: בַּיּוֹם הַהוּא. For the usage of עַתָּה as specifying a later time, see H. A. Brongers, "Bemerkungen zum Gebrauch der adverbialen wᵉʿattāh im Alten Testament," *VT* 15/3 (1965) 289–99; André Laurentin, "Weʿattâh—kai nun: Formule caractéristique des textes juridiques et liturgiques (à propos de Jean 17,5)," *Bib* 45 (1964) 168–97, 413–32. Compare Ugaritic *l ht w ʿlmh* "from now and forever," CTU 1.19 iv 5. The time reference of מֵעַתָּה וְעַד־עוֹלָם is thus contingent on its context, and so a general rendering of "perpetually" more accurately conveys its meaning.

[24] Even Targum Jonathan to the Prophets, which introduces messianic expectation into the prophecy by the addition of the word מְשִׁיחָא, nevertheless consistently renders v 5 in the perfect. See further Samson H. Levey, *The Messiah: An Aramaic Interpretation— The Messianic Exegesis of the Targum* (MHUC 2; Cincinnati: Hebrew Union College, 1974) 45–46, 142–44.

[25] LXX: Isa 10:28 (ἥξει for MT בָּא); 43:14 (ἀποστελῶ for MT שִׁלַּחְתִּי); 52:10 (ἀποκαλύψει for MT חָשַׂף). 1QIsaᵃ: Isa 2:11 (תשפלנה for MT שָׁפֵל); 11:9 (תמלאה for MT מָלְאָה).

[26] As mentioned, the reading וקרא in 1QIsaᵃ 9:5 does not constitute a change in tense.

[27] See Klein, "'Prophetic Perfect'," who attempts to catalog all of the incontrovertible cases of the prophetic perfect in MT. Rogland, *Alleged Non-Past Uses of* Qatal, 53–114, 131–34, favors explaining most cases of the prophetic perfect in terms of temporal deixis; that is, "regardless of clause type, qatal is to be understood as a relative past tense" (p. 132).

The nation has already begun to rejoice (שָׂמְחוּ לְפָנֶיךָ, v 2), and the following כִּי clauses give grounds for this celebration.[28] The first two reasons relate to the utter destruction of the reigning world superpower. A plain reading of the text shows that this final end is merely decreed, judging from the *wᵉqatal* form וְהָיְתָה in v 4. The *qatala* form הַחִתֹּתָ in v 3 refers to the same unfulfilled situation, and may be classified as a perfective serving a rhetorical function.[29] This may be compared to שָׁבַרְתִּי אֶת־עֹל מֶלֶךְ בָּבֶל in Jer 28:2, which in fact had not yet transpired as seen in vv 4, 11. The similarity in form and content between Isa 9:3–4 and 10:24–27, coupled with their consistent adoption of verbal forms, provides a compelling argument for taking the annihilation of the Assyrian juggernaut as a future prediction.[30]

Isa 9:5–6 represents a third, climactic justification for the rejoicing of the nation; namely, an apparent depiction of the birth of a king which has already transpired (יֻלַּד). Representing the consummation of the passage, this is the true focal point of the oracle, evidence that the people walking in darkness have already רָאוּ אוֹר גָּדוֹל "seen a great light" (v 1).[31] The plain future sense of תַּעֲשֶׂה־זֹּאת in the verse 6 applies strictly to the conditions of the kingdom, and not to the passage as a whole.

6.1.4. *Translation*

An investigation of the passage yields the following translation:

> (23)But there is no more gloom for him[32] who is in anguish.
> Though formerly He treated with contempt
> the land of Zebulun and the land of Naphtali,
> lately He has glorified the Way of the Sea,
> beyond the Jordan, Galilee of the nations.

---

[28] Hebrew יָגִילוּ in this verse is properly a continuing habitual action, note the preceding כַּאֲשֶׁר which makes it a typical example of something. This is a fine example of the aspectual nature of the verbal system.

[29] See Rogland, *Alleged Non-Past Uses of* Qatal, 92–113.

[30] Note the "complete destruction" (כָּלָה וְנֶחֱרָצָה) ordained in Isa 10:23, preceding the לָכֵן of v 24. The עֹשֶׂה in v 23 is incipient usage of the participle. The five *wᵉqatal* forms in Isa 10:25–27 are inverted perfects, which suggests that the sole *wᵉqatal* form in our passage, וְהָיְתָה in v 4, should be treated similarly. There is no basis for seeing the events of 701 B.C.E. in these two texts, since the "removal of the yoke" in both passages is not consonant with the historical situation following Sennacherib's third campaign.

[31] These data argue against reading הִכְבִּיד in verse 8:23 as anything other than a simple perfect.

[32] Repointed as לֹה on the basis of the pronominal suffixes in v 3.

(1)The people who walk in darkness see a great light;
upon those who dwell in a land of darkness a light shines forth.
(2)You magnify that nation, You increase [its] joy;[33]
they rejoice before You as with the jubilation of harvest time.[34]
as they exult when they are dividing the spoil.
(3)For the yoke of its burden, the bar across its shoulders,
the rod of its oppressor, You have broken as on the day of Midian,
(4)For every boot[35] tramping noisily and [each] cloak rolled in blood
shall be burnt, fuel for the flames.
(5)For a child has been born to us, a son has been given to us,
and dominion is upon his shoulders. And his name is called:[36]
Wonderful Counselor, Mighty God, Eternal Father, Prince of Peace.
(6)There shall be no end to the increase of [his] dominion and peace,
over the throne of David and over his kingdom
to make it steadfast and sustain it with justice and righteousness
henceforth, forever. The zeal of YHWH of hosts will do this.

6.1.5. *Function of Isa 9:5–6*

Among the various issues within the text evoking scholarly debate, of crucial importance for the purpose of exegesis is whether Isa 9:5–6 reflect a
birth announcement or proclamation of accession to the throne.[37] The
analysis of tenses proposed here already speak against the likelihood of a
birth announcement, as the parturition has transpired previously.[38] A key
purpose of a birth announcement throughout the Bible is to signal to the
recipient the accuracy of the divine message prior to its fulfillment, yet
the words of Isaiah expressed after the fact cannot not fulfill this function.
Hebrew ויקרא שמו in v 5 also conveys perspicuously that the following
appellations are names directly bestowed upon the individual, with no

---

[33] Following *qere* הַגּוֹי לֹו. On the restoration of this verse, see J. de Waard, *A Handbook on Isaiah* (TCT 1; Winona Lake, Ind.: Eisenbrauns, 1997) 42–43.

[34] The English tense selected in vv 1–2 is driven by the sense cf שִׂמְחוּ here.

[35] MT סְאוֹן in modern exegesis is considered cognate with Akkadian *šēnu*, "footgear," which fits better contextually than שָׁאוֹן "noise, din" as rendered by Jerome, Rashi, and the Peshitta.

[36] Repointing MT as וַיִּקְרָא, equivalent to reading iterative וקרא with 1QIsaᵃ.

[37] For the former position, see, among others, Simon B. Parker, "The Birth Announce-ment," in L. Eslinger and G. Taylor (eds.), *Ascribe to the Lord: Biblical and Other Studies in Memory of Peter C. Craigie* (JSOTSup 67; Sheffield: JSOT Press, 1988) 133–49; Laato, *Who Is Immanuel?*, 173–96; Paul D. Wegner, "A Re-examination of Isaiah IX 1–6," *VT* 42/1 (1992) 103–112.

[38] As delineated by Wegner, "Re-examination of Isaiah IX 1–6," 108, a full birth announce-ment oracle contains a declaration which precedes the upcoming childbirth, cf. Gen 16:11; 17:19; Judg 13:3; Isa 7:14; Luke 1:13, 31.

explanation of their origin as contained in formal birth oracles.[39] Regardless of the identification of the antecedent of לָנוּ in v 5, the acknowledgment via two passive verbs that a son has "been born" (יֻלַּד) and "been
given" (נִתַּן) to this party suggests that it is not the progenitor of the child.[40]
The social scope of the prophecy in any event far exceeds a parental cou-
ple as the intended audience. The sonship spoken of is thus not literal,
which obviates any need to entertain further the interpretation of the
oracle as a birth announcement.

The combination of a metaphorical birth coupled with the extravagant
titles speaks more readily to an enthronement ritual.[41] As in Ps 2:6–12,

---

[39] Cf. Gen 16:11; Isa 7:4–9, 14, noting the כִּי clause in the former. In the story of the birth
of Samson heralded by the angel of God in Judg 13, however, the name of the child is with-
held from the announcement and thus no explanation of its meaning is to be expected.
The consistency throughout forms a stark contrast with the current passage.

[40] The antecedent of the preposition לָנוּ is debated. Analysis of the prophetic corpus
yields that when the first person plural is used in the mouth of the prophet, it almost
invariably refers back to a group addressed earlier within the oracle itself. Confining ourselves to first-person verbs in First Isaiah, such use may be found in Isa 1:9 (cf. 1:2–5, 7); 1:18
(cf. v 10); 2:3, 5; 4:1; 5:18–19; 7:5–6; 9:9[10] (cf. vv 7–8[8–9]); 20:6; 22:13 (cf. vv 8–10); 25:9 (cf.
25:6–8); 26:8, 13, 17–18 (cf. 26:1); 28:15 (cf. v 14); 30:16 (cf. vv 6–7). This evidence is consonant
with the position of Alt, who sees the entirety of the passage as addressed to the northern
kingdom (הָעָם in v 1).
  However, there are also ambiguous antecedents of first-person plural forms in First Isaiah (cf. Isa 16:6; 24:16; 33:2; 38:20). The nation of Israel is excluded from being identified
with "us" in v 5 based on the unmistakable third-person references to the same in vv 1–3.
A possibility suggested by J. J. M. Roberts, "Whose Child is This? Reflections on the Speaking Voice in Isaiah 9:5," *HTR* 90/2 (1997) 115–29 is that the proclamation is being made by
the sons of God themselves, expressing their assent toward the new ruler. Although this is
feasible linguistically, the announced individual is welcomed because he is an assurance of
victory to the party receiving him. This suggests that the child has "been given" to a group
with a personal stake in the prophesied defeat, and as the dichotomy is between "us" and
"them," the antecedent of לָנוּ is most reasonably to be taken as the residents of Judah.

[41] Proposed by Gerhard von Rad, "Das judäische Königsritual," *TLZ* 72 (1947) 211–16;
Alt, "Jesaja 8, 23–9, 6," 29–49. Critics are right to take von Rad and Alt to task for claiming
that the announcement is a legal formula for adoption, in contradistinction to the view
that the Egyptian king was perceived to be physically engendered by the deity. Not only
are there no laws pertaining to adoption in the Israelite legal corpora, but the evidence
within the culture itself is meagre at best, as demonstrated in the studies of Shalom M.
Paul, "Adoption Formulae: A Study of Cuneiform and Biblical Legal Clauses," *Maarav* 2/2
(1979–80) 173–85; Jeffrey Tigay, Ben-Zion Schereschewsky and Yisrael Gilat, "Adoption,"
EncJud 1.415–20.
  I follow Roberts, "Whose Child is This?" in understanding such birth imagery as having
no connection to the legal terminology of adoption. It is rather part of the language of
divine nurture and protection which expresses in familial terms the basis of the divine-
human relationship. Its intent is to draw attention to the close bond between the respective parties, whether suzerain and vassal (2 Kgs 16:7), deity and nation (cf. Exod 4:22;
Deut 14:1; 32:18), or deity and king (Ps 2:7). The birth of a child in the royal house was insep-
arable from the idea of kingship in any case, as may be seen in the prophecy of 1 Kgs 13:2,

the divine sonship is proclaimed at the time of a king's accession and coronation, when the royal titulary is promulgated. The individual is already vested with the authority of government, as demonstrated by וַתְּהִי הַמִּשְׂרָה עַל־שִׁכְמוֹ.[42] Moreover, the people's belief that their imperial oppression had now come to an end makes no sense in the context of a birth announcement, but corresponds well with an accession oracle. Returning to Ps 2, it is only at this point that defeat of the enemies of the realm is certain (v 9, cf. Isa 9:3–4), and future blessings for the kingdom may be entertained (v 8, cf. Isa 9:6). The titles provide supporting evidence for this view, which share common characteristics with royal epithets throughout the ancient Near East.[43] Scholars are at pains to make sense of these appellations in the context of a birth oracle.[44] In any event, the argumentation here stands on its own without recourse to the controversial interpretation of this royal titulary.

6.1.6. *Literary and Historical Context*

Isa 8:23–9:6 is a direct continuation of the preceding section, Isa 8:19–22, in which the residents of the northern kingdom have appealed to the spirits of the dead in the face of a terrible calamity which had befallen the land. The fact that the southern kingdom is referenced (מַמְלַכְתּוֹ in v 6)

"A son shall be born to the house of David, Josiah by name; and on you he shall sacrifice the priests of the high places who burn incense on you, and human bones shall be burned on you."

[42] Also adduced by Irvine, *Isaiah, Ahaz, and the Syro-Ephraimitic Crisis*, 230 n. 47.

[43] Von Rad and Alt popularized the influence of Egyptian enthronement rituals on Israelite kingship, but this consensus has come under fire in recent decades as documented by Wegner, "Re-examination of Isaiah IX 1–6," 104–105 and bibliography there. In an effort to provide a more historically suitable explanation, R. A. Carlson, "The Anti-Assyrian Character of the Oracle in Is. IX 1–6," *VT* 24/2 (1974) 130–35, relates these titles to those used by Assyrian kings. Apart from *ilu qarrādu* as a close analogue to אֵל גִּבּוֹר, the remaining evidence is weakly supported or misleading.

Among the considerable evidence for Egyptian influence on the Judean coronation ritual, it has been observed by scholars such as Roberts, "Whose Child is This?" that the statement of the god Amun to king Haremhab upon his attainment of the throne, "You are my son, the heir who came forth from my flesh..." has strong affinity to the announcement of YHWH to the Davidic monarch in Ps 2:7, "You are my son, today I have begotten you." Further examples may be seen in Moshe Weinfeld, "The Roots of the Messianic Idea," in R. M. Whiting (ed.), *Mythology and Mythologies: Methodological Approaches to Intercultural Influences* (MS 2; Helsinki: The Neo-Assyrian Text Corpus Project, 2001) 283. Contemporary Egyptologists tend to see only the office as divine, as discussed in Ronald J. Leprohon, "Royal Ideology and State Administration in Pharaonic Egypt," *CANE* 1.275.

[44] Note Wegner, "Re-examination of Isaiah IX 1–6," 109–112, who devotes two full paragraphs to the weaknesses of his own interpretation.

apart from the calamity that has befallen its neighbor fixes the date of this prophecy prior to 701 B.C.E. In this case, as has been widely accepted in critical scholarship, the most attractive historical setting is the exile of part of the nation of Israel in ca. 734–732 B.C.E. during the reign of Tiglath-pileser III.[45] This is recorded in 2 Kgs 15:29, and both texts mention the land of Naphtali and the region of the Galilee. The mass deportation of this populace had never happened before, and the remaining inhabitants were resorting to whatever means of divination were at hand in order to find out what the uncertain future held for them.

It was Isaiah who stepped into this post-destruction scenario in order to reassure the houses of Ephraim and Manasseh that YHWH was still with them in their darkest hour. Whereas Tiglath-pileser had treated the land with disdain, the Lord was making it glorious once again. The nation could rejoice anew, for the rod of Assyrian supremacy would be broken by God himself.[46] There was yet another reason to justify the change in fortunes of the disheartened land of Israel: a new king who sat "upon the throne of David." Because the Assyrian juggernaut would no longer be a threat to YHWH's chosen people, the inaugurated monarch is acknowledged as a "prince of peace" whose harmonious reign will extend without limit.

If the darkest event on the horizon that can be surmised from this passage is the exile of the northern kingdom by Tiglath-pileser in ca. 734–732 B.C.E., then the prophecy should be dated within the next few years. The fall of the northern kingdom over a decade later would certainly have been a far more decisive and impactful event, yet any mention of the final doom of the house of Jacob is conspicuously absent. If the child had already been born and placed on the throne, as the oracle intimates, then the identity of the child is to be sought in a Davidic king who was crowned within this relatively narrow period of time.[47] According to the

---

[45] Advocated, most notably, by Emilio Forrer, *Die Provinzeinteilung des assyrischen Reiches* (Leipzig: J. C. Hinrichs, 1920) 59ff, 69; Alt, "Jesaja 8, 23–9, 6,"; idem, "Tiglathpilesers III. erster Feldzug nach Palästina," in *Kleine Schriften zur Geschichte des Volkes Israel* (3 vols.; Munich: C. H. Beck, 1953–59) 2.157; Emerton, "Problems in Isaiah VIII. 23," 153–56; Jesper Høgenhaven, "On the Structure and Meaning of Isaiah VIII 23B," *VT* 37/2 (1987) 218–21. For further discussion of the geographic terms in Isa 8:23, see Wilberger, *Isaiah 1–12*, 394–95; Wegner, *Kingship and Messianic Expectation in Isaiah 1–35*, 156–60.

[46] הַחְתֹּתָ in Isa 9:4. Divine deliverance is consonant with Isaiah's theology. The prophet does not consider there to be any hope in relying on human effort (cf. Ahaz calling on Assyria in Isa 7; Hezekiah relying on Egypt in Isa 30–31).

[47] There is no discrepancy here between the fact that Hezekiah was purportedly twenty-five years old when he became king (2 Kgs 18:1–2) and that he is depicted here as

reconstruction proposed here Hezekiah was coronated in 725 B.C.E., a date confined within the range of acceptable years proposed for Isaiah's oracle.

The prophecy of Isa 8:23–9:6 was most likely composed between the first exile of the northern kingdom under Tiglath-pileser III in ca. 734–732 B.C.E., and the fall of Samaria in 720. The fact that Israelite chronology pinpoints the accession year of Hezekiah in 726 B.C.E. leaves little doubt that this monarch was the intended referent of the oracle. The most significant implications for this dating are that the text should be considered as authentically Isaian, and that the prophet himself had messianic expectations. This is in line with other eighth-century prophets who similarly describe the ascendency of Judah over the north.[48]

The Judean king is seen as a reason for the troubled house of Israel to rejoice, and his rule is hyperbolically described as increasing without end. The evidence suggests that Isaiah believed that the northern and southern kingdoms would once again be reunited.[49] A possible confirmation of these hopes may be seen in 2 Chr 30, in which Hezekiah invites the northern kingdom to participate in the Passover.[50] The oracle of Isaiah ben

---

a יֶלֶד. The Hebrew word as used in the Bible can, in fact, refer to males up to the age of forty. In 1 Kings 12:8, Rehoboam consulted the "young men" (הַיְלָדִים) who had grown up with him, and in 1 Kings 14:21 Rehoboam's age is confirmed to be forty-one. For verification that the king is Davidic, confirm עַל־כִּסֵּא דָוִד in Isa 9:6.

[48] Amos 9:11–12 refers to raising up "the fallen booth of David," but the originality of this passage is disputed. I follow Wilhelm Rudolph, *Joel, Amos, Obadja, Jona* (KAT 13/2; Gütersloh: Gerd Mohn, 1971) 282; Shalom M. Paul, *Amos* (Hermeneia; Minneapolis: Fortress Press, 1991) 290–92, in favoring its authenticity, albeit with later editorial insertions. It appears that וְגָדַרְתִּי אֶת־פִּרְצֵיהֶן וַהֲרִסֹתָיו אָקִים reflects the hope of rebuilding the city of Jerusalem after its destruction in 587 B.C.E. Note the plural pronominal suffixes which lack agreement with the singular subject סֻכָּה. Excising this portion would leave the original oracle as בַּיּוֹם הַהוּא אָקִים אֶת־סֻכַּת דָּוִיד הַנֹּפֶלֶת וּבְנִיתִיהָ כִּימֵי עוֹלָם, which is grammatically coherent and retains an elegant metaphor for restoring the former glory of Davidic kingship.

William M. Schniedewind, "Jerusalem, the Late Judaean Monarchy, and the Composition of the Biblical Texts," in A. G. Vaughn and A. E. Killebrew (eds.), *Jerusalem in Bible and Archaeology: The First Temple Period* (SBLSS 18; Leiden: Brill, 2003) 391–93, argues that Hos 3:4–5 is an authentically eighth-century prophecy set in the period following the conquest of Samaria when "the Israelites shall live many days without king or prince." Just as seen in our current passage in Isaiah, the northern population would once again seek "YHWH their God and David their king (דָּוִד מַלְכָּם)," an obvious reference to the throne of Judah.

[49] A hope shared with other eighth-century prophets, see Laato, *Who Is Immanuel?*, 162 n. 8.

[50] The chronology of the book makes it appear as though Hezekiah did this early in his reign, as the incident recorded directly follows the restoration of the Temple undertaken in the king's inaugural year. Whether "those of you who escaped [and] are left from the

Amoz further dares to predict that the downfall of the Assyrian empire would materialize in the not-too-distant future. The Judean monarch, labeled as a "prince of peace," would not bloody his hands in this exercise. The Lord himself would remove the yoke of oppression from the necks of his people, leaving his chosen king to rule in justice and righteousness.

6.2. Isa 11:1–9

6.2.1. *Overview*

This prophecy of a utopian future under the rule of a righteous, God-fearing monarch is a formative passage in biblical literature. It foretells the advent of a new age which harkens back to idealistic motifs in Israelite culture, while at the same time transcending them and making them universal in scope.[51] On the one hand, the oracle plays on the positive role of the Davidic dynasty as a force for the administration of justice, dispensed swiftly and beyond cavil in accordance with the Spirit of the Lord. On the other hand, the vision of the animals recalls the primordial state in the Garden of Eden, in which beasts of prey are no longer carnivorous and may once again live in harmony with humans.[52] It is the knowledge of the Lord which acts as the binding force to maintain this state of cosmic paradise, exercised through his anointed earthly agent. This promised idyllic future era became understandably influential for the later development of messianic thought.[53]

---

hand of the kings of Assyria" (2 Chr 30:6) refers to the remnant left after the exiles of 734–732 or 720 B.C.E. will be addressed in my coverage of Chronicles.

[51] Comparison has been made to the neo-Babylonian prophecy from Uruk, published by Hermann Hunger and Stephen A. Kaufman, "A New Akkadian Prophecy Text," *JAOS* 95/3 (1975) 371–75. It similarly foretells of an ideal ruler: "A king will arise in Uruk who will provide justice in the land . . . he will renew Uruk. The gates of Uruk he will build of lapis lazuli . . . After him, his son will arise in Uruk and become master over the world . . . his dynasty will be established forever. The kings of Uruk will exercise rulership like gods."

[52] Such ideal depictions are also found in Sibylline Oracles 3.741–95; Virgil's Fourth Eclogue, and the Sumerian tales Enki and Ninhursag, Enmerkar and the Lord of Aratta. For these texts, see John J. Collins, "The Sibylline Oracles," in James H. Charlesworth (ed.), *The Old Testament Pseudepigrapha* (2 vols.; New York: Doubleday, 1983–85) 1.377–79; Moshe Weinfeld, "Jerusalem—A Political and Spiritual Capital," in J. G. Westenholz (ed.), *Capital Cities: Urban Planning and Spiritual Dimensions* (BLMJP 2; Jerusalem: Bible Lands Museum, 1998) 28–29.

[53] For the influence of Isa 11 in later literature, see Wegner, *Kingship and Messianic Expectation in Isaiah 1–35*, 260–61; John J. Collins, *The Scepter and the Star: The Messiahs of the Dead Sea Scrolls and Other Ancient Literature* (New York: Doubleday, 1995) 49–73.

6.2.2. *Literary Extent*

The identification of the borders of a literary unit is essential to its proper exegesis. In regard to the prophecy of the ideal king, the predominant view is that the oracle extends over Isa 11:1–9.[54] Others end the prophecy at v 8, or broaden it through v 10.[55] Because the shoot is mentioned only in vv 1–5, the subsequent verses which pertain to peace among animalkind and between them and humans have been viewed by some exegetes as a secondary stratum.[56] The myriad of viewpoints all stem from the desire to read the section as a unity, a task complicated by the shifting subject matter. The range of dates proposed for the textual unit, as shall be explored presently, only exacerbates the problem by opening the doors to ever later editorial activity.

Various proposals have been advanced for seeing verse 10 as a later interpolation into the text, although some of these justifications are more cogent than others.[57] The indeterminate future expressed via בַּיּוֹם הַהוּא

Messianic implications for the text itself are weighed by Randall Heskett, *Messianism within the Scriptural Scroll of Isaiah* (LHB/OTS 456; New York: T&T Clark, 2007) 38–132; Rodrigo F. de Sousa, *Eschatology and Messianism in LXX Isaiah 1–12* (LHB/OTS 516; New York: T&T Clark, 2010) 138–56.

[54] For this position, see Skinner, *Book of the Prophet Isaiah*, 102–10; Kissane, *Book of Isaiah*, 1.135–39; A. S. Herbert, *The Book of the Prophet Isaiah Chapters 1–39* (Cambridge: Cambridge University Press, 1973) 88–92; Otto Kaiser, *Isaiah 1–12: A Commentary* (2nd ed.; OTL; Philadelphia: Westminster Press, 1983) 252–61; Susan Niditch, *Chaos to Cosmos: Studies in Biblical Patterns of Creation* (Chico, Calf.: Scholars Press, 1985) 80–82; Kirsten Nielsen, *There is Hope for a Tree: The Tree as Metaphor in Isaiah* (JSOTSup 65; Sheffield: JSOT Press, 1989) 123–44.

[55] For those identifying v 8 as the end of the prophecy, see Eduard König, *Das Buch Jesaja* (Gütersloh: C. Bertelsmann, 1926) 154–62; George Buchanan Gray, *A Critical and Exegetical Commentary on the Book of Isaiah I–XXVII* (ICC; Edinburgh: T.&T. Clark Ltd., 1912) 211–28. On v 10 as inclusive to the oracle, see Shemaryahu Talmon, "The Signification of שלום and Its Semantic Field in the Hebrew Bible," in C. A. Evans and S. Talmon (eds.), *The Quest for Context and Meaning: Studies in Biblical Intertextuality in Honor of James A. Sanders* (Leiden: Brill, 1997) 108–109, 115.

[56] Eissfeldt, *Einleitung in das Alte Testament*, 428–29. Whereas vv 1–5 in his opinion is an authentic oracle of Isaiah ben Amoz because its concepts resonate with other Isaianic prophecies, the vision of future peace on Mount Zion vv 6–9 is a foreign idea, yet at home in later compositions.

[57] Willem A. M. Beuken, *Jesaja 1–12* (HTKAT; Freiburg: Herder, 2003) 315; Brevard S. Childs, *Isaiah* (OTL; Louisville: Westminster John Knox, 2000) 105–6; Ronald E. Clements, *Isaiah 1–39* (NCB Commentary; Grand Rapids: Eerdmans, 1980) 125; Kaiser, *Isaiah 1–12*, 262–63; Karl Marti, *Das Buch Jesaja* (KHC; Tübingen: J. C. B. Mohr, 1900) 114; Nielsen, *There Is Hope for a Tree*, 140; H. G. M. Williamson, *The Book Called Isaiah: Deutero-Isaiah's Role in Composition and Redaction* (Oxford: Clarendon, 1994) 66–67.

"on that day" is often appealed to as an editorial device.[58] While this may
certainly be valid in specific instances, nonetheless such cannot always be
the case, or else virtually all forward-looking prophecies, which must necessarily employ an unspecified time referent, could be classified as later
additions looking back from an exilic or post-exilic setting. It is, rather,
the incongruous aspects of the verse relative to the neighboring oracles
which speak most strongly to its secondary nature. The first is the role of
the nations, which are seemingly cast in a positive light.[59] Yet they play
no part in the exercising of justice by the ruler of the foregoing verses,
while in the vision of the reunited kingdom (vv 11–16) they are to be plun-
dered and subjugated by the gathered remnant of Israel. Moreover, they
are said to יִדְרֹשׁוּ "seek, inquire" after the root of Jesse, a metaphorical
image combining a verb and object not otherwise pressed into service in
First Isaiah.[60]

Secondly, the verse utilizes two elements to form a bridge between the
vision of the ideal ruler and that of the remnant, yet neither element is
in strict accord with its literary analog. Whereas v 10 refers to the "root of
Jesse" (שֹׁרֶשׁ יִשַׁי), the figure in v 1 is a "shoot from his roots" (נֵצֶר מִשָּׁרָשָׁיו).
Whether or not the former reference is intended to be synonymous with
or build upon the latter, the fact remains that the inexactitude of the
terminology gives pause.[61] The metaphor of the נֵס "banner, signal" is likewise broken, uniquely representing a human being despite its consistent

---

[58] H. G. M. Williamson, *A Critical and Exegetical Commentary on Isaiah 1–27, Vol. 1:
Isaiah 1–5* (ICC; London: T&T Clark, 2006) 286 n. 45. This temporal clause also comes into
play in regard to the proper translation of the verse, which is a matter of some debate as
well. On this, see J. J. M. Roberts, "The Translation of Isa 11.10," in M. Mori, H. Ogawa, and
M. Yoshikawa (eds.), *Near Eastern Studies Dedicated to H. I. H. Prince Takahito Mikasa
on the Occasion of His Seventy-fifth Birthday* (BMECCJ 5; Wiesbaden: Harrassowitz, 1991)
363–70, and the rejoinder by Jacob Stromberg, "The 'Root of Jesse' in Isaiah 11:10: Postexilic
Judah, or Postexilic Davidic King?" *JBL* 127/4 (2008) 655–56 n. 1.

[59] As noted by Stromberg "'Root of Jesse' in Isaiah 11:10," 658.

[60] First Isaiah only describes seeking YHWH or justice, cf. Isa 1:17; 8:19; 9:12[13]; 16:5; 19:3;
31:1. Inquiring from the "book of YHWH" (סֵפֶר יְהֹוָה) in Isa 34:16 is not far afield from this
idea, but this chapter is widely regarded as post-exilic in modern scholarship, see Williamson, *Book Called Isaiah*, 215–20; Claire R. Mathews, "Apportioning Desolation: Contexts
for Interpreting Edom's Fate and Function in Isaiah," in E. H. Lovering, Jr. (ed.), *Society
of Biblical Literature Seminar Papers, 1995* (Atlanta: Scholars Press, 1995) 250–66; eadem,
Defending Zion: Edom's Desolation and Jacob's Restoration (Isaiah 34–35) in Context (BZAW
236; Berlin: de Gruyter, 1995).

[61] It is just such a subtle perturbation in meaning that has led some exegetes to postulate that v 10 is not the result of careless editing, but rather reflects editorial intentionality.
This position advocates that the "root" of v 10 is a reinterpretation of the ruler in v 1 as the
post-exilic community in the afterglow of kingship. As this reading necessarily sees v 10
as secondary, it serves as independent confirmation of the ancillary nature of the verse.

use in v 12 and elsewhere as an emblem raised to the nations to accomplish the Lord's purpose.[62] Hence the secondary nature of v 10 lies not only in its lack of precision with the corresponding motifs it is intended to recall, but in the fact that these very elements form the connections with the surrounding material. With the verse excised from the chapter, the oracle flows smoothly and is more readily seen as a unified whole.[63]

Working backward from v 10, the preceding utopian vision of the animals in vv 6–9 has no express linkage to the characteristics of the divine ruler supplied in vv 1–5 and has therefore been construed as late. Literarily, however, there are no seams of an editorial insertion: the verb וְגָר at the beginning of v 6 is the grammatically correct waw-consecutive + perfect (wᵉqatal) one would expect to continue the preceding oracle, rather than the jarring בַּיּוֹם הַהוּא often argued as an editorial device. With these two passages interpreted as distinct, unrelated pericopes, the attributes of this

---

For coverage of this debate, with bibliography, see Stromberg, " 'Root of Jesse' in Isaiah 11:10," 655–57.

[62] Isa 5:26; 11:12; 18:3; 49:22; 62:10; Jer 50:2; 51:27. As observed by Gray, Isaiah I–XXVII, 225, "It remains extraordinary that a person stands like a signal or banner."

[63] Williamson, Book Called Isaiah, 125–43, makes the case for seeing vv 11–16 as part of the editorial activity of Deutero-Isaiah. Such a section, in his view, is one of several examples of free compositions authored by Deutero-Isaiah as a means to bridge the earlier oracles of First Isaiah with the message to the exiles of his own time. More recently, others have raised their voice to champion an earlier, if not authentically original, prophecy.

Weinfeld, "Jerusalem—A Political and Spiritual Capital," 27, puts forward the following points, among others, to justify an eighth-century provenance for the oracle: the three territorial units pertaining to Egypt in Isa 11:11 (Egypt, Pathros, and Kush) appear in the same order in the inscriptions of Esarhaddon but are not otherwise attested; the jealousy between Judah and Ephraim in v 13 is also known from Isa 9:20.

To this may be added the insights of J. J. M. Roberts, "Critical Reflections on The Book Called Isaiah with Particular Attention to the Second Exodus Theme (Isa 11:11–16)" (SBL Paper; Boston, Mass. 22–25 November, 2008):

- The reunification of the north and south is not reflected in post-exilic sources. The sole outlier is Zech 10, which Williamson himself has shown is modeled upon the (necessarily earlier) Isa 11:11–16.
- The diction and vocabulary differ between Isa 11:11–16 and Deutero-Isaiah with regard to the standard to the nations, the gathering of the people, and designating the farthest regions of the earth.
- The noun שְׁאָר, while prominent in First Isaiah, is never attested in Deutero-Isaiah.
- The places from which God will bring back his people in these verses are locales associated either with the Assyrian exile of the eighth century or areas whither refugees of the period may have fled.
- Deutero-Isaiah never uses the designation Ephraim, and the relations between Ephraim and Judah conveyed in Isa 11:13 subvert the reader's expectation in a characteristically Isaian style.

For further discussion, see Seth Erlandsson, "Isaiah 11:10–16 and Its Historical Background." WLQ (1974) 94–113.

leader delineated so carefully in vv 1–5 are devoid of the concomitant benefits throughout the kingdom of his just exercise of rule.

A popular methodological strategy has been to argue for the secondary nature of vv 6–9 via appeal to Isa 65:25, where the vision of the animals likewise appears: "'The wolf and the lamb (טָלֶה) shall pasture together (כְּאֶחָד), and the lion, like the ox, will eat straw. And for the snake, dust [shall be] his food. They will do no evil nor harm in all My holy mountain' says YHWH." The justification is in part statistical: the phrase הַר קָדְשִׁי "My holy mountain" occurs five times in Trito-Isaiah but only once in First Isaiah.[64] Yet Isaiah ben Amoz was certainly familiar with the conceptions of holiness and Mount Zion, and the abode of the Lord himself was *ipso facto* a holy place.[65] Rather, the references to Mount Zion and the hill of Jerusalem in the arguably authentic Isa 10:12, 32 intimate that הַר קָדְשִׁי in 11:9 is intended to bring cohesion to the broader literary unit, with the promised king bringing absolute peace to the very region which the haughty Assyrian ruler had striven so fervently to decimate.

The animal imagery of Isa 65:25 is, in fact, a concise summary of Isa 11:6–7, employing the wolf and lamb from the beginning of v 6, the verb רָעָה from the middle of the couplet, and a verbatim inclusion from the end of v 7.[66] The mention of the snake eating dust is a clear allusion to the judgment on the primordial tempter of man in Gen 3:14. Along with other passing references to the primeval history in Gen 1–11 as well as sayings from Deutero-Isaiah, the poem of Isa 65:17–25 is meant as a catena of creation motifs.[67] The evident literary borrowing points to an author who intends to recall earlier traditions rather than originate new ones. There are also reasons to question the priority of Isa 65:25 based on linguistic criteria. Hebrew כְּאֶחָד, a variant of יַחְדָּו found in Isa 11:6, has been identified as an Aramaism from כַּחְדָא. Its literal rendering "as one" has been subtly changed to connote "together," a shade of meaning attested in the

---

[64] Bernhard Duhm, *Das Buch Jesaia* (5th ed.; Göttingen: Vandenhoeck & Ruprecht, 1968) 108, 481.

[65] The reference to הַר הַקֹּדֶשׁ בִּירוּשָׁלָ͏ִם "the holy mountain of Jerusalem" in Isa 27:13 is generally not considered to be authentically Isaian, although it has been acknowledged that there is legitimate eighth-century prophetic material underlying Isa 24–27.

[66] As noted by Wegner, *Kingship and Messianic Expectation in Isaiah 1–35*, 251.

[67] Joseph Blenkinsopp, *Isaiah 55–66* (AYB 19B; New York: Doubleday, 2003) 283–90. See also J.T.A.G.M. van Ruiten, "The Intertextual Relationship between Isaiah 65,25 and Isaiah 11,6–9," in F. G. Martínez, A. Hilhorst, and C. J. Labuschagne (eds.), *The Scriptures and the Scrolls: Studies in Honour of A. S. van der Woude on the Occasion of His 65th Birthday* (VTSup 49; Leiden: Brill, 1992) 31–42.

Hebrew Bible only in Ecclesiastes, Ezra, Nehemiah, and Chronicles.[68] The designation of the lamb via Hebrew טָלֶה in Isa 65:25 is also characteristically late, with כֶּבֶשׂ as the fixed pre-exilic usage.[69]

With the proper end of the oracle established at v 9, it remains to determine its beginning. The central question is whether Isa 10:33–34 is integral to the prophecy in the following chapter, or whether their relationship is secondary due to later redaction. For those who favor seeing Isa 11:1–9 as a distinct unit, the apparent severing of the Davidic dynasty intimated in v 1 entails a later, post-exilic setting.[70] There is an acute methodological error in this approach, in that the analysis of a *crux interpretum* within the passage is used in turn to assign its literary termini. As the meaning of a text can only truly be derived from its literary context, the scholar should refrain from engaging in the exegesis of key words until the unit has been properly delimited. This reading is therefore an invalid criterion for separating Isa 10:33–34 from the oracle of the shoot.

It is also charged that chapter 11, with its depiction of a utopian rule under YHWH's anointed, is an altogether different theme than the destruction of Assyria so potently portrayed in Isa 10:33–34, which argues against seeing a direct connection between them. The change in speaker is used to support this bifurcation, with YHWH speaking in the third person in Isa 10:33–34, but in the first person (הַר קָדְשִׁי) in 11:9. The latter claim conveys a lack of appreciation for the speaking voice in prophetic oracles, which can alternate at any time between first and third person as the prophet chooses to quote the words of YHWH spoken to him or else restate that message indirectly, and is in no way an indication of the literary unity of a passage.[71] It is hence only the supposed change in

---

[68] Enno Littman, *Über die Abfassungszeit des Tritojesaia* (Freiburg: J.C.B. Mohr, 1899) 7, as noted by Lea Mazor, "Myth, History, and Utopia in the Prophecy of the Shoot (Isaiah 10:33–11:9)," in C. Cohen, A. Hurvitz and S. M. Paul (eds.), *Sefer Moshe: The Moshe Weinfeld Jubilee Volume* (Winona Lake, Ind.: Eisenbrauns, 2004) 79 n. 8.

[69] טְלָאִים occurs in the exilic Isa 40:11, another verse containing animal imagery. The noun also appears in 1 Sam 7:9, at the high point of a heavily redacted Deuteronomistic passage which suggests an exilic dating as well. On this, see F. Kyle McCarter Jr., *I Samuel* (AYB 8; Garden City, N.Y.: Doubleday, 1980) 140–51.

[70] Marti, *Das Buch Jesaja*, 110; Duhm, *Das Buch Jesaia*, 104–105; Gray, *Isaiah I–XXVII*, 215–16; Kaiser, *Isaiah 1–12*, 254; Clements, *Isaiah 1–39*, 122. For more scholars who deny Isaianic authorship, see the bibliography at Kaiser, *Isaiah 1–12*, 254 n. 22.

[71] Setting aside prophetic literature as a whole, in which the phenomenon is pervasive, choice examples in Isaiah include Isa 1:2–4, 24–28; 3:1–4; 5:3–7; 6:11–12; 10:24–26; 13:3–4, 11–13; 14:24–27, 30–32; 19:1–2; 22:25; 28:16–21; 29:1–6; 37:28–32. Upon close examination, it becomes clear that not only may the prophet freely switch between first- and third-person when relaying the Lord's message, but that God may refer to himself in the third person

subject matter which holds any true weight in justifying a textual break at
the end of chapter 10, and this assertion requires further examination.

Against this, there are several reasons to prefer Isa 10:33–34 as the true
beginning of the oracle of the shoot.[72] Grammatically, the *waw*-consecu-
tive form which begins chap. 11 cannot be the initial words of the prophecy. Although it has been claimed that the *waw*-consecutive may indeed
stand on its own at the beginning of a textual unit, without a preceding
verb there is no means by which to isolate its aspect.[73] The main clause
originates in Isa 10:33, with the word הִנֵּה. That these last two verses are
the proper introduction to the oracle is signaled by their consistent use
of aspect: note the inverted perfect (*w^{e}qatal*) and imperfect (*yiqtol*) forms
which bracket v 34, identical to those called into service in verse 11:1. The
imagery continues as well, with the severing of the lofty trees representing
the proud Assyrians balanced by the flourishing of the Judean king represented by the shoot.[74] Hence whether assessing these verses grammatically, metaphorically (the plant imagery), or in regard to their referents
(powerful heads of state), the prophecy of the ideal ruler extends over Isa
10:33–11:9.[75]

6.2.3. *The Significance of the "Shoot"*

As the predominant view in scholarship has been to partition Isa 11:1–9
from the preceding two verses, a great deal of exegetical energy has been
expended in attempting to discern the meaning of the shoot in the opening

---

as well (e.g., 6:11–12). That is, even when a prophet may be reciting direct speech from the
deity, that discourse may nonetheless contain third-person references to God.

[72] As favored by Kissane. *Book of Isaiah*, 1.133–35; Kaiser, *Isaiah 1–12*, 254; Watts, *Isaiah
1–33*, 170; Mazor, "Myth, History, and Utopia," 80. The connection between the oracle of
the shoot and Isa 10:33–34 was recognized at least as early as Johann Gottfried von Herder,
Vom Geist der ebräischen Poesie (3rd ed.; 2 vols.; Leipzig: J. A. Barth, 1825) 2.406ff.

[73] Lev 1:1 is offered as evidence of this, which begins וַיִּקְרָא אֶל־מֹשֶׁה. The lack of
expressed subject is itself a deterrent to accepting this as delimiting a new textual unit. In
fact, the grammatical subject is כְּבוֹד יְהוָה in Exod 40:35, prior to the parenthetical comment on the movement of the divine cloud in vv 36–38. A similar phenomenon is apparent
in Ezek 2:1, where וַיֹּאמֶר refers back to either כְּבוֹד יְהוָה or to קוֹל at the end of chap. 1.

[74] Nielsen, *There is Hope for a Tree*, 131.

[75] Similarly viewed by Mazor, "Myth, History, and Utopia," 80; Wegner, *Kingship and
Messianic Expectation in Isaiah 1–35*, 230–31. Wegner notes that a similar progression of
thought is found earlier in chap. 10, where the destruction of Assyria (vv 16–19) enables the
emergence of a remnant from Israel (vv 20–23). I concur with his assessment that there
is no basis for seeing the Israelites as having been cut off in Isa 10:33–34, see bibliography
at 230 nn. 69, 72.

verse.[76] This scion is stated to come forth from the גֵזַע of Jesse. Drawing on the basic meaning of "trunk, stump" for this Hebrew word available from cognate languages, a popular rendering for the first half of this verse is "a shoot will spring from the stump of Jesse."[77] With this understanding, many scholars have viewed the prophecy as originating in the dynastic aspirations of the post-destruction period, with the "stump" representing the cessation of the Davidic monarchy.[78] The imagery is consistent with that of Jer 33:15, generally accepted as post-exilic: "'In those days and at that time I will cause a righteous Branch of David to spring forth, and he shall execute justice and righteousness on the earth."[79] Rather than pointing to some indeterminate future, however, this architect of world peace in the book of Isaiah is perceived to be imminent, judging from the

---

[76] The identity of the shoot in scholarship falls into two broad categories, based on one's dating of the passage: Davidic king or Messianic figure, eschatological David. The shoot has been identified with Josiah—sprouting forth from the stump of his father who had been felled (assassinated, 2 Kgs 21:19–23)—by Jacques Vermeylen, *Du prophète Isaïe à l'apocalyptique: Isaïe I–XXXV, miroir d'un demi-millénaire d'expérience religieuse en Israël* (2 vols.; Paris: J. Gabalda, 1977–78) 1.274, 282; Sweeney, *Isaiah 1–39*, 204–205; idem, "Jesse's New Shoot in Isaiah 11: A Josianic Reading of the Prophet Isaiah," in R. D. Weis and D. M. Carr (eds.), *A Gift of God in Due Season. Essays on Scripture and Community in Honor of James A. Sanders* (JSOTSup 225; Sheffield: Sheffield Academic Press, 1996) 103–118; idem, *King Josiah of Judah: The Lost Messiah of Israel* (Oxford: Oxford University Press, 2001) 321. The oracle was composed in tribute to the relatively young and weak leader upon his accession, in contrast to the fall of the Assyrian king in Isa 10:33–34.

Another, more controversial, position likens the stump to the nation of Judah, with the shoot signifying the remnant in Isa 10:20–22, see John T. Willis, *Isaiah* (Austin: Sweet, 1980) 202–203; John H. Hayes and Stuart A. Irvine, *Isaiah the Eighth Century Prophet: His Times and His Preaching* (New York: Abingdon, 1987) 212–13, Wegner, *Kingship and Messianic Expectation in Isaiah 1–35*, 232–33.

[77] For cognate data, see Arabic جِذْع, "the trunk of a palm tree" in Lane 2.396; "stem; trunk; stump, tree stump; torso" in Wehr 139; Syriac ܓܘܼܙܥܵܐ, "rod, trunk" in Michael Sokoloff, *A Syriac Lexicon* (Winona Lake, Ind.: Eisenbrauns, 2009) 213; "the trunk or stump of a felled tree," in J. Payne Smith (ed.), *Compendious Syriac Dictionary* (Oxford: Oxford University Press, 1903) 63.

[78] Cf. Jer 23:5–6; 33:14–22; Ezek 37:24–28; Zech 3:8; 6:12. Typical are statements such as that of Kaiser, *Isaiah 1–12*, 255, 254, "The Davidic dynasty is compared to a tree, all that is left of which is a stump…At all events, the expectation of the renewal of the kingdom from the roots of the dynasty points to a time at which the David[sic] dynasty had ceased to rule."

[79] The post-exilic date of this prophecy in MT Jer 33:14–26, centered on the Levitical priests and Davidic kingship, is virtually assured due to its text-critical minus in LXX, the longest such section of missing text. For further evidence of its lateness, see William L. Holladay, *Jeremiah 2: A Commentary on the Book of the Prophet Jeremiah, Chapters 26–52* (Hermeneia; Minneapolis: Fortress Press, 1989) 227–31.

incipient use of the participle מְסָעֵף in Isa 10:33.[80] Another distinguishing characteristic from post-destruction oracles is the lack of reference to the dual roles of king and priest prevalent during this period, and evident in the Jeremian passage just cited.[81] The primary features which link these two texts, then, are the plant imagery and proper exercise of the charge as a Davidic king.

These two combined aspects derive directly from the ancient Near Eastern relationship between kingship and the cosmic tree of life.[82] This tree represented the divine world order to be maintained by the sovereign as the representative of the gods. This association was so close that in imperial art the king could often be substituted as the human personification of the cosmic tree, thus depicting him as the consummate embodiment of divine order in mankind, in essence the perfect image of the deity. The need to prevent chaos legitimated the king's dominion, and exemplified why piety and blameless conduct were crucial to successful rule.[83]

The employment of the tree as a metaphor for kingship is seen in biblical prophetic literature in the "righteous branch" (צֶמַח צַדִּיק) of Jer 23:5–6; 33:14–16, and the "apex of the cedar, its topmost shoot" (אֶת־צַמֶּרֶת הָאֶרֶז אֵת רֹאשׁ יְנִיקוֹתָיו) of Ezek 17:3–4. Royal connections to vegetation are attested elsewhere in Isaiah. The word נֵצֶר in the first verse of

---

[80] Contrast with other examples, cf. יָמִים בָּאִים in Jer 23:5; בְּיָמָיו (v 6); יָמִים בָּאִים in Jer 33:14; בַּיָּמִים הָהֵם (vv 15, 16).

[81] Jer 33:18, 21–22. Theocratic rule in this period was typically perceived as distributed between these complementary offices, although the fusion of these respective roles is very old. See the following selection of articles in John Day (ed.), *King and Messiah in Israel and the Ancient Near East: Proceedings of the Oxford Old Testament Seminar* (JSOTSup 270; Sheffield: Sheffield Academic Press, 1998): John Baines, "Ancient Egyptian Kingship: Official Forms, Rhetoric, Context," 16–53; W. G. Lambert, "Kingship in Ancient Mesopotamia," 54–70; John Day, "The Canaanite Inheritance of the Israelite Monarchy," 72–90; Deborah W. Rooke, "Kingship as Priesthood: The Relationship between the High Priesthood and the Monarchy," 187–208.

[82] Favored by Ivan Engnell, *Studies in Divine Kingship in the Ancient Near East* (2nd ed.; Oxford: Blackwell, 1967) 28ff (first ed. 1943); Geo Widengren, *The King and the Tree of Life in Ancient Near Eastern Religion* (Uppsala: Lundequistska Bokhandeln, 1951); idem, *Sakrales Königtum im Alten Testament und im Judentum* (Stuttgart: W. Kohlhammer, 1955) 56; Helmer Ringgren, *The Messiah in the Old Testament* (SBT 18; London: SCM Press, 1961) 31; Nielsen, *There is Hope for A Tree*, 132; Simo Parpola, "The Assyrian Tree of Life: Tracing the Origins of Jewish Monotheism and Greek Philosophy," *JNES* 52/3 (1993) 167–68. It is to be regretted the weight that some commentators have placed on the criticism of this motif by Sigmund Mowinckel, *He That Cometh. The Messiah Concept in the Old Testament and Later Judaism* (trans. G. W. Anderson; Oxford: Basil Blackwell, 1956) 453ff.

[83] For these two prominent qualities in Assyrian royal inscriptions, see Marie Joseph Seux, *Épithètes royales akkadiennes et sumériennes* (Paris: Letouzey & Ané, 1967) 20–21.

our prophecy is expressly equated with the Babylonian king in Isa 14:19.[84] As in Isaiah, the cedars of Lebanon were emblematic of royal majesty, to the extent that the dynastic seat could be succinctly designated as "Lebanon" (Jer 22:6, 23), and the royal residence as "the house of the forest of Lebanon" (1 Kgs 7:2).[85] The metaphor provides the basis for Jotham's oracle in Judg 9:8–15, in which the candidates for anointing approached by the populace are likened to various trees. Such pervasive exercising of metonymy throughout the biblical corpus at once gives pause to concluding that the phrase גֵּזַע יִשַׁי is intended as a mere discontinuation of the Davidic line.

Linguistically, while glosses from other languages are helpful in establishing the general nuance of a word, its precise definition is best obtained from comparative data within the same language whenever possible. It should be noted at the outset that the indisputable meaning of "stump" is conveyed elsewhere in Isaiah via the word מַצֶּבֶת, based on its having been cast down (שַׁלֶּכֶת).[86] There are only two other occurrences of גֵּזַע in the Hebrew Bible. In the first instance, the meaning is readily apparent:

$$\text{אַף בַּל־נִטָּעוּ אַף בַּל־זֹרָעוּ אַף בַּל־שֹׁרֵשׁ בָּאָרֶץ גִּזְעָם}$$

Isa 40:24   Scarcely have they been planted, scarcely have they been sown, scarcely has their גֵּזַע taken root in the earth.

Here the meaning of גֵּזַע cannot be associated with "stump": there is no intimation of a fallen tree, but rather something that is buried underground and responsible for the germination of the plant. Rather than referring to something which has been prematurely severed or has ceased to exist, גֵּזַע rather connotes something alive and virile.

The second attestation is found in the book of Job:

---

[84] Nielsen, *There is Hope for a Tree*, 132. It has been suggested that there is a close connection in royal ideology between the imagery of a young tree and the portrayal of the king as a symbol of fertility (Ps 72), see Keith W. Whitelam, "Jesse," *AYBD* 3.772.

[85] In the case of the latter, the name is primarily derived from the fact that cedar was used in its construction. For further examples of the application of "Lebanon" in royal contexts, see Judg 9:15; 1 Kings 5:13[4:33]; 2 Kgs 14:9; Song 5:15.

[86] Isa 6:13, כָּאֵלָה וְכָאַלּוֹן אֲשֶׁר בְּשַׁלֶּכֶת מַצֶּבֶת, "Like a terebinth or oak whose stump remains when it is felled."

Job 14:7–9

כִּי יֵשׁ לָעֵץ תִּקְוָה אִם־יִכָּרֵת (7)   (7)"For there is hope for a tree: if it be cut
וְעוֹד יַחֲלִיף וְיֹנַקְתּוֹ לֹא תֶחְדָּל: down, that it will sprout again, and its
shoots will not fail.

אִם־יַזְקִין בָּאָרֶץ שָׁרְשׁוֹ וּבֶעָפָר (8)   (8)If its roots grow old in the ground and
יָמוּת גִּזְעוֹ: (9)מֵרֵיחַ מַיִם יַפְרִחַ   its גֶּזַע rots in the dust, (9)at the scent of
וְעָשָׂה קָצִיר כְּמוֹ־נָטַע: water it will flourish and put forth sprigs
like a seedling."

The positive imagery intended by Job in this passage is structured around two independent clauses beginning with אִם "if." At first blush, the rendering of "stump" for גֶּזַע would seem to be justified based on poetic parallelism, as the tree mentioned in v 7 has expressly been cut down. However, the word omitted in the second couplet due to the phenomenon of gapping or ellipsis is "tree," by virtue of the fact that עֵץ precedes the conditional. It is hence this lexical element specifically rather than the conception of a stump which is to be carried over from the first bicolon.

The proper sense of גֶּזַע may be found within the same cola in v 8, where it is internally parallel to שָׁרְשׁוֹ. Both grammatical elements refer to the life-giving portion of a tree, which in this instance is in danger of decomposing due to dehydration. Whereas the tree in v 7 has been toppled, the גֶּזַע in vv 8–9 is afflicted with drought. The poetic parallelism is intended to contrast a man-made versus natural demise for the plant, which nonetheless potentially yields the same hopeful result.[87] The particle אִם thus establishes two hypothetical situations in regard to the tree which substitute rather than build upon each other, and so their relationship is paradigmatic rather than syntagmatic.[88]

This reading may be further justified by looking at other selections from Job which similarly contain conditional clauses marked with אִם. In direct poetic discourse within the book, אִם serves to establish mutually distinct theoretical instances, as may be seen in the following examples:

---

[87] The other, implicit, contrasts are in regard to location (above ground versus below ground), and swift quietus versus slow. This conclusion is entertained and then summarily dismissed by David J. A. Clines, *Job 1–20* (WBC 17; Dallas: Word Books, 1989) 328, in commenting on vv 8–9: "The picture of the felled tree is presumably continued. It is possible that the tree here is another tree to that of v 7, one that simply withers and dies of old age; גזעו could be 'its stem, trunk.' rather than 'its stump'. More likely, however, the picture is of a tree cut down, which thereafter begins to decay and wither by natural process."

[88] The linguistic notions of paradigmatic and syntagmatic relationships are applied to biblical poetry by Adele Berlin, *The Dynamics of Biblical Parallelism* (Bloomington, Ind.: Indiana University Press, 1985) 72–80, 90–91.

Job 33:32–33	If you have anything to say, answer me…
	If not, listen to me; keep silent, and I will teach you wisdom.
Job 35:6–7	If you have sinned, what do you accomplish against Him?…
	If you are righteous, what do you give to Him?

Job 31:13–40 provides another extensive case study, as Job defends his righteousness with a stream of hypothetical transgressions:

Job 31:13	If I have despised the claim of my male or female slaves…
v 16	If I have kept the poor from [their] desire…
v 19	If I have seen anyone perish for lack of clothing…
v 20	If his loins have not thanked me…
v 21	If I have lifted up my hand against the orphan…
v 24	If I have put my confidence [in] gold…
v 25	If I have gloated because my wealth was great…
v 26	If I have looked at the sun when it shone…

The many other illustrations of this same phenomenon throughout the book of Job make manifest that the allusion to the tree in chap. 14 contains two separate means of illustrating the same point.[89] As with Isa 40:24, the presentation of גֶּזַע is consistent: the part of the plant directly comparable to the root (שֹׁרֶשׁ) from which shoots sprout forth. Rather than stump, then, a better rendering for this viable, fecund vegetation would be "stem, stock."[90]

The flora metaphorically envisioned here is not vestigial nor has it been truncated, as seen by the direct contrast it forms with the judgment inflicted upon the Assyrian empire by the Lord in the preceding two verses. Far from being lopped off (מְסָעֵף), brought low (יִשְׁפָּלוּ), cut down (וְנִקַּף) or felled (יִפּוֹל), the institution of kingship in Isa 11:1 is still alive and flourishing, and thus consonant with the time of the monarchy itself. The deliberate antithesis with the prideful nature of the king of Assyria should not be overlooked, a quality symbolized by great stature that must

---

[89] Job 6:12; 9:15–16, 19, 27–31; 11:7–12 (cf. vv 7, 10); 20:6–19 (cf. vv 6, 12); 27:14–17 (cf. vv 14, 16); 31:5–10 (cf. vv 5, 7, 9), which Robert Gordis, *The Book of Job* (New York: Jewish Theological Seminary of America, 1978) 345–46, clarifies as three separate cases: cheating in business, coveting and taking the property of others, committing adultery; 31:13–40; 33:32–33; 35:6–7; 36:11–12; 37:13.

[90] LXX further undergirds this interpretation, rendering both גֶּזַע and שֹׁרֶשׁ as ῥίζα. As de Sousa comments, "This rendering of גזע could have been influenced by the presence of ῥίζα at the end of the verse, but the equivalence גזע/ῥίζα is also attested at 40:24, which could indicate that the translator simply understood the Hebrew term to mean 'root'" (*Eschatology and Messianism in LXX Isaiah 1–12*, 143).

necessarily be brought low. The heights of the trees at the end of chapter 10 are thus of great import leading into chapter 11, where the king depicted as a stem or root "will delight in the fear of the Lord." The closeness to the ground, the source of vitality for all organic life, has come to signify the measure of haughtiness or humility of these rulers before God. A reading which adheres to the translation "stump" and sees an interruption or cessation of the Davidic line does not attend to the artistry of the vision.[91] There is furthermore no basis for the cause of this striking down of the Judean monarch, as the entire literary unit extending back to Isa 10:5 portrays Yнwн himself fighting on behalf of his people, with the Assyrian army held in abeyance and ostensibly unable to reach the capital city of Jerusalem. The prophecy assures divine protection for Zion and its chosen messiah.

This contention may be further buttressed by Neo-Assyrian inscriptions which describe the king as coming forth from the root-stock of the royal line.[92] That this is the intent of the imagery in this verse may be seen both in the reference to Jesse in the opening description, the fount of legitimate kingship in Judah, as well as through the use of פֻּארָה two verses earlier in Isa 10:33. This *hapax legomenon* is cognate to the Akkadian epithet *per'u*, "branch" employed in Assyrian royal inscriptions.[93] Whereas its original purpose was to aggrandize the strength of the emissary of Aššur to rule unto the extents of the realm with an iron fist, the designation has been

---

[91] Such an interpretation undermines the position of Vermeylen, *Du prophète Isaïe*, 1.274, 282, that the shoot refers to Josiah, as the גֵּזַע does not signify a fallen king.

[92] As cited by Moshe Weinfeld, "The Protest against Imperialism in Ancient Israelite Prophecy," in S. N. Eisenstadt (ed.), *The Origins and Diversity of Axial Age Civilizations* (Albany: State University of New York Press, 1986) 182; idem, "Jerusalem—A Political and Spiritual Capital," 30. Examples include:
- Sargon: "precious branch (*per'u*) of Aššur, of royal lineage, of ancient stock"
- Esarhaddon: "precious branch (*per'u*) of Aššur, of royal lineage, of ancient stock"
- Nebuchadnezzar I: "offspring of Enmeduranki, king of Sippar, a branch of Nippur of ancient stock"

Modern English maintains this idea very well, in that something may be designated as an "offshoot" of something else, from which it "stems."

[93] *CAD* P, 12.416–18, s.v. *pir'u* "shoot, offshoot, leaf; offspring, descendant"; *AHw* 2.856, s.v. *per'u(m)*, *perḫu*, "Sproß, Nachkomme." The nominal form is from *parā'u*, "to sprout." The notion also appears in the propagandistic royal title *zēr šarrūti dārû* "lasting seed of kingship," an ancient claim to divine parentage extending back to the Ur III dynasty of the late third millennium B.C.E. For further discussion, see W. G. Lambert, "The Seed of Kingship," in P. Garelli (ed.), *Le Palais et la Royauté, Archéologie et Civilisation* (RAI 19; Paris: P. Geunther, 1974) 427–40; Barbara N. Porter, *Images, Power, and Politics: Figurative Aspects of Esarhaddon's Babylonian Policy* (Philadelphia: American Philosophical Society, 1993) 122 n. 265.

turned on its head by Isaiah ben Amoz and used to symbolize the down-fall of the tyrannical juggernaut. This reversal is made complete by juxta-posing the end of imperial dominion with the wellspring of the house of David originating in Jesse. Such a stylistic technique is commonly credited to the eighth-century prophet, and justifies attributing to him as well the vision of the ideal king in Isa 10:33–11:9.[94]

6.2.4. *Literary and Historical Context*

Looking beyond the pronouncement of the emerging shoot to the oracle as a whole, there are other factors which point to an eighth-century set-ting.[95] The demarcation of the literary unit has immediate implications for its provenance, as the pattern of divine overthrow of imperial oppres-sion followed by a Davidic ruler emerging to lead his people with justice and righteousness was seen previously in Isa 8:23–9:6, a text which by all indications is an authentically Isaian oracle.[96] The originality of Isa 10:33–34 has likewise been upheld due to the phrase הָאָדוֹן יְהוָה צְבָאוֹת, a title common in other Isaianic material.[97]

The concerns of the text also bespeak an eighth-century setting. It is a characteristically Deuteronomic concept that judging is to be done fairly (בְּצֶדֶק), a notion attested only once in all of the other legal corpora.[98] It

---

[94] Ably highlighted by Peter Machinist, "Assyria and Its Image in the First Isaiah," *JAOS* 103/4 (1983) 719–37. Note that this observation also cements the justification for see-ing Isa 10:33–34 as the beginning of the vision of the ideal king.

[95] A pertinent methodological error in dating texts is raised by Benjamin D. Som-mer, "Dating Pentateuchal Texts and the Perils of Pseudo-Historicism," in T. B. Dozeman, K. Schmid and B. J. Schwartz (eds.), *The Pentateuch: International Perspectives on Current Research* (FAT 78; Tübingen: Mohr Siebeck, 2011) 85–108; namely, postulating the date of a text by comparing its ideas to those of a particular time period. While his main point is certainly valid, there are instances in which such a comparative method still has merit. In the case of Isa 10:33–11:9 presented here, an eighth-century date has already been suggested by internal literary analysis. To compare ideas and themes in order to provide additional argumentation is therefore of value, much in the same way that stylistic variations among the Pentateuchal documents should never be used as a criterion for separation, but may nonetheless be employed after-the-fact in order to verify source-critical results. Historical comparisons are still valid as long as they are only used as supporting, not primary, evi-dence in the dating of a biblical text.

[96] Also noted by Wegner, *Kingship and Messianic Expectation in Isaiah 1–35*, 249, who concludes "It is difficult to know when the arrangement of the present passage actually occurred, but vv. 33f. and 11:1–9 portray some significant similarities to other authentic Isaianic materials."

[97] Nielsen, *There is Hope for a Tree*, 129.

[98] Deut 1:16; 16:18; Jer 11:20; cf. Deut 25:1; 2 Sam 15:4; 1 Kgs 8:32, and throughout Psalms. The sole outlier is the Holiness Legislation of Lev 19:15. As I date this literary layer to roughly the same period as the oldest stratum of Deuteronomic law, this verse should

is this standard to which Isaiah appeals in his condemnation of Jerusalem in the opening chapter of the book, promising that when YHWH restores her judges, she would be called "the city of righteousness."[99] This ideal for equanimity in legal proceedings is exercised by the shoot over both the poor (דַּלִּים) and the afflicted (עַנְוֵי־אָרֶץ), demonstrating a concern for social justice amply attested elsewhere in Deuteronomy and the prophetic literature of the day.[100] The faultless implementation of מִשְׁפָּט by the king, coupled with his living in "the fear of YHWH" (יִרְאַת יְהוָה, Isa 11:2–3) are two points stressed in the law of the king in Deut 17:14–20.[101] Finally, the universal impact of this righteousness and fairness which stems directly from judicious application of the instruction of YHWH harkens back to the Temple vision of Isa 2:1–5, another utopian oracle which follows on from a decidedly negative allocution (Isa 1:10–31) and may be shown to be authentically Isaian.[102]

---

actually be seen as evidence of its antiquity. These two legal corpora are in essence merely reflections of each other with different emphases. Whereas the Holiness Legislation is a southern, priestly composition infused with philanthropic laws influenced by the north, Deuteronomy is an originally northern, non-cultic composition infused with priestly laws influenced by the south.

[99] Isa 1:26, cf. v 21.

[100] Isa 10:2; Amos 2:7; 4:1; 5:11; 8:6. In Deuteronomy, cf. Deut 10:18; 14:29; 16:11, 14; 24:17, 19–21; 26:12–13; 27:19.

[101] Note also that the law in Deuteronomy ends with the stated aim "that his heart may not be lifted up (above his countrymen)," which aligns well with reading the stock (גֵּזַע) as being in part a measure of the ruler's humility.

[102] It is the contention of Marvin A. Sweeney, "Micah's Debate with Isaiah," *JSOT* 93 (2001) 111–24, that not only is Mic 4:1–5 to be given priority over Isa 2:2–5, but that the prophecy "is an exilic or post-exilic composition that has been employed in both prophetic books" (p. 112). His premise, then, is that an originally independent and appreciably late oracle found its way into two different prophetic books whose respective literary settings date back to the same period. Had the oracle turned up in both an early and a late prophetic book (e.g., First Isaiah and Haggai), one might more readily suspect an insertion into the earlier work. But its occurrence in the books of two eighth-century prophets shows that the later editors thought it belonged there, see Francis I. Andersen and David Noel Freedman, *Micah* (AYB 24E; New York: Doubleday, 2000) 413–25.
I follow Hans Wildberger, *Isaiah 1–12: A Commentary* (trans. Thomas H. Trapp; Continental Commentary; Minneapolis: Fortress Press, 1991) 85–87, in assigning textual priority to Isa 2, as well as in considering it to be an authentic prophecy. On the basis of expansion alone, Mic 4:1–5 looks to be an extended form of Isa 2:2–5. The popular saying in Mic 4:4, "under his vine and under his own fig tree" appears in 1 Kgs 5:5, where it better fits the context. Baruch J. Schwartz, "Torah from Zion: Isaiah's Temple Vision (Isaiah 2:1–4)," in A. Houtman, M. J. H. M. Poorthuis, and J. Schwartz (eds.), *Sanctity of Time and Space in Tradition and Modernity* (Leiden: Brill, 1998) 15, notes that the visibility of the Temple from afar concurs with the Isaian motif of the "banner to the nations," which the nations are to see and to proceed in its direction (cf. Isa 5:26; 11:12; 13:2; 18:3; 33:23). Hebrew תּוֹרָה "teaching,

Isa 8:23–9:6 has already been presented as an eighth-century messianic vision, and whether or not similar prophecies in Amos 9:11–15; Hos 2:2; 3:4–5; Mic 5:1–3 [Eng. 2–4] are accepted as originating in this period, it is meaningful that these harmonious messages are all placed in the mouths of prophets contemporaneous with Isaiah.[103] The oracle of the shoot in Isa 10:33–11:9 would seem to be anchored in the years immediately following the conquest of the northern kingdom, based on the Assyrian judgment leveled in Isa 10:9, "Is not Samaria like Damascus?"[104] This socio-political context provides an appropriate background for the renewed expectancy in a revitalized Davidic kingdom encompassing all the tribes of Jacob.[105] Placed in its proper historical setting, the universal scope of the Judean monarch's influence, coupled with his role as a just ruler, forms an antithetical counterpart to the draconian hegemony of the Assyrian empire.[106] This concurs with other studies which date the rise of universal monotheism to this period.[107]

---

instruction" is an important concept in Isaiah, cf. Isa 1:10; 2:3; 5:24; 8:16, 20; 24:5; 30:9, etc. It does not occur elsewhere, however, in the book of Micah.

Commentators have noticed that Mic 4:5, "Though all the peoples walk each in the name of his god," conflicts with the idea of universalism in the preceding verses. Micah desires to limit the influence and involvement of the nations in Jerusalem, thus taking Isaiah's radical idea of universal recognition of the God of Israel and converting it into a more conventional belief. This is further suggested by the lack of "all" in Mic 4:1, and by the fact that judgment in Mic 4:3 is handled from afar; i.e., the nations do not physically come to Jerusalem.

[103] Lofty aspirations pertaining to kingship cannot be a purely (post-)exilic phenomenon, owing to material widely acknowledged to be from the 10th–9th centuries B.C.E. such as Gen 49:10 in Jacob's blessing and the vision of the star and the scepter in Num 24:17–19.

[104] The mention of the conquest of the fall of Carchemish is another temporal indicator, being dated to 717 B.C.E. by Hayim Tadmor, "The Campaigns of Sargon II of Assur: A Chronological-Historical Study," *JCS* 12 (1958) 22–40 (Issue 1), 94 (Issue 3). Sargon variously dates its capture to his fourth or fifth *palû* (718–717 B.C.E.).

[105] Schniedewind, "Jerusalem and the Composition of the Biblical Texts," 390–93.

[106] Weinfeld, "Protest against Imperialism," 170, concurs, citing a three-fold structure in Isa 10:5–11:10, "[t]he most outspoken anti-imperialistic document of Isaiah":

    "a. The protest against Assyrian dominion and its crimes (10:5–15)

    b. The destruction of Assyria (10:16–34)

    c. The rise of the divine ruler and world salvation (11:1–10`)."

[107] The Assyrian empire has been credited with the rise of universal monotheism by scholars such as Baruch Levine, "Assyrian Ideology and Israelite Monotheism," *Iraq* 67/1 (2005) 411–27. The position taken here with regard to kingship dovetails with his assessment that "universal monotheism is to be seen as a religious response to empire" (p. 411). Christopher R. Seitz, "First Isaiah," *AYBD* 3.478, observes: "It can be no accident that classical prophecy also emerged at this period (i.e., 8th-century), taking on a certain distinctive profile but sharing a belief that the God of Israel was also the God of the nations and the cosmos (Amos 1–2; Hosea 11–13; Micah 7; Zeph 2:5–15)."

A timeframe after the fall of Samaria would once again isolate Hezekiah as the ideal candidate to be identified with the shoot, and confirm that Isaiah was not speaking abstractly of a theoretical ruler reigning at some indefinite time. The even loftier depictions of the messianic age supplied by the prophet over against those in Isa 8:23–9:6 were warranted in terms of the political situation. As the kingdom of Israel had now fallen, reunification was now feasible with a corresponding gathering of the remnant (vv 11:11–16), and retribution could justifiably be taken against Assyria for its arrogance (vv 10:12–19). The Lord of hosts was just about ready to bring low the highest bough (מְסָעֵף פֻּארָה, v 10:33), and the anointed leader whom YHWH had established—חִזְקִיָּהוּ, hence his name—would be the one the lead his people.[108] In sum, there are many reasons to argue for the originality of the oracle in Isa 10:33–11:9, and such a vision could quite plausibly have arisen out of the circumstances in the late eighth century. Although an additional case has been made for Hezekiah as the one in whom Isaiah placed his hopes, further evidence must be marshaled in support of this position.[109]

---

[108] The reign of Hezekiah as an ideal ruler is a fitting testament to Isaiah's characteristic reversals of imagery. The shoot from the stock of Jesse would replace the bough (פֻּארָה) to be lopped off by YHWH, his fear of the Lord offsetting the haughtiness of the dethroned imperial king (Isa 10:33–11:2). Instead of inveighing against a populace who "deprive the needy of justice and rob the poor of my people of [their] rights" (Isa 10:2), Hezekiah would be a "wonderful counselor" (v 9:6), who "with righteousness will judge the poor, and decide with fairness for the afflicted of the earth" (v 11:4). Isaiah had foreseen his world torn apart by conflict: "Their root will become like rot and their blossom blow away as dust, for they have rejected the law of YHWH of hosts and despised the word of the Holy One of Israel" (v 5:24). This would be replaced by an idyllic era in which "they will not hurt or destroy in all my holy mountain, for the earth will be full of the knowledge of YHWH as the waters cover the sea" (v 11:9). A people condemned by their deity would now be forgiven, such that their divinely ordained dispersion to the ends of the earth would be replaced by an unrivaled ingathering (Isa 11:11–16). The messianic reign of Hezekiah would undo the most significant deleterious aspects of Isaiah's present world.

[109] A further intimation that Isaiah had Hezekiah in mind may be found in the *rab šāqê*'s taunt against the king before the walls of Jerusalem (2 Kgs 18:20/Isa 36:5):

אָמַרְתָּ אַךְ־דְּבַר־שְׂפָתַיִם עֵצָה וּגְבוּרָה לַמִּלְחָמָה

Do you think that empty talk is counsel and strength for war?
The accusation that Hezekiah was only interested in "empty talk" aligns with the Isaianic description of him as a peaceable leader, and the fact that Jerusalem was delivered meant that the Judean ruler did indeed have "counsel and strength." Other than in the speech of the *rab šāqê*, the only other occurrence of עֵצָה וּגְבוּרָה is in Isa 11:2, which claims that the shoot shall be imbued with רוּחַ עֵצָה וּגְבוּרָה. As the Isaian tradents of Sennacherib's third campaign were intent upon accentuating the greatness of Hezekiah by inserting intentional connections back to Isa 7 and the meeting with Ahaz, it is not unreasonable that they tied into additional relevant material from this prophetic collection.

6.3. Isa 7 and the Sign of Immanuel

6.3.1. *Overview*

While the sheer volume of academic literature published on Sennacherib's third campaign has arguably consumed many forests, the distinction of the most exegetical energy spent in regard to a single verse may well be awarded to Isa 7:14.[110] The sign to the Judean king Ahaz in the form of a newborn child was given in the context of the Syro-Ephraimitic war. Rezin of Damascus and Pekah of Israel struck an alliance in order to depose Ahaz for his failure to join their anti-Assyrian coalition. Due to the influence of this verse on the development of messianism and later Christology, the sheer number of questions that could be posed are legion, meriting an extensive monograph in its own right. In the interests of space, my attention will be focused on one of the most divisive interpretive cruxes in biblical literature: the identity of the infant Immanuel.

It is a fair question at the outset of such an exegetical undertaking to inquire as to whether such a question would have been relevant to the intended audience of the prophecy. It is, after all, the birth of the newborn rather than his identity which substantiates that the Lord will stand behind the house of David at such a vexing time. As with other cases of the prophetic naming of children preserved in Isaiah and Amos, it is the promise invoked by the name which is paramount and not who bore it.[111]

---

[110] While there can be no question of an exhaustive bibliography, one should start with the abundant literature cited in Wildberger, *Isaiah 1–12*, 279–318, and Sweeney, *Isaiah 1–39*, 143–64. The following are additional studies on the Immanuel sign, apart from the standard commentaries: Cyrus H. Gordon, "'Almah in Isaiah 7:14," *JBR* 21 (1953) 106; J. Barton Payne, "Right Questions About Isaiah 7:14," in M. Inch and R. Youngblood (eds.), *The Living and Active Word of God. Studies in Honor of Samuel L. Schultz* (Winona Lake, Ind.: Eisenbrauns, 1983) 75–84; Michael E. W. Thompson, "Isaiah's Sign of Immanuel," *ExpTim* 95/3 (1983) 67–71; Christoph Dohmen, "Das Immanuelzeichen. Ein jesajanisches Drohwort und seine inneralttestamentliche Rezeption," *Bib* 68/3 (1987) 305–29; Ernst Haag, "Das Immanuelzeichen in Jesaja 7," *TTZ* 100 (1991) 3–22; H. G. M. Williamson, *Variations on a Theme: King, Messiah and Servant in the Book of Isaiah* (Carlisle, Cumbria: Paternoster Press, 1998) 73–112; Murray R. Adamthwaite, "Isaiah 7:16: Key to the Immanuel Prophecy," *RTR* 59/2 (2000) 65–83; Joel Edmund Anderson, "Isaiah 7:14. Identity and Function within the Bookend Structure of Proto-Isaiah" (Ph.D. diss.; University of Pretoria, 2008); John J. Collins, "The Sign of Immanuel," in J. Day (ed.), *Prophecy and the Prophets in Ancient Israel: Proceedings of the Oxford Old Testament Seminar* (LHB/OTS 531; New York: T&T Clark, 2010) 225–44.

[111] Conversely, names of characters within biblical narratives were often omitted due to the appelation being secondary to the role that individual played in the story, such as the name of Abraham's servant in Gen 24. Nor does Scripture always present a single

Yet there are cases in which a text is directly concerned with a certain issue but does not provide all of its details because they would have been readily known to the people of the time, such as the rationale behind various laws which have been lost to us over the intervening millennia.

Isaiah ben Amoz had someone particular in mind when proclaiming the oracle, because he designates it as a "sign" (אוֹת) by which Ahaz could confirm the Lord's promise.[112] The names selected for the children throughout the Syro-Ephraimite conflict were for the express purpose of instilling widespread confidence in the saving actions of the deity. Thus the entire community was cognizant of who they were, and in the case of Immanuel this intentional wider identification is expressly mentioned via the second masculine plural suffix: לָכֵן יִתֵּן אֲדֹנָי הוּא לָכֶם אוֹת.[113] Hence it is the fact that there was no disputation at the time as to the identity of Immanuel which obviated the need to preserve such superfluous information.[114] Having resolved that such an inquiry is indeed of interpretive merit, the scholar must nevertheless readily admit that there is no way to ascertain the identity of Immanuel with absolute certainty. In such a situation, the best that can be hoped for is to assess the strongest possibilities and to see where the bulk of the available evidence lies.

6.3.2. *The Identity of Immanuel*

Because the dialogue at the conduit of the upper pool is expressly between Ahaz and Isaiah—although the latter's son Šeʿar-yašub was present as

---

unambiguous stance on a matter, such as the double tradition of the extent of the conquest as being both complete and incomplete.

[112] In prophetic passages, an אוֹת provides a guarantee of the truth of the prophetic word, and is always of a very specific nature. The man of God who prophesies to Eli tells him that his sons will die on the very same day as a "sign to you" (וְזֶה־לְּךָ הָאוֹת, 1 Sam 2:34). Jeremiah tells the Judeans who have sought refuge in Egypt that they will meet their end by sword and famine, and that the capture of Pharaoh Hophra by his enemies is intended to serve as a "sign to you" (וְזֹאת־לָכֶם הָאוֹת, Jer 44:29). When Hezekiah is near death, Isaiah has the shadow on the stairway move back ten steps as a sign to him "that YHWH will do this thing that He has spoken." 2 Kgs 20:9; Isa 38:7–8. These examples, and many more like them, demonstrate that a "sign" was something experiential that was intended to be verified by the receiving party.

[113] Isa 7:14.

[114] Karl Budde, the progenitor of the *Denkschrift* hypothesis, argued that the assumption of so much prior knowledge on the part of the reader was a testimony to its Isaianic authorship: "Everything [in Isaiah 7] reflects the immediate present, the discussion between individuals whose personal interests are involved, between persons who are totally informed about matters. Only the prophet himself can be made responsible for such a depiction of events" ("Das Immanuelzeichen und die Ahaz-Begegnung Jesaja 7," *JBL* 52 [1933] 39).

well—the referenced mother of the child is logically presumed to be the wife of either the king or the prophet.[115] While from a grammatical standpoint the intended referent of הָעַלְמָה need not be restricted in such a manner, she necessarily must have been known to Ahaz in order for him to verify the אוֹת promised by YHWH.[116] The primary argument in favor of Immanuel being the son of Isaiah rests on the fact that the prophet bore two other children who are expressly his—Šeʿar-yašub and Maher-šalal-ḥaš-baz—whose names were also used as sign acts at the height of the Syro-Ephraimitic war as a means of consolation to Judah.[117] For some, this is decisive.[118] The oracle in Isa 8:1–4 is a close parallel to the Immanuel sign, and as Isaiah's wife is clearly the mother of the child there, it suggests that the prophet is also referring to her when speaking to Ahaz. That Immanuel may be a direct descendant of Isaiah is strengthened by appeal to Isa 8:18, in which the prophet states: "See, I and the children whom YHWH has given me are signs and portents in Israel from YHWH of hosts, who dwells on Mount Zion." Analogy has likewise been made to the prophet Hosea: just as he bore three children as a means to communicate the Lord's message to his people, Isaiah was likewise instructed to give prophetically significant names to the same typological number of offspring.

These data are suggestive, but ultimately inferential. While the other two children are explicitly stated to be sons of Isaiah, Immanuel is not, and this fact alone is telling. Since the wife of the prophet was soon to conceive Maher-šalal-ḥaš-baz as described in Isa 8:3, Immanuel must be

---

[115] There are more extreme positions such as that of L. G. Rignell, "Das Immanuelszeichen: Einige Gesichtspunkte zu Jes. 7," StTh 11 (1957) 112ff, who posits that Immanuel represents the new Israel. Such suggestions have already been weighed by previous scholarship and will not be discussed here.

[116] The "sign" has implications for the interpretation of הָעַלְמָה in Isa 7:14. Although the use of the definite article in Biblical Hebrew for the most part closely mirrors that of English, its use when an unknown participant is being introduced for the first time (e.g., הַחֲמֹר in Exod 4:20) is less understood. On this, see Peter Bekins, "The Use of the Definite Article for Frame-Based Reference in Biblical Hebrew" (Midwest SBL Regional Paper; Valparaiso, Ind., 13 Feb 2010). While grammatically the employment of the definite article permits in certain cases an indefinite discourse reference, the appearance of הָעַלְמָה in the context of אוֹת indicates that Isaiah was indeed identifying a particular individual.

[117] Isa 7:3; 8:3. Ibn Ezra and Rashi favored this interpretation.

[118] E.g., J. J. M. Roberts, "Isaiah and His Children," in A. Kort and S. Morschauser (eds.), Biblical and Related Studies Presented to Samuel Iwry (Winona Lake, Ind.: Eisenbrauns, 1985) 198. Although there is nothing in the biblical text which states that the prophetess in Isa 8:3 was the wife of Isaiah, the fact of their sexual union makes this identification the most plausible. For those who would rather keep this point open, הַנְּבִיאָה may be considered otherwise without any ramifications on my conclusions.

the child of another woman, or else the events of chap. 8 must be projected further into the future.[119] Yet the brief timeframe of the war with Aram and Ephraim makes it unlikely that Isaiah's wife would have had sufficient opportunity to bear another child in addition to Maher-šalal-ḥaš-baz; as with the sons of Hosea, some two years of weaning would have had to take place before the next child was conceived. There should also be some respect for the fact that the mother of Immanuel (הָעַלְמָה) in Isa 7:14 is not designated in the same way as the mother of the prophetic child (הַנְּבִיאָה) in v 8:3. If the latter verse, spoken in the first person, represents Isaiah's preferred way to refer to his spouse, it requires explanation as to why he would choose a different, decidedly more ambiguous epithet to refer to her in his momentous proclamation to Ahaz.

Here one begins to see indications that indeed only a royal child could be intended. The aspect of the verb הָרָה in v 7:14 intimates that the young woman was already pregnant, and judging by the likely inchoative sense of the following participle יֹלֶדֶת was soon to give birth. With this reading, the designation הָעַלְמָה is more readily understandable: Ahaz would soon become aware through social contact, if he wasn't already, of someone in his life who was pregnant. If the prophetess were the mother an express declaration would be necessary, but if the child were to be born under the auspices of Ahaz then the mother would be self-evident. This further suggests that הָעַלְמָה has been employed by Isaiah with precision, which gives credence to the suggestion of the *Religionsgeschichtliche Schule* that the word is meant to recall the cognate *ǵalmatu* in Ugaritic literature.[120] There it is used as an epithet for the virgin Anat or as an abstract designation for a goddess who gives birth to a child, most notably in KTU 1.24:7, *hl ǵlmt tld bn* "Behold! The damsel bears a son."[121]

It is well documented that the statement "YHWH is with" someone is a general expression of divine assurance and was an integral part of the Zion theology as articulated in Ps 46:8, 12 [Eng. 7, 11], "YHWH of hosts is

---

[119] As noted by Wildberger, *Isaiah 1–12*, 102; Collins, "Sign of Immanuel."

[120] Jesper Høgenhaven, *Gott und Volk bei Jesaja. Eine Untersuchung zur biblischen Theologie* (Leiden: E. J. Brill, 1988) 89–90; Mowinckel, *He That Cometh*, 114. In ancient Near Eastern myth, varying designations for 'young girl' or 'virgin' are applied to many goddesses, see Bob Becking, "Virgin," *DDD* 890–91. For extensive literature on previous studies of this controversial word, see Christoph Dohmen, "עַלְמָה," *TDOT* 11.154–56.

[121] For further discussion of this cuneiform line, see Wolfram Herrmann, *Yariḫ und Nikkal und der Preis der Kuṯarāt-Göttinen, ein kultisch-magischer Text aus Ras Schamra* (BZAW 106; Berlin: A. Töpelmann, 1968) 7; M. C. A. Korpel, *A Rift in the Clouds: Ugarit and Hebrew Descriptions of the Divine* (UBL 8; Münster: Ugarit-Verlag, 1990) 291.

with us, the God of Jacob is our refuge."[122] But this connection is most prominent in relation to the monarchy, where it conveys pervasively the well-being of YHWH's anointed as exemplified by the following:[123]

- David's rise to greatness is attributed to divine providence, as we are repeatedly told that "YHWH was with him" (cf. 1 Sam 16:18; 18:12, 14, 28; 2 Sam 5:10).
- In the initial promise to David in 2 Sam 7, the Lord tells him "I have been with you (וָאֶהְיֶה עִמְּךָ) wherever you have gone" (v 9).
- Nathan was receptive to the plan of David to build a house for his God, saying "Go, do all that is in your mind, for YHWH is with you" (כִּי יְהוָה עִמָּךְ, 2 Sam 7:3).
- At the time of royal succession, Benaiah the son of Jehoiada proclaims "As YHWH has been with my Lord the king, so may He be with Solomon!" (1 Kgs 1:37)
- In 1 Kgs 11:38, YHWH promises Jeroboam through Ahijah the prophet that if he listens to the Lord's commandments and walks in His ways as David did, "then I will be with you" (וְהָיִיתִי עִמָּךְ).

It is important to note that the sign was specifically intended to counter the threat of Rezin and Pekah to replace Ahaz with "the son of Tabeel" (Isa 7:5–6). This is expressly what the Lord says shall not come to pass (v 7), and hence the portent accorded to "the house of David" to assure continuance of the regal line could only come through a son of Ahaz, and not through a named child of the prophet. That is, it was the child himself, not simply his name, which made manifest that "God is with us."[124] If Immanuel was indeed a royal child, then each of the three children

---

[122] Cf. Exod 3:12; Judg 6:12; 1 Kgs 8:57; Jer 1:8; Ruth 2:4. See Sweeney, *Isaiah 1–39*, 155.

[123] For recent summaries, see Collins, "Sign of Immanuel." His survey also covers the covenantal language of David's house and kingdom being made firm (נֶאֱמָן) forever. There are also variations on this usage which are arguably admissible as well, as when the Lord says of David "My faithfulness and steadfast love shall be with him" (Ps 89:22), or when the rulers of Judah proclaim "Is not YHWH in our midst?" (הֲלוֹא יְהוָה בְּקִרְבֵּנוּ) in Mic 3:11. For my purposes, I have opted to demonstrate that the literal expression alone is amply attested.

[124] The significance of the name Immanuel in Isa 8:8, 10 is debated, but would seem to support his identification as a royal child. For Childs, *Isaiah*, 68–69, the use of Immanuel in these verses shows "many clear indications that it was understood messianically by the tradents of the Isaiah tradition." Joseph Blenkinsopp, *Isaiah 1–39* (AYB 19; New York: Doubleday, 2000) 233–34, makes the case that a royal child is intended because the sign is addressed to Ahaz. He also considers that "O Immanuel" in v 8 is a transparent reference to Hezekiah.

intended as sign acts related to mutually distinct aspects of the political situation: Šeʿar-yašub the fate of the people, Maher-šalal-ḥaš-baz the fate of the foreign kings, and Immanuel the Davidic dynasty.

With the weight of evidence leaning in favor of the possibility that Immanuel was a son of Ahaz, the final step is to ascertain the likelihood that the child was later enthroned as Hezekiah.[125] The most glaring obstacle is once again biblical chronology, and the problematic lineage of Ahaz: if Hezekiah was 25 years old when he became king (2 Kgs 18:2), yet his father only reigned 16 years (v 16:2), then Hezekiah was born before Ahaz ever became king. For many scholars, these data are sufficient to dispel any possibility of equation between Immanuel and Hezekiah, which swings the pendulum in favor of Immanuel as a prophetic child.

However, this issue has already been independently addressed, and its findings are that not only was Hezekiah in all likelihood the son of Ahaz, but that Hezekiah's age is suspect for reasons quite apart from the question of genealogy.[126] This chronological datum was not meticulously kept: there are no ages provided for monarchs of the northern kingdom, and even for some in the southern kingdom—Saul, Solomon, Abijam, Asa, and Athaliah—these data are simply omitted. If such details were not preserved, they may well have been mechanically filled in, or perhaps changed for political reasons.[127] It is extraordinary that Hezekiah's regnal data—25 years old when he began his reign of 29 years—are identical to those of Amaziah, an extremely rare statistical event which does not otherwise occur in Judean chronology.[128] In summation, there are many

---

[125] For previous scholarship, see Laato, *Who Is Immanuel?*, 139–44.

[126] The ages at enthronement of Jotham through Hezekiah contain the unique occurrence in Judean chronology of being round numbers (25, 20, and 25, respectively), conspicuously so in light of the coronation ages of all kings subsequent to Hezekiah: Manasseh (12 years, 2 Kgs 21:1); Amon (22 years, v 21:19); Josiah (8 years, v 22:1); Jehoahaz (23 years, v 23:31); Jehoiakim (25 years, v 23:36); Jehoiachin (18 years, v 24:8); Zedekiah (21 years, v 24:18).
Moreover, the age of 25 years is preserved no less than four times throughout the Judean list of royal records, while the next most common age (22) appears only twice, after which all ages provided for the rulers are unique. The kings aged 25 years are Amaziah (2 Kgs 14:2), Jotham (v 15:33), Hezekiah (v 18:2), and Jehoiakim (v 23:36). The monarchs aged 22 years are Ahaziah (2 Kgs 8:26) and Amon (v 21:19).

[127] It is telling that prior to the revolt of Jehu, four of the eight Judean kings—David, Rehoboam, Jehoshaphat, and Jehoram—were over 30 years of age when they began to reign, and as ages are not provided for the other four kings, this is a one-hundred percent totality: David (30 years, 2 Sam 5:4); Rehoboam (41 years, 1 Kgs 14:21); Jehoshaphat (35 years, v 22:42); Jehoram (32 years, 2 Kgs 8:17). After the revolt of Jehu, there are none.

[128] 2 Kgs 14:2; 18:2. Both rulers also happen to precede monarchs with extended, and otherwise unique, reigns of over fifty years.

different ways of approaching such numerical conundrums, but all forms of analysis reinforce the notion that although the years of reign for the divided kingdom are on the whole very reliable, the ages attributed to the kings at their enthronement do not commend themselves to historical reconstruction.

One of the strongest cases textually that may be made for Hezekiah as the throne name of the youth Immanuel is in 2 Kgs 18:7, which succinctly states "YHWH was with him (יְהוָה עִמּוֹ)." Not only is this description a direct wordplay on the name Immanuel, but of all the Judean kings, only Hezekiah and David (2 Sam 5:10) have their reigns directly evaluated in this manner by the Deuteronomistic historian. Should this be dismissed as mere coincidence, only these two rulers are stated to have prospered (הִשְׂכִּיל) due to the Lord's watchful guidance. Compare the assessment of Hezekiah above with that of David:

1 Sam 18:14	And David in all his ways was prospering (מַשְׂכִּיל),
(David)	for YHWH was with him (וַיהוָה עִמּוֹ)
2 Kgs 18:7	And YHWH was with him (יְהוָה עִמּוֹ);
(Hezekiah)	wherever he went he prospered (יַעְכִּיל).

Such indications have underscored the conclusions of recent monographs that it was Hezekiah, not Josiah, who was rightfully acknowledged as the 'second David' in the history of Israel.[129] The unique accolade of being so closely compared to the forerunner of the royal dynasty is in itself reason enough to take seriously the prospect that Hezekiah was truly considered to be the manifestation among his own people of "God with us."

A sign of continuance for the Davidic line would also have been paramount if the account of 2 Chr 28:7 is correct, in which Maaseiah the son of Ahaz is reported to have been slain by a valiant Ephraimite warrior named Zichri. Because the details of this war between Ahaz and Pekah of Israel are characteristically devoid of the Chronicler's most prominent theological motifs, in particular that individual reward or punishment is divinely predicated upon one's moral integrity, it is reasonable to see in this self-contained unit vestiges of an earlier source.[130] In this case, the

---

[129] Notably Iain W. Provan, *Hezekiah and the Books of Kings: A Contribution to the Debate about the Composition of the Deuteronomistic History* (BZAW 172; Berlin: Walter de Gruyter, 1988). This possibility will be more fully explored in my final chapter.

[130] Sara Japhet, *I & II Chronicles: A Commentary* (OTL; Louisville: Westminster/John Knox, 1993) 899–900.

express age of Maaseiah is not given yet no chronological calculations are necessary; the fact that he is sufficiently mature to go to war at the time of the Syro-Ephraimite conflict rules him out as the child Immanuel. If Maaseiah was the eldest son and heir to the throne, his death would have cast serious doubts upon the line of succession for all of Judah if Ahaz had borne no other children.

If the age of Hezekiah as given in the annalistic records may be called into question, how old would he have been at his accession if he is to be identified with Immanuel? The swift response of Tiglath-pileser III to the plea of Ahaz for help is generally dated to 734 B.C.E., when Arvad and Gaza were taken and Egyptian interference was soundly blocked.[131] This particular pocket of anti-Assyrian resistance was not put down until 732, when the second of two successive campaigns was undertaken to Damascus in order to make Rezin's kingdom an imperial vassal. Ahaz had not yet made this appeal according to the narrative of Isa 7, and it would have taken the Assyrian military at least one campaign season (palû) to respond.[132] As Immanuel had presumably already been conceived and was

---

[131] ND400 and ND4301+4305, published respectively by D. J. Wiseman, "Two Historical Inscriptions from Nimrud," *Iraq* 13 (1951) 21–28; idem, "A Fragmentary Inscription of Tiglath-pileser III from Nimrud," *Iraq* 18 (1956) 117–29. English translations and analysis of the texts may be found in Irvine, *Isaiah, Ahaz, and the Syro-Ephraimitic Crisis*, 44–62, who dates the action taken against Tyre to a subsequent campaign.

The appeal of Ahaz is dated to this year based on his inclusion in a list of tribute bearers (Summary Inscription 7), inferentially assigned to 734 B.C.E. by Hayim Tadmor, *The Inscriptions of Tiglath-pileser III King of Assyria* (Jerusalem: Israel Academy of Sciences and Humanities, 1994) 268. For editions and translations, see the bibliography at Mordechai Cogan, *The Raging Torrent: Historical Inscriptions from Assyria and Babylonia Relating to Ancient Israel* (Jerusalem: Carta, 2008) 59–60.

[132] Irvine, *Isaiah, Ahaz, and the Syro-Ephraimitic Crisis*, 70, is forced to compress the events of the onset of the war in order to fit his chronology. With Pekah's coup in Samaria dated by him to Tishri 734, he concludes: "If the campaign followed sometime after Pekah's rise to the Israelite throne, the forces of Tiglath-pileser would have invaded the area late in 734 or early in 733." There are two issues with this reconstruction. First, unlike Sennacherib, Tiglath-pileser is not known to have committed his troops during winter. Second, military responses took time and had to be planned. The anti-Assyrian coalition of the Syrian coastal cities which Tiglath-pileser crushed in 738, for instance, had formed the previous year while he was otherwise occupied with quelling Urartian influence in Ulluba, see A. Kirk Grayson, "Assyria: Tiglath-pileser III to Sargon II (744–705 B.C.)," in J. Boardman et al. (eds.), *The Cambridge Ancient History Second Edition, Volume III Part 2: The Assyrian and Babylonian Empires and other States of the Near East, from the Eighth to the Sixth Centuries B.C.* (Cambridge: Cambridge University Press, 1991) 74–76.

The extensive campaign through Philistia and down to Egypt in 734 B.C.E. was designed to cut off military aid to the rebelling states. With the reinforcements of Egypt as the primary concern of the first foray into the region after the revolt, even the effort to quell the uprising was planned by Tiglath-pileser to span multiple campaign seasons. The Assyrian

about to be born, his birth would have been no later than 735 B.C.E., the latest year in which Ahaz could have summoned aid. Hezekiah was thus approximately ten years old at his coronation in 725, and was co-regent with his father for another three years before becoming sole ruler around age thirteen.[133] Having obtained sufficient tutelage to be able to serve as sovereign on his own, the Bible rightly makes no more comment as to his youth than it does of Manasseh, who acceded to the throne at the tender age of twelve.[134]

Considering that the accession oracle of Isa 8:23–9:6 is most suitable to the reign of Hezekiah, the juxtaposition of the Immanuel prophecy with this coronation announcement lends credence to this linkage having been in the minds of the editors of this prophetic material.[135] If later Jewish interpretation of Immanuel as Hezekiah bears any weight whatsoever, it pushes the preponderance of evidence in the same direction.[136] Note that as with other birth stories in the Hebrew Bible such as those of Moses and Samson, the circumstances of their origin heralded something deeper about their lives' work, and they subsequently reached their apotheosis fulfilling these roles within the biblical text.

This observation has profound implications. If the child Immanuel (his given name) is indeed the monarch Hezekiah (his throne name), it would

---

response was thus not done in haste. The anti-Assyrian coalition was active as early as 735 B.C.E., at which time Ahaz signaled his need for assistance. His recorded tribute in 734 does not directly represent the entreaty to his overlord (2 Kgs 16:8), otherwise one must explain how Tiglath-pileser happened to be campaigning in the west when Ahaz made his overture. Rather, it represents a pledge of subservience to the Assyrian king for responding to his entreaty (v 10), made previously.

[133] Because Ahaz was in his 12th year in the first year of Hoshea (2 Kgs 17:1), and ruled for 16 years (2 Kgs 16:2), then Ahaz was only in his 14th year in the 3rd year of Hoshea, which is also the first year of Hezekiah (2 Kgs 18:1). Thus years 14–16 of Ahaz are equivalent to the first three regnal years of Hezekiah.

[134] 2 Kgs 21:1. This is also a reasonable age in terms of the dynastic succession. According to the biblical chronology, Hezekiah gave birth to Manasseh at age 42, being 54 years old (25 years of age + 29 years of reign) at his death when Manasseh became king at 12. According to the reconstruction given here, in which Hezekiah was some 15 years younger, Manasseh was born when Hezekiah was approximately 27.

[135] Against Laato, *Who Is Immanuel?*, 194–96, 305–306, who sees Isa 9:5–6 as the birth announcement of Immanuel, whose identity was unknown to the prophet. This is at once problematic: Isaiah himself had foretold the birth of the child and knew that the mother was already pregnant. If the son of Amoz was predicting that Immanuel would ascend to the throne, then he was likewise cognizant of the fact that the child was a son of Ahaz.

[136] Justin, *Dialogue with Trypho*, 43; *Exodus Rabbah* 18:5, as discussed in Tryggve Kronholm, "Den kommande Hiskia," *SEÅ* 54 (1989) 109–17; Antti Laato, *A Star is Rising* (ISFCJ 5; Atlanta: Scholars Press, 1997) 123–25; Martin Rehm, *Der königliche Messias im Licht der Immanuel-Weissagungen des Buches Jesaja* (Kevelaer: Butzon & Bercker, 1968) 83–84.

justify the lofty expectations accorded to him by Isaiah at his accession: Immanuel was the first royal child to be employed as a divine sign. As such children were intended to be evidence of the veracity of God's word through the prophet, his name alone would have lent itself to a measure of anticipation of deliverance among the populace. From the moment that Judah escaped the clutches of its northern neighbors just as Isaiah had foretold, Immanuel's unshakeable renown as a sovereign deliverer, the quintessence of "God with us," was immortalized in Israelite history.[137]

6.4. CONCLUSION

The oracle of Isa 8:16–9:6 has its provenience in the eighth century, as has been widely recognized, proclaimed by the prophet Isaiah concerning the northern kingdom ca. 725 B.C.E. in the aftermath of exile by Tiglath-pileser III. The temporal qualities of הָרִאשׁוֹן and הָאַחֲרוֹן in v 8:23 suggest that the passage is pre-exilic, and form a contrast pointing to a reversal of dire circumstances for Israel. The end of the Assyrian empire so vividly portrayed in Isa 9:3–4 is a future prediction to be accomplished by the Lord himself, the first express reason given as to why the people should rejoice. Another basis for exultation is the announcement of the corona-tion of a new ruler, in whom authority has already been vested as seen in the phrase וַתְּהִי הַמִּשְׂרָה עַל־שִׁכְמוֹ. The Judean enthronement proce-dure has been influenced by Egyptian ritual, despite the undue weight that has been placed on the royal titulary. The receipt of the child by the community evinces that the sonship here is metaphorical, and the similarities with Ps 2:7–12 further affirm that this passage is not a birth announcement. As YHWH himself would be responsible for defeating the Assyrian, this anointed one would exercise just and peaceful rule over a vast dominion. In terms of the chronology of the period, Hezekiah is the only suitable candidate to fulfill the prophecy, having taken the throne

---

[137] It is important to recognize that the destruction of Assyria stemmed directly from Isaiah's messianic beliefs. If the prophet truly believed in a ideal age overseen by a right-eous ruler, then that kingdom could not arrive before the reigning empire had been put down. Likewise, if Isaiah thought that Hezekiah was this divinely appointed deliverer, then Assyria would surely be destroyed while he was enthroned. Thus Isaiah foresaw the Assyr-ian army attacking Judah soon after the Syro-Ephraimitic crisis (Isa 7:17; 8:5–8; 10) and being divinely routed in a spectacular manner that would usher in a new messianic era (Isa 9:3–4[4–5]; 10:33–34).

of his father Ahaz in 725 B.C.E. after the incursions by Tiglath-pileser yet
while the northern kingdom remained a viable polity.

The vision of the shoot and of a utopian future in Isa 11:1–9 properly
begins in verse 10:33 with the proud Assyrians likened to colossal trees
felled by the Lord of hosts. In a stylistic reversal characteristic of Isaiah
ben Amoz, the Davidic royal line will continue unabated. Hebrew גֶּזַע יִשַׁי
in v 1 is used to refer to the root-stock of the royal line, the wellspring
of kingship originating with Jesse. It strongly contrasts with פֻּארָה in the
preceding verse, a tongue-in-cheek nod to Neo-Assyrian *per'u* "branch"
used in royal inscriptions as a metaphor for kingship. An eighth-century
literary context is indicated by the professed viability of the Davidic line
in the face of Assyrian domination, and secondarily by its affinity to Deuteronomic law in terms of impartial judgment and concern for the needy.
Its idyllic setting is a fitting *volte-face* by Isaiah of the inexorably powerful
totalitarian regime, and its messianic overtones comport with the message of other contemporary prophets. The ostensible historical context,
soon after the fall of Samaria, points to Hezekiah as the most plausible
referent for the shoot, and the only other use of the phrase עֵצָה וּגְבוּרָה
in the Hebrew Bible is in a quote about him on the lips of the *rab šāqê* in
2 Kgs 18:20/Isa 36:5.

The infant Immanuel mentioned in Isa 7:14 is better seen as a royal
child rather than as the offspring of the prophet. He is not explicitly
claimed by Isaiah as his son, whereas his other two children are, and the
prophetess had already conceived Maher-šalal-ḥaš-baz around this time.
The mother is not designated in the same manner as הַנְּבִיאָה, and the lack
of specificity in regard to הָעַלְמָה suggests that this was a young woman
close to Ahaz. The statement that "Yhwh is with" someone has strong
overtones with the monarchy, and a prophetic sign to assuage the concerns of Ahaz in regard to the continuance of the Davidic line would have
been more meaningful employed on a child of the royal house. Chronology once again favors the identification of Hezekiah as the throne name
for Immanuel, as his recorded age at succession may be called into question, while his projected age of thirteen as sole ruler is sufficiently mature.
Such an explanation would clarify the editorial note that "Yhwh was with
him" in 2 Kgs 18:7, and legitimates the lofty expectations for his kingdom
in Isa 8:23–9:6; 11:1–9.

PART THREE

HEZEKIAH IN CHRONICLES

CHAPTER SEVEN

THE HISTORICAL RELIABILITY OF 2 CHR 29–30

Of the Chronicler's reports concerning the kings of Judah, that of Hezekiah in 2 Chr 29–32 is the most extensive. While most of the material found in 2 Kgs 18–20 has been employed for the new account, about seventy percent of the Chronicler's treatment of Hezekiah has no parallel in Kings. There are various issues which arise in the process of analyzing this unique material. Based on the innate suspicion by scholars of the historical accuracy of the Chronicler's presentation due to his tendency to glorify kings who were pious, how reliable is the extensive attention given to the cultic reforms and reorganization of the Jerusalem temple and its personnel, as well as the detailed account of Hezekiah's economic buildup and civil strength? Which portions of the Chronicler's account should be assigned to an earlier source, and which were composed *de novo* for inclusion in the book? The overriding purpose of looking at the depiction of Hezekiah in Chronicles is to determine whether it contains genuine historical information, or whether this is largely a fictional depiction determined by the Chronicler's agenda.

The historical reliability of the book of Chronicles is a central question in biblical research, occasioned by its parallel yet divergent account of Israelite history in Samuel through Kings.[1] From the beginning of modern critical study of the Bible, its historical value has been negatively assessed. The basis for this pejorative evaluation stemmed indirectly from the date of authorship of the Pentateuch and its documents which occupied the efforts

---

[1] Among the most extensive studies dealing with the history of research of Chronicles' historical reliability are Matt Patrick Graham, *The Utilization of 1 and 2 Chronicles in the Reconstruction of Israelite History in the Nineteenth Century* (SBLDS 116; Atlanta: Scholars Press, 1990); Kai Peltonen, *History Debated: The Historical Reliability of Chronicles in Pre-Critical and Critical Research* (2 vols.; PFES 64; Helsinki: Finish Exegetical Society, 1996). For a more concise survey of the pre-critical period, see Thomas Willi, *Die Chronik als Auslegung. Untersuchungen zur literarischen Gestaltung der historischen Überlieferung Israels* (FRLANT 106; Göttingen: Vandenhoeck & Ruprecht, 1972) 12–47, and for the modern period, Sara Japhet, "The Historical Reliability of Chronicles: The History of the Problem and its Place in Biblical Research," *JSOT* 33 (1985) 83–107; Rodney K. Duke, *The Persuasive Appeal of the Chronicler: A Rhetorical Analysis* (JSOTSup 88; Sheffield: Almond Press, 1990) 11–29.

of 19th-century scholarship. Because the depiction of pre-exilic Israel as recorded in the Former Prophets exhibits only scant affinity with the laws of the Torah, the Deuteronomistic History was considered to be a more authentic and trustworthy account than that preserved in Chronicles. That the latter evinces a close adherence to the precepts of the Torah, particularly in regard to worship, was deemed a pellucid indicator of its inaccuracy and tendentiousness.[2]

It was the flourishing of archaeological discoveries in the Near East during the second half of the 19th century which signaled a change in attitudes toward Chronicles. Historians who had been limited previously in their reconstructions of Israelite history to the biblical text alone were now able to bring external sources to bear in their research. As a result, more careful methodology began to be employed by scholars. Initially, these studies were directed toward material unique to Chronicles which did not bear the characteristic imprint of its author, but it came to be recognized that even those passages which exhibited his distinctive theological views could nevertheless preserve authentic events.[3] Historical credence has been given to portions of the genealogical data, war reports, building texts, administrative and geopolitical reform accounts, and so forth.[4] With present-day exegesis of the book no longer moored to the question of whether or not historical sources were preserved by the Chronicler, the discussion has now turned to the extent of these reports and their manner of employment.

Limiting ourselves specifically to the Chronicler's account of Hezekiah in 2 Chr 29–32, there are additional reasons to be skeptical. The author devotes more space to recounting the reign of Hezekiah than to any other king in the divided monarchy—only David and Solomon are allotted more

---

[2] Wilhelm M. L. de Wette, *Beiträge zur Einleitung in das Alte Testament*, Band 1: *Historisch-kritische Untersuchung über die Bücher der Chronik* (Halle: Schimmelpfennig, 1806); Karl H. Graf, "Das Buch der Chronik als Geschichtsquelle," in *Die Geschichtlichen Bücher des Alten Testaments* (Leipzig: T.O. Weigel, 1866) 114–247; Julius Wellhausen, *Prolegomena zur Geschichte Israels* (6th ed.; Berlin: W. de Gruyter, 1905) 165–223. For various attempts to defend the reliability of Chronicles in the face of this established opinion, see the bibliography at Japhet, "Historical Reliability of Chronicles," 101 nn. 13–17.

[3] For examples of the former, more conservative approach, see the bibliography at Japhet, "Historical Reliability of Chronicles," 103 nn. 40–41; 104 n. 44. For an example of the latter, see William F. Albright, "The Judicial Reform of Jehoshaphat," in S. Lieberman (ed.), *Alexander Marx Jubilee Volume on the Occasion of His Seventieth Birthday* (New York: Jewish Theological Seminary of America, 1950) 61–82.

[4] Reference the excellent selection of articles in M. Patrick Graham, Kenneth G. Hoglund and Steven L. McKenzie (eds.), *The Chronicler as Historian* (JSOTSup 238; Sheffield: Sheffield Academic Press, 1997).

attention. The assessment of his reign is unabashedly glowing, and only a solitary verse casts any aspersions on him at all.[5] Despite its dependence on the parallels in Kings, the major events in chap. 32—the blockade of Jerusalem, the political taunt of Sennacherib's servants before the walls of Jerusalem, the intercession of Isaiah, the destruction of the Assyrian army, Hezekiah's illness and recovery, and the visit of the Babylonian delegation—are all drastically curtailed and reinterpreted affixed with the Chronicler's ideological stamp. The preoccupation of the author with the king's cultic reforms is evident throughout the preceding three chapters which find no analogue in the book of Kings. The dearth of comparative material within the Deuteronomistic History in regard to Hezekiah's restoration of the Temple (chap. 29), celebration of the Passover (chap. 30), and subsequent cultic initiatives (chap. 31), coupled with the Chronicler's well-known predilection for cultic matters, has placed the historicity of these recorded events in doubt. These facts warrant caution in approaching the four chapters dedicated to this regent.[6]

7.1. The Rededication of the Temple (2 Chr 29)

7.1.1. *Authorship*

The account of Hezekiah's reign begins with the immediate use of the king's name, the first and only time that the Chronicler does so in his presentation of a ruler.[7] The fronting is deliberate, a clear departure from the author's consistent usage of separating the regent's age from his length

---

[5] 2 Chr 32:25, indebted to the Deuteronomistic story of Hezekiah's illness in Kings. The visit from the Babylonian envoys is assessed as follows by Mark A. Throntveit, "The Relationship of Hezekiah to David and Solomon in the Books of Chronicles," in M. P. Graham, S. L. McKenzie and G. N. Knoppers, *The Chronicler as Theologian: Essays in Honor of Ralph W. Klein* (JSOTSup 371; London: T&T Clark, 2003) 106–107, "By adding a note stating 'God left him to himself, in order to try him and to know all that was in his heart' (v. 31b), the Chronicler has positively reinterpreted his *Vorlage* to present a blemish as a beauty mark."

[6] As the intent of this chapter is to identify potential historical material within the Hezekiah narrative of Chronicles, a detailed linguistic analysis of this account is beyond the purview of this study. For such an approach to these texts, see, for instance, Joachim Fries, *"Im Dienst am Hause des Herrn": Literaturwissenschaftliche Untersuchungen zu 2 Chr 29–31. Zur Hiskijatradition in Chronik* (ATSAT 60; St. Ottilien: EOS-Verlag, 1998).

[7] William Johnstone, *1 and 2 Chronicles, Volume 2: 2 Chronicles 10–36. Guilt and Atonement* (JSOTSup 254; Sheffield: Sheffield Academic Press, 1997) 189.

of reign by בְּמָלְכוֹ.[8] The proclivity of the Chronicler for Hezekiah would satisfactorily account for this deviation from expected word order, but there would appear to be another factor at work as well. A leitmotif in the book of Chronicles is the king's establishment of his reign.[9] Whereas the Deuteronomistic History expresses "to establish" via the roots כּוֹן (1 Kgs 2:12, 46), קוּם (1 Kgs 9:5), and חָזַק (cf. 2 Kgs 14:5, *qal*; 15:19, *hifil*), the Chronicler's preference is to employ הִתְחַזַּק to convey this action.[10] By utilizing the *hitpael*, the Chronicler expresses that a true king establishes his reign through his own actions. Such an understanding explicates the author's commitment to detailing the martial, administrative, and judicial reforms of Judah's monarchs, interests beyond the purview of the Deuteronomistic historian for whom maintenance and purity of the cult are the foremost concerns. The promoting of Hezekiah's name in his introductory verse betokens him as the ruler *par excellence* in this regard, with the following four chapters detailing the initiatives undertaken by the dynast to secure his rule.

This observation accounts for Hezekiah's first official act of repairing and cleansing the Temple as having been enacted "in the first year of his reign, in the first month": a dedicated ruler would work to secure his kingdom from the moment he was officially enthroned.[11] It likewise connotes his obedience to the deity and solicitude for his holy dwelling.[12] From the conquest of Samaria by Sargon II to the reconstruction of Babylon by Esarhaddon—both events anachronistically credited to them in their accession years (*rēš šarrūti*)—the practice of advancing significant accomplishments to the first regnal year of a monarch was a common

---

[8] 2 Chr 12:13; 20:31; 21:5, 20; 22:2; 24:1; 26:3; 27:1, 8; 28:1; 33:1, 21; 34:1; 36:2, 5, 9, 11. The introductory formula for the reign of Amaziah in 25:1 employs מָלַךְ אֲמַצְיָהוּ after the king's age rather than בְּמָלְכוֹ, but this variation only serves to underscore the unique nature of the fronting of Hezekiah's name.

[9] Johnstone, *2 Chronicles 10–36*, 189.

[10] 2 Chr 1:1; 12:13; 13:8; 17:1; 27:6. Verse 13:21 is another, more questionable, example.

[11] The wordplay on Hezekiah's name within the chapter has been noted, such as the notice that the king repaired (וַיְחַזְּקֵם) the doors of the Temple in v 3. Such paronomasia also undergirds the importance of the theme under discussion here.

[12] Martin Noth, *Überlieferungsgeschichtliche Studien* (Halle: M. Niemeyer, 1943) 157–58. Based on the understanding presented here, there is no basis for the proposal that Hezekiah instituted a new "reform era" calendar, as suggested by Max Vogelstein, *Biblical Chronology I: The Chronology of Hezekiah and his Successors* (Cincinnati: Hebrew Union College, 1944) 2–6; idem, *Fertile Soil: A Political History of Israel under the Divided Kingdom* (New York: American Press, 1957) 72–74.

literary technique in ancient Near Eastern historiography.[13] What is significant about these Mesopotamian parallels is that the historicity of the events themselves is not in question, and in fact the advancing of their dates may be argued as verification of their authenticity: the most salient achievements of a ruler were selected as the means to commend him and his exercise of power. Thus although the date in 2 Chr 29:3 is of little historical value, it has no bearing on the verisimilitude of the concomitant imputed events, which must be independently assessed.

Most of the chapter appears to be a free composition of the Chronicler, imbued with his worldview and devoid of any reliance on an older source.[14] The commissioning of the Levites in vv 5–10, for instance, is a speech of the Chronicler spoken through the mouth of Hezekiah.[15] Its overriding purpose is to persuade, calling attention to the direct outworking of God's pattern of retribution through establishment of a direct cause-and-effect relationship between past actions and present circumstances.[16] The process

---

[13] For further examples, see Hayim Tadmor, "The Inscriptions of Nabunaid: Historical Arrangement," in H. G. Güterbock and T. Jacobsen (eds.), *Studies in Honor of Benno Landsberger on his Seventy-Fifth Birthday* (AS 16; Chicago: Oriental Institute of the University of Chicago, 1965) 351–63. For the phenomenon in Chronicles, see Mordechai Cogan, "Tendentious Chronology in the Book of Chronicles," *Zion* 45 (1980) 165–72 [Hebrew]; idem, "The Chronicler's Use of Chronology as Illuminated by Neo-Assyrian Royal Inscriptions," in J. H. Tigay (ed.), *Empirical Models for Biblical Criticism* (Philadelphia: University of Pennsylvania Press, 1985) 197–209.

[14] Critical opinions on the unity of the chapter are surveyed by H. G. M. Williamson, *1 and 2 Chronicles* (NCB Commentary; Grand Rapids: Wm. B. Eerdmans 1982) 351–52.

[15] The opening of the speech with the imperative "Listen to me!" (שְׁמָעוּנִי) is a Chronistic formula, cf. 1 Chr 28:2; 2 Chr 13:4; 15:2; 20:20; 28:11; 29:5, as noted by Sara Japhet, *I & II Chronicles: A Commentary* (OTL; Louisville: Westminster/John Knox, 1993) 917. The Hebrew word אוּלָם "porch, vestibule" is used in vv 7, 17 and elsewhere in Chronicles as a metonym for the entire Temple, cf. 1 Chr 28:11; 2 Chr 8:12; 15:8; 29:17, Japhet, *I & II Chronicles*, 918. In 1 Kgs 6:3, it is clearly an architectural component of the Temple itself (הָאוּלָם עַל־פְּנֵי הֵיכַל הַבַּיִת).

The form of trespass is מַעַל "disloyalty, infidelity," (v 29:6) which is the archetypal sin in Chronicles, yet both verb and associated noun are wholly absent from Samuel-Kings. See *HALOT* 2.613; Helmer Ringgren, "מָעַל," *TDOT* 8.460–63. Johnstone, *2 Chronicles 10–36*, 191. The verb occurs in 1 Chr 2:7; 5:25; 10:13; 2 Chr 12:2; 26:16, 18; 28:19 22; 29:6; 30:7; 36:14, and the noun in 1 Chr 9:1; 10:13; 2 Chr 28:19; 29:19; 33:19; 36:14.

The rejection of Yhwh is signified by עָזַב (v 6), a verb used sparingly of forsaking the divine commandments in Kings, but which attains far greater prominence in Chronicles. In Kings, עָזַב is used in this context only eight times, in 1 Kgs 9:9; 11:33; 18:18; 19:10, 14; 2 Kgs 17:16; 21:22; 22:17. In Chronicles, this number almost doubles, to fifteen. Such stylistic markers identify this key section on the commissioning of the priests and Levites as a creation of the Chronicler himself.

[16] Although this pattern of retribution is inherent in the Chronicler's theology, it is not absolute, as observed by Ehud Ben Zvi, "A Sense of Proportion An Aspect of the Theology of the Chronicler," *SJOT* 9 (1995) 37–51. Hezekiah's discourse is indicative of rhetorical

of cleansing is also replete with distinctive Chronistic elements. It follows closely on the details of Hezekiah's oration in true command-fulfillment fashion, with literary connections to the preceding reign of Ahaz.[17] Finally, the ceremony celebrating the restoration of Temple service is evidently Chronistic in origin as well.[18]

---

speeches elsewhere in classical and ancient Near Eastern literature, which are typically placed on the lips of focal characters within the narrative in order to express the views of the author. See the bibliography at Mark A. Throntveit, "The Chronicler's Speeches and Historical Reconstruction" in *Chronicler as Historian*, 227 n. 9.

This may be confirmed by the distribution of the royal speeches in Chronicles which have no counterpart in the synoptic material of Samuel-Kings. All fifteen of these identified addresses are spoken either by rulers judged favorably by the Chronicler, or else by ambivalent rulers during a pious span of their reigns. See Rex Mason, *Preaching the Tradition: Homily and Hermeneutics after the Exile* (Cambridge: Cambridge University Press, 1990) 134–35. Even more nuanced studies of Chronicles, written in an era of greater appreciation for the value of the material for historical reconstruction, have overwhelmingly confirmed that the Chronicler functions as a theologian rather than historian in these addresses. For recent studies on these speeches in Chronicles, see Throntveit, "Chronicler's Speeches and Historical Reconstruction," 226 n. 8.

[17] The repair of the Temple by Hezekiah is officially undertaken by the priests and Levites בְּאֶחָד לַחֹדֶשׁ הָרִאשׁוֹן "on the first [day] of the first month" (v 17); that is, they began their task on the very day of their commissioning. This builds upon the leitmotif highlighted earlier of swift response due to fastidious care for the deity which has often justified the transposition of acclaimed royal initiatives to the beginning of a king's reign. The priests and Levites are commanded in v 5 to consecrate themselves and thereafter the Temple (הִתְקַדְּשׁוּ וְקַדְּשׁוּ אֶת־בֵּית יְהוָה), which they proceed to do as instructed (וַיִּתְקַדְּשׁוּ, v 15; לְקַדֵּשׁ...וַיָּחֵלּוּ, v 17). The physical act of cleansing (טָהֵר) in vv 15–16, 18 is in strict compliance with the directive in v 5 to "carry out the uncleanness (הַנִּדָּה) from the Holy Place."

The report of the priesthood to the king after the sanctification has been concluded (v 19) refers back to the repudiation of the cultic utensils by Ahaz in 2 Chr 28:24. The verb וַיְקַצֵּץ in 2 Chr 28:24 is likely taken from the author's *Vorlage* in 2 Kgs 16:17, but there is no corresponding reference to cultic vessels (כֵּלִים). The combination of these two words in chap. 29, then, are an intentional reference back to the Chronicler's own presentation of the faithlessness of Ahaz in the prior chapter.

In both of these sections Ahaz is said to have been faithless (בְּמַעֲלוֹ, v 19; לִמְעוֹל; v 28:22), a Chronistic terminological marker. That this information is included in the priests' notification to the monarch imparts that it was a component of the charge initially given to them, specifically in order to remove the wrath of YHWH on Judah which forced the captivity of its citizens (vv 6–9). This divine wrath and deportation of captives transpired, according to the Chronicler, during the Syro-Ephraimite war owing to the abominable sins of Ahaz (2 Chr 28:1–6, 8).

[18] The prophets are emphasized as bearing the Lord's commandments (v 29:25), an aggrandizing of prophetic authority consistent with the theology of the Chronicler elsewhere that treatment of the deity is reflected in how one responds to the prophets. Compare 2 Chr 20:20, in which trust in the prophets equates to trust in YHWH, with 36:16, where despising them is tantamount to mocking the deity directly. See further William M. Schniedewind, "Prophets and Prophecy in the Books of Chronicles," in *Chronicler as Historian*, 204–24.

The use of numbers throughout the chapter is yet another means of unifying the material. The king rises early on the seventeenth day of the month, the next morning after being informed of the Temple's readiness (vv 17–20). It is yet another example of the alacrity exhibited previously by both the priesthood (v 17) and the king (v 3) in addressing the neglect of the sanctuary ascribed to Ahaz. The number of animals commanded to be slaughtered for the sin offering is stated to be "seven bulls, seven rams, seven lambs, and seven male goats."[19] This typologically significant number is also reflected in the seven Levitical families enumerated in vv 12–14, with the traditional houses of Gershon, Kohath and Merari joined with four additional families in order to achieve the desired total.[20] The purification of the Temple is carried out according to the same numerology, with each of the two stages completed in eight, or seven+one days.[21]

In the summary statement of v 3, Hezekiah is said to have "opened the doors of the house of YHWH and repaired them." The claim that Ahaz had closed the Temple of the Lord, thereby halting Yahwistic worship, has been rightfully subjected to critical scrutiny. The parallel account in 2 Kgs 16:10–18 leaves the distinct impression that sacrifices and offerings to YHWH continued unabated, and cannot be readily reconciled with the report in

---

The use of musical accompaniment during the burnt offering (vv 26–28) is meant to recall the practice instituted by David in 1 Chr 23:4–5; 2 Chr 7:6, and the instruments themselves are expressly referred to as כְּלֵי דָוִיד מֶלֶךְ־יִשְׂרָאֵל (v 27). The active participation of the people in v 31 recalls the transformation of royal and cultic events elsewhere in Chronicles into popular ones, which in this case renews the fidelity toward worship just as under Solomon's rule. Compare the Hebrew rendering of v 35 with 2 Chr 8:16, both employing the same verb וַתִּכּוֹן, "establish, restore."

[19] How each of these groups of seven animals could be equally allotted "for the royal household and for the sanctuary and for Judah" is not readily apparent. The solution of Jacob Milgrom, "Hezekiah's Sacrifices at the Dedication Services of the Purified Temple (2 Chr 29:21–24)," in A. Kort and S. Morschauser (eds.), *Biblical and Related Studies Presented to Samuel Iwry* (Winona Lake, Ind.: Eisenbrauns, 1985) 159–61, is to have them all offered up for *each* beneficiary, yielding a total of 3×(7+7+7+7), or 12×7 sacrificial animals.

The typological number twelve aligns well with other texts that prescribe sacrifices for the dedication of the altar, most notably Num 7:87–88 which shares the same combination of sacrifices. That the text here obfuscates the relevance of the number twelve for the sake of accentuating the number seven is weighty evidence that the narrative of the Temple cleansing has been structured around this value.

[20] Japhet, *I & II Chronicles*, 920–21.

[21] The x+1 pattern in the Hebrew Bible is detailed in Yair Zakovitch, "The Pattern of the Numerical Sequence Three-Four in the Bible" (Ph.D. diss.; The Hebrew University of Jerusalem, 1977) [Hebrew]. The numerological pattern established throughout the chapter casts doubt on the suggestion of Japhet, *I & II Chronicles*, 923, that the duration of eight days may be historical. The later literary examples from 2 Macc 2:12; 10:6, cannot be separated from the influence of Chronicles.

Chronicles. That the Deuteronomist—for whom royal adherence to the commandments of God and to proper worship were of such paramount importance that the evaluation of each king on these terms is uniformly included in the opening regnal formula—would pass over in silence the egregious nature of such a contravention is by all accounts unthinkable. There must be another means to account for the abrupt dichotomy in the versions. The initial charge is laid on Ahaz in 2 Chr 28:24, "he closed the doors of the house of the Lord," followed in exaggerated fashion by "he made altars for himself in *every* corner (בְּכָל־פִּנָּה) of Jerusalem, and in *each and every* city (וּבְכָל־עִיר וָעִיר) of Judah he made high places."[22] The hyperbolic usage here, coupled with the earlier accusation borrowed from 2 Kgs 16:4 that Ahaz sacrificed and burned incense "on the high places, on the hills and under *every* green tree (כָּל־עֵץ רַעֲנָן)" (2 Chr 28:4), provides the key to understanding the Chronicler's intent: the apostasy of Ahaz in turning to the gods of Damascus was absolute and thus could not encompass Yahwistic worship.[23] The closing of the Temple doors is thus evidence of a theological viewpoint having been imposed on the author's *Vorlage*, and cannot be accepted as historically valid.

7.1.2. *Material*

With the origin of chap. 29 resting firmly in the hands of the Chronicler and the closure of the Temple by Ahaz summarily dismissed as a retrojection of the author's unequivocal attitude toward cultic worship, it remains to ask whether there is any concrete historical reality which lies behind the purification and rededication of the Temple under Hezekiah as described in the chapter. If one were to follow most modern method-

---

[22] The expression וּבְכָל־עִיר וָעִיר is the Chronicler's means of articulating that every single city in Judah, without exception, housed a high place erected at the king's command. This means of qualifying כֹּל is consistent with linguistic evidence elsewhere that this Hebrew word, as in English, does not necessarily mean 'all', but rather an extensive, representative amount. One may observe this in the plagues narrative, for instance, in which "all" of the livestock are destroyed multiple times over (Exod 9:4, 6, 19, 25; 12:12, 19). Also after the plague of hail has shattered every plant and tree of the field (וְאֶת־כָּל־עֵץ הַשָּׂדֶה...כָּל־עֵשֶׂב הַשָּׂדֶה, v 9:25), the locusts thereafter "ate every plant of the land and all of the fruit of the trees that the hail had left" (v 10:15). The usage in Chronicles, therefore, is precise and not redundant.

[23] Observed independently by Japhet, *I & II Chronicles*, 918: "Rather, the description reflects a peculiar Chronistic view of the vicissitudes of the Lord's worship, which diverges considerably from that of the Deuteronomist. Its leading principle is that of the mutual exclusivity of idolatry and the worship of the Lord, and entails the complete cancellation of the one during the prevalence of the other."

ologies employed in identifying historical material in Chronicles, the only permissible conclusion is that there is none in this chapter: the episode has no parallel in Kings, conforms to the author's ideology, and cannot be substantiated directly by any extrabiblical evidence.[24]

Yet the Chronicler is nonetheless a historiographer, and has chosen certain constraints within which to compose his history.[25] For all Judean kings, he adheres not only to the genealogy but also to the regnal data for length of rule, age at accession, and birth mother as preserved in the Deuteronomistic History, even in the case of the protracted 55-year reign of the wicked king Manasseh with its resulting theological tensions.[26] The corresponding burial formula has been preserved as well, containing the three key components (a) "So X slept with his fathers"; (b) the burial location; (c) "And his son X became king in his place." It is these two fixed termini, which ultimately go back to early annalistic records, that the Chronicler has chosen to provide the overarching framework for his presentation of the reign of Hezekiah.

A telling detail is the reference to "all Israel" in v 24. There is a palpable literary tension here with v 21, in which the rededication ceremony is expressly said to be for Judah.[27] The attempt has been made to harmonize

---

[24] According to the generalized criteria provided in Andrew G. Vaughn, *Theology, History, and Archaeology in the Chronicler's Account of Hezekiah* (ABS 4; Atlanta: Scholars Press, 1999) 170–71, "An aspect of the Chronicler's account is held to be factually suspect if a) it is not found in Kings, b) is consistent with the ideological or theological agenda of the Chronicler, and c) is not verifiable with extrabiblical, historical data."

[25] Respecting the role of the Chronicler as an ancient historian serves as a counterpoint to scholarship that perceives the book as essentially fictionalized history. See further Kenneth G. Hoglund, "The Chronicler as Historian: A Comparativist Perspective," in *Chronicler as Historian*, 19–29; Ehud Ben Zvi, "About Time: Observations about the Construction of Time in the Book of Chronicles," *HBT* 22 (2000) 17–31; idem, "Shifting the Gaze: Historiographic Constraints in Chronicles and their Implications," in J. A. Dearman and M. P. Graham, *The Land that I Will Show You: Essays on the History and Archaeology of the Ancient Near East in Honour of J. Maxwell Miller* (JSOTSup 343; Sheffield: Sheffield Academic Press, 2001) 38–60.

[26] The sole outlier in terms of age is the lack of correspondence in 2 Chr 36:9; 2 Kgs 24:8, although this is generally dismissed as a scribal error, see Japhet, *I & II Chronicles*, 1067. As noted by Zvi, "Shifting the Gaze," this close adherence in itself is significant, for there are frequent expansions and omissions with regard to the prophets and high priests in comparison with Samuel-Kings.

[27] Exegetes have sought to use this as evidence of literary layers within the chapter, with an older Chronistic narrative having undergone secondary expansion. See Adolf Büchler, "Zur Geschichte der Tempelmusik und der Tempelpsalmen," *ZAW* 19 (1899) 109–14; Adam C. Welch, *The Work of the Chronicler. Its Purpose and Its Date* (London: Oxford University Press, 1939) 103–108; David L. Petersen, *Late Israelite Prophecy: Studies in Deutero-Prophetic Literature and in Chronicles* (Missoula, Mont.: Scholars Press, 1977) 77–85.

the two geographic designations, with "all Israel" being a metonymy for
Judah.[28] Yet virtually every one of the 46 occurrences of כֹּל יִשְׂרָאֵל in
Chronicles refers either to the territory occupied by all twelve tribes or to
the northern kingdom alone.[29] More consequential is the fact that Hezekiah's reform narrative extending over 2 Chr 29–31 is considered to be a
substantial unity, and the subsequent four attestations of כֹּל יִשְׂרָאֵל in
2 Chr 30:1, 5, 6; 31:1 unquestionably pertain to the geographic area of
the former Israelite kingdom or else the combined nations of Judah and
Israel.[30] What seems to be in view, then, is a situation in which a contingent from the north has joined the throng of participants concentrated
from the tribes of Judah and Benjamin. The more diverse representation
of attendees warranted a broader purview for the sin offering in v 21.[31]
As the mention of כֹּל יִשְׂרָאֵל is not otherwise emphasized within the
chapter, and at the same time reflects the historical reality of northerners
who settled in Jerusalem following the Assyrian invasions of the region, it
suggests that elements of the episode of the cleansing of the Temple are
grounded in the knowledge of events of the eighth century.

Despite the Chronicler's hyperbolic claim of total retreat from Yahwistic
worship by Ahaz, discussed earlier, the parallel account of his reign in the
Deuteronomistic History nonetheless does corroborate the incorporation
of foreign elements into the cult. This opens him up to censure by the Deuteronomistic historian, who evaluates the reign of king Ahaz with greater
severity than that of any other king of Judah who preceded him. Up until
this point, the previous denouncement of equivocally viewed kings is ste-

---

[28] Wilhelm Rudolph, *Chronikbücher* (HAT 21; Tübingen: J.C.B. Mohr, 1955) 294, who
favored the unity of the chapter. As countered by H. G. M. Williamson, *Israel in the Books
of Chronicles* (Cambridge: Cambridge University Press, 1977) 127, "However, the king's command in v. 24 stresses by word order (*ky lkl yśr'l 'mr hmlk h'wlh whht't*) that the offering was
to cover an unexpectedly wider group of people, implying a correction of what the priests
had thought to be the case (v. 21)."

[29] 2 Chr 11:3 contains a clear reference to כֹּל יִשְׂרָאֵל as the territory of Judah and Benjamin. Other likely references to the kingdom of Judah may be found in 2 Chr 11:13; 12:1;
24:5; 28:23. The mention of "all Israel" in 35:3 is debated. For exclusive designations of the
northern kingdom, cf. 2 Chr 13:4, 15; 18:16.

[30] 2 Chr 30:6 contains the only reference to the northern kingdom as כֹּל יִשְׂרָאֵל in
the Hezekiah arc. According to Williamson, *Israel in the Books of Chronicles*, 126–30; idem,
1 and 2 Chronicles, 357, the consistent usage of the expression following the fall of the
northern kingdom is "to stress the completeness of the people."

[31] As argued by Milgrom, "Hezekiah's Sacrifices"; Williamson, *1 and 2 Chronicles*, 357. If
the suggestion of Milgrom is correct that the number of sacrifices listed in v 21 is actually
12x7, then the twelve tribes were originally in view from the beginning of the ceremony
and hence Hezekiah had not "changed his mind concerning the beneficiaries of the sacrifice" ("Hezekiah's Sacrifices," 159).

reotypically characterized by "He did right in the eyes of YHWH, yet the high places were not removed."[32] For the first and only time in the regnal formulae of a Judean king, a ruler with no ties to the northern kingdom is nonetheless said to have "walked in the way of the kings of Israel" (2 Kgs 16:3).[33] This damning accusation at once recalls the formulaic language applied to ruling kings of Samaria perceived as wicked: "He did evil in the eyes of YHWH, and followed the sins of Jeroboam the son of Nebat."[34] He is the first king said to have "made his son pass through the fire" (v 3), a technical term for child sacrifice.[35] He is the only king of whom it

---

[32] For these equivocal evaluations, cf. 1 Kgs 15:11, 14; 22:43; 2 Kgs 12:3–4[2–3]; 14:3–4; 15:3–4, 34–35.

[33] This is also said of the Judean king Jehoram in 2 Kgs 8:18, but in this case his ties to the polity of Israel are expressly stated: "for the daughter of Ahab became his wife."

[34] For these negative evaluations, cf. 2 Kgs 3:2–3; 13:2, 11; 14:24; 15:9, 18, 24, 28. The reign of Jehu conveys aspects of both evaluations, being both praised (2 Kgs 10:30) and compared to Jeroboam (vv 29, 31).

[35] This expression only occurs three additional times in Kings, as practiced by the Israelites (2 Kgs 17:17), by Manasseh (21:6), and supposedly ended as a worship rite by Josiah (23:10), "that no man might make his son or his daughter pass through the fire for Molech." Scholarship has long been divided on the proper understanding for both לְהַעֲבִיר אֶת־בְּנוֹ בָּאֵשׁ and מֹלֶךְ. The interpretations have fallen into three categories:

1. Hebrew מֹלֶךְ refers to a sacrificial rite, based on the name *mlk* found in Punic inscriptions. The expression "to cause (someone) to pass through the fire" is terminology for child sacrifice, practiced in ancient Israel to YHWH until it was ultimately forbidden by such laws as Lev 20:2–5; Deut 12:31; 18:10. See Otto Eissfeldt, *Molk als Opferbegriff im Punischen und Hebräischen und das Ende des Gottes Moloch* (Halle: M. Niemeyer, 1935); Hans-Peter Müller, "מֹלֶךְ *mólek,*" TDOT 8.375–88; Klaas A. D. Smelik, "Moloch, Molekh, or Molk-Sacrifice? A Reassessment of the Evidence concerning the Hebrew Term Molekh," *SJOT* 9 (1995) 133–42; Paul G. Mosca, "Child Sacrifice in Canaanite and Israelite Religion: A Study in Mulk and מלך" (Ph.D. diss.; Harvard University, 1975); Francesca Stavrakopoulou, *King Manasseh and Child Sacrifice: Biblical Distortions of Historical Realities* (BZAW 338; Berlin: Walter de Gruyter, 2004) 283–99.

2. Molech refers to the foreign god Baal-Hadad, possibly preserved in a corrupted form through the name Adrammelech (2 Kgs 17:31). Hebrew לְהַעֲבִיר אֶת־בְּנוֹ בָּאֵשׁ does not connote child sacrifice, but rather a rite dedicating an individual to cultic service of the deity. See Moshe Weinfeld, "The Worship of Molech and of the Queen of Heaven and its Background," *UF* 4 (1972) 133–54.

3. Molech is the name of a Canaanite deity to be associated with Mesopotamian Malik, who has chthonic qualities. "To cause (someone) to pass through the fire" does indeed signify child sacrifice, as may be verified by Jer 7:31; 19:5; 32:35; Ezek 16:21; 20:26, 31; Ps 106:37–38. See George C. Heider, *The Cult of Molek. A Reassessment* (JSOTSup 43; Sheffield: JSOT Press, 1985); idem, "Molech," *DDD* 581–85; John Day, *Molech. A God of Human Sacrifice in the Old Testament* (UCOP 41; Cambridge: Cambridge University Press, 1989); Baruch J. Schwartz, *The Holiness Legislation: Studies in the Priestly Code* (Jerusalem: Magnes Press, 1999) 187–203 [Hebrew].

This study concurs with the latter position. For further discussion and bibliography, see the relevant articles in Karin Finsterbusch et al. (eds.), *Human Sacrifice in Jewish and Christian Tradition* (Numen 112; Leiden: Brill, 2007).

is said, "He sacrificed and burned incense on the high places and on the hills and under every green tree" (v 4), a sweeping condemnation picked up by the Chronicler in 2 Chr 28:4.[36] By means of the assessment that "He did not do what was right in the eyes of YHWH" (v 2), Ahaz becomes the first king in the history of the kingdom of Judah whose reign is categorically denigrated.[37]

It is also credible that substantial changes were made to the Temple complex during the reign of Ahaz. In approximately 734 B.C.E. while Tiglath-pileser III was in the course of putting down the anti-Assyrian rebellion of Israel and Aram, king Ahaz journeyed to Damascus to pay his respects to his overlord. It was during this political visit that Ahaz became taken with the design of an altar he saw there, perhaps at the Aramaean temple of Adad-Rimmon, and had its design sent back to Jerusalem for reconstruction by the high priest Uriah. It was given pride of place in the Temple courtyard, directly in front of the sanctuary normally occupied by the bronze altar. The latter was repositioned on the north side of the newly introduced altar, being relegated to personal use by the king.[38] The heavy indemnity paid by Ahaz to Tiglath-pileser for his assistance was made possible by accessing the treasuries of both the Temple and the king's personal residence, and by removing significant quantities of bronze from the courtyard of the sanctuary. The frames were removed from the ten movable lavers used for the purification of worshippers and the cleansing of the courtyard after sacrifices, the bronze oxen were stripped from the "sea" which they supported, and the enigmatic מוּסַךְ הַשַּׁבָּת was detached.[39] The account in Kings leaves little doubt that whether due to

---

[36] Contrast the lesser charge leveled at Solomon in 1 Kgs 3:3.

[37] This may account for the fact that the name Ahaz is only preserved in the Bible as a hypocoristicon, excluding the divine name. The ostensible pattern of alternating fidelity by kings Ahaz through Josiah could be claimed as the inducement for this degrading characterization; that is, the reign of Ahaz is limned in such an unfavorable manner in order to highlight the faithfulness of Hezekiah, and vice versa. However, the fact that the book of Kings does not pick up on these egregious acts in the reign of Hezekiah—seen more clearly in the balanced dichotomy between Manasseh and Josiah—speaks against the depiction of Ahaz as being wholly fabricated.

[38] 2 Kgs 16:10–16. The god Adad-Rimmon was worshipped at the primary shrine in Damascus, and is mentioned in 2 Kgs 5:18. For discussion of the altar, see Mordechai Cogan and Hayim Tadmor, *II Kings* (AYB 11; New York: Doubleday, 1988) 192–93.

[39] 2 Kgs 16:8, 17–18. Based on MT, Hebrew מוּסַךְ הַשַּׁבָּת would seem to be a covered awning (from the root מסך, "to cover, screen") spanning from the king's house to the Temple. LXX τὸν θεμέλιον τῆς καθέδρας has been rendered as מוּסַד הַשֶּׁבֶת "seat of the dais" in James A. Montgomery, *A Critical and Exegetical Commentary on the Books of Kings* (ICC; New York: Charles Scribner's Sons, 1951) 464, and both "seat" and "sabbath" appear

influence or obligation, appreciable alterations were made by Ahaz to the shrine of YHWH in the course of his dealings with Assyria.[40]

Thus Hezekiah quite plausibly inherited a situation in which the purity of the cult had been sullied and the seat of the deity had been essentially vandalized. His own attitude toward the cult is reflected in the summation of the Deuteronomistic historian for whom this was the utmost concern: "He did right in the eyes of YHWH, according to all that his father David had done" (2 Kgs 18:3/2 Chr 29:2). If the Temple had indeed been ransacked and non-Yahwistic elements had been introduced into the cult, an assessment such as "He held fast to YHWH and did not depart from following him but kept his commandments" (2 Kgs 18:6) can only have validity if Hezekiah had made a concerted effort to rectify these religious concerns. The likelihood that Hezekiah undertook a religious reform has been previously argued in this study, independent of the extensive account in Chronicles. It is inconceivable that a purgation of the cult would not have begun with the Temple itself, especially in view of the extensive changes purportedly enacted by Ahaz shortly before Hezekiah's reign. The bronze serpent Nehushtan reported in 2 Kgs 18:4 was presumably in the precincts of the Temple, and its removal and destruction is consonant with the more extensive operation described in Chronicles.

The mention of "all Israel" in 2 Chr 29:24 is an implicit signal of northern participation at the rededication ceremony, and as such it is reasonable to postulate a direct linkage between the northern kingdom and the revitalization of the Temple. The attacks on Judah by Israel, Aram, and Edom give grounds for the decisions made by Ahaz in regard to the cult, both the need to plunder the Temple compound to obtain sufficient wealth as an inducement for aid from Tiglath-pileser, and the impetus to appeal to foreign gods for resolution to the crisis from the divine realm.[41] Both of these

---

as a doublet for שבת in the Lucianic recension. For the history of interpretation, see M. J. Mulder, "Was war die am Tempel gebaute 'Sabbathalle' in I Kön. 16, 18?" in W. C. Delsman et al. (eds.), *Von Kanaan bis Kerala: Festschrift für Prof. Mag. Dr. Dr. J. P. M. van der Ploeg* (AOAT 211; Neukirchen: Neukirchen-Vluyn, 1982) 161–72.

[40] The appeal to Tiglath-pileser III appears in 2 Kgs 16:7–9, 17–18; 2 Chr 28:16–21. 2 Kgs 16:17–18, although separated from the earlier description of defacing the Temple in v 8, should be read in conjunction with it owing to מִפְּנֵי מֶלֶךְ אַשּׁוּר at the end of v 18.

[41] The allegation that Ahaz "made his son pass through the fire" may be seen as a desperate act of invocation under exigent circumstances, based on the pericope in 2 Kgs 3:26–27. There, king Mesha of Moab sacrifices his eldest son during the heat of battle against the Israelites, with the expeditious effect that "a great wrath came upon Israel." The passage is remarkable for its candid portrayal of the success of an appeal to a foreign god, while at the same time offering no theological critique. As with consulting the dead in 1 Sam 28:3–19,

aspects are consistently presented in both Kings and Chronicles, with the end result that both the Temple and cult were adversely affected during a time of national crisis. The conditional nature of the covenant between God and Israel had been stressed by northern prophets in the years before the fall of Samaria, and the reality of exile would have only legitimized for Hezekiah the need to purify the cult in order to appease a vengeful deity. The Assyrian incursions into the north had already induced exiles from the region to resettle in Judah, and owing to their increasing numbers a strong worship center was needed to counter the strategic position of the nearby central sanctuary at Bethel.[42] The revitalization of the Temple was a calculated political maneuver directly related to the closure of Yahwistic shrines elsewhere, assuring the priority and economic well-being of the all-important sanctuary in Jerusalem.

In conclusion, the Chronicler has artfully presented the events of this biblical chapter in accordance with his distinctive ideological outlook, as seen notably in the dating of the Temple's restoration from the very first day of Hezekiah's accession, the speech which is addressed to the priesthood as a commission for their task and yet is a thinly veiled exhortation to repentance directed toward the wider community, and the rededication ceremony which evokes the fidelity of worship recorded under Solomon. While there can be no question that the narrative as a whole is pregnant with theological motivation, this does not exclude the possibility that it may nevertheless contain a historical kernel. This has been shown in regard to other royal propaganda in the ancient Near East containing accomplishments that have been moved early into a king's reign, and the Chronicler himself has demonstrably constructed his unique version of Israel's monarchic period within certain well-defined constraints imposed by his archival sources. By applying the criterion of historical verisimilitude within these established parameters to the likelihood of foreign elements being introduced into the Yahwistic cult by Ahaz, coupled with

---

the Hebrew Bible testifies to the efficacy of these practices without giving them sanction. See further John Barclay Burns, "Why Did the Besieging Army Withdraw (II Reg 3,27)?" *ZAW* 102 (1990) 187–94; Stavrakopoulou, *King Manasseh and Child Sacrifice*, 176–77.

[42] The tactical location of Bethel—formerly Luz (cf. Gen 35:6; Judg 1:23)—is evidenced by its vacillation in political ownership, situated as it was on the border between the northern and southern kingdoms. In the book of Joshua, it was initially allotted to the tribe of Benjamin (Josh 18:22), but was acquired by Ephraim according to the Deuteronomistic addition at the beginning of Judges (vv 1:22–26, cf. 1 Chr 7:28). It was variously in the hands of Israel (Jeroboam I, 1 Kgs 12:28–33), then Judah (Abijah, 2 Chr 13:19), and Israel once again (by the time of Jeroboam II, 2 Kgs 23:17, 19; Jer 48:13; Hos 10:15; Amos 3:14; 4:4; 5:5–6; 7:10, 13), before finally reverting to Judah after the Assyrian conquest (Ezra 2:28; Neh 7:32; 11:31).

the indispensable role that the Temple would have played as the center-piece of a subsequent renewal of worship—independently substantiated elsewhere—it is reasonable to assert that the Temple was both renovated and cleansed as part of Hezekiah's religious reform.[43]

7.2. THE PASSOVER (2 CHR 30)

7.2.1. *Summary Statement*

There has been a great deal of scholarly discussion in regard to the historic-ity of the Passover as recorded in 2 Chr 30.[44] Certainly it cannot be denied that various elements of the chapter are either anachronistic or have been created with authorial intent. The ceremonial singing by the Levites in v 21 has been deemed to be reflective of the Chronicler's own time, as well as the sacrificing of peace offerings during the Feast of Unleavened Bread in v 22.[45] The celebration of the feast for an additional seven days is highly reminiscent of the weeks' extension granted at the original dedication of the Temple under Solomon.[46] Popular participation in the *pesaḥ* sacrifice is consonant with the author's worldview elsewhere in transforming for-mal events from the royal and cultic sphere into the public domain.[47]

---

[43] Some critical applications of verisimilitude to Chronicles are discussed by Gary N. Knoppers, "History and Historiography: The Royal Reforms," in *Chronicler as Historian*, 187. It is a criterion rejected by Thomas L. Thompson, *Early History of the Israelite People: From the Written and Archaeological Sources* (SHANE 4; Leiden: Brill, 1992) 388.

[44] For previous scholarship on the unity of the chapter, see Simon J. De Vries, *1 and 2 Chronicles* (FOTL 11; Grand Rapids: Eerdmans, 1989) 378. In the context of the last plague in Exod 12–13, the meaning of the root פסח has been contested as meaning "to limp, skip" (cf. 1 Kgs 18:21, 26) or else "to protect" (Isa 31:5). The debate, with bibliography, is supplied in William H. C. Propp, *Exodus 1–18* (AYB 2; New York: Doubleday, 1998) 401. Although it has no bearing on the conclusions of this study, the latter rendering is to be preferred. The misleading term 'Passover' is employed in this section solely to yield to its prevalence in English.

[45] Judah B. Segal, *The Hebrew Passover from the Earliest Times to A.D. 70* (London: Oxford University Press, 1963) 19.

[46] 2 Chr 7:8–9. As the intent of the prolonged celebration in 2 Chr 30:23–27 is to recall the seven-day extension to Solomon's original dedication of the Temple (v 26), any con-nection here drawn to the Passover of Josiah is tenuous. It is not necessary, then, to claim "2 Chr. 30 appears to attempt deliberately to outdo the Passover of 2 Chr. 35 by adding a further seven days of festival" (Segal, *Hebrew Passover*, 19).

[47] Japhet, *I & II Chronicles*, 929, as seen, for instance, in the enthronement of David in which the food was consumed by all the people (1 Chr 12:40–41), and in the free-will contributions for the building of the Temple during the enthronement of Solomon (1 Chr 29:6–9).

One reason for discounting the observance of this celebration in the time of Hezekiah has been the ostensible contradiction created by the conspicuously similar recapitulation pertaining to the Passover of Josiah. According to v 30:26 "since the days of Solomon the son of David, king of Israel, there had been nothing like this (לֹא כָזֹאת) in Jerusalem." Yet of Josiah's observance it is stated:

2 Chr 35:18   There had not been celebrated a Passover like it (לֹא־נַעֲשָׂה פֶסַח כָּמֹהוּ) in Israel since the days of Samuel the prophet; nor had any of the kings of Israel celebrated such a Passover as Josiah did with the priests, the Levites, all Judah and Israel who were present, and the inhabitants of Jerusalem.[48]

2 Kgs 23:22   Such a Passover had not been celebrated (כִּי לֹא נַעֲשָׂה כַּפֶּסַח הַזֶּה) from the days of the judges who judged Israel, nor in all the days of the kings of Israel and of the kings of Judah.

It should be noted that by means of the relative particle (כְּ(מוֹ)), neither of these remembrances of the Passover in any way claim that there has been a cessation of the cultic ritual.[49] The issue is hence not whether the Pass-

---

[48] The summary description of Josiah's Passover in Chronicles is loosely, but ultimately, taken from the more succinct account in Kings. The clear reliance of Chronicles on Kings as a source for this episode may be verified by the verse that immediately follows in both books:

2 Chr 35:19   בִּשְׁמוֹנֶה עֶשְׂרֵה שָׁנָה לְמַלְכוּת יֹאשִׁיָּהוּ נַעֲשָׂה הַפֶּסַח הַזֶּה:
2 Kgs 23:23   כִּי אִם־בִּשְׁמֹנֶה עֶשְׂרֵה שָׁנָה לַמֶּלֶךְ יֹאשִׁיָּהוּ נַעֲשָׂה הַפֶּסַח הַזֶּה לַיהוָה בִּירוּשָׁלִָם:

Both claim that such a Passover had not been celebrated (לֹא נַעֲשָׂה) since the time of the judges. In Kings this era is expressly stated to be מִימֵי הַשֹּׁפְטִים אֲשֶׁר שָׁפְטוּ אֶת־יִשְׂרָאֵל, while in Chronicles this reference point is anchored to מִימֵי שְׁמוּאֵל הַנָּבִיא. The Chronicler selectively skips over the period of the judges in his presentation of Israelite history, with brief mention only in 1 Chr 17:6, 10, and so the variant in Kings must be given priority. As Samuel was both a prophet and the last judge of Israel before the establishment of the monarchy (cf. 1 Sam 3:20; 19:20 as prophet; 1 Sam 7:15 as judge), the Chronicler is affirming that the observance of the Passover in the time of Josiah was unlike anything that had happened since the days of the judges, while at the same time emphasizing the prophetic role of Samuel which is more relevant to the author's interests. Although by necessity this timeframe mandates that there was no prior king who had observed the cultic ritual in such a manner, Chronicles, following Kings, redundantly affirms that וְכָל־מַלְכֵי יִשְׂרָאֵל לֹא־עָשׂוּ כַּפֶּסַח.

[49] As claimed by A. D. H. Mayes, *Deuteronomy* (NCB; London: Oliphants, 1979) 256, "According to 2 Kg. 23:21f., however, Passover was not celebrated by Israel from the days of the judges until the time of Josiah." 2 Chr 35:18 rebuts this point explicitly: וְכָל־מַלְכֵי יִשְׂרָאֵל לֹא־עָשׂוּ כַּפֶּסַח אֲשֶׁר־עָשָׂה יֹאשִׁיָּהוּ "nor had any of the kings celebrated *such* a Passover as Josiah did." If the true intent were to convey non-observance, Biblical Hebrew has two ways to express a distinction without peer: by either providing a time reference expressing totality, or else by omitting a temporal citation altogether. For examples of the

over had always been celebrated, but in what manner. In the Hezekiah narrative, what sets the ceremony apart is the unified celebration. The chapter opens with the invitation "sent to all Israel and Judah," a proclamation circulated "throughout all Israel from Beersheba even to Dan" (v 30:5). Although the summons is rebuffed, it is nevertheless highly effective: there were "many people gathered at Jerusalem . . . a very large assembly" (v 13).[50] Prior to the summary statement, the imagery of a restored religious community is once again reinforced by "the whole assembly decided to celebrate [the feast] another seven days" (v 23), and "all the assembly of Judah rejoiced . . . and all the assembly that came from Israel" (v 25).[51] This is the basis for the temporal anchor "since the days of Solomon the son of David," a point during the united monarchy before the division of the tribes.

This reasoning, however, has been mechanically applied to the corresponding synopsis of the Josian Passover.[52] As a result, the claim of the latter must *ipso facto* render that of the former null and void: if a centralized celebration was novel in Josiah's time, then the Hezekian assertion, along with the associated Passover as a whole, is highly suspect. The *pesaḥ* ceremony in the Josiah account, however, has an altogether different emphasis. In describing the ritual itself the people are never mentioned, and there is not even a whisper of a summons to appear. It is not until v 35:17, immediately preceding the summary, that "the sons of Israel" are

---

former, cf. Josh 10:14 (לֹא הָיְתָה כָּזֹאת לְפָנָיו וְאַחֲרָיו הַהוּא כַּיּוֹם הָיָה לֹא) and 1 Sam 4:7 (לֹא הָיְתָה כָּזֹאת). For the latter, see 1 Kgs 21:25 (רַק לֹא־הָיָה כְאַחְאָב אֶתְמוֹל שִׁלְשֹׁם).

Hence the Passover could very well have been commemorated during the monarchic period prior to the reign of Hezekiah, and was in all likelihood. The observance of the *pesaḥ* sacrifice on at least an infrequent basis is supported by the condemnation כִּי לֹא לָרֹב עָשׂוּ כַּכָּתוּב "for they had not celebrated it in great numbers as written" (2 Chr 30:5); that is, the Passover had indeed been kept on some schedule, but not in the requisite manner. The rendering "in great numbers" is preferred for לָרֹב rather than "often" as suggested by Japhet, *I & II Chronicles*, 940–41: an increase in attendees is precisely the aim of the verse, and none of the 36 occurrences of לָרֹב in Chronicles is employed in a temporal sense.

[50] Even the number of people who had not properly consecrated themselves is described as רַבַּת בַּקָּהָל (v 17) and מַרְבִּית הָעָם (v 18).

[51] "Although the term *qāhāl* is quite common in Chronicles, it is most frequent in the Hezekiah pericope, thirteen times in all" (Japhet, *I & II Chronicles*, 928).

[52] So, for instance, Jeffrey Tigay, *Deuteronomy: The Traditional Hebrew Text with the New JPS Translation* (JPS Commentary; Philadelphia: Jewish Publication Society, 1996) 154: "According to the book of Kings and Chronicles, before Josiah enforced the law of centralization there had been no united celebration of the festival since the days of the chieftains and Samuel (2 Kings 23:22; 2 Chron. 35:18)."

even stated to be in attendance.[53] In this verse and the following, the sheer number is not even emphasized: rather than grandiloquent references to a multitude or a great assembly, the expression employed is (םי)אָצְמִּנַה "those who were present."[54] Instead, the chapter has two overriding priorities: the prominent role of the Levites and adherence of both king and clergy to the divine commandments.[55]

That a centralized observance is secondary to the Josiah account may be confirmed by the covenant ceremony preceding the reform in 2 Chr 34:29–32, limited to "all who were present in Jerusalem and Benjamin." This passage is originally from the version in the book of Kings, and even there a united celebration by the combined tribes is not in the mind of the Deuteronomist, as made clear by 2 Kgs 23:21, "Then the king commanded all the people saying, 'Celebrate the Passover to YHWH your God as it is written in the book of the covenant.'" In this verse, "all the people" refers back to vv 1–3, where the book of the covenant is read to the congregation. Those gathered are "all the elders of Judah and of Jerusalem" (v 1), with not a single denizen of Israel mentioned.[56] Just as the purpose of the reform credited to Josiah was to bring the cult into conformance with Deuteronomic law, the ambition of vv 1–3, 21–22 is to show how Judah, and only Judah, faithfully entered into a covenant "to walk after YHWH, and to keep His commandments and His testimonies and His statutes with all [his] heart and [his] soul, to carry out the words of this covenant that were written in this book" (v 3). The Chronicler, by treating the inclusion of the people as an addendum to the account, correctly preserves the spirit of the earlier tradition.

Once the distinction between the two summary accounts is recognized, and it is apparent that their basis of comparison is not the same, the observance of one ceremony in a particular manner does not preclude the other. The very fact of their mutual inclusion at only a few chapters remove from each other testifies that they were not viewed as conflicting.

[53] For which reason Japhet states "this passage serves in the present context as a kind of 'addendum'" (*I & II Chronicles*, 1054).

[54] Recognized by De Vries, *1 and 2 Chronicles*, 415, "According to this verse, Josiah made no special effort... to bring in worshipers in great numbers and from afar; his Passover is just for "the people who were present." I would take exception, however, to his claim that Hezekiah likewise did not exert himself.

[55] The former aspect has been pointed out by scholars such as Rudolph, *Chronikbücher*, 325; Williamson, *1 and 2 Chronicles*, 407; Johnstone, *2 Chronicles 10–36*, 254, but the latter point has not been sufficiently appreciated.

[56] Again in v 2, "every man of Judah and all the inhabitants of Jerusalem."

Moreover, the notice regarding Hezekiah's Passover does not appear to stem from an ancient source. As the additional seven days of assembly in 2 Chr 30:23–26 are reminiscent of the extension to the original dedication of the Temple in vv 7:8–10, the direct mention of its builder via "since the days of Solomon" in chap. 30 should be credited directly to the Chronicler. The very author of one of these synopses would be expected to avoid creating any kind of discrepancy between them, especially as the Chronicler is known to harmonize incompatible traditions in order to present a more cohesive view of Israelite history.[57] Thus in terms of history, the Passover as celebrated in the eighteenth year of Josiah does not exclude an earlier observance in the time of Hezekiah. It is therefore inaccurate to claim on the basis of the novelty of the account in 2 Chr 35:18 that the Passover in the time of Hezekiah is a mere retrojection and "can scarcely be historical."[58]

7.2.2. *Other Historical Objections*

The interchangeable use within 2 Chr 30 of the terms Passover (פֶּסַח, vv 1–2) and the Feast of Unleavened Bread (חַג הַמַּצּוֹת, v 13) has been asserted as signifying an advanced stage of the liturgical calendar and thus an indicator of lateness.[59] These two מוֹעֲדִים were thought to have been celebrated separately over the bulk of the monarchical period, and only combined under the Deuteronomic reform which necessitated that the Passover likewise be regarded as a pilgrimage festival with mandated observance at a central sanctuary.[60] Their combined portrayal as seen in the time of Hezekiah is thus anachronistic. Various literary layers of the account have been posited, with an older, pre-Chronistic account of the observance of the Feast of Unleavened Bread supplemented by the Chronicler with references to the Passover in keeping with the cultic practices of his own day.[61]

---

[57] Harmonization was a common technique employed by the Chronicler to resolve the numerous traditions with which he was presented. This, along with other examples of inner-biblical interpretation, are presented in Isaac Kalimi, *The Reshaping of Ancient Israelite History in Chronicles* (Winona Lake, Ind.: Eisenbrauns, 2005) esp. 156–57.

[58] Shigeyuki Nakanose, *Josiah's Passover: Sociology and the Liberating Bible* (The Bible & Liberation Series; Maryknoll, N.Y.: Orbis, 1993) 6, following Segal, *Hebrew Passover*, 16–19.

[59] Segal, *Hebrew Passover*, 19, 228; Japhet, *I & II Chronicles*, 948.

[60] Ernst Kutsch, "Erwägungen zur Geschichte der Passafeier und des Massotfestes," *ZThK* 55 (1958) 1–35, as implied by Deut 16:1–8.

[61] Herbert Haag, "Das Mazzenfest des Hiskia," in H. Gese and H. P. Rüger (eds.), *Wort und Geschichte. Festschrift für Karl Elliger zum 70. Geburtstag* (AOAT 18; Kevelaer: Butzon

A survey of biblical texts demonstrates that a rigid distinction between the two cannot be maintained. The word חַג, cognate to Arabic حَجّ, generally speaking refers to a journey for religious purposes.[62] Hence wherever the *pesah* sacrifice and Hebrew חַג appear in the same context, there is an express, not implicit, correlation with the Feast of Unleavened Bread. This association is plainly expressed in the exilic Ezek 45:21, "In the first [month], on the fourteenth day of the month, you shall have the *Passover* (הַפֶּסַח), a *feast* (חַג) of seven days; unleavened bread shall be eaten." After the prescription for the *pesah* ritual in Exod 12:1–13, in commemoration of God's slaying of the firstborn in the land of Egypt, the Lord commands through Moses and Aaron on the *fourteenth* day of the month, "*This day will be a memorial to* you, and you shall celebrate (חַגֹּתֶם) it [as] a feast (חַג) to YHWH" (v 14).[63] The Passover sacrifice is referred to as זֶבַח חַג in Exod 34:25, literally "sacrifice of the (pilgrimage) feast."[64] Its analogue in the Covenant Code of Exod 23:18 contains the injunction "you shall not leave until morning the fat of My festal sacrifice" (חֵלֶב־חַגִּי). Here the *pesah* sacrifice is technically considered part of the feast (חַג) because of its consumption on the fifteenth day of the month, which may be confirmed by the first half of the verse "You shall not offer the blood of My sacrifice with leavened bread." In each of these examples, the *pesah* sacrifice is observed at the time of the feast, after the pilgrimage has already been made to the local sanctuary. These texts, composed in various periods

---

& Bercker, 1973) 87–94; Williamson, *1 and 2 Chronicles*, 364–65. Haag actually posits up to four different layers, taking into account redactors and glosses. An English translation of his reconstructed oldest core layer may be found in De Vries, *1 and 2 Chronicles*, 378–79.

[62] For Arabic حَجّ, cf. Lane 2.514; Wehr 183–84, which relates to the annual pilgrimage to Mecca to encircle to *Kaaba* stone.

[63] Typically assigned to P, see Samuel Rolles Driver, *The Book of Exodus* (Cambridge: Cambridge University Press, 1918) 87–93; Propp, *Exodus 1–18*, 354, 373–80. It has also been classified as H by Joel S. Baden, "Identifying the Original Stratum of P: Theoretical and Practical Considerations," in S. Shectman and J. S. Baden (eds.), *The Strata of the Priestly Writings. Contemporary Debate and Future Directions* (AThANT 95; Zürich: Theologischer Verlag, 2009) 13–29. The day in question is the fourteenth of Nisan because the instructions are necessarily given prior to their fulfillment by the community in v 28. The strict adherence by the Israelites to the prescribed ritual as indicated in this verse means that they performed the sacrifice dutifully "between the evenings" on the fourteenth day (v 6), and hence the day to be commemorated as a feast (v 14) is entirely separate from the Feast of Unleavened Bread.

[64] As noted by Menahem Haran, *Temples and Temple-Service in Ancient Israel* (2nd ed.; Winona Lake, Ind.: Eisenbrauns, 1985) 341–43. Despite the traditional assignment of the legal code in Exod 34 to J, which would make it one of the earliest biblical law corpora, it is better seen as the latest as argued by Shimon Bar-On, "The Festival Calendars in Exodus XXIII 14–19 and XXXIV 18–26," *VT* 48/2 (1998) 161–95.

including some that are arguably pre-Deuteronomic, maintain a binding connection between the Passover and the Feast of Unleavened Bread. To contend that the Chronicler's usage evinces an exclusively later practice is therefore without merit.

Another objection in the same vein stems from the academic consensus on the date of composition of Deuteronomy. According to this view, the celebration of the Passover at the central sanctuary is a requirement known only from Deut 16:5–8, and as the origin of this legal corpus is closely linked with its discovery in the Temple during the eighteenth year of Josiah, such a prescription could not have been known as early as the reign of Hezekiah.[65] The findings previously presented in this book call such a conclusion into question, favoring that the impetus for Deuteronomy is rather to be tied to the reform efforts of Hezekiah in the aftermath of the fall of the northern kingdom.[66] The presuppositions relating to the dating of Deuteronomy, then, are not a sound basis for denying the historicity of the Passover observance in 2 Chr 30.

7.2.3. Correspondence to Josiah's Passover and Deuteronomy

If the Chronicler's account of the Passover during the reign of Hezekiah is truly imaginary and merely inspired by its undisputed observance under Josiah, then literary dependence of the former upon the latter should be demonstrable, and chap. 30 should likewise bear the hallmarks of adherence to Deuteronomic legislation. If, however, the details in the Hezekiah narrative correspond neither to the festival laws of Deuteronomy nor to the account of Josiah's Passover in 2 Chr 35, then the material must stem from elsewhere.

---

[65] Rudolph, *Chronikbücher*, 299; Edward Lewis Curtis and Albert Alonzo Madsen, *A Critical and Exegetical Commentary on the Books of Chronicles* (ICC; New York: Charles Scribner's Sons, 1910) 471, "Since Hezekiah was held to have been a reformer equally with Josiah, it was felt he too must have celebrated in a similar manner the Passover." It is the contention of Anthony Phillips, *Ancient Israel's Criminal Law: A New Approach to the Decalogue* (Oxford: Basil Blackwell, 1970) 167–79; idem, "A Fresh Look at the Sinai Pericope," *VT* 34 (1984) 39–52 (Part 1, Issue 1), 282–94 (Part 2, Issue 3), that Hezekiah's celebration of the Passover lies behind Exod 34:18–26, created by the redactor of the J and E sources (or "Proto-Deuteronomists") as the climax to the pre-Priestly Sinai tradition complex.

[66] The salient points for this association involve the inveighing of the northern prophets against the multiplying of altars and pillars, who also shared a pronounced iconoclastic tendency; the logical correspondence between a return to God and the revitalization of the covenant in the aftermath of northern exile; the lack of adherence to Deuteronomic law in the centralization efforts of Hezekiah, unlike the reform of Josiah; the finding of the law book in 2 Kgs 22:8 implies a pre-existing document.

The most general similarity between the two descriptions of the Passover in Chronicles is that they are both observed at the central sanctuary. This at once would seem to recall the requirement of Deut 16:5–6, which demands in absolute terms that "You are not permitted (לֹא תוּכַל) to offer the passover sacrifice within any of your towns that YHWH your God is giving you, but at the place that YHWH your God will choose to cause His name to dwell, only there shall you offer the passover sacrifice."[67] But the proclamation of Hezekiah is not in accord with this divine injunction. Instead, it is brought home repeatedly that the deed was not mandated by the Lord's commandments, but rather was entirely at the prerogative of Hezekiah himself: וַיִּשְׁלַח יְחִזְקִיָּהוּ (2 Chr 30:1), וַיִּיָּעַץ הַדָּבָר בְּעֵינֵי הַמֶּלֶךְ (v 4), וַיֵּלְכוּ הָרָצִים...כְּמִצְוַת הַמֶּלֶךְ (v 6). Even when the plan is credited to a wider body of individuals as in v 2, "The king and his officials and all the assembly of Jerusalem took counsel," this only accentuates the rationale of the plan as being distinct from a covenantal edict. The summons sent out by couriers throughout the extent of the kingdom is entirely voluntary, as observed by the notice in vv 10–11 that many subjects ridicule the request and refuse to comply. The commandment (מִצְוָה) of the king in v 6 does not refer to the content of the transmitted message, but pertains rather to the context of the emissaries' commission.[68]

---

[67] Scholarship continues to investigate the precise nuance of לְשַׁכֵּן שְׁמוֹ שָׁם. The *piel* of שכן is popularly understood as "to cause to dwell," but in light of the potential Akkadian cognate idiom *šuma šakānu* the Deuteronomic phrase may be translated "to place/establish His name." Used in the literary genre of building inscriptions, it indicates ownership by the placement of one's name upon an object. Under either interpretation, the traditional view of Gerhard von Rad, *Studies in Deuteronomy* (SBT 9; London: SCM Press, 1953) 38–39 remains valid, whereby the Deuteronomic conception of the deity is transcendent rather than immanent, a god who dwells in heaven rather than in the Temple enthroned between the cherubim.

For studies which survey this so-called Name theology, see S. Dean McBride, "The Deuteronomic Name Theology," (Ph.D. diss.; Harvard University, 1969); Tryggve N. D. Mettinger, *The Dethronement of Sabaoth: Studies in the Shem and Kabod Theologies* (CB 18; CWK Gleerup, 1982) 41–45; Ian Wilson, *Out of the Midst of Fire: Divine Presence in Deuteronomy* (SBLDS 151; Atlanta: Scholars Press, 1995) 1–15; Sandra L. Richter, *The Deuteronomistic History and the Name Theology: lᵉšakkēn šᵉmô šām in the Bible and the Ancient Near East* (BZAW 318; Berlin: Walter de Gruyter, 2002) 1–40.

[68] This commandment in v 12 is said to be בִּדְבַר יְהוָה "by the word of YHWH." Rather than placing the source of the royal proclamation in the divine realm, the Chronicler here is making a strong case for the opposite. As in 2 Chr 29:15, the word of the Lord is seen to be enacted through the authority of the king and his princes, as recognized by James D. Newsome Jr., "Toward a New Understanding of the Chronicler and His Purposes," *JBL* 94/2 (1975) 204; Sara Japhet, *The Ideology of the Book of Chronicles and its Place in Biblical Thought* (BEATAJ 9; 2nd ed.; Frankfurt am Main: Peter Lang, 1997) 234–39.

If there were any compulsion behind the invitation to come to Jerusalem for the Passover, one would expect to find it in the formal declaration of the couriers given in vv 6–9. At first blush, it might seem that this coercion is exercised in v 8, "Yield yourselves to YHWH and come to His sanctuary...and serve YHWH your God." But not only is this utterance on behalf of Hezekiah completely devoid of Deuteronomic idiom, it contains no mention whatsoever of the Passover. Upon closer examination, the speech has no direct connection to the upcoming *pesaḥ* sacrifice or to the pilgrimage Feast of Unleavened Bread, but has broader interests. The entreaty, not commandment, to return to the Temple to worship in vv 8–9 is balanced by the admonition in vv 6–7 that it is this very failure to do so which brought about the Assyrian conquest of the northern kingdom. The sanctuary itself has been eternally sanctified (מִקְדָּשׁוֹ אֲשֶׁר הִקְדִּישׁ לְעוֹלָם, v 8), and so rejection of the Jerusalem cult by their ancestors who "acted unfaithfully toward YHWH" (מָעֲלוּ בַּיהוָה, v 7) resulted in their captivity and destruction (וַיִּתְּנֵם לְשַׁמָּה).[69] The exhortation in this chapter to come to the Temple to worship is thus not concerned in the slightest with adhering to Deuteronomic law, but represents the Chronicler's broader theology in regard to the sanctity of the Temple. As with the closing chapters of the book, exile has been inextricably linked with the abandonment of Temple worship.

An examination of the Passover offerings in the respective traditions reveals them to be substantively different. Josiah liberally contributes provisions expressly from his personal holdings (אֵלֶּה מֵרְכוּשׁ הַמֶּלֶךְ) in 2 Chr 35:7—flocks of lambs, young goats, and bulls—as do his officials (שָׂרָיו, v 8) and the officers of the Levites (שָׂרֵי הַלְוִיִּם, v 9). The lambs and goats are in each case said to be for the *pesaḥ* offerings (לַפְּסָחִים), their enumeration bracketed on the one hand by Josiah's command to slaughter the *pesaḥ* in v 6, and on the other by the priests' compliance (וַיִּשְׁחֲטוּ הַפֶּסַח) in vv 10–11. The subsequent celebration of the Feast of Unleavened Bread is given a curt mention in v 17, with no reference whatsoever to any sort of royal benefaction. Hezekiah, by contrast, is not said to have made

---

[69] This harkens back to the speech made by the Judean king Abijah in 2 Chr 13:4–12 during the reign of Jeroboam, condemning the polity of Israel for their golden calves, and for driving out the priests of YHWH and installing illegitimate ones (vv 8–9). Those who have not abandoned the Lord have the sons of Aaron ministering as priests and the Levites attending their charge (vv 10–11). The ominous conclusion of Abijah that the sons of Israel will not succeed has immediate repercussions in its own context, but at the same time foreshadows the fulfillment announced by Hezekiah's couriers.

any contribution to the offerings for Passover or the Feast of Unleavened Bread, leaving the distinct impression that the *pesaḥ* animals slaughtered in 2 Chr 30:15 have been provided by the assembly gathered at Jerusalem.[70] Instead, the king and his officials make available propitiary beasts for the additional seven days of extended celebration (vv 23–24).[71]

The sacrificial animals related to the Passover in the Chronicler's account of Josiah also mention bovines. In 2 Chr 35:7 they are not stated to be לַפְּסָחִים, but are only listed afterwards as וּבָקָר שְׁלֹשֶׁת אֲלָפִים. This distinction is maintained throughout the preparation of the two kinds of sacrifices in v 13, in which after the *pesaḥ* is offered, "the holy offerings (הַקֳּדָשִׁים) they boiled in pots and in cauldrons and in pans and carried them quickly to all of the people." Because the bulls are uniformly differentiated from the *pesaḥ* offerings, the bringing of the *pesaḥ* from the flock is in strict accord with the commandments of Exod 12:3, 5, 21. But as sacred offerings are not demanded in addition to the *pesaḥ*, the inclusion of bovines (בָּקָר) can only stem from the influence of Deut 16:2, where the Passover is to brought "from the flock or the herd" (צֹאן וּבָקָר).[72] The nonconformity of the various Passover injunctions is clearly felt by the Chronicler, who has presented his own intrepretation aimed at harmonizing their respective content.[73] The *pesaḥ* offerings as described in

---

[70] Japhet, *I & II Chronicles*, 949, "The phrasing 'they...brought' would indicate that these were their own offerings (cf. for example, Lev. 2.8; 4.4; 5.12; Deut. 12.6, 11)." This personal sacrificing is also in accord with Exod 12:3, 21, which stipulates that each household was to slay its own animal.

[71] The ratio of flocks of sheep and goats to bulls is maintained in Josiah's version at roughly 10:1. Josiah offers 30,000 from the flocks and 3,000 bulls (10:1, 2 Chr 35:7), his officials provide 2,600 from the flocks and 300 bulls (8.67:1, v 8), and the officers of the Levites 5,000 from the flocks and 500 bulls (10:1, v 9). While this proportion also holds true for Hezekiah's officers, for the king himself the Chronicler specifies "1,000 bulls and 7,000 sheep/goats" (v 30:24). This 7:1 ratio manifests the same typological number appearing throughout the previous chapter to signify completeness, and thus Hezekiah's wholehearted devotion to serving the Lord. Such a detail tells against its literary dependence on the Josianic version.

[72] Tigay, *Deuteronomy*, 152, posits the two most likely scenarios for the variance between Exodus and Deuteronomy: (1) the earlier domestic rite was for smaller individual households whereas Deuteronomy permits the sharing of a larger animal among households at the central sanctuary; (2) the earlier ordinance reflects ownership of primarily sheep and goats, while domestication of cattle had become common by the time of Deuteronomy.

[73] Halakhic exegesis would later rule in favor of the Chronicler's solution, as seen in the *midrash halakha* on Deut 16:2, "צֹאן ובקר—since the Passover is taken only from the sheep or the goats, why does the Torah say צֹאן ובקר here? צֹאן for the Passover sacrifice and בקר for the festive offering" (*Sifre, Re'eh*, 16.2; ed. Finkelstein, §129, p. 187). The bulls are thus analogous to the שׁלמי חגיגה, or peace-offering sacrifices, presented on the eve of Passover together with the *pesaḥ* (*Mishnah Ḥagigah*, 1).

the Chronicler's account of Josiah have been appreciably impacted by Deuteronomic thought, yet this influence cannot be detected within the Hezekiah tradition, where the bulls are noticeably lacking and hence reconciliation with Deuteronomic law is not required.

Not only in terms of the offerings, but also in the manner of slaughtering there is a stark dichotomy between the two Passover accounts. In 2 Chr 35:11, it is the Levites who perform this function under the direct command of Josiah (v 6). This is in conformance with the expectation in Deuteronomy that a ceremony at the central sanctuary entails ritual discharge by the priesthood. By contrast, the laity slaughter their own *pesaḥ* animals in v 30:15, with the third-person plural verb וַיִּשְׁחֲטוּ having as its antecedent עַם־רָב in v 13. This interpretation is reinforced by the fact that the Levites only step in to perform the slaying of the *pesaḥ* for those who are unclean (v 17). This procedure adheres to the prescription in Exod 12:21–27, in which Moses instructs the elders of Israel to "Go and take for yourselves lambs according to your families, and slay the Passover lamb" (v 21).[74] The Passover ascribed to Hezekiah reflects its older observance as a domestic rite, whereas that recorded under Josiah has necessarily evolved as dictated by centralization. The tradition preserved in 2 Chr 30 thus suggests itself as preceding the Deuteronomic reform, and the attribution there of the slaughtering to the laity is all the more remarkable owing to the importance of the priesthood for the Chronicler.[75]

A final difference in regard to the Passover offerings between the two accounts is the manner of preparation. According to the Priestly source in Exod 12:8, the meat of the *pesaḥ* was to be צְלִי־אֵשׁ "roasted with fire"; that is, cooked whole on a spit over an open fire or perhaps in a pit in the ground. This specification is reinforced in the subsequent verse which proscribes alternate means of achieving the same end: "Do not eat any of it raw (נָא) or boiled at all in water (וּבָשֵׁל מְבֻשָּׁל בַּמָּיִם), but rather

---

[74] This, in turn, provides the justification for seeing the assembly as having provided their own animals rather than the king or the clergy: the slaughtering was attended to personally because the animal belonged to the individual.

[75] The move toward reducing the participation of the laity in sacrificial ritual is acutely evident in the exilic book of Ezekiel. The exclusive performance of such sacred duties by the priesthood is indicative of the book's desire to maintain the sanctity of the Temple. This is in jarring discord with the Priestly injunction of Exod 12:1–13, in which the domestic nature of the Passover rite is reiterated in the killing of the lamb by "the assembly of the congregation of Israel" (v 6). Here the Priestly Code evinces its pre-exilic date, and thus its resemblance to the Hezekian Passover in Chronicles.

roasted with fire."[76] Deuteronomy, however, avoids the verb צָלָה "to roast" altogether, and instead enjoins וּבִשַּׁלְתָּ (Deut 16:7).[77] The Chronicler, faced with two competing traditions, once again harmonizes them into וַיְבַשְּׁלוּ הַפֶּסַח בָּאֵשׁ (2 Chr 35:13), with the ends of the statement coming from Deuteronomy and Exodus, respectively. That boiling is intended even here is upheld by the context of the subsequent sentence: וְהַקֳּדָשִׁים בִּשְּׁלוּ בַּסִּירוֹת וּבַדְּוָדִים וּבַצֵּלָחוֹת, "They boiled the sacred offerings in pots, in cauldrons, and in pans." The preparation of the Passover sacrifice in the Chronicler's account of Josiah is thus steeped in Deuteronomic legislation, yet such details are once again absent from the corresponding version of Hezekiah.

The fact that the boiling in 2 Chr 35:13 was done כַּמִּשְׁפָּט "according to the ordinance" evinces that such details were integrated into the Chronicler's presentation of Josiah's Passover in order to corroborate his adherence to correct ritual according to recognized sources of authority. In v 4, the Levites are to prepare themselves בִּכְתָב דָּוִיד מֶלֶךְ יִשְׂרָאֵל וּבְמִכְתַּב שְׁלֹמֹה בְנוֹ "following the written directions of king David of Israel and the written directions of his son Solomon." In v 6, they are exhorted לַעֲשׂוֹת כִּדְבַר-יְהוָה בְּיַד-מֹשֶׁה, "to do according to the word of YHWH by Moses." When the service has been prepared, both the priests and Levites station themselves כְּמִצְוַת הַמֶּלֶךְ "according to the command of the king" (v 10). The burnt offerings are set aside for presenting to the Lord כַּכָּתוּב בְּסֵפֶר מֹשֶׁה "as it is written in the book of Moses" (v 12), followed by the aforementioned reference in v 13 to boiling the *pesaḥ* properly. The singers in v 15 are in their positions כְּמִצְוַת דָּוִיד "according to the command of David" and former ministering Levites. The summation of the ceremony, with its associated burnt offerings, claims that everything was

---

[76] Exod 12:9. Driver, *Book of Exodus*, 91, cites the conjecture of August Dillman, *Die Bücher Exodus und Leviticus* (HAT 12; Leipzig: S. Hirzel, 1880), that because the fat of the sacrifice was forbidden to be consumed (Lev 3:17; 7:23–25) and had not in this case been previously removed, roasting ensured that any adipose tissue would drip down and be engulfed in the flames. This means of handling the fat is analogous to its being incinerated on the altar as enjoined for the peace-offering, cf. Lev 3:3–5, 9–11, 14–16.

[77] The precise nuance of the verb וּבִשַּׁלְתָּ in this verse has been needlessly debated due to the broader sense of the root *bšl* in Akkadian, as seen in Tigay, *Deuteronomy*, 155. Elsewhere in the Hebrew Bible, however, the D stem of בשל is uniformly "to boil," cf. Exod 23:19; 2 Kgs 4:38; Ezek 24:4–5. Deuteronomy maintains this sense as well: לֹא-תְבַשֵּׁל גְּדִי בַּחֲלֵב אִמּוֹ (Deut 14:21). Even if one were to accept that the definition of וּבִשַּׁלְתָּ here is not limited to boiling but instead encompasses a wider range of meanings, this nonetheless affirms that the regulation of cooking the *pesaḥ* in Deuteronomy is more lenient, and therefore in conflict with that in Exodus.

done כְּמִצְוַת הַמֶּלֶךְ יֹאשִׁיָּהוּ "according to the command of king Josiah"
(v 16). The sheer pervasiveness of these reminders of proper observance
in the Passover celebration of Josiah serve to accentuate its conformance
with earlier prescriptions and legal stipulations.[78]

In the Passover account of Hezekiah there are only three references
which denote such compliance, and they are all of a decidedly different type. The closest analogue to those previously surveyed is found in
2 Chr 30:16, where the sacerdotal hierodules are stationed at their posts
כְּמִשְׁפָּטָם כְּתוֹרַת מֹשֶׁה אִישׁ־הָאֱלֹהִים. Whenever מִשְׁפָּט is used with a
third-person suffix and human antecedent a previous tradition is implied,
so that the Hebrew should be rendered "according to their custom," and
this is indeed echoed in modern translations of this verse.[79] A legal precedent is nonetheless cited for the inception of this clerical procedure,
"according to the law of Moses, man of God," reminiscent of כְּמִשְׁפָּטָם
בְּיַד אַהֲרֹן אֲבִיהֶם in 1 Chr 24:19. By this means, the Chronicler is able
to bolster long-established customs with ultimately divine sanction. The
same practice of stationing the clergy during the Passover of Josiah in
v 35:10 is rather said to be at the command of the king, and so the notice
in verse 30:16 should be understood more as a generalizing reference.[80]

The other two appeals to legal authority in describing the Passover
of Hezekiah disclose that it was, in fact, *not* followed properly. In 2 Chr
30:18, a multitude of people had not sanctified themselves prior to the
festival, with the result that אָכְלוּ אֶת־הַפֶּסַח בְּלֹא כַכָּתוּב "they ate the
pesaḥ otherwise than prescribed." The king subsequently seeks to pardon
them before the Lord as they are לֹא כְּטָהֳרַת הַקֹּדֶשׁ "not in accordance
with the purification [rules] of the sanctuary" (v 19).[81] Here strict hewing

---

[78] Emphasizing, once again, that this was the manner of observance intended by the
summary statement in v 18. Japhet, *I & II Chronicles*, 1048, states "This is the most variegated and comprehensive appeal to authority in any single pericope, with very clear
delineations of the various aspects of ritual and their respective sources of authority." Such
notices of adherence recall Josiah's injunction in 2 Kgs 23:21 to the people, "Celebrate the
Passover to YHWH your God as it is written in this book of the covenant."

[79] NAS95 has "after their custom," NRSV "their accustomed [posts]." Cf. 1 Kgs 5:8[4:28];
18:28; 2 Kgs 17:34, 40; 1 Chr 6:17[32]; 24:19. Note in 2 Kgs 17:34, 40 that the מִשְׁפָּט is in
contradistinction to divine law, such that employing legal terminology for its translation
is unwarranted.

[80] Williamson, *1 and 2 Chronicles*, 369–70, states: "[T]his is a purely general reference to
the priestly sections of the Pentateuchal law which assume the prominence of the cultic
officials on all such occasions."

[81] The authority of the king has been expanded in Chronicles, based on the preposi-
tional phrase "according to the commandment of the king by the words of the Lord" in
2 Chr 29:15. Although the decision to cleanse the Temple was solely at the initiative of

to ceremonial rite has been subsumed under the willingness of the people
to humble themselves and to return to worship YHWH at his holy dwelling, thus fulfilling the prayer of Solomon at the dedication of the Temple in v 7:14.[82] This is a far cry from the scrupulous adherence to legal
mandate throughout כָּל־עֲבוֹדַת יְהוָה lauded in the Passover of Josiah
(v 35:16). The deviation from prescribed ritual in the *pesaḥ* celebration of
Hezekiah highlights a fundamental disparity in the presentation of the
respective monarchs.

These numerous, marked differences cannot be reconciled if the Chronicler were attempting a mere retrojection of the Passover celebration of
Josiah into the reign of Hezekiah. One would expect them to correspond
more closely in regard to their details, but upon closer examination they
only have highly generalized associations with each other. The paucity of
evidence for, and moreover digressions from, Deuteronomic law in the
Hezekian version is in glaring contradistinction to the assiduous attention
to the same under the auspices of Josiah. The account of 2 Chr 35 betrays
its clear dependence on both Deuteronomy and the Deuteronomistic History, whereas the account of Hezekiah's Passover is indebted to neither of
them.[83] There is thus only one reasonable conclusion: Josiah's Passover in
Chronicles was not the basis for that of Hezekiah.

7.2.4. *Source Material*

A key question remains, however: is there an older source which underlies
the description of Hezekiah's Passover, or has it been wholly composed
by the Chronicler in accordance with his desired portrayal of this king?
There is a deliberate literary motivation in the opening chapters of the
Hezekiah narrative in Chronicles to undo all of the profane religious activity of king Ahaz, with the goal of restoring the people, the land, and most
importantly, the Temple, to their perceived ideal in the era of Solomon.
This speaks to authorial intent rather than to direct reliance on a historical source. To compound the issue, the *pesaḥ* celebration under Josiah

---

Hezekiah in v 10 ("Now it is in my heart..."), it is subsequently given divine sanction
without any express revelation. As interpreted by Japhet, *I & II Chronicles*, 922, "The king,
then, is the transmitter of the Lord's will and represents his authority."

[82] For more on the correlation between the elements of repentance in 2 Chr 30:18–20
and Solomon's prayer, see Williamson, *1 and 2 Chronicles*, 370.

[83] This section has focused on Deuteronomic influence in the Chronicler's version of
the Passover of Josiah. For indications of dependence on the Deuteronomistic History, cf.
2 Chr 34:29–32 / 2 Kgs 23:1–3; 2 Chr 35:16, 18–19 / 2 Kgs 23:21–23.

has clear antecedents in both Deuteronomy and Kings, so that the lack of correspondence with Hezekiah's Passover could simply be dismissed as evidence that the Chronicler has spun the latter out of whole cloth.[84] If the exegete also takes into account how well the details of the Hezekian version endorse the Chronicler's own ideology in regard to such broader themes as retribution and repentance, matters beyond the scope of this book, the case for the chapter being an original composition becomes compelling indeed.[85]

Against this, there are several factors which point to an authentic historical source behind the chapter. The fact that Deuteronomy is not in clear evidence in the *pesah* ritual itself is a telling omission. The Chronicler's propensity, as noted, is to harmonize multiple, conflicting traditions in order to respect and preserve their mutual authority. Because the Chronicler is well aware of the Deuteronomic laws governing the Passover, that fact that he does not make Hezekiah subject to them—the very king whom he essays to portray as completely subservient to God and his laws—suggests that their exclusion should not be sought in the literary intent of the historian, but rather in a non-Deuteronomic source used as the basis for the narrative.

A second aspect is the rationale for celebrating the Passover in Jerusalem. This section has demonstrated that the *pesah* ceremony of 2 Chr 30 was not centrally observed in order to adhere to Deuteronomic law, but has been cast by the Chronicler as an attempt to draw the beleaguered north back into what he views as proper Yahwistic worship. Once the decision by "the king and his officials" to assemble in Jerusalem for the Passover has been uncoupled from the prominent theme of centralization in Deuteronomy, the ideologically prompted description of the Chronicler nonetheless rings true as a socio-political event intended to unify the tribes. This aligns with the reconstruction offered in this study of Hezekiah's reform efforts in the aftermath of the fall of Samaria.

---

[84] Curtis and Madsen, *Books of Chronicles*, 470–71, "Nothing of this event is mentioned in 2 K., and as here described it is probably a purely imaginative occurrence, suggested by the Passover under Josiah (2 K. 23²¹)."

[85] Whether or not historical sources underly the Passover accounts of Hezekiah and Josiah, both narratives as they have come down to us are ultimately the finished product of the Chronicler's own hand. From this standpoint, comparative studies of these respective celebrations which emphasize the author's interests in both the cult and the unification of Israel are likewise beneficial, see Hee-Sook Bae, *Vereinte Suche nach JHWH: Die Hiskianische und Josianische Reform in der Chronik* (BZAW 355; Berlin: Walter de Gruyter, 2005).

The invitation extended to the north to partake in the Passover festival has been widely recognized as a potentially authentic element. The chapter as a whole is structured around the mutual participation of the northern and southern kingdoms at a common feast, with an appeal for those "left from the hand of the kings of Assyria" (v 6) to rejoin their brethren in religious worship. The population shift from the north to the south is well documented in the archaeological record, and the rapid expansion of Jerusalem during the last quarter of the eighth century—a highly organized program of constructing homes, fortification walls, and protected access to vital water sources—would not have been necessary unless king Hezekiah had himself encouraged the former denizens of Israel to take up residence in the southern capital. The tone of the narrative suggests that the invitation, and hence the Passover celebration in question, occurred after the fall of the northern kingdom. Yet according to the chronology advocated in this book, this did not occur until 720 B.C.E., the sixth regnal year of Hezekiah. Since the consensus of scholarship is that the attribution of these events to the first regnal year of Hezekiah by the Chronicler cannot be historically accurate, the resulting anachronism of the invitation is best explained as deriving from the author's deliberate reordering of the timeline of events in the source upon which he drew.

There is also the matter of the scope of the royal summons and its rejection by the north. According to v 10, the king's couriers passed "from city to city in the country of Ephraim and Manasseh, even as far as Zebulun."[86] The territory of Zebulun is typically situated in the Galilean highlands alongside the Kinneret, based on the explicit geographic boundaries of the tribe established in Josh 19:10–16.[87] This is far south of the northern limit of the total region apportioned to the twelve tribes according to the book of Joshua, which extended as far as Sidon. It therefore suggests a more plausible range of travel for the messengers from the

---

[86] The tribal boundaries of Ephraim are delineated in Josh 16:5–10. It represents one of the southernmost territories among the northern tribes, situated north of Benjamin's tribal allotment and incorporating the city of Gezer. Manasseh was centrally located between Asher to the north and Ephraim to the south, with Issachar on the east and the Mediterranean Sea on the west (Josh 17:7–12).

[87] For the boundaries of Zebulun according to archaeologists, see Yohanan Aharoni, *The Land of the Bible: A Historical Geography* (Philadelphia: Westminster Press, 1979) 237.

southern kingdom than the stereotypical merism "throughout all Israel from Beersheba even to Dan" in v 5.[88]

The repudiation of the invitation to come to Jerusalem for the Passover in v 10 is equally unexpected, "but they laughed them to scorn and mocked them." On the one hand, there is no reason whatsoever for the Chronicler to detract from his thoroughly laudable portrayal of Hezekiah, who has diligently worked to ensure that the Temple and its worship have been suitably restored.[89] Moreover, the Chronicler has previously alluded to the northern kingdom's contrite attitude toward the south in the aftermath of the Syro-Ephraimitic war, and the presumption proceeding from the impassioned candor of Hezekiah's speech is that those who have suffered so much at the hands of the Assyrian empire will respond favorably to the entreaty.[90] The brief notice of demurral is at odds with the otherwise unified conception of the kingdoms which is one of the Chronicler's chief ideological aims in the presentation of these chapters. This bespeaks a pre-exilic source with accurate knowledge of the state of affairs of Judah in the eighth century.

The same logic applies to the initiative taken by Hezekiah to pardon those who are unclean in vv 17–20, a personal decision that casts a long

---

[88] One could argue that the other references to the extent of the proclamation in the chapter ("to all Israel and Judah," vv 1, 6; "throughout all Israel from Dan to Beersheba," v 5) relay that a sweeping, all-inclusive act is intended, and therefore the range of the couriers' travel in v 10 must be interpreted as a merism for the geographical extent of the northern kingdom. This would accord well with the selection of tribes from Asher, Manasseh, and Zebulun in v 11, concerning which Japhet comments, "each time the Chronicler mentions the northern tribes, he cites a representative section, thus producing a varied literary effect" (I & II Chronicles, 946).

Such a reading should be avoided, however, for several reasons. First, the geographic regions delimited do not exhibit a representative distribution across the cumulative territory of Israel, but are contiguous territories limited to the southern and central sections. Secondly, Hebrew עַד "as far as" restricts the northern progress of the couriers, and to harmonize this with the stock, comprehensive expressions earlier in the chapter does not respect the polyvalence of the text. Finally, the second half of v 10, to be discussed next, has been widely defended as having an historical kernel. This fact should not be overlooked when conducting exegesis of the immediately preceding material. These observations commend that it is v 10 which represents the earlier, more reliable tradition, with the expansive descriptions elsewhere as later idealizations.

[89] As noted by J. Rosenbaum, "Hezekiah's Reform and the Deuteronomistic Tradition," HTR 72 (1979) 35–36, 41–42; Anson F. Rainey, "The Chronicler and his Sources—Historical and Geographical," in Chronicler as Historian, 46, if this were a purely fictional account by the Chronicler, it does a disservice to his efforts to depict Hezekiah's reign as comparable to or surpassing that of Josiah.

[90] 2 Chr 28:9–15 and 30:6–9, respectively.

shadow over the aggrandized depiction of the king by the Chronicler. As has been discussed previously, this procedure is in direct violation of all laws of purification, which adamantly refuse to accept anyone within the precincts of the holy sanctuary who is not in a state of readiness for worship.[91] The decision by Hezekiah to permit these worshippers to celebrate the Passover despite the legal proscription contravenes the Chronicler's glowing assessment of him in 2 Chr 29:2, "He did right in the sight of YHWH, according to all that his father David had done." The very notion that someone who feared the Lord, respected the sanctity of the Temple, and had just days before commanded the priesthood to "carry the uncleanness from the holy place" (v 29:5) would then turn around and actively instigate its renewed pollution is remarkable. Such recorded behavior is all the more astounding in view of the Chronicler's fidelity to the Priestly document, which upholds that sustained contamination of the sanctuary, even in its outer precincts, threatens to compel the deity to leave his dwelling and depart from his people.[92]

Certainly the priesthood would never have countenanced such an action, and there is thus some legitimacy to the notion that the exploit was discharged directly by the king. In both Passover accounts, the king oversees the festivities, and so it is reasonable to presume that he rather than the priests would have had authority to decide who could attend. The performance of Hezekiah's Passover, moreover, does not tout its rote adherence to recognized authorities, and the quarter shown to the prospective worshippers in chap. 30 is in accord with the different emphasis placed on the festival there. The sovereign's ability to personally enable them to partake of the *pesaḥ* sacrifice may be substantiated by the priestly and prophetic attributes attached to Hezekiah by the Chronicler, features which are entirely lacking in the presentation of Josiah: he employs priestly

---

[91] Reverence for the sanctuary and warnings against its profanation may be seen in Lev 12:4; 16:33; 19:30; 20:3; 21:12, 23; 26:2. Impurity is a generalized category for a broad range of polluting acts, on which see David P. Wright, "The Spectrum of Priestly Impurity," in G. A. Anderson and S. M. Olyan (eds.), *Priesthood and Cult in Ancient Israel* (JSOTSup 125; Sheffield: JSOT Press, 1991) 150–181.

[92] The deity physically resides within the sanctuary in the ideational framework of the Holiness Code, whereas Deuteronomy emphasizes that only his Name dwells there. It is therefore a procedural imperative in priestly theology to ensure the cleanliness of the sancta. Impurity defiles the land, according to Lev 20:22, and so striving for holiness by adhering to YHWH's commandments ensures not only that the people will remain in the land—an extension of the Lord's sanctuary—but that God's presence will abide among his people. For these conceptions, see Jan Joosten, *People and Land in the Holiness Code* (VTSup 67; Leiden: E.J. Brill, 1996).

language "you have consecrated yourself to the Lord," and intercedes for and obtains healing for the people.[93] This reflects early monarchic practice in which the crowned ruler officiates at inaugural ceremonies, and often adopts the role of a priest.[94] For these various reasons, the resolve to pardon "*many* in the assembly" (רַבַּת בַּקָּהָל) in these verses may well reflect an underlying remembrance of historical events. Their inclusion by the Chronicler is due to the chapter's overarching theme of the restoration of worship between the divided kingdoms: the incorporation of the wider community into the festival was deemed by the historian to be more meritorious under the circumstances than hewing to legal precedent.

7.2.5. *The Second Month*

The final, and most controversial, pillar of support for a historical source underlying the Passover account of Hezekiah is the postponement of the celebration until "the second month." Consonant with the lack of adherence to Israelite law elsewhere in the reform of Hezekiah, there is no legal exemplar for this action. Although attention is customarily drawn to the extenuating circumstances in Num 9:9–14 for keeping the Passover on the fourteenth day of the second month, the criteria there enumerated—a worshipper who is unclean or away on a journey—would have precluded many of the very people who were permitted to partake of the *pesah* sacrifice as described in Chronicles.[95] Because this law forbids someone in a state of impurity from participating, it is in fact the antithesis of the situation presented in 2 Chr 30.[96] The delaying of this ancient tradition

---

[93] 2 Chr 29:31; 30:18–20; Cf. Gen 20:7, 17; Num 21:7; Deut 9:20, 26; 1 Kgs 13:6.

[94] For other kings who assumed priestly functions during inaugural ceremonies, note 2 Sam 6:17–18 (David); 1 Kgs 8:63 (Solomon); 1 Kgs 12:32 (Jeroboam); 2 Kgs 16:12–13 (Ahaz). See further the bibliography at chap. 6 n. 81.

[95] Interpreters who see such a connection include Julian Morgenstern, "The Three Calendars of Ancient Israel," *HUCA* 1 (1924) 63–64; Immanuel Benzinger, *Die Bücher der Chronik* (Tübingen: J.C.B. Mohr, 1901) 123; Curtis and Madsen, *Books of Chronicles*, 472; Frederick L. Moriarty, "The Chronicler's Account of Hezekiah's Reform," *CBQ* 27 (1965) 405; De Vries, *1 and 2 Chronicles*, 379, following Judson R. Shaver, "Torah and the Chronicler's History Work" (Ph.D. diss.; University of Notre Dame, 1983) 158–64.

[96] If there truly were any connection between the injunction in Numbers and the situation outlined in Chronicles, then by all rights Hezekiah should have forbidden those impure from partaking in the festival, and held another, postponed ceremony in the subsequent month. These facts demonstrate that impurity was not at issue in Chronicles. A similar conclusion is reached by Simeon Chavel: "The two texts, then, describe two fundamentally different phenomena unlinked by any relationship, historical, analogical or other" ("The Second Passover, Pilgrimage, and the Centralized Cult," *HTR* 102/1 [2009] 10).

for the whole community is of an entirely different order, and demands further scrutiny.

The most cogent defense of the Passover celebration in the second month as a genuine historical remembrance has been on the basis of the liturgical calendars of the divided kingdoms. According to this view, Jeroboam I originally adjusted the festival calendar of the northern kingdom by one month at the time of the secession of the northern tribes, in order to disrupt the synchronism of the feasts between Israel and Judah and to bring the cultic festivals more in line with Ephraimite agricultural seasons.[97] Hezekiah's invitation to the people of Israel to come to Jerusalem for the Passover was met with derision and mockery according to the biblical account precisely because the celebration was a month early by northern time reckoning. The king subsequently realized that a unified liturgical calendar was imperative to restore cultic worship between north and south, and instituted a policy whereby the Ephraimite system was given prominence. The denizens of the northern kingdom consequently acquiesced, resulting in the great assembly at the Temple in the second month.

Setting aside the exegetical issues that a lasting change to the festival calendar would entail in the monarchic period, this proposal is not in accord with the biblical text. There is no report of two separate summons having been issued to Israel, one requesting an appearance in the first month and another, emended proclamation conceding the second. The disdain shown by the northern tribes in v 10 is in response to the invitation to celebrate the Passover in the second month, not the first, a fixed date that was agreed upon by both the king and the princes before the sole declaration was ever promulgated. The reasons put forward in v 3 as the rationale for the observance in the second month make manifest that the decision stemmed entirely from exigent circumstances. Its timing was thus a unique, one-time postponement rather than a permanent calendrical adjustment.[98]

If the performance of the *pesaḥ* ritual in the second month were truly intended as a measure to reunite the kingdoms, this policy could only have had disastrous consequences. Assuming for a moment that the north

---

[97] Shemaryahu Talmon, "Divergences in Calendar-Reckoning in Ephraim and Judah," *VT* 8/1 (1958) 48–74.

[98] As recognized by Talmon, "Calendar-Reckoning," 62, "But it is probable that this was a solitary occurrence. Hezekiah's plan to unite Ephraim with Judah did not materialize and it seems that eventually he reverted to the Judaean calendar while the northern tribes kept to their own system of time-reckoning."

did indeed have a festival calendar that was misaligned with that of the south by one month, favoring the liturgical system of Israel would doubtless have alienated Judah. As the southern kingdom had now been shown to be the righteous nation chosen by God by virtue of the destruction and exile of the north, what ire would Hezekiah have drawn from his own people by favoring the calendar of those who had not been deemed obedient to the covenant of their fathers? As a political maneuver, it would be a poorly received one, but Hezekiah—based on what has been reconstructed elsewhere in regard to his dealings with Israel—was unlikely to make such a blunder. The Chronicler, in any event, did not perceive the northern kingdom as valid, and so would not have condoned the idea of adopting its calendar.[99]

For some exegetes, the shifting of the *pesaḥ* ritual to the month of Ziv/Iyyar is a purely literary construct, a change necessitated by the Chronicler's decision to aggrandize the piety of Hezekiah by dating the renovation of the Temple to the month of Aviv/Nisan at the very beginning of his reign.[100] Yet Hezekiah could only be perceived as less than pious by being compared to both David and Solomon, and at the same time failing to respect the schedule of a ceremony upheld by both of his paradigmatic predecessors. On the contrary, the Chronicler is acutely aware that the timing for the ages-old observance is not in accord with tradition, and readily admits to the deviation: כִּי לֹא יָכְלוּ לַעֲשֹׂתוֹ בָּעֵת הַהִיא "for they could not keep it at its proper [lit. that] time" (2 Chr 30:3). This echoes another causative clause in the negative in v 5, which is similarly perceived as an evil and thus meriting comment. The entire foundation for the counsel taken by the king and his princes is grounded on the need to determine a course of action in the face of the inability to keep the Passover at its appointed time in the first month.

It is just this delicate balancing act performed by Hezekiah which lends the narrative a measure of historical authenticity. If the celebration of Passover in this chapter were a mere retrojection of that under Josiah, it should rightly have been kept at the prescribed time "on the fourteenth (day) of the first month" (2 Chr 35:1). If the observance in the time of Hezekiah were a complete fabrication, it would have served the Chronicler's

---

99 William Hamilton Barnes, *Studies in the Chronology of the Divided Monarchy of Israel* (HSM 48; Atlanta: Scholars Press, 1991) 158, further suggests that "there would have been a real need for such a calendrical concession only if the Northern Kingdom (and its calendar) were still in existence."

100 De Vries, *1 and 2 Chronicles*, 372–73.

authorial needs in idealizing Hezekiah just as well, if not better, to have the cleansing of the Temple transpire over two numerologically laden durations of seven days rather than eight as in 2 Chr 29:17, with the contaminant material removed by the fourteenth of the month and the *pesaḥ* ritual observed at its rightful time "between the evenings" by an obedient, God-fearing ruler. The very fact that the postponement does not attempt to make recourse to the law of the second Passover in Num 9:9–14 by way of harmonization suggests that the events are anchored in reality rather than literary creativity.

The question then remains: if the Passover celebration in the time of Hezekiah is historical, what was the unorthodox situation which gave rise to its delay until the second month? Two explanations are ready to hand in 2 Chr 30:3, "because the priests had not consecrated themselves in sufficient numbers, nor had the people been gathered to Jerusalem." However, these straightforward motives appear highly artificial. Stating that there were too few priests in readiness for the task falls afoul of v 29:34, where the same situation does not impede the ceremony due to the assistance of the Levites. The latter pretext is no more than circular reasoning: if the people had not yet assembled in Jerusalem, then they had previously known not to make the pilgrimage in the first month because the festival had already been delayed. To say that the Passover had to be deferred until the second month for the reason given is tantamount to comparing the ritual to a popular event only held when there are sufficient attendees. Even in the law of the second Passover in Num 9:9–14—hence its name in scholarship alluding to two ceremonies in two consecutive months— the *pesaḥ* ritual was still observed at its proper time on the fourteenth day of the first month regardless of who might be unqualified to attend. Moreover, its rationale to prevent defilement of the sanctuary does not hold according to the events recorded in 2 Chr 30, since the unclean are in no way deterred from partaking of the sacrifice. Thus the issue of cleanliness, pivotal to sanctioning the second Passover in the original law, has no bearing on the postponement in the account of Hezekiah.

For the entire community to be impelled to wait to keep the Passover has only one explanation: the Temple itself was not in readiness. At the appointed time of the Passover the precincts of the Temple were undergoing both cleansing and renovation, not in Hezekiah's first regnal year as claimed in 2 Chr 29:3, but in the aftermath of the fall of Israel as suggested by the timeline of the current chapter. The northern tribes had been made refugees of war owing to the Assyrian invasions into the territory, and many former residents were streaming into Judah for protection within

Hezekiah's well-established kingdom. The initiative taken by the ruler to restore the sanctuary was part of his broader program of religious reform, a carefully orchestrated policy aimed at uniting the remaining tribes around the cultic center of Jerusalem. As the Chronicler plainly states in 2 Chr 30:2–3 after the rededication of the Temple, "Then the king and his officials and all the assembly in Jerusalem took counsel to keep the Passover in the second month because they could not keep it at its proper time."[101] The postponement was not effectuated in order to change the liturgical calendar as a means of appeasing the north, but rather to rectify an extraordinary situation by resuming normal worship as soon as was feasible.[102] The account as it stands presents Hezekiah not as trying to break with tradition, but striving to preserve it.

7.3. Conclusion

While it cannot be denied that the account of Hezekiah in the book of Chronicles bears the distinct impress of its author, the narrative exhibits cogent evidence of reliance on earlier source material. The Chronicler has framed his exposition of the rule of Hezekiah within the defined parameters of older annalistic records, preserving the regnal data for his length of rule, age at accession, birth mother, and burial formula. The cleansing of the Temple in the first month of Hezekiah's reign follows the ancient Mesopotamian practice of fronting epoch-making achievements by revered monarchs, and the fact that available ancient Near Eastern analogues pertain to actual events is noteworthy at the outset. The reference to כֹּל יִשְׂרָאֵל in 2 Chr 29:24 rightfully refers to the polity of Judah and Israel as elsewhere in the reform account, and its resulting literary tension with Judah in v 21 speaks to knowledge of the Assyrian displacement of the northern population in the eighth century. That the Temple complex

---

[101] The remainder of the latter verse, a purpose clause subordinated to a purpose clause, is likely an addition inserted by later tradents more concerned than the Chronicler to justify this egregious impropriety. The Chronicler's lack of concern over the matter is reflected in his recording of Hezekiah himself as being behind the decision to move the festival as well as to dispatch the proclamation announcing the fact. For later rabbinic debate over the seriousness of this transgression, cf. *b. Sanhedrin* 12a–12b; *b. Berakhot* 10b; *j. Nedarim* 6.13. With the potential insertion excised, the narrative reads as a more natural continuation of chap. 29.

[102] In this case, Num 9:11 could well have provided the king and his officials with the appropriate date for the resumption of the feast, one legally sanctioned which would provoke the least discord among the populace.

had fallen into some degree of disrepair is undergirded within the Deuteronomistic History by the categorical indictments of idolatry heaped upon
Ahaz, as well as the recorded drastic modifications made to the sanctuary
and courtyard to accommodate his overlord Tiglath-pileser III. The reform
of Hezekiah, which has been independently established and reflects the
monarch's solicitude toward the cult as attested in 2 Kgs 18:3–6, would
logically have begun with the Temple itself. Such an undertaking is historically plausible after Israel's covenant with YHWH had been called into
question with the fall of the northern kingdom, and the massive influx of
refugees would have made paramount the need for a revitalized place of
worship at the heart of a rapidly emerging economic center.

It is a mistake to dismiss facilely the historicity of Hezekiah's Passover
as a retrojection of its better-documented counterpart set in the time of
Josiah. The assertion by scholars that Josiah's Passover had not been celebrated since "the time of the judges" (2 Kgs 23:22, cf. 2 Chr 35:18) does
not respect that an entirely different manner of observance is being highlighted within each respective summary statement. Neither the combined
use of פֶּסַח and חַג הַמַּצּוֹת, nor the unfounded consensus that the date
of composition of Deuteronomy should be associated with the reign of
Josiah, precludes the possibility of a *pesah* ritual observed in the days of
Hezekiah.

A close examination of 2 Chr 30 reveals that the text has no literary
dependence on the corresponding Josiah accounts, nor adheres to Deuteronomic law. The invitation sent by couriers throughout the kingdom
does not require observance at the central sanctuary as dictated by
Deut 16:5–6, and has been shaped instead by the Chronicler's theology of
exile. The Passover account of Josiah is at pains to show at every step that
everything was performed in accord with Deuteronomic legislation, from
the butchering of the *pesah* by the priests, to the preparation of the sacrifice by boiling, even to the inclusion of bovines. The latter two elements
are notably absent from Hezekiah's observance, and the slaughtering of
the animals by the laity in 2 Chr 30:15 conforms to the oldest tradition of
the Passover as a domestic rite. Legal authority is a subsidiary element
here, and is invoked twice to underscore that the people were, in fact, not
in accordance with prescribed ritual.

Despite its independence from the account of Josiah's Passover, the
celebration in the time of Hezekiah should not be reckoned as a mere
literary invention of the Chronicler. His tendency to meld competing traditions is evident throughout his work, and it strains credulity to propose
that within an original composition he would choose to emphasize Heze-

kiah's nonfulfillment of Deuteronomic legislation in regard to such a time-honored festival. The invitation to the north is sensible from a political standpoint, and the staunch refusal of many to attend is not something the Chronicler would have invented. The partaking of the *pesah* by the assembly likewise rings true as an historical event, being at odds with attested purification laws and the dangers inherent within the Priestly document of defiling the abode of the deity, even as it reinforces the pre-exilic notion of the king functioning in the role of priest. The postponement of the Passover until the second month was not a concession to the supposedly divergent cultic calendar in the north, but was in all likelihood driven by the Temple's inaccessibility at the prescribed time.

CHAPTER EIGHT

THE HISTORICAL RELIABILITY OF 2 CHR 31–32

The task of identifying potential historical sources behind the Chroni-cler's work continues here with the latter two chapters of the account of Hezekiah. Chapter 31 represents the conclusion of the reform narrative, transpiring after the renovation of the Temple and the observance of Pass-over. It contains a brief report of the religious reformation as instituted throughout Hezekiah's kingdom, followed by elaboration of the commu-nity's contributions on behalf of the priesthood.

The versions of Sennacherib's campaign, Hezekiah's illness, and the visit of the Babylonian envoys in chapter 32 exhibit a clear literary affin-ity with their Deuteronomistic *Vorlage* in 2 Kings 18–20. The retelling of these events is drastically curtailed, which makes the various Chronistic additions in these texts all the more consequential. As the parallels in Kings have been independently assessed in this study, attention will be focused on the material unique to Chronicles.

8.1. The Reform and the Portions (2 Chr 31)

8.1.1. *The Reform*

The opening verse of 2 Chr 31 is often read in concert with the preced-ing chapter, the final act of the extended fourteen-day celebration of the Feast of Unleavened Bread. Although the Masoretes chose to separate this material from the foregoing by means of a *parašah pᵉtuḥah* (פ), the introductory וּכְכַלּוֹת כָּל־זֹאת, followed by כָּל־יִשְׂרָאֵל הַנִּמְצָאִים, suggests a closer literary relationship:[1]

---

[1] This Masoretic marker later influenced the division of the biblical text into separate chapters during the Middle Ages. The exact content of chapters sometimes differs among the various textual witnesses due to divergent conceptions of one particular verse, which then cause a difference in numbering. Among the examples cited by Emanuel Tov, *Textual Criticism of the Hebrew Bible* (2nd ed.; Minneapolis: Fortress Press, 1992) 4, the verse "At that time, declares the Lord, I will be…" sometimes appears as the last verse of Jeremiah 30 (30:25), and sometimes as the first verse of chapter 31. These two representations of the same text are based on a different way of understanding the verse in its context.

2 Chr 31:1

וּכְכַלּוֹת כָּל־זֹאת יָצְאוּ כָל־יִשְׂרָאֵל
הַנִּמְצְאִים לְעָרֵי יְהוּדָה וַיְשַׁבְּרוּ הַמַּצֵּבוֹת
וַיְגַדְּעוּ הָאֲשֵׁרִים וַיְנַתְּצוּ אֶת־הַבָּמוֹת וְאֶת־
הַמִּזְבְּחֹת מִכָּל־יְהוּדָה וּבִנְיָמֶן וּבְאֶפְרַיִם
וּמְנַשֶּׁה עַד־לְכַלֵּה וַיָּשׁוּבוּ כָל־בְּנֵי יִשְׂרָאֵל
אִישׁ לַאֲחֻזָּתוֹ לְעָרֵיהֶם:

Now when all this was finished, all Israel who were present went out to the cities of Judah and broke down the pillars, cut down the Asherim, and pulled down the high places and the altars throughout all Judah and Benjamin, and in Ephraim and Manasseh, until they had destroyed them all. Then all the people of Israel returned to their cities, all to their individual properties.

As has been widely noted, this verse bears a strong resemblance to 2 Kgs 18:4, which also mentions the removal of the high places (הֵסִיר אֶת־הַבָּמוֹת), the breaking of the sacred pillars (וְשִׁבַּר אֶת־הַמַּצֵּבֹת), and the cutting down of the Asherim (וְכָרַת אֶת־הָאֲשֵׁרָה). Yet the lack of verbal correspondence and word order between the two precludes any demonstration of direct literary dependence.[2] Since the Chronicler doubtless had access to some form of the book of Kings, however, the verse as we have it represents the historian's own perspective on the same iconoclastic movement.

This brief report signals the end of the schematized purgation of foreign elements from the Israelite cult in ever-expanding concentric circles, beginning with the Temple in chap. 29, moving to the environs of Jerusalem in 2 Chr 30:14, and finally throughout the countryside. The eradication here is corporate as opposed to the individual actions enumerated in Kings, continuing the same democratized notion which has been a leitmotif of the Hezekian arc in Chronicles. The collective accordingly acts on a variety of cultic objects in the plural: pillars, Asherim, high places and altars. The reference to the solitary Nehushtan mentioned in the Deuteronomistic History could have been excised for this reason, or else because

---

"Certain elders of Israel came to me" forms the first verse of Ezekiel 14, but in the editions of Cassuto and Ginsberg it appears as the last verse of chapter 13—in accordance with the notation of the "closed section" indicated after this verse, 13:24. Likewise, the verse starting with the words "Early in the morning Laban arose..." appears as the last verse of Gen 31 (31:55) in the edition of Koren, but as the first verse of chap. 32 in other editions.

[2] Note the closer conformance of this verse to 2 Chr 14:2[3] during the reign of king Asa.

its presumed location in the Temple was not the emphasis of the reform movement in question.[3]

The geographical extents mentioned in the verse have also been idealized: Judah and Benjamin ably represent the kingdom of Judah, while Ephraim and Manasseh as the two largest northern tribal territories are a merism for the polity of Israel.[4] Because these regions are traversed by "all Israel who were present," the Chronicler envisions the reform as encompassing the full extent of a reunified kingdom such as it was perceived in the days of Solomon.[5] The concluding phrase וַיָּשׁוּבוּ כָל־בְּנֵי יִשְׂרָאֵל אִישׁ לַאֲחֻזָּתוֹ recalls the utopian notion of the jubilee, in which the land would revert back to its original owner in the fiftieth year so that he may "return to his property" (שָׁב לַאֲחֻזָּתוֹ, Lev 25:27–28).[6] As a result, neither the widespread active participation nor the expansive borders may be taken at face value. Furthermore, the credible notice in 2 Chr 30:10 of the rife dissent to restoring common tribal worship in Jerusalem raises serious complications: the attendees of the Temple festival could not simply have gone throughout the hinterlands wreaking havoc on religious sites. Civil unrest and ultimately full-scale tribal conflict would have erupted. Only a royal edict to enact the reform is plausible, operating largely within the confines of Hezekiah's kingdom of Judah.[7] The reformation of the

---

[3] These are other alternatives to the equally reasonable solution that the bronze serpent was omitted out of pietistic consideration for Moses, see, e.g., H. G. M. Williamson, *1 and 2 Chronicles* (NCB Commentary; Grand Rapids: Wm. B. Eerdmans, 1982) 372. The unrestrained optimism seen here will also inhere in the overflowing of the people's portion in vv 9–10.

[4] That Zebulun is also included in 2 Chr 30:10 is another subtle indication that "Ephraim and Manasseh" there is not, in fact, a simple merism. Note further the inclusion of בָּאָרֶץ in the same verse, which suggests a precise, localized territory. The mere inclusion of such geographical references does not determine their meaning, but rather how they are used.

[5] The Solomonic borders are given in 1 Kgs 8:65 as "from the entrance of Hamath (לְבֹא חֲמָת) to the brook of Egypt." Hebrew לְבֹא חֲמָת has also been construed as the name of a city, but under either interpretation it functions as a geographic marker in modern Syria for the northern boundary of the land apportioned to Israel (Num 34:7–9; Josh 13:5; 2 Kgs 14:25; Ezek 47:16), see Tom F. Wei, "Hamath, Entrance of," *AYBD* 3.36–37. Here too, the king is accompanied by כָל־יִשְׂרָאֵל עִמּוֹ "all Israel with him."

[6] William Johnstone, *1 and 2 Chronicles, Volume 2: 2 Chronicles 10–36. Guilt and Atonement* (JSOTSup 254; Sheffield: Sheffield Academic Press, 1997) 200.

[7] Under the purview of this reform would plausibly have been northern sanctuaries sufficiently close to serve as an enticement to southern residents, such as the shrine at Bethel. As articulated by Moshe Weinfeld, "Cult Centralization in Israel in the Light of a Neo-Babylonian Analogy," *JNES* 23 (1964) 206, "The calves and high places of Beth-el had, since Jeroboam's time, represented a principal obstacle to the purification of the Israelite cult and to the political unification of Judah and Israel and the kings who extended their influence over the areas of the north had, in all probability, attempted to undermine

Yahwistic cult was thus not a groundswell movement, nor did it cover the full extent of Israel.[8]

8.1.2. *Distribution of the Portions*

The portions (מָנוֹת) designated in support of the Temple are furnished in vv 3–10. The material contributions incumbent upon the ruler and the people are delineated in vv 3–6, which are once again not new measures imposed within the cultic system but rather renewals of former conventions deemed to have been discontinued by Ahaz. There is a clear division of responsibility in this passage, with the king providing the Temple offerings whereas the people are to assume ownership of the requirements of the priesthood.[9] While the organization of the maintenance of the holy precincts is only scantily documented in the biblical record, this would indeed seem to reflect Israelite praxis prior to the return from exile. Both David and Solomon are presumed to have offered sacrifices from their own holdings in public ceremonies, and Ezekiel prescribes this role as

---

the status of this 'king's sanctuary' and its cult. It is therefore possible that Hezekiah had already conspired against this northern cultic center even though it is only in the days of Josiah that we hear of its actual destruction."

[8] The uniqueness of the Chronicler's portrayal is underscored by Sara Japhet, *I & II Chronicles: A Commentary* (OTL; Louisville: Westminster/John Knox, 1993) 962, who notes: "[I]t is the only instance in the Bible where a popular religious reform is indicated." The historicity of the Hezekian reform has been assessed in this study independently of the book of Chronicles, and has upheld its legitimacy in the light of both archaeological and biblical evidence. Whatever historical kernel may potentially lie behind this verse, however, has been sufficiently obscured by the Chronicler's ideological flourishes. The destruction of the pillars, high places and altars are juxtaposed as polar opposites to the prior unfaithfulness of Ahaz in 2 Chr 28:2–4, 24–25. The location of this episode within the narrative framework of the Hezekiah arc further points out the author's theological agenda. In the following verse, the king "appointed the divisions of the priests and the Levites by their divisions, each according to his service." This action represents the last stage in reinstating the liturgical system which had been previously suspended under Ahaz, according to the Chronicler's theological perspective. It brings to a conclusion the establishment of the service of the house of YHWH as summarized in 2 Chr 29:35, and signifies for the author the full reversal of the deleterious effects imposed on the Temple by Ahaz in verse 28:24.

[9] The antecedent of the concluding relative clause in v 4, לְמַעַן יֶחֶזְקוּ בְּתוֹרַת יְהוָה, is ambiguous. Raymond B. Dillard, *2 Chronicles* (WBC 15; Waco, Texas: Word Books, 1987) 247, 250, argues that יֶחֶזְקוּ refers to the priesthood, "so that they could devote themselves to the law of Yahweh." Japhet counters that this "presses the limits of its normal usage" (*I & II Chronicles*, 964), and favors the purpose clause as referring to the people. YHWH expresses this notion of being resolute in keeping the commandments in regard to Solomon (1 Chr 28:7).

the obligation of "the prince."[10] On the other hand, the "priests' due from the people" (מִשְׁפַּט הַכֹּהֲנִים מֵאֵת הָעָם) is specified in Deut 18:3, and in Ezek 44:30 a blessing is promised upon the house of the worshipper who provides the first of his produce to the priest. This also mirrors Persian policy, for Darius decrees that the state treasury should be used to cover expenses for the various offerings, yet makes no allowance for supporting the clergy.[11] By the Second Temple period, the absence of a local sovereign meant that the citizenry had to be assessed a tax to cover all aspects of Temple maintenance including that of the regular sacrifices, and this system is reflected in Neh 10:33–40 [Eng. 32–39]. The portion provided by the king in 2 Chr 31:3, therefore, stems from earlier tradition and is given credence by its inability to serve as a viable model for the Chronicler's contemporary audience.[12]

In conformance with the leitmotif of communal unity which runs throughout the Hezekiah narrative, there is an overwhelming response on the part of the people. The obligatory portion due to the priests and Levites is commanded of "the people who lived in Jerusalem" in v 4, but the tithes are brought in by "the people of Israel and Judah who lived in the cities of Judah" (v 6). This is an explicit reference to former denizens of the northern kingdom who now dwell in the south, which accurately reflects the historical situation after the fall of Samaria. This is to be contrasted with "the people of Israel" who bring in their tithes and first fruits in v 5, who presumably still reside in the north.[13] This interpretation is reinforced by the portions of the respective groups: only those who inhabit the cities of Judah contribute the tithe of cattle and sheep. This accords with Deut 14:23–26, which requires "the firstborn of your herd or flock" from those who live close to the Temple, but for those whom "the distance is so great for you that you are not able to bring [the tithe]," an exemption is made. Even the stockpiling of these עֲרֵמוֹת "heaps" from the

---

[10] Cf. 2 Sam 6:17; 24:25; 1 Kgs 3:4, 15; 8:64; 9:25; 1 Chr 16:37–40; 2 Chr 8:12–13; Ezek 45:17, 22; 46:2.

[11] Ezra 6:9–10. As noted by H. G. M. Williamson, *Ezra, Nehemiah* (WBC 16; Waco, Texas: Word Books, 1985) 82, these offerings supplied by Darius are strictly limited to the daily sacrifices and do not include the sabbath, new moon, or annual festivals. In Ezra 7:24, although Artaxerxes permits the priesthood to be exempt from regular taxes, he does not actively make any provision for them (Japhet, *I & II Chronicles*, 961).

[12] Insofar as the kingdom of Yehud no longer had a king of its own to supply sacrifices, nor was this extensive responsibility incumbent upon the ruling authorities of the time.

[13] Pace Williamson, *1 and 2 Chronicles*, 375. As has been widely noted, the firstfruits of honey in this verse is not expressly decreed in Pentateuchal law, but is implied by Lev 2:11–12.

third to seventh months in 2 Chr 31:7 has been acknowledged as being not only an accurate reflection of Pentateuchal law but also of the agricultural calendar.[14] In short, these verses in Chronicles not only provide evidence of the population shift in the eighth century but also conform to Deuteronomic law, and so should be assigned to a source close in time to that of Hezekiah.[15]

In verses 12–13, oversight of the Temple storerooms for these various portions is delegated to Conaniah the Levite, his brother Shimei, and ten others. In verses 14–19, Kore and six other Levites under his supervision are given responsibility for apportioning the contributions. These two sections comprise respective stages in the distribution of gifts to the clergy: the collection is handled locally at the central sanctuary, and thereafter dispersed to priests and Levites both in Jerusalem and outlying provincial towns. The extensive detail alone devoted to the differing standards of eligibility between Levites and priests speaks against outright contrivance. The sophistication of the registration involved, coupled with a marked deviation from expected narrative style, point to reliance on an administrative document.[16]

It is the determination of a date for this organizational record in vv 14–19 which is more difficult to pin down, a task exacerbated by the onerous sentence structure of the passage. The characteristic *waw*-consecutive is completely absent, replaced by a series of nominal clauses spread across six verses. The first and last verses of the text form independent, self-contained units, but the intervening vv 15–18 constitute a single prolix and discursive sentence which must be carefully dissected. Verse 15 contains a list of six Levites under the authority of Kore son of Imnah, followed by their designated function: לָתֵת לַאֲחֵיהֶם בְּמַחְלְקוֹת "to apportion to their brothers by divisions." The verse ends with כַּגָּדוֹל כַּקָּטָן, denoting that no favoritism was shown by the Levites in their duty of faithfully distributing the מָנוֹת. Verse 16 begins with מִלְּבַד "besides,

---

[15] Some might claim that indications of Deuteronomic law could be argued as evidence of lateness for the passage; that is, if the earliest core of Deuteronomy is thought to have been composed sometime during the reign of Hezekiah or Manasseh, then the date of this material in Chronicles could conceivably be any time thereafter. On the other hand, its conformance to a historical situation known at the time of Hezekiah also permits these verses to be seen as reflecting the eighth century, with necessary provisions made for contemporary circumstances which would only later be incorporated into the laws of Deuteronomy. This aligns with the view discussed earlier (chap. 4 n. 88) that such customs were in practical use in Israel before they become sanctioned law.

[16] The unusual syntax is noted by Japhet, *I & II Chronicles*, 969.

apart from", marking an adverbial clause which specifies an exception in how the dispersion of the contributions was to be handled.[17] It spans the entirety of the verse, with לְכָל־הַבָּא לְבֵית־יְהוָה functioning in apposition to לִזְכָרִים, as widely recognized.

The sentence continues in MT with וְאֵת at the opening of v 17, a simple conjunctive *waw* coupled with the direct object marker. But the direct object of the verb לָתֵת in verse 15 is logically תְּרוּמַת יְהוָה וְקָדְשֵׁי הַקֳּדָשִׁים, carried forward from the earlier use of the same verb in v 14. The appearance of וְאֵת here is further compounded by the subsequent הִתְיַחֵשׂ הַכֹּהֲנִים "those [genealogically] enrolled of the priests,' which reads as a continuation of the previous list of personnel, and therefore an indirect object. In any event, הִתְיַחֵשׂ הַכֹּהֲנִים makes no sense as the direct object of לָתֵת, something which must be doled out. It is not surprising, therefore, that it has been recommended to emend וְאֵת to זֹאת based on LXX οὗτος, so that verse 17 forms a logical break between the preceding topic of the priests and the following devoted to the Levites: "this is the enrollment of the priests according to their father's houses."[18] On several grounds, however, this is a dubious suggestion.[19]

---

[17] מִלְּבַד consistently signals separation or distinction, cf. בַּד I. *HALOT* 1.108–109. The translations "besides" (NJPS) and "except" (NRSV) are consonant with this interpretation, while "without regard to" (NAS95) is further afield. The latter rendering comes from the attempt to separate הִתְיַחְשָׂם לִזְכָרִים, but this should not be done. In Chronicles, the *hitpael* of יחשׂ with a 3rd m.pl. suffix signals the group being genealogically enrolled, while the following substantive prefixed by לְ stipulates the means of agency. Thus in 1 Chr 4:33, the terse וְהִתְיַחְשָׂם לָהֶם is more fully translated as "their [the people's] enrollment was according to them [the settlements]," and in 1 Chr 7:5 we read הִתְיַחְשָׂם לַכֹּל "their [the mighty men's] enrollment was according to all [the families of Issachar]." Hence in our verse under consideration, the proper rendering is "their enrollment was according to males from three years old and upward."

[18] Japhet, *I & II Chronicles*, 971.

[19] The demonstrative particle זֹאת is routinely pressed into service in priestly documents as either the heading or conclusion to a section. For headings, cf. Exod 12:43; Lev 6:2, 7, 18; 7:1. For conclusions, cf. Lev 7:35, 37; 11:46. In this instance, the enrollment of priests has already been referenced in the preceding verse, so v 17a cannot function as an introductory heading.

Yet neither can it serve as a conclusion. The remainder of the verse forms a nominal clause which lacks a verb, with the subsequent וּלְהִתְיַחֵשׂ (v 18) being a new clause signaled by the copulative *waw* and an infinitive construct prefixed with לְ. Without a main verb to govern וְהַלְוִיִּם, there is no way grammatically to form the sentence "And the Levites… were enrolled along with all their children…' as demanded by Japhet, *I & II Chronicles*, 972. It is curious that she provides no explicit translation for the verb itself, instead rendering the Hebrew immediately preceding and following.

The Levites, rather, must be part of the same list of clergy receiving the promised portions along with the priests, a point echoed in the consistent reference to both groups as בְּמִשְׁמְרוֹתָם כְּמַחְלְקוֹתֵיהֶם "in their duties according to their divisions." The priests and

How, then, is אֵת֙ to be understood? As the preceding verse is a parenthetical comment on those who would not be receiving portions from
the authoritative body in question, v 17 is a continuation of לַאֲחֵיהֶם in
v 15. The reference "to their brethren" is intended to be all-encompassing,
based on the inclusive כַּגָּדוֹל כַּקָּטָן. The priests and the Levites in v 17 provide express clarification of this totality. The opening וְאֵת is thus an appo-
sitional marker, designating not an additional group via the introductory
conjunctive *waw*, but reinforcing an earlier, repeated element, in this case
לַאֲחֵיהֶם in v 15.[20] In Late Biblical Hebrew, וְאֵת is typically employed in
verbose lists along with ל, a consideration which makes it all the more
applicable to our diffuse sentence in question.[21]

"Those registered of the priests...and the Levites" thus fills out the
description of the task of apportioning delegated to those wielding
responsibility in v 15. Their entire households are to be included in the
distribution as well. In v 18, וּלְהִתְיַחֵשׂ בְּכָל־טַפָּם נְשֵׁיהֶם וּבְנֵיהֶם וּבְנוֹתֵיהֶם,
refers to "those enrolled among all of their [the priests' and Levites'] little

---

Levites are also listed together in v 19 precisely in regard to the reception of portions
(לָתֵת מָנוֹת), which casts doubt on any proposal which seeks to wedge an earlier grammatical break between them. To posit a summary statement at this point in the document
disrupts the flow of the text and needlessly obfuscates its meaning.

[20] JM §125j provides Exod 1:14b as an example of אֵת "before a noun in apposition to a
noun with a preposition." There is no grammatical requirement that the preposition ל be
carried over into 2 Chr 30:17, as it is routinely dropped after the initial element in a list.
In 1 Chronicles alone, cf. 1 Chr 15:11; 23:6–7; 24:27; 25:9, 11, 19, 23–31. It is furthermore of no
syntactical consequence that the copulative-*waw* precedes אֵת, as this construction may
still mark apposition, see 1 Chr 5:26. The construction identified here is technically classified by GKC §131k as permutation, which "*defines* the preceding substantive (or pronoun,
see below), in order to prevent any possible misunderstanding."

[21] JM §125j, l, citing examples for both אֵת and ל employed in enumerations. It is manifest by the shared grammatical characteristics of these two particles that in late Biblical
Hebrew their functions began to coalesce. In Chronicles, therefore, it is not surprising to
them vary stylistically.

A straightforward example may be seen in 2 Chr 23:1, where וְאֶת־מַעֲשֵׂיָהוּ is preceded by
the grammatically equivalent לַעֲזַרְיָהוּ. The lengthy enumeration of plans for the Temple
which David passed on to his son in 1 Chr 28:11–18 begins with לֶחָצְרוֹת in v 12, and proceeds with objects marked by ל across vv 12–14. Throughout vv 15–18, the list continues
but with items marked inconsistently, including וְאֶת־הַזָּהָב מִשְׁקָל לְשֻׁלְחֲנוֹת הַמַּעֲרֶכֶת at
the beginning of v 16.

In 1 Chr 16:37–40, וַיַּעֲזָב־שָׁם לִפְנֵי אֲרוֹן בְּרִית־יְהוָה לְאָסָף וּלְאֶחָיו mark both "Asaph" and
"his relatives" with the accusative ל. In the next verse, the list continues with none of the
objects marked at all, and finally in v 39 we read וְאֵת צָדוֹק. Whether or not v 39 is thought
to begin a new list of cultic functionaries, the direct object marker here is grammatically
equivalent to the accusative ל previously.

children, their wives, their sons and their daughters."[22] Whether priest, Levite, or associated family member, receipt of the Temple contributions was not automatically granted but required proof of registration. The list having been completed, the final subordinate clause mentioning faithful consecration refers back to the manner in which the original six Levites performed these assigned duties. The proposed translation of vv 14–19 in its entirety is included in Appendix B.

With this understanding, 2 Chr 31:14–19 distinguishes three different groups responsible for the distribution of the portions brought by the people, serving respectively in the Temple at Jerusalem (v 14), in the cities of the priests (vv 15–18), and their associated pasture lands (v 19).[23]

---

[22] Hebrew וּלְהִתְיַחֵשׂ בְּכָל־טַפָּם in v 18 maintains the list of indirect objects from earlier in the passage, and has the same sense as וּלְכָל־הִתְיַחֵשׂ בַּלְוִיִּם "and to everyone registered among the Levites" in the subsequent verse. Here the use of כֹּל followed by the infinitive construct fills the role more commonly taken up by the participle, followed by the preposition בְּ which in conjunction with הִתְיַחֵשׂ connotes a subgroup.

The syntax of כֹּל + infinitive construct is very rare in Biblical Hebrew, and outside of Ezra and Chronicles it appears exclusively in temporal clauses, cf. Gen 30:41; Deut 4:7; 1 Kgs 8:52; Ezra 1:6; 1 Chr 23:31; 2 Chr 31:19. The reading כָּל־עֻנּוֹתוֹ "all his affliction" (a *pual* inf. const. from ענה) in Ps 132:1 should probably be emended to עַנְוֹתִי (pl. of עֲנָוה) "his submissiveness/devotion", see Moshe Weinfeld, "The Covenant of Grant in the OT and in the ANE," *JAOS* 90/2 (1970) 187; Mitchell Dahood, *Psalms III, 101–150* (AYB 17A; Garden City, N.Y.: Doubleday, 1970) 3.243 (who renders עֲנָוה as "triumph").

[23] Japhet, *I & II Chronicles*, 970, favors emending MT בְּעָרֵי הַכֹּהֲנִים "in the cities of the priests" (v 15) to בְּיַד הַכֹּהֲנִים "under the authority of the priests' (compare 2 Chr 23:18) based on LXX διὰ χειρὸς τῶν ἱερέων. She declares that MT "is impossible at this point in the text" for the following reasons:

"(a) it creates a contradiction within the passage itself, ascribing to the priests 'in the cities' (v. 15) the office actually executed in the Temple …

(b) it also creates an unnecessary doublet to v. 19, where the priests in their cities are explicitly referred to, with the full designation of these cities …

(c) finally, with this rendering, the passage overlooks the most important constituent of the priesthood, the priests of Jerusalem."

In regard to (a), there is no contradiction with v 16, which in its entirety is a disjunctive clause raising an exception (מִלְּבַד) for those who serve at the Temple. This stated exception limits the scope of the indirect object in v 15 (לְאֲחֵיהֶם) and thus attributes nothing to the priests in the cities.

There is no doublet as professed in (b). Hebrew בִּשְׂדֵי מִגְרַשׁ עָרֵיהֶם is not equivalent to the priestly cities, although some translations perpetuate this inaccuracy (see the JPS translation "their towns with their adjoining fields"). A literal translation is "in the fields of the pasture lands of their cities"; that is, the meadowlands surrounding the cities, a separate geographical region from the cities themselves. Grammatically, the JPS translation is manifestly in error: עָרֵיהֶם is in construct with מִגְרַשׁ, and not the reverse; there is only one plural pronominal suffix available; the context requires "in" for Hebrew בְּ, not "with".

Lastly, the priests of Jerusalem are not overlooked as asserted in (c). They are expressly mentioned in v 16, "everyone who entered the house of YꜪWH for his daily obligations." Their apportionment is expressly handled by Kore the Levite in v 14, which is further justification for retaining the MT in v 15 as designating priests elsewhere.

The sanctuary was the sole repository of the heaps resulting from the gen-
erosity of the people, and this ample supply is evidenced in the response
of Azariah the chief priest in v 10 that the priests and Levites had eaten to
satiety of the contributions brought into the Temple. This explains why
no distributions are made in the cities of the priests for "everyone who
entered the house of YHWH for his daily obligations" (v 16): actively serving priests were already entitled to portions rendered at the sanctuary,
and thus there was no need for redistribution to these same individuals
in the outlying, provincial areas.

This leaves two segments of the clergy in the cities which are eligible
to receive portions: priests who did not actively serve at the Temple, and
the more numerous Levites, both of whom fall under the purview of v 17.[24]
These same two sacerdotal classes are the focus of those handling dis-
bursements in the surrounding pasture lands of the priestly cities in v 19,
again with the presumed exception of actively serving priests. In v 18, the
immediate family is included for those priests and Levites in the cities of
the priests, and may be extended to the analogous situation of the pasture
lands in the next verse.[25] By means of handling these three groups across
three different types of regional centers of dispersion, it was possible
for the Levites to distribute "to their brothers by divisions, whether young
or old" (v 15).

8.1.3. *Historical Analysis of the Portions*

Everything in this passage is in strict accord with Pentateuchal law. Both
priests and Levites were permitted recipients of apportionments at the
Temple. Priests were entitled to קָדְשֵׁי הַקֳּדָשִׁים derived from offerings to
YHWH, and as such were only to be consumed in the sanctuary precincts

---

[24] The enrollment of Levites from twenty years and up in this verse conflicts with the
age requirements of 25–50 in Num 8:24–25 (H), and the census in 1 Chr 23:3 presumes
an age of thirty. In the Second Temple period this age may well have been 20 years, see
Ezra 3:8. One explanation is to posit that there were multiple traditions in place for the
Levite regarding necessary maturation prior to service. Another is to view the age of 20
years as a harmonization by the Chronicler to the practices of his own time, which has
no bearing on the date of the underlying source in our passage. The latter position intimates the antiquity of the prerequisite in the Holiness Legislation, as one would expect the
Chronicler to follow its requirements directly if H were roughly contemporary.

[25] Just as the context implies that actively serving priests were exempt in the surrounding pasturelands. Hence there was no "male only" rule for the priests and a "general
enrollment" rule for the Levites, as maintained by Japhet, *I & II Chronicles*, 972. Under her
proposal, one is left to wonder how priests provided for their own families.

where they served.[26] Priests were also allocated the first fruits of the land and every devoted thing (חֵרֶם), which could be shared with other family members.[27] Verse 5 states that וּמַעְשַׂר הַכֹּל לָרֹב הֵבִיאוּ, "They [the people] brought in abundantly the tithe of all." The tithe is the portion assigned to the Levites under priestly law, and it was permitted to be shared with the household.[28] According to this legislation, all of the various offerings and contributions were permissible for consumption by their respective households, except for the קָדְשֵׁי הַקֳדָשִׁים, and for that reason the portions also belonged to the family members of both priests and Levites as described in v 18. Deuteronomy, significantly, maintains this distinction of allotting the first fruits to the priest and the tithe to the Levite.[29] The

---

[26] Num 18:8–10, which pertain to the "most holy things" (קָדְשֵׁי הַקֳדָשִׁים).

[27] Num 18:11–19, which describe the "lesser" holy offerings (תְּרוּמֹת הַקֳדָשִׁים).

[28] Num 18:21–32. Verse 31 clarifies that the tithe is intended for the Levitical households.

[29] Deut 18:3–5 (priest); 14:27–29; 26:12 (Levite), cf. Neh 10:38 [37]. The triennial tithe for the Levite—erroneously designated "the second tithe" in later tradition—is not in accord with the centralized collection of the portions described in 2 Chr 31, since "you shall deposit [it] within your gates" (הִנַּחְתָּ בִּשְׁעָרֶיךָ, Deut 14:28). Its parameters likewise conflict in several respects with the regular tithes of Deut 12, which were both to be brought and consumed "before YHWH your God" (vv 5–7). The admonition against eating the tithe elsewhere clearly applies to the Levite as well: "You are not allowed to eat within your gates (בִּשְׁעָרֶיךָ) the tithe … but rather before YHWH your God you shall eat it in the place which YHWH your God will choose, you and your son and daughter, and your male and female servants, and the Levite who is within your gates" (vv 12:17–18).
Even if this could be harmonized with the tithe of the third year to permit the Levite special privilege away from the sanctuary, this exemption would not extend to the alien, orphan, and widow who are likewise permitted to "eat and be satisfied" (v 14:29). This is not a concession to distance as we find in v 12:21; for worshippers who lived too far from the Temple to transport the tithe, it was to be exchanged for money which was then to be spent on perishables consumed, as before, in the presence of the Lord (vv 14:22–26). It has recently been argued that a residual amount of the triennial tithe was indeed partaken of at the central sanctuary, see Ian Wilson, "Central Sanctuary or Local Settlement? The Location of the Triennial Tithe Declaration (Dtn 26,13–15)," *ZAW* 120/3 (2008) 323–40.
The purpose of each contributive act is likewise diametrically opposed. The regular tithe has a retrospective intent: "You will rejoice in all your undertakings in which YHWH your God has blessed you" (v 12:7). The triennial tithe, however, bears an anticipatory motivation, "in order that YHWH your God may bless you in all the work of your hand which you do" (v 14:29). While one could rationalize these variations as stemming solely from the humanitarian nature of the latter, the tithing legislation as found in Deut 14:22–29 introduces other changes to the laws in Deut 12 including the ability to exchange the tithe for money. Deut 12:21 makes an allowance for remote worshippers in the specific case of slaughtering, but even here there is no concern for monetary conversion. In chap. 12, the Israelite is warned, "be careful that you do not forsake the Levite as long as you live in your land" (v 19), yet no mention is made of any specific additional provision.
The cumulative evidence suggests that Deut 14:22–29 may represent a later innovation within Deuteronomic law. The older, centralized articulation of the tithing commandments in Deut 12:15–19 would then remain in close correspondence to the administrative document in 2 Chr 31:4–19. For further studies on the triennial tithe, see the bibliography of

congruence between the priestly and Deuteronomic legislation in this regard, mutually followed by the Chronicler, may point to an underlying historical kernel.

As to historical plausibility, Hezekiah's preparation of storage chambers and appointing of Temple staff for their supervision and maintenance (vv 11, 13) are not depicted in hyperbolic terms and lack the infusion of any theologically motivated words highlighting his faithfulness in this regard. These practical measures taken to ensure the livelihood of the clergy present a highly credible representation of the socio-economic problems within the cult which would have arisen due to the Deuteronomic reform. The act of centralization effectively closed the provincial sanctuaries and put their serving Levites out of work, entailing a system of rotation for the opportunity to discharge one's duties at the Temple in Jerusalem.[30] The intent of Deut 18:1–8 is to grant those Levites who serve at the central sanctuary their right to sustenance along with their fellows, commanding that "they shall eat like portions."[31] The repeated exhortations through-

---

Duane L. Christensen, *Deuteronomy 1:1–21:9* (WBC 6A; rev. ed.; Nashville: Thomas Nelson, 2001) 297–98.

[30] Note 1 Chr 9:25, in which Levites were brought in regularly from "their villages" (חַצְרֵיהֶם) in order to exercise their functions.

[31] Following the interpretation of Rodney K. Duke, "The Portion of the Levite: Another Reading of Deuteronomy 18:6–8," *JBL* 106/2 (1987) 193–201. The focus is rather upon the Levite's right to serve in the view of Raymond Abba, "Priests and Levites in Deuteronomy," *VT* 27/3 (1977) 266, a differing interpretation which nonetheless honors the distinction between priests and Levites. The ubiquitous phrase הַכֹּהֲנִים הַלְוִיִּם in Deuteronomy is not a means of identifying priests and Levites coevally, but rather emphasizes that the only proper priest is one who is Levitical in his ancestral background, see Richard D. Nelson, *Deuteronomy: A Commentary* (OTL; Louisville: Westminster John Knox, 2002) 231.

Although it is a contentious point, Deuteronomy is indeed cognizant of the sacerdotal classes of priest versus Levite. In every instance in which the book alludes to something that the Lord has previously stated or promised, the reference is to an earlier specific, written source:
– Deut 1:8; 4:31; 6:10, 18, 23; 7:8, 12–13; 8:1, 18; 9:5; 10:11; 11:9, 21; 26:3; 28:11; 30:20; 31:7, 21, 23; 34:4. Cf. Gen 12:7; 13:15, 17; 15:7, 18; 17:8; 24:7; 26:3–4; 28:4, 13; 35:12; 48:4; Exod 6:4, 8.
– Deut 1:10–11; 6:3; 13:18[17]. Cf. Deut 10:22; 28:62; Gen 13:16; 15:5; 22:17; 26:4, 24; 48:4; Ex 32:13.
– Deut 1:34–35; 2:14. Cf. Num 14:20–23, 26–35.
– Deut 2:1. Cf. Exod 14:2.
– Deut 4:21. Cf. Num 20:12.
– Deut 1:21; 6:19; 9:3; 31:3. Cf. Deut 1:8; Exod 23:27–31; 34:11.
– Deut 11:25. Cf. Exod 23:27.
– Deut 12:20; 19:8. Cf. Exod 34:24 (J). There is no direct reliance on Exod 23:31 (E).
– Deut 15:6. Cf. Gen 12:2; 22:17; 26:3, 24.
– Deut 26:18; 29:12[13]. Cf. Exod 19:5.
– Deut 26:19; 28:9. Cf. Deut 7:6; 14:2; Exod 19:6.
– Deut 26:15; 27:3; 31:20; Cf. Exod 3:8, 17; 13:5; 33:3; Lev 20:24.

out Deuteronomy to care for the Levite "who is in your gates" bring into sharp relief the severity of the issue.[32] The only group assured of receiving their due portions after the closure of the heretofore legitimate sanctuaries were actively serving priests at the Temple, the very group exempted from receiving any distribution outside of the capital according to 2 Chr 31:16. The basis of the whole process was accurate enrollment of the priests, Levites, and their families, and Hezekiah indeed oversaw such genealogical lists as confirmed by 1 Chr 4:41, הַכְּתוּבִים בְּשֵׁמוֹת בִּימֵי יְחִזְקִיָּהוּ מֶלֶךְ־יְהוּדָה.

The mention of עָרֵי הַכֹּהֲנִים in v 15 were the outlying cities in which the remote priests and Levites were to receive their portions, the so-called Levitical cities. This is what should reasonably be expected from an administrative standpoint, as it would not be practical for the collected contributions to be allocated for all, or even most, of the larger habitations throughout the land. These municipalities, which were purely places of residence rather than cultic centers, are mentioned in Deut 18:6 in regard to a Levite who "comes from any of your towns throughout Israel where he resides."[33] The reality of these cities, let alone their historical setting, has been a matter of long-standing debate in scholarship, the conclusions typically colored by assuming a post-exilic date for the priestly compositions in the Bible. Approached from other angles, however, the locus of evidence is concentrated sometime around the eighth century.[34] Resettling the Levites would have been a sound, if not

---

The same logic must apply, therefore, in regard to Deut 10:9; 18:2, both of which affirm that the Levites have no portion or inheritance (חֵלֶק וְנַחֲלָה) among Israel, but rather יְהוָה הוּא נַחֲלָתוֹ. This decree appears only in the Holiness Legislation of Num 18:20, "You shall have no inheritance (לֹא תִנְחָל) in their land nor own any portion (חֵלֶק) among them; I am your portion and your inheritance (חֶלְקְךָ וְנַחֲלָתְךָ) among the sons of Israel" (cf. Num 18:24). This determination has implications not only for Deuteronomy's understanding of the priesthood, but also for the relative ordering of these two Pentateuchal layers.

[32] These urgings to care for the Levite are found in Deut 12:19; 14:27, 29. Other passages indicative of the same problem are Deut 12:12, 18; 16:11, 14; 26:11–13, as well as the previously mentioned 18:1–8.

[33] Menahem Haran, *Temples and Temple-Service in Ancient Israel* (2nd ed.; Winona Lake, Ind.: Eisenbrauns, 1985) 112–31, presents a cogent case that viewing the Levitical cities solely as places of residence explains the omissions of such established cultic centers as Jerusalem and Nob from the lists of Josh 21:1–42. Anathoth, one of the priestly cities according to Josh 21:18, is the place to which the high-priest Abiathar returned after being dismissed by Solomon (1 Kgs 2:26).

[34] The proposed dates for the list of Levitical cities in Josh 21 have been wide-ranging, although recent studies have gravitated toward the post-exilic period. Among the suggestions are the following:

essential, policy decision for simplifying the maintenance of the clergy in light of both the efforts at centralization and the population shift to Jerusalem.[35] The more heavily fortified among these cities could have served double duty as provisional shelters for the citizenry in general, faced with the ever-present threat of Assyrian incursion.[36] In the final analysis, 2 Chr 31:14–19 is imbued with characteristics which are best explained as stemming from a pre-exilic source.

- the early conquest period, see Yehezkel Kaufmann, *The Biblical Account of the Conquest of Palestine* (Jerusalem: Magnes Press, 1953) 40–46; Mark W. Bartusch, *Understanding Dan: An Exegetical Study of a Biblical City, Tribe and Ancestor* (JSOTSup 379; London: Sheffield Academic Press, 2003) 98–104.
- the united monarchy of the tenth century, see William F. Albright, "The List of Levitical Cities," in *Louis Ginzberg Jubilee Volume: On the Occasion of His Seventieth Birthday* (New York: American Academy for Jewish Research, 1945) 49–73; Benjamin Mazar, "The Cities of the Priests and the Levites," in *Congress Volume, Oxford 1959* (VTSup 7; Leiden: E.J. Brill, 1960) 193–205; Yohanan Aharoni, *The Land of the Bible: A Historical Geography* (Philadelphia: Westminster Press, 1979) 301–305.
- the eighth century, see John L. Peterson, "A Topographical Surface Survey of the Levitical 'Cities' of Joshua 21 and 1 Chronicles 6" (Th.D. diss.; Chicago Institute of Advanced Theological Studies and Seabury-Western Theological Seminary, 1977) 701; Haran, *Temples and Temple-Service in Ancient Israel*, 112–31; Robert G. Boling, "Levitical Cities: Archaeology and Texts," in Kort and Morschauser (eds.), *Biblical and Related Studies Presented to Samuel Iwry*, 23–32.
- the Josianic reform of the seventh century, see Albrecht Alt, "Bemerkungen zu einigen judäischen Ortslisten des Alten Testaments," in idem, *Kleine Schriften zur Geschichte des Volkes Israel* (3 vols.; Munich: C.H. Beck, 1953–59) 2.289–305; Nadav Na'aman, *Borders and Districts in Biblical Historiography: Seven Studies in Biblical Geographical Lists* (JBS 4; Jerusalem: Simor, 1986) 207.
- the post-exilic period, see Julius Wellhausen, *Prolegomena zur Geschichte Israels* (6th ed.; Berlin: W. de Gruyter, 1905) 159–61; Martin Noth, *Das Buch Josua* (2nd ed.; HAT I/7; Tübingen: J.C.B. Mohr, 1953); John R. Spencer, "The Levitical Cities: A Study of the Role and Function of the Levites in the History of Israel" (Ph.D. diss.; University of Chicago, 1980); idem, "Levitical Cities," *AYBD* 4.310–11; Gösta W. Ahlström, *Royal Administration and National Religion in Ancient Palestine* (SHANE 1; Leiden: E.J. Brill, 1982) 52–55; Richard D. Nelson, *Joshua: A Commentary* (OTL; Louisville: Westminster John Knox, 1997) 238–41; Ehud Ben Zvi, "The List of the Levitical Cities," *JSOT* 54 (1992) 77–106.

[35] For a discussion of the Levitical pastureland surrounding these cities as an exercise in realistic planning, see Jacob Milgrom, *Numbers: The Traditional Hebrew Text with the New JPS Translation* (JPS Commentary; Philadelphia: Jewish Publication Society, 1989) 435–37.

[36] Plausibly suggested by Baruch Halpern, "Jerusalem and the Lineages in the Seventh Century BCE: Kinship and the Rise of Individual Moral Liability," in B. Halpern and D. W. Hobson (eds.), *Law and Ideology in Monarchic Israel* (JSOTSup 124; Sheffield: JSOT Press, 1991) 26. Nadav Na'aman, "Hezekiah's Fortified Cities and the *LMLK* Stamps," *BASOR* 261 (1986) 17, observes that the fortified cities mentioned in Chronicles were "manned with garrisons and furnished with arms (see 2 Chr 11:12; 17:2, 19; 26:14; 33:14)."

8.2. The Invasion of Sennacherib (2 Chr 32)

8.2.1. *Hezekiah's Defensive Measures (vv 3–6)*

Of all the chapters within the Hezekian arc of Chronicles, chapter 32 has received the most scholarly attention due to its transformation of the parallel tradition in 2 Kings. It consists of the accounts of Sennacherib's campaign, Hezekiah's illness, and the visit of the Babylonian envoys, albeit in an appreciably abbreviated form. The various deviations from the earlier source material have been extensively detailed elsewhere. All of these additions, omissions, instances of rephrasing, and so forth, have been satisfactorily explicated on the basis of the Chronicler's literary method and hence need not be repeated. As the dependence of these reports on the Deuteronomistic History is beyond question, the primary task of this investigation—to identify reliance on earlier sources—has already yielded affirmative results. My inquiry shall instead focus on those sections of the chapter which have no counterpart in Kings, namely vv 3–6, 7–8, and 27–30.[37]

Verses 3–6 introduce an element noticeably lacking in the parallel account of 2 Kings: tactical measures implemented by Hezekiah faced with the inevitability of Assyrian reprisal.[38] The Chronistic authorship is unmistakeable, carrying forward elements previously noted in the Hezekian arc such as וַיִּוָּעַץ "and he took counsel," and the mass accord of the

---

[37] As observed by Paul K. Hooker, *First and Second Chronicles* (WeBC; Louisville, Kent.: Westminster John Knox, 2001) 262, one of the primary reasons for the extensive coverage of Hezekiah's activities in regard to the Temple, reform and administrative control of the portions is to accentuate the righteous aspects of the king as a counterpoint to the events of the current chapter. According to the Chronicler's ideology, incursions by foreign kings are a form of divine retribution for sinfulness, as former treatments of the Judean monarchs make manifest, cf. 2 Chr 12:2–4 (Shishak), 28:1–2 (Syro-Ephraimite war), 28:16–20 (Edomites and Philistines); 29:6–8; 30:7 (Assyria).

It is the author's intent to distance the reader from such a notion in the present instance, however, by opening the chapter with "after these acts of faithfulness." The Chronicler is acutely aware of the cognitive dissonance between his theology and history, and the fact that he chose to incorporate earlier material which conflicted with his worldview says much about his literary approach: regardless of the tendentious character manifest throughout the Chronicler's work, he was still a historian who both harnessed and was heedful of his sources.

[38] Only 2 Kgs 20:20 mentions the redirecting of the external conduit of water within the walls of the city, and even this detail is not directly credited to Hezekiah as a strategy relating to the blockade.

people.[39] It could be claimed that this information is suspect due to the Chronicler's interest elsewhere in building programs and economic projects, combined with his desire to aggrandize Hezekiah.[40] But these details are at once realistic and compelling, lacking any theological flourishes such as prayers, prophetic consolation, or even mention of the deity.[41] They are specific, well suited to the situation at hand, and lack hyperbole. They further contain elements that are unique among the Chronicler's statements concerning royal building projects.[42]

The archaeology supporting these preparations in readiness for Sennacherib's third campaign has been surveyed previously. Water supplies were distinct vulnerabilities for city populations during wartime, and

---

[39] The rhetorical question in v 4 does not otherwise appear in the Hezekiah narrative in Chronicles, but is a literary device employed throughout the book, typically prefaced with הֲלֹא or לָמָה, cf. 1 Chr 19:3; 21:3, 17; 22:18; 2 Chr 13:5, 9; 16:8; 18:17; 20:6–7, 12; 24:20; 25:15–16, 19; 28:10; 32:4, 10–13.

[40] Among the skeptics is Robert North, "Does Archaeology Prove Chronicles' Sources?" in H. N. Bream, R. D. Heim, and C. A. Moore (eds.), *A Light Unto My Path: Old Testament Studies in Honor of Jacob M. Myers* (GTS 4; Philadelphia: Temple University Press, 1974) 375–79, who conceives of this entire description as a fictional extrapolation by the Chronicler from the material at his disposal in Kings.

[41] By contrast, we find a characteristic Chronistic response to the imminent assault of the Ammonites and Moabites against the righteous Jehoshaphat in 2 Chr 20. In this instance, he "was afraid and turned his attention to seek YHWH, and proclaimed a fast throughout all Judah" (v 3). The whole of Judah comes together in the next verse "to seek help from YHWH." Once gathered, Jehoshaphat delivers a public prayer in vv 6–12, declaring the Lord's greatness in assisting Israel in the past, and soliciting deliverance by anticipating the judgment of its enemies. It is only after prophetic assurance from Jahaziel the son of Zechariah (vv 14–17) that Jehoshaphat is able to act.

[42] A key factor which differentiates the activities recorded for Hezekiah from his predecessors is their specificity: they are immediately relevant to the current context. Prior notices refer often to the building of towers and fortified towns, occasionally manned with soldiers, cf. 2 Chr 11:5 (Rehoboam); 14:5–7[6–8] (Asa); 17:2, 12–13 (Jehoshaphat); 26:9–10 (Uzziah); 27:3–4 (Jotham). Although Sennacherib is said to have "invaded Judah and besieged the fortified cities" (32:1), the very Judean king who would certainly have made such preparations for regional fortifications and distributed manpower is not described in the same generalized terms.

Instead the focus shifts to Jerusalem, the epicenter of the crisis, with pertinent data relating to water supplies, particular municipal structures, and military organization. As noted by Japhet, *I & II Chronicles*, 982, "This is in fact the only case in the Bible where this topic is referred to—the active diversion of a water supply from an invading enemy." Only Hezekiah is credited with strengthening the Millo (v 5, cf. 1 Chr 11:8), and constructing weapons (שֶׁלַח, v 5, cf. 2 Chr 23:10). The term שָׂרֵי מִלְחָמוֹת "military officers" (v 6) is unique not only to Chronicles but to the entirety of the Hebrew Bible. These are indications that the Chronicler has not felt the need to credit Hezekiah with construction achievements comparable to those of his peers, and the striking use of vocabulary when other, stock terminology is more readily available does not smack of someone who is creatively filling in details.

restricting their access from invading armies while maintaining adequate quantities for the incarcerated inhabitants of a city under siege was of the utmost importance.[43] The description in v 4 of stopping up the springs which flowed through the region was a drastic yet intelligible decision under the circumstances to make this vital resource unobtainable by the Assyrian army, while redirecting proximal sources within the fortifications of the city. The prophet Isaiah alludes to this process when he chides, "And you collected the waters of the lower pool" (Isa 22:9). The paleography of the Siloam Tunnel inscription has likewise been verified to date from the eighth century via comparative evidence, and its protected, underground channel is more conducive to military application than to royal aggrandizement.[44]

The imposing rampart of the seven-meter-wide Israelite city wall in Jerusalem, better known as the Broad Wall, is recognized as having been built in the eighth century B.C.E. due to its stratigraphy and pottery. Located on the northern side of the Upper City, it was used to fortify the city's weakest flank along the Transversal Valley. The wall bears evidence of having been hastily erected, as it cut through earlier structures within the settlement on the Western Hill. The dire situation is recorded in Isa 22:10, "Then you counted the houses of Jerusalem and tore down the houses to fortify the wall." Other pronounced similarities between these two passages affirm the accuracy of their content. The בִּקְיעֵי עִיר־דָּוִד "breaches in the city of David" (Isa 22:9) have been equated with הַחוֹמָה הַפְּרוּצָה "the wall that had been broken down" (2 Chr 32:5), which Hezekiah would have reinforced to protect the capital.[45] These two texts also refer to a second defensive bulwark—הַחוֹמָה אַחֶרֶת in Chronicles— constructed as necessary to safeguard the water supply: "And you made a

---

[43] Jan Simons, *Jerusalem in the Old Testament: Researches and Theories* (Leiden: E. J. Brill, 1952) 168, notes the deliberate blocking of water outlets leading to the Kidron valley in the late monarchic period.

[44] Williamson, *1 and 2 Chronicles*, 380, rightly observes that the construction of Hezekiah's tunnel is not mentioned in this verse, and is skeptical "that so large an undertaking could have been completed in time after the immediate Assyrian threat had become known." The assault on Hezekiah's kingdom, however, was a problem of his own making: his very actions triggered the retaliation by Sennacherib, and so served as his forewarning. The construction of the Siloam tunnel is best viewed as a peacetime project shouldered by Hezekiah with the full awareness of its inevitable wartime significance. This conclusion aligns well with the mention of the digging of the tunnel in v 30 and 2 Kgs 20:20, both apart from any siege countermeasures.

[45] Hans Wildberger, *Isaiah 13–27: A Continental Commentary* (trans. Thomas H. Trapp; Continental Commentary; Minneapolis: Fortress Press, 1997) 368.

reservoir between the two walls (בֵּין הַחֹמֹתַיִם) for the waters of the old pool" (Isa 22:11). As this natural water source had previously served as an irrigation system for the royal gardens, this double circumvallation is ostensibly the same one referenced in 2 Kgs 25:4, "the gate between the two walls by the king's garden."[46]

The allocution against Hezekiah's practices in Isa 22:8–11 establishes that the son of Amoz placed no faith in human measures because they were tantamount to a lack of trust in the Lord's ability to deliver his people.[47] The actions preserved in Isaiah's fulmination prove that Hezekiah did indeed resolve himself to military readiness, and independently affirm our passage in Chronicles. Furthermore, vv 3–6 create a marked contrast with Hezekiah's address to the people immediately following. In both form and content, verses 7–8 are entirely Chronistic in origin.[48] The rhetorical speech placed in the mouth of Hezekiah here asserts that there is no need for fear or dismay, and yet no lethargic lack of concern would justify the decisions arrived at between the king and his officers and warriors, or their need to take counsel in the first place.

The peroration promises, "With us is YHWH our God to help us and to fight our battles."[49] While the Chronicler is of the belief that the Lord alone will deliver Zion—and human effort is indeed never mentioned or intimated in the speech—the creation of weapons and shields, and the organization of a conscript army anticipate the eventuality of flesh-and-blood conflict.[50] While laudable attempts have been made to reconcile these polarized positions, no effort need be made.[51] As with the inclusion

---

[46] Philip J. King and Lawrence E. Stager, *Life in Biblical Israel* (Louisville: Westminster John Knox, 2001) 213–18.

[47] This pillar of Isaiah's ideology may also be seen in Isa 30:12; 31:1, employing the root בטח used prominently in the speech of the *rab šāqê*. This stance would serve as an explanation for the omission of royal preparations in the account of the Jerusalem blockade in Kings, which has been argued as having originated in prophetic circles.

[48] See the elements noted by Japhet, *I & II Chronicles*, 977.

[49] The wording recalls the prophecy of Jahaziel given to Jehoshaphat in 2 Chr 20:15, but the first-person usage here in the mouth of Hezekiah bespeaks authorial intentionality in playing on the name Immanuel.

[50] Verified again by Isa 22:8–11.

[51] Williamson, *1 and 2 Chronicles*, 380, readily acknowledges that "this paragraph seems to stand in contrast to the insistence on complete trust in God's power to deliver expressed both in Hezekiah's address immediately following (vv. 7–8) and in the miraculous manner of the deliverance later on." His solution for resolving this theological impasse is to suggest its incorporation "on the basis of the Chronicler's conviction that part of the blessing which faithful kings enjoyed was their success in building operations."

While this is plausible, other considerations mitigate against this suggestion. The Chronicler details various constructions set up by Hezekiah in vv 27b–29a, ranging from treasuries

of Sennacherib's invasion itself, the military preparations undertaken in vv 3–6 demonstrate the inevitable clash between the author's ideology and recorded history. The fact of these literary tensions within the chapter, combined with both the archaeological and comparative textual evidence, indicate that vv 3–6 have their origin in an historical source.[52]

8.2.2. Hezekiah's Achievements (vv 27–30)

The last section of material with no parallel in Kings is found in vv 27–30, which summarize Hezekiah's economic projects and achievements. It serves as the denouement for the king's reign, positioned immediately prior to the retelling of the visit of the Babylonian envoys in order to aid in offsetting its originally negative characterization of the ruler. Its analysis is compounded by the literary function of the text as an encapsulation of Hezekiah's grandeur. On the one hand, the recounting of such diverse embodiments of extravagant wealth has been pressed into service by the Chronicler in order to sustain his conviction that a king's prosperity emanates from his faithfulness. This perspective is formulated in no uncertain

and storehouses to entire cities. This text makes an explicit correlation between the king's faithfulness and his prosperity, and as such it is the proper exemplar of the Chronicler's ideology in this regard. Secondly, vv 3–6 convey clearly that Hezekiah's decision to fortify the city was made out of sheer necessity. This is a situation diametrically opposed to the building efforts of Rehoboam in 2 Chr 11:5–12, for example, in which defensive measures taken during peacetime assured continued protection. Hezekiah's resolute maneuvers, on the other hand, leave the reader with the quandary of how to see the incursion of a foreign ruler into Judah—elsewhere the marker for a sinful act by God's anointed—as an instrument of blessing. The Chronicler himself is well aware of this tension, or else would not have chosen to follow it with the rhetorical speech.

[52] The Chronicler in some cases chose to incorporate traditions or sources which were in direct opposition to his own worldview. The most notable is the separation of the kingdom of Israel under Jeroboam, succinctly reported in 2 Chr 10:16, "So all Israel departed to their tents." Another tradition is that of David's census in 1 Chr 21:1–22:1, a skillfully retold narrative of the older story preserved in 2 Sam 24:1–25. As noted by Hooker, *First and Second Chronicles*, 85, "In the hands of the Chronicler, the story of David's census and the plague that followed become the occasion for the selection of the Temple site, thus adding to the mounting theme of David as the founder of Israel's faith.'

In each of these instances, the Chronicler has availed himself of the long-standing technique in biblical authorship known as reinterpretation. The earlier traditions were well-known and could not be avoided, but they could be understood differently. As explained generally by Yair Zakovitch, *Introduction to Inner-Biblical Interpretation* (Even-Yehuda: Reches, 1992) 12 [Hebrew], "The written story copes with the rejected tradition by making subtle changes which fit the ideological views of the author, and thus enable it worthy to 'enter into the community of the Lord'. So while on the one hand the author struggles to conform the rejected tradition to his personal religious, spiritual, and ethical outlook, he endeavors to preserve its likeness, such that it will earn the trust of the public regarding the tradition."

terms in v 29: "For God had given him very great possessions." On the other hand, these epitomes of affluence all find their complement in earlier depictions of king Solomon. The strong correlation drawn between the two monarchs in this pivotal, closing section, coupled with the lack of extra-biblical evidence in regard to the various details therein, increases the likelihood that a number of these details may have been incorporated to shore up their similarity while aggrandizing Hezekiah.

In broad terms, the image presented of Hezekiah's kingdom in this text conforms to what may be reconstructed archaeologically of his economic buildup and vast wealth. The model proposed for the *lmlk* jars as a means of revenue generation during a time of substantial agricultural proliferation fits well with the description of "storehouses for the yield of grain, wine, and oil" (v 28).[53] These depositories (מִסְכְּנוֹת) would also have been necessary as a means to set aside the contributions of the populace on behalf of the priesthood in vv 31:5–6. The Siloam Tunnel is accurately described in v 30, and its attribution to Hezekiah has been defended previously. The adherence to certain facts of the period in question arguably stems from some form of historical remembrance, if not from a written source.[54]

8.3. Conclusion

The brief account of the reform in 2 Chr 31:1 is a Chronistic interpretation of the independently substantiated event. The division of responsibility between king and community with regard to the portions in vv 3–10 reflects pre-exilic usage, and the differentiation in contributions based on the distance from the central sanctuary is in accord with Deuteronomic law. Verses 12–19 are widely recognized as having their origin in an administrative document, but ascertaining a date for this passage is integrally connected with the translation of the lengthy sentence in vv 15–18. As interpreted in this book, the text delineates the manner of distribution to enrolled priests and Levites, including their respective families, wherever they happen to reside. The passage aligns with Pentateuchal law in regard to the receipt of apportionments by all classes of religious functionary, including the permissibility of consumption by their associated house-

---

[53] Extensively detailed in Andrew G. Vaughn, *Theology, History, and Archaeology in the Chronicler's Account of Hezekiah* (ABS 4; Atlanta: Scholars Press, 1999).

[54] Also defended by Vaughn, pp. 173–81.

holds. The procedure is a microcosm of the Deuteronomic reform, and taking into account the debated issue of the Levitical cities, points to a historical context in the eighth century B.C.E. The pre-exilic nature of the source is bolstered by comparison with the later implementation of this practice in Neh 10:38–39 [Eng. 37–38].

The very inclusion of Sennacherib's third campaign in 2 Chr 32 is a testament to the Chronicler's respect for his historical sources, conflicting directly as it does with his well-known theology of retribution. The practical and unembellished defensive maneuvers set into motion by Hezekiah in vv 3–6 include the stoppage of water supplies and fortification of the city walls. These measures may be verified in part by archaeology, and by comparison with the eighth-century Isaianic oracle in Isa 22:8–11. The human initiative in these verses is in stark contrast to the Chronistic speech in vv 7–8, and substantiates the authenticity of the military preparations. While the summation of Hezekiah's reign in vv 27–30 is meant to magnify the king and to draw comparison with the grandeur of Solomon, the constructed storehouses nonetheless dovetail well with the use of the *lmlk* jars as an economic program, and the attribution of the Siloam Tunnel to the son of Ahaz need not be doubted.

CHAPTER NINE

HEZEKIAH AS A SECOND DAVID/SOLOMON

Having assessed the historical reliability of the Hezekian account in Chronicles, it will be prudent to investigate the development of this tradition. The terse praise directed toward him in the book of Kings is a far cry from his prominent depiction in Chronicles, and this disparity requires elucidation. The effusive picture of Hezekiah limned in the book of Chronicles, along with the degree of attention his reign receives and the magnitude of accomplishments laid at his feet by the author, leaves no doubt that his kingship is positioned as the high point of this literary work.

Both David and Solomon are explicitly referenced in the presentation of his reign, and the identification of other possible allusions to them has raised debate as to which of his predecessors the Chronicler intends Hezekiah to embody as a second incarnation.[1] Although there is a cogent case that may be made for Hezekiah as either a second David or Solomon, it is more apposite to see him as epitomizing both.[2] The comparisons to one dynastic forefather cannot be maintained to the exclusion of the other, and this mediating position is more in harmony with recent scholarship which argues for the reigns of David and Solomon in the book of Chronicles as a unity.[3]

---

[1] Major proponents of seeing Hezekiah as a second David have been Rudolf Mosis, *Untersuchungen zur Theologie des chronistischen Geschichtswerkes* (FTS 92; Freiburg: Herder, 1973) 164–69, and Raymond B. Dillard, *2 Chronicles* (WBC 15; Waco, Texas: Word Books, 1987) 245, 251, 257–58. Notable advocates of Hezekiah as a second Solomon are Andrew G. Vaughn, *Theology, History, and Archaeology in the Chronicler's Account of Hezekiah* (ABS 4; Atlanta: Scholars Press, 1999) 173–81; H. G. M. Williamson, *Israel in the Books of Chronicles* (Cambridge: Cambridge University Press, 1977) 119–25.

[2] Following the intermediate position of Mark A. Throntveit, "The Relationship of Hezekiah to David and Solomon in the Books of Chronicles," in M. P. Graham, S. L. McKenzie and G. N. Knoppers, *The Chronicler as Theologian: Essays in Honor of Ralph W. Klein* (JSOTSup 371; London: T&T Clark, 2003) 105–21.

[3] Otto Plöger, "Reden und Gebete in deuteronomistischen und chronistischen Geschichtswerk," in W. Schneemelcher (ed.), *Festschrift für Günther Dehn zum 75. Geburtstag am 18. April 1957* (Neukirchen: Kreis Moers, 1957) 35–49; Roddy L. Braun, "Solomonic Apologetic in Chronicles," *JBL* 92/4 (1973) 503–16; idem, "Solomon, the Chosen Temple Builder: The Significance of 1 Chronicles 22, 28, and 29 for the Theology of Chronicles," *JBL* 95/4 (1976) 581–90; H. G. M. Williamson, "The Accession of Solomon in the Books of Chronicles," *VT* 26/3 (1976) 351–61.

Part of this equation is due to the author's *Vorlage* in the book of Kings. There one finds that Hezekiah is compared favorably to David, "He did right in the sight of YHWH, according to all that his father David had done" (2 Kgs 18:3). It is not surprising, then, to find this juxtaposition preserved verbatim in 2 Chr 29:2, along with other implicit allusions elsewhere to the archetypal dynast noted throughout this study.[4]

More deserving of comment is the thoroughgoing likening of Hezekiah to Solomon in Chronicles. The extension of the feast during the rededication of the Temple in 2 Chr 30:23 recalls that of Solomon in vv 7:8–10, and v 30:26 expressly mentions "Solomon the son of David." The enumeration of the burnt offerings to be provided by Solomon in 2 Chr 2:3 [Eng. 4] is closely echoed by v 31:3. There are also striking similarities between Hezekiah and Solomon in describing the success of their righteous endeavors.[5] In these instances, there is no clear dependency on the extant Deuteronomistic History: the Hezekiah narrative there contains no obvious Solomonic references, and the builder of the Temple is himself assessed negatively in his old age, "Solomon did what was evil in the sight of YHWH, and did not follow YHWH fully, as David his father [had done]" (1 Kgs 11:6). As one of the purposes of this book is to trace the development of the Hezekiah tradition, it is necessary to examine how his characterization came to be so fully developed from its decidedly more muted complement in the book of Kings.

---

[4] Hezekiah gathers the Levites (2 Chr 29:4) just as David had done (1 Chr 15:4). Hebrew עִם־לְבָבִי "it has been in my mind" (2 Chr 29:10) harkens back to David's resolve in 1 Chr 22:7, both occurrences related to acts of rapprochement with the deity. Hezekiah renews Davidic institutions in 2 Chr 29:25–30, where David is mentioned four times (compare v 29; 1 Chr 29:20). The phrase מִבְּאֵר שֶׁבַע וְעַד־דָּן is only used of Hezekiah's proclamation and of David's census (cf. 2 Chr 30:5; 1 Chr 21:2). The concord of the community with both Hezekiah and David is signaled by the expression לֵב אֶחָד "of one mind," cf. 2 Chr 30:12; 1 Chr 12:39[38]. The provision for storerooms in 2 Chr 31:11–14 recalls 1 Chr 9:26; 23:28; 26:22; 28:12. The strengthening of the Millo in Chronicles is undertaken only by Hezekiah (2 Chr 32:5) and David (1 Chr 11:8). YHWH saves (וַיּוֹשַׁע) Hezekiah in 2 Chr 32:22, highly reminiscent of 1 Chr 18:6, 13; 11:14.

[5] Cf. 2 Chr 7:11; 31:20–21. Note more subtle examples such as the testing (לְנַסֹּתוֹ) of Hezekiah by Merodach-baladan in 2 Chr 32:31, recalling the queen of Sheba's testing of Solomon in 1 Kgs 10:1. For further examples and discussion, see Williamson, *Israel in the Books of Chronicles*, 119–25; Baruch Halpern, "Sacred History and Ideology: Chronicles' Thematic Structure—Indications of an Earlier Source," in R. E. Friedman (ed.), *The Creation of Sacred Literature: Composition and Redaction of the Biblical Text* (UCNES 22; Berkeley: University of California Press, 1981) 50; Simon J. De Vries, *1 and 2 Chronicles* (FOTL 11; Grand Rapids: Eerdmans, 1989) 386.

9.1. The Dynastic Promises to David and Solomon

9.1.1. *Conditional and Unconditional Material*

The terminating chapter of Solomon's legacy in the Deuteronomistic History casts a long shadow over his previous accomplishments, yet these aspersions on his character are conspicuously lacking in the book of Chronicles. The fact that the latter work does not recognize the legitimacy of the northern kingdom readily accounts for the expunging of the divine sentence on Solomon to split the tribes in the book of Kings. The incorporation of this judgment, which was to be delayed until after Solomon's passing, would further contradict the Chronicler's philosophy of immediate retribution, and so the rhapsodic portrayal of the son of David by this author is understood by commentators to be the result of rigorous whitewashing.[6]

While it is beyond cavil that there has been a systematic refinement in the book of Chronicles of the image of Solomon as a founder of the Jerusalem cult, the basis for this enhanced reputation is not so straightforward. The inimical record of Solomon's idolatry in 1 Kgs 11 has been placed at the end of his reign, with his heart turning away in his old age to the worship of the gods of other nations.[7] His moral demise, however, is blamed directly on the influence of the foreign wives which he had married during the course of his rule, the very association with them of which is vehemently proscribed.[8] Solomon, then, had lived for several decades in violation of the law. Following the pronouncement from God that the kingdom would be torn from Solomon due to his syncretism, the antagonists Hadad the Edomite, Rezon the son of Eliada, and Jeroboam are all said to have risen up against him. Yet each of these characters is chronologically misplaced, and should properly be situated earlier in Solomon's reign.[9] Literarily, the division of the kingdom at this culminating

---

[6] Braun, "Solomonic Apologetic in Chronicles."

[7] 1 Kgs 11:4.

[8] 1 Kgs 11:1–2, based on Deut 12:28–31.

[9] Hadad the Edomite is listed as the first adversary (שָׂטָן) of Solomon after the Lord's promise to tear away the kingdom from him (vv 11:14–22), yet the story of Hadad's flight to Egypt is incited by events which occurred under David and Joab. At this point Hadad is but a young boy (נַעַר קָטֹן) and the return to his homeland is occasioned by their death (v 21).

Rezon, the second antagonist, is said to have been "an adversary to Israel *all* the days of Solomon" (v 25). As for Jeroboam, the justification for his rebellion is that Solomon built the Millo (v 11:27). This transpired earlier during Solomon's reign, in tandem with

point comes as no surprise to the reader, who, like Solomon, has been apprised repeatedly in no uncertain terms that only through strict obedience to the Lord's commandments will the divine promise be fulfilled: "If you will walk before Me as your father David walked, in integrity of heart and uprightness... then I will establish the throne of your kingdom over Israel forever" (1 Kgs 9:4–5).[10]

This is far removed from the all-important Davidic covenant given in 2 Sam 7.[11] There the Lord appears to David, and solemnly promises without stipulation: "Your house and your kingdom shall endure before Me forever; your throne shall be established forever" (2 Sam 7:16). Solomon, too, is already assured eternal dynasty as David's heir: "He shall build a house for My name, and I will establish the throne of his kingdom forever" (v 13). Yet from the very moment that the mantle of kingship is passed from father to son, David charges Solomon that his dominion is conditioned on compliance with "what is written in the Law of Moses... so that YHWH may carry out His promise which He spoke concerning me." (1 Kgs 2:3–4). The unconditional covenant of grant, with perpetual efficacy, has been reduced to a generation-by-generation litmus test of obsequiousness.[12] The latest, most detailed reminder of this proviso in 1 Kgs 9:4–9, given by God to Solomon soon after he has completed building the Temple, can only serve as foreshadowing the inevitable coming fall. It is also telling that whereas the unconditional promise to David is given relatively early in his reign, Solomon is reminded of his obligation to YHWH's statutes late in his life, and held accountable for his actions unto death. The clustering of the conditional dynastic promises solely within the reign of Solomon, coupled with the closing detrimental evaluation of his reign, serves only the political schism: despite all that the king had already accomplished, Solomon was set up to fail.

---

the construction of the Temple and his own residence, cf. 1 Kgs 9:15, 24. At this point in his reign, even according to the Deuteronomistic redaction, Solomon was still obedient to YHWH's will (note the equivalent timeframe provided in vv 9:1, 10, juxtaposed with the conditional material in vv 3–9).

[10] Cf. 1 Kgs 2:2–4; 8:25.

[11] Also preserved in Ps 89:19–37.

[12] Such an irrevocable charter in the ancient Near East is known as a land grant, see Moshe Weinfeld, "The Covenant of Grant in the Old Testament and in the Ancient Near East," *JAOS* 90 (1970) 184–203; idem, *Deuteronomy and the Deuteronomic School* (Oxford, 1972) 74–81; Frank M. Cross, *Canaanite Myth and Hebrew Epic* (Cambridge, Mass.: Harvard University Press, 1973) 237–65; Jon D. Levenson, "On the Promise to the Rechabites," *CBQ* 38 (1976) 508–14.

The antithetical conditional and unconditional nature of these dynastic promises has been the focus of redaction-critical studies within the Deuteronomistic History. There have been two primary positions to account for this duality. The first view is based on a temporal differentiation. The unqualified form only makes sense in the context of a thriving Davidic dynasty and must be pre-exilic, whereas the conditional form is aware of the political situation in the aftermath of exile.[13] The unconditional promises relate to the so-called "נִיר material," which pledge that the Davidic line will retain the throne of Judah regardless of the behavior of its rulers.[14] After the fall of Jerusalem and the end of Judean kingship in 587 B.C.E., these assurances were necessarily qualified by redactional insertions into the Deuteronomistic History to bring the נִיר material in line with historical reality.[15]

The other exegetical stance has been to distinguish between the two types based on their conception of kingship: the unconditional promises relate to dynasty in the abstract and affirm that the Davidic charter is indeed irrevocable, while the conditional formulae qualify only the extent of the kingdom. With this understanding, both aspects lack awareness of the Babylonian conquest and should be properly assigned to the pre-exilic period.[16] The purpose of the stipulations reiterated to Solomon throughout his reign is to legitimize the division of the Israelite kingdom: while David

---

[13] Iain W. Provan, *Hezekiah and the Books of Kings: A Contribution to the Debate about the Composition of the Deuteronomistic History* (BZAW 172; Berlin: Walter de Gruyter, 1988) 99–113. His conclusions are built on the research of Cross, *Canaanite Myth and Hebrew Epic*, 276–89, whose literary strata are popularly known as Dtr¹ (Josianic) and Dtr² (exilic). For Cross, the older, unconditional theme is highlighted by David's faithfulness and desire to establish the cult, symbols of fidelity which are contrasted by Jeroboam's apostasy in establishing the rival shrines of Dan and Bethel. These regimes are counterposed at the outset in regard to their devotion to the Yahwistic cult. Jeroboam is told by prophets that the descendants of David would be chastised only for a season, and that Josiah would be the one to defile the altar of Bethel by burning upon it the bones of its serving high priests (1 Kgs 11:39; 13:1–3, cf. vv 33–34). These dual aspects of the unconditional theme coalesce in the reign of Josiah, the quintessential Davidide who escapes all criticism (2 Kgs 22:2; 23:25) and through his reform destroys the abominable cultic site at Bethel (v 23:15). The conditional material may be seen most readily in 2 Kgs 21:2–15; 22:15–20, composed with the intent to fashion "a document relevant to exiles for whom the bright expectations of the Josianic era were hopelessly past" (*Canaanite Myth and Hebrew Epic*, 285).

[14] 1 Kgs 15:4–5; 2 Kgs 8:19.

[15] 1 Kgs 2:4; 6:12; 8:25; 9:4–5; 11:38.

[16] Baruch Halpern, *The First Historians: The Hebrew Bible and History* (San Francisco: Harper & Row, 1988) 157–75, following Richard Elliott Friedman, *The Exile and Biblical Narrative: The Formation of the Deuteronomistic and Priestly Works* (HSM 22; Chico, Calif.: Scholars Press, 1981) 12–13; Richard D. Nelson, *The Double Redaction of the Deuteronomistic History* (JSOTSup 18; Sheffield: JSOT Press, 1981) 99–105. See also Steven L. McKenzie, *The*

is assured of an "enduring house" despite the behavior of his progeny, that lineage is not guaranteed sovereignty over all Israel.[17] The apostasy of Solomon is that he worshipped such foreign gods as Ashtoreth, Milcom, and Chemosh, and constructed high places to some of these בָּהָר אֲשֶׁר עַל־ פְּנֵי יְרוּשָׁלָם "on the mount which faces Jerusalem" (1 Kgs 11:7). It was not until the reform of Josiah that these abominations were finally removed "which [were] before Jerusalem (אֲשֶׁר עַל־פְּנֵי יְרוּשָׁלָם)... which Solomon the king of Israel built" (2 Kgs 23:13). Josiah's reign, then, is responsible for the incorporation of the conditional dynastic material into older written sources extolling the inviolability of the Davidic covenant. This was part of a radical state policy to legitimize the complete extirpation of foreign cults which purportedly had been poisoning the Judean kingdom since the time of Solomon.[18]

Both of these views still hold considerable academic sway, but for the discussion at hand it is not necessary to resolve this impasse. Rather than becoming embroiled in the differences between these positions, it is sufficient to note what they have in common: the conditional material postdates the reign of Hezekiah. The direct correlation between the longevity of the Davidic dynasty and the adherence of its kings to YHWH's ordinances, whether part of a Josianic or (post-)exilic redaction, is not thought to have been present while Hezekiah was on the throne. The implications for this interpretation are profound. On the one hand, the present text of Kings does not accurately convey how Solomon would have been perceived in the eighth century B.C.E., a scant two hundred years after his dominion over a united Israel. This, in turn, has ramifications for reconstructing the attitude surrounding the rule of Hezekiah himself.

Trouble With Kings: The Composition of the Book of Kings in the Deuteronomistic History (VTSup 42; Leiden: E. J. Brill, 1991) 137–38, 151–52.

[17] Most clearly articulated in 1 Kgs 11:31–39, in which the kingdom is torn from Solomon and given to Jeroboam. Even as YHWH pledges that "my servant David will have a fiefdom always before me in Jerusalem" (v 36), and that Jeroboam has the potential for "an enduring house" (v 38), it is the Lord's prerogative to determine the extent of dominion for his anointed ruler.

[18] The link between these Solomonic reports and the Josianic court is advocated by Norbert Lohfink, "Die Bundesurkunde des Königs Josias," *Bib* 44 (1963) 261–88; Weinfeld, *Deuteronomy and the Deuteronomic School*, 168–69; Cross, *Canaanite Myth and Hebrew Epic*, 274–89; Halpern, *First Historians*, 154–55.

9.1.2. *The Depiction of Solomon*

If one can momentarily disregard the stipulations given to Solomon pertaining to kingship, closely tied as they are to the account of his apostasy in Kings, then there should still be remnants of a positive appraisal of his character. This turns out to be the case: there are perceptible indications of a pro-Solomonic source underlying his negative evaluation.[19] On his death-bed, David makes his son responsible for his unfinished business with Joab and Shimei, and Solomon dutifully takes up his father's cause and executes the blood-purge against them.[20] It is in the process of doing this that Solomon asserts that it is YHWH "who has established me and set me on the throne of David my father, and who has made me a house as He promised," in direct fulfillment of the Davidic covenant in 2 Sam 7:12–13.[21] At the conclusion of the account, Solomon declares that "the throne of David shall be established before YHWH forever," to which the narrator adds "Thus the kingdom was established in the hands of Solomon."[22] At Gibeon, it is said that "Solomon loved YHWH, walking in the statutes of his father David."[23] The appended peccadillo of his sacrifices at the high places garners no mention from the Lord who appears to him thereafter in a dream, granting him "a wise and discerning heart" so that "the wisdom of God was in him to administer justice."[24] Solomon tells Hiram that "YHWH my God has given me rest on every side; there is neither adversary nor misfortune."[25] He was "greater than all the kings of the earth in riches and in wisdom," because according to the queen of Sheba, the Lord "delighted in you to set you on the throne of Israel."[26] The process of building the Temple and the king's house takes place over twenty years, according to Kings, and throughout all this time the son of David is not said to have faltered before the Lord in any way.[27] He is promised length of reign if he will only keep God's statutes and commandments, and his

---

19 Halpern, "Chronicles' Thematic Structure," 47–48.

20 1 Kgs 2:5–9, 28–34, 36–46.

21 1 Kgs 2:24. Although it is typical to provide chapter and verse in the main body of a work after a direct citation, I have opted to forego this guideline for readability in paragraphs which frequently excerpt the biblical text.

22 1 Kgs 2:45–46.

23 1 Kgs 3:3.

24 1 Kgs 3:3–28, esp. vv. 3, 11–13, 28.

25 1 Kgs 5:18[4], cf. 5:4[4:24].

26 1 Kgs 10:23, 9.

27 1 Kgs 9:10.

forty years as king only testifies to his success in this regard.[28] After the completion of these building projects, the Lord appears to Solomon and says that he has heard the king's prayer, and as a result "I have consecrated this house which you have built by putting My name there forever, and My eyes and My heart will be there perpetually."[29] Thus the book of Kings preserves an earlier tradition which was favorable to Solomon and placed full assurance in his receipt of the Davidic promise.

This perspective is in line with the oldest dynastic oracles, in which the endurance of the kingdom was not dependent on compliance to the Lord's statutes by successive generations, but rather on the obedience of a single individual, the sole anointed ruler to whom the promise was made. The first appearance of this divine pledge is made known in retrospect when the judge Samuel confronts Saul for his rash action at Gilgal: "You have acted foolishly. You have not kept the commandment of YHWH your God, which He commanded you, for now YHWH would have established your kingdom over Israel forever. But now your kingdom shall not endure."[30] The prophet Ahijah articulates the same contract with Jeroboam in 1 Kgs 11:38.

God's covenant with David in 2 Sam 7 strikes the reader as more or less spontaneous, placed literarily a little over a chapter after the son of Jesse has been crowned king over Israel. The divine pledge is nowhere said to have been occasioned by David's faithfulness, but this is, in fact, the case. The abiding presence of the Lord with David attests to his character in the texts which precede the covenant, and his adherence to God's commandments is repeatedly affirmed thereafter in Kings.[31] In other words, the Davidic covenant was implicitly provisional as well, but those requirements had already been met: there would have been been no divine promise if the son of Jesse had not already shown himself righteous in the Lord's eyes. In the Saul narrative as well, the reader only learns of the contingent nature of kingship after his actions have already determined

---

[28] 1 Kgs 3:14.

[29] 1 Kgs 9:3.

[30] 1 Sam 13:13–14.

[31] For the preceding material, cf. 1 Sam 16:13; 18:12, 14, 28; 26:8; 2 Sam 4:9. One should also note that the deity responds to David's oracular inquiries in 1 Sam 23:2, 4, 12; 30:8; 2 Sam 2:1, as well as sends him a prophet in 1 Sam 22:5 to avert disaster. For the confirmation of David's faithfulness in the book of Kings, cf. 1 Kgs 3:14; 9:4; 11:4, 6, 33, 38; 14:8; 15:3, 11; 2 Kgs 14:3; 16:2; 18:3.

the outcome.[32] Thus the oldest form of the dynastic promise was inherently conditional, but its stipulations did not extend past the generation of the recipient. Saul was assured an eternal dynasty if he had only obeyed God's commandments, but his disobedience tore the kingdom from him; David was obedient to God's commandments and therefore his kingdom was eternally assured. This was the understanding of the dynastic covenant in the time of Hezekiah.

Chronicles preserves this older conception of an eternal dynasty conditioned upon the obedience of a single ruler, but a key difference lies in its referent: it is Solomon rather than David upon whom the promise hinges: "Your son Solomon is the one who shall build My house and My courts, for I have chosen him to be a son to Me, and I will be a father to him. I will establish his kingdom forever if he resolutely performs My commandments and My ordinances, as is done now" (1 Chr 28:6–7).[33] As in Kings, the book of Chronicles concentrates all of the qualified statements of dynastic continuance within the reign of Solomon. Yet whereas the former work intends this conditional material to build toward the schism of the kingdom due to Solomon's apostasy, the latter composition has the son of David succeed in all his undertakings.[34] The Chronicler depicts

---

[32] The fact that Solomon and Jeroboam are expressly informed of their requirements beforehand is merely a literary device to presage the fact that they will not, in fact, succeed in meeting them.

[33] As the dual nature of the dynastic promises obtains even in the more homogeneous books of Chronicles, the question becomes how they were understood by the author. For Sara Japhet, *The Ideology of the Book of Chronicles and its Place in Biblical Thought* (BEATAJ 9; 2nd ed.; Frankfurt am Main: Peter Lang, 1997) 445–91, the Davidic promise was essentially perceived as conditional. This may be seen in the omission of 2 Sam 7:14b in the Chronicler's *Vorlage*, which she views as assuring the dynasty despite the king's behavior. The subsequent inclusion of conditional material from Kings (1 Kgs 2:4; 8:25; 9:5; cf. 1 Chr 22:11–13; 28:7–9; 2 Chr 6:16; 7:17–20) verifies that the historian aligned with this conception of the promise. Her position does not countenance that the conditions of kingship are relegated solely to Solomon, and she must summarily dismiss subsequent material which upholds the eternality of the covenant (2 Chr 13:5; 21:7; 23:3).

A different perspective is offered by H. G. M. Williamson, "Eschatology in Chronicles," *TynBul* 28 (1977) 115–54; idem, "The Dynastic Oracle in the Books of Chronicles," in A. Rofé and Y. Zakovitch (eds.), *Isac Leo Seeligmann Volume. Essays on the Bible and the Ancient World* (3 vols.; Jerusalem: E. Rubenstein, 1983) 3.305–18. As the reigns of David and Solomon are treated as a unity by the Chronicler, most notably for the purpose of establishing the Temple and its service, the dynastic promise must be fulfilled by both of them. Whereas David is the recipient of the oracle from Nathan, its concerns and conditions devolve upon Solomon. That these stipulations were successfully fulfilled in the lifetime of Solomon and do not attach to subsequent generations may be seen in 2 Chr 1:9; 6:17, 42. This is the position followed in this study.

[34] The negative evaluation of Solomon's reign in Kings, in fact, implicitly testifies to the tradition preserved in Chronicles: if the Deuteronomist needed to substantiate the

Solomon as exemplifying the closest relationship attainable between king and deity, just as seen in the underlying source material in Kings.

It is well established that the reigns of David and Solomon are presented as a unified event in Chronicles, largely due to the significance for the author of the Temple and the establishment of the cult.[35] To this may be added the importance of the dynastic oracles. The Chronicler understood the eternality of the Davidic covenant, but at the same time was cognizant of the conditional material in his *Vorlage* concerning generational obedience beginning with Solomon. His solution was to reinterpret the latter texts in terms of the former, with the son of David passing all of the requisite tests demanded of him in order to eternally establish the kingdom. This ingenious solution provided an additional impetus for combining the regnal narrative of both kings into one. The promises relating to the establishment of a "secure house"—both genealogically and architecturally—were given to David, but Solomon was the one through whom they were to be fulfilled: "He shall build for Me a house, and I will establish his throne forever" (1 Chr 17:12).[36] By this means of inner-biblical interpretation, shifting the ultimate recipient of the covenant from David to his son, the Chronicler was able to remain true to both the earlier, positive traditions of Solomon within the Deuteronomistic History, as well as to the older attested form of the dynastic covenant.[37]

---

schism by attributing sin to a Judean king, why not select Rehoboam, the king at the time? Because Solomon's obedience would have assured the covenant forever, and with both David and Solomon holding fast to God's commandments it would have been theologically difficult to justify tearing the kingdom away from Rehoboam. Instead, Solomon must be the king to fall away, thus indirectly verifying the tradition of an unqualified Davidic dynasty.

There is also the fact that Solomon is not made directly responsible for his actions, but rather "his wives turned his heart away" (1 Kgs 11:3–4). In this, there is some respect for the Solomonic tradition, a desire to reinterpret while yet remaining true. The fact that the apostasy is said to have occurred when he was old also points in this direction: there is no attempt to detract from what Solomon accomplished earlier in his reign. As articulated by Halpern, *First Historians*, 153, "Even in reversing the older view of Solomon as the archetype of a successful monarch, the historian in 1 Kings 11 does not violate his sources. Instead, he reinterprets them. The sources are a mold into which the historian injects his concerns."

[35] See references at n. 3.

[36] The interpretation of these dynastic oracles has direct implications for reconstructing the Chronicler's ideology toward kingship in his own day. For a survey of these views, see Brian E. Kelly, *Retribution and Eschatology in Chronicles* (JSOTSup 211; Sheffield: Sheffield Academic Press, 1996) 135–85.

[37] The possibility has been entertained that Chronicles may in fact preserve the earlier tradition, see Henri van den Bussche, "Le texte de la prophétie de Nathan sur la dynastie davidique (II Sam., VII, I Chron., XVII)," *ETL* 24 (1948) 354–94; Halpern, "Chronicles'

9.2. The Pro-Solomonic Source of Chronicles

It would appear that the Chronicler had access to both the book of Kings as well as more extensive versions of some of its underlying sources. The dependence of the book of Chronicles on Kings is beyond question, but there are additional indications that the historian has made a concerted effort to adhere to this latter, earlier source material.[38] Several marks of divine favor which are considered to be characteristic of the Chronicler are in fact evident in the opening books of the Deuteronomistic History. Victory at war is the most evident aspect, central to the conquest narrative in the book of Joshua, and recurrent in the cycle of retribution-reconciliation throughout Judges such as Ehud, Deborah, Gideon and Samson.[39] This military success carries over into the Saul-David narrative, in which the son of Jesse prevails over his enemies due to the hand of YHWH.[40] In the book of Kings, this manifestation of human faithfulness essentially disappears.[41] It continues unabated, however, in the book of Chronicles, where one finds the kings of Judah—Abijah, Asa, Jehoshaphat, Amaziah, Uzziah, Jotham, and Hezekiah—regularly seeking the Lord and being delivered from their foes.[42]

Sennacherib's invasion within the respective histories is a notable case study. The deliverance of Jerusalem cannot be said to be part of this same overarching theme in the book of Kings, as the motivation for the Lord's intervention rests not upon the righteousness of the king, but is rather a requisite response to the direct reproach of YHWH.[43] The correlation

---

Thematic Structure," 43 n. 15. This is problematic, however, in light of the unconditional pledge of dynasty to Solomon in 1 Chr 17:11–14, followed thereafter by the conditional material in, e.g., vv 28:6–7. As there is no case to be made here for redactional layers within the dynastic promises of Chronicles, this dichotomy is best explained as stemming from the effort of the historian to reconcile the traditions within his sources.

[38] The discussion which follows here elaborates on the research of Halpern, "Chronicles' Thematic Structure," 36–43.

[39] Josh 6; 8:1–29; 10–12; Judg 3:26–30; 4–5; 7:19–22; 11:29, 32–33; 14:19; 15:14–16; 16:23–30.

[40] 1 Sam 18:5, 27–28; 19:8; 23:1–5, 8–12; 30:7–9, 18–19; 2 Sam 3:18; 4:9; 5:7–10, 17–20, 23–25; 8:1–14 (cf. vv 6, 14); 22:1.

[41] During the reign of Solomon this motif does not directly apply, as his conflicts with neighboring nations are positioned as divine reprisal for his idolatry. The rout of the Arameans in 2 Kgs 7:5–7 is not technically a battle, as there is no opposing Israelite force. The only passage in Kings which retains this motif is 2 Kgs 13:3–5, which is highly reminiscent of the cycle of oppression and deliverance found in Judges.

[42] Abijah (2 Chr 13:13–18); Asa (14:5, 8–13[6, 9–14]); Jehoshaphat (20, esp. vv 27, 29); Amaziah (25:7–10, 11–13); Uzziah (26:5–7); Jotham (27:5–6); Hezekiah (32:1–23).

[43] 2 Kgs 19:4, 6, 15–16, 21–24, 32–34. The final verse expressly omits Hezekiah as a reason for the Lord's involvement, tying back instead to the Davidic covenant.

between the faithfulness of Hezekiah and victory over Assyria is readily discernible in the book of Chronicles, however.[44] Although the original Israelite account of the third campaign is not of a piece stylistically with the preceding stories of divine rescue in Joshua-Samuel, the Chronicler has nonetheless recast the tale in such a way as to bring it in line with this theme. This is an attention to detail which speaks to the author's concern for his sources.

Spoliation is another prominent harbinger of divine blessing within the Deuteronomistic History. As a standard practice in ancient Near Eastern warfare, it was expected that the possessions of the subjugated were to be divided among their conquerors: "to the victor go the spoils."[45] Joshua and the united tribes raid the goods of several Canaanite cities during the conquest, a practice which continues in the time of the judges whenever Israel is fortunate enough to rise up against her oppressors.[46] These instances are commonly repeated throughout the story arcs of Saul and David, where they become a touchstone for each leader's military prowess.[47] The accumulation of enemy wealth was thus commonplace,

---

[44] Note the introductory "after these acts of faithfulness" in 2 Chr 32:1. The Lord's deliverance of "Hezekiah and the inhabitants of Jerusalem" stems not from affront at the words of the Rabshakeh but rather from the solicitous prayer of both king and prophet (vv 20–22).

[45] Some of the most ancient poems in the Hebrew Bible preserve this conception, cf. Gen 49:27; Exod 15:9; Judg 5:30. The receipt of spoil is clearly positioned as a mark of divine favor in Exod 3:21–22; 12:35–36, when the Lord promises that the Israelites will be permitted to plunder the Egyptians for their "articles of silver and gold, and clothing." The universality of this wartime practice is what makes the abstention of Abram so profound in Gen 14:22–23. For cases in which the accumulated wealth of the Temple became loot for Israel's enemies, cf. 1 Kgs 14:25–28; 2 Kgs 14:11–14; 24:13; Jer 15:13; 17:3; Dan 1:2; 2 Chr 12:2–12; 36:18.

[46] Josh 8:2, 27; 11:14; 22:8; Judg 5:30; 8:24–26.

[47] 1 Sam 14:30, 32, 36; 15:19–21; 30:16, 19–20, 22, 26; 2 Sam 3:22; 8:12; 12:30. Occasionally items were forbidden to be taken as plunder as a result of their being חֵרֶם, a potentially contagious quality or state which sets things apart from human use, cognate to Arabic حَرُمَ, "to be forbidden, prohibited; declare sacred, taboo" (Lane 2.553–57; Wehr 201–202). The practice is ancient and not confined to Israel. On the 9th-century Mesha Stele, the king boasts as having made ḥerem to Ashtar-Chemosh seven thousand Israelite residents of Nebo, see COS 2.137–38 and bibliography there.

For studies, see C. H. W. Brekelmans, De ḥerem in het Oude Testament (Nijmegen: Centrale Drukkerij, 1959); idem, "Le ḥerem chez les prophètes du royaume du Nord et dans le Deutéronome," in J. Coppens, A. Descamps and É. Massaux (eds.), Sacra Pagina. Miscellanea biblica Congressus Internationalis Catholici de re biblica (2 vols.; BETL 12/13; Gembloux: J. Duculot, 1959) 1.377–83; Sa-Moon Kang, Divine War in the Old Testament and in the Ancient Near East (BZAW 177; Berlin: Walter de Gruyter, 1989) 80–84; Philip D. Stern, The Biblical ḥerem: A Window on Israel's Religious Experience (BJS 211; Atlanta: Scholars Press, 1991); Norbert Lohfink, "חָרַם," TDOT 5.180–99; J. P. U. Lilley, "Understanding the Ḥerem," TynBul

and perceived in Israelite culture as a perfectly acceptable religious act involved in Holy War.

It is somewhat surprising, then, that twenty-five of the twenty-six occurrences of Hebrew שָׁלָל "plunder, spoil" in the Deuteronomistic History are all crammed into the books of Joshua through Samuel. Similarly, four of the five attestations of the root בָּזַז "to plunder" appear in these same books. In the book of Kings, spoliation is suddenly no longer associated with Israelite military practice.[48] The procedure is still carried out, however, in the book of Chronicles. Asa despoils all of the cities around Gerar, carrying away "very much plunder."[49] Jehoshaphat needs three full days to remove the bountiful spoils of Ammon, Moab, and Edom.[50] Amaziah acquires much plunder from the Edomites, and the Israelites raid the property of their Judahite brothers during the Syro-Ephraimitic war.[51] The ubiquitousness of this martial policy in the ancient world leads to distinct expectations as to the literary contexts in which it should occur, and the absence of it throughout the remainder of Kings gives pause. This raises suspicion of the tendentious nature of the Deuteronomist in regard to his sources, while supporting the accuracy of such references in Chronicles.

The other half of this military equation is the receipt of tribute (מִנְחָה). Coercion of payment from those forced into submission is as old as the recorded history of the Near East, and was an integral economic component of warfare.[52] David is said to have received tribute from both the Moabites and the Arameans, because "YHWH gave victory (וַיֹּשַׁע) to David wherever he went."[53] At the height of his kingdom, Solomon received payment from "all the kingdoms from the Euphrates to the land of the Philistines, even

---

44/1 (1993) 169–77; Richard D. Nelson, "*ḥerem* and the Deuteronomic Social Conscience," in M. Vervenne and J. Lust (eds.), *Deuteronomy and Deuteronomic Literature. Festschrift C.H.W. Brekelmans* (BETL 133; Leuven: Leuven University Press, 1997) 39–54; Meir Malul, "Taboo," *DDD* 824–27; Yair Hoffmann, "The Deuteronomistic Concept of the Herem," *ZAW* 111/2 (1999) 196–210; Moshe Greenberg, "Herem," *EncJud* 9.10–13.

[48] The sole attestation of שָׁלָל in the book of Kings is in 2 Kgs 3:23, where it is used in reference to Moab, not Israel. The lone occurrence of בָּזַז in Kings may be found in the prophetic story of the rout of the Arameans, in 2 Kgs 7:16.

[49] 2 Chr 14:13–14[14–15]. Many of the animals taken as plunder are subsequently sacrificed in 15:11.

[50] 2 Chr 20:25.

[51] 2 Chr 25:9–10, 13; 28:8, 15.

[52] See the various examples in William James Hamblin, *Warfare in the Ancient Near East to 1600 BC: Holy Warriors at the Dawn of History* (London: Routledge, 2006) 47, 61–62, 70, 78, 91, 114, 119, 201, 210–12, 232–33, 242–44, 258, 262, 319, 333, 341, 345, 349, 375–76, 398–401, 414, 429, 469, 485.

[53] 2 Sam 8:2, 6.

to the border of Egypt."[54] Such gifts could also be rendered voluntarily as a sign of respect. Toi of Hamath sends "articles of silver, gold, and bronze" to David after he has defeated the army of a mutual foe, and numerous riches are bestowed upon Solomon by those who sought his presence.[55] Yet within the Deuteronomistic History, the only mention of an Israelite king after Solomon who receives any form of tribute is in the (post-)exilic account of Merodach-baladan's visit to Hezekiah.[56] The book of Chronicles, on the other hand, contains the aforementioned references within the reigns of David and Solomon, as well as additional ones. Jehoshaphat is rendered tribute from Judah, Philistia, and the Arabs, the Ammonites do the same for Uzziah, and "Many brought tribute to YHWH, to Jerusalem, and gifts to Hezekiah, king of Judah, and he was exalted in the sight of all the nations thereafter."[57] The more consistent application of this ancient practice from the tribal through the monarchic period is precisely what one would expect from an overarching history of the nation.

Royal building programs are another hallmark of the Chronicler's style. The inclusion of these economic projects was long seen as a wholesale fabrication, an attempt to create artificial prosperity for those kings favored by the author. More recent research coupled with archaeological data has, however, upheld that these terse entries do indeed have an air of authenticity and reflect a historical reality.[58] But this detailing of fortifications and public works was already present in the Chronicler's *Vorlage*. David is said to have placed troops or garrisons (נְצִבִים) in both Aram and Edom.[59] Both of these references are preserved in Chronicles, as well as the garrisons stationed by Jehoshaphat throughout the cities of Judah and Ephraim.[60] The 40,000 horse stalls credited to Solomon in Chronicles come directly from First Kings, as does the procuring of the horses themselves from Egypt and Kue.[61] The meticulous preparations for the building of the Temple—from the 150,000 men who quarried the stone in the

---

[54] 1 Kgs 5:1[4:21].

[55] 2 Sam 8:10; 1 Kgs 10:24–25.

[56] 2 Kgs 20:12. All other references in the book of Kings are either to foreign kings who render tribute to prophets (Hazael to Elisha, 2 Kgs 8:8–9), or to Israelite kings who served in their capacity as vassals to Assyria (Hoshea to Shalmaneser V, 2 Kgs 17:3–4).

[57] Cf. 2 Chr 17:5, 11 (Jehoshaphat); 26:8 (Uzziah); 32:23 (Hezekiah).

[58] Anson F. Rainey, "The Chronicler and his Sources—Historical and Geographical," in M. P. Graham, K. G. Hoglund and S. L. McKenzie (eds.), *The Chronicler as Historian* (JSOTSup 238; Sheffield: Sheffield Academic Press, 1997) 48–55.

[59] 2 Sam 8:6, 14.

[60] 1 Chr 18:6, 13; 2 Chr 17:2.

[61] 2 Chr 9:25 / 1 Kgs 5:6[4:26]; 2 Chr 1:16 / 1 Kgs 10:28.

mountains and transported them as far as Jerusalem, to the kors of wheat and oil negotiated as payment to Hiram king of Tyre for the cut timber of Lebanon, floated down on rafts by sea—are quite in line with the Chronicler's interest in royal projects elsewhere, but in fact were previously recorded in Kings.[62] Solomon is credited with having constructed storage cities, which are likewise recorded in Chronicles as well as attributed to subsequent kings, including Hezekiah as discussed earlier.[63] Despite these attestations in Samuel and Kings, the interest there in building programs and fortifications is evanescent after the account of Solomon.[64] In light of this, the continued and extensive coverage of this topic in Chronicles throughout the reigns of the kings of Judah—including Rehoboam, Asa, Jehoshaphat, Uzziah, Jotham, Hezekiah, Manasseh, and Josiah—is more in accord with the preceding narrative and seems in no way out of place.[65] As other, independent studies affirm that the building project notices in the book of Chronicles derive from older texts, it is most logical to assign them to the same conglomerate source material which underlies the former portion of the Deuteronomistic History.

Another, more debatable, factor deserving consideration is territorial expansion. This demonstrable mark of divine favor is the foundation for the entire book of Joshua, as the Lord aids the tribes of Israel in acquiring the Promised Land. During the period of the monarchy, it becomes a reliable bellwether for the piety of a given king. In the book of Samuel, David is instructed to establish his rule in Hebron, and soon thereafter captures the stronghold of Zion and makes it his capital city.[66] Under Solomon, the dominion of the Davidides reaches its greatest extent, "from the Euphrates [to] the land of the Philistines and to the border of Egypt ... everything west of the Euphrates."[67] Thereafter, interest in expansion wanes and the

---

[62] Compare 1 Kgs 5:29[15] / 2 Chr 2:1[2], 16–17[17–18]; 1 Kgs 5:22–23[8–9] and 2 Chr 2:14–15[15–16]; 1 Kgs 5:25[11] and 2 Chr 2:9[10].

[63] 1 Kgs 9:19; 2 Chr 8:4, 6; 16:4; 17:12; 32:28. The dependency of Chronicles on the book of Kings in regard to Solomon's accomplishments is indisputable.

[64] The notice of the ships constructed by Jehoshaphat in 1 Kgs 22:49[48] (cf. 2 Chr 20:36) could be argued as belonging to this same archival source as could the accomplishments of Azariah in 2 Kgs 14:22, 25. If so, this merely begs the question as to the paucity of similar material in the accounts of other kings during the divided monarchy.

[65] These reports may be found in 2 Chr 11:5–12 (Rehoboam); 14:5–7[6–8] (Asa); 17:2, 12–13; 21:2–3 (Jehoshaphat); 26:9–10 (Uzziah); 27:3–4 (Jotham); 32:2–6, 27–30 (Hezekiah); 33:14–16 (Manasseh); 34:11–13 (Josiah).

[66] 2 Sam 2:1–3; 5:6–9.

[67] 1 Kgs 5:1, 4[4:21, 24].

only Judean notices pertain to territorial decline or threats to the realm.[68] While the book of Chronicles dutifully maintains this record of regional loss preserved in its *Vorlage*, as with the ebb and flow of royal faithfulness, the theme of expansion necessarily continues as well.[69] Abijah captures several cities of Jeroboam, Asa is said to have taken cities in the hill country of Ephraim, and finally Hezekiah is able to lay claim to territory in the north by virtue of his heralds sent "through the country of Ephraim and Manasseh, even as far as Zebulun."[70]

The foregoing manifestations of divine favor are all encapsulated within the rest motif, signified by the nouns שָׁלוֹם and בֶּטַח, *qal* שָׁקַט, and *hifil* הֵנִיחַ.[71] It is the centerpiece of the culminating statement for the conquest narrative: "So Joshua took the whole land, according to all that YHWH had spoken to Moses...thus the land had rest (שָׁקְטָה) from war."[72] Its all-encompassing nature is conveyed via מִסָּבִיב, "roundabout, on every side."[73] During the period of the judges, it is evidence of the Lord's protection in times of Israel's faithfulness, typically in the form "And the land had rest forty years."[74] Rest is a key point leveraged by Samuel as he briefly recounts the mighty acts of the Lord during his anti-monarchic speech: "Then YHWH ... delivered you from the hands of your enemies all around (מִסָּבִיב), so that you lived in safety" (בֶּטַח).[75] Prior to the bestowing of the Davidic covenant, we are told that "YHWH had given him rest roundabout

---

[68] The loss and reacquisition of Ramah recorded in 1 Kgs 15:17–22 represent a territorial stalemate. The border fortresses at Geba and Mizpah mentioned in v 22 are both in Benjaminite territory, and hence do not signify expansion. For Judean military defeats, see 2 Kgs 3:21–27; 12:18–19[17–18]; 14:13–14; 16:5–9. Israel suffers the same in 2 Kgs 10:32–33; 13:2–3.

[69] The Judean reports mentioned previously in Kings are preserved in 2 Chr 12:2, 9; 16:1–6; 24:23–24; 25:23–24; 28:5–8, with only the exceptional story of the Moabite victory over Israel (2 Kgs 3:21–27) omitted.

[70] 2 Chr 13:19; 15:8; 30:10. Japhet, *Ideology of the Book of Chronicles*, 299–304, claims that Chronicles exhibits a process of steady territorial expansion by the southern kingdom. Josiah's Passover represents the pinnacle of geographical annexation in the divided monarchy, covering "all the lands belonging to the sons of Israel" (2 Chr 34:6–7, 33). As rightly countered by Williamson, *Israel in the Books of Chronicles*, 99–101, "it seems improbable that Josiah's reform is meant to be a development from this point of view over that of Hezekiah, for in 2 Chr. 30:5 'they established a decree to make proclamation throughout all Israel, from Beersheba even to Dan'. Evidently, according to the Chronicler, Hezekiah's interests were no less limited than Josiah's."

[71] The latter is also attested as הִנִּיַח under the influence of Aramaic, cf. JM §80p; GKC §72ee.

[72] Josh 11:23, reflected in another document at v 14:15.

[73] Cf. Josh 21:44; 23:1, which permits comparison with the verb נָצַל, "to deliver save," as in Judg 8:34.

[74] Cf. Judg 3:11, 30 (eighty years); 5:31; 8:28.

[75] 1 Sam 12:11.

from all his enemies."[76] The dominion of Solomon, of course, typifies the most serene expression of this idyll: "He had peace (שָׁלוֹם) on all sides. So Judah and Israel lived in safety (לָבֶטַח), from Dan even to Beer-sheba, all of them under their vines and fig trees, all the days of Solomon."[77]

Once again, this preeminent literary motif abruptly tails off in the Deuteronomistic History after the account of Solomon's reign.[78] In the book of Chronicles, the conception is more tightly integrated into the narrative, and receives the same weight accorded to it in the pre-monarchic texts. Because David had shed "much blood upon the earth," he is forbidden to build the Temple for the Lord. His son is granted this honor instead, who is foretold to be "a man of rest." He is given the portentous name Solomon (שְׁלֹמֹה) at this time, for "peace and quiet (שָׁלוֹם וָשֶׁקֶט) I shall bestow on Israel in his days."[79] Throughout ancient Mesopotamia, care of the gods and their temples was a means to maintain cosmic order, and this philosophy inheres in the prerequisite of peace prior to construction. This correlation between Israel's rest and that of the deity is upheld in David's proclamation that "Yнwн, the God of Israel, has given rest to His people, and He dwells in Jerusalem forever."[80] The Temple is subsequently referred to as place of rest by both David (בֵּית מְנוּחָה) and Solomon (לְנוּחֶךָ).[81] Perfect reciprocity is thus attained: David desires to build God a house, and in return the anointed king is given a "house" (progeny); just as the Lord grants Israel rest, so Solomon provides the deity with a resting place. The rest motif achieves cosmic order on multiple levels.

In Chronicles, moreover, the theme does not end with the united monarchy but undergoes further development.[82] During the first thirty-five years of the reign of Asa there was no one at war with him, כִּי־הֵנִיחַ יְהוָה לוֹ "because Yнwн had given him rest."[83] Similarly, "the kingdom of Jehoshaphat was at peace (וַתִּשְׁקֹט), for his God gave him rest on all sides" (וַיָּנַח לוֹ אֱלֹהָיו מִסָּבִיב).[84] After Athaliah has been put to death and

---

[76] 2 Sam 7:1, although possibly a late insertion due to the competing tradition that David could not build the temple for being involved in wars, see P. Kyle McCarter Jr., *II Samuel* (AYB 9; Garden City, N.Y.: Doubleday, 1984) 191.

[77] 1 Kgs 5:4–5[4:24–25], and reaffirmed in 1 Kgs 5:18[4].

[78] A notable exception is 2 Kgs 11:20, as read by Halpern, "Chronicles' Thematic Structure," 41.

[79] 1 Chr 22:8–9.

[80] 1 Chr 23:25.

[81] 1 Chr 28:2 and 2 Chr 6:41, respectively.

[82] Halpern, "Chronicles' Thematic Structure," 40–42.

[83] 2 Chr 14:5[6]. Cf. 2 Chr 14:1, 5–7[2, 6–8]; 15:15, 19.

[84] 2 Chr 20:30.

Jehoiada makes a covenant between himself and the people of the land, "the city was at rest" (שָׁקָטָה).[85] The rest motif reaches its apogee in the victory over Sennacherib's army. Here it is said that the Lord saved Hezekiah and the inhabitants of Jerusalem from the king of Assyria, and "He gave them rest on every side."[86] The book of Chronicles exhibits a more cohesive history in regard to peace and rest, particularly in light of the significance of this theme, than the jarring cessation one finds in the Former Prophets.

There are many other examples of concepts or vocabulary within the Deuteronomistic History which, although their distribution falters or effectively ends sometime after the Solomonic narrative, they nonetheless persist within the book of Chronicles. The root שָׂמַח "to rejoice" occurs 17 times in Joshua-Kings, with only two attestations falling in the time of the divided monarchy.[87] In Chronicles, there are not only additional usages in the accounts of David and Solomon, but also in the reigns of Asa, Jehoshaphat, Joash, and Hezekiah.[88] The expression הָיָה עִם־לְבַב "to have in mind" is used in Kings of the relationship with the deity only in regard to David and Solomon, but in Chronicles the application is widened to include Asa and Hezekiah.[89] In Kings, only Solomon is said to have had "riches and honor" (עֹשֶׁר וְכָבוֹד).[90] This mark of divine favor is exhibited not only by Solomon in Chronicles, but also by David, Jehoshaphat and Hezekiah.[91]

One explanation for these recurrent expressions and motifs in Chronicles is to claim that the author has selected them from his *Vorlage* and has

---

[85] 2 Chr 23:21. This verse is drawn from 2 Kgs 11:20, the only example of this usage after the reign of Solomon in Kings.

[86] 2 Chr 32:22, reading MT וַיְנַהֲלֵם מִסָּבִיב "he guided them on every side" as וַיָּנַח לָהֶם מִסָּבִיב, based on LXX κατέπαυσεν αὐτοὺς κυκλόθεν and Vulgate.

[87] Judg 9:13, 19; 19:3; 1 Sam 2:1; 6:13; 11:9, 15; 19:5; 2 Sam 1:20; 1 Kgs 1:40, 45; 4:20; 5:21[7]; 8:66; 2 Kgs 11:14, 20.

[88] 1 Chr 16:10, 31; 29:9 (David); 2 Chr 6:41 (Solomon); 15:15 (Asa); 20:27 (Jehoshaphat); 24:10 (Joash); 29:36; 30:25 (Hezekiah).

[89] 1 Kgs 8:17–18 / 2 Chr 6:7–8 (David and Solomon); 2 Chr 16:9; 29:10 (Asa and Hezekiah).

[90] 1 Kgs 3:13, cf. v 11, 10:23. The abrupt literary break in Kings is apparent not only when looking at particular words and motifs, but also when looking at the book as a whole. The Lord is active in the books of Joshua through Samuel, intent on delivering the nation by periodically choosing select individuals for his purpose. Within the books of Kings the whole complex is suddenly reversed, with the focus now shifted to Israel's response to God's faithfulness. YHWH typically acts or speaks indirectly through his prophets, or not at all.

[91] 1 Chr 29:28 (David); 2 Chr 1:12 (Solomon, cf. v 9:22); 17:5; 18:1 (Jehoshaphat); 32:27 (Hezekiah).

chosen to elaborate on them for his ideological ends. This position falters, however, in light of the fact that these themes do not extend to the end of the work; specifically, almost without exception, they are curtailed or disappear altogether after the reign of Hezekiah.[92] No one after Hezekiah is said to have "riches and honor." He is the final ruler to חָזַק "take hold" of his kingship in some way, a verb applied since the reign of David.[93] Hezekiah is the last king to receive tribute, and his proclamation to "all Israel from Beer-sheba unto Dan" represents the full extent of territorial expansion. He is the final anointed ruler "to have in mind" to do something to retain a rapport with God, and he and his people are the last to rejoice. His reign is the last to see victory at war and the salvation of the Lord. In sum, after Hezekiah, the literary complex of prosperity, victory, and rest as a mark of divine favor is no longer present. Thereafter, the Lord no longer directly intervenes in order to save his people.[94]

It could be claimed that the downturn in Judah's fortunes after the reign of Hezekiah is to blame for the absence of these concepts subsequently. Obviously in Kings, this argument cannot hold because these literary motifs trail off after the reign of Solomon. But even in Chronicles this position is problematic, as both Manasseh and Josiah are viewed positively.[95] Josiah "walked in the ways of his ancestor David; he did not

---

[92] Building projects are a seemingly notable exception, as one sees with the record of Manasseh in 2 Chr 33:14 and the remodeling of the Temple by Josiah in vv 34:8–13 (cf. 2 Kgs 22:3–7). There are two points that should be made here. First of all, as with the regnal data of the kings, archival records would not cease at the time of compilation of a national history. The recording of this information is coterminous with the kingdom itself, in contrast to theological themes or ideas within a select presentation of that history which serve to delimit one author's contribution from another. My concern here is primarily with the latter, not the former.

Secondly, these supposed anomalies are themselves relevant. Josiah is not credited with any fortification projects despite his many accolades and decades-long reign. Similarly in regard to his predecessor, it has been observed by Ehud Ben Zvi, "The Chronicler as Historian: Building Texts," in Graham et al. (eds.), *Chronicler as Historian*, 139, that "Chr does not claim that Manasseh built or rebuilt any town in Judah (see 2 Chron. 33.12–17). In fact, Chr does not report any royal building activity in Judah's countryside after Hezekiah." Even here, the kingdom of Hezekiah shows a demonstrable divergence literarily from what follows.

[93] Only Ahaziah and Ahaz are exempt from this pattern. For the other references, see Halpern, "Chronicles' Thematic Structure," 49.

[94] Halpern, "Chronicles' Thematic Structure," 41, sees וַיּוֹשַׁע יְהוָה אֶת־יְחִזְקִיָּהוּ in 2 Chr 32:22 as forming an inclusio with וַיּוֹשַׁע יְהוָה לְדָוִיד בְּכֹל אֲשֶׁר הָלָךְ in 1 Chr 18:6, 13.

[95] This fact has ramifications for the view of Peter Welten, *Geschichte und Geschichtsdarstellung in den Chronikbüchern* (WMANT 42; Neukirchen-Vluyn: Neukirchener Verlag, 1973), who concludes that the *Festungen* notices in the book are by and large creations of the Chronicler to theologically qualify those kings whom he favors. This stance does not

turn aside to the right or to the left," and Manasseh as well "entreated Yʜwʜ his God and humbled himself greatly before the God of his fathers."[96] The reign of Manasseh in Chronicles does not incur the divine judgment that is imposed in 2 Kgs 21:10–15, and consequently is insufficient to explain why the reign of Hezekiah represents the end of so many aspects that had been crucial to the presentation of Israelite historiography since Joshua, and even before.[97] The basis for this sharp break should be sought, therefore, not in the ideological motivations of the Chronicler, but in the sources utilized in the composition of his history.

9.3. The Hezekian Provenance of the Source Material

This suspicion may be corroborated by yet another line of evidence which not only supports the notion that the Chronicler has faithfully adhered to his sources, but also that Hezekiah's reign originally signaled the end of an older version of Israelite history. The naming of the queen mother in the accession formula is not present in Chronicles subsequent to Hezekiah, and is more likely due to reasons relating to the author's sources than to any theological basis.[98] Some of these patterns are evident in both historiographies. With regard to the burial or death formula in Kings, subsequent

---

provide a satisfactory explanation for the lack of any martial building activities assigned to the favored Josiah, or to earlier pious kings such as Abijah and Joash.

However, the noticeable lack of fortification projects after Manasseh is understandable if most of the building reports in Chronicles are instead derived from historical records, as claimed in this study. Note the conclusions drawn concerning Stratum 10 of Jerusalem, which dates to the last half of the seventh century: "[I]t comes as no surprise that this final phase was *not* marked by the construction of new fortifications. There is neither archaeological evidence nor biblical evidence that Josiah or any of the subsequent kings undertook any major fortification projects in Jerusalem" (Lynn Tatum, "Jerusalem in Conflict: The Evidence for the Seventh-Century B.C.E. Religious Struggle over Jerusalem," in A. G. Vaughn and A. E. Killebrew (eds.), *Jerusalem in Bible and Archaeology: The First Temple Period* [SBLSS 18; Leiden: Brill, 2003] 299).

[96] 2 Chr 34:2; 33:12.

[97] Consider how profound this change is in relation to Josiah, for instance. If these identified literary motifs were truly from the hand of the Chronicler, it is alarming that neither his wealth nor his honor are mentioned at all, he does not call upon God for aid, and neither is he delivered in his time of distress. Yʜwʜ does not give him rest, nor fight for him against his enemies, yet his rule is unreservedly endorsed. As summarized by Halpern, "Chronicles' Thematic Structure," 49–50, "This is peculiar: an author who reports as frequently as does Chronicles that Yhwh entreated will not rebuke, that Yhwh, once sought, will not repudiate (1 Chron 28:9; 2 Chron 15:2; 28:11; 30:6, 8, 9; 14:6, etc.), is not the author to produce the story of Josiah's death."

[98] On this, see Halpern, "Chronicles' Thematic Structure"; Steven L. McKenzie, *The Chronicler's Use of the Deuteronomistic History* (HSM 33; Atlanta: Scholars Press, 1985) 175.

to king Ahaz the notices that the king was "buried with his fathers" (וַיִּקָּבֵר עִם־אֲבֹתָיו) and "in the city of David" (בְּעִיר דָּוִד) are completely lacking.[99] Hezekiah is also included in this scheme in the book of Chronicles, but neither work provides this information subsequently.[100] Such variation is best explained as marking a change in scribal convention rather than reflecting a change in actual burial practice.

References which state that a particular object or practice is in existence עַד הַיּוֹם הַזֶּה have been recognized as editorial comments which indicate the time of the author. This stylistic narrative device is pervasive throughout the Deuteronomistic History, until it abruptly ends in the last verse of 2 Kgs 17. The termination of this technique thus coincides with events contemporaneous with the beginning of Hezekiah's reign. On a related note, the reconstruction of the chronology of the latter kings of Judah offered in this study has concluded that whereas the regnal data of Hezekiah necessitate a brief co-regency with his father Ahaz—evident as well with several of the preceding Judean kings—no co-regencies need be posited subsequent to the fall of the northern kingdom.[101] This fact lends additional weight to the suggestion that the first edition of the book of Kings ended with the reign of Hezekiah.

This has already led some researchers to aver that Hezekiah is the 'second David' that the judgment formulae employed throughout the book of Kings are tailored to foreshadow.[102] The statement of incomparability

---

As noted in my study of the relationship between Ahaz and Hezekiah, only Asa, Jehoram, and Ahaz omit the name of the queen mother among the kings of Judah.

[99] Howard Ray Macy, "The Sources of the Books of Chronicles: A Reassessment" (Ph.D. diss.; Harvard University, 1975) 139–42. Much of his work builds on that of Helga Weippert, "Die 'deuteronomistischen' Beurteilungen der Könige von Israel und Juda und das Problem der Redaktion der Königsbücher," *Bib* 53 (1972) 301–39, who concentrates on the regnal formulae in Kings. The first of her three identified redactions included the Judean kings Jehoshaphat to Ahaz, and the Israelite kings Joram to Hoshea. Hezekiah's reign was part of the second redaction, which constituted the framework for the former.

[100] For the deviating burial formulae, cf. 2 Kgs 21:18 / 2 Chr 33:20 (Manasseh); 2 Kgs 21:23, 26 / 2 Chr 33:24–25 (Amon); 2 Kgs 23:30 / 2 Chr 35:24 (Josiah).

[101] Despite the continuing efforts as seen in Leslie McFall, "Some Missing Coregencies in Thiele's Chronology," *AUSS* 30/1 (1992) 35–58. Synchronisms between the divided kingdoms are not the only means to detect a co-regency: if the total lengths of reign for the latter kings of Judah had exceeded the remaining number of years for the kingdom itself, it would be necessary to postulate co-regencies for some of those rulers. As it turns out, this is not the case.

[102] Provan, *Hezekiah and the Books of Kings*. For others who argue for a pre-exilic Hezekian edition of Kings, see Baruch Halpern and David S. Vanderhooft, "The Editions of Kings in the 7th–6th Centuries B.C.E." *HUCA* 62 (1991) 179–244; Erik Eynikel, *The Reform of King Josiah and the Composition of the Deuteronomistic Historian* (OTS 33; Leiden: Brill, 1996).

rendered of Hezekiah in 2 Kgs 18:5, "After him there was none like him among all the kings of Judah, nor [among those] who were before him," has long been noted as being difficult to reconcile with the similar assessment of Josiah in v 23:5. The most logical conclusion to draw is that the two evaluations did not originally stand together. The sweeping defeat of the Philistines by Hezekiah in 2 Kgs 18:8 recalls the success of David in 2 Sam 5:25. The description of Hezekiah in 2 Kgs 18:7 could be seen as an inclusio to the appraisal of David in 1 Sam 18:14, and is also plausible as a vestigial recollection of Solomon.[103] This impression is strengthened by the fact that within the Deuteronomistic History, these are the only three rulers of whom it is said "YHWH was with him."[104] Subsequent to Hezekiah, this close relationship to the divine is never invoked, thereby closing the circle of rapprochement which extended back to the united monarchy.

It is, moreover, a fundamental theological issue for the Deuteronomist that the high places have not been taken away, and the only reason for the incessant repetition of this nonfulfillment is to augur the rectification of this misdeed.[105] Hezekiah is the first king to remove the high places, and the positioning of this notice within the judgment formula—precisely as seen with his many, failed predecessors—conveys that is he, not Josiah, who was originally envisioned as the archetypal reformer of the cult.[106] By removing the perceived obstacles to true Yahwistic worship, his actions ensured that Jerusalem would remain secure and the Davidic covenant would continue.[107] This echoes the faithfulness of David, used as the basis for comparison in the judgment formulae for all Kings in connection with

---

[103] לְמַעַן תַּשְׂכִּיל אֵת כָּל־אֲשֶׁר תַּעֲשֶׂה וְאֵת כָּל־אֲשֶׁר תִּפְנֶה שָׁם, 1 Kgs 2:3.

[104] 1 Sam 18:14; 1 Kgs 1:37; 2 Kgs 18:7. This should not be seen as contradictory to the observation made earlier in my analysis of the identification of Immanuel that "only Hezekiah and David (2 Sam 5:10) have their reigns directly evaluated in this manner by the Deuteronomistic Historian." In the case of Solomon, the expression is not couched in an unequivocal statement, but rather in a blessing conveyed with the jussive יְהִי.

The implications of the expression "YHWH was with him" for Zionist theology have previously been considered in regard to the identity of Immanuel, and it does not go too far to speculate that both 2 Kgs 18:7 (יְהוָה עִמּוֹ) and 2 Chr 32:7–8 (עִמָּנוּ יְהוָה) engage in wordplay with Hezekiah's given name.

[105] Prior notices only seem to be building toward this moment, cf. 1 Kgs 15:14; 2 Kgs 12:4[3]; 14:4; 15:4, 35; 18:4.

[106] This interpretation, naturally, has important ramifications for the historicity of Hezekiah's reform itself. As with the motivation to situate accomplishments earlier in the reign of a monarch, there would be little basis for portraying Hezekiah as the culmination of the Davidic ideal if he had not, in fact, truly effectuated the key feats credited to him.

[107] Francolino J. Gonçalves, *L'expédition de Sennachérib en Palestine dans la littérature hébraïque ancienne* (Études bibliques, New Series 7; Paris: Librairie Lecoffre, 1986) 430–31, has also identified parallels within his delineation of the B₁ source and the story of David

the cult, and also recalls the attitude toward right worship highlighted in the construction and dedication of the Temple by Solomon. Although the interconnections between David, Solomon, and Hezekiah are more pronounced in Chronicles, they are still palpable in the existing form of Kings.

While these many foregoing literary observations might carry little weight when assessed individually, their collective effect is to compellingly suggest that the book of Chronicles has utilized an originally pro-Solomonic source which extended from David to Hezekiah. The likening of Hezekiah to both David and Solomon in Chronicles is therefore highly implausible as an authorial creation, but should rather be perceived as a manifestation of the original attitude inherent in its underlying source material. In the academically prioritized book of Kings however, Hezekiah could not be compared to Solomon. Just as the schism mandated that the image of Solomon had to be toned down in order to account for what was seen as divine judgment, so the exile necessitated a more subdued picture of the reign of Hezekiah.[108] It is precisely for this reason that 2 Kgs 20 was argued as an exilic, Deuteronomistic addition to serve as the denouement of the Hezekiah narrative. Both rulers are given otherwise deferential presentations up until the end, when their respective reigns are abruptly sullied by exploits in their old age. Both receive allocutions directly from a prophet which postpone their respective judgments, yet in each case an end to their kingdom is irrevocably assured. Even in Kings, Hezekiah is indirectly a second Solomon.

The key Isaianic oracles which foretold of an ideal ruler, hinted at by other contemporary prophets such as Amos and Hosea have previously been argued as having an eighth-century context in the reign of Hezekiah. They already imbue the son of Ahaz with qualities previously exemplified only in the descriptions of Solomon's kingdom.[109] Just as Solomon

---

and Goliath in 1 Sam 17. For a brief rebuttal to the notion of Josiah as a second David, see Provan, *Hezekiah and the Books of Kings*, 114–17.

[108] Rainey, "The Chronicler as Historian," 54, suggests that Manasseh may have been commensurately vilified in Kings for the same reason, with Chronicles preserving the more accurate recollection.

[109] These characteristics have previously been mentioned as having older Mesopotamian origins, see Moshe Weinfeld, "The Roots of the Messianic Idea," in R. M. Whiting (ed.), *Mythology and Mythologies: Methodological Approaches to Intercultural Influences* (Melammu Symposia 2; Helsinki: The Neo-Assyrian Text Corpus Project, 2001) 279–87; idem, "Jerusalem—A Political and Spiritual Capital," in J. G. Westenholz (ed.), *Capital Cities: Urban Planning and Spiritual Dimensions. Proceedings of the Symposium Held on May 27–29, 1996, Jerusalem, Israel* (BLMJP 2; Jerusalem: Bible Lands Museum, 1998) 25–35.

was given rest on all sides from his enemies, the quintessential ruler will not have to enter into battle as David did, but will have YHWH to deliver him. The destruction of the Assyrian army in Isa 9:2–4 [Eng. 3–5] stems solely from God himself, "You shall break the yoke of their burden and the staff on their shoulders, the rod of their oppressor, as at the battle of Midian." Consonant with the rest motif, Isaiah perceives this individual as "the prince of peace," who shall have "no end to the increase of his government or of peace," to the extent that "the wolf will dwell with the lamb."[110] The expansion of dominion mentioned here recalls Solomon, who had "ruled over all the kingdoms from the River [to] the land of the Philistines and to the border of Egypt."[111] In both instances, breadth of territory is to be bestowed upon the one chosen of God. Furthermore, Solomon is given "a wise and discerning heart," such that "the wisdom of God was in him to administer justice."[112] Similarly, the prophet envisions Hezekiah as a "wonderful counselor" who will uphold his kingdom "with justice and righteousness."[113] These divine attributes imparted to a chosen anointed ruler are eloquently stated in Isa 11:2, "The Spirit of YHWH will rest on him, the spirit of wisdom and understanding, the spirit of counsel and strength, the spirit of knowledge and the fear of YHWH." If Hezekiah was already viewed as the fulfillment of the Solomonic ideal in the eighth century, then his depiction in Chronicles only substantiates the historical accuracy of the account.

It is clear that Chronicles is cognizant of the earlier tradition of Hezekiah in Kings as a second David, as well as his more muted characterization there and in the impactful prophecies by Isaiah as a Solomon *redivivus*. The Chronicler's understanding of what constitutes an anointed ruler favored by God, and his belief that Hezekiah had indeed historically attained such a sublime status, necessitated subtle changes in some of his source material. One example is the omission of the notice in 2 Kgs 18:8, "He defeated the Philistines as far as Gaza and its territory, from watchtower to fortified city." Despite the accolade of Hezekiah as successful in battle, it created an insurmountable contradiction with the coeval ideology of Isaiah in regard to a messianic ruler: one who will not be a fierce warrior but who will be given rest by the Lord and will not need to enter into combat. By the same token, Hezekiah does not become

---

[110] Isa 9:5–6[6–7]; 11:6–9.
[111] 1 Kgs 5:1[4:21], cf. v 5:4[4:24].
[112] 1 Kgs 3:11–12, 28.
[113] Isa 9:5–6[6–7].

directly embroiled with Sennacherib at the time of the blockade of Jerusalem. The Judean monarch does not attempt to buy off the Sargonid, nor does he tear his clothes at his plight as recounted in Kings.[114] Rather, he reassures the populace that "with us is YHWH our God to help us and fight our battles," and his prayer is answered when both he and Isaiah cry out to heaven for salvation.[115] For the Chronicler, the type of sovereign which he felt Hezekiah exemplified, an impression rooted directly in the prophetic literature of the eighth century, meant that the son of Ahaz could not have engaged his foes militarily as recorded in Kings. Thus in Chronicles, these particular events never occurred.

The Chronicler, then, did not represent Hezekiah as an ideal ruler on a mere whim, but rather his sources, some of those contemporaneous with the reign of Hezekiah, already conveyed this distinct impression.[116] The overall aggrandized presentation of his rule in the book of Chronicles is what one would expect if these earlier sources do indeed date from the time of the monarch himself. His court would be partial to presenting him as a second David or Solomon, the first king since the united monarchy to embody all the principal attributes of divine favor: wealth, honor, faithful maintenance of the cult, tribute, victory over his foes, and territory which once again encompassed the northern tribes. The vindication that Jerusalem was the true, unassailable abode of YHWH, affirmed in three historically profound and irrefutable events—the Syro-Ephraimitic war, the fall of Samaria, and the defeat of Sennacherib—could only have raised the expectation that the Lord was with Zion and his messiah. Many of the details which emerge from cautious reconstruction of the Hezekiah arc in Chronicles are historically plausible and cast serious doubt on the notion

---

[114] 2 Kgs 18:13–16; 19:1, cf. Isa 36:1; 37:1.

[115] 2 Chr 32:7, 20.

[116] That is, whereas Hezekiah's prominence is typically classified as part and parcel of the Chronicler's ideology, it ultimately stems from his sources. This may be demonstrated elsewhere, most notably in the Chronicler's disposition toward divine justice which Japhet, *Ideology of the Book of Chronicles*, 156–65, terms "the imperative of reward and punishment." No longer is there ancestral merit, the generational punishment encapsulated in the expression "the sins of the fathers," cf. Exod 20:5–6; 34:7; Lev 26:39; Deut 5:9–10; Lam 5:7; Isa 65:7; Jer 32:18; Ezek 18:2. Rather, there is solely individual responsibility requited within that person's lifetime, an idea advanced by the prophets in Jer 31:29–30; Ezek 18 (as clarified by Helmer Ringgren, "אָב," *TDOT* 1.13–14, Deut 24:16 deals with civil penal law, not divine retribution). Jeremiah and Ezekiel were adamant that the older perception was outmoded and no longer held a place in Israelite theodicy, and accordingly it is stricken from the Chronicler's history. Thus while the author's modifications to his *Vorlage* represent alignment to his worldview on one level, they also manifest an effort to judiciously maintain the accuracy of the various traditions at his disposal.

of his resplendent kingdom as a mere post-exilic retrojection. In tandem with all of the evidence that has been amassed in these chapters pertaining to source material underlying the Hezekiah narrative, this leads to the bold but cogent assertion that it is the book of Chronicles, not Kings, which better preserves the picture of the historical Hezekiah.[117]

9.4. CONCLUSION

Hezekiah is cast in no uncertain terms in the book of Chronicles as a second David and Solomon, but this correlation is not a literary creation of its author. The correspondence to David is already established in the book of Kings, and the censorious portrayal of Solomon has been traced in scholarship to redactional layers of the Deuteronomistic History which postdate the reign of Hezekiah. The Chronicler maintains the earliest reconstructed form of the dynastic covenant in the Former Prophets, eternal in nature and conditional upon the obedience of the individual. Both David and Solomon are responsible for its receipt and fulfillment in Chronicles, however, an artifact of the author's portrayal of these two kings as a unified event.

Independent of the dynastic promises, a pro-Solomonic source may be reconstructed which has been more carefully preserved in the book of Chronicles. Many key themes within the Deuteronomistic History that may be identified as manifestations of divine favor—victory in war, spoliation, tribute, royal building programs, territorial expansion, and most consequentially the rest motif—are present throughout the books of Joshua, Judges and Samuel, yet typically abate after the presentation of the united monarchy without explanation. In Chronicles, these motifs extend into the narratives of the divided kingdom, reaching their apotheosis in the account of Hezekiah. As other, annalistic records likewise terminate at this point in Israelite history—the naming of the queen mother, the burial formulae, and chronological evidence of co-regency—all literary

---

[117] The argumentation of these chapters, then, adopts a stance toward Chronicles that is counter to the "free, parabolic depiction of history" of Welten, *Geschichte und Geschichtsdarstellung*, 205–206: "With the books of Chronicles the historiography of Israel enters an entirely new stage; no more are traditions being collected and reworked; no more are earlier works being re-edited. The Chronicler writes history from beginning to end, anew and independently." These conclusions have already been challenged by others such as Kelly, *Retribution and Eschatology*, 111–34, who attributes to earlier sources a range of texts relating to reward and punishment.

indications are that the book of Kings originally concluded with the reign
of Hezekiah.

The son of Ahaz was already made incomparable to his predecessor
David in 2 Kgs 18:5, and his rightful place as successor was assured for
the Deuteronomist in his removal of the high places. This assessment was
ultimately toned down in the book of Kings for the same reason of that
of Solomon; namely, the illustrious nature of their rule could not be reconciled theologically with the subsequent end of their respective kingdoms. The likening of Hezekiah to Solomon, however is still present in
the eighth-century messianic oracles of Isaiah ben Amoz, in terms of territory, rest, and divine wisdom. All these data affirm that pre-exilic sources
underly the book of Chronicles, a historiographical work which has dutifully preserved, not invented, the belief in Hezekiah as an ideal ruler. The
Hezekiah of tradition was firmly rooted in the Hezekiah of history.

SUMMARY AND FUTURE DIRECTIONS

The Judean king Hezekiah came to the throne during one of the most tumultuous periods in the history of the nation. The last half of the eighth century B.C.E. had given rise to the expectation of a return to the halcyon golden age of the Davidic dynasty, as boldly proclaimed by the prophets Hosea, Amos, Micah, and Isaiah. This ideal encompassed the notions of a united kingdom with expanded territorial borders, divine protection from all enemies, and a ruler who exhibited the qualities of wise, just rule as exemplified by David and Solomon. Part of this longing was motivated by the reduction of the northern kingdom to a vassal state at the hands of the inexorable Assyrian empire. The loss of sovereignty and concomitant deportation of the population had cast Israel's covenant with YHWH in jeopardy, and the prophets were insistent that a strong corrective was needed for the nation's rampant social injustice and syncretistic idolatry. In the southern kingdom, the reign of Ahaz had marked the nadir of Yahwistic worship for the nation, with the introduction of foreign elements into the cult and substantial modifications made to the Temple complex. The divided kingdom was at war with itself, which would soon prompt Ahaz to turn to his imperial masters for aid.

It was into this maelstrom that Hezekiah was born in ca. 735 B.C.E. to his parents Ahaz and Abijah, under the birth name Immanuel: "God is with us." Isaiah used the child as a divine sign to signal to the wavering Ahaz that YHWH would prolong the Davidic dynasty despite Judah's dire circumstances at the time. The Syro-Ephraimite alliance was disrupted by direct Assyrian intervention, with the result that Immanuel was cast in the eyes of the nation as a harbinger of deliverance, literal proof of God's presence among his people. The son of Amoz, moreover, boldly proclaimed that this king's accession would harken a new golden age for both kingdoms, while at the same time signaling the cataclysmic end of the Assyrian empire.[1] The expectations were lofty for the youth who took the throne in 725 B.C.E. at approximately ten years of age, and his throne name חִזְקִיָּהוּ alludes to the belief that YHWH had firmly established his rule.[2] Counseled by advisors and learning directly from his father dur-

---

[1] Isa 8:16–9:6.

[2] Note the usage in 2 Kgs 14:5, and the *hitpael* forms in Chronicles.

ing their three-year co-regency, Hezekiah was an able statesman when he became sole monarch ca. 722 B.C.E. around the age of thirteen.

This year saw the beginning of Shalmaneser V's siege against the northern capital of Samaria, as a reprisal for Hoshea's refusal to pay tribute and decision to forge diplomatic ties with Egypt.[3] Although Hezekiah was not involved in this initial act of insurgency, he soon chose to come to the aid of Israel during the pivotal juncture of the death of Shalmaneser and the formidable political issues faced by Sargon II securing his dominion in his first regnal year.[4] In an effort to consolidate imperial resistance, Hezekiah launched an assault against pro-Assyrian cities in Philistia, retaking territory in the Shephelah and Negev lost to the Philistines under Ahaz.[5] This was an act of open rebellion, and in 720 B.C.E. Sargon countered swiftly by conquering Samaria and deporting the northern populace.[6] He also campaigned in Judah at this time, reasserting control over the region and subsequently declaring himself to be "the subduer of the land of Judah which was far away."[7] Hezekiah was forced to capitulate and assist Assyria militarily, his ambitions to break away from the inexorable grasp of the imperial threat held in abeyance.[8]

In the meantime, social conditions within the realm necessitated a redirected royal focus. Many northerners who were not deported moved southward into Judah, and Hezekiah, who had previously backed Samaria in its time of distress, once again extended his hand to draw those who had been displaced by war back into his kingdom. This humanitarian crisis of appropriately biblical proportions was for Hezekiah both a challenge and an opportunity. Territory and influence were up for grabs in the north, and the son of Ahaz immediately instigated large-scale programs aimed at accommodating this unprecedented population shift while elevating Jerusalem into a regionally prominent urban center. The capital expanded rapidly from the older Jebusite hamlet on the eastern ridge to cover the southwestern hill, including residential dwellings to the north and along the eastern slopes of the City of David. There was substantial economic development in the Judean Shephelah and the Negev, including agricultural buildup to increase food production. The storage jars which

---

[3] 2 Kgs 17:4.
[4] 2 Kgs 18:7.
[5] 2 Kgs 18:8; 2 Chr 28:17–18.
[6] For these various sources, see chap. 1 n. 19.
[7] Cf. the Azekah inscription and line 8 of the Nimrud inscription.
[8] ND 2765; ND 2608.

had been part of a pre-existing system of distribution became an essential model for supporting increased trade and generating tax revenue. Their designation as *lmlk*, "royal property," assured that money from their use flowed appropriately into the state treasury, even as their seal impressions reminded the populace that Hezekiah was justly providing for their needs.

The religious reform instituted by Hezekiah was a shrewd political move aimed at achieving the same ends. The swelling population in the environs of Jerusalem meant that the Temple needed to become the religious center of the nation, countenancing no rivals in prominent installations such as Bethel. With rural sanctuaries forcibly and permanently closed, their revenues were redirected to the Judean capital, bolstering the dominance of the king to the detriment of clan leadership elsewhere. Centralization was a logical move to promote reunification of the tribes, as was the invitation extended to those who yet remained in the north to join their brethren in Jerusalem for the Passover. Hezekiah's naming of his son Manasseh points to the same political aim.[9] The removal of pagan elements from the Yahwistic cult was in keeping with prophetic allocutions in the north, where the patriarchal covenants had been called into question by conquest and exile. An unfortunate by-product of these programs was the disenfranchisement of priests and Levites beyond Jerusalem, to which Hezekiah responded by allocating storage rooms within the precincts of the sanctuary and by having publicly-sponsored portions collected there. These contributions were subsequently redistributed throughout the system of Levitical cities for consumption by cultic functionaries and their families based on genealogical enrollment. All of these initiatives would soon become central tenets of the book of Deuteronomy.[10]

In the eyes of many Judeans, the conquest of Israel legitimated the southern kingdom and Hezekiah's rule. The messianic expectations of Isaiah became correspondingly more idyllic in the aftermath of the fall

---

[9] For additional evidence that Hezekiah was motivated to integrate northern refugees into his kingdom, William M. Schniedewind points to his son's arranged marriage to a family from Jotbah in Galilee (2 Kgs 21:19, see "Jerusalem, the Late Judaean Monarchy, and the Composition of the Biblical Texts," in A. G. Vaughn and A. E. Killebrew eds., *Jerusalem in Bible and Archaeology: The First Temple Period* [SBLSS 18; Leiden: Brill, 2003] 380).

[10] Not necessarily during the reign of Hezekiah, see Robert R. Wilson, "Deuteronomy, Ethnicity, and Reform: Reflections on the Social Setting of the Book of Deuteronomy," in J. T. Strong and S. S. Tuell (eds.), *Constituting the Community: Studies on the Polity of Ancient Israel in Honor of S. Dean McBride Jr.* (Winona Lake, Ind.: Eisenbrauns, 2005) 107–23. This proposed reconstruction does not pertain to the older northern traditions preserved within the book such as the covenant ceremony in Deut 27, which predate the fall of Samaria.

of Samaria, with the peacefulness of Hezekiah's kingdom extended even to animalkind, the dispersed tribes reunited from the four corners of the earth, and the destruction of the arrogant warmonger Assyria irrevocably ordained.[11] The city and the nation underwent a period of burgeoning economic growth and prosperity, in what may aptly be termed a national renaissance.[12] There was extensive literary activity during these years, including genealogical records and the transcription of proverbs, as well as the codification and preservation of eighth-century prophetic material.[13] Impelled in part by dramatic changes including the end of the northern kingdom, the compilation of the historiography of the early monarchy was authorized at this time, merging the northern and southern accounts of national memory into a unified narrative.[14] As one who had dutifully maintained the Temple and the cult, enlarged the city, ruled with justice, expanded national borders, and reunited and sustained the people, Hezekiah was in many respects seen as a second David and Solomon. This national history rightfully culminated with him, extolling his accomplishments and vindicating his reign.

Several overlapping factors lay behind Hezekiah's fateful decision to rebel once more against Assyria, including an epidemic which had ravaged the empire, the unanticipated death of Sargon II on the battlefield in

---

[11] Isa 10:33–11:16.

[12] Beyond the economic buildup mentioned earlier, recall the more elaborate burial tombs carved from rock to the east of the City of David.

[13] See, respectively, 1 Chr 4:41; Prov 25:1; and the superscriptions to the prophetic books. For the collection of eighth-century prophetic material as a Hezekian program, see Baruch Halpern, "'Brisker Pipes than Poetry': The Development of Israelite Monotheism," in J. A. Neusner, B. A. Levine and E. S. Frerichs (eds.), *Judaic Perspectives on Ancient Israel. Festschrift H. L. Ginsberg* (Philadelphia: Fortress Press, 1987) 77–115. The documented increase in scribal practice and literacy in the late eighth century B.C.E. made this an opportune period for literary creation which significantly impacted the growth of Scripture, as documented in David W. Jamieson-Drake, *Scribes and Schools in Monarchic Judah* (JSOTSup 109; Sheffield: Almond Press, 1991); Schniedewind, "Jerusalem and the Composition of the Biblical Texts," 375–93. On the increase in literacy during the period, see William M. Schniedewind, *How the Bible Became a Book: The Textualization of Ancient Israel* (Cambridge: Cambridge University Press, 2004). The notice in Prov 25:1 which records the copying of proverbs by the scribes of Hezekiah is widely accepted as biblical evidence of scribal schools at this time. For further studies relating to this debate, see Michael V. Fox, *Proverbs 1–9* (AYB 18A; New York: Doubleday, 2000) 7–8.

[14] Israel Finkelstein and Neil Asher Silberman, "Temple and Dynasty: Hezekiah, the Remaking of Judah and the Rise of Pan-Israelite Ideology," *JSOT* 30/3 (2006) 275–79. I am of the opinion that the J, E, and P narratives all continue into the Deuteronomistic History, recounting events up until their respective dates of authorship. They are not to be separated by the same methods as within the Pentateuch, however, because the process of editing these respective collections was altogether different.

705 B.C.E., and Sennacherib's loss of control of Babylon in his first regnal year. Prior to his Babylonian coup of 703 B.C.E., Merodach-baladan II sent a delegation to Judah to discuss an alliance, his very presence in the small, far-flung nation attesting to Hezekiah's status as a military ally.[15] Hezekiah may have spearheaded the regional revolt himself, becoming directly involved with Philistine cities sworn on oath to Assyria and accepting the loyalist king Padî from the Ekronites.[16] The Siloam Tunnel had been constructed over several of the preceding years for just this eventuality, and additional fortifications such as the Broad Wall were added to prepare the city for attack.[17] In his rage, Sennacherib tore through the Judean countryside, undaunted by the clash with Egyptian forces at Eltekeh. The chief cupbearer was dispatched to the blockaded capital of Jerusalem in order to negotiate a surrender, and Hezekiah was resigned to offer tribute to Sennacherib as a token of fealty. His gift had to be conveyed to Nineveh by couriers, however, owing to the abrupt withdrawal of the Assyrians from the campaign for reasons unrelated to military defeat. In his subsequent annals, Sennacherib would respectfully characterize Hezekiah as "tough and powerful."[18]

The remaining five years of Hezekiah's reign were focused on recovering from the decimation of his kingdom, with total destruction of many key cities. Despite the desolation, the escape of Jerusalem from Assyrian clutches was seen as divine deliverance, and the inviolability of Zion became inextricably intertwined with Hezekiah's faithfulness. Both of these facets were magnified by Isaian tradents, who credited the angel of the Lord with the routing of the Assyrian army in keeping with Isaiah's earlier prophecies of direct, divine retribution.[19] The Chronicler would go on to preserve his positive aspects as they were essentially transmitted in the national history composed during his own reign. For the exilic Deuteronomist, the Zion ideology and the ascendant rule of Hezekiah could not be theologically reconciled with the fall of Jerusalem to Babylonia little more than a century hence, and thus the account of his reign was brought in line with political reality by making him personally responsible for the

---

[15] Sennacherib's personal leadership of this western campaign suggests the same. This chronology follows that suggested by John A. Brinkman, "Merodach-Baladan II," in *Studies Presented to A. Leo Oppenheim, June 7, 1964* (Chicago, 1964) 31–33.

[16] Rassam 42, 46b–48; OIP ii 73–77, iii 14–17.

[17] 2 Chr 32:2–6; Isa 22:8–11.

[18] *šepṣu mitru*, Bull 1, line 21; Bulls 2–3, line 21.

[19] 2 Kgs 19:35 / Isa 37:36, cf. Isa 9:3–4[4–5]; 10:17–19, 33–34.

nation's undoing.[20] Later tradition would nonetheless envision Hezekiah as a type of ideal future ruler.[21]

This portrait of Hezekiah requires a re-examination of some positions currently entrenched in biblical scholarship. First and foremost is the extent of influence in the authorship of the Hebrew Bible under king Josiah, whose reign has been credited for such works as the pre-exilic redactions of Deuteronomy, the Deuteronomistic History, and First Isaiah. With the reign of Hezekiah compellingly established as the height of economic prosperity and literary creativity in the history of the nation of Israel, it must be asked whether some of these attributions have been drawn perfunctorily to the time of Josiah.[22] The scope and aims of the Hezekian program, according to the findings of this study, should have implications for how the scholar approaches these crucial biblical texts.

The conclusions raised by this book also having a strong bearing on the historical reconstruction of the priesthood. The distinction made between

---

[20] 2 Kgs 20:12–19; secondarily, Isa 39.

[21] Note the statement of Rabbi Johanan ben Zakkai: "Prepare a throne for Hezekiah, king of Judah, who is coming" (*b. Berakhot* 28b). According to Samson H. Levey, *The Messiah: An Aramaic Interpretation—The Messianic Exegesis of the Targum* (MHUC 2; Cincinnati: Hebrew Union College, 1974) 154 n. 33, "Johanan's statement is especially significant, for it was he who salvaged what little he could in 70 C.E." Note also *j. Sotah* 9:17 [24c]; *j. Avodah Zarah* 3:1 [42c], in which Rabbi Eliezer ben Hyrcanus is said to have seen upon his death bed the same vision which his teacher Rabbi Johanan ben Zakkai saw just before dying: that of king Hezekiah of Judah. See further Jacob Neusner, *A Life of Rabban Yohanan ben Zakkai, ca. 1–80 C.E.* (Leiden: E. J. Brill, 1962) 172ff; Aharon Agus, *The Binding of Isaac & Messiah: Law, Martyrdom and Deliverance in Early Rabbinic Religiosity* (Albany: State University of New York: 1988) 207–21.

For Moshe Aberbach, "Hezekiah King of Judah and Rabbi Judah the Patriarch—Messianic Aspects," *Tarbiz* 53/3 (1984) 353–71 [Hebrew], the statements of Bar Kappara that God had intended Hezekiah to be the Messiah (*b. Sanhedrin* 94a) and of Rabbi Hillel that "Israel has no Messiah, for they have already consumed him in the days of Hezekiah" (99a) are to be related to messianic speculation surrounding the patriarch Rabbi Judah I. The name Hezekiah was substituted for that of the patriarch for reasons of prudence.

[22] Among those studies which have tended to take a pan-Josianic approach to the biblical text, see Antti Laato, *Josiah and David Redivivus* (CB 33; Stockholm: Almqvist & Wiksell International, 1992); Marvin A. Sweeney, *King Josiah of Judah: The Lost Messiah of Israel* (Oxford: Oxford University Press, 2001). The questionable nature of this position may be seen in Sweeney's stated purpose for the Josianic redaction of First Isaiah, "which focused on the restoration of Judah in the aftermath of the Assyrian collapse, and which employed Hezekiah, in contrast to Ahaz, as the ideal Davidic model for the reign of King Josiah" (*Isaiah 1–39 with An Introduction to Prophetic Literature* [FOTL 16; Grand Rapids: Eerdmans, 1996] 154).

As this book represents my own response to this approach, there need be no point-by-point rebuttal here. Instead, see the reviews of Laato by George M. Landes, *JBL* 113/3 (1994) 519–21; H. G. M. Williamson, *VT* 43/4 (1993) 573–74, and of Sweeney by John Van Seters, *JAOS* 122/1 (2002) 118–19; Steven L. McKenzie, *RBL* 02/2003.

priests and Levites in regard to the allocation of portions calls into question the well-entrenched notion that this sacerdotal division was not palpable until the exile.[23] Even for those scholars who appreciate the subtle differences in their respective offices as expressed in the laws of Deuteronomy, this historical watershed must be pushed back from the reign of Josiah by almost a century. The fact that the Temple contributions and the Levitical cities both materialize in the Holiness Legislation suggests the origin of this literary stratum in the eighth century, with the Priestly Code being correspondingly antecedent.[24] It remains for future scholarship to anchor these insights on a more sure footing.

Positing a national history composed during the reign of Hezekiah warrants an investigation of the relationship of this work to the J document of the Pentateuch. The Yahwist material is notably pro-Davidic in its stance, analogous to the material in Kings which depicts Hezekiah as the rightful successor to the dynasty's eponymous ancestor.[25] It, too, contains references to Assyria, Nineveh, and Calah which mandate a historical setting when the empire was dominant in the ancient Near East.[26] A recent linguistic analysis has affirmed its pre-exilic provenance.[27] Notable similarities have long been detected between J and Deuteronomistic texts, and the work of the Yahwist historian has been dated by some scholars to the seventh century B.C.E.[28] What connection, if any, this document has to the royal court of Hezekiah remains to be clarified.

In terms of chronology, there is a pressing need to redress the regnal record of the divided kingdom. Insufficient attention has been paid to clear indicators of co-regency in Israelite archival data which permit a highly reliable reconstruction of the monarchic reigns. Modern attempts at establishing this timeline have yielded questionable results by placing

---

[23] As claimed by Julius Wellhausen, *Prolegomena zur Geschichte Israels* (6th ed.; Berlin: W. de Gruyter, 1905) 115–45.

[24] This reasoning was already suggested by the perpetuation of the *pesah* sacrifice as a domestic rite in Exod 12, which would be impracticable after the decree of centralization.

[25] The so-called messianic prophecy of Gen 49:10 is relevant in this regard.

[26] Gen 2:14; 10:11–12; 25:18.

[27] Richard M. Wright, *Linguistic Evidence for the Pre-exilic Date of the Yahwistic Source* (LHB/OTS 419; London: T&T Clark, 2005).

[28] Lothar Perlitt, *Bundestheologie im Alten Testament* (Neukirchen-Vluyn: Neukirchener Verlag, 1969); Hans Schmid, *Der sogenannte Jahwist* (Zürich: Theologischer Verlag, 1976). For dates proposed by other scholars, see Wright, *Linguistic Evidence*, 162–63. The idea that the Pentateuchal sources extend into the historical books is no longer popular, but for a select bibliography see Iain W. Provan, *Hezekiah and the Books of Kings: A Contribution to the Debate about the Composition of the Deuteronomistic History* (BZAW 172; Berlin: Walter de Gruyter, 1988) 2 n. 9.

too much emphasis on reconciling the biblical record with other ancient Near Eastern documents. What is sorely needed is an analysis which enables the chronology of the northern and southern kingdoms to stand on its own, as a means to appreciate how ancient Israel envisioned its own history.

There is certainly more that may be said with regard to Israelite historiography. The findings of this study suggest that the tarnishing of the character of Solomon in the Deuteronomistic History is directly related to the paucity of Solomonic qualities in the corresponding account of Hezekiah. While attention is typically focused in biblical scholarship on the exilic Deuteronomist, a more thorough understanding of his pre-exilic counterpart would enable greater precision in delineating the various redactional layers within this extensive work, as well as permit more informed reconstructions of the monarchic period. Given the priority assigned to the Chronistic record in this particular case study, the extent and reliability of the Chronicler's sources should continue to be sought, even as they are mined for the underpinnings of that historian's own ideology.

Another matter is the extent of messianic or royalist thought in the pre-exilic period. Sanguine depictions of the future in prophetic literature are predominantly viewed as creations of the (post)-exilic period, but this book has provided a plausible basis for these aspirations in the prominent royal ideology of the eighth century. To advance a later, conjectural historical context for a propitious vision does not preclude the possibility of an earlier, more apposite social setting. The subject of exile in particular must be delicately handled due to its multiple occurrences in the historically brief duration of a century and a half.[29] It must be remembered that the deportations in the eighth century were the first to be experienced by the Israelite tribes, and that by the larger and more powerful northern kingdom. Reading conceivably pre-exilic texts with an awareness of both deportation and the expectations for the existing Davidic dynasty will lead to additional prospective historical settings for their composition.

By implication, the rise of universalism in Israelite religious thought should be re-examined in light of this study. The ideology of Isaiah, which

---

[29] As aptly stated by J. J. M. Roberts, "Critical Reflections on The Book Called Isaiah with Particular Attention to the Second Exodus Theme (Isa 11:11–16)" (SBL Paper; Boston, Mass. 22–25 November, 2008): "I am inclined to think that the impact of the Babylonian exile has so dominated the thought of modern scholars that they have failed to truly appreciate the enormous impact of the Assyrian exile of both northerners and many Judeans (over 250,000 according to Sennacherib) in the late eighth century."

advocates that the supreme rulers of the ancient world are but instruments in the hands of YHWH, has been acknowledged as a religious
response to empire.[30] As a goal of iconic politics was to dethrone foreign
gods and to place the local deity securely in his temple, the centralization of Hezekiah could be justifiably tied to this heightened monotheistic
conception. When considered in tandem with prophetic judgment on a
national level—as exemplified in the oracles against the nations and the
Day of the Lord passages—the transformation of Yahwistic religion in the
later monarchic period was understandably profound.

The final quarter of the eighth century B.C.E. was in some respects
the most volatile time in the history of the Israelite nation, and it was
just these exigent circumstances and Hezekiah's response to them which
ensured his legacy. His efforts to incorporate the northern tribes after
the fall of Samaria unified the nation on an ethnological level, just as
his authorization of a national history did on a cultural level. He was
esteemed for his feats in waterworking, and admired for his preservation
of prophetic and wisdom collections. The expansion of Jerusalem and his
far-ranging economic programs identified him as a true shepherd of his
people. His sweeping cultic reform ensured an essential, common religious identity for his diverse subjects, enacting laws which earned him
the renown of judging his people with justice and righteousness. He was
also a shrewd and widely respected military leader, personally acknowledged by the supreme imperial ruler of the ancient world at the time.
Despite the aggrandized reputation given to David and Solomon as the
fountainhead of the Davidic dynasty, Hezekiah by all accounts surpassed
their achievements and deservedly accepted the comparison to his fore-
runners. Few men have done more in one lifetime to immortalize their
place on the world stage. It is only appropriate that biblical scholarship
has finally come to recognize his well-deserved status as the greatest king
in the history of Israel.

---

[30] Baruch Levine, "Assyrian Ideology and Israelite Monotheism," *Iraq* 67/1 (2005) 411–27.

APPENDIX A

SENNACHERIB'S BLOCKADE OF JERUSALEM
(THE JUDEAN VIEW—2 KGS 18:13–19:37)

Source A (Chronistic Record—2 Kgs 18:13–16)

(18:13)Now in the fourteenth year of King Hezekiah, Sennacherib king of
Assyria came up against all the fortified cities of Judah and seized them.
(14)Then Hezekiah king of Judah sent to the king of Assyria at Lachish, saying, "I have done wrong. Withdraw from me; whatever you impose on
me I will bear." So the king of Assyria required of Hezekiah king of Judah
three hundred talents of silver and thirty talents of gold. (15)Hezekiah gave
[him] all the silver which was found in the house of YHWH, and in the
treasuries of the king's house. (16)At that time Hezekiah cut off [the gold
from] the doors of the temple of YHWH, and [from] the doorposts which
Hezekiah king of Judah had overlaid, and gave it to the king of Assyria.

Source B₁ (Prophetic Account 1–2 Kgs 18:17a, 26–36; 19:1–9a, 36–37)

(18:17a)Then the king of Assyria sent the *rab šāqê* from Lachish to Jerusalem with a large army.[1] So he went up and came to Jerusalem. (26)Then
Eliakim the son of Hilkiah, and Shebnah and Joah, said to the *rab šāqê*,
"Speak now to your servants in Aramaic, for we understand [it]; and do
not speak with us in Judean in the hearing of the people who are on the
wall." (27)But the *rab šāqê* said to them, "Has my master sent me only to
your master and to you to speak these words, [and] not to the men who
sit on the wall, [doomed] to eat their own dung and drink their own urine
with you?"

(28)Then the *rab šāqê* stood and cried with a loud voice in Judean, saying, "Hear the word of the great king, the king of Assyria. 29)"Thus says the
king, 'Do not let Hezekiah deceive you, for he will not be able to deliver
you from my hand; (30)nor let Hezekiah make you trust in YHWH, saying,
"YHWH will surely deliver us, and this city will not be given into the hand
of the king of Assyria." (31)'Do not listen to Hezekiah, for thus says the king
of Assyria, "Make your peace with me and come out to me, and eat each

---

[1] This emended version is taken from Isa 36:2, in which only the *rab šāqê* appears.

of his vine and each of his fig tree and drink each of the waters of his own cistern, (32)until I come and take you away to a land like your own land, a land of grain and new wine, a land of bread and vineyards, a land of olive trees and honey, that you may live and not die." But do not listen to Hezekiah when he misleads you, saying, "YHWH will deliver us." (33)'Has any one of the gods of the nations delivered his land from the hand of the king of Assyria? (34)'Where are the gods of Hamath and Arpad? Where are the gods of Sepharvaim, Hena and Ivvah? Have they delivered Samaria from my hand? (35)'Who among all the gods of the lands have delivered their land from my hand, that YHWH should deliver Jerusalem from my hand?'" (36)But the people were silent and answered him not a word, for the king's commandment was, "Do not answer him."

(19:1)And when King Hezekiah heard, he tore his clothes, covered himself with sackcloth and entered the house of YHWH. (2)Then he sent Eliakim who was over the household with Shebna the scribe and the elders of the priests, covered with sackcloth, to Isaiah the prophet the son of Amoz.

(3)They said to him, "Thus says Hezekiah, 'This day is a day of distress, rebuke, and rejection; for children have come to birth and there is no strength to [deliver]. (4)'Perhaps YHWH your God will hear all the words of *rab šāqê*, whom his master the king of Assyria has sent to reproach the living God, and will rebuke the words which YHWH your God has heard. Therefore, offer a prayer for the remnant that is left.'" (5)So the servants of King Hezekiah came to Isaiah.

(6)Isaiah said to them, "Thus you shall say to your master, 'Thus says YHWH, "Do not be afraid because of the words that you have heard, with which the servants of the king of Assyria have blasphemed Me. (7)"Behold, I will put a spirit in him so that he will hear a rumor and return to his own land. And I will make him fall by the sword in his own land."'" (8)Then the *rab šāqê* returned and found the king of Assyria fighting against Libnah, for he had heard that the king had left Lachish. (9a)When he heard [them] say concerning Tirhakah king of Kush, "Behold, he has come out to fight against you," (36)so Sennacherib king of Assyria departed and returned [home], and lived at Nineveh. (37)It came about as he was worshiping in the house of Nisroch his god, that Adrammelech and Sharezer killed him with the sword; and they escaped into the land of Ararat. And Esarhaddon his son became king in his place.

Source B₂ (Prophetic Account 2–2 Kgs 18:17b–25, 37; 19:9b–35)

(18:17b)Then the king of Assyria sent the *tartānu* and the *rab ša-rēši* and the *rab šāqê* from Lachish to King Hezekiah with a large army to Jerusalem. And they went up, and they came and stood by the conduit of the upper pool, which is on the highway of the fuller's field. (18)When they called to the king, Eliakim the son of Hilkiah, who was over the household, and Shebnah the scribe and Joah the son of Asaph the recorder, came out to them.

(19)Then the *rab šāqê* said to them, "Say now to Hezekiah, 'Thus says the great king, the king of Assyria, "What is this security in which you trusted? (20)"You say (but [they are] only empty words), '[I have] counsel and strength for the war.' Now on whom do you rely, that you have rebelled against me? (21)"Now behold, you rely on the staff of this crushed reed, [even] on Egypt; on which if a man leans, it will go into his hand and pierce it. So is Pharaoh king of Egypt to all who rely on him. (22)"But if you say to me, 'We trust in YHWH our God,' is it not He whose high places and whose altars Hezekiah has taken away, and has said to Judah and to Jerusalem, 'You shall worship before this altar in Jerusalem'? (23)"Now therefore, come, make a bargain with my master the king of Assyria, and I will give you two thousand horses, if you are able on your part to set riders on them. (24)"How then can you repulse one official of the least of my master's servants, and rely on Egypt for chariots and for horsemen? (25)"Have I now come up without YHWH's approval against this place to destroy it? YHWH said to me, 'Go up against this land and destroy it.' " ' "

(37)Then Eliakim the son of Hilkiah, who was over the household, and Shebna the scribe and Joah the son of Asaph, the recorder, came to Hezekiah with their clothes torn and told him the words of *rab šāqê*.

(19:9b)[The king of Assyria] sent messengers again to Hezekiah saying, (10)"Thus you shall say to Hezekiah king of Judah, 'Do not let your God in whom you trust deceive you saying, "Jerusalem will not be given into the hand of the king of Assyria." (11)'Behold, you have heard what the kings of Assyria have done to all the lands, destroying them completely. So will you be spared? (12)'Did the gods of those nations which my fathers destroyed deliver them, [even] Gozan and Haran and Rezeph and the sons of Eden who [were] in Telassar? (13)'Where is the king of Hamath, the king of Arpad, the king of the city of Sepharvaim, and [of] Hena and Ivvah?' "

(14)Then Hezekiah took the letter from the hand of the messengers and read it, and he went up to the house of YHWH and spread it out before YHWH. (15)Hezekiah prayed before YHWH and said, "O YHWH, the God of Israel, who are enthroned [above] the cherubim, You are the God, You alone, of all the kingdoms of the earth. You have made heaven and earth. (16)"Incline Your ear, O YHWH, and hear; open Your eyes, O YHWH, and see; and listen to the words of Sennacherib, which he has sent to reproach the living God. (17)"Truly, O YHWH, the kings of Assyria have devastated the nations and their lands (18)and have cast their gods into the fire, for they were not gods but the work of men's hands, wood and stone. So they have destroyed them. (19)"Now, O YHWH our God, I pray, deliver us from his hand that all the kingdoms of the earth may know that You alone, O YHWH, are God."

(20)Then Isaiah the son of Amoz sent to Hezekiah saying, "Thus says YHWH, the God of Israel, 'Because you have prayed to Me about Sennacherib king of Assyria, I have heard [you].' (21)"This is the word that YHWH has spoken against him: 'She has despised you and mocked you, The virgin daughter of Zion; She has shaken [her] head behind you, The daughter of Jerusalem! (22)'Whom have you reproached and blasphemed? And against whom have you raised [your] voice, And haughtily lifted up your eyes? Against the Holy One of Israel! (23)'Through your messengers you have reproached the Lord, And you have said, "With my many chariots I came up to the heights of the mountains, To the remotest parts of Lebanon; And I cut down its tall cedars [and] its choice cypresses. And I entered its farthest lodging place, its thickest forest. (24)"I dug [wells] and drank foreign waters, And with the sole of my feet I dried up All the rivers of Egypt."

(25)'Have you not heard? Long ago I did it; From ancient times I planned it. Now I have brought it to pass, That you should turn fortified cities into ruinous heaps. (26)'Therefore their inhabitants were short of strength, They were dismayed and put to shame; They were as the vegetation of the field and as the green herb, As grass on the housetops is scorched before it is grown up. (27)'But I know your sitting down, And your going out and your coming in, And your raging against Me. (28)'Because of your raging against Me, And because your arrogance has come up to My ears, Therefore I will put My hook in your nose, And My bridle in your lips, And I will turn you back by the way which you came.

(29)'Then this shall be the sign for you: you will eat this year what grows of itself, in the second year what springs from the same, and in the third year sow, reap, plant vineyards, and eat their fruit. (30)'The surviving remnant of the house of Judah will again take root downward and bear fruit upward. (31)'For out of Jerusalem will go forth a remnant, and out of Mount Zion survivors. The zeal of YHWH will perform this. (32)'Therefore thus says YHWH concerning the king of Assyria, "He will not come to this city or shoot an arrow there; and he will not come before it with a shield or throw up a siege ramp against it. (33)"By the way that he came, by the same he will return, and he shall not come to this city," ' declares YHWH. (34)'For I will defend this city to save it for My own sake and for My servant David's sake.' " (35)Then it happened that night that the angel of YHWH went out and struck 185,000 in the camp of the Assyrians; and when men rose early in the morning, behold, all of them were dead.

TRANSLATION OF 2 CHRONICLES 31:14–19

(14)וְקוֹרֵ֨א בֶן־יִמְנָ֤ה הַלֵּוִי֙ הַשּׁוֹעֵ֣ר לַמִּזְרָ֔חָה עַ֖ל נִדְב֣וֹת הָאֱלֹהִ֑ים לָתֵת֙ תְּרוּמַ֣ת יְהוָ֔ה וְקָדְשֵׁ֖י הַקֳּדָשִֽׁים׃

(14)And Kore the son of Imnah the Levite, the keeper of the eastern [gate, was] over the freewill offerings of God, to apportion the contributions for YHWH and the most holy things.

(15)וְעַל־יָד֡וֹ עֵ֣דֶן וּ֠מִנְיָמִן וְיֵשׁ֨וּעַ וּֽשְׁמַעְיָ֜הוּ אֲמַרְיָ֣הוּ וּשְׁכַנְיָ֗הוּ בְּעָרֵי֙ הַכֹּ֣הֲנִ֔ים בֶּאֱמוּנָ֖ה לָתֵ֣ת לַאֲחֵיהֶ֑ם בְּמַחְלְק֖וֹת כַּגָּד֥וֹל כַּקָּטָֽן׃ (16)מִלְּבַ֞ד הִתְיַחְשָׂ֣ם לִזְכָרִ֗ים מִבֶּ֨ן שָׁל֤וֹשׁ שָׁנִים֙ וּלְמַ֔עְלָה לְכָל־הַבָּ֣א לְבֵית־יְהוָ֗ה לִדְבַר־י֤וֹם בְּיוֹמוֹ֙ לַעֲב֣וֹדָתָ֔ם בְּמִשְׁמְרוֹתָ֖ם כְּמַחְלְקוֹתֵיהֶֽם׃ (17)וְאֵ֨ת הִתְיַחֵ֤שׂ הַכֹּהֲנִים֙ לְבֵ֣ית אֲבוֹתֵיהֶ֔ם וְהַלְוִיִּ֗ם מִבֶּ֨ן עֶשְׂרִ֤ים שָׁנָה֙ וּלְמָ֔עְלָה בְּמִשְׁמְרוֹתֵיהֶ֖ם בְּמַחְלְקוֹתֵיהֶֽם׃ (18)וּלְהִתְיַחֵ֗שׂ בְּכָל־טַפָּ֧ם נְשֵׁיהֶ֛ם וּבְנֵיהֶ֥ם וּבְנוֹתֵיהֶ֖ם לְכָל־קָהָ֑ל כִּ֥י בֶאֱמוּנָתָ֖ם יִתְקַדְּשׁוּ־קֹֽדֶשׁ׃

(15)Under his authority [were] Eden, Miniamin, Jeshua, Shemaiah, Amariah and Shecaniah in the cities of the priests, to distribute faithfully [the portions] to their brothers by divisions, whether old or young (16)(with the exception of those registered of males from three years old and upward, everyone who entered the house of YHWH for his daily obligations, for their work in their duties according to their divisions): (17)those registered of the priests according to their fathers' households, and [registered of] the Levites from twenty years old and upwards, by their duties [and] by their divisions, (18)along with those registered among all their little children, their wives, their sons and their daughters, for the whole assembly, for in their faithfulness they kept themselves holy.

(19)וְלִבְנֵי֩ אַהֲרֹ֨ן הַכֹּהֲנִ֜ים בִּשְׂדֵ֨י מִגְרַ֤שׁ עָרֵיהֶם֙ בְּכָל־עִ֣יר וָעִ֔יר אֲנָשִׁ֕ים אֲשֶׁ֥ר נִקְּב֖וּ בְּשֵׁמ֑וֹת לָתֵ֣ת מָנ֗וֹת לְכָל־זָכָר֙ בַּכֹּ֣הֲנִ֔ים וּלְכָל־הִתְיַחֵ֖שׂ בַּלְוִיִּֽם׃

(19)Also for the sons of Aaron the priests in the pasture lands of their cities, in each and every [priestly] city, [there were] men who were designated by name to distribute portions to every male among the priests and to everyone registered among the Levites.

BIBLIOGRAPHY

Abba, Raymond. "Priests and Levites in Deuteronomy," *VT* 27/3 (1977) 257–67.

Abel, Félix-Marie. *Géographie de la Palestine* (2 vols.; Paris: Lecoffre, 1933–38).

Aberbach, Moshe. "Hezekiah King of Judah and Rabbi Judah the Patriarch—Messianic Aspects," *Tarbiz* 53/3 (1984) 353–71. [Hebrew, citation below]

Abusch, Tzvi. "The Socio-Religious Framework of the Babylonian Witchcraft Ceremony *Maqlû*: Some Observations on the Introductory Section of the Text, Part 1," in idem (ed.), *Riches Hidden in Secret Places. Ancient Near Eastern Studies in Memory of Thorkild Jacobsen* (Winona Lake, Ind.; Eisenbrauns, 2002) 27–32.

Achenbach, Reinhard. "Jabâ und Atalja: zwei jüdische Königstöchter am assyrischen Königshof? Zu einer These von Stephanie Dalley" *BN* 113 (2002) 29–38.

Ackerman, Susan. *Under Every Green Tree: Popular Religion in Sixth-Century Judah* (Atlanta: Scholars Press, 1992).

Ackroyd, Peter R. "An Interpretation of the Babylonian Exile: A Study of II Kings 20, Isaiah 38–39," *SJT* 27 (1974) 329–52. Reprinted in idem, *Studies in the Religious Tradition of the Old Testament* (London: SCM Press, 1987) 152–71.

———. "Isaiah 36–39: Structure and Function," in W. C. Delsman et al. (eds.), *Von Kanaan bis Kerala: Festschrift für Prof. Mag. Dr. Dr. J. P. M. van der Ploeg O.P. zur Vollendung des siebzigsten Lebensjahres am 4. Juli 1979* (AOAT 211; Neukirchen-Vluyn: Neukirchener Verlag, 1982) 3–21. Reprinted in idem, *Studies in the Religious Tradition of the Old Testament*, 105–20.

———. "The Biblical Interpretation of the Reigns of Ahaz and Hezekiah," in W. B. Barrick and J. R. Spencer (eds.), *In the Shelter of Elyon: Essays on Ancient Palestinian Life and Literature in Honor of G.W. Ahlström* (JSOTSup 31; Sheffield: JSOT Press, 1984) 247–59.

Adamthwaite, Murray R. "Isaiah 7:16: Key to the Immanuel Prophecy," *RTR* 59/2 (2000) 65–83.

Agus, Aharon. *The Binding of Isaac & Messiah: Law, Martyrdom and Deliverance in Early Rabbinic Religiosity* (Albany: State University of New York, 1988) 207–221.

Aharoni, Yohanan. "The Chronology of the Kings of Israel and Judah," *Tarbiz* 21 (1950) 92–100. [Hebrew, citation below]

———. "Arad: Its Inscriptions and Temple," *BA* 31 (1968) 2–32.

———. "The Horned Altar of Beer-sheba," *BA* 37 (1974) 2–6.

———. "Excavations at Tel Beer-sheba, Preliminary Report of the Fifth and Sixth Seasons, 1973–1974," *TA* 2 (1975) 146–68.

———. *Investigations at Lachish: The Sanctuary and the Residency (Lachish V)* (Tel Aviv: Institute of Archaeology, 1975).

———. *The Archaeology of Eretz Israel: From the Prehistoric Beginnings to the End of the First Temple Period* (ed. Miriam Aharoni; trans. Anson F. Rainey; Philadelphia: Westminster, 1978). [Hebrew, citation below]

———. *The Land of the Bible: A Historical Geography* (Philadelphia: Westminster Press, 1979).

Aharoni, Miriam, and Yohanan Aharoni. "The Stratification of Judahite Sites in the 8th and 7th Centuries B.C.E.," *BASOR* 224 (1976) 73–90.

Ahlström, Gösta W. *Royal Administration and National Religion in Ancient Palestine* (SHANE 1; Leiden: E.J. Brill, 1982).

Albertz, Rainer. *A History of Israelite Religion in the Old Testament Period* (2 vols.; trans. J. Bowden; OTL; Louisville: Westminster/John Knox, 1992). Originally published as *Religionsgeschichte Israels in alttestamentlicher Zeit* (Das Alte Testament Deutsch; Göttingen: Vandenhoeck & Ruprecht, 1992).

Albright, William F. "Researches of the School in Western Judaea," *BASOR* 15 (1924) 2–11.
———. "The Administrative Division of Israel and Judah," *JPOS* 5 (1925) 17–54.
———. Review of A. T. Olmstead, *History of Palestine and Syria to the Macedonian Conquest.* *JQR* 24/4 (1934) 363–76.
———. *The Excavation of Tell Beit Mirsim, Vol. III: The Iron Age* (AASOR; New Haven: American Schools of Oriental Research, 1943).
———. "The Chronology of the Divided Monarchy of Israel," *BASOR* 100 (1945) 16–22.
———. "The List of Levitical Cities," in *Louis Ginzberg Jubilee Volume: On the Occasion of His Seventieth Birthday* (New York: American Academy for Jewish Research, 1945) 49–73.
———. "The Judicial Reform of Jehoshaphat," in S. Lieberman (ed.), *Alexander Marx Jubilee Volume on the Occasion of His Seventieth Birthday* (New York: Jewish Theological Seminary of America, 1950) 61–82.
———. "New Light from Egypt on the Chronology and History of Israel and Judah," *BASOR* 130 (1953) 4–11.
———. *The Biblical Period from Abraham to Ezra* (rev. ed.; New York: Harper & Row, 1963).
Alt, Albrecht. "Beiträge zur historischen Geographie und Topographie des Negeb, III: Saruhen, Ziklag, Horma, Gerar," *JPOS* 15 (1935) 294–324. Reprinted in idem, *Kleine Schriften zur Geschichte des Volkes Israel* (3 vols.; Munich: C.H. Beck, 1953–59) 3.409–435.
———. "Jesaja 8, 23–9, 6. Befreiungsmacht und Krönungstag," in W. Baumgartner (ed.), *Festschrift Alfred Bertholet zum 80. Geburtstag gewidmet* (Tübingen: Mohr/Siebeck, 1950) 29–49. Reprinted in idem, *Kleine Schriften zur Geschichte des Volkes Israel,* 2.206–25.
———. "Bemerkungen zu einigen judäischen Ortslisten des Alten Testaments," in idem, *Kleine Schriften zur Geschichte des Volkes Israel,* 2.289–305.
———. "Tiglathpilesers III. erster Feldzug nach Palästina," in idem, *Kleine Schriften zur Geschichte des Volkes Israel,* 2.150–62.
Amiran, Ruth. "The Necropolis of Jerusalem in the Time of the Monarchy," in *Judah and Jerusalem: The Twelfth Archaeological Convention* (Jerusalem: Israel Exploration Society, 1957) 65–72. [Hebrew, citation below]
Andersen, Francis I., and David Noel Freedman. *Micah: A New Translation with Introduction and Commentary* (AYB 24E; New York: Doubleday, 2000).
Anderson, George W. "Some Observations on the Old Testament Doctrine of the Remnant," *TGUOS* 23 (1969–70) 1–10.
Anderson, Joel Edmund. "Isaiah 7:14. Identity and Function within the Bookend Structure of Proto-Isaiah" (Ph.D. diss.; University of Pretoria, 2008).
Ariel, Donald T., and Alon De Groot. "The Iron Age Extramural Occupation at the City of David and Additional Observations on the Siloam Channel," in Donald T. Ariel (ed.), *Excavations at the City of David 1978–1985 Directed by Yigal Shiloh, Vol. V: Extramural Areas* (Qedem 40; Jerusalem: Institute of Archaeology, Hebrew University of Jerusalem, 2000) 155–69.
Ashmore, James Philip. "The Social Setting of the Law in Deuteronomy" (Ph.D. diss.; Duke University, 1995).
Aubin, Henry Trocmé. *The Rescue of Jerusalem: The Alliance between Hebrews and Africans in 701 B.C.* (New York: Soho Press, 2002).
Avigad, Nahman. "New Light on the MSH Seal Impressions," *IEJ* 8 (1958) 115–19.
———. *Discovering Jerusalem: Recent Archaeological Excavations in the Upper City* (Nashville: Thomas Nelson, 1983).
Avigad, Nahman, and Hillel Geva. "Iron Age II Strata 9–7," in Hillel Geva (ed.), *Jewish Quarter Excavations in the Old City of Jerusalem Conducted by Nahman Avigad, 1969–1982, Vol. 1: Architecture and Stratigraphy – Areas A, W and X-2, Final Report* (Jerusalem: Israel Exploration Society, 2000) 44–82.
Avigad, Nahman, and Benjamin Sass. *Corpus of West Semitic Stamp Seals* (Jerusalem: Israel Academy of Sciences & Humanities, 1997).
Baden, Joel S. "Identifying the Original Stratum of P: Theoretical and Practical Considerations," in S. Shectman and J. S. Baden (eds.), *The Strata of the Priestly Writings.*

Contemporary Debate and Future Directions (AThANT 95; Zürich: Theologischer Verlag, 2009) 13–29.

Bae, Hee-Sook. *Vereinte Suche nach JHWH: Die Hiskianische und Josianische Reform in der Chronik* (BZAW 355; Berlin: Walter de Gruyter, 2005).

Bahat, Dan. "Was Jerusalem Really That Large?" in A. Biran and J. Aviram (eds.), *Biblical Archaeology Today, 1990: Proceedings of the Second International Congress on Biblical Archaeology, Jerusalem, June 1990* (Jerusalem: Israel Exploration Society, 1993) 581–84.

Baines, John. "Ancient Egyptian Kingship: Official Forms, Rhetoric, Context," in J. Day (ed.), *King and Messiah in Israel and the Ancient Near East: Proceedings of the Oxford Old Testament Seminar* (JSOTSup 270; Sheffield: Sheffield Academic Press, 1998) 16–53.

Baker, Heather D. "Marduk-apla-iddina," *PNAE* 2/II, 705–11.

Baltzer, Klaus. *Deutero-Isaiah: A Commentary on Isaiah 40–55* (trans. M. Kohl; Hermeneia; Minneapolis: Fortress Press, 2001).

Bar-On, Shimon. "The Festival Calendars in Exodus XXIII 14–19 and XXXIV 13–26," *VT* 48/2 (1998) 161–95.

Barkay, Gabriel. "Jerusalem of the Old Testament Times: New Discoveries and New Approaches," *BAIAS* 5 (1985–86) 33–34, 40–41.

——. "The Iron Age II–III," in A. Ben-Tor (ed.), *The Archaeology of Ancient Israel* (trans. R. Greenberg; New Haven: Yale University Press, 1992) 302–73.

——. "Ramat Rahel," *NEAEHL* 4.1261–67.

——. "Excavations at Ketef Hinnom in Jerusalem," in H. Geva (ed.), *Ancient Jerusalem Revealed* (2nd ed.; Jerusalem: Israel Exploration Society, 2000) 85–105.

——. "Royal Palace, Royal Portrait? The Tantalizing Possibilities of Ramat Rahel," *BAR* 32/5 (Sept.–Oct. 2006) 34–44.

Barker, Margaret. "Hezekiah's Boil," *JSOT* 95 (2001) 31–42.

Barnes, William Hamilton. *Studies in the Chronology of the Divided Monarchy of Israel* (HSM 48; Atlanta: Scholars Press, 1991).

Barnett, Richard D., Erika Bleibtrau and Geoffrey Turner. *Sculptures from the South-West Palace of Sennacherib at Nineveh* (2 vols.; London: British Museum Press, 1998).

Barney, Kevin L. "Enallage in the Book of Mormon," *JBMS* 3/1 (1994) 113–147.

Barton, George A. *Archaeology and the Bible* (Philadelphia: American Sunday-School Union, 1916).

Bartusch, Mark W. *Understanding Dan: An Exegetical Study of a Biblical City, Tribe and Ancestor* (JSOTSup 379; London: Sheffield Academic Press, 2003)

Beaulieu, Paul-Alain. "An Episode in the Fall of Babylon to the Persians," *JNES* 52/4 (1993) 241–61.

Beckerath, Jürgen von. "Ägypten und der Feldzug Sanheribs im Jahre 701 v. Chr.," *UF* 24 (1992) 3–8.

Becking, Bob. *The Fall of Samaria: An Historical and Archaeological Study* (SHCANE 2; Leiden: E.J. Brill, 1992).

——. "Virgin," *DDD* 890–91.

Begg, Christopher T. "The Literary Criticism of Deut 4,1–40: Contributions to a Continuing Discussion," *ETL* 56 (1980) 10–55.

——. "2 Kings 20:12–19 as an Element of the Deuteronomistic History," *CBQ* 48 (1986) 27–38.

——. "The Deuteronomistic Retouching of the Portrait of Hezekiah in 2 Kgs 20,12–19," *BN* 38/39 (1987) 7–13.

——. "'Sennacherib's Second Palestinian Campaign': An Additional Indication," *JBL* 106/4 (1987) 685–86.

Begrich, Joachim. *Die Chronologie der Könige von Israel und Juda und die Quellen des Rahmens der Königsbücher* (BHT 3; Tübingen: J.C.B. Mohr, 1929).

Bekins, Peter. "The Use of the Definite Article for Frame-Based Reference in Biblical Hebrew" (Midwest SBL Regional Paper; Valparaiso, Ind., 13 Feb 2010).

Benzinger, Immanuel. *Die Bücher der Chronik* (Tübingen: J.C.B. Mohr, 1901).

Beuken, Willem A. M. *Jesaja 1–12* (HTKAT; Freiburg: Herder, 2003).

Blenkinsopp, Joseph. *Isaiah 1–39: A New Translation with Introduction and Commentary* (AYB 19; New York: Doubleday, 2000).

——. *Isaiah 55–66: A New Translation with Introduction and Commentary* (AYB 19B; New York: Doubleday, 2003).

Bliss, F. J., and R. A. S. Macalister. *Excavations in Palestine during the Years 1898–1900* (London: Committee of the Palestine Exploration Fund, 1902).

Boling, Robert G. "Levitical Cities: Archaeology and Texts," in A. Kort and S. Morschauser (eds.), *Biblical and Related Studies Presented to Samuel Iwry* (Winona Lake, Ind.: Eisenbrauns, 1985) 23–32.

Borger, Riekele. *Babylonisch-assyrische Lesestücke* (2nd ed.; 3 vols; AnOr 54; Roma: Pontificium Institutum Biblicum, 1979).

Borowski, Oded. "Hezekiah's Reforms and the Revolt Against Assyria," *BA* 58/3 (1995) 148–55.

Braun, Roddy L. "Solomonic Apologetic in Chronicles," *JBL* 92/4 (1973) 503–16.

——. "Solomon, the Chosen Temple Builder: The Significance of 1 Chronicles 22, 28, and 29 for the Theology of Chronicles," *JBL* 95/4 (1976) 581–90.

Brekelmans, C. H. W. *De ḥerem in het Oude Testament* (Nijmegen: Centrale Drukkerij, 1959).

——. "Le ḥerem chez les prophètes du royaume du Nord et dans le Deutéronome," in J. Coppens, A. Descamps and É. Massaux (eds.), *Sacra Pagina. Miscellanea biblica Congressus Internationalis Catholici de re biblica. Actes du Congrès International Catholique des Sciences Bibliques, Bruxelles-Louvain 1958* (2 vols.; BETL 12/13; Gembloux: J. Duculot, 1959) 1.377–83.

Brettler, Marc Zvi. "2 Kings 24:13–14 as History," *CBQ* 53 (1991) 541–52.

——. *The Creation of History in Ancient Israel* (London: Routledge, 1995).

Bright, John. *A History of Israel* (4th ed.; Louisville: Westminster John Knox, 2000).

Brinkman, John A. "Merodach-Baladan II," in *Studies Presented to A. Leo Oppenheim, June 7, 1964* (Chicago, 1964) 6–53.

——. "Sennacherib's Babylonian Problem: An Interpretation," *JCS* 25/2 (1973) 89–95.

——. "Marduk-apla-iddina," RlA 7.374–75.

——. *Prelude to Empire: Babylonian Society and Politics, 747–626 B.C.* (Philadelphia: University Museum, 1984).

Brodsky, Harold. "Bethel," *AYBD* 1.710–12.

Brongers, H. A. "Bemerkungen zum Gebrauch der adverbialen w^e'attāh im Alten Testament," *VT* 15/3 (1965) 289–99.

Broshi, Magen. "The Expansion of Jerusalem in the Reigns of Hezekiah and Manasseh," *IEJ* 24 (1974) 21–26. Reprinted in *Israel Exploration Journal Reader* (2 vols.; New York: Ktav, 1981) 2.880–85, and idem, *Bread, Wine, Walls and Scrolls* (JSPSup 36; London: Sheffield Academic Press, 2001) 174–80.

——. "Estimating the Population of Ancient Jerusalem," in *Bread, Wine, Walls and Scrolls*, 110–20. Originally published as "La population de l'ancienne Jérusalem," *RB* 82 (1975) 5–14.

Broshi, Magen, and Israel Finkelstein. "The Population of Palestine in Iron Age II," *BASOR* 287 (1992) 47–60. Originally published in Hebrew as "The Population of Palestine in 734 BCE," *Cathedra* 58 (1990) 3–24. [Citation below]

Büchler, Adolf. "Zur Geschichte der Tempelmusik und der Tempelpsalmen," *ZAW* 19 (1899) 96–133, 329–44; *ZAW* 20 (1900) 97–135.

Budde, Karl. "Das Immanuelzeichen und die Ahaz-Begegnung Jesaja 7," *JBL* 52 (1933) 22–54.

Budge, E. A. Wallis. *A History of Egypt, from the End of the Neolithic Period to the Death of Cleopatra VII. B.C. 30, Vol. 6: Egypt Under the Priest-Kings and Tanites and Nubians* (BEC 14; London: Kegan Paul, Trench, Trübner & Co., 1902).

Burns, John Barclay. "Why Did the Besieging Army Withdraw (II Reg 3,27)?" *ZAW* 102 (1990) 187–94.

Burrows, Millar. "The Conduit of the Upper Pool," *ZAW* 70 (1958) 221–27.

van den Bussche, Henri. "Le texte de la prophétie de Nathan sur la dynastie davidique (II Sam., VII, I Chron., XVII)," *ETL* 24 (1948) 354–94.

Cahill, Jane M. "Jerusalem at the Time of the United Monarchy: The Archaeological Evidence," in A. G. Vaughn and A. E. Killebrew (eds.), *Jerusalem in Bible and Archaeology: The First Temple Period* (SBLSS 18; Leiden: Brill, 2003) 13–80.

Camp, Ludger. *Hiskija und Hiskijabild: Analyse und Interpretation von 2 Kön 18–20* (MThA 9; Altenberge: Telos, 1990).

Carena, Omar. *Il resto di Israele. Studio Storico-Comparativo delle Inscrizioni Reali Assire e dei Testi Profetici sul Tema del resto* (SRB 13; Bologna: Edizioni Dehoniane, 1985).

Carlson, R. A. "The Anti-Assyrian Character of the Oracle in Is. IX 1–6," *VT* 24/2 (1974) 130–35.

Carr, David M. *Reading the Fractures of Genesis: Historical and Literary Approaches* (Louisville: Westminster John Knox, 1996).

Cazelles, Henri. "587 ou 586?" in C. L. Meyers and M. O'Connor (eds.), *The Word of the Lord Shall Go Forth: Essays in Honor of David Noel Freedman in Celebration of His Sixtieth Birthday* (Winona Lake, Ind.; Eisenbrauns, 1983) 427–35.

Chavel, Simeon. "The Second Passover, Pilgrimage, and the Centralized Cult," *HTR* 102/1 (2009) 1–24.

Chen, Doron, Shlomo Margalit and Bargil Pixner. "Mount Zion: Discovery of Iron Age Fortifications Below the Gate of the Essenes," in H. Geva (ed.), *Ancient Jerusalem Revealed* (2nd ed.; Jerusalem: Israel Exploration Society, 2000) 76–81.

Childs, Brevard S. *Isaiah and the Assyrian Crisis* (SBT II/3; London: SCM Press, 1967).

——. *Isaiah* (OTL; Louisville: Westminster John Knox, 2000).

Christensen, Duane L. *Deuteronomy 1:1–21:9* (WBC 6A; rev. ed.; Nashville: Thomas Nelson, 2001).

Claburn, W. Eugene. "The Fiscal Basis of Josiah's Reforms," *JBL* 92/1 (1973) 11–22.

Clements, Ronald E. *God and Temple: The Idea of the Divine Presence in Ancient Israel* (Philadelphia: Fortress Press, 1965).

——. *Isaiah and the Deliverance of Jerusalem. A Study of the Interpretation of Prophecy in the Old Testament* (JSOTSup 13; Sheffield: JSOT Press, 1980).

——. *Isaiah 1–39* (NCB Commentary; Grand Rapids: Eerdmans, 1980).

——. "The Prophecies of Isaiah and the Fall of Jerusalem in 587 B.C.," *VT* 30/4 (1980) 421–36.

——. "The Isaiah Narrative of 2 Kings 20:12–19 and the Date of the Deuteronomic History," in A. Rofé and Y. Zakovitch (eds.), *Isac Leo Seeligmann Volume. Essays on the Bible and the Ancient World* (3 vols.; Jerusalem: E. Rubinstein, 1983) 3.209–20.

——. "שָׁעַר, šā'ar," *TDOT* 14.272–86.

Clines, David J. A. *Job 1–20* (WBC 17; Dallas: Word Books, 1989).

Clover, R., *The Sabbath and Jubilee Cycle* (2nd ed.; Garden Grove, Calif.: Qadesh La Yahweh Press, 1995).

Cogan, Mordechai. *Imperialism and Religion: Assyria, Judah and Israel in the Eighth and Seventh Centuries B.C.E.* (SBLMS 19; Missoula, Mont.: Scholars Press, 1974). Published under the name Morton Cogan.

——. "Tendentious Chronology in the Book of Chronicles," *Zion* 45 (1980) 165–72. [Hebrew, citation below]

——. "The Chronicler's Use of Chronology as Illuminated by Neo-Assyrian Royal Inscriptions," in J. H. Tigay (ed.), *Empirical Models for Biblical Criticism* (Philadelphia: University of Pennsylvania Press, 1985) 197–209.

——. "Judah under Assyrian Hegemony: A Reexamination of *Imperialism and Religion*," *JBL* 112/3 (1993) 403–414.

——. "Into Exile: From the Assyrian Conquest of Israel to the Fall of Babylon," in Michael D. Coogan (ed.), *The Oxford History of the Biblical World* (New York: Oxford University Press, 1998) 242–75.

——. *I Kings: A New Translation with Introduction and Commentary* (AYB 10; New York: Doubleday, 2000).

——. *The Raging Torrent: Historical Inscriptions from Assyria and Babylonia Relating to Ancient Israel* (Jerusalem: Carta, 2008).

Cogan, Mordechai and Hayim Tadmor. *II Kings: A New Translation with Introduction and Commentary* (AYB 11; New York: Doubleday, 1988).

Coggins, Richard. "What Does 'Deuteronomistic' Mean?" in J. Davies, G. Harvey, and W. G. E. Watson (eds.), *Words Remembered, Texts Renewed: Essays in Honour of John F.A. Sawyer* (JSOTSup 195; Sheffield: Sheffield Academic Press, 1995) 135–48. Reprinted in L. S. Schearing and S. L. McKenzie (eds.), *Those Elusive Deuteronomists: The Phenomenon of Pan-Deuteronomism* (Sheffield: Sheffield Academic Press, 1999) 22–35.

Cohen, Chaim. "Neo-Assyrian Elements in the First Speech of the Biblical *Rab-šāqê*," IOS 9 (1979) 32–48.

Collins, John J. "The Sibylline Oracles," in James H. Charlesworth (ed.), *The Old Testament Pseudepigrapha* (2 vols.; New York: Doubleday, 1983–85) 1.317–472.

——. *Daniel* (Hermeneia; Minneapolis: Fortress, 1993).

——. *The Scepter and the Star: The Messiahs of the Dead Sea Scrolls and Other Ancient Literature* (New York: Doubleday, 1995).

——. "The Sign of Immanuel," in John Day (ed.), *Prophecy and the Prophets in Ancient Israel: Proceedings of the Oxford Old Testament Seminar* (LHB/OTS 531; New York: T&T Clark, 2010) 225–44.

Conrad, Diethelm. "Einige (archäologische) Miszellen zur Kultgeschichte Judas in der Königszeit," in A. H. J. Gunneweg and O. Kaiser (eds.), *Textgemäss: Aufsätze und Beiträge zur Hermeneutik des Alten Testaments. Festschrift für Ernst Würthwein zum 70. Geburtstag* (Göttingen: Vandenhoeck & Ruprecht, 1979) 28–32.

Conrad, Edgar W. "The Royal Narratives and the Structure of the Book of Isaiah," *JSOT* 41 (1988) 67–81.

——. *Reading Isaiah* (OBT; Minneapolis: Fortress Press, 1991).

Coogan, Michael D. "Canaanite Origins and Lineage: Reflections on the Religions of Ancient Israel," in P. D. Miller, P. D. Hanson, and S. D. McBride (eds.), *Ancient Israelite Religion: Essays in Honor of Frank Moore Cross* (Philadelphia: Fortress Press, 1987) 115–24.

Cross, Frank M. "Judean Stamps," *Eretz-Israel* 9 (1969) 20–27*.

——. *Canaanite Myth and Hebrew Epic: Essays in the History of the Religion of Israel* (Cambridge, Mass.: Harvard University Press, 1973).

——. "King Hezekiah's Seal Bears Phoenician Imagery," *BAR* 25/2 (Mar.–Apr. 1999) 42–45, 60.

Dahood, Mitchell. *Psalms III, 101–150: A New Translation with Introduction and Commentary* (AYB 17A; Garden City, N.Y.: Doubleday, 1970).

Dalley, Stephanie. "Nineveh, Babylon and the Hanging Gardens: Cuneiform and Classical Sources Reconciled," *Iraq* 56 (1994) 45–58.

——. "Yabâ, Atalyā and the Foreign Policy of Late Assyrian Kings," *SAAB* 12/2 (1998) 83–98.

——. "More about the Hanging Gardens," in L. Al-Gailani Werr et al. (eds.), *Of Pots and Plans: Papers on the Archaeology and History of Mesopotamia and Syria Presented to David Oates in Honour of his 75th Birthday* (Cambridge: MacDonald Institute, 2002) 67–73.

——. "Recent Evidence from Assyrian Sources for Judaean History from Uzziah to Manasseh," *JSOT* 28/4 (2004) 387–401.

——. "The Identity of the Princesses in Tomb II and a New Analysis of Events in 701 BC," in J. E. Curtis et al. (eds.), *New Light on Nimrud: Proceedings of the Conference on Nimrud 11th–13th March 2002* (London: British School of Archaeology in Iraq, 2008) 171–76.

Damerji, M. S. B., ed. *Gräber assyrischer Königinnen aus Nimrud* (JRGZM 45; Mainz: Verlag des Römisch-Germanischen Zentralmuseums, 1999).

Davies, Philip R. *In Search of 'Ancient Israel'* (JSOTSup 148; Sheffield: Sheffield Academic Press, 1992).

Davies, Philip R. and David M. Gunn, eds. "*A History of Ancient Israel and Judah*: A Discussion of Miller-Hayes (1986)," *JSOT* 39 (1987) 3–63.

Day, John. *Molech. A God of Human Sacrifice in the Old Testament* (UCOP 41; Cambridge: Cambridge University Press, 1989).

——. "The Canaanite Inheritance of the Israelite Monarchy," in idem (ed.), *King and Messiah in Israel and the Ancient Near East: Proceedings of the Oxford Old Testament Seminar* (JSOTSup 270; Sheffield: Sheffield Academic Press, 1998) 72–90.

Day, John, ed. *King and Messiah in Israel and the Ancient Near East: Proceedings of the Oxford Old Testament Seminar* (JSOTSup 270; Sheffield: Sheffield Academic Press, 1998).

Delitzsch, Franz. *Biblical Commentary on the Prophecies of Isaiah, Vol. I* (Edinburgh: T.&T. Clark, 1892).

——. *Jesaja* (5th ed.; TVG; Giessen: Brunnen, 1984). Reprint of the 3rd ed. of Leipzig: Dörflin & Franke, 1879.

Deutsch, Richard R. *Die Hiskiaerzählungen. Eine formgeschichtliche Untersuchung der Texte Js 36–39 und 2R 18–20* (Basel: Basileia, 1969).

Deutsch, Robert. *Messages from the Past: Hebrew Bullae from the Time of Isaiah Through the Destruction of the First Temple* (Tel Aviv: Archaeological Center Publications, 1997) [Hebrew, citation below]. An updated, English translation was published in 1999.

——. "Lasting Impressions: New Bullae Reveal Egyptian-Style Emblems on Judah's Royal Seals," *BAR* 28/4 (Jul.–Aug. 2002) 42–51, 60.

Dever, William G. Review of A. D. Tushingham, *Excavations in Jerusalem 1961–1967, Vol. 1. AJA* 93/4 (1989) 610–12.

——. "Social Structure in Palestine in the Iron II Period on the Eve of Destruction," in T. E. Levy (ed.), *The Archaeology of Society in the Holy Land* (New York: Facts on File, 1995) 416–30.

——. *Did God Have a Wife? Archaeology and Folk Religion in Ancient Israel* (Grand Rapids: Eerdmans, 2005).

Dillard, Raymond B. *2 Chronicles* (WBC 15; Waco, Texas: Word Books, 1987).

Dillman, August. *Die Bücher Exodus und Leviticus* (HAT 12; Leipzig: S. Hirzel, 1880).

Dion, Paul-Eugène. "Sennacherib's Expedition to Palestine," *EgT* 20 (1989) 5–25.

Diringer, David. "On Ancient Hebrew Inscriptions Discovered at Tell Ed-Duweir (Lachish)—II," *PEQ* 73/3 (1941) 89–109, pls. VI–XI.

——. "The Royal Jar-Handle Stamps of Ancient Judah," *BA* 12/4 (1949) 70–86.

Dohmen, Christoph. "עַלְמָה," *TDOT* 11.154–63.

——. "Das Immanuelzeichen. Ein jesajanisches Drohwort und seine inneralttestamentliche Rezeption," *Bib* 68/3 (1987) 305–29.

Donner, Herbert. *Israel unter den Völkern. Die Stellung der klassischen Propheten des 8. Jahrhunderts v. Chr. zur Aussenpolitik der Könige von Israel und Juda* (VTSup 11; Leiden: E. J. Brill, 1964).

——. *Geschichte des Volkes Israel und seiner Nachbarn in Grundzügen* (2 vols.; GAT 4; Göttingen: Vandenhoeck & Ruprecht, 1984–86).

Drews, Robert. "The Babylonian Chronicles and Berossus," *Iraq* 37 (1975) 39–55.

Driver, Godfrey Rolles. "Isaianic Problems," in G. Wiessner (ed.), *Festschrift für Wilhelm Eilers* (Wiesbaden: Otto Harrasowitz, 1967) 43–57.

Driver, Samuel Rolles. *The Book of Exodus* (Cambridge: Cambridge University Press, 1918).

——. *A Treatise on the Use of the Tenses in Hebrew and Some Other Syntactical Questions* (4th ed.; Grand Rapids: Eerdmans, 1998). [First published London Oxford University Press, 1874; 3rd ed. 1892]

Dubovský, Peter. *Hezekiah and the Assyrian Spies: Reconstruction of the Neo-Assyrian Intelligence Services and its Significance for 2 Kings 18–19* (BibOr 49; Rome: Pontifical Biblical Institute, 2006).

Duhm, Bernhard. *Das Buch Jesaia* (5th ed.; Göttingen: Vandenhoeck & Ruprecht, 1968).

Duke, Rodney K. "The Portion of the Levite: Another Reading of Deuteronomy 18:6–8," *JBL* 106/2 (1987) 193–20:.

——. *The Persuasive Appeal of the Chronicler: A Rhetorical Analysis* (JSOTSup 88; Sheffield: Almond Press, 1990).

Edelman, Diana. "Hezekiah's Alleged Cultic Centralization," *JSOT* 32/4 (2008) 395–434.

Edelstein, Gershon, and Ianir Milevski. "The Rural Settlement of Jerusalem Re-evaluated: Surveys and Excavations in the Reph'aim Valley and Mevasseret Yerushalayim," *PEQ* 126 (1994) 2–23.

Eichrodt, Walther. *Der Herr der Geschichte: Jesaja 13–23 und 28–39* (BAT 17,2; Stuttgart: Calwer, 1967).

Eissfeldt, Otto. *Molk als Opferbegriff im Punischen und Hebräischen und das Ende des Gottes Moloch* (Halle: M. Niemeyer, 1935).

——. *Einleitung in das Alte Testament* (3rd ed.; Tübingen: J.C.B. Mohr, 1964). Translated by P. R. Ackroyd as *The Old Testament: An Introduction* (New York: Harper & Row, 1965).

Emerton, J. A. "Some Linguistic and Historical Problems in Isaiah VIII. 23," *JSS* 14 (1969) 151–75.

Engnell, Ivan. *Studies in Divine Kingship in the Ancient Near East* (2nd ed.; Oxford: Blackwell, 1967). First ed. Uppsala: Almqvist & Wiksells, 1943.

Eph'al, Israel. "On Warfare and Military Control in the Ancient Near Eastern Empires: A Research Outline," in H. Tadmor and M. Weinfeld (eds.), *History, Historiography and Interpretation: Studies in Biblical and Cuneiform Literatures* (Jerusalem: Magnes Press, 1983) 88–106.

——. "Ways and Means to Conquer a City, Based on Assyrian Queries to the Sungod," in S. Parpola and R. M. Whiting (eds.), *Assyria 1995: Proceedings of the 10th Anniversary Symposium of the Neo-Assyrian Text Corpus Project, Helsinki, September 7–11, 1995* (Helsinki: Neo-Assyrian Text Corpus Project, 1997) 49–53.

Erlandsson, Seth. "Isaiah 11:10–16 and Its Historical Background," *WLQ* (1974) 94–113. Originally published as "Jesaja 11:10–16 och dess historiska bakgrund," *SEÅ* 36 (1971) 24–44.

Etz, Donald V. "The Genealogical Relationships of Jehoram and Ahaziah, and of Ahaz and Hezekiah, Kings of Judah," *JSOT* 71 (1996) 39–53.

Evans, Carl D. "Judah's Foreign Policy from Hezekiah to Josiah," in C. D. Evans, W. W. Hallo, and J. B. White (eds.), *Scripture in Context: Essays on the Comparative Method* (Pittsburgh: Pickwick Press, 1980) 157–78.

Evans, Paul S. *The Invasion of Sennacherib in the Book of Kings. A Source-Critical and Rhetorical Study of 2 Kings 18–19* (VTSup 125; Leiden: Brill, 2009).

Eynikel, Erik. *The Reform of King Josiah and the Composition of the Deuteronomistic History* (OTS 33; Leiden: E.J. Brill, _1996).

Fabry, Heinz-Josef. "נחשת," *TDOT* 9.370–80.

Fales, Frederick Mario, ed. *Assyrian Royal Inscriptions: New Horizons in Literary, Ideological, and Historical Analysis. Papers of a Symposium held in Cetona (Siena) June 26–28, 1980* (Rome: Istituto per L'Oriente, 1981).

Finkelstein, Israel, and Neil Asher Silberman. *The Bible Unearthed: Archaeology's New Vision of Ancient Israel and the Origin of Its Sacred Texts* (New York: Simon and Schuster, 2001).

——. "Temple and Dynasty: Hezekiah, the Remaking of Judah and the Rise of Pan-Israelite Ideology," *JSOT* 30/3 (2006) 259–85.

Finsterbusch, Karin et al., eds. *Human Sacrifice in Jewish and Christian Tradition* (Numen 112; Leiden: Brill, 2007).

Fishbane, Michael. *Biblical Interpretation in Ancient Israel* (Oxford: Clarendon Press, 1985).

Fohrer, Georg. *Das Buch Jesaja* (3 vols.; ZBK; Zürich: Zwingli, 1960–64).

Forrer, Emilio. *Die Provinzeinteilung des assyrischen Reiches* (Leipzig: J. C. Hinrichs, 1920).

Fowler, Mervyn D. "The Excavation of Tell Beer-sheba and the Biblical Record," *PEQ* 114 (1982) 7–11.

——. "Excavated Incense Burners," *BA* 47 (1984) 183–86.

Fox, Michael V. *Proverbs 1–9: A New Translation with Introduction and Commentary* (AYB 18A; New York: Doubleday, 2000).

Fox, Nili Sacher. *In the Service of the King. Officialdom in Ancient Israel and Judah* (HUCM 23; Cincinatti: Hebrew Union College Press, 2000).

Frahm, Eckart. *Einleitung in die Sanherib-Inschriften* (AfOB 26; Vienna: Institut für Orientalisk der Universität, 1997).

——. "Sīn-aḫḫē-eriba" *PNAE* 3/I, 1113–27.

Freedman, David Noel. "The Babylonian Chronicle," *BA* 19/3 (1956) 49–60.

Fried, Lisbeth S. "The High Places (*Bāmôt*) and the Reforms of Hezekiah and Josiah: An Archaeological Investigation," *JAOS* 122/3 (2002) 437–65.

Friedman, Richard Elliott. *The Exile and Biblical Narrative: The Formation of the Deuteronomistic and Priestly Works* (HSM 22; Chico, Calif.: Scholars Press, 1981).

Fries, Joachim. *«Im Dienst am Hause des Herrn»: Literaturwissenschaftliche Untersuchungen zu 2 Chr 29–31. Zur Hiskijatradition in Chronik* (ATSAT 60; St. Ottilien: EOS-Verlag, 1998).

Fritz, Volkmar. "Where is David's Ziklag?" *BAR* 19/3 (May–Jun. 1993) 58–61, 76.

Fuchs, Andreas. *Die Inschriften Sargons II. aus Khorsabad* (Göttingen: Cuvillier, 1994).

——. *Die Annalen des Jahres 711 v. Chr. nach Prismenfragmenten aus Ninive und Assur* (SAAS 8; Helsinki: Neo-Assyrian Text Corpus Project, 1998).

Fullerton, Kemper. "The Invasion of Sennacherib," *BibSac* 63 (1906) 577–634.

Gadd, C. J. "Inscribed Prisms of Sargon II from Nimrud," *Iraq* 16 (1954) 173–201.

Gadegaard, Niels H. "On the So-Called Burnt Offering Altar in the Old Testament," *PEQ* 110 (1978) 35–45.

Galil, Gershon. "The Babylonian Calendar and the Chronology of the Last Kings of Judah," *Bib* 72 (1991) 367–78. An updated version appears in idem, *Chronology of the Kings of Israel and Judah*, 108–26.

——. "Conflicts between Assyrian Vassals," *SAAB* 6 (1992) 55–63.

——. "Judah and Assyria in the Sargonid Period," *Zion* 57 (1992) 111–33. [Hebrew, citation below]

——. "The Last Years of the Kingdom of Israel and the Fall of Samaria," *CBQ* 57 (1995) 52–65. An updated version appears in idem, *Chronology of the Kings of Israel and Judah*, 83–97.

——. "A New Look at the 'Azekah Inscription'," *RB* 102 (1995) 321–29.

——. *The Chronology of the Kings of Israel and Judah* (SHCANE 9; Leiden: E.J. Brill, 1996).

Gallagher, William R. *Sennacherib's Campaign to Judah: New Studies* (SHCANE 18; Leiden: Brill, 1996).

Gardiner, Alan. *Egypt of the Pharaohs: An Introduction* (Oxford: Clarendon Press, 1961).

Gelb, Ignace J. "Makkan and Meluḫḫa in Early Mesopotamian Sources," *RA* 64 (1970) 1–8.

Gesenius, D. Wilhelm. *Der Prophet Jesaia* (4 vols.; Leipzig, 1820–29).

Geva, Hillel. "Western Jerusalem at the End of the First Temple Period in Light of the Excavations in the Jewish Quarter," in A. G. Vaughn and A. E. Killebrew (eds.), *Jerusalem in Bible and Archaeology: The First Temple Period* (SBLSS 18; Leiden: Brill, 2003) 183–208.

Gibson, Shimon. "Ancient Jerusalem's Rural Landscape," *BAIAS* 3 (1983–84) 30–35.

——. "The 1961–1967 Excavations in the Armenian Garden, Jerusalem," *PEQ* 119 (1987) 81–96.

Gibson, Shimon, and Gershon Edelstein. "Investigating Jerusalem's Rural Landscape," *Levant* 17 (1985) 139–55.

Ginsberg, H. L. "MMŠT and MṢH," *BASOR* 109 (1948) 20–22.

——. "An Unrecognized Allusion to Kings Pekah and Hoshea of Israel," *Eretz-Israel* 5 (1958) 61*–65*.

——. *The Israelian Heritage of Judaism* (New York: Jewish Theological Seminary, 1982).

Gitin, Seymour. "The *lmlk* Jar-Form Redefined: A New Class of Iron Age II Oval-Shaped Storage Jar," in A. M. Maeir and P. de Miroschedji (eds.), *"I Will Speak the Riddles of Ancient*

Times": Archaeological and Historical Studies in Honor of Amihai Mazar on the Occasion of His Sixtieth Birthday (2 vols.; Winona Lake, Ind.: Eisenbrauns, 2006) 2.505–24.

Glassner, Jean-Jacques. *Mesopotamian Chronicles* (SBLWAW 19; Atlanta: Scholars Press, 2004).

Goldberg, Jeremy. "Two Assyrian Campaigns against Hezekiah and Later Eighth Century Biblical Chronology," *Bib* 80/3 (1999) 360–90.

Gomes, Jules Francis. *The Sanctuary of Bethel and the Configuration of Israelite Identity* (BZAW 368; Berlin: Walter de Gruyter, 2006).

Gonçalves, Francolino J. *L'expédition de Sennachérib en Palestine dans la littérature hébraïque ancienne* (Études bibliques, New Series 7; Paris: Librairie Lecoffre, 1986).

Gordis, Robert. *The Book of Job* (New York: Jewish Theological Seminary of America, 1978).

Gordon, Cyrus H. "Almah in Isaiah 7:14," *JBR* 21 (1953) 106.

Grabbe, Lester L. "Introduction," in idem (ed.), *'Like a Bird in a Cage': The Invasion of Sennacherib in 701 BCE* (JSOTSup 363; London: Sheffield Academic Press, 2003) 3–20.

———. "Two Centuries of Sennacherib Study: A Survey," in idem (ed.), *'Like a Bird in a Cage': The Invasion of Sennacherib in 701 BCE*, 20–36.

———. "Of Mice and Dead Men: Herodotus 2.141 and Sennacherib's Campaign in 701 BCE," idem (ed.), *'Like a Bird in a Cage': The Invasion of Sennacherib in 701 BCE*, 119–40.

———. *Ancient Israel: What Do We Know and How Do We Know It?* (London: T&T Clark, 2007).

Grabbe, Lester L., ed. *'Like a Bird in a Cage': The Invasion of Sennacherib in 701 BCE* (JSOTSup 363; London: Sheffield Academic Press, 2003).

———. *Can a 'History of Israel' Be Written?* (JSOTSup 245; Sheffield: Sheffield Academic Press, 1997).

Graf, Karl H. *Die Geschichtlichen Bücher des Alten Testaments* (Leipzig: T.O. Weigel, 1866).

Graham, Matt Patrick. *The Utilization of 1 and 2 Chronicles in the Reconstruction of Israelite History in the Nineteenth Century* (SBLDS 116; Atlanta: Scholars Press, 1990).

Graham, M. Patrick, Kenneth G. Hoglund and Steven L. McKenzie, eds. *The Chronicler as Historian* (JSOTSup 238; Sheffield: Sheffield Academic Press, 1997).

Gray, George Buchanan. *A Critical and Exegetical Commentary on the Book of Isaiah I–XXVII* (ICC; Edinburgh: T.&T. Clark Ltd., 1912).

Gray, John. "The Canaanite God Horon," *JNES* 8/1 (1949) 27–34.

———. *I & II Kings* (2nd ed.; OTL; London: SCM, 1970). First ed. 1964.

Grayson A. Kirk. *Assyrian and Babylonian Chronicles* (TCS 5; Locust Valley, NY: J.J. Augustin, 1975).

———. "Assyria: Tiglath-pileser III to Sargon II (744–705 B.C.)," in J. Boardman et al. (eds.), *The Cambridge Ancient History Second Edition, Volume III Part 2: The Assyrian and Babylonian Empires and other States of the Near East, from the Eighth to the Sixth Centuries B.C.* (Cambridge: Cambridge University Press, 1991) 71–102.

———. "Assyria: Sennacherib and Esarhaddon (704–669 B.C.)," in J. Boardman et al. (eds.), *The Cambridge Ancient History Second Edition, Volume III Part 2*, 103–41.

———. "Assyrian Rule of Conquered Territory in Ancient Western Asia," *CANE* 2.959–68.

Greenberg, Moshe. "Ḥerem," *EncJud* 9.10–13.

Grena, G. M. *Lmlk—A Mystery Belonging to the King, Vol. 1* (Redondo Beach, Cal.: 4000 Years of Writing History, 2004).

Groves, Joseph W. *Actualization and Interpretation in the Old Testament* (SBLDS 86; Atlanta: Scholars Press, 1987).

Haag, Ernst. "Das Immanuelzeichen in Jesaja 7," *TTZ* 100 (1991) 3–22.

Haag, Herbert. "La campagne de Sennachérib contre Jérusalem en 701," *RB* 58 (1951) 348–59.

———. "Das Mazzenfest des Hiskia," in H. Gese and H. P. Rüger (eds.), *Wort und Geschichte. Festschrift für Karl Elliger zum 70. Geburtstag* (AOAT 18; Kevelaer: Butzon & Bercker, 1973) 87–94.

Hackett, Jo Ann, et al. "Defusing Pseudo-Scholarship: The Siloam Inscription Ain't Hasmonean," *BAR* 23 (Mar.–Apr. 1997) 41–50, 68.

Hallo, William W. "Cult Statue and Divine Image: A Preliminary Study," in W. W. Hallo, J. C. Moyer, and L. G. Perdue (eds.), *Scripture in Context II: More Essays on the Comparative Method* (Winona Lake, Ind.: Eisenbrauns, 1993) 1–18.

Halpern, Baruch. "Sacred History and Ideology: Chronicles' Thematic Structure—Indications of an Earlier Source," in R. E. Friedman (ed.), *The Creation of Sacred Literature: Composition and Redaction of the Biblical Text* (UCNES 22; Berkeley: University of California Press, 1981) 35–54. Reprinted in idem, *From Gods to God* (FAT 63; Tübingen: Mohr Siebeck, 2009) 202–227.

——. " 'Brisker Pipes than Poetry': The Development of Israelite Monotheism," in J. A. Neusner, B. A. Levine and E. S. Frerichs (eds.), *Judaic Perspectives on Ancient Israel. Festschrift H. L. Ginsberg* (Philadelphia: Fortress Press, 1987) 77–115. Reprinted in idem, *From Gods to God*, 13–56.

——. *The First Historians: The Hebrew Bible and History* (San Francisco: Harper & Row, 1988).

——. "Jerusalem and the Lineages in the Seventh Century BCE: Kinship and the Rise of Individual Moral Liability," in B. Halpern and D.W. Hobson (eds.), *Law and Ideology in Monarchic Israel* (JSOTSup 124; Sheffield: JSOT Press, 1991) 11–107. Reprinted in idem, *From Gods to God*, 339–424.

Halpern, Baruch, and David S. Vanderhooft. "The Editions of Kings in the 7th–6th Centuries B.C.E." *HUCA* 62 (1991) 179–244.

Hamblin, William James. *Warfare in the Ancient Near East to 1600 B.C.: Holy Warriors at the Dawn of History* (London: Routledge, 2006).

Handy, Lowell K. "Hezekiah's Unlikely Reform," *ZAW* 100/1 (1988) 111–115.

Haran, Menahem. "Behind the Scenes of History: Determining the Date of the Priestly Source," *JBL* 100/3 (1981) 321–33. Originally published in Hebrew in *Zion* 45 (1980) 1–20.

——. *Temples and Temple-Service in Ancient Israel: An Inquiry into Biblical Cult Phenomena and the Historical Setting of the Priestly School* (2nd ed.; Winona Lake, Ind.: Eisenbrauns, 1985).

Hardmeier, Christof. *Prophetie im Streit vor dem Untergang Judas: Erzähl-kommunikative Studien zur Entstehungssituation der Jesaja- und Jeremia-erzählungen in II Reg 18–20 und Jer 37–40* (BZAW 187; Berlin: 1990).

Hasel, Gerhard F. *The Remnant: The History and Theology of the Remnant Idea from Genesis to Isaiah* (AUM 5; Berrien Springs, Mich.: Andrews University, 1972).

——. " 'Remnant' as a Meaning of *'aḥarît*," in L. T. Geraty (ed.), *The Archaeology of Jordan and Other Studies* (Berrien Springs, Mich.: Andrews University Press, 1986) 511–524.

Hayes, John H. "The Tradition of Zion's Inviolability," *JBL* 82/4 (1963) 419–26.

——. "On Reconstructing Israelite History," *JSOT* 39 (1987) 5–9.

Hayes, John H. and Paul K. Hooker. *A New Chronology for the Kings of Israel and Judah and Its Implications for Biblical History and Literature* (Atlanta: John Knox, 1988).

Hayes, John H. and Jeffrey K. Kuan. "The Final Years of Samaria (730–720 BC)," *Bib* 72/2 (1991) 153–81.

Heider, George C. *The Cult of Molek. A Reassessment* (JSOTSup 43; Sheffield: JSOT Press, 1985).

——. "Molech," *DDD* 581–85.

Hendel, Ronald S. "The Date of the Siloam Inscription: A Rejoinder to Rogerson and Davies," *BA* 59/4 (1996) 233–37.

Herbert, A. S. *The Book of the Prophet Isaiah Chapters 1–39* (Cambridge: Cambridge University Press, 1973).

von Herder, Johann Gottfried. *Vom Geist der ebräischen Poesie: Eine Anleitung für die Liebhaber derselben und der ältesten Geschichte des menschlichen Geistes* (3rd ed.; 2 vols.; Leipzig: J. A. Barth, 1825). [English edition *The Spirit of Hebrew Poetry* (2 vols.; trans. James Marsh; Burlington: Edward Smith, 1833).

Herr, Larry G. "The Iron Age II Period: Emerging Nations," *BA* 60/3 (1997) 114–83.

Herrmann, Siegfried. *A History of Israel in Old Testament Times* (2nd ed.; trans. J. Bowden; London: SCM Press, 1981).

Herrmann, Wolfram. *Yariḫ und Nikkal und der Preis der Kuṭarāt-Göttinen, ein kultisch-magischer Text aus Ras Schamra* (BZAW 106; Berlin: A. Töpelmann, 1968).

Herzog, Ze'ev. "The Temple at Arad and Its Parallels," in idem, *Arad: The Arad Fortresses* (Tel Aviv: Hakkibutz Hammeuchad, 1997) 182–209. [Hebrew, citation below]

———. "The Date of the Temple at Arad: Reassessment of the Stratigraphy and the Implications for the History of Religion in Judah," in A. Mazar (ed.), *Studies in the Archaeology of the Iron Age in Israel and Jordan* (JSOTSup 331; Sheffield: Sheffield Academic Press, 2001) 156–78.

———. "The Fortress Mound at Tel Arad: An Interim Report," *TA* 29 (2002) 3–109.

Herzog, Ze'ev, et al. "The Israelite Fortress at Arad," *BASOR* 254 (1984) 1–34.

Herzog, Ze'ev, Anson F. Rainey, and Shmuel Moshkovitz. "The Stratigraphy of Beer-sheba and the Location of the Sanctuary," *BASOR* 225 (1977) 49–58.

Heskett, Randall. *Messianism within the Scriptural Scroll of Isaiah* (LHB/OTS 456; New York: T&T Clark, 2007).

Hess, Richard S. "Issues in the Study of Personal Names in the Hebrew Bible," *CR:BS* 6 (1998) 169–92.

Hestrin, Ruth and Michal Dayagi. "A Seal Impression of a Servant of King Hezekiah," *IEJ* 24 (1974) 27–29.

Hoffmann, Hans D. *Reform und Reformen: Untersuchungen zu einem Grundthema der deuteronomistischen Geschichtsschreibung* (AThANT 66; Zürich: Theologischer Verlag, 1980).

Hoffmann, Yair. "The Deuteronomistic Concept of the Herem," *ZAW* 111/2 (1999) 196–210.

Hoffmeier, James K. "Egypt's Role in the Events of 701 B.C. in Jerusalem," in A. G. Vaughn and A. E. Killebrew (eds.), *Jerusalem in Bible and Archaeology: The First Temple Period* (SBLSS 18; Leiden: Brill, 2003) 219–34.

———. "Egypt's Role in the Events of 701 B.C.: A Rejoinder to J. J. M. Roberts," in *Jerusalem in Bible and Archaeology*, 285–89.

Hoffmeier, James K. and Alan Millard, eds. *The Future of Biblical Archaeology: Reassessing Methodologies and Assumptions. The Proceedings of a Symposium August 12–14, 2001 at Trinity International University* (Grand Rapids: Eerdmans, 2004).

Høgenhaven, Jesper. "On the Structure and Meaning of Isaiah VIII 23B," *VT* 37/2 (1987) 218–21.

———. *Gott und Volk bei Jesaja. Eine Untersuchung zur biblischen Theologie* (Leiden: E.J. Brill, 1988).

Holladay, John S. "Religion in Israel and Judah Under the Monarchy: An Explicitly Archaeological Approach," in P. D. Miller, P. D. Hanson, and S. D. McBride (eds.), *Ancient Israelite Religion: Essays in Honor of Frank Moore Cross* (Philadelphia: Fortress Press, 1987) 249–99.

Holladay, William L. *Jeremiah 2: A Commentary on the Book of the Prophet Jeremiah, Chapters 26–52* (Hermeneia; Minneapolis: Fortress Press, 1989).

Honor, Leo L. *Sennacherib's Invasion of Palestine: A Critical Source Study* (New York: Columbia University Press, 1926).

Hooker, Paul K. "The Kingdom of Hezekiah: Judah in the Geo-political Context of the Late Eighth Century BCE" (Ph.D. diss.; Emory University, 1993).

———. *First and Second Chronicles* (WeBC; Louisville, Kent.: Westminster John Knox, 2001).

Hooker, Paul K. and John H. Hayes. "The Year of Josiah's Death: 609 or 610 BCE?" in J. A. Dearman and M. P. Graham (eds.), *The Land that I Will Show You: Essays on the History and Archaeology of the Ancient Near East in Honour of J. Maxwell Miller* (JSOTSup 343; Sheffield: Sheffield Academic Press, 2001) 96–103.

Horn, Siegfried H. "The Chronology of King Hezekiah's Reign," *AUSS* 2 (1964) 40–52.

———. "Did Sennacherib Campaign Once or Twice against Hezekiah?" *AUSS* 4 (1966) 1–28.

Huesman, John. "The Infinitive Absolute and the *Waw*+Perfect Problem," *Bib* 37 (1956) 410–34.

Hughes, Jeremy. *Secrets of the Times: Myth and History in Biblical Chronology* (JSOTSup 66; Sheffield: Sheffield Academic Press, 1990).

——. "Post-Biblical Features of Biblical Hebrew Vocalization," in S. E. Balentine and J. Barton (eds.), *Language, Theology, and the Bible: Essays in Honour of James Barr* (Oxford: Clarendon Press, 1994) 67–80.

Hunger, Hermann and Stephen A. Kaufman. "A New Akkadian Prophecy Text," *JAOS* 95/3 (1975) 371–75.

Hutter, Manfred. *Hiskija König von Juda: Ein Beitrag zur Judäischen Geschichte in Assyrischer Zeit* (GrTS 6; Graz: Universität Graz, 1982).

Irvine, Stuart A. *Isaiah, Ahaz, and the Syro-Ephraimitic Crisis* (SBLDS 123; Atlanta: Scholars Press, 1990).

Jacobs, Paul and Oded Borowski. "Notes and News: Tell Halif, 1992," *IEJ* 43 (1993) 66–70.

Jacobsen, Thorkild, and Seton Lloyd. *Sennacherib's Aqueduct at Jerwan* (OIP 24; Chicago: University of Chicago Press, 1935).

Jamieson-Drake, David W. *Scribes and Schools in Monarchic Judah: A Socio-Archeological Approach* (JSOTSup 109; Sheffield: Almond Press, 1991).

Japhet, Sara. "The Historical Reliability of Chronicles: The History of the Problem and its Place in Biblical Research," *JSOT* 33 (1985) 83–107. Reprinted in eadem, *From the Rivers of Babylon to the Highlands of Judah. Collected Studies on the Restoration Period* (Winona Lake, Ind.; Eisenbrauns, 2006) 117–36. Originally published in Hebrew, citation below.

——. *I & II Chronicles: A Commentary* (OTL; Louisville: Westminster/John Knox, 1993).

——. *The Ideology of the Book of Chronicles and its Place in Biblical Thought* (BEATAJ 9; 2nd ed.; Frankfurt am Main: Peter Lang, 1997). [First edition published in 1989]

——. "The Concept of the «Remnant» in the Restoration Period. On the Vocabulary of Self-definition," in F.-L. Hossfeld and L. Schwienhorst-Schönberger (eds.), *Das Manna fällt auch heute noch. Beiträge zur Geschichte und Theologie des Alten, Ersten Testaments. Festschrift für Erich Zenger* (HBS 44; Freiburg: Herder, 2004) 340–361.

Jenkins, Allan K. "Hezekiah's Fourteenth Year: A New Interpretation of 2 Kings xviii 13–xix 37," *VT* 26/3 (1976) 284–98.

Johnstone, William. *1 and 2 Chronicles, Volume 2: 2 Chronicles 10–36. Guilt and Atonement* (JSOTSup 254; Sheffield: Sheffield Academic Press, 1997).

Joines, Karen R. "The Bronze Serpent in the Israelite Cult," *JBL* 87/3 (1968) 245–46.

Joosten, Jan. *People and Land in the Holiness Code: An Exegetical Study of the Ideational Framework of the Law in Leviticus 17–26* (VTSup 67; Leiden: E.J. Brill, 1996).

——. "The Disappearance of Iterative WEQATAL in the Biblical Hebrew Verbal System," in S. E. Fassberg and A. Hurvitz (eds.), *Biblical Hebrew in Its Northwest Semitic Setting: Typological and Historical Perspectives* (Jerusalem: Hebrew University Magnes Press, 2006) 135–47.

Kaiser, Otto. *Isaiah 1–12: A Commentary* (2nd ed.; OTL; Philadelphia: Westminster Press, 1983). First English edition 1972. Second edition originally published as *Das Buch des Propheten Jesaja, Kapitel 1–12* (5th ed.; ATD 17; Göttingen: Vandenhoeck and Ruprecht, 1981).

Kalimi, Isaac. *The Reshaping of Ancient Israelite History in Chronicles* (Winona Lake, Ind.: Eisenbrauns, 2005).

Kamil, Ahmed. "Inscriptions on Objects from Yaba's Tomb in Nimrud," in M.S.B. Damerji (ed.), *Gräber assyrischer Königinnen aus Nimrud* (JRGZM 45; Mainz: Verlag des Römisch-Germanischen Zentralmuseums, 1999) 13–18.

Kang, Sa-Moon. *Divine War in the Old Testament and in the Ancient Near East* (BZAW 177; Berlin: Walter de Gruyter, 1989).

Kataja, Laura, and Robert Whiting, eds. *Grants, Decrees and Gifts of the Neo-Assyrian Period* (SAA 12; Helsinki: Helsinki University Press, 1995).

Katz, Hayah. *"A Land of Grain and Wine . . . A Land of Olive Oil and Honey"—The Economy of the Kingdom of Judah* (Jerusalem: Yad Ben-Zvi, 2008). [Hebrew, citation below]

Kaufmann, Yehezkel. *The History of Israelite Religion: From Ancient Times to the End of the Second Temple* (8 vols.; Tel Aviv: Bialik Institute-Dvir, 1937–56). [Hebrew, citation below]

——. *The Biblical Account of the Conquest of Palestine* (Jerusalem: Magnes Press, 1953). [2nd ed. 1985]

Kelly, Brian E. *Retribution and Eschatology in Chronicles* (JSOTSup 211; Sheffield: Sheffield Academic Press, 1996).

Kelm, George L. and Amihai Mazar. "Three Seasons of Excavations at Tell Batash—Biblical Timnah," *BASOR* 248 (1982) 1–36.

Kennicott, Benjaminus. *Vetus Testamentum Hebraicum: cum variis lectionibus* (2 vols.; Oxonii: e typographeo Clarendoniano, 1776–80). [Reprinted New York: Olms-Weidmann, 2003]

Kenyon, Kathleen M. "The Date of the Destruction of Iron Age Beer-sheba," *PEQ* 108 (1979) 63–64.

Kilian, Rudolf. "Der Rest in der Verkündigung Jesajas" in idem, *Jesaja 1–39* (EdF 200; Darmstadt: Wissenschaftliche Buchgesellschaft, 1983) 27–39.

Killebrew, Ann E. "Biblical Jerusalem: An Archaeological Assessment," in A. G. Vaughn and A. E. Killebrew (eds.), *Jerusalem in Bible and Archaeology: The First Temple Period* (SBLSS 18; Leiden: Brill, 2003) 329–45.

King, Philip J., and Lawrence E. Stager. *Life in Biblical Israel* (Louisville: Westminster John Knox, 2001).

Kissane, Edward J. *The Book of Isaiah* (2 vols.; Dublin: Browne & Nolan, 1941–43).

Kitchen, Kenneth A. *Ancient Orient and Old Testament* (Chicago: Inter-Varsity Press, 1966).

——. *Pharaoh Triumphant: The Life and Times of Ramesses II, King of Egypt* (Warminster, England: Aris & Phillips, 1982).

——. "Egypt, the Levant and Assyria in 701 BC," in M. Görg (ed.), *Fontes atque Pontes: Eine Festgabe für Hellmut Brunner* (ÄAT 5; Wiesbaden: Harrassowitz, 1983) 243–53.

——. *The Third Intermediate Period in Egypt (1100–650 B.C.)* (2nd ed.; Warminster, England: Aris & Phillips, 1986).

——. Review of William R. Gallagher, *Sennacherib's Campaign to Judah, New Studies. JSS* 47/1 (2002) 133–36.

——. "Egyptian Interventions in the Levant in Iron Age II," in W. G. Dever and S. Gitin (eds.), *Symbiosis, Symbolism, and the Power of the Past: Canaan, Ancient Israel, and Their Neighbors from the Late Bronze Age through Roman Palaestina* (Winona Lake, Ind.: Eisenbrauns, 2003) 113–32.

——. *On the Reliability of the Old Testament* (Grand Rapids: Eerdmans, 2003).

Kittel, Rudolf. *Geschichte des Volkes Israel, 2. Band: Das Volk in Kanaan* (2nd ed.; Gotha: Friedrich Andreas Perthes, 1909).

Klein G. L. "The 'Prophetic Perfect'," *JNSL* 16 (1990) 45–60.

Kletter, Raz. "Temptation to Identify: Jerusalem, *mmšt*, and the *lmlk* Jar Stamps," *ZDPV* 118 (2002) 136–49.

Kloner, Amos, and David Davis. "A Burial Cave of the Late First Temple Period on the Slope of Mount Zion," in H. Geva (ed.), *Ancient Jerusalem Revealed* (2nd ed.; Jerusalem: Israel Exploration Society, 2000) 107–10.

Knauf, Ernst Axel. "King Solomon's Copper Supply," in E. Lipiński (ed.), *Phoenicia and the Bible: Proceedings of the Conference held at the University of Leuven on the 15th and 16th of March 1990* (OLA 44; Leuven: Peeters, 1991) 167–86.

——. "Hezekiah or Manasseh? A Reconsideration of the Siloam Tunnel and Inscription," *TA* 28 (2001) 281–87.

——. "History, Archaeology, and the Bible," *TZ* 57/2 (2001) 262–68.

——. "Who Destroyed Beersheba II?" in U. Hübner and E. A. Knauf (eds.), *Kein Land für sich allein: Studien zum Kulturkontakt in Kanaan, Israel/Palästina und Ebirnâri für Manfred Weippert zum 65. Geburtstag* (OBO 186; Freiburg: Universitätsverlag, 2002) 181–95.

———. "701: Sennacherib at the Berezina," in L. L. Grabbe (ed.), *Like a Bird in a Cage': The Invasion of Sennacherib in 701 BCE* (JSOTSup 363; London: Sheffield Academic Press, 2003) 141–49.

Knohl, Israel. *The Sanctuary of Silence: The Priestly Torah and the Holiness School* (Minneapolis: Fortress Press, 1995).

Knoppers, Gary N. "History and Historiography: The Royal Reforms," in M. P. Graham, K. G. Hoglund and S. L. McKenzie (eds.), *The Chronicler as Historian* (JSOTSup 238; Sheffield: Sheffield Academic Press, 1997) 178–203.

König, Eduard. *Das Buch Jesaja* (Gütersloh: C. Bertelsmann, 1926).

Konkel, August H. "The Sources of the Story of Hezekiah in the Book of Isaiah," *VT* 43/4 (1993) 462–82.

van der Kooij, Arie. "Das assyrische Heer vor den Mauern Jerusalems im Jahr 701 v. Chr," *ZDPV* 102 (1986) 93–109.

———. "The Story of Hezekiah and Sennacherib (2 Kings 18–19): A Sample of Ancient Historiography," in J. C. de Moor and H. F. van Rooy (eds.), *Past, Present, Future: The Deuteronomistic History and the Prophets* (OTS 44; Leiden: Brill, 2000) 107–19.

Korpel, Marjo Christina Annette. *A Rift in the Clouds: Ugarit and Hebrew Descriptions of the Divine* (UBL 8; Münster: Ugarit-Verlag, 1990).

Kronholm, Tryggve. "Den kommande Hiskia," *SEÅ* 54 (1989) 109–17.

Kuenen, Abraham. *Historisch-kritische Einleitung in die Bücher des alten Testaments, I/1* (Leipzig: Otto Schulze, 1885).

Kuhrt, Amélie. *The Ancient Near East c. 3000–330 BC* (2 vols.; London: Routledge, 1995).

Kwasman, Theodore, and Simo Parpola. *Legal Transactions of the Royal Court of Nineveh, Part I: Tiglath-Pileser through Esarhaddon* (SAA 6; Helsinki: Helsinki University Press, 1991).

Laato, Antti. "New Viewpoints on the Chronology of the Kings of Juda and Israel," *ZAW* 98 (1986) 210–21.

———. *Who Is Immanuel? The Rise and the Foundering of Isaiah's Messianic Expectations* (Åbo: Åbo Academy Press, 1988).

———. *Josiah and David Redivivus: The Historical Josiah and the Messianic Expectations of Exilic and Postexilic Times* (CB 33; Stockholm: Almqvist & Wiksell International, 1992).

———. *A Star is Rising: The Historical Development of the Old Testament Royal Ideology and the Rise of the Jewish Messianic Expectations* (ISFCJ 5; Atlanta: Scholars Press, 1997).

Lambert, Wilfred G. "The Seed of Kingship," in P. Garelli (ed.), *Le Palais et la Royauté, Archéologie et Civilisation* (RAI 19; Paris: P. Geunther, 1974) 427–40.

———. "Kingship in Ancient Mesopotamia," in J. Day (ed.), *King and Messiah in Israel and the Ancient Near East: Proceedings of the Oxford Old Testament Seminar* (JSOTSup 270; Sheffield: Sheffield Academic Press, 1998) 54–70.

Landes, George M. Review of Antti Laato, *Josiah and David Redivivus: The Historical Josiah and the Messianic Expectations of Exilic and Postexilic Times. JBL* 113/3 (1994) 519–21.

Lapp, Paul W. "Late Royal Seals from Judah," *BASOR* 158 (1960) 11–22.

Lasswell, Harold D., Daniel Lerner, and Hans Speier, eds. *Propaganda and Communication in World History, Vol. 1: The Symbolic Instrument in Early Times* (Honolulu: University Press of Hawaii, 1979).

Laurentin, André. "*We'attâh—kai nun*: Formule caractéristique des textes juridiques et liturgiques (à propos de Jean 17,5)," *Bib* 45 (1964) 168–97, 413–32.

Layton, Scott C. *Archaic Features of Canaanite Personal Names in the Hebrew Bible* (HSM 47; Atlanta: Scholars Press, 1990).

Leclant, Jean, and Jean Yoyotte. "Notes d'histoire et de civilisation éthiopiennes: À propos d'un ouvrage récent," *BIFAO* 51 (1952) 1–39.

van Leeuwen, Cornelius. "Sanchérib devant Jérusalem," *OTS* 14 (1965) 245–72.

Lemche, Niels P. "Is it Still Possible to Write a History of Israel?" *SJOT* 8 (1994) 165–90.

Lemche, Niels P., and Thomas L. Thompson. "Did Biran Kill David? The Bible in the Light of Archaeology," *JSOT* 64 (1994) 3–22.

Leprohon, Ronald J. "Royal Ideology and State Administration in Pharaonic Egypt," *CANE* 1.273–87.

Levenson, Jon D. "On the Promise to the Rechabites," *CBQ* 38 (1976) 508–14.

Levey, Samson H. *The Messiah: An Aramaic Interpretation—The Messianic Exegesis of the Targum* (MHUC 2; Cincinnati: Hebrew Union College, 1974).

Levine, Baruch. "Assyrian Ideology and Israelite Monotheism," *Iraq* 67/1 (2005) 411–27.

Levine, Louis D. "Sennacherib's Southern Front: 704–689 B.C.," *JCS* 34/1,2 (1982) 28–58.

——. "Preliminary Remarks on the Historical Inscriptions of Sennacherib," in H. Tadmor and M. Weinfeld (eds.) *History, Historiography, and Interpretation: Studies in Biblical and Cuneiform Literatures* (Jerusalem: Magnes Press, 1983) 58–75.

Lewy, Julius. *Forschungen zur alten Geschichte Vorderasiens* (MVAG 29/2; Leipzig: J. C. Hinrichs, 1925).

——. "Sanherib und Hizkia," *OLZ* 31 (1928) 150–63.

Licht, Jacob. "Biblical Historicism," in H. Tadmor and M. Weinfeld (eds.), *History, Historiography and Interpretation: Studies in Biblical and Cuneiform Literatures* (Jerusalem: Magnes Press, 1983) 107–20.

Lie, Arthur G. *The Inscriptions of Sargon II, King of Assryia. Part 1: The Annals* (Paris: Librairie orientaliste Paul Geuthner, 1929).

Lilley, J. P. U. "Understanding the Ḥerem," *TynBul* 44/1 (1993) 169–77.

Lipschits, Oded, Omer Sergi and Ido Koch. "Royal Judahite Jar Handles: Reconsidering the Chronology of the *lmlk* Stamp Impressions," *TA* 37/1 (2010) 3–32.

Littman, Enno. *Über die Abfassungszeit des Tritojesaia* (Freiburg: J.C.B. Mohr, 1899).

Liverani, Mario. "Kitru, Katāru," *Mesopotamia* 17 (1982) 43–66.

Liwak, Rüdiger. "Die Rettung Jerusalems im Jahr 701 v. Chr," *ZTK* 83 (1986) 137–66.

Lloyd, Alan B. *Herodotus Book II* (3 vols.; EPRO 43; Leiden: E. J. Brill, 1975–88).

Lohfink, Norbert F. "Die Bundesurkunde des Königs Josias," *Bib* 44 (1963) 261–88.

——. "חָרַם," *TDOT* 5.180–99.

——. "Was There a Deuteronomistic Movement?" in L. S. Schearing and S. L. McKenzie (eds.), *Those Elusive Deuteronomists: The Phenomenon of Pan-Deuteronomism* (JSOTSup 268; Sheffield: Sheffield Academic Press, 1999) 36–66.

Long, Burke O. "On Finding the Hidden Premises," *JSOT* 39 (1987) 10–14.

——. *2 Kings* (FOTL 10; Grand Rapids: Eerdmans, 1991).

Long, V. Philips, ed. *Israel's Past in Present Research: Essays on Ancient Israelite Historiography* (SBTS 7; Winona Lake, Ind.: Eisenbrauns, 1999).

Lowery, Richard H. *The Reforming Kings: Cults and Society in First Temple Judah* (JSOTSup 120; Sheffield: JSOT Press, 1991).

Lubetski, Meir. "King Hezekiah's Seal Revisited," *BAR* 27/4 (Jul.–Aug. 2001) 44–51, 59.

Luckenbill, Daniel David. *The Annals of Sennacherib* (OIP 2; Chicago: University of Chicago, 1924).

Lundbom, Jack R. *Jeremiah 21–36: A New Translation with Introduction and Commentary* (AYB 21B; New York: Doubleday, 2004).

——. *Jeremiah 37–52: A New Translation with Introduction and Commentary* (AYB 21C; New York: Doubleday, 2004).

Maag, Victor. "Erwägungen zur deuteronomischen Kultzentralisation," *VT* 6/1 (1956) 10–18.

Macadam, M. F. Laming. *The Temples of Kawa: Oxford University Excavations in Nubia* (2 vols.; London: Oxford University Press, 1949).

Machinist, Peter. "Assyria and Its Image in the First Isaiah," *JAOS* 103/4 (1983) 719–37.

——. "Palestine, Administration of (Assyrian and Babylonian Administration)," *AYBD* 5.69–81.

——. "The *rab šāqēh* at the Wall of Jerusalem: Israelite Identity in the Face of the Assyrian 'Other'," *HS* 41 (2000) 151–168.

Macy, Howard Ray. "The Sources of the Books of Chronicles: A Reassessment" (Ph.D. diss.; Harvard University, 1975).

Magonet, Jonathan. "Jonah, Book of," *AYBD* 3.936–42.

Malul, Meir. "Taboo," *DDD* 824–27.

Marcus, Ralph. *Josephus, Jewish Antiquities: Books IX–XI* (LCL; Cambridge, Mass: Harvard University Press, 1958).

Mariottini, Claudemiro Francisco. "The Problem of Social Oppression in the Eighth Century Prophets" (Ph.D. diss., The Southern Baptist Theological Seminary, 1983).

Marti, Karl. *Das Buch Jesaja* (KHC; Tübingen: J.C.B. Mohr, 1900).

Martin, W. J. "'Dischronologized' Narrative in the Old Testament," in *Congress Volume, Rome 1968* (VTSup 17; Leiden: E.J. Brill, 1969) 179–86.

Mason, Rex. *Preaching the Tradition: Homily and Hermeneutics after the Exile* (Cambridge: Cambridge University Press, 1990).

Massmann, Ludwig. "Sanheribs Politik in Juda. Beobachtungen und Erwägungen zum Ausgang der Konfrontation Hiskias mit den Assyrern," in U. Hübner and E. A. Knauf (eds.), *Kein Land für sich allein: Studien zum Kulturkontakt in Kanaan, Israel/Palästina und Ebirnâri für Manfred Weippert zum 65. Geburtstag* (OBO 186; Freiburg: Universitätsverlag, 2002) 167–80.

Mathews, Claire R. "Apportioning Desolation: Contexts for Interpreting Edom's Fate and Function in Isaiah," in E. H. Lovering, Jr. (ed.), *Society of Biblical Literature Seminar Papers, 1995* (Atlanta: Scholars Press, 1995) 250–66.

———. *Defending Zion: Edom's Desolation and Jacob's Restoration (Isaiah 34–35) in Context* (BZAW 236; Berlin: de Gruyter, 1995).

Mattingly, Gerald L. "An Archaeological Analysis of Sargon's 712 Campaign against Ashdod," *NEASB* 17 (1981) 47–64.

Mayer, Walter. *Politik und Kriegskunst der Assyrer* (ALASP 9; Münster: Ugarit-Verlag, 1995).

———. "Sennacherib's Campaign of 701 BCE: The Assyrian View," in L. L. Grabbe (ed.), *'Like a Bird in a Cage': The Invasion of Sennacherib in 701 BCE* (JSOTSup 363; London: Sheffield Academic Press, 2003) 168–200.

Mayes, A. D. H. *Deuteronomy* (NCB; London: Oliphants, 1979).

Mazar, Amihai. "The Spade and the Text: The Interaction between Archaeology and Israelite History Relating to the Tenth-Ninth Centuries BCE," in H. G. M. Williamson (ed.), *Understanding the History of Ancient Israel* (PBA 143; Oxford: Oxford University Press, 2007) 143–71.

Mazar, Amihai, David Amit, and Zvi Ilan. "The 'Border Road' between Michmash and Jericho and the Excavations at Ḥorvat Shilḥah," *Eretz-Israel* 17 (1984) 236–50, pls. 21–24. [Hebrew, citation below]

Mazar, Benjamin. "The Cities of the Territory of Dan," *IEJ* 10 (1960) 65–77.

———. "The Cities of the Priests and the Levites," in *Congress Volume. Oxford 1959* (VTSup 7; Leiden: E.J. Brill, 1960) 193–205.

———. "Jerusalem," *EncBib* 3.791–837.

Mazor, Lea. "Myth, History, and Utopia in the Prophecy of the Shoot (Isaiah 10:33–11:9)," in C. Cohen, A. Hurvitz and S. M. Paul (eds.), *Sefer Moshe: The Moshe Weinfeld Jubilee Volume* (Winona Lake, Ind.: Eisenbrauns, 2004) 73–90.

McBride, S. Dean. "The Deuteronomic Name Theology," (Ph.D. diss.; Harvard University, 1969).

McCarter Jr., P. Kyle. *I Samuel: A New Translation with Introduction and Commentary* (AYB 8; Garden City, N.Y.: Doubleday, 1980).

———. *II Samuel: A New Translation with Introduction and Commentary* (AYB 9; Garden City, N.Y.: Doubleday, 1984).

McCurdy, James Frederick. *History, Prophecy and the Monuments or Israel and the Nations* (3 vols.; London: Macmillan Company, 1894–1901).

McFall, Leslie. *Enigma of the Hebrew Verbal System: Solutions from Ewald to the Present Day* (Sheffield: Almond Press, 1982).

———. "Did Thiele Overlook Hezekiah's Coregency?" *BibSac* 146 (1989) 393–404.

———. "Some Missing Coregencies in Thiele's Chronology," *AUSS* 30/1 (1992) 35–58.

McKay, John W. *Religion in Judah under the Assyrians 732–609 BC* (SBT 2/26; London: SCM Press, 1973).

McKenzie, Steven L. *The Chronicler's Use of the Deuteronomistic History* (HSM 33; Atlanta: Scholars Press, 1985).

———. *The Trouble With Kings: The Composition of the Book of Kings in the Deuteronomistic History* (VTSup 42; Leiden: E.J. Brill, 1991).

———. Review of Marvin A. Sweeney, *King Josiah of Judah: The Lost Messiah of Israel. RBL* 02/2003.

Melugin, Roy F. *The Formation of Isaiah 40–55* (BZAW 141; Berlin: W. de Gruyter, 1976).

Melville, Sarah C. "Neo-Assyrian Royal Women and Male Identity: Status as a Social Tool," *JAOS* 124/1 (2004) 37–57.

Mettinger, Tryggve N. D. *The Dethronement of Sabaoth: Studies in the Shem and Kabod Theologies* (CB 18; Lund: CWK Gleerup, 1982).

Meyer, Lester V. "Remnant," *AYBD* 5.669–71.

Milgrom, Jacob. "Hezekiah's Sacrifices at the Dedication Services of the Purified Temple (2 Chr 29:21–24)," in A. Kort and S. Morschauser (eds.), *Biblical and Related Studies Presented to Samuel Iwry* (Winona Lake, Ind.: Eisenbrauns, 1985) 159–61.

———. *Numbers: The Traditional Hebrew Text with the New JPS Translation* (JPS Commentary; Philadelphia: Jewish Publication Society, 1989).

———. "Does H Advocate the Centralization of Worship?" *JSOT* 88 (2000) 59–76.

———. *Leviticus 17–22: A New Translation with Introduction and Commentary* (AYB 3A; New York: Doubleday, 2000).

Millard, Alan R. "The Old Testament and History: Some Considerations," *FT* 110/1,2 (1983) 34–53.

———. "Sennacherib's Attack on Hezekiah," *TynBul* 36 (1985) 61–77.

———. *The Eponyms of the Assyrian Empire 910–612 B.C.* (SAAS 2; Helsinki: Neo-Assyrian Text Corpus Project, 1994).

Miller, J. Maxwell, and John H. Hayes. *A History of Ancient Israel and Judah* (2nd edition; Louisville: Westminster John Knox, 2006).

Miller, Patrick D. "Meter, Parallelism, and Tropes: The Search for Poetic Style," *JSOT* 28 (1984) 99–106.

———. *The Religion of Ancient Israel* (London: SPCK, 2000).

Mommsen, Hans, Isadore Perlman and Joseph Yellin. "The Provenience of the *lmlk* Jars," *IEJ* 34 (1984) 89–113.

Montgomery, James A. *A Critical and Exegetical Commentary on the Books of Kings* (ICC; New York: Charles Scribner's Sons, 1951).

Moore, Carey A. *Daniel, Esther and Jeremiah: The Additions* (AYB 44; Garden City, N.Y.: Doubleday, 1977).

Morgenstern, Julian. "The Three Calendars of Ancient Israel," *HUCA* 1 (1924) 13–78.

Moriarty, Frederick L. "The Chronicler's Account of Hezekiah's Reform," *CBQ* 27 (1965) 399–406.

Mosca, Paul G. "Child Sacrifice in Canaanite and Israelite Religion: A Study in Mulk and מלך" (Ph.D. diss.; Harvard University, 1975).

Mosis, Rudolf. *Untersuchungen zur Theologie des chronistischen Geschichtswerkes* (FTS 92; Freiburg: Herder, 1973).

Mowinckel, Sigmund. *He That Cometh. The Messiah Concept in the Old Testament and Later Judaism* (trans. G. W. Anderson; Oxford: Basil Blackwell, 1956). Reprint Grand Rapids: Eerdmans, 2005.

Le Moyne, Jean. "Les deux ambassades de Sennachérib à Jérusalem: Recherches sur l'évolution d'une tradition," in *Mélanges bibliques rédigés en l'honneur d'André Robert* (Paris: Bloud & Gay, 1957) 149–53.

Mulder, M. J. "Was war die am Tempel gebaute 'Sabbathalle' in II Kön. 16, 18?" in W. C. Delsman et al. (eds.), *Von Kanaan bis Kerala: Festschrift für Prof. Mag. Dr. Dr. J. P. M.*

van der Ploeg O.P. zur Vollendung des siebzigsten Lebensjahres am 4. Jui 1979 (AOAT 211; Neukirchen: Neukirchen-Vluyn, 1982) 161–72.

Müller, Hans-Peter. "מֹלֶךְ *mólek*," *TDOT* 8.375–88.

Na'aman, Nadav. "Sennacherib's 'Letter to God' on his Campaign to Judah," *BASOR* 214 (1974) 25–39.

———. "Sennacherib's Campaign to Judah and the Date of the *lmlk* Stamps," *VT* 29/1 (1979) 61–86.

———. "The Brook of Egypt and Assyrian Policy on the Border of Egypt," *TA* 6 /1–2 (1979) 68–90.

———. "The Inheritance of the Sons of Simeon," *ZDPV* 96 (1980) 136–52.

———. "Historical and Chronological Notes on the Kingdoms of Israel and Judah in the Eighth Century B.C.," *VT* 36/1 (1986) 71–92. Reprinted in idem, *Ancient Israel's History and Historiography: The First Temple Period. Collected Essays, Volume 3* (Winona Lake, Ind.: Eisenbrauns, 2006) 236–255.

———. "Hezekiah's Fortified Cities and the *LMLK* Stamps," *BASOR* 261 (1986) 5–21. Reprinted in idem, *Ancient Israel and Its Neighbors: Interaction and Counteraction. Collected Essays, Volume 1* (Winona Lake, Ind.: Eisenbrauns, 2005) 153–78.

———. *Borders and Districts in Biblical Historiography: Seven Studies in Biblical Geographical Lists* (JBS 4; Jerusalem: Simor, 1986).

———. "The Historical Background to the Conquest of Samaria (720 B.C.)," *Bib* 71/2 (1990) 206–25.

———. "The Kingdom of Judah under Josiah," *TA* 18 (1991) 3–71. Reprinted in idem, *Ancient Israel and Its Neighbors: Interaction and Communication. Collected Essays, Volume 1,* 329–98.

———. "Ahaz's and Hezekiah's Policy Toward Assyria in the Days of Sargon II and Sennacherib's Early Years," *Zion* 59/1 (1994) 5–30. [Hebrew, citation below]

———. "Hezekiah and the Kings of Assyria," *TA* 21 (1994) 235–54. Reprinted in idem, *Ancient Israel and Its Neighbors: Interaction and Communication. Collected Essays, Volume 1,* 98–117.

———. "The Historical Portion of Sargon II's Nimrud Inscription," *SAAB* 8/1 (1994) 17–20.

———. "The Debated Historicity of Hezekiah's Reform in the Light of Historical and Archaeological Research" *ZAW* 107 (1995) 179–95. Reprinted in idem, *Ancient Israel's History and Historiography: The First Temple Period. Collected Essays, Volume 3,* 274–90.

———. "The Contribution of the Amarna Letters to the Debate on Jerusalem's Political Position in the Tenth Century B.C.E.," *BASOR* 304 (1996) 17–27. Reprinted in idem, *Ancient Israel's History and Historiography: The First Temple Period. Collected Essays, Volume 3,* 1–17.

———. "No Anthropomorphic Graven Image: Notes on the Assumed Anthropomorphic Cult Statues in the Temples of YHWH in the Pre-Exilic Period," *UF* 31 (1999) 391–415. Reprinted in idem, *Ancient Israel's History and Historiography: The First Temple Period. Collected Essays, Volume 3,* 311–338.

———. "The Abandonment of Cult Places in the Kingdoms of Israel and Judah as Acts of Cult Reform," *UF* 34 (2002) 585–602.

———. "Updating the Messages: Hezekiah's Second Prophetic Story (2 Kings 19.9b-35) and the Community of Babylonian Deportees," in L. L. Grabbe (ed.), *'Like a Bird in a Cage': The Invasion of Sennacherib in 701 BCE* (JSOTSup 363; London: Sheffield Academic Press, 2003) 201–20.

———. "When and How Did Jerusalem Become a Great City? The Rise of Jerusalem as Judah's Premier City in the Eighth-Seventh Centuries B.C.E." *BASOR* 347 (2007) 21–56.

———. "The Growth and Development of Judah and Jerusalem in the Eighth Century B.C.E.: A Rejoinder," *RB* 116 (2009) 321–35.

Nakhai, Beth Alpert. *Archaeology and the Religions of Canaan and Israel* (ASOR Books 7; Boston: ASOR, 2001).

Nakanose, Shigeyuki. *Josiah's Passover: Sociology and the Liberating Bible* (The Bible & Liberation Series; Maryknoll, N.Y.: Orbis, 1993).

Naveh, Joseph. "Khirbet al-Muqanna'—Eqron: An Archaeological Survey," *IEJ* 8 (1958) 87–100, 165–70.

Nelson, Richard D. *The Double Redaction of the Deuteronomistic History* (JSOTSup 18; Sheffield: JSOT Press, 1981).

———. "*ḥerem* and the Deuteronomic Social Conscience," in M. Vervenne and J. Lust (eds.), *Deuteronomy and Deuteronomic Literature. Festschrift C.H.W. Brekelmans* (BETL 133; Leuven: Leuven University Press, 1997) 39–54.

———. *Joshua: A Commentary* (OTL; Louisville: Westminster John Knox, 1997).

———. *Deuteronomy: A Commentary* (OTL; Louisville: Westminster John Knox, 2002).

Neusner, Jacob. *A Life of Rabban Yohanan ben Zakkai, ca. 1–80 C.E.* (Leiden: E.J. Brill, 1962).

Newman, Judith H. *Praying by the Book: The Scripturalization of Prayer in Second Temple Judaism* (SBLEJL 14; Atlanta: Scholars Press, 1999).

Newsome Jr., James D. "Toward a New Understanding of the Chronicler and His Purposes," *JBL* 94/2 (1975) 201–17.

Nicholson, Ernest W. "The Centralisation of the Cult in Deuteronomy," *VT* 13/4 (1963) 380–89.

———. "Current 'Revisionism' and the Literature of the Old Testament," in J. Day (ed.), *In Search of Pre-exilic Israel. Proceedings of the Oxford Old Testament Seminar* (JSOTSup 406; London: T&T Clark, 2004) 1–22.

Niditch, Susan. *Chaos to Cosmos: Studies in Biblical Patterns of Creation* (Chico, Calif.: Scholars Press, 1985).

Nielsen, Kjeld. *Incense in Ancient Israel* (VTSup 38; Leiden: E.J. Brill, 1986).

Nielsen, Kirsten. *There is Hope for a Tree: The Tree as Metaphor in Isaiah* (JSOTSup 65; Sheffield: JSOT Press, 1989).

Noble, Paul R. "The Remnant in Amos 3–6: A Prophetic Paradox," *HBT* 19/2 (1997) 122–147.

Norin, Stig. "An Important Kennicott Reading in 2 Kings xviii 13," *VT* 32/3 (1982) 337–38.

———. "The Age of the Siloam Inscription and Hezekiah's Tunnel," *VT* 48/1 (1998) 37–48.

North, Robert. "Does Archaeology Prove Chronicles' Sources?" in H. N. Bream, R. D. Heim, and C. A. Moore (eds.), *A Light Unto My Path: Old Testament Studies in Honor of Jacob M. Myers* (GTS 4; Philadelphia: Temple University Press, 1974) 375–401.

Noth, Martin. *Überlieferungsgeschichtliche Studien* (Halle: M. Niemeyer, 1943).

———. *Das Buch Josua* (2nd ed.; HAT I/7; Tübingen: J.C.B. Mohr, 1953).

———. *The History of Israel* (2nd ed.; London: Adam & Charles Black, 1960).

O'Brien, Mark A. *The Deuteronomistic History Hypothesis: A Reassessment* (OBO 92; Freiburg: Universitätsverlag, 1989).

Ockinga, Boyo G. "Hiskias 'Prahlerei.' Ein Beitrag zur Interpretation von 2 Könige 20, 12–19/ Jesaja 39, 1–8," in M. Görg (ed.), *Fontes atque Pontes: Eine Festgabe für Hellmut Brunner* (ÄAT 5; Wiesbaden: O. Harrassowitz, 1983) 342–46.

———. "The Inviolability of Zion—A Pre-Israelite Tradition?" *BN* 44 (1988) 54–60.

Oded, Bustenay. *Mass Deportations and Deportees in the Neo-Assyrian Empire* (Wiesbaden: Reichert, 1979).

Oestreicher, Theodor. *Das deuteronomische Grundgesetz* (BFCT 27/4; Gütersloh: C. Bertelsmann, 1923).

Ofer, Avi. "'All the Hill Country of Judah': From a Settlement Fringe to a Prosperous Monarchy," in I. Finkelstein and N. Na'aman (eds.), *From Nomadism to Monarchy: Archaeological and Historical Aspects of Early Israel* (Jerusalem: Yad Izhak Ben-Zvi, 1994) 92–121.

Ollenburger, Ben C. *Zion the City of the Great King: A Theological Symbol of the Jerusalem Cult* (JSOTSup 41; Sheffield: JSOT Press, 1987).

Olley, John W. "'Trust in the 'Lord': Hezekiah, Kings, and Isaiah," *TynBul* 50/1 (1999) 59–77.

Olmstead, A. T. E. *Assyrian Historiography: A Source Study* (Columbia, Mo.: University of Missouri, 1916).

———. *History of Assyria* (New York: C. Scribner's Sons, 1923).

———. *History of Palestine and Syria to the Macedonian Conquest* (New York: C. Scribner's Sons, 1931).

Olyan, Saul. *Asherah and the Cult of Yahweh in Israel* (SBLMS 34; Atlanta: Scholars Press, 1988).

Parker, Barbara. "Administrative Tablets from the North-West Palace, Nimrud," *Iraq* 23/1 (1961) 15–67.

Parker, Richard A. "The Length of the Reign of Amasis and the Beginning of the Twenty-Sixth Dynasty," *MDAIK* 15 (1957) 208–12.

Parker, Richard A. and Waldo H. Dubberstein. *Babylonian Chronology: 626 B.C.–A.D. 75* (Providence: Brown University Press, 1956). Previously published as *Babylonian Chronology: 626 B.C.–A.D. 45* (2nd ed.; SAOC 24; Chicago: University of Chicago Press, 1946).

Parker, Simon B. "The Birth Announcement," in L. Eslinger and G. Taylor (eds.), *Ascribe to the Lord: Biblical and Other Studies in Memory of Peter C. Craigie* (JSOTSup 67; Sheffield: JSOT Press, 1988) 133–49.

Parpola, Simo. *Neo-Assyrian Toponyms* (AOAT 6; Kevelaer: Butzon & Bercker, 1970).

———. *The Correspondence of Sargon II, Part I: Letters from Assyria and the West* (SAA 1; Helsinki: University of Helsinki Press, 1987).

———. "The Assyrian Tree of Life: Tracing the Origins of Jewish Monotheism and Greek Philosophy," *JNES* 52/3 (1993) 161–208.

Parrot, André. *Nineveh and the Old Testament* (2nd ed.; SBA 3; trans. B E. Hooke; New York: Philosophical Library, 1955).

Paul, Shalom M. *Studies in the Book of the Covenant in the Light of Cuneiform and Biblical Law* (VTSup 18; Leiden: E. J. Brill, 1970).

———. "Adoption Formulae: A Study of Cuneiform and Biblical Legal Clauses," *Maarav* 2/2 (1979–80) 173–85. Reprinted in *Divrei Shalom. Collected Studies of Shalom M. Paul on the Bible and the Ancient Near East, 1967–2005* (Leiden: Brill, 2005) 109–19.

———. *Amos* (Hermeneia; Minneapolis: Fortress Press, 1991).

Payne, J. Barton. "Right Questions About Isaiah 7:14," in M. Inch and R. Youngblood (eds.), *The Living and Active Word of God. Studies in Honor of Samuel L. Schultz* (Winona Lake, Ind.: Eisenbrauns, 1983) 75–84.

Pečírková, Jana. "The Administrative Methods of Assyrian Imperialism," *ArOr* 55 (1987) 162–75.

Peltonen, Kai. *History Debated: The Historical Reliability of Chronicles in Pre-Critical and Critical Research* (2 vols.; PFES 64; Helsinki: Finish Exegetical Society, 1996).

Perlitt, Lothar. *Bundestheologie im Alten Testament* (Neukirchen-Vluyn: Neukirchener Verlag, 1969).

Person, Raymond E. *The Kings-Isaiah and Kings-Jeremiah Recensions* (BZAW 252; Berlin: W. de Gruyter, 1997).

Petersen, David L. *Late Israelite Prophecy: Studies in Deutero-Prophetic Literature and in Chronicles* (Missoula, Mont.: Scholars Press, 1977).

Peterson, John L. "A Topographical Surface Survey of the Levitical 'Cities' of Joshua 21 and 1 Chronicles 6: Studies on the Levites in Israelite Life and Religion" (Th.D. diss.; Chicago Institute of Advanced Theological Studies and Seabury-Western Theological Seminary, 1977).

Petrie, William M. Flinders. *A History of Egypt From the XIXth to the XXXth Dynasties* (London: Methuen & Co., 1905).

Phillips, Anthony. *Ancient Israel's Criminal Law: A New Approach to the Decalogue* (Oxford: Basil Blackwell, 1970).

———. "A Fresh Look at the Sinai Pericope," *VT* 34 (1984) 39–52 (Part 1, Issue 1), 282–94 (Part 2, Issue 3). Reprinted in idem, *Essays on Biblical Law* (JSOTSup 344; Sheffield: Sheffield Academic Press, 2002) 25–48.

Pfaff, Heide-Marie. *Die Entwicklung des Restgedankens in Jesaja 1–39* (EHS 561; Frankfurt am Main: Peter Lang, 1996).

Plöger, Otto. "Reden und Gebete im deuteronomistischen und chronistischen Geschichtswerk," in W. Schneemelcher (ed.), *Festschrift für Günther Dehn zum 75. Geburtstag am*

18. April 1957 (Neukirchen: Kreis Moers, 1957) 35–49. Reprinted in idem, *Aus der Spätzeit des Alten Testaments: Studien. Zu seinem 60. Geburtstag am 27.11.1970* (Göttingen: Vandenhoeck & Ruprecht, 1971) 50–66.

Porter, Barbara N. *Images, Power, and Politics: Figurative Aspects of Esarhaddon's Babylonian Policy* (Philadelphia: American Philosophical Society, 1993).

Preuss, Horst D. *Deuteronomium* (EdF 164; Darmstadt: Wissenschaftliche Buchgesellschaft, 1982).

Priese, Karl-Heinz. "The Kingdom of Kush: The Napatan Period," in S. Wenig (ed.), *Africa in Antiquity: The Arts of Ancient Nubia and the Sudan* (2 vols.; Brooklyn: Brooklyn Museum, 1978) 75–88.

Propp, William H. C. *Exodus 1–18: A New Translation with Introduction and Commentary* (AYB 2; New York: Doubleday, 1998).

———. *Exodus 19–40: A New Translation with Introduction and Commentary* (AYB 2A; New York: Doubleday, 2006).

Provan, Iain W. *Hezekiah and the Books of Kings: A Contribution to the Debate about the Composition of the Deuteronomistic History* (BZAW 172; Berlin: Walter de Gruyter, 1988).

Provan, Iain, V. Philips Long, and Tremper Longman III. *A Biblical History of Israel* (Louisville: Westminster John Knox, 2003).

von Rad, Gerhard. "Das judäische Königsritual," *TLZ* 72 (1947) 211–16. Translated into English as "The Royal Ritual in Judah," in idem, *The Problem of the Hexateuch and Other Essays*, 222–31.

———. *Studies in Deuteronomy* (SBT 9; London: SCM Press, 1953).

———. "The Deuteronomic Theology of History in I and II Kings," in idem (ed.), *The Problem of the Hexateuch and Other Essays* (trans. E. W. Trueman Dicken; Edinburgh: Oliver & Boyd, 1966) 205–21.

Radner, Karen. "Atalia," *PNAE* 1/II, 433.

Rainey, Anson F. "Taharqa and Syntax," *TA* 3 (1976) 38–41.

———. "Beer-Sheva Excavator Blasts Yadin—No Bama at Beer-Sheva," *BAR* 3/3 (Sept. 1977) 18–21, 56.

———. "Wine from the Royal Vineyards," *BASOR* 245 (1982) 57–62.

———. "Hezekiah's Reform and the Altars at Beer-sheba and Arad," M. D. Coogan, J. C. Exum, and L. E. Stager (eds.), *Scripture and Other Artifacts: Essays on the Bible and Archaeology in Honor of Philip J. King* (Louisville: Westminster John Knox, 1994) 333–54.

———. "The Chronicler and his Sources—Historical and Geographical," in M. P. Graham, K. G. Hoglund and S. L. McKenzie (eds.), *The Chronicler as Historian* (JSOTSup 238; Sheffield: Sheffield Academic Press, 1997) 30–72.

Rawlinson, George. *The Five Great Monarchies of the Ancient Eastern World* (4 vols.; London: John Murray, 1864).

Rawlinson, Henry C. *A Commentary on the Cuneiform Inscriptions of Babylonia and Assyria* (London: John W. Parker, 1850).

Reade, Julian. "Ideology and Propaganda in Assyrian Art," in M. T. Larsen (ed.), *Power and Propaganda: A Symposium on Ancient Empires* (Mesopotamia 7; Copenhagen: Akademisk Forlag, 1979) 329–43.

Redford, Donald B. *Egypt, Canaan, and Israel in Ancient Times* (Princeton: Princeton University Press, 1992).

Rehm, Martin. *Der königliche Messias im Licht der Immanuel-Weissagungen des Buches Jesaja* (Kevelaer: Butzon & Bercker, 1968).

Reich, Ronny. "The Ancient Burial Ground in the Mamilla Neighborhood, Jerusalem," in H. Geva (ed.), *Ancient Jerusalem Revealed* (2nd ed.; Jerusalem: Israel Exploration Society, 2000) 111–18.

Reich, Ronny, and Eli Shukron. "Light at the End of the Tunnel," *BAR* 25/1 (Jan.–Feb. 1999) 22–33, 72.

———. "The System of Rock-Cut Tunnels near Gihon in Jerusalem Reconsidered," *RB* 107/1 (2000) 5–17.

——. "The Urban Development of Jerusalem in the Late Eighth Century B.C.E.," in A. G. Vaughn and A. E. Killebrew (eds.), *Jerusalem in Bible and Archaeology: The First Temple Period* (SBLSS 18; Leiden: Brill, 2003) 209–18.

——. "On the Original Length of Hezekiah's Tunnel: Some Critical Notes on David Ussishkin's Suggestions," in in A. M. Maeir and P. de Miroschedji (eds.), *"I Will Speak The Riddles Of Ancient Times" Archaeological and Historical Studies in Honor of Amihai Mazar on the Occasion of his Sixtieth Birthday* (Winona Lake, Ind.: Eisenbrauns, 2006) 2.795–800.

——. "A Fragmentary Palaeo-Hebrew Inscription from the City of David, Jerusalem," *IEJ* 58/1 (2008) 48–50.

Rendtorff, Rolf. "Israels 'Rest'. Unabgeschlossene Überlegungen zu einem schwierigen Thema der alttestamentlichen Theologie,", in A. Graupner, H. Delkurt, and A. B. Ernst (eds.), *Verbindungslinien. Festschrift für Werner H. Schmidt zum 65. Geburtstag* (Neukirchen-Vluyn: Neukirchener Verlag, 2000) 265–279.

Reviv, Hanoch. "The History of Judah from Hezekiah to Josiah," in A. Malamat (ed.), *The World History of the Jewish People. The Age of the Monarchies: Political History, Vol. 4/1* (Jerusalem: Massada Press, 1979) 193–204.

Rey, Charles Fernand. *In the Country of the Blue Nile* (London: Duckworth, 1927). Reprinted New York: Negro Universities Press, 1969.

Richter, Sandra L. *The Deuteronomistic History and the Name Theology: ľšakkēn šᵉmô šām in the Bible and the Ancient Near East* (BZAW 318; Berlin: Walter de Gruyter, 2002).

Rignell, L. G. "Das Immanuelszeichen. Einige Gesichtspunkte zu Jes. 7," *StTh* 11/1 (1957) 99–119.

Ringgren, Helmer. *The Messiah in the Old Testament* (SBT 18; London: SCM Press, 1961).

——. "אָב," *TDOT* 1.1–19.

——. "מָעַל," *TDOT* 8.460–63.

Roberts, J. J. M. "Isaiah and His Children," in A. Kort and S. Morschauser (eds.), *Biblical and Related Studies Presented to Samuel Iwry* (Winona Lake, Ind.: Eisenbrauns, 1985) 193–203.

——. "The Translation of Isa 11.10," in M. Mori, H. Ogawa, and M. Yoshikawa (eds.), *Near Eastern Studies Dedicated to H. I H. Prince Takahito Mikasa on the Occasion of His Seventy-fifth Birthday* (BMECCJ 5; Wiesbaden: Harrassowitz, 1991) 363–70.

——. "Whose Child is This? Reflections on the Speaking Voice in Isaiah 9:5," *HTR* 90/2 (1997) 115–29. Reprinted in idem, *The Bible and the Ancient Near East: Collected Essays* (Winona Lake, Ind.: Eisenbrauns, 2002) 143–56.

——. "The Davidic Origin of the Zion Tradition," *JBL* 92 (1973) 329–44. Reprinted in idem, *Bible and the Ancient Near East: Collected Essays*, 313–30.

——. "Zion in the Theology of the Davidic-Solomonic Empire," in T. Ishida (ed.), *Studies in the Period of David and Solomon and Other Essays. Papers Read at the International Symposium, Tokyo, 5–7 December, 1979* (Winona Lake, Ind.: Eisenbrauns, 1982) 93–108. Reprinted in idem, *Bible and the Ancient Near East: Collected Essays*, 331–47.

——. "Egypt, Assyria, Isaiah, and the Ashdod Affair: An Alternative Proposal," in A. G. Vaughn and A. E. Killebrew (eds.), *Jerusalem in Bible and Archaeology: The First Temple Period* (SBLSS 18; Leiden: Brill, 2003) 265–83.

——. "Critical Reflections on The Book Called Isaiah with Particular Attention to the Second Exodus Theme (Isa 11:11–16)" (SBL Paper; Boston, Mass. 22–25 November, 2008).

Robinson, Edward. *Biblical Researches in Palestine and the Adjacent Regions. A Journal of Travels in the Years 1838 & 1852* (2nd ed.; 3 vols.; London: John Murray, 1856). Originally published as *Biblical Researches in Palestine, Mount Sinai and Arabia Petraea: A Journal of Travels in the Year 1838* (3 vols.; Boston: Crocker & Brewster, 1841).

Robinson, Theodore H. and W. O. E. Oesterley. *A History of Israel* (2 vols.; Oxford: Clarendon Press, 1932).

Rofé, Alexander. "Israelite Belief in Angels in the Pre-exilic Period as Evidenced by Biblical Traditions" (Ph.D. diss.; Jerusalem: Hebrew University, 1969). [Hebrew]

Rogerson, John, and Philip R. Davies. "Was the Siloam Tunnel Built by Hezekiah?" *BA* 59 (1996) 138–49.

Rogland, Max. *Alleged Non-Past Uses of* Qatal *in Classical Hebrew* (Assen: Royal Van Gorcum, 2003).

Römer, Thomas C. "The Book of Deuteronomy," in S. L. McKenzie and M. P. Graham (eds.), *The History of Israel's Traditions: The Heritage of Martin Noth* (JSOTSup 182; Sheffield: JSOT Press, 1994) 178–212.

Römer, Thomas C. and Albert de Pury. "Deuteronomistic Historiography (DH): History of Research and Debated Issues," in A. de Pury, T. C. Römer, and J.-D. Macchi (eds.), *Israel Constructs Its History: Deuteronomistic History in Recent Research* (JSOTSup 306; Sheffield: JSOT Press, 2000) 24–141.

Rooke, Deborah W. "Kingship as Priesthood: The Relationship between the High Priesthood and the Monarchy," in J. Day (ed.), *King and Messiah in Israel and the Ancient Near East: Proceedings of the Oxford Old Testament Seminar* (JSOTSup 270; Sheffield: Sheffield Academic Press, 1998) 187–208.

Rosenbaum, Jonathan. "Hezekiah's Reform and the Deuteronomistic Tradition," *HTR* 72.1/2 (1979) 23–43.

Rosenberg, Stephen. "The Siloam Tunnel Revisited," *TA* 25 (1998) 116–30.

Rost, Paul, ed. *Die Keilschrifttexte Tiglat-Pilesers III nach den Papierabklatschen und Originalen des Britischen Museums* (2 vols., Leipzig: E. Pfeiffer, 1893).

Rowley, Harold H. "Zadok and Nehushtan," *JBL* 58/2 (1939) 113–41.

——. "Hezekiah's Reform and Rebellion," *BJRL* 44/2 (1962) 395–431. Reprinted in idem, *Men of God: Studies in Old Testament History and Prophecy* (London: Thomas Nelson, 1963) 98–132.

Rudman, Dominic. "Is the Rabshakeh also among the Prophets? A Rhetorical Study of 2 Kings XVIII 17–35," *VT* 50/1 (2000) 100–10.

Rudolph, Wilhelm. "Sanherib in Palästina," *PJ* 25 (1929) 59–80.

——. *Chronikbücher* (HAT 21; Tübingen: J.C.B. Mohr, 1955).

——. *Joel, Amos, Obadja, Jona* (KAT 13/2; Gütersloh: Gerd Mohn, 1971).

van Ruiten, J. T. A. G. M. "The Intertextual Relationship between Isaiah 65,25 and Isaiah 11,6–9," in F. G. Martínez, A. Hilhorst, and C. J. Labuschagne (eds.), *The Scriptures and the Scrolls: Studies in Honour of A. S. van der Woude on the Occasion of His 65th Birthday* (VTSup 49; Leiden: Brill, 1992) 31–42.

Ruprecht, Eberhard. "Die ursprüngliche Komposition der Hiskia-Jesaja-Erzählungen und ihre Umstrukturierung durch den Verfasser des deuteronomistischen Geschichtswerkes," *ZTK* 87 (1990) 33–66.

Russell, John Malcolm. *The Writing on the Wall: Studies in the Architectural Context of Late Assyrian Palace Inscriptions* (MC 9; Winona Lake, Ind.: Eisenbrauns, 1999).

Saggs, H. W. F., "Historical Texts and Fragments of Sargon II of Assyria. 1: The 'Aššur Charter,'" *Iraq* 37/1 (1975) 11–20, pl. ix.

——. *The Nimrud Letters, 1952* (CTN 5; London: British School of Archaeology in Iraq, 2001).

Sayce, A. H. "The Ancient Hebrew Inscription Discovered at the Pool of Siloam in Jerusalem," *PEFQS* (1881) 141–54.

Schmid, Hans. *Der sogenannte Jahwist* (Zürich: Theologischer Verlag, 1976).

Schniedewind, William M. "The Problem with Kings: Recent Study of the Deuteronomistic History," *RSR* 22/1 (1996) 22–27.

——. "Prophets and Prophecy in the Books of Chronicles," in M. P. Graham, K. G. Hoglund and S. L. McKenzie (eds.), *The Chronicler as Historian* (JSOTSup 238; Sheffield: Sheffield Academic Press, 1997) 204–24.

——. "Jerusalem, the Late Judaean Monarchy, and the Composition of the Biblical Texts," in A. G. Vaughn and A. E. Killebrew (eds.), *Jerusalem in Bible and Archaeology: The First Temple Period* (SBLSS 18; Leiden: Brill, 2003) 375–93.

——. *How the Bible Became a Book: The Textualization of Ancient Israel* (Cambridge: Cambridge University Press, 2004).

Schrader, Eberhard. *Cuneiform Inscriptions and the Old Testament* (2 vols.; trans. O. C. Whitehouse; London: Williams and Norgate, 1885–88).

Schultz, Michael, and Manfred Kunter. "Erste Ergebnisse der anthropologischen und paläopathologischen Untersuchungen an den menschlichen Skelettfunden aus den neuassyrischen Königinnengräbern von Nimrud," in M.S.B. Damerji (ed.), *Gräber assyrischer Königinnen aus Nimrud* (JRGZM 45; Mainz: Verlag des Römisch-Germanischen Zentralmuseums, 1999) 85–128.

Schwartz, Baruch J. "Torah from Zion: Isaiah's Temple Vision (Isaiah 2:1–4)," in A. Houtman, M.J.H.M. Poorthuis, and J. Schwartz (eds.), *Sanctity of Time and Space in Tradition and Modernity* (Leiden: Brill, 1998) 11–26.

——. *The Holiness Legislation: Studies in the Priestly Code* (Jerusalem: Magnes Press, 1999). [Hebrew, citation below]

Scurlock, JoAnn. "Neo-Assyrian Battle Tactics," in G. D. Young et al. (eds.), *Crossing Boundaries and Linking Horizons: Studies in Honor of Michael C. Astour on His Eightieth Birthday* (Bethesda: CDL, 1997) 491–517.

Segal, Judah B. *The Hebrew Passover from the Earliest Times to A.D. 70* (London: Oxford University Press, 1963).

Seitz, Christopher R. *Zion's Final Destiny: The Development of the Book of Isaiah. A Reassessment of Isaiah 36–39* (Minneapolis: Fortress Press, 1991).

——. Review of Christof Hardmeier, *Prophetie im Streit vor dem Untergang Judas: Erzählkommunikative Studien zur Entstehungssituation der Jesaja- und Jeremia-erzählungen in II Reg 18–20 und Jer 37–40*. *JBL* 110 (1991) 511–13.

——. "First Isaiah," *AYBD* 3.472–88.

Sellin, Ernst. *Introduction to the Old Testament* (trans. W. Mortgomery; London: Hodder & Stoughton, 1923). Originally published as *Einleitung in das Alte Testament* (Leipzig: Quelle & Meyer, 1910).

Van Seters, John. *Abraham in History and Tradition* (New Haven: Yale University Press, 1975).

——. Review of Marvin A. Sweeney, *King Josiah of Judah: The Lost Messiah of Israel*. *JAOS* 122/1 (2002) 118–19.

Seux, Marie Joseph. *Épithètes royales akkadiennes et sumériennes* (Paris: Letouzey & Ané, 1967).

Shai, Itzhack and Aren M. Maeir. "The Pre-*LMLK* Jars: A New Class of Iron Age IIA Storage Jars," *TA* 30 (2003) 108–23.

Shanks, Hershel. "Yigael Yadin Finds a Bama at Beer-Sheva," *BAR* 3/1 (Mar. 1977) 3–12.

——. "The Mystery Nechushtan," *BAR* 33/2 (Mar.–Apr. 2007) 58–63.

Shaver, Judson R. "Torah and the Chronicler's History Work" (Ph.D. diss.; University of Notre Dame, 1983). Published as *Torah and the Chronicler's History Work: An Inquiry into the Chronicler's References to Laws, Festivals, and Cultic Institutions in Relationship to Pentateuchal Legislation* (BJS 196; Atlanta: Scholars Press, 1989).

Shea, William H. "Sennacherib's Second Palestinian Campaign," *JBL* 104/3 (1985) 401–18.

——. "Jerusalem under Siege: Did Sennacherib Attack Twice?" *BAR* 25/6 (Nov.–Dec. 1999) 36–44, 64.

Shiloh, Yigal. "The Population of Iron Age Palestine in the Light of a Sample Analysis of Urban Plans, Areas, and Population Density," *BASOR* 239 (1980) 25–35.

——. *Excavations at the City of David I* (Qedem 19; Jerusalem: Institute of Archaeology, 1984).

——. "Judah and Jerusalem in the Eighth-Sixth Centuries B C.E.," in S. Gitin and W. G. Dever (eds.), *Recent Excavations in Israel: Studies in Iron Age Archaeology* (AASOR 49; Winona Lake, Ind.: Eisenbrauns, 1989) 97–105.

Simons, Jan. *Jerusalem in the Old Testament: Researches and Theories* (Leiden: E.J. Brill, 1952).

Skinner, John. *The Book of the Prophet Isaiah Chapters I–XXXIX* (2nd ed.; Cambridge: Cambridge University Press, 1915). First ed. 1896.

Smelik, Klaas A. D. "Distortion of Old Testament Prophecy: The Purpose of Isaiah xxxvi and xxxvii," in *Crises and Perspectives: Studies in Ancient Near Eastern Polytheism, Biblical Theology, Palestinian Archaeology and Intertestamental Literature* (OTS 24; Leiden: E.J. Brill, 1986) 70–93.

———. "King Hezekiah Advocates True Prophecy. Remarks on Isaiah xxxvi and xxxvii//II Kings xviii and xix," in idem, *Converting the Past. Studies in Ancient Israelite and Moabite Historiography* (OTS 28; Leiden: E.J. Brill, 1992) 93–128.

———. "Moloch, Molekh, or Molk-Sacrifice? A Reassessment of the Evidence concerning the Hebrew Term Molekh," *SJOT* 9 (1995) 133–42.

Smith, George. *History of Assurbanipal* (London: Williams and Norgate, 1871).

———. *History of Sennacherib* (London: Williams and Norgate, 1878).

Smith, George Adam. *Jerusalem, the Topography, Economics and History from the Earliest Times to A.D. 70* (2 vols.; London: Hodder and Stoughton, 1908).

Smith, Mark S. "Ugaritic Studies and Israelite Religion: A Retrospective View," *NEA* 65/1 (2002) 17–29.

———. *The Early History of God: Yahweh and the Other Deities in Ancient Israel* (2nd ed.; Grand Rapids: Eerdmans, 2002). First ed. 1990.

Smith, J. Payne, ed. *Compendious Syriac Dictionary. Founded Upon the Thesaurus Syriacus of R. Payne Smith* (Oxford: Oxford University Press, 1903).

Smith, Sidney. "Sennacherib and Esarhaddon," in J. B. Bury, S. A. Cook, and F. E. Adcock (eds.), *The Cambridge Ancient History, Vol III: The Assyrian Empire* (1st ed.; Cambridge: Cambridge University Press, 1925) 61–87.

von Soden, Wolfram. "Sanherib vor Jerusalem 701 v. Chr.," in H.-P. Müller, *Bibel und Alter Orient. Altorientalische Beiträge zum Alten Testament von Wolfram von Soden* (BZAW 162; Berlin: Walter de Gruyter, 1985) 149–57. Originally published in R. Stiehl and G. A. Lehmann (eds.), *Antike und Universalgeschichte. Festschrift Hans Erich Stier zum 70. Geburtstag am 25. Mai 1972* (FCSup 1; Münster: Aschendorff, 1972) 43–51.

Sokoloff, Michael. *A Syriac Lexicon: A Translation from the Latin, Correction, Expansion, and Update of C. Brockelmann's Lexicon Syriacum* (Winona Lake, Ind.: Eisenbrauns, 2009).

Sommer, Benjamin D. "Dating Pentateuchal Texts and the Perils of Pseudo-Historicism," in T. B. Dozeman, K. Schmid and B. J. Schwartz (eds.), *The Pentateuch: International Perspectives on Current Research* (FAT 78; Tübingen: Mohr Siebeck, 2011) 85–108.

de Sousa, Rodrigo F. *Eschatology and Messianism in LXX Isaiah 1–12* (LHB/OTS 516; New York: T&T Clark, 2010).

Spalinger, Anthony J. "The Year 712 B.C. and Its Implications for Egyptian History," *JARCE* 10 (1973) 95–101.

———. "The Foreign Policy of Egypt Preceding the Assyrian Conquest," *CdÉ* 53 (1978) 22–47.

Spencer, John R. "The Levitical Cities: A Study of the Role and Function of the Levites in the History of Israel" (Ph.D. diss.; University of Chicago, 1980).

———. "Levitical Cities," *AYBD* 4.310–11.

Spieckermann, Hermann. *Juda unter Assur in der Sargonidenzeit* (Göttingen: Vandenhoeck & Ruprecht, 1982).

Spiegelberg, Wilhelm. *Die Glaubwürdigkeit von Herodots Bericht über Ägypten im Lichte der ägyptischen Denkmäler* (Heidelberg: C. Winter, 1926).

Stackert, Jeffrey. *Rewriting the Torah: Literary Revision in Deuteronomy and the Holiness Legislation* (FAT 52; Tübingen: Mohr Siebeck, 2007).

Stade, Bernhard. "Miscellen. 16. Anmerkungen zu 2 Kö. 15–21," *ZAW* 6 (1886) 156–89.

Stade, Bernhard, and Friedrich Schwally. *The Book of Kings* (SBOT; Leipzig: J.C. Hinrichs, 1904).

Stager, Lawrence E. "The Archaeology of the Family in Ancient Israel," *BASOR* 260 (1985) 1–35.

Stamm, Johann Jakob. *Die Akkadische Namengebung* (MVAG 44; Leipzig: J.C. Hinrichs, 1939).

Starkey, James L. "Excavations at Tell Ed Duweir," *PEQ* 69 (1937) 228–41.

Stavrakopoulou, Francesca. *King Manasseh and Child Sacrifice: Biblical Distortions of His-torical Realities* (BZAW 338; Berlin: Walter de Gruyter, 2004).

Steiner, Margreet. "The Archaeology of Ancient Jerusalem," *CR:BS* 6 (1998) 143–68.

Stern, Ephraim. "Limestone Incense Altars," in Y. Aharoni (ed.), *Beer-Sheba I: Excavations at Tel Beer-Sheba, 1969–1971 Seasons* (Givatayim-Ramat Gan: Peli Printing Works Ltd., 1973) 52–53, pls. 29, 52.

——. *Archaeology of the Land of the Bible, Vol. 2: The Assyrian, Babylonian, and Persian Periods (732–332 B.C.E.)* (New York: Doubleday, 2001).

Stern, Philip D. *The Biblical ḥerem: A Window on Israel's Religious Experience* (BJS 211; Atlanta: Scholars Press, 1991).

Stromberg, Jacob. "The 'Root of Jesse' in Isaiah 11:10: Postexilic Judah, or Postexilic Davidic King?" *JBL* 127/4 (2008) 655–69.

Swanson, Kristin A. "Hezekiah's Reform and the Bronze Serpent" (Ph.D. diss.; Vanderbilt University, 1999).

——. "A Reassessment of Hezekiah's Reform in Light of Jar Handles and Iconographic Evidence," *CBQ* 64 (2002) 460–69.

Sweeney, Marvin A. "Sargon's Threat against Jerusalem in Isaiah 10,27–32," *Bib* 75/4 (1994) 457–70.

——. *Isaiah 1–39 with an Introduction to Prophetic Literature* (FOTL 16; Grand Rapids: Eerd-mans, 1996).

——. "Jesse's New Shoot in Isaiah 11: A Josianic Reading of the Prophet Isaiah," in R. D. Weis and D. M. Carr (eds.), *A Gift of God in Due Season. Essays on Scripture and Community in Honor of James A. Sanders* (JSOTSup 225; Sheffield Sheffield Academic Press, 1996) 103–118.

——. "Micah's Debate with Isaiah," *JSOT* 93 (2001) 111–24.

——. *King Josiah of Judah: The Lost Messiah of Israel* (Oxford: Oxford University Press, 2001).

Tadmor, Hayim. "Chronology of the Last Kings of Judah," *JNES* 15/2 (1956) 226–30.

——. "The Campaigns of Sargon II of Assur: A Chronological-Historical Study," *JCS* 12 (1958) 22–40 (Issue 1), 77–100 (Issue 3).

——. "The Sin of Sargon," *Eretz-Israel* 5 (1958) 150–63. [Hebrew, citation below]

——. "Hezekiah," *EncBib* 3.95–99. [Hebrew]

——. "Chronology," *EncBib* 4.245–310. [Hebrew]

——. "The Inscriptions of Nabunaid: Historical Arrangement," in H. G. Güterbock and T. Jacobsen (eds.), *Studies in Honor of Benno Landsberger on his Seventy-Fifth Birthday* (AS 16; Chicago: Oriental Institute of the University of Chicago, 1965) 351–63.

——. "Philistia under Assyrian Rule," *BA* 29/3 (1966) 86–102.

——. "Judah from the Fall of Samaria to the Fall of Jerusalem," in H. H. Ben-Sasson (ed.), *A History of the Jewish People* (Cambridge, Mass.: Harvard University Press, 1976) 139–58.

——. "The Chronology of the First Temple Period: A Presentation and Evaluation of the Sources," in A. Malamat (ed.), *The World History of the Jewish People, First Series: Ancient Times. The Age of the Monarchies: Political History, Vol. 4/1* (Jerusalem: Massada Press, 1979) 44–60, 318–20.

——. "Treaty and Oath in the Ancient Near East: A Historian's Approach," in G. M. Tucker and D. A. Knight (eds.), *Humanizing America's Iconic Book: Society of Biblical Literature Centennial Addresses 1980* (Chico, Calif.: Scholars Press, 1982) 125–52.

——. "Autobiographical Apology in the Royal Assyrian Literature," in H. Tadmor and M. Weinfeld (eds.), *History, Historiography and Interpretation: Studies in Biblical and Cuneiform Literatures* (Jerusalem: Magnes Press, 1983) 36–57.

——. "Rab-sārîs or Rab-shakeh in 2 Kings 18," in C. L. Meyers and M. O'Connor (eds.), *The Word of the Lord Shall Go Forth: Essays in Honor of David Noel Freedman in Celebration of His Sixtieth Birthday* (Winona Lake, Ind.: Eisenbrauns, 1983) 279–85.

——. *The Inscriptions of Tiglath-pileser III King of Assyria* (Jerusalem: Israel Academy of Sciences and Humanities, 1994).

——. "Sennacherib's Campaign to Judah: Historiographical and Historical Considerations," *Zion* 50 (1985) 65–80. [Hebrew, citation below]

——. "Propoganda, Literature, Historiography: Cracking the Code of the Assyrian Royal Inscriptions," in S. Parpola and R. M. Whiting (eds.) *Assyria 1995: Proceedings of the 10th Anniversary Symposium of the Neo-Assyrian Text Corpus Project. Helsinki, Spetember 7–11, 1995* (Helsinki: Neo-Assyrian Text Corpus Project, 1997) 325–38.

——. "World Dominion: The Expanding Horizon of the Assyrian Empire," in L. Milano et al. (eds.), *Landscapes: Territories, Frontiers and Horizons in the Ancient Near East: Papers presented to the XLIV Rencontre Assyriologique Internationale Venezia, 7–11 July 1997. Part 1: Invited Lectures* (HANEM 3/1; Padova: Sargon, 1999) 55–62.

Tadmor, Hayim, and Mordechai Cogan. "Ahaz and Tiglath-Pileser in the Book of Kings: Historiographic Considerations," *Bib* 60 (1979) 491–508. Originally published in Hebrew, citation below.

——. "Hezekiah's Fourteenth Year: The King's Illness and the Babylonian Embassy," *Eretz-Israel* 16 (1982) 198–201. [Hebrew, citation below]

Talmon, Shemaryahu. "Divergences in Calendar-Reckoning in Ephraim and Judah," *VT* 8/1 (1958) 48–74. Reprinted as "The Cult and Calendar Reform of Jeroboam I," in *King, Cult and Calendar in Ancient Israel. Collected Studies* (Jerusalem: Magnes Press, 1986) 113–139.

——. "The Signification of שלום and Its Semantic Field in the Hebrew Bible," in C. A. Evans and S. Talmon (eds.), *The Quest for Context and Meaning: Studies in Biblical Inter-textuality in Honor of James A. Sanders* (Leiden: Brill, 1997) 75–115.

Tallqvist, Knut L. *Assyrian Personal Names* (ASSF 43/1; Helsinki, 1914).

Tatum, Lynn. "Jerusalem in Conflict: The Evidence for the Seventh-Century B.C.E. Religious Struggle over Jerusalem," in A. G. Vaughn and A. E. Killebrew (eds.), *Jerusalem in Bible and Archaeology: The First Temple Period* (SBLSS 18; Leiden: Brill, 2003) 291–306.

Tawil, Hayim. "The Historicity of 2 Kings 19:24 (= Isaiah 37:25): The Problem of *Ye'ōrê Māṣôr*," *JNES* 41/3 (1982) 195–206.

Tetley, M. Christine. "The Date of Samaria's Fall as a Reason for Rejecting the Hypothesis of Two Conquests," *CBQ* 64/1 (2002) 59–77.

——. *The Reconstructed Chronology of the Divided Kingdom* (Winona Lake, Ind.: Eisenbrauns, 2005).

Thiel, Winfried. "Athaliah," *AYBD* 1.511–12.

——. "Omri," *AYBD* 5.17–20.

Thiele, Edwin R. "The Chronology of the Kings of Judah and Israel," *JNES* 3/3 (1944) 137–86.

——. "The Question of Coregencies Among the Hebrew Kings," in E. C. Hobbs (ed.), *A Stubborn Faith. Papers on the Old Testament and Related Subjects Presented to Honor William Andrew Irwin* (Dallas: Southern Methodist University Press, 1956) 39–52.

——. "Coregencies and Overlapping Reigns among the Hebrew Kings," *JBL* 93 (1974) 174–200.

——. *The Mysterious Numbers of the Hebrew Kings* (new rev. ed.; Grand Rapids: Zondervan, 1983).

Thompson, Michael E. W. "Isaiah's Sign of Immanuel," *ExpTim* 95/3 (1983) 67–71.

Thompson, Thomas L. *The Historicity of the Patriarchal Narratives: The Quest for the Historical Abraham* (BZAW 133; Berlin: W. de Gruyter, 1974).

——. *Early History of the Israelite People: From the Written and the Archaeological Sources* (SHANE 4; Leiden: Brill, 1992).

Thompson, Thomas L., ed. *Jerusalem in Ancient History and Tradition* (JSOTSup 381; London: T&T Clark International, 2003).

Throntveit, Mark A. "The Chronicler's Speeches and Historical Reconstruction," in M. P. Graham, K. G. Hoglund and S. L. McKenzie (eds.), *The Chronicler as Historian* (JSOTSup 238; Sheffield: Sheffield Academic Press, 1997) 225–45.

——. "The Relationship of Hezekiah to David and Solomon in the Books of Chronicles," in M. P. Graham, S. L. McKenzie and G. N. Knoppers, *The Chronicler as Theologian: Essays in Honor of Ralph W. Klein* (JSOTSup 371; London: T&T Clark, 2003) 105–21.

Tigay, Jeffrey. *Deuteronomy: The Traditional Hebrew Text with the New JPS Translation* (JPS Commentary; Philadelphia: Jewish Publication Society, 1996).

Tigay, Jeffrey, Ben-Zion Schereschewsky, and Yisrael Gilat. "Adoption," *EncJud* 1.415–20.

Timm, Stefan. *Moab zwischen den Mächten. Studien zu historischen Denkmälern und Texten* (ÄAT 17; Wiesbaden: Harrassowitz, 1989).

Todd, E. W. "The Reforms of Hezekiah and Josiah," *SJT* 9 (1956) 288–93.

Tov, Emanuel. *Textual Criticism of the Hebrew Bible* (2nd ed.; Minneapolis: Fortress Press, 1992).

———. *The Text-Critical Use of the Septuagint in Biblical Research* (2nd ed.; JBS 8; Jerusalem: Simor, 1997).

Tufnell, Olga. *Lachish III: The Iron Age* (2 vols.; London: Oxford University Press, 1953).

———. "Hazor, Samaria, and Lachish: A Synthesis," *PEQ* 91 (1959) 90–105.

Tushingham, A. Douglas. "A Royal Israelite Seal (?) and the Royal Jar Handle Stamps," *BASOR* 200 (1970) 71–78 (part one) and *BASOR* 201 (1971) 23–35 (part two).

———. *Excavations in Jerusalem 1961–1967, Vol. 1* (Toronto: Royal Ontario Museum, 1985).

———. "The Western Hill of Jerusalem: A Critique of the 'Maximalist' Position," *Levant* 19 (1987) 137–43.

———. "New Evidence Bearing on the Two-Winged *LMLK* Stamp,' *BASOR* 287 (1992) 61–65.

Uehlinger, Christoph. "Clio in a World of Pictures—Another Look at the Lachish Reliefs from Sennacherib's Southwest Palace at Nineveh," in L. L. Grabbe (ed.), *'Like a Bird in a Cage': The Invasion of Sennacherib in 701 B.C.E.* (JSOTSup 363; London: Sheffield Academic Press, 2003) 221–305.

Umoren, Gerald Emem. *The Salvation of the Remnant in Isaiah 11:1–12: An Exegesis of a Prophecy of Hope and Its Relevance Today* (Boca Raton, Fl.: Dissertation.com, 2007).

Unger, Merrill F. *Archeology and the Old Testament* (Grand Rapids: Zondervan, 1954).

Ussishkin, David. "The Syro-Hittite Ritual Burial of Monuments," *JNES* 29/2 (1970) 124–28.

———. "The Original Length of the Siloam Tunnel in Jerusalem " *Levant* 8 (1976) 82–95.

———. "The Destruction of Lachish by Sennacherib and the Dating of the Royal Judean Storage Jars," *TA* 4 (1977) 28–57.

———. "Excavations at Lachish, 1973–77: Preliminary Report" *TA* 5 (1978) 1–97.

———. "Answers at Lachish," *BAR* 5/6 (Nov.–Dec. 1979) 16–39.

———. *The Conquest of Lachish by Sennacherib* (Tel Aviv: Institute of Archaeology, 1982).

———. "The Date of the Judean Shrine at Arad," *IEJ* 38/3 (1988) 142–57.

———. "The Level V 'Sanctuary' and 'High Place' at Lachish. A Stratigraphic Analysis" in C. G. den Hertog, U. Hübner and S. Münger (eds.), *Saxa Loquentur: Studien zur Archäologie Palästinas/Israels. Festschrift für Volkmar Fritz zum 65. Geburtstag* (AOAT 302; Münster: Ugarit-Verlag, 2003) 205–11.

———. "The Water Systems of Jerusalem during Hezekiah's Reign," in M. Weippert and S. Timm (eds.), *Meilenstein: Festgabe für Herbert Donner zum 16. Februar 1995* (ÄAT 30; Wiesbaden: Harrassowitz Verlag, 1995) 289–307. Originally published in *Cathedra* 70 (1994) 3–28, Hebrew citation below.

———. "Archaeology of the Biblical Period: On Some Questions of Methodology and Chronology of the Iron Age," in H. G. M. Williamson (ed.), *Understanding the History of Ancient Israel* (PBA 143; Oxford: Oxford University Press, 2007) 131–41.

Vaughn, Andrew G. *Theology, History, and Archaeology in the Chronicler's Account of Hezekiah* (ABS 4; Atlanta: Scholars Press, 1999).

———. "Palaeographic Dating of Judean Seals and Its Significance for Biblical Research," *BASOR* 313 (1999) 43–64.

Vaughn, Andrew G., and Ann E. Killebrew, eds. *Jerusalem in Bible and Archaeology: The First Temple Period* (SBLSS 18; Leiden: Brill, 2003).

Vaughn, Patrick H. *The Meaning of 'bāmâ' in the Old Testament. A Study of Etymological, Textual and Archaeological Evidence* (SOTS 3; Cambridge: Cambridge University Press, 2009).

de Vaux, Roland. *Jerusalem and the Prophets* (Cincinnati: Hebrew Union College Press, 1965).

——. "Jérusalem et les prophètes," *RB* 73 (1966) 481–509.

Vermeylen, Jacques. *Du prophète Isaïe à l'apocalyptique: Isaïe I–XXXV, miroir d'un demi-millénaire d'expérience religieuse en Israël* (2 vols.; Paris: J. Gabalda, 1977–78).

Vogelstein, Max. *Biblical Chronology* (Cincinnati: Hebrew Union College, 1944).

——. *Fertile Soil: A Political History of Israel under the Divided Kingdom* (New York: American Press, 1957).

De Vries, Simon J. *1 and 2 Chronicles* (FOTL 11; Grand Rapids: Eerdmans, 1989).

Vriezen, T. C., and A. S. van der Woude. *Ancient Israelite and Early Jewish Literature* (trans. Brian Doyle; Leiden: Brill, 2004).

de Waard, Jan. *A Handbook on Isaiah* (TCT 1; Winona Lake, Ind.: Eisenbrauns, 1997).

Waddell, W. G. *Herodotus Book II* (London: Bristol Classical Press, 1998).

Wade, George W. *The Book of the Prophet Isaiah* (London: Methuen & Co., 1911).

Waltke, Bruce K. and M. O'Connor. *An Introduction to Biblical Hebrew Syntax* (Winona Lake, Ind.: Eisenbrauns, 1990).

Warren, Charles. "Phoenician Inscription on Jar Handles," *PEQ* 2 (1870) 372.

Watts, John D. W. *Isaiah 1–33* (WBC 24; Waco, Texas: Word Books, 1985).

Wegner, Paul D. "A Re-examination of Isaiah IX 1–6," *VT* 42/1 (1992) 103–112.

——. *An Examination of Kingship and Messianic Expectation in Isaiah 1–35* (Lewiston, N.Y.: Edwin Mellen, 1992).

——. "What's New in Isaiah 9:1–7?" in D. G. Firth and H. G. M. Williamson (eds.), *Interpreting Isaiah. Issues and Approaches* (Downers Grove, Ill.: InterVarsity Press, 2009) 237–49.

Wei, Tom F. "Hamath, Entrance of," *AYBD* 3.36–37.

Weinfeld, Moshe. "Cult Centralization in Israel in the Light of a Neo-Babylonian Analogy," *JNES* 23 (1964) 202–12.

——. "The Covenant of Grant in the Old Testament and in the Ancient Near East," *JAOS* 90 (1970) 184–203.

——. *Deuteronomy and the Deuteronomic School* (Oxford: Clarendon Press, 1972).

——. "The Worship of Molech and of the Queen of Heaven and its Background," *UF* 4 (1972) 133–54.

——. "Divine Intervention in War in Ancient Israel and in the Ancient Near East," in H. Tadmor and M. Weinfeld (eds.), *History, Historiography, and Interpretation: Studies in Biblical and Cuneiform Literatures* (Jerusalem: Magnes Press, 1983) 121–47.

——. "Zion and Jerusalem as Religious and Political Capital: Ideology and Utopia," in R. E. Friedman (ed.), *The Poet and the Historian: Essays in Literary and Historical Biblical Criticism* (HSS 26; Chico, Calif.: Scholars Press, 1983) 75–115.

——. "The Protest against Imperialism in Ancient Israelite Prophecy," in S. N. Eisenstadt (ed.), *The Origins and Diversity of Axial Age Civilizations* (Albany: State University of New York Press, 1986) 169–82, 510–11.

——. *Deuteronomy 1–11: A New Translation with Introduction and Commentary* (AYB 11; New York: Doubleday, 1991).

——. "Jerusalem—A Political and Spiritual Capital," in J. G. Westenholz (ed.), *Capital Cities: Urban Planning and Spiritual Dimensions. Proceedings of the Symposium Held on May 27–29, 1996, Jerusalem, Israel* (BLMJP 2; Jerusalem: Bible Lands Museum, 1998) 15–40.

——. *From Joshua to Josiah: Turning Points in the History of Israel from the Conquest of the Land until the Fall of Judah* (Jerusalem: Magnes Press, 1992). [Hebrew, citation below].

——. "The Roots of the Messianic Idea," in R. M. Whiting (ed.), *Mythology and Mythologies: Methodological Approaches to Intercultural Influences. Proceedings of the Second Annual Symposium of the Assyrian and Babylonian Intellectual Heritage Project. Held in Paris, France, October 4–7, 1999* (MS 2; Helsinki: The Neo-Assyrian Text Corpus Project, 2001) 279–87.

Weippert, Helga. "Die 'deuteronomistischen' Beurteilungen der Könige von Israel und Juda und das Problem der Redaktion der Königsbücher," *Bib* 53 (1972) 301–39.

Weissert, Elnathan. "Creating a Political Climate: Literary Allusions to Enūma Eliš in Sennacherib's Account of the Battle of Halule," in H. Waetzoldt and H. Hauptmann (eds.), *Assyrien im Wandel der Zeiten* (HSO 6; Heidelberg: Heidelberger Orientverlag, 1997) 191–202.

Welch, Adam C. *The Work of the Chronicler. Its Purpose and Its Date* (London: Oxford University Press, 1939).

Wellhausen, Julius. *Prolegomena zur Geschichte Israels* (Berlin, 1883; 5th ed.; Berlin: W. de Gruyter, 1905). Originally published as *Geschichte Israels, Band 1: Prolegomena*. Translated into English as *Prolegomena to the History of Ancient Israel* (trans. J. S. Black and A. Menzies; Edinburgh, 1885; repr. New York, 1957).

Welsby, Derek A. *The Kingdom of Kush: The Napatan and Meroitic Empires* (London: British Museum Press, 1996).

Welten, Peter. *Die Königs-Stempel: Ein Beitrag zur Militärpolitik Judas unter Hiskia und Josia* (Wiesbaden: Otto Harrassowitz, 1969).

———. *Geschichte und Geschichtsdarstellung in den Chronikbüchern* (WMANT 42; Neukirchen-Vluyn: Neukirchener Verlag, 1973).

de Wette, Wilhelm M. L. "Dissertatio critico-exegetica qua Deuteronomium a prioribus pentateuchi libris diversum, alius cuiusdam recentioris auctoris cpus esse monstratur" (Ph.D. diss.; Jena, 1805).

———. *Beiträge zur Einleitung in das Alte Testament*, Band 1: *Historisch-kritische Untersuchung über die Bücher der Chronik* (Halle: Schimmelpfennig, 1806). Also published as *Kritischer Versuch über die Glaubwürdigkeit der Bücher der Chronik mit Hinsicht auf die Geschichte der mosaischen Bücher und Gesetzgebung* (Halle: Schimmelpfennig, 1806).

Whitehouse, Owen C. *Isaiah I–XXXIX* (New Century Bible; New York: Oxford University Press, 1905).

Whitelam, Keith W. "Jesse," *AYBD* 3.772.

Whitley, C. F. "The Language and Exegesis of Isaiah 8 16–23," *ZAW* 90/1 (1978) 28–43.

Widengren, Geo. *The King and the Tree of Life in Ancient Near Eastern Religion* (Uppsala: Lundequistska Bokhandeln, 1951).

———. *Sakrales Königtum im Alten Testament und im Judentum* (Stuttgart: W. Kohlhammer, 1955).

Wildberger, Hans. *Isaiah 1–12: A Commentary* (trans. Thomas H. Trapp; Continental Commentary; Minneapolis: Fortress Press, 1991). Originally published as *Jesaja, Kapitel 1–12* (2nd ed.; Biblischer Kommentar; Neukirchen-Vluyn: Neukirchener Verlag, 1980).

———. *Isaiah 13–27: A Continental Commentary* (trans. Thomas H. Trapp; Continental Commentary; Minneapolis: Fortress Press, 1997). Originally published as *Jesaja, Kapitel 13–27* (Biblischer Kommentar; Neukirchen-Vluyn: Neukirchener Verlag, 1978).

———. *Isaiah 28–39: A Continental Commentary* (trans. Thomas H. Trapp; Continental Commentary; Minneapolis: Fortress Press, 2002). Originally published as *Jesaja, Kapitel 28–39* (Biblischer Kommentar; Neukirchen-Vluyn: Neukirchener Verlag 1982).

Willi, Thomas. *Die Chronik als Auslegung. Untersuchungen zur literarischen Gestaltung der historischen Überlieferung Israels* (FRLANT 106; Göttingen: Vandenhoeck & Ruprecht, 1972).

Williamson, H. G. M. "The Accession of Solomon in the Books of Chronicles," *VT* 26/3 (1976) 351–61.

———. "Eschatology in Chronicles," *TynBul* 28 (1977) 115–54.

———. *Israel in the Books of Chronicles* (Cambridge: Cambridge University Press, 1977).

———. *1 and 2 Chronicles* (NCB Commentary; Grand Rapids: Wm. B. Eerdmans, 1982).

———. "The Dynastic Oracle in the Books of Chronicles," in A. Rofé and Y. Zakovitch (eds.), *Isac Leo Seeligmann Volume. Essays on the Bible and the Ancient World* (3 vols.; Jerusalem: E. Rubenstein, 1983) 3.305–18.

———. *Ezra, Nehemiah* (WBC 16; Waco, Texas: Word Books, 1985).

———. Review of Antti Laato, *Josiah and David Redivivus: The Historical Josiah and the Messianic Expectations of Exilic and Postexilic Times*. *VT* 43/4 (1993) 573–74.

——. *The Book Called Isaiah: Deutero-Isaiah's Role in Composition and Redaction* (Oxford: Clarendon Press, 1994).

——. "Hezekiah and the Temple," in M. V. Fox et al. (eds.), *Texts, Temples, and Traditions: A Tribute to Menahem Haran* (Winona Lake, Ind.: Eisenbrauns, 1996) 47–52.

——. *Variations on a Theme: King, Messiah and Servant in the Book of Isaiah. The Didsbury Lectures 1997* (Carlisle, Cumbria: Paternoster Press, 1998).

——. *A Critical and Exegetical Commentary on Isaiah 1–27, Vol. 1: Isaiah 1–5* (ICC; London: T&T Clark, 2006).

Williamson, H. G. M., ed. *Understanding the History of Israel* (PBA 143; Oxford: Oxford University Press, 2007).

Willitts, Joel. "The Remnant of Israel in 4QpIsaiah^a (4Q161) and the Dead Sea Scrolls," *JJS* 57/1 (2006) 11–25.

Wilson, Ian. *Out of the Midst of Fire: Divine Presence in Deuteronomy* (SBLDS 151; Atlanta: Scholars Press, 1995).

——. "Central Sanctuary or Local Settlement? The Location of the Triennial Tithe Declaration (Dtn 26,13–15)," *ZAW* 120/3 (2008) 323–40.

Wilson, Robert R. "Deuteronomy, Ethnicity, and Reform: Reflections on the Social Setting of the Book of Deuteronomy," in J. T. Strong and S. S. Tuell (eds.), *Constituting the Community: Studies on the Polity of Ancient Israel in Honor of S. Dean McBride Jr.* (Winona Lake, Ind.: Eisenbrauns, 2005) 107–23.

Wiseman, D. J. *Chronicles of Chaldaean Kings (626–556 B.C.) in the British Museum* (London: Trustees of the British Museum, 1961).

Winckler, Hugo. *Die Keilschrifttexte Sargons, Vol. 1* (Leipzig: Eduard Pfeiffer, 1889).

——. *Die Keilinschriften und das Alte Testament* (3rd ed.; Berlin: Reuther & Reichard, 1903).

Winter, Irene. "Royal Rhetoric and the Development of Historical Narrative in Neo-Assyrian Reliefs," *SVC* 7/2 (1981) 2–38.

Wright, David P. "The Spectrum of Priestly Impurity," in G. A. Anderson and S. M. Olyan (eds.), *Priesthood and Cult in Ancient Israel* (JSOTSup 125; Sheffield: JSOT Press, 1991) 150–181.

Wright, Richard M. *Linguistic Evidence for the Pre-exilic Date of the Yahwistic Source* (LHB/OTS 419; London: T&T Clark, 2005).

van der Woude, A. S. "Jesaja 8, 19–23a als literarische Einheit," in J. van Ruiten and M. Vervenne (eds.), *Studies in the Book of Isaiah: Festschrift Willem A.M. Beuken* (BETL 132; Leuven: Leuven University Press, 1997) 129–36.

Würthwein, Ernst. *Die Bücher der Könige. 1. Kön. 17–2. Kön. 25.* (ATD 11/2; Göttingen: Vandenhoeck & Ruprecht, 1984).

Yadin, Yigael. "Beer-sheba: The High Place Destroyed by King Josiah," *BASOR* 222 (1976) 5–17.

Yamada, Shigeo. "Notes on the Genealogical Data of the Assyrian King List," *Eretz-Israel* 27 (2003) 265*–275*.

Young, Rodger C. "When Did Jerusalem Fall?" *JETS* 47/1 (2004) 21–38.

Younger Jr., K. Lawson. "The Fall of Samaria in Light of Recent Research," *CBQ* 61/3 (1999) 461–82.

——. "Yahweh at Ashkelon and Calah? Yahwistic Names in Neo-Assyrian," *VT* 52/2 (2002) 207–18.

——. "Assyrian Involvement in the Southern Levant at the End of the Eighth Century B.C.E.," in A. G. Vaughn and A. E. Killebrew (eds.), *Jerusalem in Bible and Archaeology: The First Temple Period* (SBLSS 18; Leiden: Brill, 2003) 235–63.

Yurco, Frank J. "Sennacherib's Third Campaign and the Coregency of Shabaka and Shebitku," *Serapis* 6 (1980) 221–40.

——. "The Shabaka-Shebitku Coregency and the Supposed Second Campaign of Sennacherib against Judah: A Critical Assessment," *JBL* 110/1 (1991) 35–45.

Zadok, Ran. *The Pre-Hellenistic Israelite Anthroponymy and Prosopography* (OLA 28; Leuven: Peeters, 1988).

Zakovitch, Yair. "The Pattern of the Numerical Sequence Three-Four in the Bible" (Ph.D. diss.; The Hebrew University of Jerusalem, 1977). [Hebrew, citation below]

——. *Introduction to Inner-Biblical Interpretation* (Even-Yehuda: Reches, 1992). [Hebrew, citation below]

——. "Elijah and Elisha in the 'Praise of Israel's Great Ancestors' (Ben Sira 47:36–48:19)," in M. Garsiel et al. (eds.), *Studies in Bible and Exegesis, Vol. 5. Presented to Uriel Shimon* (Ramat Gan: Bar Ilan University Press, 2000) 163–77. [Hebrew, citation below]

Zerafa, P. "Il Resto di Israele nei Profeti preesilici," *Angelicum* 49 (1972) 3–29.

Zevit, Ziony. *The Religions of Ancient Israel: A Synthesis of Parallactic Approaches* (London: Continuum, 2001).

Zimhoni, Orna. "Two Ceramic Assemblages from Lachish Levels III and II," *TA* 17 (1990) 3–52.

——. *Studies in the Iron Age Pottery of Israel: Typological, Archaeological and Chronological Aspects* (Tel Aviv: Institute of Archaeology, 1997).

Zvi, Ehud Ben. "Who Wrote the Speech of the Rabshekeh and When?" *JBL* 109/1 (1990) 79–92.

——. "The List of the Levitical Cities," *JSOT* 54 (1992) 77–106.

——. "A Sense of Proportion: An Aspect of the Theology of the Chronicler," *SJOT* 9 (1995) 37–51. Reprinted in idem, *History, Literature and Theology in the Book of Chronicles* (London: Equinox, 2006) 160–73.

——. "The Chronicler as Historian: Building Texts," in M. Patrick Graham, Kenneth G. Hoglund and Steven L. McKenzie (eds.), *The Chronicler as Historian* (JSOTSup 238; Sheffield: Sheffield Academic Press, 1997) 132–49. Reprinted in idem, *History, Literature and Theology in the Book of Chronicles*, 100–116.

——. "About Time: Observations about the Construction of Time in the Book of Chronicles," *HBT* 22 (2000) 17–31. Reprinted in idem, *History, Literature and Theology in the Book of Chronicles*, 144–57.

——. "Shifting the Gaze: Historiographic Constraints in Chronicles and their Implications," in J. A. Dearman and M. P. Graham, *The Land that I Will Show You: Essays on the History and Archaeology of the Ancient Near East in Honour of J. Maxwell Miller* (JSOTSup 343; Sheffield: Sheffield Academic Press, 2001) 38–60. Reprinted in idem, *History, Literature and Theology in the Book of Chronicles*, 78–99.

משה אברבך, "חזקיהו מלך יהודה ורבי יהודה הנשיא: הקשרים משיחיים", תרביץ נג/ג (תשמ"ד) 71–353.

יוחנן אהרוני, "כרונולוגיה של מלכי יהודה וישראל", תרביץ כא (תש"י) 100–92.

יוחנן אהרוני, ארכאולוגיה של ארץ ישראל (ירושלים: שקמונה, 1978).

דוד אוסישקין, "מפעלי המים של ירושלים בימי חזקיהו" קתדרה 70 (1994) 28–3.

מגן ברושי וישראל פינקלשטיין, "מניין אוכלוסי ארץ-ישראל בשנת 734 לפנה"ס," קתדרה 58 (1990) 24–3.

גרשון גליל, "היחסים בין יהודה לאשור בימי סרגון ב'," ציון 57/2 (1992) 133–111.

רוברט דויטש, מסרים מן העבר: בולות עבריות מימי ישעיהו ועד חורבן בית ראשון (תל אביב: ספרי מרכז ארכאולוגי, 1997).

זאב הרצוג, "המקדש בערד ומקבילותיו", בתוך: ערד: תל המצודות בערד (תל אביב: הקיבוץ המאוחד, 1997) 209–182.

משה ויינפלד, מידושע ועד יאשיהו: תקופות מפנה בתולדות ישראל מההתנחלות ועד חורבן בית ראשון (ירושלים: מאגנס, 1992).

יאיר זקוביץ, "הדגם דספרותי שלושה-ארבעה במקרא" (עבודה לשם קבלת התואר דוקטור; האוניברסיטה העברית בירושלים, 1977).

יאיר זקוביץ, מבוא לפרשנות פנים מקראית (אבן-יהודה: רכס, 1992).

יאיר זקוביץ, "אליהו ואלישע בשבח אבות עולם (בן סירא מז ,לו-מח, יט)," בתוך: עיוני מקרא ופרשנות כרך ה. מנחת ידידות והוקרה לאוריאל סימון (ערכו מ' גרסיאל ואחרים; רמת גן: אוניברסיטת בר-אילן, 2000) 177–163.

שרה יפת, "המהימנות ההסטורית של ספר דברי הימים, לתולדות מחקר הבעיה ומקומה בחקר המקרא," י' זקוביץ וא' רופא (עורכים), ספ־ יצחק אריה זלינגמן, ב (ירושלים: תשמ"ג) 346–327.

מרדכי כוגן, "שימוש כרונולוגי מכוון בספר דברי הימים," ציון מה (תש"ם) 172–165.

חיה כץ, 'ארץ דגן ותירוש...ארץ זית יצהר ודבש': הכלכלה בממלכת יהודה בימי הבית הראשון (ירושלים: יד בן-צבי, 2008).

עמיחי מזר, דוד עמית, צבי אילן, "דרך הגבול שבין מכמש ליריחו וחפירות חורבת שילחה," ארץ-ישראל 17 (תשמ"ד) 250–236, לוחות 24–21.

נדב נאמן, "מדיניותם של אחז וחזקיהו כלפי אשור בימי סרגון ובראשית ימי סנחריב," ציון 59/1 (תשנ"ד) 30–5.

רות עמירן, "שני קברים בירושלים מתקופת מלכי יהודה", בתוך: יהודה וירושלים: הכינוס הארצי השנים-עשר לידיעת הארץ (ירושלים: החברה לחקירת ארץ-ישראל ועתיקותיה, תשי"ז) 72–63.

יחזקאל קויפמן, תולדות האמונה הישראלית: מימי קדם עד סוף בית שני (תל אביב: מוסד ביאליק-דביר, 56–1937).

ברוך שורץ, תורת הקדושה: עיונים בחוקה הכוהנית שבתורה (ירושלים: מאגנס, 1999).

חיים תדמור, "חטאו של סרגון," ארץ-ישראל 5 (תשי"ט) 163–150.

חיים תדמור, "מלחמת סנחריב ביהודה: בחינת היסטוריוגראפיות והיסטוריות," ציון 50 (תשמ"ה), 80–65.

מרדכי כוגן וחיים תדמור, "אחז ותגלת-פלאסר בספר מלכים: בחנים היסטוריוגרפיים", ארץ-ישראל 14 (תשל"ח) 61–55.

חיים תדמור ומרדכי כוגן, "מאירועי שנת ארבע-עשרה לחזקיהו: מחלת המלך וביקור המשלחת הבבלית," ארץ-ישראל 16 (1982, תשמ"ב) 201–198.

AUTHOR INDEX

Abba, R.   246n31
Abel, F.-M.   96n16
Aberbach, M.   290n21
Abusch, T.   79n56
Achenbach, R.   29n70, 30n71, 32n82
Ackerman, S.   116n82
Ackroyd, P. R.   106n50, 124n2, 135n33
Adamthwaite, M. R.   181n110
Adcock, F. E.   72n27
Agus, A.   290n21
Aharoni, M.   96n17
Aharoni, Y.   11nn4–5, 12n7, 52n61, 53n65,
    93n3, 95n15, 96n17, 97nn19, 21, 98n23,
    99n26, 224n87, 248n34
Ahlström, G. W.   91n1, 110n63, 248n34
Albertz, R.   92n2, 116n82, 117n86
Albright, W. F.   10n3, 51n56, 52nn57, 61,
    66n10, 81n63, 196n3, 248n34
Alt. A.   96n16, 153n3, 160nn40–41, 161n43,
    162n45, 248n34
Amiran, R.   45n32
Amit, D.   52n59
Andersen, F. I.   178n102
Anderson, G. A.   226n91
Anderson, G. W.   132n26
Anderson, J. E.   181n110
Ariel, D. T.   45n35, 47n42
Ashmore, J. P.   115n78
Aubin, H. T.   67n11, 75n35
Avi-Jonah, M.   43n28
Avigad, N.   1n1, 35n11, 43n28, 46n39,
    47nn42, 44, 53n61, 54n70
Aviram, J.   44n31

Baden, J. S.   214n63
Bae, H.-S.   223n85
Bahat, D.   44n31, 46n37
Baines, J.   172n81
Baker, H. D.   69n15
Balentine, S. E.   103n40
Baltzer, K.   156n16
Bar-On, S.   214n64
Barkay, G.   43n28, 44n30, 45n32, 53n61
Barker, M.   144n53
Barnes, W. H.   10n2, 12n7, 13n8, 229n99
Barnett, R. D.   42n24, 63n6
Barney, K. L.   105n44
Barr, J.   3n3, 5n9

Barrick, W. B.   105n50
Barton, G. A.   66n10
Barton, J.   103n40
Bartusch, M. W.   248n34
Baumgartner, W.   153n3
Beaulieu, P.-A.   111n65
Becking, B.   13n8, 14n12, 15nn15–16, 16n19,
    17n25, 38–39n14, 184n120
Begg, C. T.   67n10, 105n44, 135n34
Begrich, J.   10n2
von Beckerath, J.   73n27, 74n32
Bekins, P.   183n116
Ben-Sasson, H. H.   6n10
Ben-Tor, A.   44n30
Benzinger, I.   227n95
Berlin, A.   174n88
Beuken, W. A. M.   165n57
Biran, A.   44n31
Bleibtrau, E.   42n24, 63n6
Blenkinsopp, J.   69n13, 133n27, 134n30,
    168n67, 185n124
Bliss, F. J.   50n53
Boardman, J.   37n15, 67n10, 69n16, 188n132
Boling, R. G.   248n34
Borger, R.   30n71, 77n46, 85n80
Borowski, O.   53n65, 91n1, 92n2
Braun, R. L.   257n3, 259n6
Bream, H. N.   259n40
Brekelmans, C. H. W.   268n47
Brettler, M. Z.   3n3, 145n54
Bright, J.   67n11, 71n20, 109n59
Brinkman, J. A.   69nn15–16, 130n18,
    289n15
Brodsky, H.   114n75
Brongers, H. A.   157n23
Broshi, M.   44n30, 46n37, 47nn42, 44
Büchler, A.   203n27
Budde, K.   182n114
Budge, E. A. W.   66n10
Burns, J. B.   208n41
Burrows, M.   138n41
Bury, J. B.   72n27
van den Bussche, H.   266n37

Cahill, J. M.   49n49
Camp, L.   91n1
Carlson, R. A.   161n43
Carr, D. M.   142n47, 171n76

Cazelles, H. 18n27
Charlesworth, J. H. 164n52
Chavel, S. 227n96
Chen, D. 44n31
Childs, B. S. 72n25, 131n20, 135n34,
    137nn39–40, 139n44, 142n49, 143n51,
    149n64, 165n57, 185n124
Christensen, D. L. 246n29
Claburn, W. E. 114n76
Clements, R. E. 132n26, 134n32, 135n34,
    142n49, 145n54, 165n57, 169n70
Clines, D. J. A. 174n87
Clover. R. 75n36
Cogan, M. 13n8, 15nn18–19, 16n19, 17n25,
    18n26, 20nn35–36, 21n40, 36n4,
    38nn10–11, 39nn14–15, 40n17, 69n16,
    72n24, 73n27, 80n60, 91n1, 106nn48, 50,
    107n53, 109n60, 110n64, 111n65, 125n4,
    126n6, 128n12, 129n12, 130n18, 147n58,
    188n131, 199n13, 206n38
Coggins, R. 2n2
Cohen, Ch. 128n12, 129n13, 169n68
Collins, J. J. 149n63, 164nn52–53, 181n110,
    184n119, 185n123
Conrad, D. 102n37, 114n77
Conrad, E. W. 128n11
Coogan, M. D. 96n16, 116n82
Cook, S. A. 72n27
Coppens, J. 268n47
Cross, F. M. 1n1, 53n63, 54n70, 107n54,
    156n20, 260n12, 261n13, 262n18
Curtis, E. L. 215n65, 223n84, 227n95
Curtis, J. E. 31n78

Dahood, M. 243n22
Dalley, S. 28n64, 29nn66, 70, 31nn78–80,
    41nn20–22, 42n24, 48n48, 50n52, 80n61,
    109n60, 130n18
Damerji, M. S. B. 28n64. 31n79
Davies, J. 2n2
Davies, P. R. 3n3, 4nn6–7, 44n29, 49n51
Davis, D. 45n32
Day, J. 3n3, 172n81, 181n110, 205n35
Dayagi, M. 1n1
Dearman, J. A. 23n44, 203n25
Delitzsch, F. 115n80, 127n10, 131nn19–20
Delkurt, H. 132n26
Delsman, W. C. 124n2, 207n39
Descamps, A. 268n47
Deutsch, Robert. 1n1
Deutsch, Richard. R. 142n49
Dever, W. G. 43–44n29, 44n30, 52n56,
    74n33, 115n80, 116n82
Dillard, R. B. 238n9, 257n1

Dillman, A. 220n76
Dion, P.-E. 67n11, 74n32, 118n87, 142n49
Diringer, D. 51n56, 52n57
Dohmen, C. 181n110, 184n120
Donner, H. 36n4, 91n1
Dozeman, T. B. 177n95
Drews, R. 73n28
Driver, G. R. 154n9
Driver, S. R. 103n38, 115n80, 156n20,
    214n63, 220n76
Dubberstein, W. H. 18n29, 20n35,
    21n39
Dubovský, P. 128n12
Duhm, B. 168n64, 169n70
Duke, R. K. 195n1, 246n31

Edelman, D. 92n1, 94nn8–9, 95n12,
    96n17, 100nn32–33, 101n34, 111nn65–66,
    112nn69–70, 113nn71–72
Edelstein, G. 45n34
Eichrodt, W. 66n10
Eisenstadt, S. N. 131n19
Eissfeldt, O. 128n11, 156n21, 165n56,
    205n35
Emerton, J. A. 154nn10–11, 162n45
Engnell, I. 172n82
Eph'al, I. 80n61
Erlandsson, S. 167n63
Ernst, A. B. 132n26
Eslinger, L. 159n37
Etz, D. V. 25n51
Evans, C. A. 165n55
Evans, C. D. 39n14
Evans, P. S. 137n40
Exum, J. C. 96n16
Eynikel, E. 118n87, 277n102

Fabry, H.-J. 102n36
Fales, F. M. 6n2
Fassberg, S. E. 103n40
Finkelstein, I. 45nn33–34, 46n37, 47n42,
    91n1, 98n25, 114n75, 288n14
Finsterbusch, K. 205n35
Firth, D. G. 155n13
Fishbane, M. 4n6
Fohrer, G. 66n10
Forrer, E. 162n45
Fowler, M. D. 96nn16, 18
Fox, M. V. 124n1, 288n13
Fox, N. S. 51n54–56, 53n62, 54nn69–70,
    57nn79, 81–82
Frahm, E. 24n48, 38n13, 39nn14–15, 61n2,
    69n15, 77n46, 79n54, 85n80
Freedman, D. N. 20n36, 178n102

Frerichs, E. S.   288n13
Fried, L. S.   92n1, 94n10, 97nn20, 22
Friedman, R. E.   135n32, 258n5, 261n16
Fries, J.   197n6
Fritz, V.   96n16
Fuchs, A.   16n19, 17n23, 37n9, 38n10,
    39n14, 129n12
Fullerton, K.   66n10, 70n19, 112n69

Gadd, C. J.   16n19
Gadegaard, N. H.   96n18
Galil, G.   1on2, 11n6, 13n8, 14n14, 18n27,
    39nn14–15
Gallagher, W. R.   61n1, 72nn25–26,
    74n32, 77n43, 78n48, 79nn54–55, 80n61,
    81nn64–65, 82nn65–66, 85nn80–81,
    86n82, 128n12, 130n17, 137n40
Gardiner, A.   75n39
Garelli, P.   176n93
Garsiel M.   127n9
Gelb, I. J.   76n40
Geraty, L. T.   132n26
Gese, H.   213n60
Gesenius, D. W.   123n1, 150n65
Geva, H.   43n28, 44nn30–31, 45nn32, 34,
    46n37, 47n43
Gibson, S.   44n31, 45n34
Gilat, Y.   160n41
Ginsberg, H. L.   52n61, 115n78, 154nn8, 11
Gitin, S.   50n53, 52n56, 55n72, 74n33
Glassner, J-J.   20n35
Goldberg, J.   39n14, 67n10
Gomes, J. F.   114n75
Gonçalves, F. J.   1on2–3, 11n5, 69n16,
    91n1, 104n43, 105n46, 110n63, 123n1,
    124n3, 125n4, 129n13, 149n62, 278n107
Gordis, R.   175n89
Gordon, C. H.   181n110
Görg, M.   72n23, 144n53
Grabbe, L. L.   3n3, 61n2, 62nn3–4, 63n6,
    64n7, 72nn25–26, 81n65, 137n40
Graf, K. H.   117n86, 196n2
Graham, M. P.   23n44, 118n87, 195n1,
    196n4, 197n5, 203n25, 257n2, 270n58,
    275n92
Graupner, A.   132n26
Gray, G. B.   165n55, 167n62, 169n70
Gray, J.   67n10, 102n36, 108n56, 138n41
Grayson, A. K.   14n12, 18n29, 19n30, 20n35,
    36n4, 37nn5, 8, 67n10, 69n16, 73n27,
    78n50, 83n71, 188n132
Greenberg, M.   269n47
Grena, G. M.   1n1, 50n53
De Groot, A.   45n35, 47n42

Groves, J. W.   135n33
Gunkel, H.   5n12
Gunn, D. M.   3n3
Gunneweg, A. H. J.   132n37
Güterbock, H. G.   199n13

Haag, E.   181n110
Haag, H.   66n10, 213–14n61
Hackett, J. A.   49n51
Hallo, W. W.   39n14, 11n65
Halpern, B.   46n38, 53n65, 91n1, 110n63,
    114n74, 248n36, 258n5, 261n16, 262n18,
    263n19, 266nn34, 37, 267n38, 273nn78,
    82, 275nn93–94, 276nn97–98, 277n102,
    288n13
Hamblin, W. J.   269n52
Handy, L. K.   91n1, 110nn61–62
Hanson, P. D.   99n26, 116n82
Haran, M.   91n1, 103n39, 117n86, 214n64,
    247n33, 248n34
Hardmeier, C.   124n1, 139n44, 142n48
Harvey, G.   2n2
Hasel, G. F.   132n26, 133n28
Hauptmann, H.   82n65
Hawkins, J. D.   4_n23
Hayes, J. H.   5n9, 1on2, 13n8, 23n44, 38n12,
    39n14, 41n20, 46n38, 50n52, 91n1, 117n84,
    134n32, 171n76
Heider, G. C.   205n35
Heim, R. D.   250n40
Hendel, R. S.   49n51
Herbert, A. S.   165n54
von Herder, J. G.   170n72
Herr, L. G.   46n41
Herrmann, S.   8on60
Herrmann, W.   184n121
den Hertog, C. G.   98n24
Herzog, Z.   91n1, 93nn4–6, 94n10, 95n11,
    97n19, 114n75
Heskett, R.   165n53
Hess, R. S.   24n47
Hestrin, R.   1n1
Hilhorst, A.   168n67
Hobbs, E. C.   23n46
Hobson, D. W.   46n33, 91n1, 248n36
Hoffman, H. D.   91n1, 102n37, 118n87
Hoffmann, Y.   269n47
Hoffmeier, J. K.   3n3, 38n10, 74n34
Høgenhaven, J.   162n45, 184n120
Hoglund, K. G.   196n4, 203n25, 270n58
Holladay, J. S.   99n26
Holladay, W. L.   171n79
Hooker, P. K.   1on2, 13n8, 23n44, 40n18,
    41n20, 249n37, 253n52

Honor, L. L.   61nn1–2, 67n11, 72n24, 77n47, 112n69
Horn, S. H.   12n6, 67nn10–11
Hossfeld, F.-L.   132n26
Houtman, A.   178n102
Hübner, U.   65n8, 80n61, 96n17, 98n24
Huesman, J.   103nn38, 40
Hughes, J.   18n27, 103n40, 125n5
Hunger, H.   164n51
Hurvitz, A.   103n40, 169n68
Hutter, M.   69n16, 147n58

Ilan, Z.   52n59
Inch, M.   181n110
Irvine, S. A.   36n4, 106n50, 154n8, 161n42, 171n76, 188nn131–32
Ishida, T.   135n32
Jacobs, P.   92n2
Jacobsen, T.   48n48, 199n13
Jamieson-Drake, D. W.   44n29, 288n13
Japhet, S.   132n26, 187n130, 195n1, 196nn2–3, 199n15, 201nn20–21, 202n23, 203n26, 209n47, 211nn49, 51, 212n53, 213n59, 216n68, 218n70, 221n78, 222n81, 225n88, 238nn8–9, 239n11, 240nn14, 16, 241nn18–19, 243n23, 244n25, 250n42, 252n48, 265n33, 272n70, 281n116
Jenkins, A. K.   11n5, 70n19
Jeremias, A.   66n10
Johnstone, W.   197n7, 198n9, 199n15, 212n55, 237n6
Joines, K. R.   102n36
Joosten, J.   103n40, 226n92

Kaiser, O.   102n37, 165n54, 165n57, 169n70, 170n72, 171n78
Kalimi, I.   4n6, 213n57
Kamil, A.   29n69
Kang, S.-M.   268n47
Kataja, L.   29n67
Katz, H.   47n43
Kaufmann, S. A.   164n51
Kaufmann, Y.   111n68, 248n34
Kelly, B. E.   266n36, 282n117
Kelm, G. L.   51n56
Kennicott, B.   148n62
Kenyon, K. M.   96n17
Kilian, R.   132n26
Killebrew A. E.   38n10, 43nn27–29, 44n31, 45nn33–35, 46n39, 74n34, 79n53, 130n17, 148n61, 163n48, 276n95, 287n9
King, P. J.   48n47, 97n22, 252n46
Kissane, E. J.   131n20, 153n4, 165n54, 170n72

Kitchen, K. A.   3n3, 61n1, 72n23, 74nn31, 33, 75nn34–35, 37
Kittel, R.   116n82
Klein, G. L.   156n20, 157n27
Kletter, R.   52n60, 53n61, 55n70, 56n76, 57n79
Kloner, A.   45n32
Knauf, E. A.   3n3, 44n29, 49n51, 65n8, 80n61, 81n65, 83n71, 96n17
Knight, D. A.   79n56, 130n18
Knohl, I.   118n86
Knoppers, G. N.   197n5, 209n43, 257n2
Koch, I.   52n59, 53n65, 55nn72–73, 56nn75, 77
König, E.   165n55
Konkel, A. H.   124n1, 136n36, 149n63, 150n65
van der Kooij, A.   71n22, 80n61
Korpel, M. C. A.   184n121
Kort, A.   183n118, 201n19, 248n34
Kronholm, T.   189n136
Kuan, J. K.   13n8
Kuenen, A.   117n86
Kuhrt, A.   13n11, 37n5
Kunter, M.   29n67
Kutsch, E.   213n60
Kwasman, T.   29n67

Laato, A.   13n8, 124n1, 152n2, 159n37, 163n49, 186n125, 189nn135–36, 290n22
Labuschagne, C. J.   168n67
Lambert, W. G.   172n81, 176n93
Landes, G. M.   290n22
Lane, E. W.   171n77, 214n62, 268n47
Lapp, P. W.   54n70
Larsen, M. T.   105n45
Lasswell, H. D.   105n45
Laurentin, A.   157n23
Layton, S. C.   31n82
Leclant, J.   74n31, 75n35, 76n41
van Leeuwen, C.   61n2, 67n10
Lemche, N. P.   44n29
Leprohon, R. J.   161n43
Lerner, D.   105n45
Levenson, J. D.   260n12
Levey, S. H.   157n24, 290n21
Levine, B. A.   131n23, 179n107, 288n13, 293n30
Levine, L. D.   61n2, 78n51
Levy, T. E.   44n29
Lewy, J.   11n5, 19n31
Licht, J.   3n3
Lie, A. G.   17n23
Lieberman, S.   196n3

Lilley, J. P. U. 268n47
Lipschits, O. 52n59, 53n65, 55nn72–73, 56nn75, 77
Lipiński, E. 44n29
Littman, E. 169n68
Liverani, M. 130n17
Liwak, R. 69n16
Lloyd, A. B. 72n23, 73n27
Lloyd, S. 48n48
Lohfink, N. F. 2n2, 262n18, 268n47
Long, B. O. 3n3, 126n6
Long, V. P. 3n3
Longman III, T. 3n3
Lovering E. H. 166n60
Lowery, R. H. 91n1, 110n61, 111n66
Lubetksi, M. 57n79
Luckenbill, D. D. 1n1, 24n48, 30nn71, 74, 61n2, 66n10, 79n54, 85n80, 130n18
Lundbom, J. R. 19n32, 153n5
Lust, J. 269n47

Maag, V. 112n69, 113n71
Macadam, M. F. L. 74n31, 75n34
Macalister, R. A. S. 50n53
Macchi, J.-D. 118n87
Machinist, P. 36n4, 61n1, 84n76, 128n12, 142n49, 177n94
Macy, H. R. 277n99
Madsen, A. A. 215n65, 223n84, 227n95
Maeir, A. M. 49n50, 50n53, 55n72
Magonet, J. 149n63
Malamat, A. 10n2, 110n63
Malul, M. 269n47
Marcus, R. 73n28
Margalit, S. 44n31
Mariottini, C. F. 115n80
Marti, K. 165n57, 169n70
Martin, W. J. 81n65
Martínez, F. G. 168n67
Mason, R. 200n16
Massaux, É. 268n47
Massmann, L. 80n61
Mathews, C. R. 166n60
Mattingly, G. L. 37n8
Mayer, W. 61n2, 67n12, 80n61, 81n62, 85n80
Mayes, A. D. H. 210n49
Mazar, A. 5n11, 51n56, 52n59, 91n1
Mazar, B. 81n63, 138n41, 248n34
Mazor, L. 169n68, 170n72, 170n75
McBride, S. D. 99n26, 116n82, 216n67
McCarter Jr., P. K. 169n69, 273n76
McCurdy, J. F. 66n10
McFall, L. 9n1, 12n6, 156n17, 277n101

McKay, J. W. 91n1, 102n37, 103n38, 104n41, 109n60, 115n80, 116n83
McKenzie, S. L. 2n2, 118–19n87, 196n4, 197n5, 257n2, 261n16, 270n58, 276n98, 290n22
Melugin, R. F. 124n2
Melville, S. C. 28n65
Mettinger, T. N. D. 216n67
Meyer, L. V. 132n26, 133n27
Meyers, C. L. 18n27, 141n45
Milano, L. 36n2, 78n52
Milevski, Ianir 45n34
Milgrom, J. 99nn28–29, 101n34, 103n39, 117–18n86, 137n38, 201n19, 204n31, 248n35
Millard, A. R. 3n3, 13n10, 14n13, 77n45, 78n50, 84nn72–73
Miller, J. M. 38n12, 39n14, 41n20, 46n38, 50n52, 91n1, 117n84
Miller, P. D. 92n2, 99n26, 116n82, 153n5
de Miroschedji, P. 49n50, 50n53
Mommsen, H. 51n54, 52n61, 53n62, 54n68
Montgomery, J. A. 11n5, 61n1, 206n39
de Moor, J. C. 71n22
Moore, C. A. 149n63, 250n40
Morgenstern, J. 227n95
Mori, M. 166n58
Moriarty, F. L. 227n95
Morschauser, S. 183n118, 201n19, 248n34
Mosca, P. G. 205n35
Moshkovitz, S. 97n19
Mosis, R. 257n1
Mowinckel, S. 172n82, 184n120
Moyer, J. C. 111n65
Le Moyne, J. 66n10
Mulder, M. J. 207n39
Müller, H.-P. 78n49, 205n35
Münger, S. 98n24

Na'aman, N. 5n11, 10n3, 11n5, 12n6, 13n8, 14n12, 15nn16–17, 38nn13–14, 39nn14–16, 40n16, 45n34, 47n42, 52n61, 53nn62, 64, 54nn66–67, 70, 81n63, 92n1, 94n9, 95n12, 96nn16–17, 99n27, 100nn29, 32, 102nn35, 37, 104n44, 107n53, 117n85, 119–20n91, 137n40, 142n49, 147n59, 148n60, 248nn34, 36
Nakanose, S. 213n58
Nakhai, B. A. 98n22
Naveh, J. 81n63
Nelson, R. D. 246n31, 248n34, 261n16, 268n47
Neusner, J. A. 288n13, 290n21

Newman, J. H.   149n63
Newsome Jr., J. D.   216n68
Nicholson, E. W.   3n3, 5n9, 67n10,
   112nn69–70, 113n71, 115nn77–78, 81
Niditch, S.   165n54
Nielsen, K.   99n29, 165n54, 165n57,
   170n74, 172n82, 173n84, 177n97
Noble, P. R.   133n28
Norin, S.   49n51, 149n62
North, R.   250n40
Noth, M.   2n2, 66n10, 96n16, 198n12,
   248n34

O'Brien, M. A.   119n87
O'Conner, M.   18n27, 141n45, 154n12
Ockinga B. G.   135n32, 144n53
Oded, B.   40n19
Oesterley, W. O. E.   110n63
Oestreicher, T.   108n57, 109nn59–60,
   111n68
Ofer, A.   45n34
Ogawa, H.   166n58
Ollenburger, B. C.   135n32
Olley, J. W.   129n13
Olmstead, A. T. E.   13n8, 16n20, 66n10,
   109n60
Olyan, S. M.   102n36, 116n82, 226n91
Oppenheim, A. L.   80n60

Parker, B.   30n72
Parker, R. A.   18n29, 20n35, 21n39, 74n30
Parker, S. B.   159n37
Parpola, S.   15n14, 29n67, 30n74, 78n49,
   80n61, 105n45, 172n82
Parrot, A.   66n10
Paul, S. M.   117n86, 160n41, 163n48,
   169n68
Payne, J. B.   181n110
Pečírková, J.   36n4
Peltonen, K.   195n1
Perdue, L. G.   111n65
Perlitt, L.   291n28
Perlman, I.   51n54
Person, R. E.   124n1
Petersen, D. L.   203n27
Peterson, J. L.   248n34
Petrie, W. M. F.   66n10
Pfaff, H.-M.   132n26
Phillips, A.   215n65
Pixner, B.   44n31
Plöger, O.   257n3
Poorthuis, J. H. M.   178n102
Porter, B.n176n93
Preuss, H. D.   118n87

Priese, K.-H.   73n29
Propp, W. H. C.   209n44, 214n63
Provan, I. W.   3n3, 118n87, 187n129, 261n13,
   277n102, 279n107, 291n28
de Pury, A.   118n87

von Rad, G.   145n55, 160n41, 161n43,
   216n67
Radner, K.   31n79
Rainey, A. F.   50n53, 52n61, 56n74, 74n34,
   96nn16–17, 97n19, 225n89, 270n58,
   279n108
Rawlinson, G.   66n10, 109n60
Rawlinson, H. C.   77n43
Reade, J.   105n45
Redford, D. B.   74n32, 75n36
Rehm, M.   189n136
Reich, R.   45nn32, 35, 48n46, 49nn50–51
Rendtorff, R.   132n26
Reviv, H.   110n63
Rey, C. F.   76n39
Richter, S. L.   216n67
Rignell, L. G.   183n115
Ringgren, H.   172n82, 199n15, 281n116
Roberts, J. J. M.   38n10, 134n32, 148n61,
   160nn40–41, 161n43, 166n58, 167n63,
   183n118, 292n29
Robinson, E.   49n49
Robinson, T. H.   110n63
Rofé, A.   72n24, 135n34, 265n33
Rogers, R. W.   66n10
Rogerson, J.   49n51
Rogland, M.   156n20, 157n27, 158n29
Römer, T. C.   118n87
Rooke, D. W.   172n81
van Rooy, H. F.   71n22
Rosenbaum, J.   109n59, 119n91, 225n89
Rosenberg, S.   49n51
Rost, P.   38n14
Rowley, H. H.   11n4, 12n7, 61n1, 66n10,
   67n11, 74n32, 91n1, 102n36, 109n59,
   112n70
Rudman, D.   128n12
Rudolph, W.   66n10, 163n48, 204n28,
   212n55, 215n65
Rüger, H. P.   213n61
van Ruiten, J.   153n3, 168n67
Ruprecht, E.   147n58
Russell, J. M.   79n54

Saggs, H. W. F.   15n19, 41nn21–23
Sass, B.   1n1, 35n1
Sayce, A. H.   49n51
Schearing, L. S.   2n2

Schereschewsky, B.-Z.   160n41
Schmid, H.   291n28
Schmid, K.   177n95
Schneemelcher, W.   257n3
Schniedewind, W. M.   44n31, 119n87,
    163n48, 179n105, 200n18, 287n9, 288n13
Schrader, E.   66n10
Schultz, M.   29n67
Schwally, F.   137n39
Schwartz, B. J.   177n95, 178n102, 205n35
Schwartz, J.   178n102
Schwienhorst-Schönberger, L.   132n26
Scurlock, J.   80n61
Segal, J. B.   209nn45–46, 213nn58–59
Seitz, C. R.   125n4, 135n33, 137n40, 142n48,
    179n107
Sellin, E.   115n78
Sergi, O.   52n59, 53n65, 55nn72–73,
    56nn75, 77
Seters, J. V.   4n5, 290n22
Seux, M. J.   172n83
Shai, I.   55n72
Shanks, H.   97n19, 112n69
Shaver, J. R.   227n95
Shea, W. H.   39n14, 67nn10, 12, 74n32,
    76n42
Shectman, S.   214n63
Shiloh, Y.   46n37, 51n56
Shukron, E.   45n35, 48n46, 49nn50–51
Silberman, N. A.   45nn33–34, 91n1, 98n25,
    114n75, 288n14
Simons, J.   43n28, 48n45, 49n49, 251n43
Skinner, J.   112n69, 131n20, 156n20, 165n54
Smelik, K. A. D.   74n32, 124n2, 127n9,
    134n31, 137n40, 205n35
Smith, G.   1n1, 6n2, 75n36, 79n54, 85n80
Smith, G. A.   66n10
Smith, J. P.   171n77
Smith, M. S.   92n2, 110n63, 116n82
Smith, S.   72n27
von Soden, W.   78n49
Sokoloff, M.   171n77
Sommer, B. D.   177n95
de Sousa, R. F.   165n53, 175n90
Spalinger, A. J.   38n10, 74n32
Speier, H.   105n45
Spencer, J. R.   106n50, 248n34
Spieckermann, H.   91n1, 102n37, 103n38,
    109n60
Spiegelberg, W.   72n26
Stackert, J.   118n86
Stade, B.   137nn39–40, 139n44
Stager, L. E.   46n41, 48n47, 96n16, 97n22,
    252n46

Stamm, J. J.   30n73
Starkey, J. L.   51n56
Stavrakopoulou, F   205n35, 208n41
Steiner, M.   43n23
Stern, E.   64n7, 65n9, 97n19
Stern, P. D.   268n47
Stromberg, J.   166nn53–59, 167n61
Strong, J. T.   115n78, 287n10
Swanson, K. A.   102n56, 103n38, 112n69
Sweeney, M. A.   37n7, 119n91, 124n1,
    131n20, 153n4, 171n76, 178n102, 181n110,
    185n122, 290n22

Tadmor, H.   3n3, 10n2, 13nn8–9, 14n14,
    15n18, 17nn22, 24–25, 19n33, 20nn36–37,
    21nn38, 40, 22n41, 35n1, 36nn2–3, 38n10,
    39nn14, 16, 40n17, 61nn1–2, 66n10, 72n24,
    73n27, 77n44, 78n52 79n56, 80n61,
    82n67, 84n73, 85n79, 91n1, 105n45,
    106nn48, 50, 111n65, 126n6, 128n12,
    130n18, 137n38, 141n45, 147n58, 179n104,
    188n131, 199n13, 206n38
Tallqvist, K. L.   31n81
Talmon, S.   165n55, 228nn97–98
Tatum, L.   46n39, 50n52, 276n95
Tawil, H.   48n48
Taylor, G.   159n37
Tetley, M .C.   10n2, 11nn4–5, 13n8
Thiel, W.   31n76
Thiele, E. R.   10n3, 13n18, 23n46, 69n16
Thompson, M. E. W.   18n110
Thompson, T. L.   4n5, 44n29, 45n34,
    209n43
Throntveit, M. A.   197n5, 200n16,
    257n2
Tigay, J. H.   40n17, 160n41, 199n13, 211n52,
    218n72, 220n77
Timm, S.   39n14, 49n49
Todd, E. W.   103n38, 109n59, 112n69
Török, L.   75n38
Tov, E.   143n50, 157n22, 235n1
Tucker, G. M.   79n56, 130n18
Tuell, S. S.   115n78, 287n10
Tufnell, O.   50n53, 51n56, 54n70
Turner, G.   42n24, 63n6
Tushingham, A. D.   44nn30–31, 52n59,
    57n79

Uehlinger, C.   63n6
Umoren, G. E.   132n26
Unger, M. F.   66n10
Ussishkin, D.   49nn49–50, 50n52, 51n56,
    52n57, 53n65, 63nn5–6, 94n7,
    98nn24–25, 100n30–31

Vanderhooft, D. S.   277n102
Vaughn, A. G.   38n10, 43nn27–29, 44n31, 45nn34–35, 46n39, 47n43, 50n53, 51n54, 52nn58–59, 54n69, 55nn71–73, 56nn76–77, 57nn78, 81–82, 64n7, 66n9, 74n34, 79n53, 130n17, 148n61, 163n48, 203n24, 254nn53–54, 257n1, 276n95, 287n9
Vaughn, P. H.   97n22
de Vaux, R.   67n10
Vermeylen, J.   171n76, 176n91
Vervenne, M.   153n3, 269n47
Vogelstein, M.   11n5, 198n12
De Vries, S. J.   209n44, 212n54, 214n61, 227n95, 229n100, 258n5
Vriezen, T. C.   49n51

de Waard, J.   159n33
Waddell, W. G.   72n23
Wade, G. W.   11n6
Waetzoldt, H.   82n65
Waltke, B. K.   154n12
Warren, C.   50n53
Watson, W. G. E.   2n2
Watts, J. D. W.   155n16, 170n72
Wegner, P. D.   152n2, 155n13, 159nn37–38, 161nn43–44, 162n45, 164n53, 168n66, 170n75, 171n76, 177n96
Wehr, H.   171n77, 214n62, 268n47
Wei, T. F.   237n5
Weinfeld, M.   3n3, 61n2, 79n56, 80n61, 84n73, 91n1, 105nn44, 46, 106n49, 110n63, 111n65, 115nn78–79, 116nn82–83, 119nn88–90, 128n10, 129n13, 131n19, 135n32, 137n38, 161n43, 164n52, 167n63, 176n92, 179n106, 205n35, 237n7, 243n22, 260n12, 262n18, 279n109
Weippert, H.   277n99
Weippert, M.   49n49
Weis, R. D.   171n76
Weissert, E.   82n65
Welch, A. C.   203n27
Wellhausen, J.   66n10, 91n1, 115n80, 117–18n86, 196n2, 248n34, 291n23
Welsby, D. A.   76n39
Welten, P.   50n53, 53nn61–62, 275n95, 282n117
Wenig, S.   73n29
Werr, L.   48n48
Westenholtz, J. G.   164n52, 279n109
de Wette, W. M. L.   118n87, 196n2
White, J. B.   39n14
Whitehouse, O. C.   11n6

Whitelam, K. W.   173n84
Whiting, R. M.   29n67, 80n61, 105n45, 161n43, 279n109
Whitley, C. F.   154n12, 155n15
Widengren, G.   172n82
Wiessner, G.   154n9
Wildberger, H.   61n1, 124n1, 126n7, 127n8, 131n20, 135n33, 145n55, 149n64, 150n65, 162n45, 178n102, 181n110, 184n119, 251n45
Willi, T.   195n1
Williamson, H. G. M.   3n3, 5n11, 100n31, 124n1, 135n33, 136n37, 149n64, 155n13, 165n57, 166nn58, 60, 167n63, 181n110, 199n14, 204nn28, 30–31, 212n55, 214n61, 221n80, 222n82, 237n3, 239nn11, 13, 251n44, 252n51, 257nn1, 3, 258n5, 265n33, 272n70, 290n22
Willis, J. T.   171n76
Willitts, J.   132n26
Wilson, I.   216n67, 245n29
Wilson, R. R.   115n78, 287n10
Winckler, H.   14n14, 38n11
Winter, I.   105n45
Wiseman, D. J.   18n29, 19n30, 20n35, 188n131
van der Woude, A. S.   49n51, 153n3
Wright, D. P.   226n91
Wright, R. M.   291nn27–28
Würthwein, E.   91n1

Yadin, Y.   96n18, 97n19
Yamada, S.   25n52
Yellin, J.   51n54
Yoshikawa M.   166n58
Young, G. D.   80n61
Young, R. C.   18n27
Youngblood, R.   181n110
Younger Jr., K. L.   13n8, 15n19, 17n25, 29n70, 30nn71–72, 75, 37nn7, 9, 38n10, 39n14, 40n16, 41n21, 79n53, 80n61, 81n65, 82n66, 85n78, 86n82, 130n17
Yoyotte, J.   74n31, 75n35, 76n41
Yurco, F. J.   67n12, 73n28, 74n31, 75n34, 76n40

Zadok, R.   29n70
Zakovitch, Y.   4n7, 127n9, 135n34, 201n21, 253n52, 265n33
Zevit, Z.   92n2, 111n66
Zimhoni, O.   55n70, 98n24
Zvi, E. B.   128n12, 199n16, 203nn25–26, 248n34, 275n92

SCRIPTURE INDEX

Ancient Near East

ABL 301   129n12
ABL 403   129n12
Annals of Sargon   16–17, 18n26, 37n6
  lines 53–57   17n23
Annals of   1, 30n74, 61n2,
  Sennacherib   66–67, 71, 76, 78–83,
  (see also Oriental   85
  Institute Prism,
  Rassam Cylinder)
Aššur Charter   15n19
  (K. 1349)
  lines 16–28   17n24
Azekah Inscription   38–41, 58, 65, 67,
                                69n16, 286n7

Babylonian Chronicle 1   14–17, 32
  i 27–32   14
  i 28   14–15n14
  ii 5'   83n71
  ii 6'   78n50
  iv 16   73n27
Babylonian Chronicle 5 (BM 21946)
                                18, 22nn41, 43
  obverse,   19n30
    lines 1–5
  reverse,   20
    lines 11–13
Bellino Cylinder   77, 77n45
BM 21901   23n44
Bull Inscription (Sargon)   16n19
Bull Inscriptions (Sennacherib)
  1, line 21   85n80, 289n18
  2 and 3, line 21   30n71, 85n80, 289n18
  4, lines 19–20   79n54

Cylinder Inscription (Sargon)   16n19

Enki and Ninhursag   164n52
Enmerkar and the
  Lord of Aratta   164n52
Enūma Eliš   30n74, 81–82n65
Eponym Chronicle   16n21

Great Summary Inscription (Sargon)
                    16, 16n19, 17n21

Kawa stela   74, 74nn31, 34
Khorsabad Annals   16n19, 17
  hall 2, pl. 2,   17n21
    lines 11–17
KTU 1.24
  line 7   184

Lachish Letter 6
  line 1   154n11

Mesha stela   268n47

ND 400   188n131
ND 2608   41, 58, 286n8
ND 2765   41, 58, 286n8
ND 4301+4305   188n131
Nimrud Inscription
  line 8   38, 58, 286n7
Nimrud Prisms, D and E   16n19, 17n21
  lines 46–48   17n22
Nineveh Prism (VI.b)
  lines 25–33   37–38n10
  line 31   129n12

Oriental Institute Prism
  ii 45   111n66
  ii 73–77   289n16
  ii 73–iii 11   82n66
  ii 78–iii 5   71n21
  ii 78–83   76, 76n40, 83n70,
                    87n84
  ii 78–81   130n17
  iii 14–17   289n16
  iii 18–27   113n70
  iii 18–23   80n58
  iii 32–34   110n62
  iii 46   24n48

Palace Door no. 4 (Sargon)   16n19

Rassam Cylinder   77, 77n46
  line 34   111n66
  lines 36–38   79n54
  line 42   289n16
  lines 43–45   71n21

lines 43–44	76, 76n40, 83n70, 87n84	SAA 6, Text 143	29n67
line 43	82n66, 130n17	Seal of Shebanyau	35, 35n1
lines 46–48	289n16	Small Summary Inscription (Sargon)	16n19
lines 49–51	80n58, 113n70	Summary Inscription (Tiglath-pileser III)	
line 53	110n62		
line 58	24n48	7:r.11′	36n3
iv 86–87	95n11		
		Uruk Prophecy	164n51

Hebrew Bible/Old Testament

Genesis		31:55/32:1	236n1
1–11	168	32:33 [Eng. 32]	4n6
2:14	291n26	33:17	157n22
3:14	168	34:5	103n40
10:11–12	291n26	35:6	4n6, 208n42
11:9	157n22	35:12	246n31
12:2	246n31	36:31	4n6
12:6	4n6	37:3	103n40
12:7	246n31	38:5	103n40
13:15–17	246n31	48:4	246n31
14:14	4n6	48:9	26n54
14:22–23	268n45	48:16	26n54
15:5	246n31	49:10	179n103, 291n
15:7	246n31	49:23	103n38
15:13	145n55	49:27	268n45
15:18	246n31	50:11	157n22
16	145n55		
16:6	145n55	Exodus	
16:11	159n38, 160n39	1:11–12	145n55
17:8	246n31	1:13–14	145n55
17:16	26n54	1:14	242n20
17:19	159n38	3:8	246n31
17:20	26n54	3:12	185n122
19:22	157n22	3:17	246n31
20:7, 17	227n93	3:21–22	268n45
22:17	26n54, 246n31	4:20	183n116
24	181n111	4:22	160n41
24:7	246n31	6:4, 8	246n31
24:60	26n54	9:4, 6, 19, 25	202n22
25:18	291n26	10:15	202n22
25:30	157n22	12–13	209n44
26:3–4	246n31	12	291n24
26:4, 24	26n54, 246n31	12:1–14	214
27:36	157n22	12:1–13	219n75
28:3	26n54	12:3, 5	218
28:4, 13	246n31	12:8	219
28:14	26n54	12:9	220n76
29:34	157n22	12:12, 19	202n22
30:6	26n54	12:21–27	219
30:20	26n54	12:21	218
30:41	243n22	12:28	214n63
31:48	157n22	12:35–36	268n45

12:43	241n19	10:21	103n40
13:5	246n31	14:20–23, 26–35	246n31
14:2	246n31	14:39–45	109n60
15:9	268n45	18:8–10	245n26
15:23	157n22	18:11–19	245n27
19:5–6	246n31	18:20	247n31
20:5–6	281n116	18:21–32	245n28
23:18	214	18:24	247n31
23:19	220n77	20:12	246n31
23:27–31	246n31	21:7	227n93
30:1–10	99n28	21:20	103n40
32:13	246n31	24:17–19	179n103
33:3	246n31	32:1	154n12
34	214n64	33:52	118n86
34:7	281n116	34:7–9	237n4
34:11	246n31		
34:18–26	215n65	Deuteronomy	215–20
34:25	214	1:1	4n6
38:28	103n40	1:8	246n31
40:35–38	170n73	1:10–11	246n31
		1:16	177n98
Leviticus		1:21	246n31
1:1	170n73	1:34–35	246n31
2:8	218n70	2:1	246n31
2:11–12	239n13	2:12	4n6
3:3–5, 9–11, 14–16	220n76	2:21–22	4n6
3:17	220n76	3:11	4n6
4:4	218n70	4:7	243n22
5:12	218n70	4:21	246n31
6:2, 7, 18	241n19	4:31	246n31
7:1	241n19	5:9–10	281n116
7:23–25	220n76	6:3	246n31
7:35, 37	241n19	6:10, 18	246n31
11:46	241n19	6:19	246n31
12:4	226n91	6:23	246n31
16:33	226n91	6:25	115n81
17:8ff	117n86	7:5	102n35
19:15	177n98	7:6	246n31
19:30	117n86, 226n91	7:8, 12–13	246n31
20:2–5	205n35	8:1, 18	246n31
20:3	226n91	8:19	115n81
20:22	226n92	9:3	246n31
20:24	246n31	9:5	246n31
21:12, 23	226n91	9:20, 26	227n93
25:27–28	237	10:8	4n6
26:2	117n86, 226n91	10:9	247n31
26:30–31	118n86	10:11	246n31
26:39	281n116	10:18	178n100
		10:22	246n31
Numbers		11:9	246n31
7:87–88	201n19	11:13–15	115n81
8:24–25	244n24	11:21	246n31
9:9–14	227, 230	11:22–28	115n81
9:11	231n102	11:25	246n31
10:17	103n40	12:3	102n35, 103n39

12:5–7	245n29
12:6, 11	218n70
12:12	247n31
12:13	106n47
12:15–19	245n29
12:18	247n31
12:19	247n31
12:20	246n31
12:21	245n29
12:28–31	259n8
12:31	205n35
13:10	153n5
13:18–19 [Eng. 17–18]	115n81
13:18 [Eng. 17]	246n31
14:1	160n41
14:2	246n31
14:21	220n77
14:23–26	239
14:22–29	245n29
14:27	247n31
14:29	178n100, 247n31
15:4–5	115n81
15:6	246n31
16:1–8	213n60
16:2	218
16:5–8	215
16:5–6	216, 232
16:7	220
16:11, 14	178n100, 247n31
16:18	177n98
17:7	153n5
17:14–20	178
18:1–8	246, 247n31
18:2	247n31
18:3–5	245n29
18:3	239
18:6	247
18:10	205n35
18:22	145n55
19:8–9	115n81
19:8	246n31
19:28	115n81
24:16	281n116
24:17, 19–21	178n100
25:1	177n98
26:3	246n31
26:11–13	247n31
26:12–13	178n100
26:12	245n29
26:15	246n31
26:18	246n31
26:19	246n31
27	287n10
27:3	246n31
27:19	178n100
28:9	246n31
28:11	246n31
28:62	246n31
29:12 [Eng. 13]	246n31
30:1–10	115n81
30:15–20	115n81
30:20	246n31
31:3	246n31
31:7	246n31
31:20	246n31
31:21, 23	246n31
32:18	160n41
34:4	246n31
34:6	4n6
34:10	4n6
Joshua	
3–4	143n50
4:9	4n6
6	267n39
7:26	4n6, 157n22
8:1–29	267n39
8:2	268n46
8:27	268n46
8:28–29	4n6
9:1	139n42
9:27	4n6
10–12	267n39
10:14	211n49
10:27	4n6
11:1	139n42
11:14	268n46
11:16	154n12
11:23	272n72
13:5	237n4
13:13	4n6
14:14	4n6
14:15	272n72
15:26	96n16
15:35	52n61
15:48	52n61
15:55	52n61
15:63	4n6
16:5–10	224n86
16:10	4n6
17:7–12	224n86
18:22	208n42
19:2	96n16
19:10–16	224
21	247n34
21:1–42	247n33
21:23	81n63
21:44	272n73

22:8	268n46	12:11	272n75
23:1	272n73	13:13–14	264n30
		14:30, 32, 36	268n47
Judges		15:19–21	268n47
1:21	4n6	16:13	264n31
1:22–26	208n42	16:14	103n40
1:23	208n42	16:18	185
1:26	4n6	17	143n50, 279n107
3:11	272n74	17:1	52n61
3:26–30	267n39	17:38	103n38
3:30	272n74	18:5	267n40
4–5	267n39	18:12	185, 264n31
5:30	268nn45–46	18:14	185, 187, 264n31,
5:31	272n74		278n104
6:12	185n122	18:27–28	267n40
6:24	4n6	18:28	185, 264n31
7:19–22	267n39	19:5	274n87
8:24–26	268n46	19:8	267n40
8:28	272n74	19:20	210n48
8:34	272n73	22:5	264n31
9:8–15	173	23:1–5	267n40
9:13	274n87	23:2, 4	264n31
9:15	173n85	23:8–12	267n40
9:19	274n87	23:12	264n31
10:4	4n6	26:8	264n31
11:29, 32–33	267n39	27:6	4n6
13	160n39	27:9	103n40
13:3	159n38	28:3–19	132n24, 207n41
14:4	4n6	30:7–9	267n40
14:19	267n39	30:8	264n31
15:14–16	267n39	30:16	268n47
15:19	4n6, 157n22	30:18–19	267n40
16:18	103n40	30:19–20, 22	268n47
16:23–30	267n39	30:25	4n6
17–18	132n24	30:26	268n47
18:12	4n6		
19:3	274n87	2 Samuel	
		1:20	274n87
1 Samuel		2:1–3	271n66
2:1–10	149n63	2:1	264n31
2:1	274n87	3:1	246n56
2:22	103n40	3:6–21	246n56
2:30	155n13	3:18	267n40
2:34	182n112	3:22	268n47
3:20	210n48	4:3	4n6
4:7	211n49	4:9	264n31, 267n40
5:5	4n6	5:4	286n127
5:7	103n40	5:6–9	271n66
6:13	274n87	5:7–10	267n40
6:18	4n6	5:10	185, 187
7:9	169n69	5:17–20	267n40
7:15	210n48	5:20	157n22
9:9	4n6	5:23–25	267n40
11:9, 15	274n87	5:25	278

6:8	4n6
6:17–18	227n94
6:17	239n10
6:22	155n13
7	260. 264
7:1	273n76
7:3	185
7:9	185
7:12–14	26n54
7:12–13	263
7:14	265n33
8:1–14	267n40
8:2	269n53
8:6	269n53, 270n59
8:10	270n55
8:12	268n47
8:14	270n59
11:1	22n41
12:30	268n47
15:4	177n98
18:18	4n6
19:17	103n40
22:1	267n40
24:1–25	253n52
24:25	239n10
1 Kings	
1:37	185, 278n104
1:40, 45	274n87
2:2–4	260n10
2:3–4	260
2:3	278n103
2:4	26n54, 261n15, 265n33
2:5–9	263n20
2:12	198
2:24	263n21
2:26	247n33
2:27	145n55
2:28–34	263n20
2:36–46	263n20
2:45–46	263n22
2:46	198
3:3–28	263n24
3:3	206n36, 263n23
3:4	239n10
3:6	26n54
3:11–12	280n112
3:11, 13	274n90
3:14	264nn28, 31
3:15	239n10
3:28	280n112
4:19	154n12
4:20	274n87

5:1 [Eng. 4:21]	270n54, 271n67, 280n111
5:3 [Eng. 4:23]	27n58
5:4–5 [Eng. 4:24–25]	273n77
5:4 [Eng. 4:24]	263n25, 271n67, 280n111
5:5 [Eng. 4:25]	129n14, 178n102
5:6 [Eng. 4:26]	270n61
5:8 [Eng. 4:28]	221n79
5:13 [Eng. 4:33]	173n85
5:18 [Eng. 4]	263n25, 273n77
5:21 [Eng. 7]	274n87
5:22–23 [Eng. 8–9]	271n62
5:25 [Eng. 11]	27n58, 271n62
5:29 [Eng. 15]	271n62
6:3	199n15
6:12	261n15
6:32	103n38
6:35	103n40
7:2	173
8:8	4n6
8:17–18	274n89
8:25	260n10, 261n15, 265n33
8:32	177n98
8:52	243n22
8:57	185n122
8:63	227n94
8:64	239n10
8:65	237n4
8:66	274n87
9:1–10	260n9
9:3	264n29
9:4–9	260
9:4–5	261n15
9:4	264n31
9:5	198, 265n33
9:9	199n15
9:10–11	27n58
9:10	263n27
9:14	27n58
9:15	260n9
9:19	57n81, 271n63
9:21	4n6
9:24	260n9
9:25	103n40, 239n10
9:28	27n58
10:1	258n5
10:9	263n26
10:10	27n58
10:12	4n6
10:23	263n26, 274n90
10:24–25	270n55
10:28	270n61

11	259, 266n34	21:12	103n40
11:4	264n31	21:25	211n49
11:6	258, 264n31	22:7–28	127n9
11:7	262	22:38	145n55
11:12	26n54	22:42	186n127
11:31–39	262n17	22:43	205n32
11:33	199n15, 264n31	22:49 [Eng. 48]	271n64
11:38	185, 261n15, 264		
11:39	261n13	2 Kings	
12:2	139n42	2:22	4n6, 145n55
12:4	155n13	3:2–3	205n34
12:8	163n47	3:4	103n40
12:10	155n13	3:15	103n40
12:15	145n55	3:21–27	272nn68–69
12:19	4n6	3:23	269n48
12:22–24	127n9	3:26–27	132n24, 207n41
12:28–33	208n42	4:38	220n77
12:32	103n40, 227n94	4:42	27n58
13	127n9	4:44	145n55
13:1–3	261n13	5:18	206n38
13:2	160n41	7:5–7	267n41
13:6	227n93	7:16–18	145n55
13:26	145n55	7:16	269n48
13:33–34	261n13	8:8–9	270n56
14:5–10	127n9	8:16–17	28n63
14:8	264n31	8:17	186n127
14:18	145n55	8:18	31n76, 205n33
14:21	163n47, 186n127	8:19	261n14
14:23	102n35	8:22	4n6
14:25–28	268n45	8:26	31n76, 186n126
14:27	103n40	9:7	19n34
15:3	264n31	10:29–31	205n34
15:4–5	261n14	10:32–33	272n68
15:4	26n54	11:1	103n38
15:11	205n32, 264n31	11:14	274n87
15:12–13	102n35	11:20	273n78, 274nn85, 87
15:14	205n32, 278n105	12:3–4 [Eng. 2–3]	205n32
15:17–22	272n68	12:4 [Eng. 3]	278n105
15:21	139n42	12:18–19 [Eng. 17–18]	272n68
15:29–30	127n9	13:2–3	272n68
15:29	145n55	13:2	205n34
16:1–4, 7, 12	127n9	13:3–5	267n41
16:12	145n55	13:11	205n34
17:13	153n5	14:1–2	27n60
17:16	145n55	14:2	186nn126–27
18:18	199n15	14:3–4	205n32
18:21, 26	209n44	14:3	264n31
18:28	221n79	14:4	278n105
19:10	199n15	14:5	198, 286n2
19:13	139n42	14:7	4n6, 103n38
19:14	199n15	14:9	173n85
20:21	103n40	14:11–14	268n45
20:22	22n41	14:13–14	272n68
20:26	22n41	14:14	103n38

14:22	271n64	18:1–2	24n47, 162n47
14:24	205n34	18:1	1n1, 11n6, 12n6, 26n56, 189n133
14:25	127n9, 145n55, 237n4, 271n64	18:2	22, 27n62, 70n17, 125, 186
15:2	12n6	18:3–6	232
15:3–4	205n32	18:3–4	118n87
15:4	278n105	18:3	144n52, 207, 258, 264n31
15:5	24n46, 26n55	18:4	92, 101–103, 106–107, 111n67, 117n85, 119n88, 119n90, 121, 207, 236, 278n105
15:9, 18	205n34		
15:19	198		
15:24, 28	205n34		
15:29	162		
15:30	25n50, 26n56, 27n59		
15:33	25n50, 186n126	18:5–6	144n52
15:34–35	205n32	18:5	105n45, 129n14, 278, 283
15:35	278m105		
16:1	26n56, 27n59, 32	18:6	207
16:2	12n6, 24n49, 27n57, 28n63, 186, 189n133, 264n31	18:7–8	58, 278
		18:7	40, 187, 191, 278n104, 286n4
16:3–4	106n50	18:8	40, 280, 286n5
16:3	205	18:9–12	17n25, 70n18
16:4	202	18:9–10	10–11, 11n6, 12, 12n6
16:5–9	272n68		
16:5, 7–9	125, 126n6, 136	18:10	1n1
16:6	4n6	18:11	17n25
16:7–9	207n40	18:13–20:19	70, 83n68, **123–50**
16:7–8	36n3	18:13–19:37	71n22, **295–98**
16:7	160n41	18:13–16	1n1, 62, 70, 83, **123–26**, 150, 281n114
16:8	189n132, 206n39		
16:10–18	201	18:13	10–11, 11nn5–6, 12n6, 68
16:10–16	106n50, 206n38		
16:10	189n132	18:14	70n19
16:12–13	227n94	18:15–16	70n19
16:17–18	206n39, 207n40	18:17–19:37	62, 67, **126–33**
16:17	200n17	18:17	70, 70n19
17:1–6	17n25	18:19–25	104n44
17:1	12n6, 26n56, 27n59, 32, 189n133	18:19–22	105n45
		18:20	180n109, 191
17:3–4	270n56	18:21	82, 87
17:4	286n3	18:22	92, **104–108**, 111n67, 112n70, 119n90, 121
17:6	15n18, 17n25		
17:13–14	145n55	18:24	105n45
17:13	19n34	18:25	105n45
17:16	199n15	18:26–28	104n44
17:17	205n35	18:29	105n45
17:23	4n6, 19n34, 145n55	18:30	105n45
17:31	205n35	18:32	105n45
17:34	4n6, 221n79	18:33–35	105n45
17:40	221n79	19–20	127n9
17:41	4n6, 277	19:1	281n114
18–20	1n1, 195, 235	19:4, 6	267n43
18	12n6	19:9	71n21, 73–76, 87
18:1–6	117n85	19:13	70n17

19:15–16, 21–24, 32–34	267n43	23:21–22	210n49, 212
19:35	84, 289n19	23:21	119n89, 221n78, 223n84
20	107n52, **133–36**, 150, 279	23:22	210, 211n52, 232
20:1–11	11n5	23:23	210n48
20:6	11n5, 70n17, 125	23:24	108, 119n89
20:9	182n112	23:25	261n13
20:10	1n1	23:26	103n39
20:12–19	69, 290n20	23:30	277n100
20:12	69, 270n56	23:31–34	25n53
20:20	35, 49n50, 249n38, 251n44	23:31	22, 186n126
20:21	24n47	23:33	22n41
21:1	22, 186n126, 189n134	23:36	22, 186n126
21:2–15	261n13	24:2	19n34
21:3–7	102n35	24:8	22, 186n126, 203n26
21:6	205n35	24:12	19, 20n36, 22n41
21:10–15	127n9, 276	24:13–14	145n54
21:10	19n34	24:13	135, 145n55, 268n45
21:18	277n100	24:15	20n36
21:19–26	107n51	24:18–25:30	126
21:19–23	171n76	24:18	22, 186n126
21:19	22, 186n126, 287n9	25:4	48n47, 252
21:22	199n15	25:8–11	18n28
21:23, 26	277n100	25:13–17	135
22:1	22, 186n126	25:27	21
22:2	261n13		
22:3–10	119n90	Isaiah	
22:3–7	275n92	1–35	129
22:8	215n66	1:1	1n1
22:14–20	127n9	1:2–5, 7	160n40
22:15–20	261n13	1:2–4	169n71
22:14	45n36	1:9	160n40
22:17	108, 199n15	1:10–31	178
23:1–3	108, 212, 222n83	1:10	160n40, 179n102
23:2	127n9	1:17	166n60
23:3	119n89	1:18	160n40
23:4–20	113n71	1:21	178n99
23:4	48n47	1:24–28	169n71
23:5	278	1:26	178n99
23:6	102n35, 103n39	2:1–5	178
23:8	102n35, 103nn39–40, 104n41, 108n56	2:3	160n40, 179n102
23:10	205n35	2:5	160n40
23:12–13	108n55	2:8	132n25
23:13–14	102n35	2:13	133n29
23:13	262	2:20	132n25
23:14	103n38	3:1–4	169n71
23:15–17	145n55	4:1	160n40
23:15	261n13	4:2	133n27
23:17	208n42	4:3	133n27
23:19	208n42	5:3–7	169n71
23:21–23	108, 222n83	5:18–19	160n40
		5:24	179n102, 180n108
		5:26	167n62, 178n102
		6:11–12	169–70n71

6:13	173n86
7	146n59, 148, 151, 162n46, 180, **181–90**
7:1	128
7:2	128
7:3	128, 133n27, 138n41
7:4–9	128, 160n39
7:5–6	160n40
7:9	130
7:11	128
7:14	159n38, 160n39, 191
7:15–25	128n11
7:17	190n137
7:18	133n29
8:1–4	183–84
8:5–8	131n19, 190n137
8:6	49n49
8:8, 10	185n124
8:16–9:6 [Eng. 8:16–9:7]	190, 285
8:16–22	153
8:16	179n102
8:18	183
8:19–22	161
8:19	166n60
8:20	179n102
8:22	153n3
8:23–9:6 [Eng. 9:1–7]	**151–64**, 177, 179–80, 189, 191
9:2–4 [Eng. 3–5]	280
9:3–4 [Eng. 4–5]	84n75, 289n19
9:5–6 [Eng. 6–7]	280nn110, 113
9:7–9 [Eng. 8–10]	160n40
9:12 [Eng. 13]	166n60
9:20	167n63
10	190n137
10:2	178n100, 180n108
10:5–11:10	179n106
10:5–34	37n7
10:5–19	131
10:5–11	131n19
10:5–6	131n21
10:5	176
10:8–14	131n21
10:9	179
10:10–11	131n21
10:12–19	180
10:12	168
10:15	131n21
10:16–19	170n75
10:17–19	84n75, 289n19
10:19–22	133n27
10:20–23	170n75
10:20–22	133n28, 171n76
10:20	133n27
10:23	158n30
10:24–34	84n74
10:24–27	158
10:24–26	169n71
10:24	158n30
10:25–27	158n30
10:27–32	37n7
10:28 [LXX]	157n25
10:32	168
10:33–11:16	288n11
10:33–34	84n75, **169–70**, 171n76, 176–77, 179–80, 190, 289n19
10:33	172, 191
10:34	133n29
11:1–9	151, **164–180**, 191
11:2–3	178
11:2	280
11:6–9	280n110
11:10	**165–67**
11:11–16	166, **167n63**, 180
11:11	133nn27–28
11:12	167, 167n62, 178n102
11:16	133nn27–28
13:2	178n102
13:3–4	169n71
13:11–13	169n71
14:8	133n29
14:19	173
14:22	133n27
14:24–27	37n7, 131n19, 169n71
14:30–32	169n71
14:30	133n27
15:9	133n27
16:5	166n60
16:6	160n40
16:14	133n27
17:3	133nn27–28
17:6	133n27
18:3	167n62, 178n102
19:1–2	169n71
19:3	166n60
19:6–8	133n29
19:23–24	42n25
20:1	40n16
20:6	160n40
21:17	133n27
22:8–11	48n47, 252, 255, 289n17
22:8–10	160n40
22:9–10	251
22:10–11	46n40

22:13	160n40	40	134
22:25	169n71	40:11	169n69
23:3	133n29	40:24	175
23:9	155n13	41:4	153n7
23:10	133n29	42:17	132n25
24–27	168n65	43:14 [LXX]	157n25
24:5	179n102	44:6	153n7
24:6	133n27	44:28	136n35
24:12	133n27	48:12	153n7
24:16	160n40	49:22	167n62
25:6–9	160n40	52:10 [LXX]	157n25
26:1, 8, 13, 17–18	160n40	59:21	157n23
27:13	168n65	62:10	167n62
28:5	133nn27–28	65:7	281n116
28:14–15	160n40	65:17–25	168
28:16–21	169n71	65:25	**168–69**
29:1–6	169n71		
29:17	133n29	Jeremiah	
30–31	162n46	1:8	185n122
30:1–5	129n15	3	113n71
30:6–7	160n40	7:31	205n35
30:9	179n102	10:3–5	132n25
30:12	252n47	11:20	177n98
30:16	160n40	15:4	1n1
31:1	129n15, 166n60, 252n4	15:13	268n45
31:5	209n44	17:3	268n45
32:14	42n27	19:5	205n35
33:2	160n40	22:6, 23	173
33:9	133n29	23:5–6	171n78, 172
33:23	178n102	25:1	19
34:16	166n60	25:4	19n34
35:2	133n29	26:17–19	105n46
36–39	1n1, 67, **123–50**, 127	26:18–19	1n1
36–37	**126–33**	28:2	158
36:1	281n114	30:25/31:1	235n1
36:5	180n109, 191	31:29–30	281n116
36:6	87	32:18	281n116
36:7	104n42	32:35	205n35
37:1	281n114	33:14–26	171n79
37:4	133nn27–28	33:14–22	171n78
37:9	73–76, 87	33:14–16	172
37:28–32	169n71	33:15	171
37:31–32	133nn27–28	33:18, 21–22	172n81
37:31	133n27	36:4–32	137n38
37:32	133n27	39:4	48n47
37:36	84, 289n19	44:29	182n112
38:7–8	182n112	46:2	19
38:8	127n8	48:13	208n42
38–39	133–36, 150	50:2	167n62
38:5	125	50:17–20	84n76
38:20	160n40	50:17	153n5
39	290n20	51:17	132n25
39:1	69	51:27	167n62
40–66	129	51:64	126, 127n8

52	126–27
52:7	48n47
52:12–15	18n28

Ezekiel

1:2	22n41
1:28	170n73
2:1	170n73
13:24/14:1	236n1
16:21	205n35
17	130n18
17:3–4	172
18	281n116
20:26, 31	205n35
24:4–5	220n77
37:24–28	171n78
40:24	103n40
40:35	103n40
42:15	103n40
44:30	239
45:17	239n10
45:21	214
45:22	239n10
46:2	239n10
47:16	237n4

Hosea

1:1	1n1
2:2	179
3:4–5	163n48, 179
10:15	208n42
11–13	179n107

Amos

1–2	179n107
2:7	178n100
3:14	208n42
4:1	178n100
4:4	208n42
5:5–6	208n42
5:11	178n100
7:10, 13	208n42
8:6	178n100
9:11–15	179
9:11–12	163n48

Jonah

2:1–9	149n63
3:6	139n43

Micah

1:1	1n1
3:11	185n123
4:1–5	178–79n102

4:6–7	157n23
4:8	42n27
5:1–3 [Eng. 2–4]	179
7	179n107

Zephaniah

1:1	1n1
1:4–6	113n71
1:8–9	113n71
1:10–11	45n36
2:5–15	179n107
2:13–15	84n76

Haggai

2:9	153n6

Zechariah

3:8	171n78
6:12	171n78
10	167n63
10:8–12	84n76
10:10	154n12

Psalms

2:6–12	160–61
2:7–12	190
2:7	160n41, 161n43
9:10 [Eng. 9]	154n11
10:1	154n11
31:16 [Eng. 15]	154n11
46:8, 12 [Eng. 7, 11]	184
72	173n84
72:20	127n8
89:19–37	260n11
89:22	185n123
106:37–38	205n35
113:2	157n23
115:18	157n23
121:8	157n23
125:2	157n23
131:3	157n23
132:1	243n22

Job

1:1	103n40
6:12	175n89
9:15–16, 19, 27–31	175n89
11:7–12	175n89
14:7–9	174–75
20:6–19	175n89
27:14–17	175n89
31:5–10	175n89
31:13–40	175
31:40	127n8

33:32–33	175
35:6–7	175
36:11–12	175n89
37:13	175n89

Proverbs

25:1	1n1, 288n13

Ruth

2:4	185n122
3:10	153n6

Song of Songs

5:15	173n85

Ecclesiastes

1:11	153n7

Lamentations

5:7	281n11

Esther

9:24–25	103n40

Daniel

1:2	268n45
2:12–13	103n40
3:8	103n40
3:21	103n40
5:3–4	103n40
5:29	103n40
6:24	103n40
11:29	153n6

Ezra

1:6	243n22
2:16	1n1
2:28	208n42
3:8	244n24
4:10	15n14
4:24	103n40
6:1	103n40
6:9–10	239n11
6:14	103n40
7:24	239n11
8:36	103n40

Nehemiah

3:15	48n47
3:26–27	42n27
7:21	1n1
7:32	208n42
8:18	153n7
10:18 [Eng. 17]	1n1

10:33–40 [Eng. 32–39]	239
10:38–39 [Eng. 37–38]	255
10:38 [Eng. 37]	245n29
11:9	45n36
11:21	42n27
11:31	208n42
13:1	103n40
13:30	103n38

1 Chronicles

2:7	199n15
3:13	1n1
4:18	52n61
4:33	241n17
4:41	247, 288n13
5:9	154n12
5:25	199n15
5:26	242n20
6:17 [Eng. 32]	221n79
6:51–54 [Eng. 66–69]	81n63
7:5	241n17
7:21	103n40
7:28	208n42
8:7	103n40
9:1	199n15
9:25	246n30
9:26	103n40, 258n4
10:13	199n15
11:8	250n42, 258n4
11:14	258n4
12:39 [Eng. 38]	258n4
12:40–41	209n47
14:11	157n22
15:4	258n4
15:11	242n20
16:10, 31	274n88
16:37–40	239n10, 242n21
17:6	210n48
17:10	210n48
17:11–14	267n37
17:11–13	26n54
17:12	266
18:6, 13	258n4, 270n60, 275n94
19:3	250n39
20:1	22n41
21:1–22:1	253n52
21:2	258n4
21:3, 17	250n39
22:7	258n4
22:8–9	273n79

22:11–13	265n33
22:18	250n39
23:3	244n24
23:4–5	201n18
23:6–7	242n20
23:10	250n42
23:25	273n80
23:28	258n4
23:31	243n22
24:19	221
24:27	242n20
25:9, 11, 19, 23–31	242n20
26:22	258n4
28:2	199n15, 273n81
28:6–7	265, 267n37
28:7–9	265n33
28:7	238n9
28:9	276n97
28:11–18	242n21
28:11	199n15
28:12	258n4
29:9	274n88
29:20	258n4
29:28	274n91

2 Chronicles

1:1	198n10
1:9	265n33
1:12	274n91
1:16	270n61
2:1 [Eng. 2]	271n62
2:3 [Eng. 4]	258
2:9 [Eng. 10]	271n62
2:14–15 [Eng. 15–16]	271n62
2:16–17 [Eng. 17–18]	271n62
6:7–8	274n89
6:16	265n33
6:17	265n33
6:41	273n81, 274n88
6:42	265n33
7:6	201n18
7:8–10	258
7:8–9	209n46
7:11	258n5
7:14	222
7:17–20	265n33
8:4, 6	57n81, 271n63
8:12–13	239n10
8:12	199n15
8:16	201n18
9:22	274n91
9:25	270n61
10:2	139n42
10:4	155n13
10:16	253n52
11:2–4	127n9
11:3	204n29
11:5	250n42
11:5–12	253n51, 271n65
11:6–10	54n67
11:8	52n61
11:12	248n36
11:13	204n29
12:1	204n29
12:2–12	268n45
12:2–4	249n37
12:2	199n15, 272n69
12:9	272n69
12:10	103n40
12:13	198nn8, 10
13:4–12	217n69
13:4	199n15, 204n29
13:5	250n39, 265n33
13:8	198n10
13:9	250n39
13:13–18	267n42
13:15	204n29
13:19	208n42, 272n70
13:21	198n10
14:1 [Eng. 2]	273n83
14:2 [Eng. 3]	236n2
14:5–7 [Eng. 6–8]	250n42, 271n65, 273n83
14:5 [Eng. 6]	267n42, 273n83
14:6 [Eng. 7]	276n97
14:8–13 [Eng. 9–14]	267n42
14:13–14 [Eng. 14–15]	269n49
15:2	199n15, 276n97
15:8	199n15, 272n70
15:15	273n83, 274n88
15:19	273n83
16:1–6	272n69
16:4	57n81, 271n63
16:5	139n42
16:8	250n39
16:9	274n89
17:1	198n10
17:2	248n36, 250n42, 270n60, 271n65
17:5	270n57, 274n91
17:11	270n57
17:12–13	250n42, 271n65
17:12	57n81, 271n63
17:19	248n36
18:1	274n91
18:16	204n29
18:17	250n39
20	250n41, 267n42

20:6–7, 12	250n39	28:16–21	207n40
20:15	252n49	28:16–20	249n37
20:20	199n15, 200n18	28:17–18	286n5
20:25	269n50	28:18	42n26
20:27	274n88	28:19	199n15
20:30	273n84	28:22	199n15, 200n17
20:31	198n8	28:23	204n29
20:36	271n64	28:24–25	238n8
21:2–3	271n65	28:24	200n17, 202
21:5	198n8	28:27	24n47
21:6	31n76	29–32	195–97
21:7	265n33	29–31	204
21:20	198n8	29	**197–209**, 231–32, 236
22:2	31n76, 198n8	29:1	24n47, 27n62
23:1	242n21	29:2	226, 258
23:3	265n33	29:3	230
23:18	243n23	29:4	258n4
23:21	274n85	29:5	226
24:1	198n8	29:6–9	209n47
24:5	204n29	29:6–8	249n37
24:10	274n88	29:10	222n81, 258n4,
24:20	250n39		274n89
24:23–24	272n69	29:15	216n68, 221n81
25:7–10	267n42	29:17	230
25:9–10	269n51	29:18	1n1
25:11–13	267n42	29:25–30	258n4
25:13	269n51	29:27	1n1
25:15–16, 19	250n39	29:31	227n93
25:23–24	272n69	29:34	230
26:3	198n8	29:35	238n8
26:5–7	267n42	29:36	274n88
26:8	270n57	30	163, **209–32**
26:9–10	250n42, 271n65	30:1	204
26:14	248n36	30:5	204, 258n4, 272n70
26:16, 18	199n15	30:6	114n73, 164n50, 204,
27:1	198n8		276n97
27:3–4	250n42, 271n65	30:7	199n15, 249n37
27:3	42n27	30:8	276n97
27:5–6	267n42	30:9	114n73, 276n97
27:6	198n10	30:10	237, 272n70
27:8	198n8	30:12	258n4
29–32	1n1	30:14	236
28:1–6, 8	200n17	30:23	258
28:1–2	249n37	30:24	1n1
28:1	24n49, 27n57, 198n8	30:25	274n88
28:2–4	238n8	30:26	258
28:4	202, 206	31	235–48, 254–55
28:5–8	27n61, 272n69	31:1	111n67, 114n73, 204
28:7	187	31:3	258
28:8	269n51	31:5	113n70
28:9–15	225n90	31:11–14	258n4
28:10	250n39	31:14–19	299
28:11	199n15, 276n97	31:19	243n22
28:15	269n51	31:20–21	258n5

32	235, 249–55	33:19	199n15
32:1–23	267n42	33:20	277n100
32:1–5	50n52	33:21–25	107n51
32:1	268n44	33:21	198n8
32:2–6	49n50, 271n65,	33:24–25	277n100
	289n17	34:1	198n8
32:2–5	47n44	34:2	276n96
32:3–4	86n83	34:6–7	119n90, 272n70
32:5	258n4	34:8–13	275n92
32:7–8	278n104	34:11–13	271n65
32:7	281n115	34:22	45n36
32:15	1n1	34:29–32	212, 222n83
32:20–22	268n44	34:30	127n9
32:20	281n115	34:33	272n70
32:22	258n4, 274n86,	35	**209–22**
	275n94	35:1–18	119n90
32:23	270n57	35:1	229
32:25	197n5	35:3	204n29
32:27–30	271n65	35:18	232
32:27	274n91	35:24	277n100
32:28	271n63	36:1–4	25n53
32:30	35, 49n50, 50n52	36:2	198n8
32:31	258n5	36:5	198n8
32:33	24n47	36:9	22n43, 203n26
33:1	198n8	36:10	22n41
33:12	276n96	36:11	198n8
33:14–16	271n65	36:14	199n15
33:14	42n27, 248n36,	36:16	200n18
	275n92	36:18	268n45

Apocrypha

Tobit		2 Maccabees	
1:1–2	15n18	2:12	201n21
1:15	15n18	10:6	201n21

Pseudepigrapha

Sibylline Oracles	
3.741–95	164n52

Dead Sea Scrolls

1QIsaᵃ	157	9:5	157nn22, 26
2:11	157n25	11:9	157n25

New Testament

Gospel of Luke		Gospel of John	
1:13	159n38	9:7	49n49
1:31	159n38		

Hellenistic/Roman Authors

Herodotus
2.141   **71–73**, 83, 83n68

Virgil's Fourth Eclogue   164n52

Jewish/Christian Authors

Josephus, *Antiquities*
9.283–87   13n11
10.20 (10.1.4)   73n28
10.30–31   144n53

Justin, *Dialogue with Trypho*
43   189n36

Rabbinic Texts

Mishnah
Ḥagigah, 1   218n73

b. Sanhedrin
12a–12b   231n101
94a   290n21
99a   290n21

b. Berakhot
10b   231n101
28b   290n21

j. Avodah Zarah
3:1 [42c]   290n21

j. Nedarim
6.13   231n101

j. Sotah
9:17 [24c]   290n21

Exodus Rabbah
18:5   189n36

Sifre, Re'eh
16.2   218n73

SUBJECT INDEX

Aaron 214, 217n69, 299
Abiathar 247n33
Abijah (king) 208n42, 217n69, 267, 272, 276n95, 285
Abijam 186
Abiyah (queen mother) 24
Abner 146n56
Abraham/Abram 70, 145n55, 181n111, 268n45
Adad-Rimmon 206
Adapa 30n74
Adar 10, 14, 18–24, 68, 69n16, 73n27, 77
Addaru see Adar
adoption 160n41
Adrammelech 205n35, 296
Ahab 31n76, 127n9, 205n33
Ahaz 11–12n6, **24–28**, 32–33, 36, 42n26, 106, 108n55, 125, 126n6, 128, 130, 135, 143–44, 147n59, 148, 151, 162n46, 180n109, **181–91**, 200–202, 204–209, 222, 227n94, 232, 238, 255, 275n93, 277, 279, 281, 283, 285–86, 290n22
Ahaziah 25n51, 186n126, 275n93
Ahijah 127n9, 185, 264
Aḥimiti 37
Akkad 14n12, 20
Akkadian see Neo-Assyrian
Alexander the Great 75n35
altar 92–93, 95–97, 99–100, 103n39, 104, 105n45, 106–107, 108n55, 111, 114n73, 115, 117n86, 120, 201n19, 202, 206, 215n66, 220n76, 236, 238n8, 261n13, 297
Amariah (steward) 1n1
Amaziah 27, 186, 198n8, 267
Amēl-Marduk 21
Ammon 41, 78, 250n41, 269–70
Amon 22, 107n51, 151, 186n126, 277n100
Amos (prophet) 115n81, 133nn27, 28, 181, 279, 285
Amoz 2, 46n40, 123, 127–29, 131, 133, 148, 150–51, 156, 163, 165n56, 168, 177, 182, 189n135, 191, 252, 283, 285, 296, 298
Amun 161n43
Anat 184
Anathoth 247n33
annals, Assyrian 1, 13, 16–17, 18n26, 37n5, 61n1, 65–67, 71, 76n40, 78, 79nn53, 57, 81,

82nn65, 67, 83, 85, 94n9, 110n62, 130n17, 137, 289
Anšar 39–40n16
Arabic (language) 31n76, 96n16, 171n77, 214, 268n47
Arad 64, **92–95**, 96–97, 99–100, 113, 114n77, 120
Aram 20, 36, 42n23, 126n6, 133n27, 184, 206–207, 237n5, 267n41, 269–70
Aramaic 15n14, 103–104n40, 140, 168, 272n71, 295
Arbailu 77n45
archaeology 2–3, 5, 35–66, 68, 86, 92–101, 112n69, 113, 120, 196, 224, 238n8, 249–55, 270, 276n95
Arpad 17n24, 37n6, 188, 296–97
Arvad see Arpad
Asa 101, 186, 236n2, 250n42, 267, 269, 271–74, 277n98
Asaph 142n47, 242n21, 297
Ashdod 37, 38n10, 40n16, 50n52, 69n16, 70n19, 78
Asher 224n86, 225n88
Asherah 92, 101, 102n36, 103n39, 236
Ashkelon 78–79, 82
Ashtar-Chemosh 268n47
Ashtoreth 262
Assyria 5n8, 10, 12–18, 29n68, 31n78, 32, 35–42, 58, **61–87**, 94n9, 105n44, 109–113, 117, 123–50, 152, 153n5, 158, 161–64, 167n63, 168–70, 175–76, 179–80, 188, 190–91, 197, 204, 207–208, 217, 224–25, 230–31, 248, 249–53, 268, 270n56, 274, 280, 285–86, 288–89, 291, 292n29, 295–98
Assyrian king list 25
Asuhili 96n17
Aššur 14n12, 37n10, 39nn15–16, 109, 111, 129n12, 130n18, 176
Aššur-rabi II 25n53
Aššurbanipal 95n11, 129n12
Ataliah **28–31**, 33
Athaliah 29–30, 31n76, 186, 273
Av 18, 19n30
Aviv see Nisan
Azariah (king) see Uzziah
Azariah (priest) 244

Azariah (steward) 1n1
Azekah 38–41, 52n61, 54n67, 58, 64–65, 67, 69n16, 286n7
Azriyau 35–36n1
Azuri 37

Baal-Hadad 205n35
Baasha 57n81, 127n9
Babylon(ia) 14, 18–19, 20–21, 32, 37, 40n17, 51n56, 55, 65, 69, 73nn27–28, 78, 95, 102n36, 111n65, 129n12, 130n18, 133n27, 134–36, 142n48, 143–46, 150, 153n5, 164n51, 173, 197, 235, 249, 253, 261, 289–90, 292n29
Babylonian (language) 14–15n14
Babylonian Chronicle 5n8, 14–17, 18n29, 19n30, 20, 22n43, 23, 32, 73n27, 78n50, 83nn69, 71
Baruch 137n38
bāmâ 97, 107, 118n86, 236
Beer-sheba 92, 94n9, 95–97, 100n32, 101, 113n72, 120, 273, 275
Bel 21, 78
Benaiah 185
Benjamin 204, 208n42, 212, 224n86, 236–37
Berossus 73n28
Beth-Shemesh 64
Beth-zur 54n67
Bethel 114, 208, 237n7, 261n13, 287
Bir es-Seba' 96n16
Birket el-Ḥamra 48n47
Birket Silwan 49n49
bīt kāri 40n18
Bit-Yakin 69
blockade 50, 80–81, 84–85, 87, 123, 126, 133, 136, 146, 147n58, 197, 249n38, 252n47, 281, 289, 295–97
Book of the Covenant 103n39, 105n44, 117n86, 119, 212, 214, 221n78
bridge theory 133, 135n33, 145, 148, 167n63
Broad Wall 47, 86n83, 251, 289
bullae 1, 107

Calaḥ see Nimrud
Carchemish 19, 179n104
centralization 100n29, 102, 107–121, 215n66, 219, 223, 246, 248, 287, 291n24, 293
Chemosh 262
child sacrifice 106, 132n24, 205, 207n41
co-regency 10n3, 11–12n6, 23–28, 32–33, 74n34, 147, 148n61, 189, 277, 282, 286, 292
Conaniah 240

Cyprus 38n12, 79
Cyrus 111n65, 130n18, 136n35

Damascus 27, 36, 37n6, 126n6, 179, 181, 202, 206
Dan 4n6, 81n63, 211, 225, 261n13, 272n70, 273, 275
Darius 14, 239
David 1, 3n3, 25–26, 42n27, 52n61, 102n36, 143n50, 146n56, 151, 156, 159, 161nn41, 43, 162–64, 169, 171–73, 176–77, 179, 181, 185–87, 191, 196, 197n5, 201n18, 207, 209n47, 210–11, 220, 226, 227n94, 229, 238, 242n21, 253n52, 257–83, 285, 288, 290n22, 291, 293, 298
David, City of 42–43, 45, 48–49, 51n56, 58, 251, 277, 287, 288n12
Davidic convenant 26, 185n123, 260, 262–66, 267n43, 272, 278, 282
Dead Sea Scrolls 151
Debir see Khirbet Rabud
Deborah 267
Deutero-Isaiah see Second Isaiah
Deuteronomistic History 2, 62, 86, 118–19n87, 125, 131, 133, 136, 137n38, 143n50, 145, 147–48, 150–51, 196–98, 203–204, 222, 249, 258–83, 288n14, 290–92
divine abandonment 105n45, 130n18
Domla 1n1
Dor 78
Dur-Šarrukin 17n21, 78

Ea 30, 33
Edom 37n10, 78, 207, 249n37, 259, 269–70
Egypt 5n8, 17, 19, 22n42, 23n44, 31n77, 35, 37, 38n10, 40n18, 41–42, 52n57, 71–72, 73nn27–28, 74–76, 78–79, 81n65, 82, 83n69, 86–87, 102n36, 112n69, 129, 130n17, 133, 143, 145n55, 160n41, 161n43, 162n46, 167n63, 182n112, 188, 190, 214, 237n5, 259n9, 268n45, 270–71, 280, 286, 289, 297–98
Ehud 267
Ekron 39, 78–79, 81n63, 65, 82, 85, 130n17, 289
Elam 37, 69, 86
Eli 182n112
Eliada 259
Eliakim (steward) 141, 142n47, 295–97
Elijah 127n9
Elisha 127n9, 270n56
Ellipi 78

Elohist document (E)   215n65, 246n31, 288n14
Eltekeh   76, 79, 81–84, 87, 289
Elul   10n2, 18n29, 20n37, 22n41
Enmeduranki   176n92
Ephraim   see Israel, Syro-Ephraimite war
epidemic   see plague
eponym list   13–14, 16n21, 77n45
Esarhaddon   5n8, 40n17, 72, 83n69, 129n12, 167n63, 176n92, 198, 296
Esther   149n63
Euphrates   269, 271
Evil-Merodach   see Amēl-Marduk
exile   3, 18, 20n36, 21, 23, 114n73, 115, 126n6, 135, 143, 145nn54–55, 146, 148, 150, 162–63, 164n50, 167n63, 190, 208, 215n66, 217, 229, 232, 238, 261, 279, 287, 291–92
Ezekiel (prophet)   238, 281n116

Feast of Unleavened Bread   209, 213–15, 217–18, 235
first fruits   112n70, 239, 245
First Isaiah   1, 6, 86, **123–191**, 290n22

Galilee   15n18, 158, 162, 287n9
Garden of Eden   164
Gath   39
Gaza   37n6, 40–41, 78, 188, 280
Geba   272n68
Gerar   269
Gershon   201
Gezer   65, 224n86
Gibeon   263
Gideon   267
Gihon spring   48, 50
Gilgal   264
Goliath   143n50, 279n107

Hadad   259
Hagar   145n55
Halicarnassus   71
Hamath   37n6, 237n5, 270, 296–97
Hanani   127n9
Hannah   149n63
Haremhab   161n43
Harran   23n44
Hatti   20
Hazael   270n56
Hebrew (language)   14n14, 19n33, 21n38, 30, 35, 48n45, 49, 69n14, 77n44, 94n10, 102–104, 128n11, 152n1, 153–59, 163n47, 168–77, 178n102, 183n116, 191, 199n15, 201n18, 202n22, 205n35, 206n39,

210–11n49, 214, 221, 225n88, 237n5, 240–43, 250n42, 258n4, 269
Hebron   52n61, 54, 271
Hephaestus   71, 72n23
Herodotus   71–73, 83n68
Hilkiah   108, 118n87, 142n47, 295, 297
Hinnom Valley   43, 45
Hiram   263, 271
Holiness Legislation   99n28, 117–18n86, 177–78n98, 214n63, 226n92, 244n24, 247n31, 291
Hophra, Pharaoh   182n112
Hormah   see Tel Ḥalif
Horon   102n36
Hosea (prophet)   115n81, 183–84, 279, 285
Hoshea (king)   12n6, 26n56, 27, 189n133, 270n56, 277n99, 286
Huldah   108
ḥbrn   52n61
Ḥirbet ʿAbbād   52n61
Ḥirbet Šuwēkē   52n61

Iaʾ/Iadnana   see Cyprus
Ibn Ezra   183n117
idols   95, 131–32
illness   11n5, 24n46, 69, 123, 134, 136, 143, 144n53, 146–48, 150, 197, 235, 249
Immanuel   151–52, **181–91**, 252n49, 278n104, 285
Imnah   240, 299
incense   92, 95n13, 96, 97n19, 99, 101, 108, 120, 161n41, 202, 206
India   76n40
instruments   201n18
Iran   76n40
Isaiah   2, 31n78, 42, 46n40, 71n20, 84, 115n80, 123, **123–91**, 197, 251–52, 280–81, 283, 285, 288–89, 293, 296, 298
Isaiah, book of   see First Isaiah
Israel   3–5, 10, 12–18, 25, 27, 31n78, 32, 37, 40, 42, 47n44, 55, 57, 61, 92, 100–101, 106, 108n55, 112n70, 114n73, 115n77, 116, 119n88, 121, 126n6, 127n9, 131n19, 132, 136n35, 139, 145n55, 154, 160n40, 162–63, 164, 166, 167n63, 170n75, 179nn102, 107, 180–81, 183, 187, 188n132, 190, 195–96, 203–208, 210–13, 214n63, 217n69, 219–20, 223n85, 224–25, 228–32, 236–39, 240n15, 247, 250n41, 253n52, 259n9, 260–64, 267n41, 268–73, 274n90, 275–76, 277n99, 282, 285–86, 288, 290, 292–93, 297–98
Issachar   224n86, 241n17
Iyyar   229

Jahaziel 250n41, 252n49
Jehoahaz II 22, 23n44, 25, 186n126
Jehoiachin 19–23, 135, 186n126
Jehoiada 185, 274
Jehoiakim 19, 22, 23n44, 25n53, 186n126
Jehoram 28n63, 186n127, 205n33, 277n98
Jehoshaphat 57n81, 186n127, 250nn41–42,
    252n49, 267, 269–71, 273–74, 277n99
Jehu 127n9, 186n127, 205n34
Jeremiah (prophet) 126, 137n38, 142n48,
    182n112, 281n116
Jeroboam I 127n9, 185, 205, 208n42,
    217n69, 227n94, 228, 237n7, 253n52, 259,
    261n13, 262n17, 265n32, 272
Jeroboam II 127n9, 208n42
Jerome 159n35
Jerusalem 2, 10, 12, **18–21**, 23, 26n54,
    28n64, 31–32, 35, 37n7, **42–50**, 51–52,
    58, 62, 64, 68, 70–71, 80–82, 84–87, 92,
    101n34, 104, 107–108, 110, 111n66, 112,
    113n71, 114, 115n77, 116, 119, **123–50**,
    163n48, 168, 176, 178, 179n102, 180n109,
    195, 197, 202, 204, 206, 208, 210–12, 216–18,
    223–25, 228, 230–31, 237, 239–40, 243,
    246, 247n33, 250n42, 251, 252n47, 259,
    261–62, 267, 268n44, 270–71, 273–74,
    278, 281, 286–87, 289–90, 293, **295–98**
Jesse 151, 166, 171, 176–77, 180n108, 191,
    264, 267
Joab 259n9, 263
Joah 141, 142n47, 295, 297
Joash 274, 276n95
Jonah (prophet) 127n9, 149n63
Jonah ben Amittai 127n9
Joram 277n99
Jordan 4n6, 143n50, 158
Joshua (figure) 268, 272, 276
Josiah 2, 19, 22–23, 25, 51, 52n57, 54n70,
    57n80, 91n1, 93, 102, 103n39, 104, 106–108,
    117n85, 118–21, 127n9, 144, 151–52, 161n41,
    171n76, 176n91, 186n126, 187, 205, 206n37,
    209–222, 223nn84–85, 225n89, 226, 229,
    232, 238n7, 261n13, 262, 271, 272n70,
    275, 276nn95, 97, 277n100, 278, 279n107,
    290–91
Jotbah 287n9
Jotham 24–28, 33, 173, 186n126, 250n42,
    267, 271
jubilee 237
Judah 2, 19–23, 25, 27–29, 31–33, **35–150**,
    160n40, 163, 167, 171n76, 176, 183, 185n123,
    188, 190, 195, 198, 200n17, 201n19, 202–
    204, 206–208, 210–12, 225, 228–31, 236–
    37, 239, 250nn41–42, 253n51, 261, 267,

269, 270–71, 273, 275, 277–78, 285–86,
    289, 290nn21–22, 295–98

kaige-recension of LXX 149n63
Kawa 74
Ketef Hinnom 45
Khirbet el-Mukenna' see Tel Miqne
Khirbet Rabud 64
Khorsabad 16–17
Kidron Valley 48, 251n43
king's garden 48, 50, 252
Kinneret 224
Kir 126n6
Kiriath-Sefer see Khirbet Rabud
Kislimu 20
Kohath 201
Kore 240, 243n23, 299
Kue 270
Kurru 75n39
Kush 62, 73–76, 83, 87, 140, 167, 296
Kutha 95n11

Laban 37, 236n1
Lachish 44n30, 50n53, 51–52, 54, 59,
    62–63, 64–65, 68, 70, 80, 82, 92, 96n17,
    97–101, 113n72 120, 126, 141n46, 154n11,
    295–96
law 2, 4n6, 70, 99n28, 102, 103n39,
    105n44, 108, 115 117–19, 121, 145n55,
    160n41, 177–78, 180n108, 182, 191, 196,
    205n35, 211n52, 212, 214n64, 215, 217,
    219–23, 226–27 230, 231n102, 232–33,
    238n9, 239n13, 240, 244–46, 247n31, 254,
    259–60, 281n116, 291, 293
Lebanon 133, 173, 271, 298
legislation see law
Levites 114n76, 117n86, 127n9, 199, 200n17,
    209–10, 212, 217, 218n71, 219–20, 230,
    238n8, 238–48, 254, 258n4, 287, 291,
    299
Levitical cities 81n63, 117n86, 247–48,
    255, 287, 291
Libya 75
limmu-chronicle see eponym list
lmlk seals 2, 35, **50–59**, 63–65, 68, 96n17,
    112n69, 254–55, 287
Lower Pool 48–49, 251
Lucianic recension of LXX 102n36,
    207n39
Lulî 78–79
Luz 208n42
LXX 19n32, 27n57, 102n36, 103n38, 141n47,
    154n12, 157, 171n79, 175n90, 206n39, 241,
    243n23, 274n86

Maaseiah   27, 33, 187–88
Maher-šalal-ḥaš-baz   183–84, 186, 191
Makteš   45
Malik   205n35
Mampsis-Kurnub   52n61
Manasseh   22, 24, 49n51, 51n56, 96n17, 101,
    106–107, 108n55, 127n9, 144, 162, 186n126,
    189, 203, 205n35, 206n37, 224, 225n88,
    236–37, 240n15, 271–72, 275–76, 277n100,
    279n108, 287
Marcheshvan   22n43
Marduk   81n65, 130n18
Marduk-apla-iddina   see
    Merodach-baladan II
Mareshah   54n67
maximalist view   35, 43
Media   78
Mediterranean Sea   224n86
Megiddo   100n32
Meluḫḫa   see Kush
Memphis   72n23, 73n27
Merari   201
Merodach-baladan II   14n12, 37, 68–69,
    78, 86, 130n18, 144n53, 258n5, 270, 289
Mesha   207n41, 268n47
messianism   151–91, 279–81, 283, 288,
    290n21, 291n25, 292–93
Metunu   77n46
Micah (prophet)   115n80, 137n38, 179n102,
    285
Micaiah ben Imlah   127n9
Midian   159, 280
Milcom   262
Millo   250n42, 258n4, 259n9
minimalist view   43
Mišneh   45, 58
Mizpah   see Tell en-Naṣbeh
mmšt   52n61
Moab   37n10, 41, 78, 133n27, 207n41,
    250n41, 269, 272n69
Molech   205n35
Mordechai   149n63
Moresheth   see Tell Judeideh
Moses   4n6, 92, 101, 102n36, 107, 115, 189,
    214, 219–21, 237n3, 260, 272
Mount Moriah   42, 43n28
Mount Zion   132, 165n56, 168, 183
MT   6n13, 102n36, 103n38, 141n47, 154n12,
    157nn25, 27, 159nn35–36, 171n79, 206n39,
    241, 243n23, 274n86

Nabonidus   111n65
Nabopolassar   19
Nabu-naṣir   14

Nabuli   77n45
Napata   75
Naphtali   155, 158, 162
Nathan   185, 265n33
Nebat   205
Nebo   268n47
Nebuchadrezzar I   176n92
Nebuchadrezzar II   18–21, 22n41, 32
Neco II, Pharaoh   19, 22n42, 23n44,
    25n53
Negev   42n26, 47, 51, 52n61, 54, 56n74, 58,
    286–87
Nehushtan   92, 101–102, 107, 112n69, 121,
    207, 236
Neo-Assyrian   13n9, 14–15n14, 15nn16–17,
    21n38, 29, 30–31, 33, 35n1, 85,
    176nn92–93, 191 (search on CAD,
    AHW)
Nile Delta/River   72n23, 75
Nimrud   28, 31, 33, 41, 58, 291
Nineveh   15n18, 24, 42, 63, 68, 80–81, 84,
    99, 139n43, 289, 291, 296
Nippur   176n92
nîr material   259–66
Nisan/Nisânu   10n2, 14, 18–22, 24, 68,
    69n16, 77, 214n63, 229
Nob   247n33
Nubia   73–76, 83, 86n83, 87

oath   28n64, 79n56, 129n12, 130n18, 289
Omri   31
Ophel   42, 43n28
Orontes   37n7

Padî   79, 289
Palestine   11n5, 20, 36–37, 41n20, 61n1, 62,
    67, 73, 82, 114n75
Passover   163, 197, **209–33**, 272n70, 287
Pathros   167n63
patriarch   4n5, 287, 290n21
Pekah   26n56, 27, 36, 126n6, 154, 181, 185,
    187, 188n132
Pelusium   71, 72n23, 73n28
pesaḥ   see Passover
Peshitta   27n57, 102n36, 103n38, 127n8,
    154n12, 159n35
Pharaoh   19, 22n42, 25n53, 74n31, 75–76,
    86–87, 129n12, 182n112, 297
Philistia   37n10, 39, 40n18, 42n26, 51,
    77–79, 129n12, 133n27, 188n132, 270, 286
Philistine   37, 39n15, 40, 42, 58, 78, 110n62,
    249n37, 269, 271, 278, 280, 286, 289
Phoenicia   31n77, 41n20, 78–79, 102n36
Pir'u   38n10

plague   72, 78, 83, 144n53, 202n22,
    209n44, 253n52, 289
Pool of Siloam   49
Port Said   72n23
portions (מָנוֹת)   **238–48**, 249n37, 254,
    287, 291, 299
Priestly document (P)   99n28, 117–18n86,
    214n63, 215n65, 219, 226, 233, 241n19,
    288n14, 291
province   18, 36, 78, 109
Ptah   72n23, 73n27

Qarqar   37

rab šāqê   80, 82, 87, 92, 104–107, 111n66,
    112n70, 121, 128–30, 137–42, 148, 180n109,
    191, 252n47, 295–97
rabbinic literature   1, 231n101, 290n21
Rafiah   17
Ramah   272n68
Ramat Rachel   51, 53n61, 64
Ramesses II   75n35
Rashi   159n35, 183n117
reform, Deuteronomic   115–21, 213, 219,
    246, 255
reform, Hezekian   2, 11n5, 91–121, 137n38,
    195, 197, 198n12, 204, 207, 209, 215, 223,
    227, 231–32, 235–38, 249n37, 254, 278,
    287, 293
reform, Josaianic   51, 52n57, 53, 104,
    107n54, 108, 109n60, 114n76, 117n85,
    118n87, 119nn89–90, 121, 212, 215n66,
    248n34, 248n34, 261n13, 262, 272n70
Rehoboam   101, 163n47, 186n127, 250n42,
    253n51, 266n34, 271
Remaliah   126n6
remnant   132–33, 164n50, 166, 170n75,
    171n76, 180, 296, 298
rest motif   272–75, 280, 282
rēš šarrūti   21n38, 40n17, 198
Rezin   36, 126n6, 181, 185, 188
Rezon   259
Rimmon see Tel Ḥalif
Rukibtu   79

Samaria   10–11, **12–18**, 21, 23, 32, 36–37,
    40–41, 46, 50n52, 58, 68, 70n18, 131n20,
    163, 179–80, 188n132, 191, 198, 205, 208,
    223, 239, 281, 286, 287n10, 288, 293, 296
Samson   160n39, 189, 267
Samuel (judge)   210, 211n52, 264, 272
sanctuary   92–100, 101n34, 107n53, 108,
    110–11, 113–14, 118n86, 120, 201, 206, 208,

213–22, 226, 230–32, 237–38n7, 240,
    244–47, 254, 287
Sarai   145n55
Sargon   1, 11n5, 14n12, **15–18**, 29–33,
    36–42, 46, 58, 66, 68, 69n16, 76n40, 77,
    78, 79n53, 83, 129n12, 130n18, 131, 136,
    176, 179n104, 198, 281, 286, 289
Saul   3n3, 146n56, 186, 264–65, 267–68
seal impressions   1n1, 35–36n1, 50–59,
    63–65, 96n17, 107, 112n69, 287
Second Isaiah   133, 135, 136nn35, 37, 143,
    145, 148, 156n16, 167n63, 168
Semna   75
Sennacherib   1–2, 10, 11n5, 15n16, 24,
    28–30, 33, 38–39, 40, 41n20, 42, 46n38,
    47–48, 50n52, 52n59, 53, 54n69, 58,
    61–87, 92n2, 93, 94n9, 95–96, 98n24,
    99, 106n48, 110, 112, 113nn71–72, 115n77,
    120, 123–24, 126n6, 129n12, 130nn17–18,
    131, 136, 137n38, 138, 139n44, 141, 142n48,
    144n53, 146–50, 158n30, 180n109, 188n132,
    197, 235, **249–53**, 255, 267, 274, 281, 289,
    292n29, **295–98**
Sennacherib's third campaign   2, 10, 24,
    39nn14, 16, 46n38, 47nn14, 44, 48, 50,
    52n59, 53–55, **61–87**, 93, 96, 99, 106n48,
    110–14, 115n77, **123–50**, 158n30, 180n109,
    181, 197, 235, **249–53**, 255, 267–68, **289**,
    295–98 (search on campaign,
    invasion)
Sethon   73n27
Sethos   71n23
Shabako   75
Shalmaneser III   37n7
Shalmaneser IV   25n53
Shalmaneser V   12–18   32, 36, 70n18,
    270n56, 286
Sheba, queen of   258n5, 263
Shebanyau   35–36n1
Shebitku   73n27, 74n31, 75, 76n41
Shebna   137n38, 141, 142n47, 295–97
Shema/Sheba   96n16
Shemaiah   127n9, 299
Shephelah   42n26, 47, 51–54, 58, 96n17,
    286–87
Shiloh   127n9
Shimei   240, 263
Shishak   249n37
shoot   165–66, 169–80, 191
shrine   71n23, 92n2, 93–95, 97–98, 100n32,
    108, 114n75, 118n87, 120, 206n38, 207–208,
    237n7, 261n13
Sib'u   17

Sidon 79, 224
Siloam tunnel 35, **48–50**, 58, 251, 254–55, 289
Simirra 37n6
Sinai 73, 215n65
Sippar 95n11, 176n92
Sokoh 54n67
Solomon 1, 3n3, 5n11, 27n58, 42, 57n81, 76n39, 108n55, 186, 196, 201n18, 206n36, 209–11, 213, 220, 222, 227n94, 229, 237–38, 247n33, 254, 257–83, 285, 288, 292–93
spoliation 109n60, 111n65, 268–69
Sudan 75
Sumerian 13n9, 80, 164n52
syncretism 116, 259, 285
Syria see Aram
Syriac 157, 171n77
Syro-Ephraimite war 27, 33, 36, 125, 151, 181–84, 187–88, 189n132, 190n137, 200n17, 206, 225, 249n37, 269, 281, 285
śwkh 52n61
Ṣidqa 79
Šamaš-šum-ukīn 14, 129n12
Šarru-lū-dāri 79
Šeʿar-yašub 182–83, 186

Taanach 100n32
Tabalu 78
Taharqo 62, **73–76**, 82–83, 86–87, 140
Targum 102n36, 157n24
tartānu 17, 40n16, 141, 296
Tebet(u) 14, 77n44, 83n71
tefillin 31n78
Tel Batash see Timnah
Tel ʿAmal 100n32
Tel ʿErani 64
Tel Ḥalif 64, 92n2
Tel Maresha 65
Tel Miqne 81n63
Tel Seraʿ see Ziklag
Tel Sheva 65
Tel Zakariyah 65
Tell Beit Mirsim 64
Tell en-Naṣbeh 65
Tell esh-Sharîʿah see Ziklag
Tell esh-Shallaf 81n63, 82
Tell eṣ-Ṣafi 39n15, 65
Tell Jezer see Gezer
Tell Judeideh 64
Tell Melât 81n63
Tell Zafit see Tell eṣ-Ṣafi

Tell Zīf 52n61
Temple 107n53, 108, 116n82, 118n87, 119n90, 126n6, 132, 135, 136n35, 139–40, 142–43, 146, 178, 195, **197–209**, 213, 215, 216n67, 217, 219n75, 221n81, 222, 225–26, 228–33, 236–40, 242n21, 243–47, 249n37, 253n52, 258, 260, 263, 265n33, 266, 268n45, 270, 273, 275n92, 279, 285, 287–88, 291, 295
Temple Mount 5, 42n27
Tiglath-pileser III 13, 27, 36, 38n14, 40, 77, 126n6, 162–63, 188–91, 206–207, 232
Timnah 51n56, 64
Tirhakah see Taharqo
Tishri 10n2, 20n37, 22n41, 188n132
tithe 111n66, 239, 245
Toi 270
Torah 119, 196, 218n73
Transversal Valley 43, 251
tree 84, 170–77, 178n102, 191, 202, 206, 273, 296
tribute 16, 28n64, 36nn3–4, 37n10, 38, 39n15, 41, 58, 81, 111n66, 188n131, 189n132, 269–70, 275, 281–82, 286, 289
trust 42, 71, 104–105, 129, 130n17, 135, 142, 153, 200n18, 252, 295, 297
Tubaʾalu 79
Tyre 78–79, 188n131, 271
Tyropoeon Valley 44

Ugaritic 157n23, 184
universalism 179nn102, 107, 293
Upper Pool 128, 138, 140, 182
Ur III dynasty 176n93
Urartu 39n16, 41, 42n23, 188n132
Uriah 206
Uruk 164n51
Ushna 1n1
Ushu see Tyre
Uzziah 12n6, 24n46, 26, 28, 35, 36n1, 250*n42, 267, 270–71

Vulgate 103n38, 157, 274n86

Warren's Shaft 48n46
water 46 nn. 37, 40, 48–50, 58, 63, 86n83, 174, 180n108, 219, 224, 249n38, 250–52, 255, 293, 296, 298

Yabâ **31–32**
Yahwist document (J) 145n55, 214n64, 215n65, 246n31, 288n14, 291

Yau-bi'di   37n6
Yehozarah   1n1
Yehud   239n12

Zebulun   155, 158, 224, 225n88, 237n4, 272
Zechariah   24, 250n41
Zedekiah   20, 22–23, 135, 186n126

Zephaniah   1n1
Zichri   187
Ziklag   96n16
Zion tradition   134, 184, 278n104, 289
Ziv   see Iyyar
z[y]p   52n61